The Power Triangle

The Power Triangle

MILITARY, SECURITY, AND POLITICS IN REGIME CHANGE

HAZEM KANDIL

Oxford University Press is a department of the University of Oxford. It furthers the University's objective of excellence in research, scholarship, and education by publishing worldwide. Oxford is a registered trade mark of Oxford University Press in the UK and certain other countries.

Published in the United States of America by Oxford University Press
198 Madison Avenue, New York, NY 10016, United States of America.

Library of Congress Cataloging-in-Publication Data
Names: Kandil, Hazem, author.
Title: The power triangle : military, security, and politics in regime change / Hazem Kandil.
Description: New York, NY : Oxford University Press, 2016. | Includes bibliographical references and index.
Identifiers: LCCN 2015047834 | ISBN 9780190239206 (hardcover : alk. paper)
Subjects: LCSH: Regime change. | Regime change—Egypt. | Regime change—Iran. | Regime change—Turkey. | Civil-military relations—Egypt. | Civil-military relations—Iran. | Civil-military relations—Turkey. | Egypt—Politics and government—21st century. | Iran—Politics and government—21st century. | Turkey—Politics and government—21st century.
Classification: LCC JC489 .K36 2016 | DDC 321.09—dc23
LC record available at http://lccn.loc.gov/2015047834

9 8 7 6 5 4 3 2 1
Printed by Sheridan Books, Inc., United States of America

To Naheed

"I don't write about victims so much as I write about the people who have power, who exert the power, and who use the power against other people."

—Gore Vidal, *The United States of Amnesia*, 2013

CONTENTS

PREFACE

In power struggles, there are no lasting victories—only the ceaseless clash of wills. This is why regimes constantly change. Sudden, dramatic, popularly forced changes impress themselves upon us as revolutions. Less spectacular ones, brought forth by pressure and compromise, are the much less memorable reforms. Frustratingly slow rearrangements of power at the top, with limited reverberations below, are symptoms of resilience. The important thing is: regimes, defined simply as how society is ruled, are never entirely stagnant. And revolution, reform, and resilience are essentially different labels describing the same phenomenon, that is, regime change.

Yet studies of regime change have been long divided into three separate fields, depending on the speed and extent of change: revolution theory, mostly developed by sociologists; transition theory, a preferred niche for reform-minded political scientists; and the residual and exotic phenomenon of authoritarian resilience, commonly relegated to area specialists. To end this clearly unhelpful division, one must examine how regimes operate over decades, rather than just parachute onto the most exciting episodes. To quote Cambridge historian Herbert Butterfield: "History is not the study of origins; rather it is the analysis of all the mediations by which the past was turned into our present" ([1931] 1965: 3). Only long-term studies can capture revolution, reform, and resilience through a single lens.

This book presents one such attempt. It starts with a historical puzzle. In the first half of the twentieth century, officers in Iran, Turkey, and Egypt decided to pull their once great nations up by the bootstraps and shepherd them back to the path of progress. These revolutions from above were all conceived in the name of modern state building, and occurred in comparable settings only a few years apart. But despite similarities, they met different fortunes: Iran became an absolutist monarchy that was overthrown by revolution; Turkey evolved into a limited democracy through successive reforms; and Egypt metamorphosed into a resilient police state. How can we account for this divergence? While most studies of regime change highlight popular forces, I focus instead on the ruling bloc. My central claim is that these different trajectories were determined by the power struggle between the military, security, and political institutions—what I refer to as the *power triangle*. I conclude that it was political hegemony over the agents of coercion in Iran that produced a toothless monarchy vulnerable to overthrow; that the aversion of Turkey's military guardians to direct governance left a relatively autonomous space for democratic politics to develop; and that the growing security dominance in Egypt produced an exceptionally intransigent police state.

The assumption here, of course, is that the military, security, and political institutions have separate agendas, based on their varying (albeit overlapping) interests. Though partners in domination, and generally invested in regime stability, the three institutions inevitably compete over regime control in order to impose their own priorities. And it is through their conflict and collaboration that power continuously shifts within the ruling bloc, and with it the overall character of the regime. Analyzing regime change should therefore begin by demystifying relations within this triangular ruling complex. Other variables, whether class, ideology, or geopolitics, should be accounted for through their impact on these ruling institutions.

That being said, my appreciation of the impact of power struggles at the top does not contradict Pierre Bourdieu's assertion that "there is no single, final, or even correct explanation of anything, only more complete, developed, adequate explanations" (Gorski 2013: 356). I therefore see my effort as complementary. My aim is to enhance the literature on regime change, not question the multiplicity of approaches needed to grasp this intricate phenomenon. Indeed, Jack Goldstone once compared the scholarly endeavor to exploring a large plot of land, where only by mapping the various parts could we begin to imagine the whole (2003: 43). And it is the fact that so much ground has been covered with regards to class politics, ideological conflicts, and geopolitics, that drove me toward the relatively neglected area of institutional tensions within the state.

Let me end with a note on the book's structure. The preface is followed by a somehow lengthy exposition of the theoretical underpinnings of the power triangle model, and a justification of my methodological choices. And at the very end of the book, another long section reviews the literature on civil–military relations, and shows how comparing the Iranian, Turkish, and Egyptian cases hopes to contribute to it. Readers uninterested in theory, method, or academic squabbles could skip the introduction and conclusion and delve into the historical analysis that forms the core of this study. Theory and history were kept separate for the benefit of nonacademic readers, though they were certainly entwined in my mind during the research itself. Likewise, the historical chapters were divided by cases rather than themes not because I studied each country separately—few comparativists could, even if they tried—but because the density of intraregime conflicts, and the plethora of names and dates that come with it, would render interweaved narratives too confusing.

This concern for general as well as scholarly readers is inspired by Theda Skocpol's (2003) advice for social scientists to be "doubly engaged": to address audiences within and outside academia by contributing to scientific debates, on the one hand, and offering insights into real-life issues, on the other. This particularly applies to studies of power. For as Bourdieu tirelessly repeated, sociologists have a special obligation to debunk existing power arrangements by exposing how historically contingent and volatile they are; how despite their apparent rigidity, they remain permanently in flux.

Bibliography

Butterfield, Herbert. [1931] 1965. *The Whig Interpretation of History*. New York: W.W. Norton.

Goldstone, Jack A. 2003. "Comparative Historical Analysis and Knowledge Accumulation in the Study of Revolutions." In *Comparative Historical Analysis in the Social Sciences,* edited by James Mahoney and Dietrich Rueschemeyer, pp. 41–90. Cambridge, UK: Cambridge University Press.

Gorski, Philip S. 2013. "Conclusion: Bourdieusian Theory and Historical Analysis: Maps, Mechanisms, Methods." In *Bourdieu and Historical Analysis,* edited by Philip S. Gorski, pp. 327–66. London: Duke University Press.

Skocpol, Theda. 2003. "Doubly Engaged Social Science: The Promise of Comparative Historical Analysis." In *Comparative Historical Analysis in the Social Sciences,* edited by James Mahoney and Dietrich Rueschemeyer, pp. 407–28. Cambridge, UK: Cambridge University Press.

ACKNOWLEDGMENTS

Considering that this book is based on my dissertation, I must begin by thanking my supervisor Michael Mann and the other members of my doctoral committee, Rogers Brubaker, Leonard Binder, and William Roy, as well as those who offered guidance throughout my graduate career, especially Perry Anderson, Bahgat Korany, Timothy Mitchell, Jeffrey Prager, and Andreas Wimmer. But as any graduate student knows, much of the intellectual traction achieved during these formative years comes from sustained dialogue with fellow travelers. And I could not have hoped for better companions than Joshua Bloom, Wesley Hiers, Robert Jansen, Kristin Surak, and Iddo Tavory.

In the three years that have passed between the dissertation and the current manuscript, my ideas have evolved through discussions with students here at Cambridge, both my graduate students and the remarkably talented undergraduates of the Revolution, War, and Militarism course. And the final conversion from dissertation to manuscript was made possible by the enthusiastic support of my editor James Cook and his team at Oxford University Press.

I would finally like to note that writing a dissertation could be a turbulent and unsettling process. Mine was smooth sailing all along for the simple reason that my partner in this journey was a woman of great calm, prudence, warmth, and infinite generosity. To her I dedicate this book.

Introduction

FROM REVOLUTION TO REGIME CHANGE

Revolution scholars have for long made it their business to determine the requisites for successful revolts. What they implicitly meant was that regimes were normally stable and coherent, and only under exceptional circumstances become vulnerable to overthrow. Only a handful reversed this approach to regimes by "turning the problem of revolutionary causation around . . . [and] instead of treating stability as unproblematic and piling up sets of conditions that lead to revolution . . . treating stability as the problem" (Goldstone 2003: 78). By treating continuity and change as two sides of the same coin, they managed to highlight how regimes were inherently volatile, despite appearances. This is because members of the ruling bloc compete constantly for overall power, even if their conflicts rarely break out into open confrontation. This introduction lays out my reasons for conceiving regimes in this way, and my suggestions for how to study them.

Regimes as Fields of Power

"Power," Bertrand Russell famously declared, is the "fundamental concept in social science . . . in the same sense which Energy is the fundamental concept in physics" ([1938] 2004: 4). Like energy, power comes in multiple forms and can be studied from multiple perspectives. The most rewarding paradigm, in my view, is realism. Realism emphasizes how people strive to advance their interests by increasing their power. It does not suggest that everyone is constantly immersed in power struggles. Rather, that enough people participate in these struggles for long enough to provide the central dynamic of social interaction (Mann 1986: 4).[1] Or as Russell bluntly put it: "Those whose love of power is not strong are unlikely to have much influence on the course of events. . . . Love of power, therefore, is characteristic of the men who are causally important" ([1938] 2004: 6). My work builds on the insights of some of the most astute students of power relations in sociology (Michael Mann, Theda Skocpol, Charles Tilly); history (Perry Anderson, Herbert Butterfield, E. H. Carr, Alfred Cobban); and theory (from Machiavelli, Hobbes, and Clausewitz to Michel Foucault). The concepts I use, however, are mostly drawn from Pierre Bourdieu, who summarized his "realistic philosophy" (2014: 343) as follows: "When you do sociology . . . you are simply obliged to assume that people who hold power . . . act, whether they are aware of it or not, in such a way as to perpetuate or increase their power" (2014: 266).

Just as a realist would, Bourdieu places conflict at the heart of social life. No action is disinterested, even if it tries to appear so. People are predominantly concerned with securing their interests, whether ideal or material (Bourdieu 1977: 177). They achieve this by enhancing the volume and value of whichever type of power they have, in whichever social sphere they operate. Bourdieu refers to the various sources of power as *capital,* presumably because they buy people better positions. And he refers to the various arenas of power as *fields,* drawing on metaphors of the battlefield, playfield, and force field.[2] Fields are structured spaces of dominant and subordinate positions organized around one type of capital (political, military, economic, cultural, etc.). Society is a web of interlocking fields. At the apex lies the *field of power.* This is where the dominant in each field confront each other to negotiate the overall distribution of power.[3] Here, players try to impose the legitimacy of their particular species of capital in order to dominate the entire social order (Bourdieu 1996: 264–72).

And so the essence of a Bourdieusian social analysis is that power struggles pervade the entire social body. "Every society is an arena of social conflicts," as Carr previously concluded, "and those individuals who range themselves against existing authority are no less products and reflections of the society than those who uphold it" (1961: 65). Or as Foucault put it: "A battlefront runs through the whole of society, continuously and permanently. . . . There is no such thing as a neutral subject. We are all inevitably someone's adversary" (2004: 51). In fact, what holds society together, according to Bourdieu, is not interdependence, but the "sheer fact of struggle, that actors take up positions relationally, in opposition to others, and it is the system of oppositions that gives unity" (Swartz 2013: 59). As Edmund Burke once remarked, it is "the reciprocal struggle of discordant powers [that] draws out the harmony of the universe" ([1790] 1910: 33).[4]

To translate this abstract scheme into a concrete analysis of power relations, it is helpful to focus on one of the forms that Bourdieusian fields could take, that is, institutions. Since a field exists to the degree that it has an autonomous elite and logic, it is therefore strongest when institutionalized (Gorski 2013a: 329).[5] Realists, in general, think institutionally. At close inspection, their grim view of the human condition does not necessarily pertain to human nature per se, but rather to social organizations. While the drive for power originates in individuals, as classical realists maintain, it is played out through institutions. As Hobbes once reasoned, individuals circumvent differences in physical and mental capacities by working through factions that synergize individual energies ([1651] 1968: 150). Likewise, Bourdieu noted that in complex societies, relations of power are not "established directly between individuals; they are set up, in objectivity, among institutions" (1990a: 132). Institutions also occupy a favored position in Foucault's work because they offer a "fundamental point of anchorage" for power relations (2000: 339).

What Bourdieu contributed is a unique understanding of how institutions work. Although formally led from the top, institutions are not simply steered via directives. They are "collectively orchestrated without being the product of the organizing action of a conductor" (Bourdieu 1990a: 59). This is because "an institution exists twice, both in . . . the objectivity of regulations and in the subjectivity of mental structures in tune with these regulations" (Bourdieu 2014: 115). Officers and politicians, for example, acquire a set of taken-for-granted beliefs (*doxa*) and practical dispositions (*habitus*) that orient them toward advancing their interests without much reflection. Like athletes or musicians, their actions are not entirely conscious. They reflect a practical sense cultivated through repetitive training (Bourdieu 2000: 162)—what Bourdieu aptly described as a "feel for the game" (Bourdieu 1998: 25).

The same applies to strategies. Contrary to rational choice and game theorists, Bourdieu disassociated strategies from goals. He rejected the idea that "adopting a strategy means defining explicit ends in relation to which present action is organized" (2014: 241). Instead, social agents with a feel for the game are "absorbed in their affairs . . . present at the coming moment, the doing, the deed . . . which is not posed as an object of thought, as a possible aimed for project." In other words, the strategies of social agents "rarely have a true strategic intention" (Bourdieu 1998: 80–81).

Notably, some of the greatest analysts of war and revolution shared Bourdieu's appreciation of practical logic. Clausewitz described his study of war as "merely providing a rationale of the actions of every general in history" ([1832] 1989: 486). And Cobban stated unambiguously that the actions of revolutionaries are "prescribed by the need to find practical solutions to immediate problems . . . [in the] game they were playing, even if unconsciously" (1963: 152–57). This *logic of practice* is how institutional actions are synchronized, and how competition between them unfolds.

Now if fields become more tangible when they materialize as institutions, they become even more so when they assume the pyramidal form of state institutions, which include large populations, formal boundaries, and strict hierarchies (Gorski 2013a: 330–33). Another reason to focus on state institutions is that power struggles at that level are usually more pronounced since the stakes are higher. As Bourdieu held, power relations become more transparent as we move upward toward those truly invested in the game, those who "admit that the game is worth playing and that the stakes created in and through the fact of playing are worth pursuing" (1998: 77). From a Bourdieusian perspective, one should therefore focus on "this universe of agents of the state who have constituted themselves into a *state nobility* by instituting the state" (1994: 16, emphasis added), or, as he described them elsewhere, "agents who have made the state, and have made themselves into state agents in order to make themselves the holders of state power" (2014: 38).[6] Quoting Russell again: "Since men love power, and since, on average, those who achieve power love it more than most, the men who control the State . . . desire an increase of it [most than all]" ([1938] 2004: 136). Perhaps this is why Anderson pertinently remarked, that: "A 'history from above' . . . is no less essential than a 'history from below' " (1974: 11).

Immersed as he was in the French case, Bourdieu recognized the autonomy of those at the helm of a strong centralized state. He took this so much for granted that he saw no need to explicitly theorize the state until much later in his career, beginning with the College de France lectures in 1990 (Wacquant 2005: 10). Bourdieu's state looms over the field of power, and "overshadows all fields" (2014: 367). It performs three simultaneous roles: player, referee, and goalpost. As player, the state is the "field of high public office," where the "state nobility" augments statist capital—a sort of meta-capital with regulatory power over all fields (Bourdieu 2014: 91).[7] This unique state power derives from its ability to determine the relative value (or exchange rate) of the different forms of capital (Bourdieu 1993: 26).[8] As such, the state is also a referee who enforces the rules of the game in the field of power, and adjudicates between competitors (Bourdieu 1990b: 137). It follows that controlling the state—itself the product of historical struggles—grants the winner considerable leverage. Here, the state appears as a goalpost, with the field of power defined as "the space of play in which holders of various forms of capital struggle *in particular* for power over the state, that is, over the statist capital that grants power over the different species of capital" (Bourdieu and Wacquant 1992: 114–15). So while Bourdieu's sociology of the state tends to emphasize its social dominance, he also views it as a contested object and an arena of struggle.[9]

How does his view compare to others? To start with, Bourdieu (2004) regarded the state's supreme power as a product of modernity. He would agree with Anderson that only after the American and French revolutions did states develop the capacity to shape society's "collective mode of existence as a whole" (Anderson 1980: 20). More generally, Bourdieu's perception of the state as a network of fields has more in common with Foucault and Mann than state-centric theorists (Swartz 2013: 27). Like Foucault, he believed that in the modern world "power relations have come more and more under state control" so that "all other forms of power relations must refer to it" (Foucault 2000: 336–40, 347). Bourdieu would also agree with Timothy Mitchell, the foremost Foucauldian state theorist that "the line between state and society is not the perimeter of an intrinsic entity. . . . It is a line drawn internally, *within* the network of institutional mechanisms through which a certain social and political order is maintained" (Mitchell 1991: 90).[10] Yet Bourdieu certainly sided with Mann against Foucault in perceiving state power as directly "wielded by agents in defense of their interests and in support of their projects" rather than being impersonal and diffuse (Calhoun 2013: 48).

Where Bourdieu's account of the state fell short of those provided by Anderson and Mann is in its neglect of geopolitics. He was so absorbed in mapping power within the nation-state (primarily France) that he apparently forgot that one could hardly grasp power relations in Renaissance Italy or Eastern Europe without referring to Paris and Moscow, respectively. That being said, an excessive preoccupation with geopolitics could be harmful, leading postwar realists as it did to treat states as coherent and rational actors.[11] Even statist sociologists who studied intra-regime conflicts, like Skocpol (1979), blamed geopolitical crises for disrupting an otherwise unified state elite (Mitchell 1991: 88). Bourdieu again followed Mann in breaking away from these presumptions. Instead of reifying the state or assuming elite unity under normal circumstances, Mann had recast the state as a volatile object, a "polymorphous power network" that crystalizes differently depending on the interplay between various power holders. The domination of one or more forms of power (politics, military, etc.) is always temporary because any crystallization produces conflict (Mann 1986: 18–20; 1993: 82). Foucault similarly portrayed the social order as a field of "generalized war that, at particular moments, assumes the forms of peace and the state" (2000: 124). Foucault indeed went further by inverting Clausewitz's world-famous proposition that war is the continuation of politics by other means, and claiming instead "that politics is the continuation of war by other means," that "peace itself is a coded war" (Foucault 2004: 15, 51). Clausewitz himself explained that even "an absolute balance of forces cannot bring about a standstill." What appears to be a state of balance is really one where the aggrieved side is powerless to tilt the scales in its favor. "Inaction," for Clausewitz, is simply a situation where actors are "waiting for a better time to act" ([1832] 1989: 82). Power relations within the ruling bloc could therefore be best understood, borrowing Bourdieu's curious formula, as an "armed peace between 'hostile brothers'" marked by constant strife over "the dominant principle of domination" (Bourdieu 1993: 22–25).

Needless to say, when state institutions scramble to dominate the regime, they must make sure that the regime itself is not destroyed in the process. Even in revolution, the aim is "not to destroy the citadel of vested interest but to occupy it" (Cobban 1963: 116). Both the powerful and power-hungry share an interest in preserving the terrain. Of course, sometimes they fail. "Very often, the dominant can contribute to shaking the foundations of their domination because, caught up by the logic of the game . . . they can forget that they have gone a bit too far" (Bourdieu 2014: 319). These are the mistakes that make radical change possible.[12] But in general, however, the power strategies of state rulers, as Bourdieu recognized, are rarely subversive (2004: 16). Foucault likewise described antagonists in power struggles as essentially partners. They do not compete in a zero-sum game, nor do they try to obliterate one another. Since power is relational, the "the other" must be preserved throughout. Antagonistic partners therefore start from a prior consent over their respective positions in the relationship, and then proceed to modify these positions through adversarial strategies, without disrupting the relationship itself. Clausewitz expressed a similar sentiment. A battle between similar forces (such as national armies) is marked by "true polarity, since the victory of one side excludes the victory of the other." But in a battle between "different things that have a common relation external to themselves" (such as different institutions commonly serving the state), "polarity lies not in the *things* but in their relationship" ([1832] 1989: 83). Simply stated, each institution wants to dominate the relationship without abolishing the other institutions, since they all perform different functions necessary for the whole.

In short, relations within the ruling bloc are both collaborative and conflictive. State agents, in Bourdieu's terms, are "both accomplices and opponents—accomplices in the use of power, and opponents in competition for . . . the monopoly of a particular form of power which claims to be the only legitimate one" (2014: 289). One should therefore follow Foucault's advice by looking at how "the various operators of domination support one another, relate to one another, at how they converge and reinforce one another in some cases, and negate or strive to annul one another in other cases" (2004: 45). On the one hand, state rulers find themselves in a homologous position vis-à-vis their subjects: they are bound by an "*organic solidarity within the division of labor of domination*" (Bourdieu 1993: 25). On the other hand, their relationship is strained by the fact that they draw on different power sources, and therefore develop different priorities.[13] So while state rulers perceive themselves as partners in the enterprise of domination, they also realize that their institutional differences produce different views on how to employ state power: How should revenues be collected and expended? How far should opposition be tolerated? How should enemies and allies be engaged? Small and large questions on socioeconomic development, foreign affairs, armaments, repression, and so on are usually resolved in a way that benefits some institutional interests and hurts others. Negotiating a pecking order within the ruling hierarchy constantly lurks in the background. And the moment a power balance is established, it becomes open to renegotiation. State institutions extend their reach when possible, retract when necessary; they are sometimes subtle, sometimes combative, but always keen on maximizing their influence over society. The goal is to determine the *regime*, understood simply as the rules of the game in any society. It is an endless game with no ultimate winner. The following study focuses on only one part of this intricate game, the one involving the holders of coercive and political power. Below, I explain why.

Military, Security, and Politics

State theory is rich and varied. Class theorists categorize states according to mode of production, and privilege the role of the economically dominant class. The undeniable increase in state power has forced many of them to entertain some notion of relative state autonomy, though they still hold that the state's main function is to reproduce the existing socioeconomic order (Miliband 1969; Althusser 1971; Poulantzas 1973; Offe and Ronge 1982; Jessop 1990; Therborn 1982; Wright 1998; Hobsbawm 2001). In other words, they continue to perceive the state as "an institutional chameleon, able to adopt the class character of whatever class holds economic power" (Kimmel 1990: 19). Exceptional cases of state autonomy are perceived as contingent, perhaps added as qualifiers to class-based models, but rarely theorized in their own right. The agents of coercion are either considered instruments of class domination (as in classic Marxian analysis), or treated as part of the "military–industrial complex"—thus primarily an economic actor (as in the contemporary analyses of Mills 1956 and Johnson 2004). Liberals characteristically confuse reality with aspiration, envisioning states run by elected representatives, responsive to popular demands, and beholden to social values and legal norms (Lipset 1959; Easton 1965; Dahl 1977). As Mann rightly noted (1993: 46), their view of the state simply reflects "liberal democracy's view of itself"—and, as such, remains limited. In contrast to both class theorists and liberals, elitists depict history as a relentless battle between organized minorities over state power. A state, in their opinion, is an institution colonized by various power elites across time (Mosca 1939; Lenski 1965; Pareto 1968; Domhoff 1990). Elitists, in essence, "invert" class and liberal theories by visualizing power as radiating "outward from, not inward to, the state" (Mann 1993: 48). Still, elitist views of the state remain as functionalist as those of Marxists and liberals. Bourdieu and Foucault criticized them for focusing on what states do, rather than on how they work (Bourdieu 2014: 5–6; Foucault 2004: 13–14, 24).

Many historical sociologists tried to remedy that by shifting their analytical gaze from how elites conquer the state (from the outside) to how state officials (on the inside) identify with the interests of the institutions they belong to. This view reverberates through the work of both state-centered sociologists (Trimberger 1978; Skocpol 1979, 1985) and network-centered ones (Mann 1986; Tilly 1990; Collins 2009). The idea here is that studying concrete institutions with specific members and interests exposes how regimes actually function. Bourdieu's depiction of the state as an ensemble of bureaucratic institutions echoes this same view (Bourdieu and Wacquant 1992: 113). With increasing institutionalization and professionalization, state officials shift from representing the interests of their original social groups to safeguarding the state organizations they now belong to (Bourdieu 1991: 82–83, 197). Bourdieu's justification for why state rulers, as it were, dissolve into their institutions rather than remain socially separate is that the "apparatus gives everything (including power over the apparatus) to those who give it everything and expect everything from it because they themselves have nothing or are nothing outside it . . . [T]he apparatus depends most on those who most depend on it" (1991: 216). Analyzing how states work, in that case, should begin by recognizing how state institutions act *individually* to defend their interests vis-à-vis other institutions, as well as *collectively* to defend state interests.

But which state institutions should one examine? Anderson defined the state as "a centralized apparatus of coercion and administration" (1980: 24). Skocpol also saw it as "a set of administrative, policing, and military organizations," and concluded unequivocally that "administrative and coercive organizations are the basis of state power as such" (1979: 27–29).[14] Why is that? Historically, there have been two preconditions for declaring sovereignty over a designated territory and population: these were *force* to protect the land and cage its people, and *governance* to administer both. This is why coercion and politics, above all, mark the birth of states and cast a long shadow over their future.[15] Other factors doubtlessly count, but they do so mostly through enhancing these two functions. Economic assets (in the form of land, capital, or natural resources) empower state institutions by helping them sustain the populace and co-opt the most ambitious among them. Cultural assets (myths, religion, ideology, values, and norms, which all eventually find expression in laws and practices) legitimize the existing order, condition subjects to accept it, and mobilize them when necessary. A favorable geopolitical environment is similarly valuable to state power. Yet states could manage with meager economic or cultural resources and against geopolitical hostility, but never without administration and coercion. A breakdown in either of those results in state failure, not just material or ideal impoverishment or international tension.

For the sake of analytical clarity, it is therefore useful to strip states down to the bones, and focus on military, security, and politics. This is not to reduce states to these three institutions, but to simply acknowledge that they exert the most direct impact on how states are ruled, that economic, cultural, and geopolitical influences are *mediated* through the *immediate* actions of administrative and coercive agents. For while many social forces struggle away from state institutions, they find themselves in "a relationship of homology with agents involved in the bureaucratic field and in the struggles within it" (Bourdieu 2014: 368). And, by the same token, whenever state officials serve themselves, they necessarily serve the interests of some social groups rather than others (Bourdieu 2014: 113). So while all types of power are considered in this study, they are accounted for through their effect on the power relationship between the military, security, and political institutions. In Bourdieusian parlance, I capture external influences "retranslated into the internal logic" of state institutions (Bourdieu and Wacquant 1992: 105). Or as Anderson put it, I consider how social struggles are "ultimately resolved at the *political*—and not the economic or cultural—level of society" (1974: 11). My emphasis therefore is on how regimes are shaped and reshaped through the cooperation and collision of military, security, and political powers, embedded as they are in economic, cultural, and geopolitical crosscurrents.[16]

Now, let us move from abstract to concrete. My substantive model builds on the historical observation that in the Iranian, Turkish, and Egyptian coups, just as in countless other founding coups, power seizure was immediately followed by a division of labor between those who ran government, those who handled security, and those who controlled the officer corps.[17] The components of this internally differentiated bloc oscillated between cooperation and competition because their interests, while generally overlapping, remained essentially separate. The political leadership (represented by the ruling party, presidency, royal court) needs military and/or security support to preserve its power should it be forced to resort to violence, but played them off against each other to safeguard its autonomy and avoid falling hostage to any of them.[18] That is why coup leaders normally charge a group of army confidants with creating an elaborate security apparatus to coup-proof the armed forces and repress the population,[19] while at the same time making sure that rogue security agencies could be reined in using military units if needs be. The security establishment (secret police, intelligence, anti-riot forces) understands that its influence is contingent on the persistence of political autocracy and its obsession with the "enemy within," and that a transition to democracy would spell its downfall from power. As for those who remain in the military, the adverse effects of politicization on the combat readiness and public image of the officer corps are usually unsettling. Their preference is to return to the barracks at some future point after implementing the needed reforms, and re-intervene only if necessary.[20]

With these observations in mind, this study not only aims to highlight the continuous tension between the administrative and coercive apparatuses, but also the crucial distinction in the attitudes of the two wings of the coercive apparatus: the military and security.[21] Historically, military and police power have been intimately linked.[22] Otto Hintze (1975: 201) asserted that the "military state developed into the tutelary police state,"[23] and indeed many considered police states a symptom of the "*perversion and corruption*" of military politics (Koonings and Kruijt 2002: 32). But although both military and security organs could carry out coercive functions, their institutional mindset differs considerably. First of all, security forces could hardly muster a bargaining power comparable to that of the military if the state democratizes. Contrary to the centralized and hierarchical military, security agencies are usually too divided to be able to defend a unified corporate agenda vis-à-vis new rulers. Second, security officials are more likely to suffer retaliation should opposition come to power than military officers. Unlike the military, which normally represses citizens through deterrence (via communiqués, curfews, or street parades), security personnel directly administer repression (through detention, torture, summary executions), and therefore can scarcely hope for a general amnesty. Finally, while the officer corps is usually esteemed, receiving special privileges under democratic and authoritarian regimes alike (since both have external enemies), the prerogatives of security agencies under authoritarianism (with its preoccupation with internal enemies) diminishes substantially in a democracy: the extra-legal benefits that security agents receive are abrogated as soon as their extra-legal services are no longer required. To sum up, security organs are in a far more vulnerable position than the military should democratization succeed.[24]

These diverse institutional attitudes indicate that police and military states are qualitatively different. Military states are characterized by direct military governance (such as Latin American juntas) or repeated military interventions in politics (as in Turkey). What defines a police state, on the other hand, is the constant surveillance and regulation of political life with the aim of suppressing all challenges to the existing order, whether from political opposition groups or the armed forces (such as in Communist and Fascist regimes).[25] With this variation in mind, one begins to understand why military and security organs are as likely to work against each other, as they are to complement one another in politics.

Clearly, the premise here is that the military and security are not the "iron fists" or "heavy hands" of political authority, or other such metaphors that portray them as mere appendages rather than independent institutions with distinct corporate interests. Military and security officers are full partners in any ruling bloc. They work *with,* rather than *for,* politicians.[26] And while the interests of the three partners frequently coincide—thus projecting an image of unity—they are never identical. Machiavelli once wrote, "Between the armed and unarmed man no proportion holds, and it is contrary to reason to expect that the armed man should voluntarily submit to him who is unarmed, or that the unarmed man should stand secure among armed retainers" ([1532] 2004: 68–69).

It is therefore contrary to the nature of things to assume that the custodians of violence in "healthy" states function as benign pressure groups, and to treat military or security interventions in politics as alarming deviations from their normal course as professional institutions. Surely, these institutions have more at stake than other pressure groups. They identify their mission as no less than preserving the state's existence, and thus feel justified in forcing politicians' hands when it comes to countering foreign and domestic threats. And because they monopolize violence, politicians cannot simply check their influence through strictly legal means. Instead, they subordinate these mighty partners through various power arrangements. So whenever military and security officers appear to succumb to politicians, it is because the latter have either successfully balanced them against each other or surrendered enough power to keep them satisfied, not because they have been trained to learn their place in the ladder of authority and defer to their political masters.

Hence, the relationship between soldiers, spies, and statesmen is a power relation rather than a hierarchal one—even if the tense dynamics of this relationship are subtle in developed societies and crude elsewhere. Through a dizzying sequence of alliances, reversals, and confrontations within this triangular ruling complex, the balance of power constantly shifts, and with it the overall character of the regime. Political hegemony over the organs of coercion creates an impotent regime open to overthrow from below, as was the case in Iran in 1979. Military guardianship by officers with no interest in direct governance creates a relatively autonomous political space that politicians could expand gradually under the nose of the military and eventually at its expense, as in the Turkish case since 2002.[27] The dominance of the security produces a police state that effectively blocks change, such as the one that governed Egypt in 2011. This is why analyzing regimes must begin by demystifying relations within this *power triangle*.

In that sense, my objective here is not only to contribute to our understanding of Iran, Turkey, and Egypt, but also to produce a historically grounded explanatory model of how regimes change, an analytical frame of reference that is both generalizable and sensitive to variation, that is, one that does not claim that if particular conditions pertain, then a specific outcome invariably follows, but instead identifies the causal mechanisms at work and views outcomes as constantly evolving from one crystallization to another.[28] Here, comparative historical causality is key.

Comparative History and the Causes of Regime Change

States and regimes are conceptually different. The state is a constellation of institutions. It is an objective, concrete structure. A regime, on the other hand, is the outcome of institutional interactions, a reflection of their power balance at any given time. It is an ongoing process. Anderson accurately noted this dual character in his description of the social order as both "a *structure* which can be understood in terms of the inter-relationship of its parts, and a *process* which can only be understood in terms of cumulative weight of its past" (quoted in Elliot 1998: 7). Bourdieu's concept of the field of power also captures this dualism. The field of power is at once a structure, that is, a space with set hierarchies, and a process, that is, a space for struggle with continuously changing outcomes (Bourdieu and Wacquant 1992: 17).

This latter focus on process is why Bourdieu's approach is commonly described as "radically historicist" or historical realist (Swartz 2013: 31–32). He believed one could best understand states and regimes by examining their genesis and long-term trajectory (Bourdieu 1993: 41; 1994: 4). Here is the essence of "Andersonian historical sociology, intent upon the detection of long-run, long-range developmental patterns" (Elliott 1998: 161). Following in their footsteps, I adopt a primarily historical method—the method of choice for realists—conceived in the spirit of Carr's famous dictum that "the more sociological history becomes, and the more historical sociology becomes, the better for both" (1961: 84). Or, better yet, Bourdieu's radical negation that "the idea of a boundary between sociology and history has no meaning" (2014: 88).

The purpose of my historical investigation is to locate the causes of regime change. The assumption, of course, is that history contains causal regularities, and that the problem is how to extricate them from the heap of facts and intertwined patterns. In war, for instance, outcomes "seldom result from a single cause; there are usually several concurrent causes" (Clausewitz [1832] 1989: 157). Revolutions, likewise, result from a "conjuncture of distinct causal streams" (Goldstone 2003: 80). In Cobban's picturesque depiction, they arise from the "confluence of a host of contributory currents, small and great, flowing together to swell suddenly into a mighty flood" (1963: 137). Indeed, the central "truth of history," as Herbert Butterfield maintained, is that it is "the whole of the past, with its complexity of movement, its entanglement of issues, and its intricate interactions, which produced the whole of the complex present" ([1931] 1965: 19). This is why Bloch concluded his classic on historical method by asserting that "reality offers us a nearly infinite number of lines of force which all converge together upon the same phenomenon," compelling historians to discard the "fetish of single cause" for multiple "causal wave-trains" (1953: 193–94). What he meant to say is that abandoning the search for causal determination, as some historians do, is not a solution. If history appears too messy or random, as Anderson explained, "it is not because there are no determinations, but because there are too many. The historian's necessary duty . . . can only be acquitted by reconstructing the complex manifold of their actual determinations" (1980: 10). To achieve this, Bourdieu relies on *conjuncture*:

> Bourdieu is not content to reconstruct a single chain of causality but insists that we attempt to track multiple lines and levels of causation to whatever extent is practically possible. . . . [S]ociological explanation as Bourdieu conceives it consists in the effort to reconstruct a web of causal interdependence . . . map

these causal interrelationships . . . [and then] focus on the causal conjunctions, on the intersection of "independent causal series." (Gorski 2013a: 356–57)

Inspired by a realist philosophy of science, Bourdieu is less interested in establishing falsifiable laws than in identifying the "causal mechanisms that produced a given outcome, *mechanisms* being understood here as patterns or sequences of events that recur across different contexts" (Gorski 2013a: 358).[29] Indeed, Bourdieu does not provide a general law for change. His arsenal consists of sensitizing concepts, or "thinking tools," that help reconstruct complex sequences into intelligible patterns (Gorski 2013a: 328). This brings us to the idea of sequences and the patterns they generate.

State institutions, according to Bourdieu, conserve and extend "the trace of previous struggles" (2000: 127). A researcher's job is to establish how these struggles led the state down certain paths in a way that barred alternative possibilities. This approach is referred to as *path dependence*—an approach brilliantly summarized by Bourdieu as the belief that "history destroys possibilities: at every moment the space of possibilities constantly closes" (2014: 116).[30] A path-dependent account attends to how past events trigger self-reinforcing processes whose outcome could only be appreciated in the fullness of time. Pierson, one of the most rigorous appliers of path dependence, compares it to studying earthquakes. An earthquake "takes place in a very short period. . . . [T]he explanation or causal account typically offered, however, invokes a very slow-moving process—the buildup of pressure on a fault line over an extended period" (2003: 178). This is why scholars must consider the *longue durée*, the "very substantial stretch of time" that renders the whole casual chain visible (Pierson 2003: 192–97).[31]

But where should one start? Bourdieu and Foucault emphasize *genesis*: the moment when the existing power structure came to being. Indeed, Bourdieu once wrote, "Sociology as I conceive it is a genetic structuralism or a structural genesis" (2014: 87).[32] Coups are a good example. Students of militarism agree that the first seizure of power by the military constitutes an irreversible shift in civil–military relations. Henceforth, officers become prone to political intervention, and civilians regard the military as a cornerstone of political power (Vagts 1959: 22; Welch 1976: 324). Explaining how a regime turned out requires examining twists and turns extending several decades back to this original sin. This is why I examine both the foundational coups in Iran, Turkey, and Egypt and the six to eight decades that followed.

Still, path dependency methodologists recognize that self-reinforcing processes do not perpetually reproduce the same institutional positions. Occasional disruptions, like wars and revolts, offer opportunities for change.[33] Paths are thus punctuated by both equilibrium and transformation. And institutions could present either constraints or resources for change (Thelen 2003: 211–13). In fact, Bourdieu's work, despite claims to the contrary, is as much attentive to transformation as it is to reproduction (Gorski 2013b: 2). In culture, for instance, he studied continuities in schools, as well as rupture in the field of literature. On the national level, he was as alert to factors of stability in the French state as he was to the disruptive episodes of war (in Algeria) and revolt (May 1968). In other words, a good study of path dependence must be equally vigilant to long spells of stability and those critical moments when new possibilities arise. So the institutional power balance in a given state, crystalizing in a certain type of regime, is at once the result of past struggles and the springboard for future ones. To accurately gage this dynamic process, one needs to go beyond mapping institutional players and their interests to tracing how their interactions propel them forward. *Process tracing* is therefore a key complement to path dependence (Skocpol 1984b: 1; Goldstone 2003: 47–49; Mahoney 2003: 363–64).

An instinctive methodologist, Clausewitz naturally understood that the longer the causal process, the more events one needs to consider, and the more crucial the "tracing of effects back to their process" becomes ([1832] 1989: 156–59). In war, the most accentuated form of power struggle, "only a very small part of the time is occupied by action, while the rest is spent in inactivity" (Clausewitz [1832] 1989: 83). Yet as the experienced Clausewitz understood: "A state of rest and equilibrium can accommodate a good deal of activity" ([1832] 1989: 221). Adversaries in a power struggle maneuver constantly: they build up strength, collect allies, test the ground, lure each other into mistakes, and, above all, wait for favorable conditions to act (Clausewitz [1832] 1989: 541). These power strategies are crucial to explaining major changes. Going back to the example of earthquakes, numerous incremental changes might exert modest impact on the outcome we seek to explain, by their cumulative force carry forward the process to the threshold of critical change (Pierson 2003: 182). Richard Evans captured this in his advice to investigate *how* things happened, not just *why* they happened (2000: 135). Understanding the process is just as vital as explaining the overall trajectory. In Bourdieu's rendition, the power structure in any society "*depends at every moment*" on the inconclusive battles and tactical alliances between power holders (1993: 24–25). Critical junctures might be necessary to transform power relations, but it is what actors do in the interregnum that places them in a good spot to seize the opportunity and improve their position in the field of power (Bourdieu 1996b: 262).[34] In sum, critical junctures are nothing more than high pitches in ongoing power struggles. A careful analysis must therefore account for both minor maneuvers and major episodes of reconstitution.

Inevitably, all this talk of maneuver and struggle begs the question of agency: To what extent are power players the authors of their fortune? This is all the more important since this book is populated by the often called "great men of history," those exceptionally skilled and determined individuals who presumably shape events. Indeed, national histories have been written in terms of the actions of the Shah and Khomeini, Atatürk and Erdogan, Nasser and his celebrated successors and rivals. So we return to the ancient question: Do men make history?

Machiavelli weighed in early on this endemic debate. People act according to what they deem necessary, but their interpretation of *necessita* is based on their objective situation, and their success depends on their overall capacity (*virtu*) and particular circumstances (*fortuna*). Effective players, in other words, must behave "in conformity with the times" (Machiavelli [1519] 2003: 430; see also Clausewitz [1832] 1989: 100). Russell similarly believed that the way people pursue power depends on their temperament, which in turn is molded by their circumstances ([1938] 2004: 219). Anderson found this compound inherent in the term "agency" itself, which possesses "two opposite connotations . . . active initiator and passive instrument" (1980: 18). In another determined effort to transcend this agency–structure dichotomy, Carr explained how extraordinary individuals simply embody and intensify the spirit of their age:

> What seems to be essential is to recognize in the great man [of history] an outstanding individual who is at once a product and an agent of the historical process, at once the representative and the creator of social forces which change the shape of the world. . . . [T]he imaginary antithesis between society and the individual is no more than a red herring drawn across our path to confuse our thinking. (1961: 68–69)

Bourdieu provided the most systematic answer to this quandary. For him, "agents are acting, active, but it is history that acts through them, the history whose product they are" (2014: 96). Indeed, "it is only by way of interactions that structures reveal themselves" (Bourdieu 2014: 111). He explained how "structured agency" operates through the concept of *habitus*. Structures are inscribed on agents' mental and physical dispositions, and thus shape their practice. This practice is neither subjectively determined nor objectively rational. It is driven by a practical logic, by rules "mastered in a practical state without the players being able to formulate them explicitly." When agents interact, they do not act according to their own free will, nor do they consult the laws of reason. They develop "a feel for the game, a practical sense, [guided by] a habitus, by dispositions to play by . . . the implicit regularities of a game in which one has been immersed" (Bourdieu 2014: 241). In other words, agents embody structures. And this is why structures appear remarkably stable.

However, the rules that agents habitually follow are not fixed; they evolve historically as agents use them and test their limits. This explains why we observe both historical regularities (despite the independence of historical agents) and historical changes (despite the constraints of historical structures). Structural disruptions often occur during times of crises. It is during these exceptional moments that agents become aware of the possibility of behaving untypically, and thus altering the rules of the game (Bourdieu 1990: 59, 108). Of course, the question is: What causes these crises? As mentioned earlier, causes are conjunctures of several streams, most of which are outside the purview of agents. The Arab oil embargo enabled the Shah to raise oil prices and transform Iranian society. Iraq's invasion of Iran was essential to Khomeini's consolidation of power. The First World War allowed Kemal's modernizing revolution in Turkey. The creation of the European Union, and the possibility of Turkey's joining it, were crucial to the rise of Erdogan. And Israel's bewildering victory in the Six-Day War delivered the fatal blow to Nasser's seemingly successful regime.

Yet even in those times of rupture, agents remain largely constrained by past dispositions (Swartz 1998: 113). Khomeini, for example, embodied the *habitus* of the clerical field. So even when the revolutionary crisis enabled him to generate new ruling structures, he did so primarily as a cleric. Atatürk was a product of a military that has embraced Western modernity since the mid-nineteenth century. Imposing modernization from above faithfully reflected his long-ingrained disposition. Mohamed Morsi and his Muslim Brothers continued to embody the closed and subordinated nature of their organization. Even at the height of power, they mistrusted other political factions and deferred to their past tormentors in the military and security. As a result, while my analysis covers the strategies and actions of several historical actors, they are all treated as products of their institutions and structural conditions.

Now let us turn to another longstanding debate on history, that is, the role of contingency. Even if we try to determine the causal mechanisms at work, it is plain that accidents, mistakes, and the like are rife in history. In fact, this is how most of us understand history. As Clausewitz put it, "Although our intellect always longs for clarity and certainty, our nature often finds uncertainty fascinating. It prefers to day-dream in the realms of chance and luck rather than accompany the intellect on its narrow and torturous path of philosophical enquiry and logical deduction" ([1832] 1989: 86). But if we were to force ourselves to find logic in history, how could we fit all these chance occurrences? One approach is to claim that historical events are "over-determined", that is, there are "several sufficient as well as necessary causes, any one of which might have been enough to trigger the event on its own" (Evans 2000: 158). So if some waves were broken on the rock of contingency, the rest would still carry the ship to shore. Others apply historical Darwinism. Trotsky, representing a common Marxist line, explained that "the historical law is realized through the natural selection of accidents" (2007: 422). Contingencies in step with the march of history are incorporated into the causal chain, while others are cast off. In practice, most historians weave causes and contingencies into a single narrative—just as they are in real life. In the social sciences, however, this will not do. Causes need to be clearly delineated and ranked. So how could we justify privileging a handful of causal mechanisms and ignoring contingencies? Carr made the controversial suggestion that because historical studies are preoccupied with the present, they should only highlight those causal processes relevant to our current concerns:

> Just as from the infinite ocean of facts the historian selects those which are significant for his purpose, so from the multiplicity of sequences of cause and effect he extracts those, and only those, which are historically significant; and the standard of historical significance is his ability to fit them into his pattern of rational explanation and interpretation. Other sequences of cause and effect have to be rejected as accidental, not because the relation between cause and effect is different, but because the sequence itself is irrelevant. . . . Accidental causes . . . teach no lessons and lead to no conclusions. (1961: 138–40)

Butterfield and Evans rightly dismissed this. Historians must strive to understand what really happened in the past, regardless of their immediate concerns. What allows us to privilege a specific causal mechanism is our theoretical understanding of how the world operates. In Clausewitz's words, "Theory should cast a steady light on all phenomena so that we can more easily recognize and eliminate the weeds . . . keep the important and the unimportant separate" ([1832] 1989: 578). Even a professional historian, like Evans, admitted that empirical research cannot be carried out without the historian having "some basic theory of how and why things happen, some fundamental idea of human motivation and behavior, to begin with" (2000: 139). Skocpol, a keen searcher for causal regularities, insisted that interrogating history "cannot ever substitute for theoretical models or conceptual lenses in offering a meaningful portrait of how the world works" (1984a: 384).

However, this is not a license to twist historical evidence to fit our models. Just as theory directs us to which causal mechanisms to emphasize, historical evidence provides a check for theoretical speculation (Skocpol 1979: 39). History helps researchers validate, amend, or abandon their theoretical dispositions. Anderson attributed the deplorable tendency to divorce the abstract from the concrete to the belief that an "intelligible necessity only inhabits the broadest and most general trends in history, which operate so to speak 'above' the multiple empirical circumstances of specific events and institutions" (1974: 7–8). Carrying out proper research requires a continuous dialogue between theory and evidence (Carr 1961: 35; Evans 2000: 230). Skocpol illustrated this point using a metaphor from Arthur Stinchcombe: a historical sociologist builds "as a carpenter builds, adjusting the measurements as he goes along, rather than as an architect builds, drawing first and building later" (1984a: 385). Evans provided an even more compelling image of the historian's craft: "We start with a rough-hewn block of stone, and chisel away at it until we have a statue. The statue was not waiting there to be discovered, we made it ourselves, and it would have been perfectly possible for us to have made a different statue made from the one we finally created" (2000: 147). Yet the best description by far comes from Francis Bacon: "Empirics, like ants, gather and consume. The Rationalists, like spiders, spin webs out of themselves. The Bee adopts the middle course, drawing her material from the flowers of the garden or the field, but transforming it, by a faculty peculiar to herself" (1964: 131). In short, theory and history cannot be separated.

The reason why theory is of such supreme value is that historical agents themselves are usually unaware of either the drives or consequences of their own actions. Because historical change is "the result of a clash of wills," Butterfield explained, it is often "a result which often neither party wanted or even dreamed of, a result which indeed in some cases both parties would eventually have hated" ([1931] 1965: 28). The outcome being investigated, Butterfield continued, is nothing but the result of "continual interplay and perpetual collision. . . . It is the very embodiment of all the balances and compromises and adjustments that were necessitated by this interplay" ([1931] 1965: 41). As Joseph Ellis concluded after a lifelong study of the American

Revolution, "Men make history . . . but they can never know the history they are making" (2002: 4). Here, one appreciates Bourdieu's crucial distinction between practical and theoretical logic: people act unreflectively on their immediate environment, yet the long-term outcome of their complex interplay is only available to the theoretically informed social scientist (1977: 6). This is why I zigzag between my power triangle model and empirical evidence to develop a historically grounded theoretical explanation of regime change.

But in order to validate the causal hypotheses generated by this model, I combine historical analysis with comparison of a limited number of cases: three to be exact. Skocpol (1984a: 378) and Goldstone (2003: 43) prefer small case comparisons because they allow us to carefully juxtapose specific elements of each case and ascertain their effect on the outcome. This is because in historical change, particularities are extremely important—propelling Bourdieu, in one of his grand statements, to declare: "My entire scientific enterprise is indeed based on the belief that the deepest logic of the social word can be grasped only if one plunges into the particularity of an empirical reality, historically located and dated, but with the objective of constructing it as . . . an exemplary case in a finite world of possible configurations" (1998: 2).

A number of considerations determined my choice of Iran, Turkey, and Egypt. I was firstly guided by Clausewitz's concept of *absolute types*, that "in order to lend clarity, distinction, and emphasis to our ideas, only perfect contrasts, the extremes of the spectrum, [should be] included in our observations" ([1832] 1989: 517). Unlike Weber, who used abstract *ideal types* as measuring rods for empirical analysis, this nineteenth-century Prussian theorist preferred to use extreme—yet "actual fact"—historical cases to draw the boundaries of his theoretical models (Clausewitz [1832] 1989: 69). By embodying the model in its purest form, these concrete cases therefore mark its outer parameters, and facilitate future investigations into hybrid cases. Applied to this study, monarchical Iran reflects political hegemony in its most absolute form; the new Turkish republic best demonstrates military domination; and present-day Egypt is a perfect example of police states. Second, I follow Bourdieu's advice to study each of these "privileged particular cases" separately, focusing on specific institutions rather than society as a whole (Bourdieu and Wacquant 1992: 109; Bourdieu 2014: 87).[35]

Third, I apply the "method of difference," which contrasts similar cases with dissimilar outcomes (Skocpol 1984a: 378). According to Skocpol, the best comparisons start with cases that share certain essentials (1979: 40). The countries I chose have a lot in common in terms of land

and population size, geographic location, religious and ethnic homogeneity, and socioeconomic structure. I also consider them roughly within the same time span, from the second quarter of the twentieth century to the turn of the new century. Persia, the Ottoman Empire, and Egypt were three longtime pillars of the Muslim world. They were ruled by archaic monarchies, undermined internally by liberal constitutional movements, and externally by European powers (mostly British, but also French and Russian). Their development was curtailed by the depletion or exploitation of their resources, either due to occupation (Egypt), division into spheres of foreign influence (Persia), or constant war (Ottoman Turkey).[36] At the same time, European colonial powers helped them build modern armies with an eye toward maintaining regional stability. But the Great War, and the devastating Depression that followed, loosened the colonial grip. Imperial capitals were too exhausted militarily and economically to maintain territorial gains in (what soon became) modern-day Turkey, nor could they preserve control over the Egyptian and Persian governments. And so instead of continuing to serve their European patrons, the relatively developed officer corps seized power with the declared aim of achieving national independence and revolutionizing society from above using the standard tools of late modernizers: state-led socioeconomic development, and a secular nationalist ideology. The young nationalist officers who triggered these modernizing revolutions (Reza Khan in 1921, Mustafa Kemal in 1923, and Gamal 'Abd al-Nasser in 1952) thus shared comparable state-building ambitions. And yet despite these similarities, each country followed a completely different track. The comparative historical analysis at the core of this study explains why.

Finally, in terms of evidence, I rely on primary sources (interviews in Cairo, Istanbul, and with the Iranian diaspora in California, in addition to memoirs, news clips, official documents, and archival materials), supported by an extensive reexamination of the secondary literature. This latter endeavor is quite central to the revisionist account I provide since it involves substantial rearranging and re-analyzing of the evidence provided by historians and other social scientists.

The picture that emerges is one of internally differentiated ruling blocs working together to maintain their regimes, while at the same time competing for control over them. The result is ongoing power struggles, muted most of the time and explosive during times of crisis. And it is those silent maneuvers and explicit battles between the military, security, and political institutions that propel regimes down specific pathways, and ultimately determine the direction and pace of regime change.

Notes

1. The realist ontology is captured in Michael Mann's claim that "human beings are restless, purposive, and rational, striving to increase their enjoyment of the good things of life and capable of choosing and pursuing appropriate means for doing so. Or, at least, enough of them do this to provide the dynamism that is characteristic of human life" (1986: 4)—a modern rendition of Hobbes: "In the first place, I put for a generall inclination of all mankind, a perpetuall and restlesse desire of Power after power, that ceaseth only in Death" ([1651] 1968: 161–62).

2. Like a battlefield, Bourdieu's field is dominated by the preparation for and the conduct of struggle (Bourdieu and Wacquant 1992: 17). Like a playfield, players act strategically to get ahead (Bourdieu and Wacquant 1992: 118). And like a force field, each field has an objective character that arranges its elements in identifiable patterns (Bourdieu 1984: 149).

3. In one of his definitions of the field of power, Bourdieu describes it as the space for the relations of force between "agents or institutions which have in common the possession of a sufficient quantity of specific capital to occupy dominant positions within their respective fields" (1998: 34).

4. This echoes Clausewitz's understanding of the world order as "major and minor interests of states and peoples interwoven in the most varied and changeable manner. Each point of intersection binds and serves to balance one set of interests against the other. The broad effect of all these fixed points is obviously to give a certain amount of cohesion to the whole" ([1832] 1989: 373).

5. Bourdieu preferred field analysis to institutional analysis because the term "institution" implies consensus and coherence, while he was interested in tensions and contradictions (Bourdieu and Wacquant 1992: 105, 232). Sharing the same interest, my institutional analysis is carried out in the spirit of a Bourdieusian field analysis.

6. Though one must not confuse institutions with institutional elites. Bourdieu censored those who "instead of studying *structures* of power... study *populations* of agents who occupy positions of power" (1993: 19).

7. Statist capital is different from political capital, which is the capacity to mobilize public support to influence the state (Bourdieu and Wacquant 1992: 119).

8. A monarchy, for instance, assigns great value to the type of political capital accumulated by courtesans. A military dictatorship privileges the type of assets available to officers. A republic of letters, as France presents itself, prizes the holders of cultural power more than the decidedly anti-intellectual America.

9. Swartz provides a laudable summary of the Bourdieusian state as "a differentiated field of struggle situated within the broader field of power that it both attempts to regulate and is itself simultaneously the object of control by agents in the field of power. The state is a contested arena as well as an institution of control in the field of power" (2013: 144).

10. There is a clear parallel here between this Foucauldian line of thought that presents the state as "a structural effect ... not as an actual structure" (Mitchell 1991: 93–94), and Bourdieu's claim that "the state is a well-founded illusion, this place that exists because people believe it exists" (2014: 10).

11. Critiques of this view are best captured in the volumes edited by Keohane (1986) and Frankel (1996).

12. Contrary to elite theorists, who attribute political change to the weakening of elites, "I believe on the contrary that very often one of the mechanisms by which elites commit suicide relates to . . . [the] passion of internal struggles" (Bourdieu 2014: 319).

13. According to Poggi, various forms of power are embodied in distinctive institutions with distinctive platforms that normally compete over who gets to shape state and society (2001: 1–2, 23).

14. Similarly, Tilly (1990: 96) held that "a state's essential activities form a trio: *state-making*: attacking and checking competitors and challengers within the territory claimed by the state; *war-making*: attacking and checking rivals outside the territory already claimed by the state; *protection*: attacking and checking rivals of the rulers' principal allies, whether inside or outside the state's claimed territory."

15. Bourdieu saw "nothing other than arbitrariness and usurpation" in the founding of regimes, and dismissed the Constitution as "merely a founding fiction designed to disguise the act of lawless violence which is the basis of the establishment of law" (2000: 168).

16. As Skocpol noted, state institutions maneuver for power at the intersection of international and domestic pressures (1979: 32, 47).

17. I am indebted to Stepan's (1988: 30–31) distinction between the "military as government" (politicized officers running government), the "security community," and the "military as institution."

18. I agree with Poggi (2001: 30, 53) that political power is primarily grounded "in the harsh reality of physical coercion," though once in place, it "may endure with a less lavish and visible expenditure of violence." Foucault (2000: 337) also described violence as power's "primitive form, its permanent secret, and its last resource, that which in the final analysis appears as its real nature when it is forced to throw aside its mask and to show itself as it really is." As Machiavelli noted ([1532] 2004: 21), rulers must "urgently arrange matters so that when [subjects] no longer believe they can be made to believe by force."

19. Coups usually beget other coups, as was demonstrated in the case of Syria, Iraq, Algeria, the Sudan, Pakistan, Indonesia, and Ghana. Syria alone witnessed fifteen coups between 1949 and 1970.

20. Soldiers also face the dilemma of explaining why they are still in power if their coup was successful, and what makes them think they are competent to rule if it was not. Vagts mentioned in his magisterial study of militarism that "even without an express prohibition [on military participation in politics] it would appear doubtful whether officers as a type have the ability, the suppleness, the temperament, or the time for a continuous application to politics" (1959: 294).

21. Middle East experts have employed the term "police state" derogatively to condemn draconian Arab governments without really explaining what constitutes this type of state (Salamé 1994; Makiya 1998).

22. We know that the creation of the first national army in the early 1790s in France went hand-in-hand with the development of the organs of domestic repression under the Reign of Terror. This process was accelerated by the militarization of the polity following Napoleon's coup (Tilly 1993: 170–76). For differences in mission between military and police forces, see Poggi (2001: 184–85).

23. Though at the time Hintze was writing, the concept of a *polizeistaat* had not yet received the negative connotation of today, and was mostly used in reference to well-ordered polities.

24. Succinctly summarized by Geddes (1999): for the military, there is life after democracy.

25. Of course, all law-governed societies must be policed. But in "police states," coercion is not only more blatant than in democracies; it is explicitly designed to preserve the rulers in power by dominating all other institutions, including the military. The security apparatus checks military autonomy through multiple control mechanisms, such as screening recruits, monitoring officers, recommending promotions and economic payoffs, purging dissidents, in addition to isolating the army from the "political street" by relieving it from the responsibility of domestic repression. This military control model (usually via commissars) was devised during the French Revolution, and perfected by Communists.

26. "People say: 'Civil servants simply obey,'" Bourdieu, wrote, "but in fact this is not servility, there are deep interests that are beneath the threshold of consciousness, and only became apparent at critical moments" (Bourdieu 2014: 272).

27. This conclusion is consistent with quantitative studies, which demonstrate that among the authoritarian regimes erected between 1945 and 2000, security-sustained single-party regimes lasted three times as long as military-dominated ones, while personalist autocracies came somewhere in the middle (Geddes 1999).

28. As Bourdieu (2014: 27) wrote: "There is a whole empirical work to be done each time, which does not mean that the model does not hold good. The model is there as an invitation to study the variations in parameters."

29. Mahoney (2003: 363) defines causal mechanisms as the "processes and intervening variables through which an explanatory variable exerts a causal effect on an outcome variable." The essential difference between casual mechanisms and general laws is that the "degree of generality of any particular causal mechanism . . . is variable and is part of what the investigation needs to determine" (Goldstone 2003: 44).

30. According to Machiavelli ([1532] 1995: 18), "Men almost always walk along the beaten path, and what they do is almost always an imitation of what others have done before."

31. Indeed, two prominent historians recently published a manifesto demanding a return to the *longue durée* (Guldi and Armitage 2013).

32. Foucault (2004: 169) distinguishes this type of genetic history or *genealogy* from that of Machiavelli and others who simply use history as a source of examples.

33. And as Lewis Namier (1964: 36) noted, there is a "close interaction" between war and revolution, as "they shatter political structures, and open a way for each other."

34. Machiavelli believed those successful in improving their lot are the most capable, but require first some opening. Without this opportunity, their *virtu* remains untapped ([1532] 1995: 19).

35. The first part of this advice echoes an often cited statement by Marx and Engels: "Events strikingly similar, but occurring in a different historical milieu, lead to completely dissimilar results. By studying each of these evolutions separately and then comparing them, it is easy to find the key of the understanding of this phenomenon" (quoted in Carr 1961: 82).

36. Raymond Aron (1985: 274) described nineteenth-century Persia and Turkey as "semi-colonies."

Bibliography

Allison, Graham T. 1971. *Essence of Decision: Explaining the Cuban Missile Crisis.* Boston: Little, Brown and Company.

Althusser, Louis. 1971. *Lenin and Philosophy and Other Essays*. London: New Left Books.

Anderson, Perry. 1974. *Lineages of the Absolutist State*. London: Verso.

Anderson, Perry. 1980. *Arguments within English Marxism*. London: Verso.

Andreski, Stanislav. 1968. *Military Organization and Society*. Berkeley: University of California Press.

Bacon, Francis. 1964. *The Philosophy of Francis Bacon*. Liverpool, UK: Liverpool University Press.

Bloch, Marc. 1953. *The Historian's Craft*. New York: Vintage Books.

Bourdieu, Pierre. 1977. *Outline of a Theory of Practice*. Cambridge, UK: Cambridge University Press.

Bourdieu, Pierre. 1984. *Homo Acadamicus*. Paris: Minuit.

Bourdieu, Pierre. 1990a. *The Logic of Practice*. Cambridge, UK: Polity Press.

Bourdieu, Pierre. 1990b. *In Other Word: Essays Towards a Reflexive Sociology*. Stanford, CA: Stanford University Press.

Bourdieu, Pierre. 1991. *Language and Symbolic Power*. Cambridge, MA: Harvard University Press.

Bourdieu, Pierre. 1993. "From Ruling Class to Field of Power: An Interview with Pierre Bourdieu on *La Nobless d'État*." *Theory and Society* 10: 19–44.

Bourdieu, Pierre. 1994. "Rethinking the State: Genesis and Structure of the Bureaucratic Field." *Sociological Theory* 12 (1): 1–18.

Bourdieu, Pierre. 1996b. *The State Nobility: Elite Schools in the Field of Power*. Stanford, CA: Stanford University Press.

Bourdieu, Pierre. 1998. *Practical Reason*. Cambridge, UK: Polity Press.

Bourdieu, Pierre. 2000. *Pascalian Meditations*. Stanford, CA: Stanford University Press.

Bourdieu, Pierre. 2004. "From the King's House to the Reason of State: A Model of the Genesis of the Bureaucratic Field." *Constellations* 11 (1): 16–36.

Bourdieu, Pierre. 2014. *On the State: Lectures at the College de France, 1989–1992*. Cambridge, UK: Polity Press.

Bourdieu, Pierre and Loïc Wacquant. 1992. *An Invitation to Reflexive Sociology*. Chicago: University of Chicago Press.

Brooks, Risa A. 2008. *Shaping Strategy: The Civil-Military Politics of Strategic Assessment*. Princeton, NJ: Princeton University Press.

Burke, Edmund. [1790] 1910. *Reflections on the Revolution in France*. London: J. M. Dent & Sons.

Butterfield, Herbert. [1931] 1965. *The Whig Interpretation of History*. New York: W.W. Norton.

Calhoun, Craig. 2013. "For the Social History of the Present." In *Bourdieu and Historical Analysis*, edited by Philip S. Gorski, pp. 36–66. London: Duke University Press.

Carr, E. H. [1946] 2001. *The Twenty Years' Crisis, 1919–1939: An Introduction to the Study of International Relations*. New York: Perennial Press.

Carr, E. H. 1961. *What Is History?* New York: Random House.

Clausewitz, Carl von. [1832] 1989. *On War*. Princeton, NJ: Princeton University Press.

Clausewitz, Carl von. 1988. *War, Politics, and Power: Selections from* On War, *and* I Believe and Profess. Washington, DC: Regnery Gateway.

Collins, Randal. 2009. *Conflict Sociology: A Sociological Classic Updated*. London: Paradigm.

Cook, Steven. 2007. *Ruling But Not Governing: The Military and Political Development in Egypt, Algeria, and Turkey*. Baltimore, MD: John Hopkins University Press.

Dahl, Robert. 1977. *Polyarchy*. New Haven, CT: Yale University Press.

Domhoff, William. 1990. *The Power Elite and the State*. New York: Aldine de Gruyter.

Downing, Brian M. 1992. *The Military Revolution and Political Change: Origins of Democracy and Autocracy in Early Modern Europe*. Princeton, NJ: Princeton University Press.

Dunn, John. 1972. *Modern Revolutions: An Introduction to the Analysis of a Political Phenomenon*. Cambridge, UK: Cambridge University Press.

Easton, David. 1965. *A Framework for Political Analysis*. Englewood Cliffs, NJ: Prentice Hall.

Elliott, Gregory. 1998. *Perry Anderson: The Merciless Laboratory of History*. Minneapolis: University of Minnesota Press.

Evans, Richard J. 2000. *In Defense of History*, 2d ed. London: Granta Books.

Finer, Samuel E. 1962. *Men on Horseback: The Role of the Military in Politics*. London: Pall Mall Press.

Foucault, Michel. 2000. *Power: Essential Works of Foucault, 1954–1984*. New York: The New Press.

Foucault, Michel. 2004. *Society Must Be Defended: Lectures at the College De France, 1975–76*. London: Penguin.

Frankel, Benjamin. 1996. *Roots of Realism*. London: Frank Cass.

Geddes, Barbara. 1999. "Authoritarian Breakdown: Empirical Test of a Game Theoretic Argument." Paper presented at the Annual Meeting of the American Political Science Association, Atlanta, September 25, 1999.

Goldstone, Jack A. 2003. "Comparative Historical Analysis and Knowledge Accumulation in the Study of Revolutions." In *Comparative Historical Analysis in the Social Sciences*, edited by James Mahoney and Dietrich Rueschemeyer, pp. 41–90. Cambridge, UK: Cambridge University Press.

Gorski, Philip S. 2013a. "Conclusion: Bourdieusian Theory and Historical Analysis: Maps, Mechanisms, Methods." In *Bourdieu and Historical Analysis*, edited by Philip S. Gorski, pp. 327–66. London: Duke University Press.

Gorski, Philip S. 2013b. "Introduction: Bourdieu as a Theorist of Change." In *Bourdieu and Historical Analysis*, edited by Philip S. Gorski, pp. 1–18. London: Duke University Press.

Guldi, Jo and David Armitage. 2013. *The History Manifesto*. Cambridge, UK: Cambridge University Press.

Hintze, Otto. 1975. *The Historical Essays of Otto Hintze*. New York: Oxford University Press.

Hobbes, Thomas. [1651] 1968. *Leviathan*. Oxford: Oxford University Press.

Huntington, Samuel. 1968. *Political Order in Changing Societies*. New Haven, CT: Yale University Press.

Jessop, B. 1990. *State Theory: Putting the Capitalist State in Its Place*. University Park: Pennsylvania State University Press.
Johnson, Chalmers. 2004. *The Sorrows of Empire: Militarism, Secrecy, and the End of the Republic*. New York: Henry Holt.
Keohane, Robert O. 1986. *Neorealism and Its Critics*. New York: Columbia University Press.
Koonings, Kees and Dirk Kruijt (eds.). 2002. *Political Armies: The Military and Nation Building in the Age of Democracy*. New York: Zed Books.
Lenski, Gerhard. 1965. *Power and Privilege: A Theory of Social Stratification*. New York: McGraw-Hill. See especially pp. 50–72.
Lipset, Seymour M. 1959. *Political Man*. London: Mercury Books.
Machiavelli, Niccolò. [1519] 2003. *The Discourses*. London: Penguin.
Machiavelli, Niccolò. [1532] 1995. *The Prince*. Indianapolis: Hackett.
Machiavelli, Niccolò. [1532] 2004. *The Prince*. New York: Pocket Books.
Mahoney, James. 2003. "Strategies of Causal Assessment in Comparative Historical Analysis." In *Comparative Historical Analysis in the Social Sciences*, edited by James Mahoney and Dietrich Rueschemeyer, pp. 337–72. Cambridge, UK: Cambridge University Press.
Makiya, Kanan. 1998. *Republic of Fear: The Politics of Modern Iraq*. Berkeley: University of California Press.
Maniruzzama, Talukder. 1987. *Military Withdrawal from Politics: A Comparative Study*. Cambridge, MA: Ballinger Publishing.
Mann, Michael. 1986. *The Sources of Social Power*. Volume 1: *A History of Power from the Beginning to A.D. 1760*. New York: Cambridge University Press.
Mann, Michael. 1993. *The Sources of Social Power*. Volume 2: *The Rise of Classes and Nation-States, 1760–1914*. New York: Cambridge University Press.
Mearsheimer, John J. 2003. *The Tragedy of Great Power Politics*. New York: W.W. Norton.
Miliband, Ralph. 1969. *The State in Capitalist Society*. Oxford: Oxford University Press.
Mills, C. Wright. [1956] 2000. *The Power Elite*. New York: Oxford University Press.
Mitchell, Timothy. 1991. "The Limits of the State: Beyond Statist Approaches and Their Critics." *American Political Science Review* 85 (1): 77–96.
Morgenthau, Hans J. 1948. *Politics among Nations: The Struggle for Power and Peace*. New York: Alfred A Knof.
Mosca, Gaetano. 1939. *The Ruling Class*. New York: McGraw-Hill.
Namier, Lewis. 1964. *1848: The Revolution of the Intellectuals*. New York: Anchor Books.
Nordlinger, Eric A. 1977. *Soldiers in Politics: Military Coups and Governments*. Englewood Cliff, NJ: Prentice Hall.
Offe, C. and V. Ronge. 1982. "Theses on the Theory of the State." In *Classes, Power and Conflict*, edited by Anthony Giddens and David Held, pp. 249–56. London: Macmillan.
Pareto, Vilfredo. 1968. *The Rise and Fall of Elites: An Application of Theoretical Sociology*. New York: Transaction.
Perlmutter, Amos. 1974. *Egypt: The Praetorian State*. New York: Transaction.
Pierson, Paul. 2003. "Big, Slow-Moving, and Invisible: Macrosocial Processes in the Study of Comparative Politics." In *Comparative Historical Analysis in the Social*

Sciences, edited by James Mahoney and Dietrich Rueschemeyer, pp. 177–207. Cambridge, UK: Cambridge University Press.

Poggi, Gianfranco. 2001. *Forms of Power*. Cambridge, UK: Polity Press.

Poulantzas, Nicos. 1973. *Political Power and Social Classes*. London: New Left Books.

Russell, Bertrand. [1938] 2004. *Power*. London: Routledge.

Salamé, Ghassan (ed.). 1994. *Democracy Without Democrats? The Renewal of Politics in the Muslim World*. London: I.B. Tauris.

Skocpol, Theda. 1979. *States and Social Revolution: A Comparative Analysis of France, Russia, and China*. New York: Cambridge University Press.

Skocpol, Theda. 1984a. "Emerging Agendas and Recurrent Strategies in Historical Sociology." In *Vision and Division in Historical Sociology*, edited by Theda Skocpol, pp. 356–91. New York: Cambridge University Press.

Skocpol, Theda. 1984b. "Sociology's Historical Imagination." In *Vision and Division in Historical Sociology*, edited by Theda Skocpol, pp. 1–21. New York: Cambridge University Press.

Skocpol, Theda. 1985. "Bringing the State Back In: Strategies of Analysis in Current Research." In *Bringing the State Back In*, edited by Peter Evans, Dietrich Rueschemeyer, and Theda Skocpol, pp. 3–43. Cambridge, UK: Cambridge University Press.

Skocpol, Theda. 2003. "Doubly Engaged Social Science: The Promise of Comparative Historical Analysis." In *Comparative Historical Analysis in the Social Sciences*, edited by James Mahoney and Dietrich Rueschemeyer, pp. 407–28. Cambridge, UK: Cambridge University Press.

Stepan, Alfred. 1988. *Rethinking Military Politics: Brazil and the Southern Cone*. Princeton, NJ: Princeton University Press.

Swartz, David. 2013. *Symbolic Power, Politics, and Intellectuals: The Political Sociology of Pierre Bourdieu*. Chicago: University of Chicago Press.

Therborn, Göran. 1982. "What Does the Ruling Class Do When It Rules?" In *Classes, Power and Conflict*, edited by Anthony Giddens and David Held, pp. 224–48. London: Macmillan.

Thelen, Kathleen. 2003. "How Institutions Evolve: Insights from Comparative Historical Analysis." In *Comparative Historical Analysis in the Social Sciences*, edited by James Mahoney and Dietrich Rueschemeyer, pp. 208–40. Cambridge, UK: Cambridge University Press.

Tilly, Charles. 1982. *Big Structures, Large Processes, Huge Comparisons*. New York: Russell Sage Foundation.

Tilly, Charles. 1992. *Coercion, Capital, and the European State, AD 990–1990*. Oxford: Blackwell.

Tilly, Charles. 1993. *European Revolutions*. Cambridge: Blackwell

Trotsky, Leon. 2007. *My Life: An Attempt at Autobiography*. New York: Dover.

Wacquant, Loïc. 2005. *Pierre Bourdieu and Democratic Politics: The Mystery of Ministry*. Cambridge, UK: Polity Press.

Wagner, R. Harrison. 2007. *War and the State: The Theory of International Politics*. Ann Arbor: University of Michigan Press.

Walt, Stephen. 1987. *The Origins of Alliances*. Ithaca, NY: Cornell University.

Walt, Stephen. 1996. *Revolution and War*. Ithaca, NY: Cornell University.
Waltz, Kenneth. 1954. *Man, the State, and War: A Theoretical Analysis*. New York: Columbia University Press.
Vagts, Alfred. 1959. *A History of Militarism: Civilian and Military*. New York: Meridian Books.
Zegart, Amy B. 1999. *Flawed by Design: The Evolution of the CIA, JSC, and NSC*. Stanford, CA: Stanford University Press.

I | Iran

ROYALISM AND REVOLUTION

How could he then miscarry, having . . . so many trained soldiers . . . [and] ammunitions in places fortified?

—*Hobbes, Behemoth, 1681*

IRAN EARNED A DOUBLE entry in revolution literature: it was the first Islamic Revolution in the modern age, and the last "great revolution" of our time. Naturally, the Revolution was exhaustively analyzed. A little less natural was the early consensus regarding its causes. While rival theses and revisionist histories are still being advanced today to explain the great democratic and Communist revolutions, in the Iranian case scholars agree that two main factors, and a third complementary one, produced the Revolution.

First, Iran suffered from uneven development. Early works by Halliday (1979), Saikal (1980), Abrahamian (1982), later ones by Farrokh (1991) and Milani (1994), and most recently Martin (2007) and Milani (2011b) underscored middle-class frustration with the disjunction between economic and political progress—an explanation that mirrors De Tocqueville's analysis of revolution in France. As Martin (2007: 24) quipped, Iran was "an economic giant but a political dwarf." A rapidly modernizing society starved of democracy was bound to explode. Military and political experts on Iran endorse this view. General Robert E. Huyser, America's special envoy to Tehran during the Revolution, blamed the attempt to "impose twentieth-century industrialization on top of a medieval concept of rule" (1986: 294). U.S. National Security Advisor Zbigniew Brzezinski, who saw Iran turn Islamic on his watch, ascribed the revolt to the "fateful conflict between the effects of rapid socioeconomic modernization and the consequences of a highly traditional and excessively personal system of power" (1983: 366). Scholars particularly highlight how the Shah's direction of the economy, as opposed to the "depoliticized, abstract, and invisible hand of the market," made him a visible target for aggrieved Iranians (Parsa 1989: 17), and how the rupture in traditional norms drove the alienated masses into the hands of clerics (Arjomand 1988: 197).

This last point connects with the second widely held cause for the Revolution: that the Iranian masses were exceptionally imbued with ideological zeal. Pioneering works by Moaddel (1992), Dabashi (1993), and Algar (2001) brought to life the vigor of the Islamic ideology that animated the revolutionaries. Bayat (1998b) and Kurzman (2004) found unique mobilization mechanisms at work. Even the tough-minded Skocpol confessed that this incredible Revolution "forces me to deepen my understanding of the possible role of idea systems and cultural understandings in the shaping of political action" (1994: 244). At the center of all this laid the astonishing charisma of Ayatollah Khomeini. Munson (1988: 134) claimed that Khomeini's "aura enabled him to mobilize segments of Iranian (urban) society that had traditionally been apolitical and acquiescent." Algar (2001: 44) asserted more dramatically, "The historians will still be scratching their heads a hundred years from now wondering how it happened. But the Muslim when he sees this will see the kind of leadership provided by Imam Khomeini and the moral and spiritual dimensions that he gave to the Iranian revolution."

A more modest weight was assigned to geopolitics. Washington supposedly stood by while its political ally was overthrown (Keddie 1981). Although American passivity did not bring about revolution, its "non-action . . . opened the door to the full play of the internal balance of forces" (Foran 2005: 79). Of course, the testimonies of U.S. officials at the time are rife with examples of negligence and discord (Sullivan 1981; Brzezinski 1983; Sick 1985; Daugherty 2001; Precht 2004). The aggrieved Shah (Pahlavi 1980) and his loyal associates, such as chief of staff Abbas Gharabaghi (1999), actually believed Washington plotted against them.

What about repression? Few questioned the fact that Iran's repressive organs remained intact during the early phases of the revolt. Unlike its French and Russian counterparts, the Imperial Armed Forces had not been exhausted or demoralized by war, nor had they been subject to geopolitical pressures. Likewise, the notorious secret police (SAVAK) functioned just fine. On the eve of the revolt, the Iranian monarch had full control of "a thoroughly modernized army and a ruthless, omnipresent secret police force" (Skocpol 1994: 243).

So what happened? The universal answer seems to be that the angry masses swamped the coercive organs. The "military-security complex was not so much weak as overwhelmed. No system of repression is intended to deal with wholesale popular disobedience" (Kurzman 2004: 165). Some say it was ideology: "A non-violent revolution against a heavily armed dictatorship could not have taken place without remarkable cultures of opposition" (Foran 2005: 80; Axworthy 2014: 410). Or as proclaimed by a temporarily infatuated Foucault: "Ideas are more active, stronger, more resistant, more passionate than 'politicians' think," and to appreciate their power, one only needs to witness the "bursting outward of their forces" against repression (Foucault, in Afary and Anderson 2005: 3). And here, of course, Khomeini was essential in generating this unarmed torrent against a highly equipped military–security establishment (Harney 1999: 1; Algar 2001: 44). The more practically inclined point to the unprecedented level of mass participation. Repression fails when numerous groups combine their forces (Parsa 1989: 25; Ward 2009: 225). Either way, Iranians were awarded the badge of honor for exceptional bravery, as Skocpol conceded:

> [I]f ever there has been a revolution deliberately "made" by a mass-based social movement aiming to overthrow the old order, the Iranian Revolution ... surely is it. . . . An extraordinary series of mass urban demonstrations and strikes, ever growing in size and revolutionary fervor, even in the face of lethal military repression ... Their revolution did not just come; it was deliberately and coherently made. . . . It *did* matter than the Iranian crowds were willing to face the army again and again—accepting casualties much more persistently than European crowds have historically done—until sections of the military rank-and-file began to hesitate or balk at shooting into the crowds. (1994: 242, 249)

At the risk of oversimplifying their differences, Iranian Revolution scholars apparently agreed that the regime contradicted itself by preserving authoritarianism next to socioeconomic modernization, and that ideological zeal unleashed an irrepressible force. By contrast, I demonstrate that the Iranian regime was consistent with the model it had adopted. By replacing the Qajar monarchy with that of the Pahlavis, rather than declaring a republic, the 1921 coup placed Iran on a different trajectory than that of the new regimes in Turkey and Egypt. The regime evolved into an absolutist monarchy, and the court's micromanagement of the military and security made them partly unwilling and largely incapable of repressing the revolt.

So while it does matter that Iranians took to the street and risked their lives, they could not have succeeded had the regime not been vulnerable because of the relative weakness of its coercive apparatus. Explaining the Revolution therefore demands examining intraregime tensions from its creation to overthrow to reveal how political dominance caused repression to fail.

1 | A One-Man Coup

FEBRUARY 1921

Colonel Reza Khan's seizure of power in 1921 was hardly a military coup, considering that Iran had no military. The armed retainers, tribal levies, and foreign-controlled militias that existed back then were too frail and fragmented to orchestrate a coup. Regime change was prompted by British desire to place a strongman at the helm after Russia embraced Bolshevism. The so-called coup in 1921 was therefore little more than a one-man show. This chapter traces the formation of the Pahlavi regime during its first two decades—that is until Reza Shah's house of cards collapsed with the 1941 Allied invasion.

Slipping Off the Road to Republic

The Constitutional Revolution of 1906 and the ensuing civil war weakened the century-old Qajar dynasty. British fear that Iran might descend to chaos gained urgency with the Communist threat to the north. A strong man was needed to hold the country together. The best candidate was a Cossack Division colonel named Reza Khan. In his son's hagiographic account, Colonel Reza was exceptionally revered: "My father was the stuff of legends" (Pahlavi 1980: 49).[1] In truth, the 40-year-old giant was an obscure figure, an illiterate descendent of Turkish-speaking peasants (Abrahamian 1982: 117). Enlisting at the age of 14, his military record was quite unassuming, little more than petty raids against bandits. He did, however, gain some notoriety in 1918 for helping the British secure the Russian-supervised Cossack Division after conspiring to replace his commander, Colonel

Clergi, a Kerensky appointee, with his deputy, the White Russian Colonel Starroselsky.[2] He was promoted to brigadier general and given a regimental command, but soon disappointed his superiors and lost both. Yet he retained the favor of the British, who controlled Iran's southern oil-rich regions (Ward 2009: 82, 127; Cronin 2010: 15).

At the instigation of General Edmund Ironside, commander of the British forces in Persia, and with British arms and funds, Reza Khan marched on the capital with 3,000 Cossacks from the Qazvin garrison in February 1921. As instructed, he reassured the Qajar sovereign Ahmed Shah that this was not a coup, but an attempt to fortify the dynasty against Russian aggression. He then convinced the shah to form a government under the pro-British journalist Sayyid Ziya al-Din Tabatabai (Abrahamian 1982: 117–18). Reza's role was supposed to end here, especially after the cabinet appointed a gendarmerie officer as war minister. But the ambitious colonel was determined not to return to obscurity. He incited the Cossacks against the war minister, forcing the latter's resignation in April 1921, and taking up the post himself. He then turned the Qajar shah against his prime minister, ensuring his replacement in May with the weak Qavam as-Saltaneh. By the end of 1923, the confident war minister had persuaded his sovereign to take an extended vacation in Europe. And in a couple of years, Reza Khan managed through his divide-and-rule tactics, nationalistic posture, and modernization agenda to gain the support of parliamentarians, clerics, intellectuals, and officers. In December 1925, the Majles (Iranian Parliament) replaced the Qajar dynasty with the Pahlavi (Keddie 1981: 88–91).

The important thing to note here is that Reza Khan's rise to power depended less on coercion (by the modest military, or the even more modest police) than on mobilizing political support. The widespread belief that the Qajar dynasty was beyond reform certainly helped, but equally important was how he convincingly reinvented himself as a modern state-builder (Cronin 2010: 19–20). In a ceremony held in April 1926, Reza Khan, imitating his hero Napoleon, placed the crown on his own head. He now became Reza Shah.

But why did Reza choose to reproduce monarchism rather than declare a republic like other twentieth-century modernizers? He himself claimed it was to appease the clergy. Atatürk's radical secularism in Turkey gave republicanism a bad name. So after consulting clerics in the shrine-city of Qom in March 1924, he abandoned his republican ambitions (Rahnema 2000: 2). Others point to geopolitics. Besides Turkey, republics only spread in the region after the Second World War. In the 1920s, monarchism was the default option (Heikal 1981: 31). Reza also knew from the European examples he so admired that monarchs could be great modernizers, and made an extensive visit to

Turkey in 1934 to copy some of their modernization programs minus republicanism (Marashi 2003). Still, one cannot overlook Reza's personal insecurity. He was after all "a figure of marginal significance, rescued from obscurity only by immediate British strategic needs ... invisible in Iranian political and military life. . . . The blankness of [his] early life contrasts strikingly with the biographies of other nationalist officers of the period" (Cronin 2010: 14). A crown over his head went a long way toward boosting his insipid persona.

But however we justify his decision to scrap republicanism, the insignificance of the military was crucial. Even if Atatürk or Nasser wanted to become monarchs, their armies would not have accepted crowning one of their own, and becoming his obedient subjects. The weakness of the Iranian army, and the fact that Reza owed it little (as symbolized by his self-coronation), allowed him more freedom than his Turkish and Egyptian counterparts. And embracing monarchism was vital to future regime development.

Although Reza Shah adopted the mantras of modernization from above (nationalism, centralization, secularism, state-planned economy, etc.), diverging from the Turkish and Egyptian paths had long-term implications. While the political apparatus in Turkey and Egypt crystallized into a ruling party, the court represented the seat of political power in Iran. And while Atatürk and Nasser sought to legitimize their actions through ideological manifestos (such as the Six Arrows of Kemalism or Nasser's National Charter), Reza Shah, as king, had little need for ideological platforms beside the ethos of Persia's ancient glory.[3]

A more telling difference was socioeconomic. Because Atatürk and Nasser championed industry, the former tried (with limited success) to undermine the landed class, and the latter replaced large landlords with middling ones. Reza Shah, by contrast, not only strengthened landlords, but also joined them. During his decade-and-a-half in power, he went from being the son of a small landowner to becoming the country's largest landlord, with 2,000 villages (over 3 million acres) of the most fertile estates (an estimated 15 percent of Iran's arable land) and employing 235,800 peasants (Graham 1978: 55). This fortune was acquired through grants by those eager to attain royal favor, and confiscation of the land of those who fell into disfavor. Again, his humble origins show: his "mania" for acquiring land betrays "a typical peasant land hunger, albeit on a scale made possible by his own meteoric political rise" (Cronin 2010: 4). To further entrench himself with the landed aristocracy, Reza married a Qajar princess, adorned his court with noblemen, and placed the throne at the top of an extended patronage network (Abrahamian 1982: 137, 149). His promotion of landlordism kept half of Iran's cultivated land in the hands of large landowners, while 98 percent of the rural population remained landless. And regardless of his modernization rhetoric, when he was deposed, 90 percent of the workforce was still employed in agriculture; industry employed a mere 50,000 workers; and public money was directed toward Western imports (Keddie 1981: 101–03, 127; Parsa 1989: 36).

With no interest in fundamental socioeconomic reform, Reza Shah's modernization mostly extended state control over Iran's unruly provinces through 14,000 miles of new roads, and a German-built 808-mile-long Trans-Iranian Railroad from the Persian Gulf to the Caspian Sea (Ward 2009: 134). But even his attempt to increase state capacity was limited by the difficulty of extracting revenue from a landlord-based agricultural economy. And oil revenues at the time provided a meager 10 percent of state income (Keddie 1981: 102).

In the end, Reza Shah's abandonment of republicanism for the Peacock Throne "fundamentally alerted the trajectory of Iran's political development" (Cronin 2010: 21). Now, the court of an absolutist monarch occupied the center of power, and a constellation of great landlords formed its political base. But where did the military stand in this traditional structure?

The First Imperial Army

The Imperial Armed Forces was the sacred cow that consumed the largest share of the state's budget under both Pahlavi monarchs, yet did little to protect its paymasters. It was not politically disloyal, but plagued with structural weakness. To appreciate this weakness, we need to take a long view. Unlike the Turkish military, which ruled a sprawling empire until the Great War, and Egypt, which sent armies to the Levant, Arabia, sub-Saharan Africa, and Crete, before being halted at the gates of Constantinople by an alliance of European powers in 1840, Iran at the turn of twentieth century had no military. Qajar shahs relied instead on political survival tactics: fostering factional divisions, bribing tribal chiefs, holding hostages from noble families as court "guests," and so on (Ward 2009: 82).

Iran's armed forces consisted of separate militias (Cossack Brigade, gendarmerie, South Persia Rifles) alongside a humble regular force. Cossacks were initially royal bodyguards. During his 1878 visit to Russia, Nasser al-Din Shah was so impressed by the Cossacks that he asked his host, Tsar Alexander II, to provide him with some. The following year, Russians (under Lieutenant General Domantovich) built the Shah's Praetorian Guard. It was quite small, with only 700 officers and 3,000 troops in 1921. It was officered by Russians, with only 10 percent seasonal-serving Persian soldiers. And its record was mixed. Although it failed to prevent Nasser al-Din Shah's assassination in 1896, it secured the enthronement of his successor, Muzaffar al-Din. And although it failed again in preempting the riots that culminated into the 1906 Constitutional Revolution, it aided a Russian-backed royal coup in 1908, which leveled the parliament building over the head of deputies, and triggered a three-year civil war. The gendarmerie was notably different. Created in 1911 by Americans (Persia's Treasurer-General W. Morgan Shuster and Colonel J. N. Merrill) for tax-collecting purposes, it was led by nationalist officers from prominent families. With the help of Swedish instructors, it expanded its mandate to policing the countryside, which was highly appreciated by peasants, merchants, and constitutional activists. But although it was larger than the Cossacks, with 700 officers and 9,300 soldiers in 1921, it was much more dispersed. A third foreign-created unit was the 2,000-men South Persia Rifles, recruited by British General Percy Sykes in 1915 and commanded by Indians to guard oilfields. It was dismantled shortly after the Great War. In addition, Persia had, in 1921, 13,000 infantrymen scattered across the country; 5,000 artillerymen with a handful of field guns; and tribal levies serving as cavalry. Officers received no training, soldiers rarely fired a rifle, and both moonlighted as farmers and tradesmen (Ward 2009: 85–118; Cronin 1997). It was a regular force "totally incapable of fighting . . . [which] existed mostly on paper" (Ward 2009: 108).

So during the 1921 coup, Iran had only two functioning militias. Because of the gendarmerie's nationalist outlook, the British preferred the promonarchy Cossacks in their bid to impose order. But there was a backlash when Reza Khan as war minister attempted to incorporate the gendarmes into a national army. In April 1921 Colonel Muhammad Taqi Khan Pasyan, gendarmerie commander of Khorasan, formed a revolutionary government in the city of Mashhad; 4,000 revolutionaries soon joined his 200 gendarmes; and they sent the corrupt governor of Khorasan, Qavam al-Saltanah, to the capital in chains. Pasyan was everything Reza was not. The charismatic arch-republican belonged to a noble Persian family, had received a European education, and served bravely during the Great War. Reza, however, did not yield. He defiantly named Qavam al-Saltanah prime minister, and—realizing he had no military force to rely on—incited tribal chiefs and landlords against the insurrectionaries. With hastily organized tribal and peasant levies, he crushed the six-month revolution and killed Pasyan. That December gendarmes and Cossacks merged under Army Order Number One. But instead of containing their antagonism, this forced fusion exacerbated it further, leading to the army's dissolution twenty years later (Ward

2009: 130–32; Cronin 2010: 44, 97–100). The important thing to note here is that unlike Atatürk, who relied on the army to brave early challenges, and Nasser, who immediately erected a strong security apparatus to counter his enemies, Reza Khan had no reliable military or security institutions, and was forced to make due with traditional court intrigues.[4]

He tried to remedy this serious deficiency: persuading Parliament to finance a proper army; establishing a military college and a higher military council; and organizing the army into five divisions, with each stationed in a major city. He introduced conscription in 1924, with two-year compulsory service and two-and-a-half-decade reservist status. He increased the defense budget fivefold between 1926 and 1941 (swallowing half the state's budget), and expanded the army to 2,100 officers and 126,000 soldiers (Ward 2009: 132–45; Cronin 2010). He created an air force in 1924, a navy in 1932, and an army bank (Bank Sepah). And he sent officers for training to Germany, France, and Russia—though never Britain (Halliday 1979: 66).

Nonetheless, these seemingly great accomplishments paled in reality. Iran's agricultural economy could hardly sustain a modern military. Equipment was limited. The armored corps purchased 100 (mostly Czech) light and medium tanks, but cavalry remained the real strike force; the 1,000 sailors of the navy operated six vessels; and the 300 poorly trained pilots operated 245 obsolete British biplanes and 10 U.S. Hawk fighters—they were so unqualified that they "lost aircraft almost as quickly as new ones were being purchased" (Ward 2009: 142–54; Cronin 2003).

More important, the insecure Shah submitted the military to mediocre officers who owed everything to royal favor, including his 20-year-old heir, Muhammad Reza, who was appointed Special Inspector of the Armed Forces. Qualified aristocrats were celebrated in court but denied senior army commissions. As in Europe, the divorce between the military and the economically dominant class, while presumably enhancing professionalism, weakened the bond between the coercive organs and the ruling class (Halliday 1979: 67; Abrahamian 1982: 136). Adding insult to injury, the Shah's bigotry fostered an "atmosphere of arbitrary terror" within the ranks (Cronin 2003: 44). In 1929 alone, four generals were imprisoned for failing to curb tribal revolts, among them the commander of the southern army division and his chief of staff; and in 1933 the war minister himself was arrested. Charges of political disloyalty resulted in dozens of detentions, including the commander of the central army division, and the Shah's own aide-de-camp (Ward 2009: 150; Cronin 2010: 195). So behind the façade of modernization, the military remained basically "a parade-ground army, largely untried in battle and led by complacent and corrupt officers" (Ward

2009: 145). It was "militarily ineffective, structurally weak, deeply politicized, and expensive beyond the capacity of the state" (Cronin 2003: 37). Its collapse in 1941 was not entirely surprising.

The Allies rightly suspected Reza Shah of harboring Nazi sympathies, and could not risk losing Iran as a corridor to Russia. Refusing an ultimatum to support war against Germany, the defiant Shah mobilized his troops and delivered a rousing speech to defend the homeland. But the army melted once the British and Soviets invaded on August 25. The country was subdued in four days. When a furious Shah called for a meeting of his high command, only the war minister, chief of staff, and two generals showed up. Always a violent man, Reza cursed his generals, struck them with his cane, and ordered court-martials all-around. But it was too late (Ward 2009: 159–69). He abdicated on September 16, 1941, and died in exile in South Africa in July 1944. The military he left behind was as much of a wreck as the one he had inherited from the Qajars. In contrast to the militaries that rallied around Atatürk and Nasser to repel foreign aggression, the Iranian army, two decades after Reza took control, proved utterly useless.

Geopolitics: From Complacency to Defiance

After decades of coexistence between British and Russian spheres of influence in southern and northern Persia, respectively, the Bolshevik Revolution propelled Britain to tighten its grip on Tehran. General Ironside groomed Reza Khan as "an antidote to chaos" (Katouzian 2004: 2). But the ambitious colonel displayed early signs of independence, eventually breaking with London over its support for southern tribes to secure the oilfields regardless of how this undermined his centralization efforts (Cronin 2010: 194). Reza lobbied Parliament to reject an Anglo-Persian treaty in 1919; dismissed A. C. Millspaugh, the American administer of Persian finance; abrogated legal capitulations to foreigners and eliminated non-oil economic concessions; founded a national bank (Bank-e Melli) to counter the British-run Imperial Bank; nationalized the European-managed customs and telegraph offices; closed down missionary schools; and, in 1932, he boldly cancelled the 1901 D'Acry Oil Concession. Although a year later he was forced by British gunboat diplomacy to sign another slightly less unfavorable agreement (increasing Iran annual profit share from 16 percent to 20 percent), Reza demonstrated striking resolve in defending his country's interests (Abrahamian 1982: 118, 143–44).

The Shah attempted to check Britain's influence by forging a regional power bloc with Turkey, Iraq, and Afghanistan. Considering this insufficient, he turned to Germany. As the clouds of war gathered, Iran received about 1,000 German experts, and Berlin secured 41 percent of Iran's foreign trade. The Nuremberg Racial Laws acknowledged Iranians as pure Aryans, thus removing the threat of Nazi invasion, and henceforth the Shah began referring to Persia as Iran (Saikal 1980: 23–24). Reza's last acts of defiance were to reject an Allied request to use Iran as a supply route and to declare neutrality (Saikal 1980: 25).

The Shah's abdication ended the first chapter of the Pahlavi regime. Most of his achievements expired with him. The tribes regained their independence, and government control was again limited to Tehran; the economy remained as backward as ever; and the military was effectively dismantled. In the words of his 22-year-old heir: "We have returned in 1941 to the same position Iran was at in 1920" (Pahlavi 1980: 33). The only institution left was the monarchy, and the young shah was determined to preserve it. But he first had to weather a greater storm than the one that swept his father out. And this time the challenge came from within.

Notes

1. One amusing legend went as follows: "While up north with his soldiers fighting yet another gang of bandits, he swung onto his white horse and galloped toward enemy lines. Frightened at first by the sudden apparition of a giant on his white steed, the bandits were too stunned to react. Then, when they opened fire, they shot at random without taking careful aim. As a result, my father was able to spur his horse through the barrage unharmed" (Pahlavi 1980: 50).

2. The British first approached his superior, the St. Cyr–educated commander Sardar Homayun, but when he refused to take part in the plot, they turned to his second-in-command, "a man of humble background who lacked the prestige and military education of his superior" (Arjomand 1988: 60).

3. The name "Pahlavi" referred to the language of the Parthians who fought memorable battles against Rome.

4. A less critical challenge confronted Reza in January 1922, when Major Abulqasim Lahuti declared a Communist regime in Tabriz, placing power in the hands of a workers and soldiers' council. But his eleven-day mutiny was easily crushed (Cronin 2010: 101; Arjomand 1988: 61).

2 A Coup De Théâtre

AUGUST 1953

THE CONVENTIONAL ACCOUNT OF THE downfall of Prime Minister Muhammad Mosaddeq centers on the foreign-backed coup of August 1953. The belief that it was the military that saved the regime led many to expect a similar intervention in 1979. But as this chapter demonstrates, it was political divisions that sealed the prime minister's fate. Washington and London did support anti-Mosaddeq forces, and emboldened the Shah to dismiss him. Yet the military's part was remarkably insignificant in this so-called coup. Even at its weakest point, the court remained the most powerful state institution.

Mosaddeq's Few Triumphs and Fatal Blunders

In his first decade as ruler, Muhammad Reza Shah was described by an occasional visitor as a "thoroughly demoralized young man . . . shocked by what had happened to his father, appalled by the responsibilities that had been thrust upon him, bewildered by all the new faces and problems surrounding him, and conscious that he had no exceptional qualities with which to meet the challenge" (Heikal 1981: 39). Driven by insecurity, he obstructed the rise of a strong chief executive. Between 1941 and 1953, thirty-one cabinets governed Iran in rapid succession, with an average lifespan of six months (Katouzian 2004: 5). In the early 1950s, however, Parliament demanded a strong government to nationalize Iranian oil.

The price of oil had increased threefold since the Anglo-Iranian Oil Company (AIOC) monopoly agreement of 1933. The fact that AIOC paid more taxes to London than royalties to Tehran was simply infuriating. Crucially, the 50-50 percent profit-sharing formula introduced by the 1950 American-Saudi deal underscored British intransigence. And the pulse of the street was reflected in the assassination of Prime Minister Ali Razmara in March 1951 for being soft on AIOC. The following month, a coalition of deputies, calling itself the National Front, issued the Nationalization Law and nominated its spokesman, Mosaddeq, as prime minister—decisions the Shah could only ratify (Keddie 1981: 133). The new premier then went on to promise euphoric crowds, "With the oil revenues we could meet our entire budget and combat poverty, disease, and backwardness" (quoted in Saikal 1980: 39).

Evidently, Mosaddeq had not thought this through. Unlike the Suez Canal, which Nasser successfully nationalized, there were alternatives to Iranian oil. Leading Western monopolists (the amiably dubbed Seven Sisters) simply doubled Arab oil production and boycotted Tehran, reducing the latter output from 241.4 million to 10.6 million barrels (Saikal 1980: 41). Mosaddeq pleaded with Americans, only to receive a presidential note, dated June 29, stating: "It would not be fair to American taxpayers for the United States Government to extend any considerable amount of economic aid to Iran" (Eisenhower 1963: 161).[1] The stifling embargo was the first nail in Mosaddeq's tomb.

Still, the prime minister retained popular support, as demonstrated by the *siy'e tyr* uprising. On July 16, 1952, he resigned over the Shah's insistence on naming the war minister. On July 21 members of Parliament demonstrated outside the royal palace to have him reinstated. Shops closed down, transport workers and public employees went on strike, and violence was in the air. A compromise was negotiated whereby Mosaddeq would supervise the War Ministry aided by three generals chosen by the monarch. A triumphant Mosaddeq then removed royalists from his cabinet and pressured the Shah to exile conspirators from his court, including his sister Princess Ashraf (Abrahamian 1982: 272; Katouzian 2004: 10).

The tide soon turned, however. The following winter, Mosaddeq asked the Shah to surrender Crown lands to the state, and issued two agricultural reform measures: requiring 20 percent of the crop of absentee landlords to remain in their villages to benefit peasants, and abolishing free services by agricultural workers. Rumors that Mosaddeq was being advised by the Communist Hezb-e Tudeh-e Iran aggravated his traditional backers. Landowners, which constituted the largest bloc in Parliament, resented his flirtation with the lower classes. Tribal magnates cherished the Shah, especially now that the queen (Soraya) hailed from one of their biggest tribes (the Bakhtiaris). These notables had endorsed Mosaddeq in order to share power with the monarch, not to create an equal society that would rob them of wealth and privilege. Needless to say, peasants and tribesmen took their cue from their superiors. Bazaar merchants were equally hostile to Communism, which threatened their export–import business. And the clergy believed that monarchy was the pillar of Islamic rule, and saw nothing in Communism beyond atheism. The militant Feda'iyan-e Islam, which fought for an Islamic state, was even more agitated. Its radicals had accepted Mosaddeq because they blamed the Pahalvis for Iran's creeping secularization, but when he rebuffed their call to prohibit alcohol and impose the veil, they joined his growing list of enemies (Parsa 1989: 42; Azimi 2004: 80; Katouzian 2004: 14; Bayandor 2010: 75–77).

What Mosaddeq failed to understand was that his supporters wanted oil nationalization to bring prosperity; that they wanted the monarchy circumscribed not abolished; and that, despite their differences, they were universally anti-Communist. When the Shah signaled his intention to travel on vacation, Ayatollah Kashani, prominent leader of the then disintegrating National Front and its speaker of Parliament, issued a rabble-rousing declaration:

> People, be warned! Treacherous decisions have resulted in the decision of our beloved and democratic shah to leave the country. . . . You should realize that if the shah goes, whatever we have will go with him. Rise up and stop him, and make him change his mind. . . . [O]ur existence and independence depend on the very person of His Majesty Mohammed Reza Shah Pahlavi, and no one else. (Katouzian 1999: 172)

And on February 28 Mosaddeq's previous parliamentary allies joined a royalist crowd outside the Winter Palace, chanting pro-monarchy slogans and stoning Mosaddeq's motorcade. This so-called *noh'e esfand* uprising was a dress rehearsal for what lay ahead.

Mosaddeq had two options: either to reconcile himself with the traditional elite, or declare a republic and throw his lot with the Communist Tudeh, which had 25,000 disciplined members (Parsa 1989: 39). Yet he felt it was too late for reconciliation, and that he was fundamentally unprepared for revolution. The 70-year-old aristocrat, who had been a parliamentarian since 1924 and served as finance and foreign minister, was essentially a conservative establishment figure, despite his constitutional and nationalistic positions. American Foreign Secretary Dean Acheson pinned him down as "a rich, reactionary, and feudal-minded Persian" (Acheson 1969: 504). In his own memoirs, Mosaddeq confessed: "I was opposed not only to democratic, but to all kinds of republics, because a change of regime would not make for a nation's progress, and unless a nation is enlightened and has able statesmen, its affairs would be run as in this country." He then proudly added: "I issued strict orders for anyone who advocated a republic to be brought to the law" (1988: 352–53).

Naturally, Tudeh leaders suspected that the prime minister's positions were "determined by his class origins and interests," and that he would eventually substitute British for American hegemony (Azimi 2004: 69). His refusal to renew Moscow's fishing concessions in February 1953 at the same time that he was luring American investors confirmed this view (Katouzian 2004: 19). Like nationalist leaders of the time, he was using the Communist bogeyman to secure American support for reform—a tactic that backfired when Washington felt he could no longer rein in Communists (Bayandor 2010: 160). Indeed, when Mosaddeq turned down Tudeh's request to terminate oil negotiations and abolish the monarchy, the party organized a general strike (Azimi 2004: 70). Future Iranian President Hashemi Rafsanjani remembers how Tudeh's actions convinced religious activists (like himself) that Mosaddeq was losing the country to Communism (Rafsanjani 2005: 39).

Caught between the conservative rock and the radical hard place, Mosaddeq made the worst possible choice: he dissolved Parliament. His aim was to disempower his old allies, whom he rightly suspected of conspiring against him. But now he was trampling over the constitutional legitimacy he had always championed because only the Shah could dissolve Parliament. He tried to circumvent this by pressuring enough deputies to resign to prevent a quorum, but when he failed, he proceeded anyway, declaring: "A Majles that is unwilling to carry out the goals of the people in their anti-imperialist struggles must be eliminated" (Parsa 1989: 43). Now, the pendulum of constitutional legitimacy swung back to the Shah and his traditional supporters (landlords, tribal chiefs, and clerics). The enemy of royal autocracy was becoming a petty dictator. And although both left and right vowed to bring him down, it was the latter that succeeded because of Western support.

On August 3, 1953, the night Mosaddeq scheduled a face-saving referendum to endorse his dissolution of Parliament, the Shah met with a CIA representative to consider his options. Without Parliament, Mosaddeq could only be dismissed by royal decree. In issuing this decree, on August 13, the Shah was acting within his legal boundaries—though the still timid monarch preferred to travel the day it was delivered to the prime minister. Tudeh promptly took to the streets, calling for the eradication of monarchism, landlordism, tribalism, and clericalism. On August 17 party militants occupied municipal buildings hoisting red flags, statues of the Shah and his father were destroyed, and mosques were desecrated.[2] To distance himself from what he saw as unbridled radicalism, the prime minister committed his final misstep, on August 18, by banning rallies and arresting 600 Communists. So during the showdown, the following morning, the only people who could have come to his aid were off the street. And even though Tudeh's Central Committee member (and future Secretary-General) Noureddin Kianouri begged him to unleash Communists against their common enemy, it was too late (Bayandor 2010: 93–111).

On the morning of August 19, 3,000 people gathered around the bazaar. It included thugs (*zur-khaneh*) like gym owner Shaaban-bi-mokh Ja'fari, renowned hoodlum Al-Tayyeb Haj Reza'i, and several agents provocateurs. Bakhtiari tribesmen (longtime allies of the British and now the monarch's in-laws) poured into the capital to swell their ranks. The angry mob marched with clubs and knives toward Mosaddeq's residence. On their way, they seized the Telegraph and Telephone Office and Tehran Radio, and freed the Imperial Guard chief (Colonel Ne'matollah Nasiri), whom Mosaddeq had detained a couple of nights before when he delivered the royal dismissal. Military and police were paralyzed, since the now deposed prime minister claimed he was still in charge. No more than four Sherman tanks (those stationed outside the royal palace) joined the gang that sieged Mosaddeq's house. The defeated prime minister raised the white flag at 5 P.M. and eventually turned himself in. During the next few months, the victorious Shah arrested over 4,000 activists (mostly Communists), and cashiered 400 officers and 3,000 civil servants (De Bellaigue 2004: 173; Gasiorowski 2004: 253–57; Bayandor 2010: 104–12).

Two things are obvious here. First, it was a civilian uprising, triggered by political battles within the National Front, that overthrew Mosaddeq. Officers lent symbolic support—mostly through their understandable passivity in this confusing situation. Second, although rioters took the law into their own hands, they were ultimately fulfilling a perfectly legal royal edict; Mosaddeq's defiance of Parliament, the constitution, and the king made him an outlaw. In that sense, the whole episode was hardly a coup. So how did officers and foreign spies get involved?

In the Presence of Absence: The Officers of 1953

Reza Shah's abdication in 1941 had left the military in disarray. Several political factions competed for its loyalty. The new Shah showered officers with promotions (producing twice as many generals and colonels in his first twenty months than his father had done in twenty years), and packed the War Ministry with royalists (Ward 2009: 170). Tudeh created a 700-strong Communist bloc within the army,[3] and nationalist cells were organized under General Mahmoud Afshartus, Mosaddeq's future police chief (Behrooz 2000: 13). Weak and divided, the military was powerless against Mosaddeq's decision to reduce the defense budget by 15 percent, purge 136 officers (including 15 generals), transfer 15,000 soldiers to the gendarmerie, investigate corrupt officers, and declare that Iran would henceforth purchase only defensive weapons (Abrahamian 1982: 273; Cronin 2010: 262).[4]

The Shah was, in fact, so sure that the military obeyed Mosaddeq that he snubbed his sister's advice to seek Western help through U.S. General H. Norman Schwarzkopf (father of the famous commander of the 1991 Gulf War). Even when he finally met the CIA's Kermit Roosevelt in a car parked outside his palace in pitch darkness, the Shah was so worried that Roosevelt had to reassure him: "Your Majesty ... You were right to suspect that it would be dangerous to talk to Princess Ashraf or General Schwarzkopf in the palace, or even perhaps near any tree in your garden; [but] this isn't even your car" (Roosevelt 1979: 146–47; 162). Muhammad Reza's doubts were confirmed on the night of August 16 when Chief of Staff General Taqi Riahi detained the head of the Imperial Guard, Colonel Nassiri, because he delivered a royal dismissal to Mosaddeq. Worse still, the Shah had to return to Tehran, on August 22, with an Iraqi fighter escort, since he did not trust his own air force (Gasiorowski 2004: 256–57).

However, Mosaddeq's overthrow was considered a coup because the man who replaced him was a former general. So let us examine the career of his successor, General Fazlollah Zahedi. Born in 1893 to a relatively wealthy family, he was recruited to the Cossacks at the age of 13 by Colonel Reza Khan. When Reza ascended to the throne, he employed Zahedi in tribal pacification campaigns. His greatest feat was to capture Sheikh Ghazal, a British ally, after inviting him to a feast and intoxicating him. Zahedi then moved to the gendarmerie, but was so incompetent that Reza Shah had him arrested. After months in prison, he wormed his way back into royal favor, and was appointed police chief. Barely a year later, the monarch dismissed him for negligence, dramatically tearing away the stars from his uniform. A shamed Zahedi now lived as a civilian. He first opened a shoe store, and then worked for a car dealer. After much pleading, the king found him a minor administrative post. But during the Second World War, Zahedi begged for a provincial post and received command of the 9th Army in Isfahan. There, he was exposed to one of the most humiliating trials that could befall an officer:

suspected of pro-Nazi sympathies (like his monarch), Zahedi was kidnapped from his garrison by a singlehanded British agent (Fitzroy MacLean), and shipped to a British camp in Palestine for three years. In 1946, two years after he returned home, the new shah appointed him governor of Fars, then transferred him in 1949 to his former job as chief of police, and finally offered him an honorary position in the Senate. Hoping to prevent a National Front victory in the 1951 elections, he brought in Zahedi as interior minister to rig it. But with the usually incompetent Zahedi, the National Front won by a landslide. A grateful Mosaddeq kept him as interior minister, but he soon got into trouble again, shooting demonstrators (killing thirty and injuring dozens) who chanted anti-American slogans during the visit of U.S. envoy Averell Harriman. Both the Shah and Mosaddeq forced him into retirement in August 1951. After laying low for a couple of years, Zahedi tried his luck again with court, but the Shah rebuffed him. And when he was arrested on February 26, 1953, with other royalists, Mosaddeq thought him utterly harmless and let him go, at which point he went into hiding. And this is where the CIA found him (Kinzer 2003: 142–44; Milani 2008a: 496–500; Bayandor 2010: 83).

If anything, Zahedi's career demonstrates that his relationship to the military was at best tenuous. His only occupation in 1953 was that of president of the Retired Officers Club. But when Washington searched for someone to replace Mosaddeq, they hit on Zahedi's name—mainly upon the recommendation of his son Ardeshir, deputy administrator of the American aid program, and future ambassador to the United States (Rubin 1981: 84). And in return for his service, America was willing to pay $1 million in cash (Gasiorowski 2004: 257). With a former officer onboard, the CIA hoped to hatch a royalist coup. But it was not to be.

On July 21, 1953, CIA paramilitary expert George Carroll visited Tehran to assess officers' attitudes. He reported that the army had no qualms with the government, and that Zahedi had no reliable contacts—his friends occupied peripheral posts (transportation, border guards, etc.). There was also Colonel Teimur Bakhtiar, the queen's uncle, but his Kermanshah garrison was 525 kilometers west of Tehran, too far to intervene. And Colonel Nasiri's 700-strong Imperial Guard was minuscule. After meeting Zahedi, the CIA confirmed he had "no military assets," and that his network of retired officers is "inadequate for carrying out a coup" (Gasiorowski 2004: 241). Quoting from declassified documents:

> A run of the mill *coup* plan of a Latino variety . . . had been prepared. . . . It soon became clear to the planners that General Zahedi, by then retired from

the army for several years, had no significant allies, and none among the brigades. He had indicated that he could count on help from the Imperial Guard, while mentioning elements in the police and the Armed Customs Guard as well as some units from the Army Transportation branch. This was patently inadequate. (Bayandor 2010: 115–16)

This was old news to London, whose military attaché in Tehran had noted back in August 1952 that a coup was "unlikely to have much support in the army" (Azimi 2004: 76). Britain and America therefore realized the following: "MI6-CIA assets within the armed forces were too limited and, as such, incapable of assuring the military objectives" (Bayandor 2010: 86). As the operation's field leader admitted: Iranian officers cannot be relied on (Roosevelt 1979: 109).

Yet the search continued. Colonel Abbas Farzanegan, a CIA asset recruited while serving in Washington, was hastily sent to Tehran in July 1953 to find more officers for Zahedi. He called on three acquaintances: General Nader Batmanqelich, Colonel Hassan Akhavi, and Colonel Zand-Karimi. General Zahedi only met them on August 6, a few days before the operation (Gasiorowski 2004: 241–42; Bayandor 2010: 116). Alas, none of them played any role in the overthrow. Akhavi fell sick; Batmanqelich and Zand-Karimi were arrested three days prior; and Zahedi and Farzanegan hid in a CIA safe house three blocks away from the U.S. embassy (Gasiorowski 2004: 249; Bayandor 2010: 116).

The downward spiral began with the conspirators conditioning their support on a royal decree replacing Mosaddeq with Zahedi—thus divesting the whole operation of its "coup" status. When Colonel Nasiri delivered the edict to Mosaddeq at 1 A.M. on August 16, he was arrested for plotting a coup, though he barked back defensively: "Nonsense! You are the one who is guilty of dangerous action. I am simply carrying out the Shah's orders" (Roosevelt 1979: 175). He was right: the "real coup" was Mosaddeq's refusal to implement the "fully legal dismissal order signed by the sovereign" (Milani 2008a: 502). In a desperate effort, the CIA's men pleaded with forty officers for help, but they were harshly rebuffed. On the morning of August 17, operation leader Kermit Roosevelt received orders to evacuate (Gasiorowski 2004: 249–53; Bayandor 2010: 114).

With no military support, all bets were placed on the growing popular anger with Mosaddeq. CIA's hope was now limited to making sure their man (Zahedi) ended up on top. The wealthy Rashidian brothers hired thugs to kick off anti-Mosaddeq protests on August 19, and Roosevelt waited for their ranks to swell. By 4 P.M. he decided it was time to "collect the good general . . . [and] turn [him] loose to lead the crowd" (Roosevelt 1979: 178). Back at the CIA safe house, he "found the legal—about to become actual—Prime Minister of Iran sitting in what looked to me like his winter underwear. His uniform was draped over a chair beside him. . . . He rose immediately and started pulling on the uniform" (Roosevelt 1979: 193). While Zahedi was getting dressed, Roosevelt arranged his hero's entrance. Through the good offices of Deputy Police Chief Colonel Ziauddin Khalatbari (a police, not military officer) a tank was procured for Zahedi to be paraded on (Bayandor 2010: 111; Gasiorowski 2004: 255).

Finally, there is no better testament to how little influence Zahedi had in the army than what happened afterward. The new premier's first action was to telegram the Shah in Rome, begging him to return, though many friends advised him to keep the king waiting until he cultivated his own power base. Then, according to the Shah's wishes, the new cabinet was composed almost exclusively of civilians, and those officers who had cooperated with the CIA were transferred to the civilian sector. In March 1955 the Shah asked Zahedi to resign and leave Iran, and without much fuss, the ill-fated general packed his bags. He died in exile ten years later (Gasiorowski 2004: 257; Milani 2008a: 502–04). It was the court and its traditional allies that had brought down Mosaddeq, not a military cabal. And Zahedi knew it.

Operation Ajax: Pushing at an Open Door

Although the army had no role to speak of in the Mosaddeq affair,[9] British and American spies did. London could not accept Iran's oil nationalization: its postwar economy was shaky, and if it let this one slip, a wave of nationalist takeovers in its former colonies might follow. Besides, the Abadan refinery not only produced half of the Middle East's oil, but was also "the largest installation of its kind in the world. It was Britain's single largest overseas asset." Indeed, some Britons believed that Iran's oil was "rightly British oil because it had been discovered by the British, developed by British capital, and exploited through British skill and British ingenuity" (Louis 2004: 129).

Washington, on the contrary, had no qualms to start with. After the British had humiliated his father, the embittered Shah sought American support to rebuild his economy and army (Saikal 1980: 54). Millspaugh was recalled in 1942 (two decades after Reza Shah had dismissed him) and granted full control over Iranian finances (Keddie 1981: 115). Two U.S. military missions were set up, with the Imperial Armed Forces and the gendarmerie (Ward 2009: 186).[5] And after pressuring Moscow to evacuate Iran and desert its allies in Kurdistan and Azerbaijan, a grateful Shah signed a Mutual Defense Assistance Agreement with Washington (Halliday 1979: 91).

Americans naturally wanted a share of Iranian oil, but preventing a Communist government in Tehran was their first priority, especially after Ambassador Leland Morris warned in a dispatch that a pro-Soviet government will "end all possibility of an American oil concession in Iran ... [and threaten] our immensely rich oil holdings in Saudi Arabia, Bahrain, and Kuwait" (Heikal 1981: 45). An alarmed President Truman recorded in his diary, "If the Russians were to control Iran's oil, either directly or indirectly, the raw material balance of the world would undergo serious damage" (Truman 1956: 94–95). Yet Truman believed, after talks with Mosaddeq in October 1952, that nationalists could block a Communist takeover, and mediated, through his envoy Averell Harriman, between London and Tehran. CIA station chief in Tehran Roger Goiran agreed (Gasiorowski 2004: 229–31), and Defense Secretary Robert Lovett advised that Mosaddeq's departure would lead to the "absorption of Iran in the Soviet system" (Byrne 2004: 223). It helped that Mosaddeq himself was more pro-American than most regional politicians (Axworthy 2014: 49). So during their Paris meeting, on November 9, 1952, Secretary of State Dean Acheson relayed to his British counterpart that Mosaddeq was a partner, not an enemy. And in his memoirs, Acheson proudly relayed his attempt to sabotage the British "rule or ruin policy in Iran" (Acheson 1969: 602). A frustrated Anthony Eden recorded: "Our reading of the situation was different. I did not accept the argument that the only alternative to Musaddiq was communist rule" (Eden 1960: 200). So Truman sent special aide Paul Nitze to warn that if AIOC offered no concessions, the United States would bring in its own oil companies (Rubin 1981: 75).

Unfortunately, Mosaddeq's chance to curry American favor diminished with the appointment of Eisenhower's hawkish administration, with the Dulles brothers heading the State Department and the CIA; Frank Wisner as CIA director of operations; and former CIA Director General Walter Bedell Smith as undersecretary of state. What these Cold Warriors had in common was a fascination with covert operations. While Truman was not impressed with the CIA's record, Eisenhower saw black-ops as a cheap alternative to war (Byrne 2004: 223). Eisenhower's men also saw third world nationalism as a gate—not a barrier—to Communism (Rubin 1981: 56, 76).

This change of guard was only one of three changes that ended the possibility of a peaceful compromise. The second was Churchill's return to power in 1951. Labor Prime Minister Clement Attlee had vetoed plans to occupy Abadan (Operation Buccaneer), and rejected several MI6 schemes. Churchill, on the other hand, did not only champion secret operations, but had also been involved in securing Persian oil concessions during the Great War, and bragged about how he converted the Royal Navy from coal to oil without burdening the British taxpayer by relying on Middle East oil (Louis 2004: 133, 161–67). Worse still for Iran was Joseph Stalin's death in March 1953. Mosaddeq believed the bullish Soviet leader would deter Western powers from imposing their will (Mussaddiq 1988: 272). Indeed, Kermit Roosevelt noted that Stalin's death rendered "our hopes for a favorable climate" for intervention stronger than ever (Roosevelt 1979: 129).

With the geopolitical conditions set, the National Front riot against Mosaddeq, in February 1953, convinced London and Washington that he was losing control over his own camp. Eisenhower was finally ready to join Britain's long-simmering plot. MI6 had begun discussions with Kermit Roosevelt as early as November 1952 (Roosevelt 1979: 107). The following month Christopher Montague Woodhouse, the MI6 man in Tehran, and Sam Falle, the Foreign Office's oriental secretary at the embassy, presented their case in Washington (Gasiorowski 2004: 227). Knowing exactly which tune to play, they presented their plot as an attempt to block a Soviet march southward. As Woodhouse wrote, "Not wishing to be accused of trying to use the Americans to pull the British chestnuts out of the fire, I decided to emphasize the Communist threat to Iran rather than the need to recover control of the oil industry" (Kinzer 2003: 3–4).

At the time, there were two spy rings active in Tehran. The British managed the Rashidian brothers' network, which included parliamentarians, clergymen, courtiers, landlords, businessmen, journalists, and petty criminals. CIA's Donald Wilber, a Princeton-educated scholar of Islamic architecture who specialized in psychological warfare, ran another network, headed by journalists Ali Jalali and Faruq Kayvani. In May 1953 Wilber met MI6 operative Norman Darbyshire in Nicosia to coordinate their assets. Operation Ajax was drafted during a CIA–MI6 meeting in Beirut on June 13. It centered on destabilizing the country through propaganda and street agitation, and had no significant military component. Roosevelt was appointed field commander (Gasiorowski 2004: 232–37). The aim was "to provide a catalytic framework within which local political and social forces would be unleashed; the dynamics they generated would lead to [Mosaddeq's] downfall" (Bayandor 2010: 86–87). But when Mosaddeq dissolved Parliament, the hope to vote him out by his peers was destroyed, and Roosevelt had to secure a royal decree instead. And when the emissary who delivered the edict was arrested, the plan was simply aborted. Roosevelt, nonetheless, gave it another shot.

On August 16 he directed journalists Jalali and Kayvani to disseminate thousands of copies of Mosaddeq's royal dismissal in the bazaar and media outlets. He then asked the Shah, through U.S. ambassador to Baghdad, to relay the same message on radio. That night, Roosevelt used $50,000 to hire dozens of agents provocateurs to tag onto Tudeh demonstrations and attack mosques, royal symbols, and private property. Prominent ayatollahs Kashani, Behbahani, and Borujerdi were asked to summon Muslims to holy war against Communism.[6] On August 18 U.S. Ambassador Loy W. Henderson warned Mosaddeq that if he did not rein in street violence, American citizens would be deported. Still counting on U.S. support, Mosaddeq fell into the trap and gullibly cleared the streets for the mob scheduled to overthrow him the next day (Gasiorowski 2004: 251–53).

Immediately following the Shah's return, Washington provided him with a $45 million loan to stabilize the economy and, between 1953 and 1957, supplied an additional $500 million (Parsa 1989: 46–47). A grateful Shah then signed a contract with a consortium of Western oil companies in August 1954, granting Iran its coveted 50 percent profit share. And although the consortium allocated a 40 percent share to British Petroleum (the reincarnated AIOC), five U.S. companies received 8 percent each, with a total share of 40 percent (Saikal 1980: 48). Four years later, Roosevelt left the CIA to become a Gulf Oil executive (Bayandor 2010: 7).

It is worth noting that recent scholarship cast doubts over Roosevelt's Homeric exploits (Gasiorowski 2004; Bayandor 2010; Axworthy 2014). His claim to have single-handedly manipulated the August 19 crowds now appears dubious. After meeting him, on October 8, 1953, Eisenhower recorded in his diary: "I listened to his detailed report and it seemed more like a dime novel than historical fact" (Bayandor 2010: 7–8). So how important was Operation Ajax? Bill (1988: 94) and Parsa (1989: 45) insisted that anti-Mosaddeq forces would have been defeated without Western help. Azimi (2004: 89) saw this help as a "concentrated final blow delivered against a cumulatively incapacitated, fragile government"; or, as Richard Cottom wrote, it was like "pushing on an already-opened door" (quoted in Rubin 1981: 89). One of the most thorough studies of the Communist failure to protect Mosaddeq conceded that anti-royalist forces were really insignificant (Behrooz 2000: 3). And recently declassified documents maintain that "internal political dynamics more than foreign intrigues were responsible for the ultimate blow" (Bayandor 2010: 155). The ill-fated prime minister failed to recognize that monarchy was both the linchpin of oligarchic privileges, and the traditional bastion of clerics, peasants, and the petit bourgeoisie who resented secular modernity. Also, Mosaddeq's

National Front was no more than a loose coalition of parliamentarians; and while he excelled in communicating with the masses, he was a notoriously poor political broker who ultimately "stepped over the interests of virtually all elements in the power structure" (Bayandor 2010: 156–59). Though the debate rages on, it is sufficient for our purposes to see that it was Western-supported political forces, rather than the military, that counted in 1953, and that loyalty to the throne was the cornerstone of both domestic and foreign efforts.

Notes

1. Amusingly, once Mosaddeq's fell, Eisenhower approved a $23.5 million aid package to Iran, and an additional $45 million grant to help the new cabinet balance its finances (Saikal 1980: 48).

2. Some suggest that CIA-employed provocateurs inflamed the Communist riots, but Tudeh's radical campaign, launched weeks before, makes it "safe to assume that these events would have occurred with or without their [hired agents]" (Bayandor 2010: 100).

3. Their identities were exposed in September 1954: 429 of them were arrested; 37 fled the country; and the rest were cashiered (Behrooz 2000: 13).

4. A group of retired officers planned to establish a Committee to Save the Fatherland (Komiteh-e Najat-e Vatan), but their intention was to incite tribes and mullahs to rebel—a coup was not in the cards (Abrahamian 1982: 279).

5. In August 1942 West Point graduate and former head of the New Jersey State Police Colonel H. Norman Schwarzkopf took charge of the U.S. mission to Tehran. He re-separated the army and Gendarmerie (after Reza Shah's forced merger) and placed the latter under the Ministry of Interior (Ward 2009: 172).

6. Roosevelt alleges passing $10,000 to Kashani to pay the August 19 mob. In reality, "Kashani and other senior clergy did not need money to persuade them to act against Mossadeq, and their influence and connections were quite enough to bring crowds on to the street without American cash" (Axworthy 2014: 55).

3 The Road to Persepolis and Back

AUGUST 1953–JANUARY 1978

IF HISTORY OFFERS A FEW examples of how to build a vulnerable regime, what the Shah did during the following two decades of his rule would certainly occupy the top of the list. While the world's few remaining monarchs were struggling to modernize by separating themselves from governance, the Shah refashioned his monarchy along medieval (even ancient) lines. He shunned the terms "modernization" and "development" for rebuilding the Great Civilization (*Tamaddon-e Bozorg*). It was not just semantics. His goal was not to catch up with the advanced world, as Atatürk and Nasser hoped, but to reclaim Persia's ancient glory through imperial command. While his father considered himself "a patriot," Muhammad Reza imbued his rule with "a sense of divine mission" (Graham 1978: 57). More dangerously, he enhanced the power of the court over all other state institutions in a way that alienated the military and security. And while a political apparatus cannot usually coerce opposition, this was especially true in one not based on a mass-mobilizing party, but a narrow-grounded court. Once the scepter of power shook in the hands of the monarch, the whole regime began to crumble.

White Revolution, Black Reaction

In January 1963 the Shah launched his White Revolution: a six-point initiative centered on land reform and industrialization, with social benefits such as profit-sharing for workers, enfranchisement for women, and literacy and health corps for peasants. It was a token of royal benevolence, formulated away from Parliament, and legitimized through a popular referendum that won 99.9 percent approval. A thousand families had dominated the countryside, where 70 percent of Iranians lived, and the richest half of these families controlled 56 percent of arable land (Halliday 1979: 106). The Shah limited holdings to 370 acres per family, and sold the surplus (almost 20 percent of arable land) at nominal prices to 743,406 farmers (Saikal 1980: 84–85).[1] Though some families retained large holdings, "there can be no doubt that the traditional peasant-landlord relationship, which was the power basis of the landowning class ... was destroyed" (Arjomand 1988: 73). State control of religious endowments, forests, and pastoral land affected clerics and tribes in much the same way (Saikal 1980: 84–85). Power now shifted to the emerging state-run economy "in a manner designed to assure maximum profit for the royal family [and its] oligarchy" (Algar 2001: 55).

Carrying out these reforms against the wishes of Iran's countryside magnates demonstrated the court's autonomy. These magnates had fiercely opposed land reform in Parliament. One of them warned: "Talk of land distribution incites class hatred against our noble one thousand families—the families that are the main bulwarks of Iran and the recognized protectors of Islam." Another proclaimed: "Proposals for land reform may have been suitable for medieval Europe, but are in no ways applicable to Islamic Iran. For Iran, unlike Europe, never experienced feudalism. Our peasants remained free men. . . . And our landlords acted as responsible and peaceful citizens, treating the peasants as their own children" (Abrahamian 1982: 246). Yet none of them dared challenge the royal will directly.

Secret agitation against the Shah by landlords and tribal chiefs culminated in the June 1963 uprising six months after the White Revolution. In March 1963 a still-unknown Ayatollah Khomeini criticized the royal court. He was arrested for a few days, and eventually exiled for his continued insolence (Keddie 1981: 158–59). On June 5, 1963, hundreds demonstrated in Tehran and Qom against royal autocracy. It lasted for only three days since it failed to attract peasants, workers, professionals, or students who accepted royal reforms (Abrahamian 1982: 426; Parsa 1989: 51). The Shah was probably right to judge the June 1963 uprising as the last battle of dispossessed country magnates (Pahlavi 1980: 103).

As unintuitive as it might seem for a monarch to undercut the traditional supporters of monarchy, the Shah's logic for destroying independent power bases was to tie the elite exclusively to court, like the centralizing monarchs of Europe. He recognized that "centralizing power around himself ... meant depriving others ... of the power they had enjoyed for centuries" (Kian-Thiébaut 1998: 127). This was translated politically in the reduction of

Parliament representation of countryside magnates by 50 percent between 1961 and 1967. They now occupied less than a quarter of Parliament seats, and naturally flocked to court (Kian-Thiébaut 1998: 130). Unfortunately, they had to compete with another of the Shah's social creatures, "a new class, previously unknown to historians and sociologists: the petro-bourgeoisie. . . . [T]his class depended on neither social conflict (as in feudalism) nor on competition (as in industry and trade), but only on conflict and competition for the Shah's grace and favor" (Kapuscinski 2006: 64).

Where did it come from? For years, the Shah had been obsessed with securing an independent source of royal wealth. Oil revenue was his best option. Even before the crises that led to its astronomical surge in the early 1970s, Iranian oil revenue had already increased from $34 million in 1954 to $555 million in 1964. The Arab-Israeli War of 1967 almost doubled that to $958 million in 1969, and $1.2 billion in 1971. But it was the second round of that war, in October 1973, that triggered a fivefold jump to $5 billion, reaching the unfathomable figure of $20 billion in 1976 after the oil-producing countries found the nerve to defy the world market. In total, Iran's accumulated $38 billion in oil revenues between 1964 and 1977 (Abrahamian 1982: 427). The Shah's imperial ambitions seemed finally within reach. It was time to celebrate.

The first big party coincided with the first oil boom in 1967. In October of that year, the Shah held a belated crowning ceremony at the Gulistan Palace. Like his father, and Napoleon before him, he crowned himself to signify he was "beholden to nobody," and gave a short but telling speech: "I have crowned myself because now the Iranian people are living in prosperity and security. I long ago promised myself that I would never be king over a people who were beggars or oppressed. But now that everyone is happy I allow my coronation to take place" (quoted in Heikal 1981: 93). He took the title "Shahanshah" (king of kings), and amended the constitution to allow the queen to act as regent if he died before the crown prince's twentieth birthday (Alam 2008: 51). It was a demonstration of the court's growing omnipotence.

Then came the fancy-dress party that dwarfed all others. The occasion was quite imaginative (or downright silly): the commemoration of twenty-five-centuries of Persian royalty. The objective was to emphasize the continuity between Cyrus the Great, founder of the Achaemenian Empire, and the Shah. Fittingly, the site for this splendid ceremony, in October 1971, was the temple of Persepolis, erected by King Darius in the sixth century B.C.E. Like a Technicolor epic of Cecil B. de Mille, a parade of colorfully dressed warriors representing Iran's various epochs marched to the sound of music. A company of horsemen approached

Muhammad Reza in his ornate uniform to deliver a parchment, supposedly an imperial homage. The Shah replied, through a loudspeaker, "Hail Cyrus, founder of the Persian Empire. . . . On this historic day when the whole country renews its allegiance to its glorious past, I, Shahanshah of Iran, call history to witness that we, the heirs of Cyrus, have kept the promise made two thousand five hundred years ago" (quoted in Hoveyda 1980: 115–16). A total of 20 kings, 5 queens, 21 princes and princesses, 16 presidents, 3 premiers, 4 vice presidents, 2 foreign ministers, 500 foreign dignitaries, and 600 journalists from around the world attended the three-day gala, housed in sixty Parisian-designed villa-sized tents that cost Iran $200 million (Bill 1988: 183). At last the Shah felt equal to his historical European peers, bragging to confidants: "The decedents of Charlemagne came to Persepolis to pay homage to son of a corporal" (Heikal 1981: 95).

In 1977 the monarch published *Towards the Great Civilization*, which celebrated his White Revolution as the "greatest change in the history of Iran" (quoted in Hoveyda 1980: 30). And in a subsequent interview, he proclaimed, "Today our ancient land . . . is in the throes of a glorious rebirth. Our White Revolution has its roots in a similar bloodless revolution that was accomplished by the Emperor Cyrus some 2500 years ago, when he built his empire . . . within a single generation" (Hoveyda 1980: 118). If Cyrus could do it, then so could he. The Shah genuinely believed that in two decades, Iran would achieve "greater economic and conventional military strength than that deployed by Britain and France" (Saikal 1980: 138). In another interview, he stated, "I want the standard of living in Iran in ten years' time to be exactly on a level with that in Europe today. In twenty years' time we shall be ahead of the United States" (Heikal 1981: 109). And the only way to accomplish this was to strengthen the monarchy further. Fereydoun Hoveyda, Iranian diplomat and translator of the Shah's books, noted how his conception of authority harked back to Europe's past: "Three centuries after Louis XIV he was proclaiming, *L'état, c'est moi*" (1980: 87). In *My Answer to History*, the Shah was crystal clear:

> Intellectually, my education confirmed my passion for history and for the great men who had important roles in shaping it. I admired the emperor Charles V, for example, for his military genius in establishing what was then the best infantry in Europe and for giving such prestige and strength to Spain. Peter the Great unified Russia and I found his accomplishments fascinating. . . . And Catherine the Great continued the course he had set. The French, of course, were closest to my thinking. I admired the great French rulers like Henri IV and Louis XIV, the Sun King, and most of all Napoleon. (Pahlavi 1980: 64)

He flirted with the idea of creating a loyal ruling party, and experimented with one in 1975—Rastakhiz (Resurgence Party)—but it was little more than an additional route to royal favor. Indeed on the eve of the party's creation, he affirmed: "We must divide [Iranians] into two categories: those who believe in the Monarchy ... and those who don't.... A person who does not ... is a traitor. Such an individual belongs in an Iranian prison, or if he desires he can leave the country ... because he is not Iranian" (quoted in Halliday 1979: 47–48). Someone who knew the Shah before and after Persepolis highlighted his change in psyche:

> Persepolis had gone to the Shah's head ... thinking of himself as the reincarnation of Cyrus or Darius. Court ceremonial was greatly elaborated. There was continual bowing and scraping, visitors had to leave the royal presence walking backward.... He was consciously turning himself into an oriental monarch—the old Persian kings, the Egyptian pharaohs, and the Byzantine emperors all rolled into one.[2] And these monarchies, which he was setting out to imitate had in common not just the magnificent ritual of their courts, but a tradition of absolutism. That too became the hallmark of the Pahlavi monarchy. There was one man and one man alone who could make the decisions. All those around the Shah cowered in his presence, for they were all his creatures. The more he grew in stature in his own eyes, the more they seemed to diminish, for without him they were nothing. (Heikal 1981: 96)

But while it was certainly curious that the Shah became absorbed in "an imaginary world which was more real to him than reality" (Hoveyda 1980: 29), we still need to consider the implications. A diary entry, on January 12, 1971, by Court Minister (and former Prime Minister) Asadollah Alam is especially revealing, "More and more I get the impression that national affairs are uncoordinated, with no firm hand on the tiller, all because the captain himself is overworked. Every minister and high official receives a separate set of instructions direct from HIM [His Imperial Majesty] and the result is that individual details often fail to mesh with any overall framework. Thank God, the Shah is a strong man, but he's no computer" (Alam 2008: 190).

Problems began in the economic sphere. The hastily prepared White Revolution proved damaging. Landlords were pressed to invest the proceeds of their surplus land sales in industry, causing factories to mushroom from 8,520 in 1961 to an incredible 112,500 factories a decade later, with a corresponding swelling of industrial labor from 121,800 to 540,000 workers (Saikal 1980: 86). But the lack of skills and infrastructure blunted the competiveness of Iranian products (Halliday 1979: 285–86). At the same time, the explosion of independent farmers from 5 percent to 76 percent of rural society concealed the fact that 65 percent of them did not have enough land to make it on their own (Abrahamian 1982: 429). Expectedly, most sold their "uneconomic smallholdings" to agro-businesses and migrated to the cities, causing a rapid 20 percent rise in urban population (Martin 2007: 21). Tehran's population alone doubled from 2.5 to 5 million during the 1970s (Saikal 1980: 184). Worse still, land fragmentation hurt agricultural production, reducing its GNP share from 27.9 percent in 1963 to 9.3 percent in 1977, and turning Iran into a net importer of agricultural products (Kian-Thiébaut 1998: 133).

Moreover, the Shah ignored his ministers' advice not to inject the entire oil revenue into the economy (Hoveyda 1980: 79). Soon, the vultures began circling around court and global investors joined the gold rush. *Financial Times* correspondent Robert Graham recalled, "One of the most lasting impressions was to see senior executives of major international companies prepared to tolerate every indignity and discomfort, including sleeping in hotel lobbies . . . and waiting for days on favor of Iranian officials in the hope of doing business" (1978: 11). By 1976, 215 multinational corporations operated in Iran (Parsa 1989: 68). GDP jumped fivefold from $10.6 billion in 1960 to $51 billion in 1977, and the economy grew annually by 10 percent between 1963 and 1978 (Foran 2005: 75; Milani 2008b: 583). Even industry developed at a rate of 15.2 percent per annum during the decade 1965–1975—almost twice as much as it did in other developing countries (Parsa 1989: 66).

Eventually, bottlenecks developed throughout the economy. Power outages in 1977 caused 180 factories to close, and another 700 to cut down production. During that summer, a single factory endured 760 blackouts. Months-long transportation delays ruined 30 percent of Iran's agricultural produce, and derailed the entry of imported goods. In 1975, for example, 200 ships with 1 million tons of goods had to wait for 160 days to unload at one of Iran's chocked ports, which could only handle 9,000 tons a day (Kurzman 2004: 87). And it was the Shah's fault, as Kapuscinski noted in his evocative depiction:

> [The] Shah is making purchases costing billions, and ships full of merchandize are streaming toward Iran from all the continents. But when they reach the Gulf, it turns out that the small obsolete ports are unable to handle such a mass cargo (the Shah hadn't realized this). Several hundred ships line up at sea and stay there for up to six months, for which delay Iran pays the shipping companies a billion dollars annually. Somehow the ships are gradually unloaded, but then it turns out that there are no warehouses (the Shah hadn't realized). In the open air, in the desert, in nightmarish tropical heat, lie millions of tons of all sorts of cargo, half of it consisting of perishable foodstuffs and chemicals, and end up being thrown away. The remaining cargo now has to be transported into the depths of the country, and at this moment it turns out that there is no transport (the Shah

> hadn't realized).... Two thousand tractor-trailers are thus ordered from Europe, but then it turns out there are no drivers (the Shah hadn't realized). After much consultation, an airliner flies off to bring South Korean truckers.... With time and the help of foreign freight companies, however, the factories and machines purchased abroad finally reach their appointed destinations. Then comes the time to assemble them. But it turns out that Iran has no engineers or technicians (the Shah hadn't realized). From a logical point of view, anyone who sets out to create a Great Civilization ought to begin with his people. (2006: 56–57)

And yet "the people" did not really figure in the Shah's grand project. A 1974 survey by the International Labor Office reported that the richest 20 percent of Iranians accounted for 60 percent of expenditures, while the poorest 20 percent were responsible for less than 4 percent (Abrahamian 1982: 448). Another statistic showed that only 10 percent of Iranians accounted for 40 percent of consumption (Halliday 1979: 15). Worse still, the overheated economy succumbed to a double-digit inflation, raising the cost-of-living index from 100 in 1970 to 190 in 1976 (Abrahamian 1982: 497). And in 1977, inflation reached a record 30 percent (Saikal 1980: 186). What made the situation even more acute was a temporary decline in oil revenue in 1977 due to global business slowdown (Parsa 1989: 62–63).

Disaster loomed. The oil sector accounted for 38 percent of GNP in 1977, up from 17 percent a decade earlier (Halliday 1979: 138–39). Between 1963 and 1977, the share of oil in state revenues increased from 45 percent to 77 percent, while that of direct taxes rose only from 5 to 11 percent, and that of indirect taxes fell from 35 to 9 percent. And while oil funds financed 30 percent of the five-year-development plan in the 1950s, it financed 80 percent of the 1973/1978 plan (Parsa 1989: 64; Rajaee 2007: 93). Oil exports also provided 80 percent of Iran's foreign currency, which bought most imports (Rubin 1981: 131). Iran had become a rentier state "awash in petrodollars" (Skocpol 1994: 244). Yet the petro-bourgeoisie was an "unusual social phenomenon [which] produces nothing, and unbridled consumption makes up its whole occupation" (Kapuscinski 2006: 64). Iran's bubble was about to burst. Politically speaking, this was a calamity. The Shah's direct handling of the economy made him responsible for its busts and booms (Parsa 1989: 33). He was now expected to fix the mess. But where could he begin?

On the eve of the Revolution, Iran's upper class (1,000 landowners, businessmen, and senior bureaucrats), headed by the royals (63 princes and princesses), controlled 85 percent of manufacturing, foreign trade, banking, and construction. Below them came the propertied middle class (1.2 million families). Some owned land (perhaps 100,000 people). Others were employees (about 630,000 people). But half of the middle class were bazaar merchants who controlled three-quarters of Iran's wholesale trade, two-thirds of its retail trade, half of its handicraft production, one-third of imports, and one-fifth of the credit market. Then came the working class, which grew fivefold during the 1970s, to 1.27 million workers, though this figure increased to 2.4 million if the urban poor were added, and to 3.5 million if rural wage earners were thrown in as well (Abrahamian 1982: 432–34; Moaddel 1991: 317–19; Kurzman 2004: 101).

The problem was that the upper class was so tightly linked to the court that the middle and lower classes could not blame the class as a whole (landlords, industrialists, and top bureaucrats), but only the royal family. "Anyone who wanted to build a factory, open a business, or grow cotton had to give a piece of the action as a present to the Shah's family" (Kapuscinski 2006: 63). The Pahlavi family owned 137 of Iran's largest 527 industrial and financial corporations, and 10 courtiers owned another 390 of these corporations (Parsa 1989: 69–70). A breakdown of industrial ownership revealed that the royal family and its immediate associates controlled 80 percent of cement, 70 percent of tourism, 62 percent of finance, 40 percent of textiles, and 35 percent of transport (Heikal 1981: 95). The court budget was ridiculously high ($40 million in 1977), and the court minister was ranked on a par with the prime minister and treated as the most powerful man in the government. In fact, prime ministers were sometimes "promoted" to court ministers, as the examples of Asadollah Alam and Amir Abbas Hoveyda demonstrate (Graham 1978: 139). For average Iranians, "the Great Civilization, the Shah's Revolution, was above all a Great Pillage" (Kapuscinski 2006: 63).

The Shah had to move fast. In August 1976 he replaced Premier Amir Abbas Hoveyda (after a twelve-year tenure) with economist Jahangir Amouzegar to save the country from hiking inflation. One of new cabinet's first decisions was to end low-interest loans to bazaar tradesmen and small manufactures. Another was to cancel Hoveyda's secret annual fund ($11 million), which "supported" mullahs (Hoveyda 1980: 84). The Shah also decided to blame inflation on profiteers. He recruited 10,000 students in a hardnosed battle against the bazaar. Between 1975 and 1977, he fined 250,000 bazaaris, banished 23,000, imprisoned 8,000, and closed 600 shops (Abrahamian 1982: 498). He also approved redevelopment schemes that involved razing bazaars to modernize cities (Keddie 1981: 241). The Shah's alienation of the most organized fragments of the middle class, merchants and mullahs, sparked the unrest that became a revolution. But the question still remains: Why did the military allow things to get out of hand?

The Shah's Paper Tiger

When Muhammad Reza ascended the throne, his father's army had been reduced to 65,000 men. But with a defense budget that consumed half of Iran's oil revenue, the military expanded to 410,000 men.[3] By 1977 the Shah bragged about having the largest navy in the Gulf, the most advanced air force in the Middle East, and the fifth largest army in the world (Abrahamian 1982: 435–36). The Imperial Air Force was, in fact, larger than those of France or West Germany, and Iran's tank inventory was becoming as large as that of the French and twice as large as that of the British (Ward 2009: 197–98).

Defense spending increased from $67 million in 1953, when the Shah regained control from Mosaddeq, to $183 million in 1963, before the oil boom (Halliday 1979: 71; Abrahamian 1982: 420). It then multiplied 3.5 times with the oil hikes, from $900 million in 1970 to $10.6 billion in 1977 (Ward 2009: 194). Arms purchases during the last decade of the Shah's rule were estimated at $17 billion (Wahid 2009: 57). Over $12 billion were used to purchase American products, and an equal amount was earmarked for orders to be delivered by the United States in 1980 (Abrahamian 1982: 435–36). Iran had become the world's largest single purchaser of U.S. arms, and in 1977 alone it bought arms worth $5.7 billion, which was more than the entire U.S. sales to other foreign countries that year (Saikal 1980: 157–58).

Yet the Iranian stockpile was not entirely American as some believed. The army owned 860 American tanks (M-47 and M-60 Patton), but its main battle tanks were 760 British Chieftains, with another 1,450 ordered in 1977. Its 1,500 artillery pieces were divided equally between American and Soviet field guns and missiles, and its air defense missiles were Russian SAMs, with only a handful of American I-HAWKs. Army aviators flew American, British, and Italian helicopters. And although the navy was relatively more U.S.-based, it was minuscule (three destroyers and four frigates), and the Shah was in the process of buying Italian frigates and German submarines. Only the air force basked in American hardware. From 75 combat aircrafts (including F-5 Tigers) in 1965, it enlarged its portfolio to 500 jets (including F-4 Phantoms and F-14 Tomcats) in 1978.

But beneath the surface, a different picture emerged. Iranian scholar Amin Saikal cautioned that Iran's military "potential" must not be "misunderstood as military capability" (1980: 156). Others did not put it so mildly. Former U.S. officer and military historian Steven Ward described the Imperial Armed Forces as a "Crippled Giant," which only looked "Imposing on paper" (2009: 201, 205). Barry Rubin said that "poor performance and even poorer leadership were the norm" (1981: 166). Kapuscinski was even harsher: "I hesitate to use the term 'army'" when referring to the Iranian armed forces (2006: 61).

Interestingly, this was the view of American politicians. Ted Sorensen, Kennedy's advisor, complained in 1961 that the Shah demanded U.S. support for "an expensive army too large for border incidents and internal security and of no use in an all-out war . . . [like] the proverbial man who was too heavy to do any light work and too light to do any heavy work" (quoted in Halliday 1979: 92). Chairman of the Joint Chiefs of Staff General George Brown remarked mockingly that the kind of military the Shah was eager to build makes one wonder if he believes he was ruling the ancient Persian Empire (quoted in Halliday 1979: 97). U.S. military instructors in Iran warned that the military would "grind to a halt" if the buildup continued (Rubin 1981: 137). In 1977 Ambassador William H. Sullivan was asked to advise the Shah that his country "lacked the material and human infrastructure necessary to support the advanced military . . . technology [he] imported" (Hoveyda 1980: 101). A 1976 congressional staff report concluded that Iran lacked "experience in logistic and support operations and [it] does not have the maintenance capabilities, the infrastructure . . . and the construction capacity to implement its new programs. . . . Iran will not be able to absorb and operate . . . sophisticated military systems purchased from the U.S." (Saikal 1980: 186–87). Iran's buildup was equally mindboggling to its superpower neighbor to the north. In September 1976 Russian Foreign Minister Andrei Gromyko asked his Iranian counterpart: "All these arms you're equipping yourself with. . . . [W]e wonder why, and against whom. Iraq? But that is a small country. The Emirates? They don't count militarily. Saudi Arabia? It is not a threat. Then why?" (Hoveyda 1980: 99).

The first president of the Islamic Republic, Abol Hassan Bani-Sadr, who had to prepare for war with Iraq after his election in 1980, provided the best summary of the state of the armed forces:

> The man in the street considered the army a product of the superpowers. . . . [A]n official study of the army was impossible. . . . [It was a] mystery. . . . We then realized that about 90 percent of the army's power depended on this mystery. . . . Secret investigations of the army . . . revealed [that] the organization of the army . . . was based not on the necessities of terrain, climate, neighboring countries, and other armies, but on a multinational model [in the Shah's mind]. . . . [T]he soldiers did not know how to use their equipment in the field. . . . [O]ur soldiers' lack of practice prevented us from making the most of the limited resources we had. . . . How could a war be fought with an army like this, an army no longer shrouded in mystery, an army afraid of its own shadow. (1991: 105–08)

What was crucial politically was that Iranian officers shared this view. Court Minister Asadollah Alam noted in his diary, on October 8, 1973, that the Commander of the Imperial Air Force, General Khatami, "confided in me that we're ordering far more planes than we can possibly use. We simply haven't enough pilots, or the facilities to train more. Yet, despite being his brother-in-law, the Commander dares not draw the matter to HIM's attention. Instead he asked me to bring it up when an opportunity arose, being careful not to reveal who had supplied me with my information" (2008: 390). Deputy Defense Minister General Toufanian complained that although he was officially responsible for procurements, the Shah never consulted him. Not only that, but whenever he relayed the demands of the military chiefs, the Shah would yell: "The arms I choose. All the systems I choose" (quoted in Schofield 2007: 115). Military Intelligence Chief General Hassan Pakravan confided to a U.S. official that he "opposed our supplying military equipment on a scale that cut into the development budget," and hoped Washington could dissuade the monarch (Milani 2008a: 480). This feeling of powerlessness vis-à-vis the sovereign pervaded the Imperial Armed Forces on all levels. Admiral Kamyabipour, who commanded a navy frigate division in the 1970s, said, "I respected the Shah as my commander, but I have to admit that he ran a one-man show" (Kamyabipour 2011).

Here are a few examples of the problems the military faced. Let us start with the most infamous: the F-14 deal. This new fighter jet was so sophisticated that the U.S. Navy struggled to absorb it. At the same time, Iranian pilots failed to master the relatively simpler F-4s and F-5s (Ward 2009: 198, 208). When the Shah expressed interest, the Pentagon strenuously objected, explaining in a note to President Nixon, on May 12, 1972, that aside from the fact that "virtually no military exigency possible could justify this sale ... [Iran] lacked even the most basic technical skills to maintain airframes, engines, and weapons systems on much less sophisticated aircraft" (Daugherty 2001: 50). So the Shah went through the backdoor, loaning Grumman the funds required to improve the jet in return for eight out of the first batch of F-14s. William J. Daugherty, the CIA operative in Tehran, described the ludicrous result:

> In the end, the Tomcats were squandered. Fear of crashing or otherwise losing the aircraft and thus displeasing the shah made [air force] commanders unwilling to schedule aggressive training missions for the F-14s. Likewise the aircrews were hesitant to fly them in any flight or weather conditions that might be conducive to accidents lest they lose or damage the plane and bear the brunt of the shah's wrath. What was arguably the world's most sophisticated and

combat-capable aircraft was flown almost entirely in daylight hours, only when good weather permitted, and only in low-risk, straight-level missions. (2001: 50–51)[4]

Even much more modest aircrafts, such as the Bell helicopter that required ten hours of maintenance for every hour of flight, were useless because Iran had only a few good pilots and even fewer skilled technicians (Rubin 1981: 137). In a rare incident that same year, American instructors organized a strike at the Isfahan's Aviation Training School because they were being pressured by the court to pass substandard pilots with little flying experience (Halliday 1979: 98).

The navy was in a worse condition—dismissed by British naval attaché as "inefficient and understaffed" (Halliday 1979: 98). An amusing entry from the diary of Court Minister Alam describes naval performance during a maneuver attended by the Shah and foreign dignitaries, on November 5, 1972: "On the spur of the moment HIM requested that a couple of ships armed with missiles take a shot at the targets. . . . Two vessels were selected for the display. The first missed the target altogether; the second could not even get its missiles off the launch pad. A total shambles" (2008: 252). Alam then recalls an awkward meeting with the British ambassador, on June 7, 1973. The troubled diplomat explained that his government was "anxious to conclude the deal on Chieftain tanks which promises Britain employment and considerable revenue. However, I cannot help thinking that 800 tanks may be too many for Iran to cope with, given the cost of maintenance and your shortage of skilled technicians. Moreover, the tanks themselves are ill-suited to mountainous or marshy terrain such as you have" (Alam 2008: 297). Nonetheless, the Shah bought more Chieftains than Britain kept (Axworthy 2014: 84). He did not even consult his army leaders before designating the Chieftain as Iran's main battle tank (Schofield 2007: 119).

Of course, the most pervasive problem was manpower. A congressional report estimated that the air force suffered from a shortfall of 10,000 technicians (Halliday 1979: 97). In fact, Iran had more jets than trained pilots (Wahid 2009: 58). The ground forces were no better. Conscripts came from different regions and ethnic groups and could hardly communicate with each other and their commanders in Persian, let alone absorb sophisticated Western equipment (Saleh 2008: 76). Once more, the court minister captured this dismal state of affairs in a diary entry recorded after attending a parade on the outskirts of Tehran, on December 12, 1969:

> HIM reviewed the troops on horseback. . . . [The] Commander of the First Army, an infantry man in charge of today's proceedings, was unseated by his mount. How humiliating! The loose horse stepped out in front of HIM, ahead of the royal party, and worse still, television cameras broadcast the whole thing live. Elsewhere an officer stepped out of rank when passing the royal box and tried to present some sort of petition to the Shah. He was held back by security men, and it turned out that his sole request was to be sent to study electronics in the USA. (Alam 2008: 111)

But it was all essentially the Shah's doing. One Pentagon official commented that the Shah read armaments trade magazines so avidly that he knew more about the equipment than his officers (Rubin 1981: 128). "Arms dealers began to jest that the shah read their manuals in much the same way other men read *Playboy*" (Abrahamian 1982: 436). He could not care less about what his military chiefs desired. As a result, "A stream of the most fantastic orders flowed out from Tehran. How many tanks does Great Britain have? Fifteen hundred? Fine . . . I'm ordering two thousand. How many artillery pieces does the Bundeswehr have? A thousand? Good, put us down for fifteen hundred" (Kapuscinski 2006: 62). When it came to procurement, noted U.S. diplomat John Wiley, the Shah's thinking was "strictly in never never land" (Rubin 1981: 39).

In addition to all the above, Iranian officers had no combat experience. The absence of battles "permitted the Iranian army to cultivate an unusual degree of complacency regarding its own capacities" (Cronin 1997: 234). Unlike Turkey and Egypt, the Iranian army never experienced a military setback that might have inspired embittered officers to reflect on the nature of their regime. It is true that the Shah ordered logistical support for the Kurds in the 1960s, engaged in sporadic border skirmishes with Iraq in the early 1970s, and helped Oman subdue Communist insurgents in the mid-1970s, but these were low-intensity conflicts. Even when Iran occupied three islands in the Persian Gulf in 1971 following the British withdrawal, it faced no resistance (Saikal 1980: 156).

So what was the Shah up to? He answered in an interview:

> You ask me what these arms are for. I will tell you. They are because we want to be very strong in the area in which we live. . . . I live in an area which . . . [represents] the center of gravity of the world. I belong to this area; I have a stake in it which I intend to preserve. I have a function in it which I intend to exercise. I have a policy which I intend to pursue. There can be no stake, no function, no policy, which is not backed by military power. . . . The Iranian air force ought to be strong enough to protect the whole area from the Persian Gulf to the

> Sea of Japan. . . . India and Pakistan will become natural markets for Iranian industrial projects, but I shall have to protect Pakistan against Indian aggression. . . . I can assure you . . . that Iran will not be the last in the area to be a nuclear power. (Heikal 1981: 106)

At a very early meeting with the Shah, in Washington, D.C., in November 1949, U.S. Secretary of State Dean Acheson judged him as a "very impractical young man . . . full of grandiose ideas; he fancied himself a great military leader," but his belief that his country could be a great military power was "utterly fanciful and never had any basis at all" (Rubin 1981: 42). Acheson was right. Iran's military buildup was no more than a sandcastle, an impressive structure meant to enhance the prestige of the man on the Peacock Throne, a man obsessed—as was his father—with becoming a great monarch like his European heroes.

But his eagerness to develop "an outward-looking military that reflected his perception of Iran's strategic position" prevented him from providing it with arms and training fit for repressing domestic uprisings. The army had no rubber bullets, tear gas canisters, or any other riot-control gear. So when they did respond, they did so with disproportionate force, therefore inflaming popular anger even more (Hickman 1982: 3).

More importantly, the military had no autonomy. The Defense Ministry only handled administrative tasks. There was no joint chiefs of staff. Instructions passed directly from court to service chiefs and field officers (Abrahamian 1999: 73). The Shah met his chiefs *separately* every fortnight. They were not allowed to communicate without him, even on social occasions. Provincial commanders could not visit Tehran without royal authorization. In fact, when the Shah asked U.S. General Robert E. Huyser to set up Iran's command control system, "one of his principle requirements . . . was that he should be able to maintain absolute control" (Huyser 1986: 8). Two security organs reported on suspect officers: the Imperial Inspection Commission and the Second Bureau (Rokn-e Do). And the court relied on these reports not only to determine promotions, but also to ferret out cadets during entrance exams (Ward 2009: 209). Finally, military indoctrination inculcated the view that soldiers were worthless without a strong monarch (Halliday 1979: 74).

Of course, the Shah was generous with his generals, but he always made sure they knew who held the purse. Incentives were presented as royal gifts, not professional bonuses. Commanders were frequently shuffled to weaken camaraderie. And every few months, some officer was jailed on corruption charges—a reminder that he who has the power to give could also strike down at will. So in the 1960s, for instance, 5 generals and 300 colonels were put on trial; in 1974, 3 generals and 2 colonels were sentenced; in 1976 the head of the navy, his deputy, and 12 naval officers were sacked. On one occasion, in August 1969, the Shah remarked casually to his court minister, "I have received unfavorable reports on the Naval High Command. Today I ordered that every Admiral and senior officer accept early retirement. They will be replaced by new blood from amongst the younger generation" (Alam 2008: 85). In 1971 he fired Chief of Staff General Fereydoun Djam because he moved troops in response to Iraqi provocations without royal approval (Hoveyda 1980: 89). When Navy Chief Admiral Ahmad Madani dared request more autonomy for him and his colleagues, he was dismissed (Rubin 1981: 226)—later becoming Khomeini's military advisor.

One might think there is no better proof of the "*exceptional dominance* of the monarch" over his military than how he fired commanders, left and right, without much scuffle (Halliday 1979: 68). But there was worse. The Shah "scolded senior officers like a father training little children" (Ward 2009: 209). Some of the most amusing incidents were recorded in his court minister's diary. On November 18, 1972, the Shah sacked a general because "the bloody fool suggested at a meeting with the Minister of Finance that we increase the medical allowance for army personnel sent abroad for special treatment. As he put it, the expense would be a drop in the ocean compared to the profligacy of Princess Ashraf. I had to remind him that I myself paid out $30,000 to settle his private gambling debts. . . . [Then I told him] I always knew you were a clown but had no idea quite how stupid a clown you were" (Alam 2008: 257). When the air force chief suggested that the crown prince's training aircraft be painted in the same colors as every other military trainer, "HIM retorted that on the contrary, all the others must be altered to match the prince's colors" (Alam 2008: 428). Naturally enough, during a meeting of Iranian and Israeli officers, on August 17, 1972, Chief of Staff General Gholam-Reza Azhari "butted in with an appalling howler, remarking that we owe any progress we have made to one fact: that everyone here is scared rigid by HIM" (Alam 2008: 237).

Needless to say, the Shah infused the corps with family members. A few examples suffice. General Mohammed Khatmai, commander of the air force between 1957 and 1975, was his brother-in-law. General Fereydoun Djam, chief of staff between 1969 and 1971, was another. General Fathollah Minbashian, commander of the ground forces between 1969 and 1972, was the brother of yet a third brother-in-law. The Shah's brother General Gholam Reza was inspector-general of the army, and his nephew Shahriar Shafiq was a naval officer (Alam 2008: 60, 509). And then there was the meeting of November

22, 1973, when the Shah gathered his military commanders (a rare event) to instruct them to obey whoever was on the Peacock Throne: "Their orders may come from a woman or a man of tender years, but they are to be obeyed with no less respect. The safety of all your lives depends on this. . . . The men of the armed services owe nothing but blind obedience. . . . [E]ach officer puts obedience to the Shah above loyalty to fellow [officers]." The Shah then asked every commander to sign his approval at the bottom of the speech he had just delivered (Alam 2008: 334–37).

Weak and Disloyal: Security under the Shah

One of the most striking features of the Iranian regime is that until 1957 (i.e., after more than three decades of Pahlavi rule), the country had no political police or intelligence service. After the Mosaddeq debacle, the United States helped develop the National Security and Information Organization (Sazman-e Etelaat va Amniyat-e Keshvar), better know by its acronym SAVAK (Gasiorowski 2004: 257). However, SAVAK was born with a fatal weakness. As CIA agent William J. Daugherty explained: "Against all advice from the U.S. government, the shah chose to concentrate law enforcement, internal security, and foreign intelligence collection duties in SAVAK" (Daugherty 2001: 40–41). It handled dissidents, guerillas, organized crime, as well as counter-intelligence, foreign espionage, and covert operations (Halliday 1979: 77). SAVAK was therefore perpetually overstretched.

And yet the Shah kept it small. Estimates vary. The Shah said that in 1979 SAVAK had 4,000 operatives (Pahlavi 1980: 157). Journalists estimated this figure to actually be 30,000 (Graham 1978: 144). But most researchers now agree that full-time officers ranged between 3,000 and 5,000 during SAVAK's two-decade-long existence (Rubin 1981: 179; Abrahamian 1999: 104). It is true that it operated an army of informers, but those who studied the organization concluded that its claim to have recruited countless informers was a psychological ruse. The agency "shrewdly cultivated a politics of distrust so that the people were led to believe that they were being constantly watched by its numerous members" (Saikal 1980: 190). There are several examples of its manpower limitations. In 1978 SAVAK compiled a list of 124 dangerous clerics, but—as the report confessed—could not monitor them all (Kurzman 2004: 111). Similarly, SAVAK knew a lot about dissidents, but constantly "failed to penetrate their networks" (Ward 2009: 212). A more embarrassing example is when the court minister asked for a report on the political affiliations of those residing within a 1-kilometer radius around the

Shah's palaces. SAVAK not only admitted it had no such report, but also that such a broad survey was beyond its capacity. Court support helped produce a preliminary estimate.

> The results [were] incredible. . . . [T]here were literally dozens of local residents who were either ex-army officers sacked for their communist affiliations, or else related to those who were executed for the rebellion against land reform. My report came as just as much of a shock to HIM. "I must commend your initiative," he said, "but what the hell do Savak . . . think they're playing at?" (Alam 2008: 174)

More embarrassing still was what occurred during Nixon's 1972 visit. Not only were security measures a mess, but also a couple of bombs exploded near the American residence, leading the Shah to proclaim that SAVAK "couldn't so much as guard a sack of potatoes" (Alam 2008: 223). More shocking was that SAVAK had "no plans, no training, and no equipment for riot control" (Ward 2009: 210; Harney 1999: 38). Only in November 1978—almost a year into the Revolution—did the Shah request clubs, tear gas canisters, and rubber bullets from Washington, and the first shipments only arrived in December, days before his abdication (Naraghi 1999: 134). In addition, the court prevented SAVAK from developing an independent counter-insurgency arm, forcing it to rely on gendarmes in the countryside and urban police—the result being that leftist and Islamist militias increased in power and provided muscle to the Revolution (Ward 2009: 212).

In terms of counter-espionage, SAVAK's proudest moment came when its master spy-catcher (General Manuchehr Hashemi) caught a mole in the army in September 1977. But this glorious feat was overshadowed by the fact that it was the Shah who tipped him off (Milani 2008a: 465). SAVAK was not very successful on the external front either. Its botched coup against Saddam Hussein in 1969 was only one of several disastrous operations. Most distressing to the Shah was the agency's consistent failure to disrupt the activities of the Iranian diaspora—the diaspora that arranged Khomeini's stay in France during the Revolution, and produced the Islamic regime's first president and foreign minister. Nor could SAVAK intercept the cassettes carrying Khomeini's inflammatory speeches (Halliday 1979: 68).

Of course, the Shah made it worse by his choice of security chiefs. General Hassan Pakravan, SAVAK's head during the White Revolution, was a "Renaissance man . . . a humanist," described by colleagues as "a nice man [who] should have been a professor at some university." Pakravan preferred the company of intellectuals, and hoped to reconcile opposition through dialogue. Caught off-guard by the 1963 uprising, he "delivered a passionate speech on the radio, blaming the leaders of the uprising for abusing his trust and leniency." When it was over, he pleaded for clemency for the ringleaders, including Khomeini (Milani 2008a: 474–79). Inevitably, the Shah ended his four-year service. But his replacement was no other than General Ne'matollah Nasiri, the Imperial Guard commander who had walked blindly into Mosaddeq's trap in August 1953. He was dismissed in 1978 after failing to stem the gathering revolt.

The Shah also refused to grant SAVAK a blank check in dealing with opposition. Torture was a case in point. Despite SAVAK's notoriety, recent research revealed that torture was much less systematically used compared to other authoritarian settings.[5] Abrahamian affirmed that "brute force was rarely used" (1999: 2). Reza Shah had abolished torture in the 1920s, and appointed a committee (composed of a justice, finance head, and court minister, who all held law degrees from Europe) to reform the incarceration system. The year he abdicated (1941), Iran's largest prison, Qasr-e Qajar, held less than 200 political prisoners and none of them was tortured. Indeed, Iran had no maximum-security detention center before Evin prison was built in 1971, and until 1977 its maximum capacity was 1,500 prisoners (Abrahamian 1999: 25–28, 105). In the 1960s, SAVAK chief, the humanist Pakravan, not only prohibited torture, but "when he heard that an interrogator had slapped a prisoner, he moved swiftly to reprimand and demote the man" (Milani 2008a: 478). Admittedly, there were two glaring exceptions. One was the period that followed Mosaddeq's overthrow. But even Communist detainees conceded that the "barbaric practices" introduced in 1953 were hardly used afterward. Likewise, Islamist militants detained in 1956 for plotting to assassinate the prime minister confirmed that they "were not subjected to physical torture." Even the deposed prime minister's associates at the National Front were treated leniently (except for his foreign minister), and Mosaddeq himself was tried publicly and spent less than four years in prison (Abrahamian 1999: 88–89, 99). The second exception was occasioned by the resurgence of Marxist and Islamist guerillas. During intense shoot-outs between 1971 and 1976, 275 guerillas were killed in action and another 93 were tried by military tribunals and sentenced to death. But the Shah outlawed torture again in 1976 and, according to inmates, his decision changed prison conditions overnight (Abrahamian 1999: 102, 119). Rafsanjani, future president of the Islamic Republic, was detained six times for crimes no less than plotting to assassinate the king and the prime minister, and was held at several locations, including Evin and Qasr-e Qajar prisons. And although he had every reason to slander, he recorded in his memoirs that he was only physically assaulted once during his repeated detentions, and even then it was mostly a few slaps (Rafsanjani 2005: 118).[6]

Over and above, the Shah frequently reprimanded security personnel. For instance, when the agency confiscated subversive books from the Tehran University library, the Shah ordered them to return the books and apologize, adding that "such stupidity will not go unpunished" (Alam 2008: 361). When SAVAK directed the police to manhandle residents of a popular neighborhood to apprehend a drug dealer, in September 1970, the Shah sacked the police chief (Alam 2008: 171). Also, the agency's presence at Iran's Washington embassy was terminated after the ambassador (who happened to be Ardeshir Zahedi, the king's son-in-law) complained that its agents were brutish and undiplomatic (Rubin 1981: 152). Bazaar strongman Al-Tayyeb Haj Reza'i, who was key to Mosaddeq's overthrow, relayed another degrading incident in an interview. He had lined up his men to celebrate the crown prince's birth in 1960. When security officials cordoned his crew, he cried out for the Shah, who immediately chastised the security chief—"the scuffle and the Shah's rebuke were a great humiliation," Tayyeb concluded (De Bellaigue 2004: 174). It is important to note here that, unlike Egypt, the security apparatus did not control popular thugs, who remained tied to traditional bazaar networks. Crucially, the Shah disowned and purged SAVAK during the revolutionary turmoil itself, forcing it to lift censorship and release 2,700 of its 3,000 detainees (Abrahamian 1999: 120).

Predictably, security chiefs were notoriously disloyal to the Shah. Out of his seven security chiefs, four conspired against him, and the loyalty of the remaining three cannot be ascertained (Milani 2008a: 445). The first SAVAK director, General Teymur Bakhtiar, was the queen's uncle. But during a Washington visit in 1958, he requested the help of CIA's Allen Dulles and Kermit Roosevelt to topple the Shah. Later that day, he received a "verbal barrage" from Secretary of State John Foster Dulles and was humiliatingly ushered out of the State Department (Rubin 1981: 108). Undeterred, Bakhtiar tried his luck again in 1960 with president-elect John F. Kennedy, and a third time with U.S. embassy officials in May 1961. This time the Shah was informed. Bakhtiar escaped to Iraq, and his deputy and co-conspirator, General Alavi Kia, was sacked. The treacherous SAVAK chief continued to offer his services to all the Shah's enemies, from Communists to Islamists. And when he formed the Liberation Movement of Iran in Baghdad in 1970, the Shah had him assassinated (Milani 2008a: 433–36).

Then there was the head of Military Intelligence, General Valiollah Gharani, who plotted against the court and later joined Khomeini's Revolutionary Council and became the Islamic Republic's first chief of staff

(Halliday 1979: 68; Milani 2008a: 445). In January 1958 Gharani met three members of the U.S. embassy in Tehran to convince them that "the present government has no popular support and is despised by the mass of Iranian people and ... Soviets are quite openly engaged in penetrating and wooing the Iranian people.... Therefore [it] is urgent that a change in government be brought about.... [T]he Shah ... should reign and not rule" (Milani 2008a: 448). The following month, Gharani and thirty-eight accomplices were arrested, but received a light two-year sentence. He was detained again in 1963 for organizing dissidents, and was sentenced to another two years (Milani 2008a: 448–49).

The most tragic case, however, was General Hussein Fardust, the unrivaled "intelligence tsar of the Pahlavi regime," and the Shah's best friend since childhood (Milani 2008a: 438). Fardust had been banished from court, in the 1940s, for leaking information about the royal family. He was then exiled to Paris on Mosaddeq's orders because of his constant scheming. There, the KGB recruited him. Prime Minister Zahedi warned the Shah that Fardust had become a Russian spy, but the monarch still entrusted him with the country's most sensitive intelligence organ: the Imperial Inspection Commission, which was established in 1958 to monitor SAVAK and Military Intelligence. Fardust defected to Khomeini and was rewarded by heading the Islamic Republic's top security agency (SAVAMA) between 1979 and 1984—before being executed for his KGB links. He also played a critical role in convincing his protégé General Abbas Gharabaghi, the Shah's last chief of staff, not to repress the Revolution (Milani 2008a: 438–40). Fardust was finally instrumental in converting military and security officers to Khomeini's cause upon the latter's return to Iran (Axworthy 2014: 7).

All the above leads one to conclude that SAVAK's reputation was "exaggerated and misleading. SAVAK [was] clumsy ... [and] riddled with administrative and personal pettiness" (Graham 1978: 148). It was "hardly more than a glorified police force," as the French intelligence chief described it in the 1970s (Kurzman 2004: 109). Overstretched, restricted, and subject to royal distain, SAVAK was neither invested in the regime, nor capable of defending it.

Friendly Fire: Geopolitics before the Fall

America no doubt played a key role in building the Shah's Iran. But the relationship between the two was not as intimate as commonly held. Like his father, once the Shah secured the throne, he adopted a combative attitude toward his benefactors. The result was that the country that provided him with unconditional support in 1953 did so only halfheartedly in 1978.

Beginning with military aid, it was clear that the Shah's ambitions were a source of endless friction. As early as 1947, the U.S. State Department warned that the Shah's military pretensions would impoverish Iran and render it vulnerable to Communism. The Truman administration insisted that an American military umbrella, rather than a large and ineffective Iranian army, would work best (Rubin 1981: 37). However, the Shah's tenacity was such that one U.S. ambassador suggested that only "harpoon therapy [could] deflate his 'extravagant' aspirations and 'astronomical figures' for modern weapons" (Abrahamian 1999: 74). In 1959 the two countries signed a mutual defense agreement, but Eisenhower refused to supply the Shah with the equipment he desired (Rubin 1981: 102). Indeed, during the Shah's first two decades in power, total U.S. military grants amounted to $535.4 million—a modest figure by all accounts (Saikal 1980: 54). The Kennedy administration then upped the ante by pressuring Tehran to downsize the army (from 240,000 to 100,000 men), and scale down military purchases (Rubin 1981: 107). And although Lyndon Johnson agreed to raise Iran's military credit from $48 million to $300 million, this was a temporary reaction to Britain's scheduled withdrawal from the Gulf in 1971 (Halliday 1979: 93–96).

Only when Iran's oil revenues kicked in did the Shah finally manage to "have his way" with Washington (Rubin 1981: 38). The shift began with Nixon's 1972 visit. In six short years, Iran became the world's largest purchaser of American arms; built the fourth largest air force in the world; and quadrupled its military from 100,000 to 410,000 men (Halliday 1979: 93–96).[7] Whereas U.S. arms sales to Iran between 1941 and 1971 barely exceeded $1 billion, during the Shah's last eight years, delivered and future orders amounted to $19 billion (Hoveyda 1980: 98). He was obsessed with acquiring "the best equipment in the greatest quantities at the fastest possible rate" (Rubin 1981: 158).

So why did Nixon overturn "the efforts of five presidential administrations to convince the shah to moderate his arms purchases" (Daugherty 2001: 49)? One explanation was Nixon's post-Vietnam doctrine, which hoped for regional allies to counter Communism without American involvement. Iran was the default choice because of the minuscule size of the Jordanian and Arab Gulf armies, and the volatility of Egyptian, Iraqi, and Syrian militaries. A regional policeman was essential to protect the Gulf's 75 percent of non-Communist oil reserves, especially after the creation of a Marxist South

Yemen; a Communist revolt in Oman's Dhofar province; and the signing of a Soviet-Iraqi friendship agreement (Rubin 1981: 124–26).

Another explanation was that Washington was short of cash. The United States became a net importer of oil in 1970 (with 38 percent of its imports coming from the Gulf) and used arms sales to balance the bill (Rubin 1981: 130). When Tehran complained that the price of certain weapons went up 50 percent between 1973 and 1976, the Pentagon responded that Iranian oil prices tripled during the same period. Defense Secretary James Schlesinger confided, "We are going to make them pay through the nose, just as they are making us pay them through the nose" (Rubin 1981: 172).

It was also a marketing bonanza. U.S. General Ellis Williamson described Iran in the 1970s as "a salesman's dream" for arms companies; and sure enough, Tehran received over thirty corporate visitors a week—many struggling to offset post-Vietnam cutbacks. Aerospace companies marketed their jets to the Shah while they were still on the drawing board. A case in point was the sale of 250 F-18 Hornets before the Pentagon even had a chance to review it (Rubin 1981: 135, 175). Another was Grumman's offering an Iranian official a $28 million commission to expedite the $2.2 billion F-14 contract (Bill 1988: 209). A third example was how the producers of AWAC (aircraft-borne radar warning system) argued in Congress that sales to Iran would reduce the per-unit cost enough to make the system marketable to European armies. Iranian officers were not completely deluded in assuming that American companies regarded their country as a "technical dumping ground" (Rubin 1981: 168). In fact, by 1975, thirty-nine of America's top arms, electronic, and communication companies had permanent representation in Iran, including Bell Helicopter International, General Electric, Grumman Aerospace, Lockheed, McDonnell-Douglas, Northrop, and Westinghouse (Bill 1988: 209).

But regardless of what caused the U.S. policy shift, the Shah now scrambled to "use American arms in order to free himself as much as possible from any dependence on American protection" (Rubin 1981: 126). He refused to burn bridges with Moscow, writing in 1970:

> We in Iran have adopted a policy which we call a policy of independent nationalism. Its essential principles are non-interference in the internal affairs of other countries and peaceful co-existence . . . especially to countries with different political and social systems from ours. . . . [P]eace cannot be achieved without sincere respect for the principles of co-existence between different ideologies. (Pahlavi 1980: 173–74)

He also denounced Nixon's détente because it limited Iran's maneuverability: "We will simply not allow them to strike their sordid little bargains as if we had no say in the matter. Don't they realize how easily we can come to our own agreement with Russia? Iran is not some pawn to be shunted about" (Alam 2008: 82). When Egypt attacked the U.S. representative to the United Nations, in October 1970, he wondered, "Why on earth we didn't follow the Egyptian lead, and voice our grievances against America" (Alam 2008: 172–73). Then on the eve of his fateful decision to raise oil prices, in January 1973, the Shah confided to his court minister: "Nixon has the audacity to tell me to do nothing in the interest of my country until he dictates where that interest lies. At the same time he threatens me that failure to follow his so-called advice will be to jeopardize the special relations between our two countries. I say to hell with these relations" (Alam 2008: 278). He followed this with a veiled threat to Nixon's successor, Gerald Ford, "You are no doubt fully aware, My President, of my deep concern to maintain close cooperation between our two countries. However, if there were any opposition in the Congress and other circles to see Iran prosperous and militarily strong, there are many sources of supply to which we can turn, for our life is not in their hands. . . . Nothing could provoke more reaction in us than this threatening tone from certain circles and their paternalistic attitude" (letter in Alam 2008: 522). He believed Americans were out to get him, commenting sardonically on the hostile protests that greeted him in Washington in 1977, "No one bothered to answer my question: Who had paid for the anti-Shah demonstrations. The crowd was dotted with black faces and blond manes, rarely found in Iran" (Pahlavi 1980: 20). He mistrusted London even more, asking his court minister, in August 1972, to relay to the British foreign secretary that

> we were wrong to believe that the British are our friends. You are obsessed solely with your own selfish interests and treat us as a people beyond the pale. But your attitude is a matter of profound disinterest. Your democratic system has already erupted in chaos. We shall soon overtake you and in a decade you will be struggling in our wake. Perhaps then you will remember how once you treated us. (Alam 2008: 236)

In the Shah's mind, Iran and Western powers were on a collision course. He wrote: "The West created an organized front against me . . . [because] my policies diverged from theirs" (Pahlavi 1980: 22). And stated in an interview, in December 1978, that America and Britain wanted to liquidate him because they "oppose having a strong state in the region" (Naraghi 1999: 140). The Shah complained to Kissinger that the CIA was supporting revolutionary mullahs because "he was too cozy with the Soviet Union. If the Americans thought he was soft, maybe the religious people would be more stanchly anti-Communist" (Precht 2004: 10). This is why he terminated the agency's training of SAVAK in the 1960s (Daugherty 2001: 41). This is why he withdrew CIA consultants from government administrations (Heikal 1981: 101). This is why he prohibited the CIA from meeting Iranian politicians (Milani 2011a). And this is why, in 1973, he cancelled his weekly meetings with the CIA station chief (Heikal 1981: 16).

By the mid-1970s, the Shah was becoming increasingly scornful of his old Western allies. Attending a royal dinner, in 1976, Iran's UN representative Fereydoun Hoveyda watched painfully as a senator from New York had to endure the Shah's speech on America's unashamedly corrupt system. The Shah then warned in his interview with Mike Wallace on *60 Minutes*, in October 1976, that the Jewish lobby controlled American policy and media (Hoveyda 1980: 19, 155). He publically lectured Americans for their lack of "social discipline" and dismissed Britons as "lazy, undisciplined, and permissive" (Bill 1988: 192). The U.S. State Department protested in a report, on May 4, 1976, that "in recent months the Shah has permitted unusually severe criticisms of the United States in Iranian media. He has lent his own name to sweeping charges against the U.S., raising public questions about the bases of the alliance and U.S. reliability" (Bill 1988: 214). But the Shah's confidence grew in correspondence with Iran's increased oil revenues, and nothing could halt his abusive barrages (Harney 1999: 8). "He lectured London and Rome, advised Paris, scolded Madrid. The world heard him out meekly and swallowed even the bitterest admonitions because it couldn't take its eyes off the gold pyramid piling up in the Iranian desert" (Kapuscinski 2006: 55).[8]

But it was not just talk. The Shah actively undermined Western interests. The most brazen example, of course, was the oil-price hikes. Iran led the Organization of Petroleum Exporting Companies (OPEC) in raising prices after world demand tripled between 1960 and 1970—knowing that the United States and Western Europe accounted for over 50 percent of world demand. In December 1970 the Shah instigated an OPEC threat to reduce oil production by half unless the share of its members was increased. The bluff worked, leading to the Tehran Agreement of February 1971, in which the large oil companies (the Seven Sisters) succumbed to OPEC demands in order to maintain current prices. Iran observed the Arab oil embargo on pro-Israel countries during the 1973 war, and reaped huge gains. The Shah then raised the stakes, on December 23, 1973, by unilaterally abrogating the 1954 consortium agreement and nationalizing Iranian oil (Saikal 1980: 99–109, 124; Rubin 1981: 132). On the first day of the new year, the Shah announced, the price of oil would jump almost 128 percent from $5.032 a barrel to $11.651 a barrel (Pahlavi 1980: 97). The Shah ended his defiant press conference by warning industrial powers that the "era of their terrific progress and even more terrific income and wealth based on cheap oil is finished" (Kurzman 2004: 86). Reporter Robert Graham recalled how the Shah lectured rich countries:

> Well, some people are going to say this [oil hike] is going to create chaos in the industrialized world. . . . That is true, but as to the industrialized world they will have to tighten their belts, and they will have to work even harder. . . . Eventually all those children of well-to-do families who have plenty to eat at every meal, who have their own cars . . . will have to rethink all these privileges of the advanced world. (Graham 1978: 15)

When Kissinger threated that the United States would not allow oil to be turned into a political weapon, the Shah pledged to defend any country that was attacked for trying to capitalize on its natural resources (Saikal 1980: 23). He then lashed out in a press conference: "No one can dictate to us. No one can wave a finger at us, because we will wave a finger back" (Rubin 1981: 140). In fact, he asked his military chiefs to prepare for an "oil war" with Washington and London (Milani 2011a). Americans were baffled. U.S. representative to the UN John Scali cornered his Iranian counterpart Hoveyda, in January 1974, demanding: "Why have you pulled this trick? It's hard to swallow, coming from a friend" (Hoveyda 1980: 80). The Shah himself provided the answer to journalists, "Obviously, to have weapons and an army is not something which can be had free of charge, but thank God, today we can afford to purchase as many of the best weapons in the world . . . without any favors from anybody, for we pay in cash" (Saikal 1980: 157). And this was surely the case, for in November 1976, Iran struck its first oil-for-weapons deal with Britain, and laid the infrastructure for a domestic arms industry with the goal of becoming self-sufficient in two decades. During the regime's final years, Iran was producing small weapons and anti-tank missiles, and assembling helicopters and tanks. The ultimate objective was to use oil revenue to turn Iran into "a global power in its own right, before the end of the century" (Saikal 1980: 135).

To cover his back, the Shah moved "dramatically toward rapprochement with Moscow" (Rubin 1981: 108). In September 1962 the Shah prohibited the installation of U.S. bases or missiles on Iranian soil. Next came his well-publicized visit to Moscow, in the summer of 1965, to sign economic and military agreements. In exchange for $600 million worth of Iranian natural gas, the USSR constructed Iran's first steel mill complex in Isfahan together with a pipeline from north Iran to the Caucasus. Soviets also supplied $110 million worth of armored carriers and anti-aircraft guns (Saikal 1980: 95). An Iranian diplomat remembered the Shah's euphoria, "That's it! We've just signed the contract with the Russians. The steelworks that the Westerners refused us will soon stand. . . . Heavy industry will guarantee our independence!" (Hoveyda 1980: 72). He was no less excited about importing Soviet artillery, which he described as the best in the world (Huyser 1986: 202). A massive Iranian-Soviet arms deal for $414 million followed, in November 1976 (Saikal 1980: 159). That same year, the two countries concluded a trade agreement, with a complementary $280 million economic aid package. By 1977 over 15 percent of Iranian exports went to the Soviet Union, and 1,500 Russian experts were attached to civilian and military projects in Iran. In a final attempt to placate Communists, Tehran established relations with Beijing in 1971—before Nixon's visit (Halliday 1979: 262–63).

The Shah also cemented his regional ties. In 1964 he tried to convince Turkey and Pakistan to join him in a tripartite alliance separate from the Western-sponsored CENTO (Saikal 1980: 93).[9] He improved relations with India and Afghanistan; dropped Iranian claims to Bahrain; settled boundary disputes with Saudi Arabia; offered technical support to the Gulf sheikhdoms; and resumed diplomatic relations with Cairo, in August 1970, while Nasser prepared for war with Israel and cut off ties with Washington (Rubin 1981: 127). Equally important was the signing of the 1975 Algeria Accord with Saddam Hussein, pledging to terminate support for the Kurdish secessionists—against American wishes—in exchange for territorial concessions over the Shatt al-Arab waterway (Wahid 2009: 49). And he justified his compromise as follows: "We agreed to bury our differences and succeeded in ending the misunderstanding which [Western] colonialist influences had maintained between us" (Pahlavi 1980: 133).

But how could the Shah balance these Arab overtures with his reputably close links with Israel? In truth, Iran had always been careful not to offend its Arab neighbors. In 1949 the Shah only allowed a de facto recognition of Israel. The Jewish state's mission in Tehran was unofficial and low key. But by the late 1960s, his court minister's diary reveals how obsessive the Shah had become with concealing ties to Israel. According to a February 1969 entry, "Levi Eshkol, the Prime Minister of Israel, has died. I've arranged for HIM to offer condolences to the Israeli President, without risking trouble from the Arabs" (Alam 2008: 36); in May 1970, "The unofficial Israeli mission in Tehran celebrated Israel's twenty-second anniversary. HIM forbade anyone from the court or government to attend. . . . [H]e's keen that we should adopt a pro-Arab stand" (Alam 2008: 152); in April 1972, "[I] passed on a request from the Israeli envoy here, that HIM accept a visit from Prime Minister Golda Meir or from Abba Eban, the Israeli Foreign Minister. . . . 'We have nothing of importance to discuss with Israel,' said HIM, 'but if they're really determined to see me, they must bear full responsibility for keeping our meeting a secret'" (Alam 2008: 212); in December 1974, "HIM was due to receive Yitzhak Rabin, the Prime Minister of Israel. . . . I made all the necessary arrangements . . . instructing the guard how to transfer him to the Palace without arousing suspicion, and even selecting a servant to attend. . . . I picked a man of quite outstanding stupidity in the knowledge that he would be incapable of recognizing Rabin" (Alam 2008: 401).

As the revolutionary clouds gathered, it was obvious that the Shah had become a "supreme nationalist," pursuing an aggressive policy to enhance Iran's global potentials. Washington now suspected that he had been using "the shield of the West to gain the necessary time to strengthen . . . his own position" (Chubin and Zabih 1974: 15, 296). The Shah no longer considered himself "a vassal but a peer" (Hoveyda 1980: 76). Unfortunately in 1978, he learned—the hard way—that perhaps he should not have sailed too far away from Western shores. With a dependent military, an incompetent and conspiring security apparatus, and increasingly suspicious Western allies, he was entirely unprepared for revolution.

Notes

1. See Majd (2000) for details.

2. Brzezinski recorded in his diary that when he called the Shah amidst the revolutionary crisis of 1978, "I was struck, while I was waiting on the line, by the strange protocol followed at the other end in Tehran: a guard or a functionary of some sort barked out several times in aloud voice and in Iranian the Shah's full title before he actually came to the line" (1983: 365).

3. Service breakdown ran as follows: army, 200,000; Gendarmerie, 60,000; air force 100,000; navy 25,000; commandos 17,000; and Imperial Guard 8,000 (Abrahamian 1982: 436).

4. Axworthy (2014: 190) offers a spirited defense of the capacity of Iranian pilots to fly the F-14s, claiming that U.S. doubts were "based on little more than prejudice, exaggeration . . . and a certain woodenheaded inability to comprehend a different kind of war fought in an unfamiliar context." The problem is, of course, that these doubts were not just expressed by Americans, but by the head of the Iranian air force himself. The effectiveness demonstrated during the Iran-Iraq War in the 1980s was

a product of extreme necessity and does not prove they had mastered these sophisticated jets when they first received them under the Shah (an analysis of the constraints imposed by lack of training on the conduct of Iranian pilots during the first stages of the war appears in Hickman 1982: 20–21).

5. Axworthy (2014: 284) lists SAVAK's torture methods, but notes that they were used to extract information rather than force confessions (as would occur under the Islamic Republic).

6. It is also worth adding that (unlike Egypt) the regular police was prohibited from using violence against criminals in police stations (Abrahamian 1999: 1).

7. "Sales of military hardware to Iran jumped from $524 million in 1972 to $3.9 billion in 1974. . . . Between 1970 and 1978, the Shah ordered $20 billion worth of arms, which accounted for 25 percent of all United States arms sales" (Parsa 1989: 52). During his last visit to Washington, in November 1977, an unabated Shah ordered $10 billion worth of weapons (Halliday 1979: 294).

8. A disconcerting example of the Shah's bursting ego comes from his court minister's diary entry on May 26, 1973: "I had to report a request from the English royal family. Prince Philip wishes to be elected to the governing committee of the Iranian Imperial Equestrian Society. HIM was amused by this, commenting, 'In days gone by, an Iranian politician would have considered it a catastrophe if he'd been missed off the guest list to a British embassy cocktail party. Now it appears the boot is on the other foot; a request from the British royal family is filed away amongst insignificant trivia' " (Alam 2008: 294). This megalomania prompted William Simon, Nixon's secretary of the Treasury, to assert in an interview with *American Banker*, on July 15, 1973, that "the Shah is a nut" (Alam 2008: 381), and to repeat the same claim—weeks after he had ostensibly apologized to Tehran—before the Senate's Foreign Affairs Committee (Heikal 1981: 16).

9. Curiously, his father had taken a similar step with Turkey, Iraq, and Afghanistan in 1937, but nothing came of this initiative either (Saikal 1980: 155).

4 | The Coup That Never Was
JANUARY 1979

THE CENTRAL MYTH OF THE Iranian Revolution is that an exceptionally motivated population challenged one of the world's most repressive machines and its superpower patron—and won. In reality, the Imperial Armed Forces was only impressive on paper; the security apparatus was in shambles; and Washington seriously questioned the Shah's reliability. But before analyzing how the regime and its foreign ally responded to the popular demonstrations, let us first recount the events constituting the Iranian Revolution.

The Shah's confidence in his popularity tempted him to open up the political system, encouraging intellectuals to pen open letters demanding further reform (the first published in May 1977 by fifty lawyers). However, in November 1977, Ayatollah Khomeini's son was allegedly killed by SAVAK. His followers' indignation turned to rage after Information Minister Darius Homayoun—acting on royal orders—anonymously published a vicious personal attack on Khomeini in Iran's leading newspaper *Etelaat*, on January 9, 1978 (Saikal 1980: 196). This imprudent provocation sparked riots in the shrine-city of Qom, and several were killed. Thus began a series of fortieth-day mourning demonstrations, each commemorating the deaths that occurred forty days before. These spread geographically from Qom (January 9) to Tabriz (February 18) to Yazd and Kermanshah (March 28) to Tehran (May 6). The cycle was interrupted briefly in June, and then resumed in Mashhad and Isfahan in July. On August 19 the Cinema Rex complex in the city of Abadan was set on fire, killing perhaps 400 people. SAVAK tried to pin it down on Islamists, who had attacked movie theaters in the past, but the accusation did not stick.[1] The Shah appointed a liberal cabinet under Jafar Sharif-Emami, on August 27, to absorb popular anger. Emami was close to clerical circles, but he was also head of the Pahlavi Foundation and had no public credibility. On September 7 the exiled Khomeini called for a general strike. The government responded by imposing a curfew on Friday September 8, soon to be known as Black Friday. Either because they had not learned about the curfew or because they were determined to defy it, hundreds of demonstrators gathered in Tehran's Jaleh Square. Soldiers opened fire. Estimates of how many people died that day vary wildly between 40 and 4,000.[2] Oil workers threw in their hat with a series of strikes that reduced production from 6 million barrels a day to almost nil. The Revolution died down for a couple of months, but then on November 5, later known as Bloody Sunday, an unruly crowd burned and ransacked dozens of buildings, including the British embassy. The violence unnerved the Shah. On November 6 he declared martial law and appointed a military government under General Gholam-Reza Azhari. These measures invited an estimated 1 million-man march on December 11—which coincided with the somber religious festival of Ashura (Keddie 1981; Harney 1999; Kurzman 2004).

The Shah decided to abdicate. On December 30 he appointed a reforming cabinet under National Front veteran Shahpour Bakhtiar, established his Regency Council, and left Iran for the last time on January 16, 1979. After a humiliating trip, he ended up in Egypt, where he died in July 1980. Meanwhile, Khomeini returned to Iran after sixteen years of exile, on February 1—commencing the so-called *Daheh-ye Fajr*, the "ten days of dawn" that ended with revolutionary triumph on February 11. He was driven from the airport to the Behesht-e Zahra cemetery to pay tribute to the martyrs of the Revolution. There, he dismissed Bakhtiar's government as illegal, warning: "If they were to continue to stay in power, we would treat them as criminals. . . . I shall appoint my own government" (quoted in Axworthy 2014: 2). On February 5 Khomeini formed a new government under Mehdi Bazargan, founder of the liberal Freedom Movement. Khomeini noted solemnly that "this is not an ordinary government. It is a government based on the shari'a. Opposing this government means opposing the shari'a. . . . Revolt against God's government is a revolt against God" (quoted in Axworthy 2014: 5). During the cabinet's first press conference, Rafsanjani outlined Khomeini's roadmap: a referendum to endorse an Islamic republic; a Constituent Assembly to draft its constitution; then parliamentary elections.

With two rival cabinets, the revolutionary situation persisted. But on February 10, a clash between 200 Imperial Guards and mutinous air force technicians (*homofars*) aggravated Islamist and leftist militias (the Mujahidin-e Khalq and Feda'iyan-e Khalq, respectively), who occupied a machinegun factory and police stations and handed out weapons to demonstrators.

Armed protestors then forced their way into the public radio station and began issuing directives. Two days later, on February 11, the military declared its neutrality; Bakhtiar fled; and Bazargan's government was left standing. However, Bazargan proved to be Iran's Kerensky, for soon Khomeini and his men secured power (Rubin 1981; Schahgaldian 1987).

Street Politics, Court Intrigues

Emphasis on the role of Shi'ism pervades most accounts of the Iranian Revolution. Moaddel (1992: 353) underscored the "all-encompassing role played by the imageries and symbolism of Shi'i Islam in initiating and sustaining the revolutionary movement." Skocpol (1994: 247–49) agreed that Shi'a Islam was both "organizationally and culturally crucial to the making of the Iranian revolution" because it had "especially salient symbolic resources to justify resistance against unjust authority, and to legitimate religious leaders as competitors to the state." Even Foucault was so (temporarily) overtaken by it that he proclaimed: "Islam—which is not simply a religion, but an entire way of life, an adherence to a history and a civilization—has a good chance to become a gigantic powder keg, at the level of hundreds of millions of men" (quoted in Afary and Anderson 2005: 4). Indeed, Shi'a Islam was still portrayed as omnipotent decades following the Revolution, as Axworthy (2014: 410) claimed: "If a critical mass of believers among the Iranian people ever decide that the Islamic regime has become un-Islamic . . . then Iran's rulers will be gone as if they had never been more substantial than a puff of smoke."[3]

So why is Shi'ism particularly revolutionary? Wright (2000: 10) explained, "Shi'ite Islam demands that the faithful fight against injustice and tyranny, even if it means certain death." Because Islam's minority sect was born out of a political revolt in the seventh century, its followers remain exceptionally willing "to face martyrdom, indeed to welcome it"; and this "ensured that the Revolution would triumph" (Heikal 1981: 176; Algar 2001: 13–19; Axworthy 2014: 19–24). In addition, Shi'a clerics shepherd their flock more closely because they represent the infallible knowledge of the twelve holy descendants of the Prophet, as opposed to Sunni clerics, whose views are merely interpretative. They are also more financially independent because, unlike their Sunni counterparts, they resisted becoming salaried state functionaries, and continued to rely on religious offerings.[4]

Structurally and historically, however, these differences have been superficial. First, while Shi'a mullahs officially present their opinions as infallible and Sunnis do not, their effect is practically the same. On the one hand, variations among Shi'ite interpretations undermine any claim to infallibility, and on the other hand, Sunni opinions are issued with the type of scientific authority that deems them binding. Pious Muslims, regardless of their sect, faithfully follow their clerics, and it is ludicrous to assume that the Shi'ite ones are taken more seriously. Second, both Shi'a and Sunni scholars rely on religious endowments and almsgiving. Whether rulers disrupt the flow of funds is historically contingent. So before Nasser nationalized religious endowments in Egypt, for instance, Sunni clerics were as independent as Shi'as. And even in that case, generous donations usually allow them substantial independence. The third and most important flaw in the Shi'ite exceptionalism argument is historical. A quick survey of Islamic history shows that Sunnis have been more revolutionary than Shi'as—who were typically associated with political quietism and dissimulation (*taqiya*). In modern history, Azhar clerics' activism, between Napoleon's invasion of Egypt in 1798 and the national revolution of 1919, is well documented. Also, the cleric who incited the famous 1891 Tobacco Protest in Iran against the Qajars was the Sunni Jamal al-Din al-Afghani, who then went on to inspire revolution throughout the Muslim world. Finally, from the 1980s onward, Sunni and Shi'a militants have equally raised the banner of martyrdom. And the 2011 Arab revolts demonstrated that Sunnis were as willing to sacrifice their lives as Iranians had been in the 1970s.

This last claim brings us to recent research on how many Iranians made the "ultimate sacrifice." The revolutionaries themselves claimed 50,000 martyrs (Algar 2001: 139). U.S. sources brought down that number to 10,000 (Bill 1988: 236; Daugherty 2001: 65; Ward 2009: 225). This figure has been steadily declining. According to Arjomand (1988: 120), despite "wild rumors," those killed during the sixteen-month revolt were 3,000 in total—"[a] relatively small number of casualties for an upheaval of major proportions." British diplomat Desmond Harney (1999: 97), who lived through the Revolution in Tehran, recorded an overall death toll of 1,600 people. Yet scrupulous research, conducted via the Martyr Foundation's archives and the Tehran coroner's office, drastically reduced the range to between 744 and 895 dead, adding, "These may be under-accounts, but even if multiplied many times over they do not match the image of vast masses standing up to machine-gun fire" (Kurzman 2004: 71). To put this into perspective, note that Egypt's non-ideological and peaceful revolt claimed the lives of over 1,000 demonstrators in less than 18 days.

So if Shi'ism was not inherently revolutionary, did clerical organization offer demonstrators a unique advantage? Bayat argued that it was not religion per se but the clergy's "institutional capacity"—versus the "organizationally decapitated" seculars—that helped them prevail (1998b: 37). Similarly, Halliday asserted that the mosque "found itself" the center of resistance because secular platforms were repressed (1979: 19). This mosque-based institutional capacity was estimated at 80,000 mosques and 180,000 mullahs (Halliday 1979: 19). However, future research counted 5,000 major mosques and 15,000 minor ones run by 90,000 clergymen (Abrahamian 1982: 432–34; Kurzman 2004: 37, 101; Martin 2007: 23).[5] Moreover, Kurzman uncovered through ethnographic fieldwork that these mosques were not the "sanctuaries" that Islamist revolutionaries claimed. On the contrary, "mosques were considered dangerous places for oppositionists" because most clerics shunned political activism (Kurzman 2004: 39).

What about clerical radicalism? The litmus test for the revolutionary potential of Iranian clergymen was their reaction to the first Pahlavi. Reza Shah introduced new commercial, criminal, and civil codes based on French law rather than Shari'a, and restricted the judicial role of mullahs to family law; he decreed European dress, and banned the veil; he expunged Arabic vocabulary from Persian dictionaries, and enforced the use of Farsi in official documents; he revived Zoroastrian symbols and architecture, and required schoolchildren to memorize parts of the epic poem *Shahnameh,* which glorified Iran's pre-Islamic history. Most crucially, he placed religious education under the supervision of the Ministry of Education, and extended state control over religious endowments. His treatment of clerics was, to say the least, abusive. In October 1928 he arrested (and nine years later executed) the most senior cleric, Seyyed Hassan Modarres, because he rejected the Uniform Dress Law (Rahnema 2000: 3–5; Martin 2007: 14). When a princess was castigated for not covering her hair in a holy shrine, Reza Shah returned to that shrine with a hundred men, entered with their boots on, and whipped the errant mullahs (De Bellaigue 2004: 90). He outdid himself, however, in 1928. When clerics from Mashhad's Gowharshad Mosque protested against his reforms, Reza Shah attacked the mosque with 2,000 soldiers, killing about 200 mullahs and students, and dragging another 800 in chains to the capital (Zabih 1988: 84). No wonder that clerical representation in Parliament dropped from 40 percent in the 1920s to zero in 1937 (Parsa 1989: 36). Remarkably, though, clerical resistance to his rule was "most notable by its absence" (Martin 2007: 15). Pious Iranians were no less apathetic. In fact, the intellectual who mobilized revolutionary youth more than any other (Ali Shari'ati) lamented in the 1970s that Iranians suffered from spiritual poverty; that the "flames of faith have died in the hearts of the youth" (quoted in Rahnema 2000: 62). When he tried to revolutionize Shi'ism by infusing it with socialist and anti-colonial vocabulary, most clerics considered him a heretic (Naraghi 1999: 28).[6]

But although there was nothing essentially revolutionary about Shi'ite theology and institutions, Ayatollah Khomeini was certainly exceptional. In his comparative study of Islamic revolutionary trends, Munson concluded that Khomeini enjoyed "a far greater degree of charismatic authority than any other Muslim fundamentalist. . . . His messianic aura enabled him to mobilize segments of Iranian (urban) society that had traditionally been apolitical and acquiescent" (1988: 134). Yet Khomeini was not a typical Shi'ite cleric, and his blend of religion and politics was innovative and controversial. Even if Algar portrayed him as a culminating figure in a long tradition of clerical activism, he had to admit that Khomeini also "*broke sharply* with the existing tradition of the learned institution by cultivating from a quite early point radical political interest" (2001: 53; my emphasis).

As late as 1978, the critical mass within the clergy, led by the most senior authority, Ayatollah Shariatmadari, was monarchist and averse to Islamist republicanism (Hoveyda 1980: 38). Months into the Revolution, clerics remained conservative, even passive (Burns 1996: 364). Mullahs constantly ordered their followers to "keep quiet and not expose the seminaries to further repression" (Kurzman 2004: 33).[7] In the fall of 1978, the highest Shi'ite authority of the time, Ayatollah Kho'i in Najaf ("the Pope of the Shi'as"), carefully distanced himself from Khomeini (Harney 1999: 109). Two weeks before the Shah abdicated, Ayatollah Qomi in Mashhad, one of Iran's five senior clerics, published an essay in all the leading newspapers describing how Imam Reza, one of the twelve Shi'a saints, came to him in a dream to enquire "why [Iranians] were trying to destroy the only Shi'a king and the only Shi'a nation?" (Harney 1999: 118). The truth is, Khomeini's ideas "ran contrary to traditional Muslim political thought, the established practice in the seminaries, and even the position he himself had taken before" (Rajaee 2007: 90–91). His "clerics-turned-ideologues . . . brought about a revolution in Shi'ism" (Arjomand 2002: 721; Zubaida 1988; Dabashi 1993). The cloaked revolutionary icon was "entirely exceptional" (Cronin 2010: 266).

Now, if Khomeini's clerical faction was "small and unable to mobilize the population" (Parsa 1989: 218), we still need to explain who they were and how they eventually succeeded. Until September 1978, Khomeini's circle was mostly composed of former students. Rafsanjani wrote that what fascinated them about Khomeini was how radically different he was from all the other clerics (2005: 33). But the ayatollah's effect was limited, as the failed 1963 uprising demonstrates. Even the traditionally pious bazaar merchants turned their back on Khomeini's when the economy was prospering in the 1960s and early 1970s, and only rediscovered their piety after the regime undermined their economic interests (Parsa 1989: 123–24; Katouzian 1999: 175). So what changed in 1978?

Arjomand (1988: 103) and Parsa (1989: 219) argued that his vilification of the regime, rather than his representation of Islam, was what made him popular among the revolutionaries. Heikal (1981: 88), Rubin (1981: 221), and Burns (1996: 375) compared him to Lenin. His maximalist positions, his sense of timing, his inflammatory rhetoric steeled the opposition. And like the Bolshevik leader, he led his faction from the sidelines to the height of power, even if most Iranians had barely heard about his radical ideology.[8] Also like Lenin, he was a master strategist who manipulated disparate opposition groups to achieve his goals (Heikal 1981: 186; Moin 1999: 200). Others assigned more weight to charisma. Khomeini inspired the masses by "his boldness, his steadfastness, his consistency, his simplicity. This is what political leadership is about" (Harney 1999: 132). Algar, who was close to Khomeini, agreed, "Anyone who has come into the presence of Imam Khomeini has realized that this man is a kind of embodiment of the human ideal. It is by exercising a combination of moral, intellectual, political, and spiritual ability that he has come to have such a tremendous role" (2001: 42).

Even more important were his organizational skills. The reason why Khomeini rode the revolutionary crest to power with considerable agility is that his organization enabled him to move swiftly and decisively when others wavered. He ran several networks of associates. Some of them, such as Ibrahim Yazdi and Sadeq Qotbzadeh (both future foreign ministers), received military training in Cairo in the mid-1950s.[9] Others, such as future president Rafsanjani set up neighborhood *komitehs* (revolutionary committees)—1,500 in Tehran alone. A third group recruited members of Islamist and leftist guerillas that had been operating in Iran for years. And upon his return, many of these groups evolved into revolutionary militias: *Hezbollahis* to enforce Islamic law, as well as the standing *Pasdaran* and volunteer *Basij* forces to protect the new regime (Heikal 1981: 71, 166). He also avoided Washington's mistake in Iraq in 2003 by decapitating the military and security institutions, but keeping them intact and transforming them to serve his purposes.

On the political front, Khomeini created a secret Council of the Islamic Revolution in November 1977, and compiled a list of trustworthy candidates for various public posts (from ministers to mayors). He also asked the former director of the National Iranian Oil Company to draft an oil policy for the new regime (Heikal 1981: 169). In November 1978 Mehdi Bazargan and Karim Sanjabi, representing Iran's largest political movements, the Freedom

Movement and National Front, respectively, performed a symbolic pilgrimage to Paris to show that they "aligned themselves and their followers unequivocally with Khomeini" (Axworthy 2014: 120).

The month he returned to Iran, the methodical ayatollah instructed Rafsanjani to work with Ayatollah Beheshti on forming the Islamic Republic Party to unite their supporters and prepare for parliamentary elections, which the Party won in a landslide (Rafsanjani 2005: 221).[10] And before the other factions knew what hit them, Khomeini legitimized his power via two popular referendums: one at the end of March (a month after he returned from exile), which showed 98.2 percent of voters in favor of replacing the monarchy with a still-undefined Islamic Republic, and the second, in December, which approved, by 99.7 percent, a constitution establishing Islamist rule according to the principle of *velayat-e faqih* (jurist guardianship)—a principle Khomeini explored in his *Hokumat-e Eslami* (Islamic Government) in 1970.

So while the ayatollah was ideologically driven, his success derived from his ability to translate beliefs into effective strategies. As Axworthy (2014: 119) noted, "Khomeini saw the essentials. Power was the essential thing—the rest . . . would follow." A good example is how he turned the traditional fortieth-day mourning ceremonies (which also exist in the Sunni world) into occasions for protest, or as Kurzman put it, shifted "grief recovery into grief-based mobilization" (2004: 54).[11] Another example is his media savvy, especially his cassette recordings and interviews. It was partly why he moved to France during the revolutionary turmoil, where in his words: "They were kind to us and we could publicize our views extensively" (quoted in Moin 1999: 3). Indeed, Khomeini was one of the first Muslim clerics to reinvent himself as a celebrity; in his competent hands, "the first media revolution was born" (Rajaee 2007: 113).

Nonetheless, Khomeini's revolutionary crusade might have failed again (as in 1963) if the regime had not begun to crack. So why was 1978 different? Numerous accounts emphasize the plight of the urban mob: 35 percent of Tehran's population dwelled in slums, and about half of them lived as squatters (Bayat 1998b: 29).[12] Khomeini personally thanked those *mustaz'afin* (oppressed): "This momentous Islamic Revolution is indebted to the efforts of this class—the class of the deprived . . . the shanty dwellers, the class that brought about the victory of the revolution" (quoted in Bayat 1998b: 35). Yet Kazemi (1980) and Bayat (1998b) showed that they actually remained marginal until the Revolution triumphed (see also Halliday 1979: 278; Kurzman 2004: 100). A squatter told the *Washington Post*, in January 1978, "We have heard about the demonstrations, but we don't take part; to demonstrate you have to have a full stomach. . . . Whoever gives us bread and work, we will be with him" (Parsa 1989: 5). In Bayat's succinct description, the disenfranchised "cannot afford to be ideological" (1998a: 159). Halliday extended the argument to labor. Although Iran had 10.6 million workers, over half of them remained isolated in the countryside (1979: 173). So in effect, the lower classes only became important after the Shah abdicated. During his sixteen-year exile, Khomeini only referred to them eight times in his sermons—compared to fifty references to students (Bayat 1998b: 43). Their mobilization began with the construction of the new regime (Parsa 1989: 5).

Iran's popular revolt featured urban middle-class groups with different agendas (Martin 2007: 148; Cronin 2010: 265–66). Even the most active among them, the bazaar merchants, did not act as a coherent group,[13] nor did students or professionals (Parsa 1989: 10). Moreover, this middle-class uprising involved less than 10 percent of Iranians (Bayat quoted in El-Hennawy 2011: 6). The absence of the urban poor, the workers, and the peasants—in short, the most numerous, oppressed, and potentially violent groups—casts doubt over the conventional reading of the Revolution as an invincible mass revolt that overwhelmed the state's coercive organs. The Revolution might have been repressed if the Shah had not undermined the men with guns.

A contingent, yet noteworthy fact is that the Shah had been suffering lymphomatous cancer for six years, and realized by 1978 that he was a dying man (Pahlavi 1980: 11). Medication weakened his resolve. And his deteriorating condition made him primarily concerned with how to pass power to his son. If the Pahlavi dynasty was to continue, he could not tarnish the Peacock Throne by authorizing a bloodbath. Unlike 1963, he was not going to be around long enough to mitigate the effects of a ruthless crackdown. "He was afraid if he slaughtered his people in the streets and turned over to a teenager a situation he could not handle the dynasty would be swept aside" (Precht 2004: 17). Just like father stepped aside to allow the dynasty to survive under his son, the Shah abdicated peacefully to save the Crown. He spared no thought for his ruling partners, the military and security forces. An absolute monarch had no partners. They would now have to pay the price for their political subservience.

A Coup at the Eleventh Hour?

The Shah confessed to the American and British ambassadors that the military urged him to restore order through arrests and curfews, but he refused (Brzezinski 1983: 366). But if the monarch had, in fact, stifled his officers, why did they not act independently to protect the regime despite the king's wishes or immediately after he left? A common explanation is that soldiers and junior officers disobeyed their superiors: good Muslims flocked to their imam, and good Iranians fraternized with demonstrators. Yet careful examination of the attrition rate proves that desertions did not really impair the army. A month before the Shah abdicated, only 5,434 conscripts and noncommissioned officers (NCOs) had deserted (Parsa 1989: 243). General Robert E. Huyser, sent by Washington to assess the military situation, reported that as late as January 20, 1979, the desertion rate was relatively low: "The media was talking of 2,000 to 3,000 desertions each day, but this was rubbish. A more realistic figure was probably 200 to 300, out of some 450,000. This left us with far more than we could ever need" (1986: 160). Arjomand similarly maintained that the desertion rate was 100 a day in early January 1979; then 200 after the Shah departed in mid-January; and only jumped to 1,000 a day after Khomeini returned in February (1988: 121; see also Axworthy 2014: 6). Moreover, most deserters were bewildered by their sovereign's abdication, rather than sympathetic with the revolt (Harney 1999: 155; see also Halliday 1979: 293; Parsa 1989: 243; Kurzman 2004: 114; Milani 2011a). In brief, the military did not melt away: "Discipline in the ranks was maintained and the army was still largely intact. . . . [T]he incidents of the breakdown of discipline were isolated and the desertions did not amount to a fraction of the army . . . [which] held together very well, perhaps even better than could have been expected" (Arjomand 1988: 121).[14]

The most notorious en masse desertion was that of the *homafars*, the 12,000-strong corps of noncommissioned air force technicians. Revolutionary lore has them swayed by Khomeini's triumphant return, replayed on television, on February 10, at Tehran's Doshan Tappeh air base. They supposedly "broke out into demonstrations demanding the installation of an Islamic government under Imam Khomeini" (Algar 2001: 136). But there was more to it, as one could imagine. *Homafar* mutinies began on January 23, and spread to air force bases in Tehran, Shiraz, and Isfahan (Huyser 1986: 181). This corps of technicians was created in the 1970s to service Iran's expanding inventory. But the Shah refused to incorporate them into the air force because they were little more than mechanics from humble backgrounds. Witnessing firsthand the privileges of Imperial pilots, the *homafars* certainly nursed a grudge (Hickman 1982: 6). Worse, when their contracts expired, they were forcefully reenlisted, thus preventing them from capitalizing on their skills in the market (Rubin 1981: 227). Over and above, they resented General Huyser's plan to fly Iran's F-14s out of the country lest they fall into the wrong hands (Huyser 1986: 188; Zabih 1988: 44). What is noteworthy here is that these men were not part of the armed forces, had no conceivable role in repressing the revolt, and mutinied three weeks after the Shah's departure.

But if desertions cannot explain why the military faltered, then what can? Simply, the Imperial Armed Forces had no institutional autonomy, and therefore no capacity to identify and protect their collective interests. With the benefit of hindsight, RAND explained:

> Although well-equipped and numerous, the military in fact lacked the necessary *esprit de corps* that would have made it a credible political power center in Iranian politics. . . . The Shah's extensive personal control . . . emasculated the armed forces, seriously undermined the internal solidarity of the forces, and demoralized large numbers of middle-level and junior officers. . . . [T]he military lost its bearings without the King. (Schahgaldian 1987: 13–14)

As part of his mission to evaluate the cohesiveness of the Iranian military, General Huyser met the top brass during the first week of January 1979. To his surprise, the commanders predicted that the military would collapse without the Shah. He lectured them on how "as military leaders, your responsibilities are not to defend one person" (Huyser 1986: 39). Yet their response, best articulated by Deputy War Minister General Hassan Toufanian, was this: "The Shah is not just a man. He is the *country*" (Huyser 1986: 32). Long conditioned by his patrimonial command style and micromanagement of everyday military affairs, officers learned to adjust their behavior (even their thoughts) to royal expectations. American officers were often frustrated by their Iranian counterparts' aversion to decision-making, even on routine matters, to avoid royal rebuke (Ward 2009: 206). In his Tehran diary, U.K. diplomat Desmond Harney ruled out a crisis-triggered coup because Iranian officers were "terrified of responsibility" (1999: 47). The "commanding generals had little real authority over their commands. . . . [E]ach of the service chiefs reported to him on a regular basis on all matters. . . . [T]he shah made decisions on all kinds of military activity. . . . This made him the de facto commander of the individual services as well" (Hickman 1982: 4–5). The full effect of this "paralytic loyalty" became evident during the Revolution (Rubin 1981: 226). A military needs more than money and weapons; it needs a leadership capable of concerted action (Arjomand 1988: 126). This was precisely what it lacked.

Divide-and-rule tactics guided the Shah's treatment of his top brass. He fostered rivalry and resentment among generals to reduce their ability to coordinate (Arjomand 1988: 124). Indeed, he proudly confided to his court minister that foreign powers would not be able to unseat him through a coup because "my generals distrust—and lack professional respect for—one another. . . . [T]hey're too much at one another's throats to constitute a threat" (Alam 2008: 197–98). Even amidst revolution, the Shah persisted in his old ways. Iranian diplomat Fereydoun Hoveyda remembered that during his last court audience, in April 1978, "I was astonished to observe that the Shah was receiving [generals] one at a time. . . . It was often said that the Shah approved of the idea of divide and rule, but who would have thought to such an extent" (Hoveyda 1980: 28). Naturally, officers relished competing for royal favor and "never developed a corporate and independent political identity" (Cronin 2010: 262).[15] Furthermore, they had no proper structures. The War Ministry was a hollow shell, and its leaders were little more than "grand quartermasters" (Abrahamian 1999: 73). The Supreme Defense Council existed on paper, but almost never met (Ward 2009: 209). Most crucially, Iran not only lacked a joint chiefs of staff, but the Shah's suspicion of social contact between officers also prevented the establishment of an informal "old boy network" (Heikal 1981: 68; Huyser 1986: 8). In short, the inaction of commanders, the bewilderment of conscripts, and the dilemma of the officers caught in between paralyzed the whole structure.

When the Shah finally decided to form a military government, on November 5, 1978, he entrusted it to General Gholam-Reza Azhari, a weak and aging commander with a fatal heart condition (Rubin 1981: 224). The revolutionaries perceived him for the "ineffectual parlor general" that he was and were hardly deterred by his appointment (Arjomand 1988: 116). The general immediately collapsed. On November 11 U.S. Ambassador William Sullivan found him languishing under an oxygen tent in a dimly lit bedroom. The nominal military governor complained to his American visitor that although the Shah had imposed martial law, he still forbade shooting demonstrators, and reprimanded him whenever accidents occurred (Heikal 1981: 161; Arjomand 1988: 115, 120). Azhari's military government crumpled in two months, as its leader traveled to the United States for heart surgery (Rubin 1981: 228). On December 30 the Shah invited the National Front's Shahpour Bakhtiar, a respected oppositionist, to form a government.

With the clock ticking on the Pahlavi dynasty, the Shah was still determined to keep officers subordinate in hopes of returning to Iran or passing the crown to his inexperienced son (Arjomand 1988: 124). This partly showed in his hesitation over top appointments. When he asked General Azhari, the military's chief of staff, to head the government in November, his spot remained vacant until January 7. Again, royal trepidations kept the position of war minister empty until January 10. Between those two dates, on January 8, Army Commander General Gholam-Ali Oveisi fled Iran because he realized the sovereign was abandoning ship, and his position was only filled three days later—despite this being the most dangerous phase of the Revolution. The Shah's choice for chief of staff was General Abbas Gharabaghi, an Azerbaijani with a strong Turkish accent, who—as former commander of the gendarmerie—was considered an outsider by the officer corps (Rubin 1981: 239). His new war minister, General Shafqat, was junior to the service chiefs, which assured he would not be taken seriously (Huyser 1986: 25). When the new prime minister invited military strongman General Feridun Djam from Europe to take charge, the monarch strenuously objected (Ward 2009: 219). Iranian academic Ehsan Naraghi saw Djam walk out of the royal presence, on January 8, after being told he was a persona non grata (1999: 152). The embittered general commented, "My visit to Tehran convinced me that . . . there is no one from whom [the military] could receive command" (quoted in Zabih 1988: 38).

General Huyser tried to impose order via an impromptu joint chiefs of staff, created on January 9, a week before the Shah left (Huyser 1986: 41).[16] He explained to the generals that he appreciated their quandary since they were accustomed to receiving plans from court, but now they had to formulate their own plan (Huyser 1986: 48). His little speech obviously fell on deaf ears since Air Force Commander Amir Hussein Rabi'i still blamed the Americans for not saving the regime, and famously proclaimed during his trial that they "took the Shah by the tail, and threw him into exile like a dead rat" (Arjomand 1988: 114). A navy admiral—summarizing the view of his comrades—laid the blame on Washington for urging the supreme commander (the Shah) to leave, and not helping officers seize power (Kamyabipour 2011).

The truth is, U.S. National Security Advisor Zbigniew Brzezinski threw all his weight behind the Iranian military's ability to save the regime. But a briefly elated Brzezinski soon bewailed in his diary, "Alas, nothing happened. . . . [They] simply procrastinated" (1983: 363). This procrastination provoked a harsh rejoinder from Huyser during a January 10 meeting:

> "Your country is at stake. How on earth do you think you are going to pull a coup? Is there something that I don't know about, which will enable you to take control?" . . . All of them wore the same blank looks that I had always received when asking such questions. I therefore pressed harder, because I wanted to reach the bottom line—to find an answer to the one question that nagged me ever since my arrival: Did this group have secret plans for a coup that I did not know about? At last I found the answer I was looking for. Iran's military leadership was in a totally helpless state. (1986: 69)

While officers remained clueless, the farsighted Khomeini launched a charm offensive. "Do not attack the army in its breast," he instructed, "but in its heart" (Ward 2009: 216–17). As he explained in a cassette recording, "We know that the soldiers are confused, not knowing how to act, but they . . . obey their orders. How can they refuse to obey orders when they are bound by military discipline?" (Heikal 1981: 146). In September 1978 he ended a sermon by proclaiming: "I extend my hand to all those in the army, air force, and navy who are faithful to Islam and the homeland and ask them to assist us in preserving our independence" (Khomeini 1981: 236). On the day he returned, Khomeini gestured in his victory speech: "[You] noble class of military forces. . . . This is your nation. You are the nation" (Huyser 1986: 237). He also promised to empower the army, which is now the "the army of Islam" (Martin 2007: 168). On his second day in Iran, he asked officers (rhetorically), "We want you in the army to be independent. . . . Army commanders, do you want to be independent? [Or] Do you want to be the servant of others?" (Khomeini 1981: 260). And declared, on February 28, that officers and soldiers "are now in the service of Islam and the nation. The nation should support them, and do nothing that might discourage them or hurt their feelings. . . . I emphatically warn the Iranian nation that the government must have a strong national army with a mighty morale" (Hickman 1982: 10).

Khomeini typically backed words with deeds. He directed his representatives, Mehdi Bazargan and Ayatollah Beheshti, to negotiate a deal the day the Shah left. Military leaders were not only promised amnesty, but also employment under the new regime. As a sign of good faith, the top brass omitted the pledge of loyalty to the Shah from the military oath on February 6. Four days later, General Neshat, commander of the Imperial Guard, defected (Arjomand 1988: 127). And on the morning of February 11, the chief of staff convinced his top twenty-seven commanders to sign a declaration of neutrality, which was broadcast on the radio at 2 P.M. (Zabih 1988: 61).[17] Senior officers, who could have fled the country, stayed in the belief that their future was safe (Milani 2011a).

Khomeini moved cautiously. He dismissed the service chiefs but confirmed the chief of staff in his position (Huyser 1986: 277). He then appointed his military advisor, Admiral Ahmad Madani, war minister. Since the former navy chief had once occupied this position under the Shah, the appointment was met with general relief (Harney 1999: 199). By the end of his first month in power, he allowed Chief of Staff General Gharabaghi to leave for Paris and replaced him with General Muhammad Vali Gharani. The former director of Military Intelligence was again no outsider, and so no objections were raised. Khomeini followed these actions with two decisions that proved immensely popular to the rank-and-file: reducing conscription from two years to one year, and dismissing foreign instructors (Ward 2009: 225).

There were, nevertheless, some disturbing developments. The commanders of the army, the air force, the special forces, and Tehran's military governor were summarily executed in mid-February; the commanders of the navy and the deputy war minister were detained (but managed to escape to America); the commander of the Imperial Guard and the director of army aviation committed suicide to avoid imminent arrest (Heikal 1981: 178). Some of those who had fled before, such as the former army commander, were later assassinated (Arjomand 1988: 121). Then the purges began. The first purge, between mid-February 1979 and September 1980, affected 10,000 military personnel. Executions were still limited, though. Of the first 404 executions of old regime men, only 85 were military, and of those only 26 were senior officers. It was the second purge, administered by zealous War Minister Mustafa Charman, that cut deeply into the armed forces (Hickman 1982: 9). By 1986 perhaps 500 officers were executed and 23,000 military personnel purged, 17,000 of whom were officers—an estimated 45 percent of the corps (Schanahgaldian 1987: 26). The military was first reduced from 410,000 men to 238,000, and then plummeted to 120,000 by the autumn of 1980 (Ward 2009: 244; Axworthy 2014: 191).[18] Khomeini finally established the cleric-dominated Supreme Defense Council to oversee the armed forces (Martin 2007: 168). Most importantly, he established the Sepah-e Pasdaran-e Enqelab-e Eslami (Islamic Revolutionary Guard Corps) to counterweigh the regular forces (Ward 2009: 226).

Remarkably, even after Khomeini showed his true colors, even after officers realized their lives were at stake, they still failed to act in unison. According to a senior navy admiral, "We did not anticipate Khomeini's consolidation of absolute power. When we understood what he was trying to do, it was too late. He had already formed a strong militia and we did not want to plunge the country into a civil war" (Kamyabipour 2011). The most serious coup attempt, the so-called Nuzhih Plot, which was organized by a movement labeled the Patriotic Officers in July 1980, was led by exiled civilians under deposed Premier Bakhtiar in Paris, and featured a mixture of intelligence operatives, policemen, Imperial Guard members, NCOs, and at least 100 civilians, in addition to a few dozen army officers. Needless to say, the plot was foiled before it even unfolded (Ward 2009: 238–39; Schanahgaldian 1987: 23).

In conclusion, Iran's armed forces never crystalized into a coherent institution with well-defined corporate interests. Despite the Shah's modernization policies, it still acted as a medieval army expecting its monarch to personally lead it into battle. The military was not national, but royal. By structure and training, it saw itself as the servant of monarchy rather than a ruling partner. Once the Shah made his exit, the military fell to pieces—but what about the security?

Breaking the Shield

We have seen previously how unreliable the Iranian security establishment was. But whatever competence and loyalty it had left were devastated by the Shah's actions during the revolutionary crisis. Beginning in 1977, the monarch systematically distanced himself from his security men. He authorized Red Cross inspection of Iranian prisons, and allowed foreign observers to attend the trials of political prisoners, asking them to report any abuses so he could punish the wrongdoers. When the first wave of demonstrations, in January 1978, was repressed, the Shah fired the police chief and his top two aides (Harney 1999: 13). By the summer of 1978, he had dismissed three dozen SAVAK operatives, including the agency's chief, who was sacked in June and arrested in November (Ward 2009: 214). SAVAK Deputy Director General Parviz Sabeti fled the country that fall to avoid arrest (Harney 1999: 29). The martial law commander, General Gholam-Ali Oveissi, and the Tehran police chief, General Mulawi, fled to the United States the following January for the same reason (Rubin 1981: 240). The Shah appointed the popular head of the gendarmerie, General Nasser Moghadam, as SAVAK's new director, in June 1978, to administer a complete housecleaning. The appointment of Moghadam, a mild man with cordial relations with the opposition, signaled royal reluctance to clamp down on demonstrations (Hoveyda 1980: 36; Rubin 1981: 207). The court further authorized Sharif-Emami's cabinet to overhaul SAVAK; they accordingly sacked thirty-three security officials in September 1978, banned another 2,000 from traveling, released 4,000 political prisoners, lifted censorship, and threatened to try anyone involved in repression through popular tribunals (Arjomand 1988: 114–15; Parsa 1989: 56). And in his historic address to the nation, on November 5, 1978, the Shah attacked SAVAK and promised to curb its excesses (Saikal 1980: 196).

Yet even the moderate SAVAK chief believed his monarch had gone too far in accommodating opposition. He complained to a CIA official that the court has "tied our arms and the hands of the armed forces. . . . We are of course astonished as to why the Shahanshah follows these policies" (quoted in Arjomand 1988: 115). And he, expectedly, followed this complaint by sending a secret envoy to Paris, in November 1978, to negotiate a deal with Khomeini. As a result, General Moghadam himself was not harmed and much of SAVAK remained intact under the new regime—although it was renamed the Organization of the Iranian Nation's Security and Information, with the strikingly similar acronym SAVAMA (Rubin 1981: 240, 266; Zabih 1988: 37). Even more important than Moghadam's defection was that of the Shah's general security supervisor, General Hussein Fardust, who subsequently headed Khomeini's SAVAMA (Axworthy 2014: 7). It was hard to blame them, though, considering that "the awe-inspiring SAVAK [was actually] disabled by its [political] master" (Zabih 1988: 132).

Geopolitical Meltdown

Most accounts of Iranian-American relations center on what is possibly the greatest verbal blunder in history: Jimmy Carter's notorious 1977 New Year's toast at the Niavaran Palace, "Iran, because of the great leadership of the Shah, is an island of stability in a turbulent corner of the world" (Sullivan 1981: 134). This little speech supposedly implied that if Washington had not been caught unawares, it could have saved the Pahlavi monarchy.

There is a kernel of truth here. Henry Precht, the State Department's country director for Iran between 1978 and 1980, and Tehran embassy officer between 1972 and 1976, confessed: "I recall sitting in one of those meetings [at the White House] and looking around the room at the others present . . . and thinking that there was nobody in the room who knew anything about Iran except me, and I knew how inadequate my knowledge was. So we were really in the soup during this crisis" (2004: 16). Gary Sick, the National Security Council's (NSC) Iran officer—ironically, a Soviet and Chinese naval expert—described the intelligence on Iran as "dreadful" (1985: 91). Carter himself complained, "I am not satisfied with the quality of our political intelligence" (Brzezinski 1983: 367). As late as September 1978, the CIA, the Defense Intelligence Agency (DIA), and the State Department's Bureau of Intelligence and Research (INR) believed the Shah would weather the storm (Daugherty 2001: 74). The CIA, in particular, insisted that Iran was not even in a "pre-revolutionary situation" (Precht 2004: 15). Even more embarrassing was the prediction of the CIA's veteran Iran hand, Kermit Roosevelt, weeks after the Shah's abdication that the revolutionary struggle would produce another absolutist royal dynasty (1979: preface).

Besides intelligence failure, politicians typically cherry-picked. Robert Daugherty, the CIA operative in Tehran during this turbulent time, asserted,

> [Policy] preferences and desires of the senior policymakers played a larger role in the "failure" than they might wish to acknowledge. A 1979 House of Representatives review of the intelligence produced prior to the fall of the shah ascertained that "long-standing U.S. attitudes toward the shah inhibited intelligence collection, dampened policymakers appetite for analysis of the shah's position, and deafened policymakers to the warning implicit in available intelligence." (2001: 66)

As Edward Said (1997: 99–113) explained, this so-called intelligence failure was yet another example of how policymakers distorted the production of knowledge. Washington privileged think-tank researchers and area specialists who praised its success in modernizing and secularizing Iran. To suggest that Iranians might rally behind a radical cleric was dismissed as overly pessimistic. Political complacency, in other words, was as significant as intelligence failure.

There was also political bickering. The familiar divide between the State Department's doves and the NSC's hawks meant that Carter received contradictory counsel. The Shah was similarly caught in the crossfire. As Precht put it, the "poor fellow was confused by the conflicting advice. He was getting one line from Brzezinski, and another from Sullivan, and was desperate to know what to do" (2004: 17). A case in point was the so-called *nasseem-e Carteri* (Carter breeze): the president's human rights platform that emboldened Iranian oppositionists (Bayat 1998b: 36). Although the State Department supported it enthusiastically, Carter asked Ambassador Sullivan to make allowances for the Shah, on account of Brzezinski's advice (Sullivan 1981: 133). Brzezinski himself called the monarch, in November 1978, to reiterate Washington's support "without any reservation whatsoever, completely and fully, in the present crisis" (1983: 363–65). The conflict of wills reached a climax, on February 11, 1979, when Brzezinski asked Sullivan to order the senior U.S. officer in Tehran, General Gast, to help Iran's top brass stage a coup. Sullivan replied, "I can't understand you. You must be speaking Polish. General Gast is in the basement of the Supreme Commander's headquarters pinned down by gunfire and he can't save himself, much less this country" (Precht 2004: 25).

This raises the more serious accusation that the United States was "instrumental in persuading military commanders to proclaim their neutrality"

(Parsa 1989: 241). Particularly suspect here is the shady visit of Four-Star Air Force General Robert E. Huyser, deputy commander of the European Command, to Tehran ten days before the Shah departed. In his memoir, Huyser claimed that his visit aimed to impress on the high command the following: "It is extremely important for the Iranian military to do all it can to remain strong and intact in order to help a responsible civilian government function" (1986: 18). Brzezinski confirmed that Huyser's mission was "to assist the Iranian military in retaining their cohesion once the Shah left" (1983: 376). But in Iranian Chief of Staff General Gharabaghi's rendition, Huyser was dispatched to shepherd them into a settlement with Khomeini (Milani 1994: 127). More likely, as Precht admitted, Washington wanted Huyser to assess the possibility of a coup, and concluded that the Imperial Armed Forces was not up to it (2004: 25). So even if the United States had endorsed a coup to preempt Khomeini's power bid, Iranian officers could not have pulled it off.

All the above notwithstanding, a close examination of the historical evidence reveals another unexplored scenario. There had already been a backstairs debate in Washington since the early 1970s on the wisdom of retaining the Shah in light of his growing ingratitude (even hostility) toward the West. The Shah of the 1950s, whom the United States had gone to so much trouble to protect, had changed considerably. By the time Carter took office, in January 1977, there were many voices against investing so much in one man: "And what a man he was: arrogant, ambitious, and likely to create a local arms race, if not outright war" (Rubin 1981: 147). A report by the Senate Foreign Relations Committee, in August 1976, had concluded that the Shah's pretensions threatened to ignite a regional war (Rubin 1981: 173). Committee Chairman Senator Frank Church then added reassuringly, "Any government in Iran that comes to power will have to sell its oil and the only place to sell its oil is in the Western world" (Rubin 1981: 245). In other words, why support an unruly patriarch, if the same factors that made him cooperate with the United States will guide any Iranian regime?

The White House hesitated because there was "no visible strategic alternative" to the Shah (Sick 1985: 22). But in 1978, Khomeini presented such an alternative. The CIA envisioned a solution along the Saudi and Pakistani lines: a friendlier, albeit religiously conservative regime (Heikal 1981: 151; Brzezinski 1983: 358). The State Department painted Khomeini as a Gandhi-like figure who could stabilize Iran (Keddie 1981: 253; Huyser 1986: 290).[19] Then on November 9, Ambassador Sullivan cabled his dramatically titled memo, "Thinking the Unthinkable," in which he highlighted how Khomeini's faction and the army were both anti-Communist and could therefore cooperate to maintain order before Khomeini retired to a ceremonial role and passed power to a coalition government grateful for U.S. support. In sum, the Shah's fall might be in America's interest (Sullivan 1981: 201; Brzezinski 1983: 368).

Khomeini's camp helped cultivate this impression. As Bazargan, future prime minister, confessed, "There was only one way of freeing ourselves from the shah—to persuade America to abandon him" (Rubin 1981: 221). Accordingly, he presented Ambassador Sullivan, in December 1978, with a five-step roadmap to democratic transition. Sullivan was impressed, though he requested an end to anti-Western rhetoric, and a pledge not to interfere with the army, to which Khomeini's representative readily conceded (Heikal 1981: 166). In a meeting between another Khomeini aide, future Foreign Minister Ibrahim Yazdi, and Warner Zimmerman, the political counselor at the U.S. embassy in Paris, in mid-January 1979, it was agreed that Washington would restrain the Shah's generals as a sign of goodwill (Milani 1994: 125). A third associate, future President Abol Hassan Bani-Sadr, emphasized Khomeini's aversion to a "religious dictatorship dominated by the mullahs" (Bani-Sadr 1991: 1). When Americans inquired about the ayatollah's disquieting views on Islamic government, his followers dismissed them as philosophical ideals, not intended for application—ideals akin to those found in Plato's *Republic* or More's *Utopia* (Milani 2011a). Khomeini himself promised on January 1, 1979: "It would be a mistake for the American government to fear the shah's departure. . . . If the United States behaves correctly . . . we will respect them in return" (Rubin 1981: 241). In an interview with *Le Monde* before returning to Iran, he again proclaimed: "Our intention is not that religious leaders should themselves administer the state" (Wright 2000: 14).

The earliest attempt to contact Khomeini occurred in September 1978, when American academic Richard Cottam arranged a meeting in Washington between Yazdi and Precht. But the State Department got cold feet at the last moment (Precht 2004: 14). The following month, however, Yazdi connected with the CIA, which had rented a villa near the ayatollah's suburban residence at Neauphle-le-Château (Rubin 1981: 220). There were also informal contacts with the ayatollah through U.S. emissaries, such as former Attorney General Ramsey Clark (Hoveyda 1980: 182). In November the State Department overcame its timidity and arranged a dinner between Yazdi and Precht, after which the two exchanged telephone numbers and remained in touch. This meeting paved the way for Professor Cottam's visit to Tehran over Christmas to introduce the embassy staff to Khomeini's right-hand man, Ayatollah Beheshti. That December Brzezinski called Precht into his office to discuss Iran's future under Khomeini (Precht 2004: 18–21). Brzezinski reluctantly agreed to communicate with Khomeini to establish his position on a revolutionary government under military guardianship (Brzezinski 1983: 372). It was around this time that the American rhetoric began to change. On December 7 Carter announced that although he liked the Shah personally, it was up to Iranians to decide their future (Hoveyda 1980: 184). On January 10 General Huyser recommended establishing "some relationship with Khomeini," and upon receiving Washington's approval, on January 14, organized meetings between Khomeini's representatives, Bazargan and Beheshti, and the army leadership (Huyser 1986: 74, 109). Ten days later, General Huyser and Ambassador Sullivan reported on the merits of a "military-Khomeini coalition" (Arjomand 1988: 131). Days before the Shah abdicated, the Americans sent Khomeini a questionnaire, and his answers were exemplary: oil would continue to flow; Soviet influence would be checked and domestic Communists repressed; Islamists would share power with nationalists and liberals. And Carter's envoy, George Ball, confirmed that a Khomeini-blessed government would serve U.S. interests (Milani 2011a).

It is clear therefore that Washington was not entirely opposed to a post-Shah regime. "The reality of Iranian-US relations," as Halliday explained, "[lay] somewhere in the middle between the official rhetoric about Iran being a fully independent country, ready to stand up to the US if necessary, and the claims . . . that the Shah is some kind of 'agent' of Washington's" (1979: 254). And even though the Shah himself blamed the United States for undoing his dynasty (Pahlavi 1980: 14), the truth was: "*All* sides have tended to exaggerate the importance of American actions and decisions on events in Iran. . . . The fact that Washington was seeking to undermine an already shaky regime . . . explains why the 1953 operation was so simple and successful. . . . [I]n 1978 it was the shah who headed the similarly faltering and even more unpopular regime" (Rubin 1981: 254–55). No foreign power could have saved the Shah from Iran's peculiar power structure.

Reza Shah's decision in the 1920s to maintain an absolutist monarchy set Iran on a separate path from coup-installed republics (like Turkey and Egypt). Power was centralized in court at the expense of other state institutions, including the military and security. The Shah's micromanagement prevented the military from developing an independent structure and identity. And a half-empowered intelligence agency was only established in the late 1950s. Moreover, the megalomaniac monarch alienated his Western patrons without first developing the strength to survive without them. With a regime wholly centered on a medieval-styled political apparatus, the custodians of violence could hardly resist the temptation of defecting in the hope of improving their lot under a new regime. So despite Khomeini's strategic agility, and despite the Iranian opposition's impressive mobilization, the regime's structure is what made it vulnerable to overthrow long before 1979.

Notes

1. The CIA learned from its SAVAK contacts that the agency was responsible (Precht 2004: 12).

2. The authorities put the number at 87 dead, and the opposition, at the time, claims it was close to 500 (Abrahamian 1982: 516). Keddie (1981: 50) suggested that perhaps 900 people were killed; Rubin's (1981: 214) upper limit was 2,000; and Algar (2001: 76) raised the bar to 4,000. U.S. embassy sources said casualties did not exceed 125 (Precht 2004: 13); and Kurzman (2004: 75) and Axworthy (2014: 112) working off official documents a few decades later insist that the number did not exceed 80, though it was probably much less.

3. The focus on ideology has probably resulted from the nature of the new regime. Because Islamists prevailed, studies of the Revolution "tend to be circular accounts beginning with the outcome" (Parsa: 1989: 9). Not only that, but the outcome of the 1979 revolt tempted scholars to overemphasize the role of Shi'ite clerics in past revolts as well, such as the Constitutional Revolution at the turn of the century, and the 1953 uprising against Mosaddeq (Axworthy 2014 is the latest example). But Iranian clerics rarely acted in their institutional capacity as religious spokesmen. Individual clerics supported various platforms according to their political views. Also, Western ideas (notably, constitutional democracy) were more relevant to past upheavals than traditional Shi'ite themes (Afary 1996: 22–23; Martin 2007: 8). In addition, religion had often been used as a proxy for nationalism. "In the European revolutionary context, to be oppositional meant to oppose the established institutions and to rebel against one's own solidified culture, including the church. In an anticolonial context where 'the church' was under attack by domestic power-holders with strong ties to foreign powers, religion could play a part in nationalism" (Benard and Khalilzad 1984: 23–24).

4. Laymen "emulators" provide one fifth of their annual income to the ayatollahs they emulate.

5. There were 50 ayatollahs (senior scholars), 5,000 *hojjat al-Islams* (junior scholars), 10,000 theology students, and a mass of low-ranking mullahs and prayer leaders.

6. Truth be told, Ayatollah Khomeini was infuriated. He wrote in his 1944 tract *Kashf al-Asrar* (Uncovering the Secrets): "All the orders issued by the dictatorial regime of the bandit Reza Khan have no value at all. The laws passed by his parliament must be scrapped and burned. All the idiotic words that have proceeded from the brain of that illiterate soldier are rotten and it is only the law of God that will remain and resist the ravages of time" (Algar 2001: 53–54). Yet only his students read these angry words, and neither he nor they defied Reza Shah politically.

7. Foran further noted that even within the small clerical revolutionary camp, there were "at least five distinct orientations:" militant Islamism, radical liberation theology, liberal Islamism, socialist Islamism, and nationalist Islamism (2005: 80). Clerics were also divided by status. Senior scholars were keen on maintaining stability, and the politically active among them were mildly reformist. Radical views were mostly found among lower-ranking mullahs. Keddie speculated that the source of disagreement was that revolution threatened the privileges of the high clergy because its advocates were mostly lower clergy. Still, she admitted that those who outranked Khomeini considered him a populist innovator (1981: 210).

8. Burns asserted that the Revolution succeeded because its "ambiguous ideology" allowed a motely alliance of regime opponents (1996: 370). A testament to the lack of popular support for Khomeini's ideology was the fact that revolutionary tribunals executed over 10,000 Iranians for their disloyalty to the new regime, and that half a million of Iran's 40 million Shi'as emigrated shortly after the Revolution (Ward 2009: 241–42).

9. Nasser provided military training to several third world "liberation" movements (Heikal 1981: 71).

10. The Islamic Republic Party drew on the same members and networks of an earlier Khomeini-inspired body: the Combatant Clergy Association (Jame-ye Ruhaniyat-e Mobarez), which, in 1977, brought together anti-Shah clerics and *bazaaris* under Khomeini's student Ayatollah Motahhari, and included future presidents Khamenei and Rafsanjani.

11. Doubtless, strategies are most effective when they draw on established practices (Skocpol 1994: 250).

12. Though half of Iranians inhabited the countryside, peasants remained docile (Halliday 1979: 213; Milani 2008b: 583).

13. As Keddie explained, "Bazaaris are not a class in the Marxist sense, as they have different relations to the means of production; the journeymen artisan or worker in a small bazaar factory is in a different position from a banker or moneylender, who may be quite wealthy; nonetheless the expression 'bazaari' has meaning in its involvement with petty trade, production, and banking of a largely traditional or only slightly modernized nature, as well as its centering on bazaar areas. . . . These people are sometimes called 'petty bourgeois', but this term seems inadequate, as some are very rich wholesales and bankers and some are workers" (1981: 244).

14. One should remember that the soldiers served in units far from their home regions (e.g., Azerbaijanis in Tehran), so they would have had little in common with those they needed to repress (Heikal 1981: 144; Hickman 1982: 7).

15. Starting from the rank of colonel, officers communicated directly with the Shah. Milani added, "Even as a conscript, I needed a royal permission to go on vacation" (Milani 2011a).

16. It included Chief of Staff Gharabaghi, War Minister Shafqat, Deputy War Minister Toufanian, Air Force Commander Amir Hussein Rabi'i, Navy Commander Kamal al-Din Mir Habiballahi, Army Commander Badraie, and its meetings were sometimes attended by SAVAK chief Nasser Moghadam.

17. The preamble read: "To prevent disorder and further bloodshed, the army proclaims neutrality in the current political conflicts and had ordered all its units to

return to their garrisons. The Iranian army has always supported and will support the noble and patriotic people of Iran and their demands" (Parsa 1989: 247).

18. In terms of military spending, one cannot be sure what the new regime's policy would have been if it had not been for the war with Iraq. Spending was initially reduced from $9.4 billion in 1978 to $4.8 in 1979, but it increased to $16.1 billion as the war began in the fall of 1980, and during the eight years of war, it remained as high as it was under the Shah, ranging between $7.7 billion and $10.2 billion (Wahid 2009: 61).

19. Precht defends American ignorance of the implications of Khomeini's ideology: "There had never been an Islamic revolution. . . . I recall a cable coming in from the Embassy in May 1978 which identified Khomeini. . . . That the Embassy had to identify him in a cable to the Washington audience tells you something about how much we knew about Iranian internal politics and Khomeini's role" (2004: 10).

5 | Checks and Balances: The Realist Version

FEBRUARY 1979 AND AFTER

Because revolution is notoriously divisive, consolidating a revolution is infinitely more difficult than winning one. This is why Islamist success in seizing power is overshadowed by the remarkably stable regime they established. And their means to achieving stability was not consensus building, though there was some of that. Nor was it successive waves of terror and retribution, though there were plenty of those. It was mainly through institutionalizing the regime in a way that absorbed competing factions, rather than letting any of them dominate. In this sense, the Islamists applied one of democracy's central tenets: checks and balances—not through a formal separation of powers, but by allowing influential groups comparable leverage. This was first made possible by the fact that Khomeini "did not rule like a classic dictator." He created the space for competitive elites to thrive under his shadow, and often strove to persuade rather than order them (Axworthy 2014: 280). More importantly, the regime he presided over was "more thoroughly institutionalized than most in the Middle East" (Schahgaldian 1987: 104). Despite its apparent hierarchy, with a supreme jurist on top, it remained multicentral. Indeed, "factional balancing was the hallmark" of the new regime, based essentially on "a balance of power among contending ... forces" (Katzman 1993: 30, 47). As Zubaida concluded, different factions found representation because of the "existence of rival power centers within the state," making the regime "surprisingly more open and diverse ... than that of most other countries in the region" (1988: 6). More surprisingly still, this logic pervaded the political, military, and security fields.

Politics: Team of Rivals

In comparing Iran's stability to the chaos that accompanied the French and Russian revolutions, Axworthy noted that in the latter cases those who initially took power were soon displaced, whereas in the Iranian case, Khomeini provided continuity "by letting others take responsibility for government, and by allowing *them* to be displaced" (2014: 143). And he did so methodically.

The nationalists, liberals, and leftists who supported Khomeini assumed he would be content with a supervisory role for the clergy, as in the 1906 Constitution, and the shrewd ayatollah indulged their fantasies by signaling his intent to retire to Qom once the Revolution triumphed. But when an Assembly of Experts was elected in August 1979, clerics secured three-fourths of the seats, and Ayatollahs Beheshti and Montazeri, Khomeini's clerical associates, became chair and deputy-chair, respectively. Assembly meetings commenced with an inaugural letter from Khomeini demanding an Islamic constitution, and instructing secular members to defer to clerics. The constitution famously established the principle of *velayat al-faqih* (jurist guardianship) to be carried out by a *murshid 'ala* (Supreme Guide) with sweeping power, including the appointment of the heads of the armed forces and revolutionary guards; declaring war; approving presidential candidates and dismissing elected ones; and naming the head of the judiciary, directors of state media, and other public agencies. The supreme guide is appointed, supervised, and could be dismissed by a regularly elected Assembly of Experts.[1] A twelve-member Guardian Council (half supreme guide–appointed clerics and the other Parliament-elected lawyers) ensured legislations' compatibility with Islam and vetted candidates before any elections. Meanwhile, Khomeini's secret Islamic Revolutionary Council gave birth to an Islamic Republic Party (IRP), in the spring of 1979, which secured over half the seats of the first revolutionary Parliament (130 seats out of 241) in May 1980. Hashemi Rafsanjani, Khomeini's chief political aide, was elected speaker, and remained so for a decade. No less significant politically was Khomeini's transformation of the Pahlavi Foundation, which operated 300 factories, 100 construction companies, 90 agricultural enterprises, and 1000 apartment buildings, into a Bonyad-e Mostazafan (Foundation for the Oppressed) to extend patronage to new regime supporters (Katzman 1993: 41; Axworthy 2014: 160–80).

Now Islamists adopted the curious technique of pushing their revolutionary partners to the top, one after the other, then pushing them over. Khomeini first urged the nationalists to disown their leader Shahpur Bakhtiar for accepting the premiership from the Shah. National Front members heeded the ayatollah's call in order not to spoil their chances of sharing power. Nevertheless, Islamists blamed them for Bakhtiar's Nuzhih coup plot of July 1980 and raided their offices, arrested their members, and closed down their newspaper. Those who survived sought clemency by staying on the sidelines. Next came the liberals. Khomeini entrusted Mehdi Bazargan with the provisional government. The head of the Freedom Movement focused on reconciling Iran with the West. But on November 4, 1979, three days after he met U.S. National Security Advisor Brzezinski in Algiers, zealous youth calling themselves "Students in the Line of the Imam [Khomeini]" occupied the American embassy, which Khomeini had christened the "nest of spies." Losing face and abandoned by Khomeini, Bazargan resigned, allowing his liberal followers to be hounded out of office (Axworthy 2014: 150–85).

Khomeini now turned to the left. Abol Hassan Bani-Sadr, the self-styled leftist intellectual who had joined the ayatollah in exile, was elected president in January 1980. In return for Khomeini's blessing, he accepted the Islamist nominee for the premiership, Ali Rajai. Yet with 76.4 percent of the vote, Bani-Sadr felt he had a popular mandate to lead, and offered himself as the lightening rod of anti-clerical resistance. To protect his back, he allied himself with the left-leaning militia Mujahedin-e Khalq , and—more dangerous still—drew on his position as commander-in-chief to entrench himself with professional officers and turn them against the Islamist militias. Soon enough, evidence exposing Bani-Sadr's CIA links in Paris emerged from the occupied U.S. embassy. And even though Khomeini had blessed these links, the sage of Qom remained silent. A smear campaign followed. And accusations of a presidential plot to use the army to crush Islamists added fuel to the fire. On June 10, 1981, Khomeini stripped Bani-Sadr of his powers as commander-in-chief. Ten days later, he was impeached in a stormy session in Parliament. Fearing imminent arrest, the beleaguered president fled to Paris. In exile, Bani-Sadr continued to conspire with his Mujahedin-e Khalq supporters. When the Islamist Ali Rajai was voted president with 88 percent of the vote, he and the new prime minister (Javad Bahonar) were duly assassinated on August 30. The Mujahedin retaliation, however, proved futile, as Islamists put forward an even stronger presidential candidate. In October 1981 Ali Khamenei, head of the Islamic Republic Party, secured 95 percent of the vote. Mir Hussein Musavi, the editor of *Jomhuri-ye Eslami,* the party's newspaper, became prime minister. And the political duo reigned until Khomeini's death, eight years later (Axworthy 2014: 210–16).[2]

However, as soon as Islamists dominated the political scene, their suppressed differences emerged. Socioeconomic policy proved the most divisive.

Conservatives, led by President Khamenei, supported the free market—a position reflecting the interests of the bazaar. Prime Minister Musavi aligned with the radicals in advocating redistribution and regulation—a position attractive to the popular classes and the growing bureaucratic elite. And because the political arena had become effectively Islamized, both factions appealed to religious values: the sanctity of private property, on the one hand, and social justice, on the other (Zubaida 1988: 6). A table-tennis routine ensued, whereby radicals would toss bills on land reform, labor protection, or nationalizing foreign trade, only to have them vetoed by Guardian Council conservatives, with Khomeini refusing to endorse either since "the revolution was a fusion of conservative and radical ideas, intimately mixed" (Axworthy 2014: 242).

The stakes were high because of the opportunities that the Revolution created. Landowners and bazaar merchants were scrambling to replace the old regime capitalists who fled with the Shah. Peasants and workers, eager to claim the Revolution, resisted. The fall of 1979 witnessed 300 outbreaks of rural violence. Some 15,000 associations sprang up to organize poor farmers. And when conservatives watered down the land reform bill tabled by Parliament radicals, peasant revolts swept the countryside, in March 1980, forcing a revised bill in mid-April that allocated 245,000 hectares to small and landless farmers. Eight months later, however, the law was suspended, and landowners reclaimed much of what they had lost. Likewise, a bill to nationalize foreign trade was stuck in Parliament for nineteen months before being issued in April 1982, and then retracted by the Guardian Council that fall. Workers were in a tighter position. Not only was the new regime wary of Communists (and thus labor unions), but also Iranian industries were small and scattered in a way that hindered national organization. Initially, however, they succeeded through strikes, especially in the oil sector, to press their cause. Between 1979 and 1982, about 80 percent of the economy was nationalized; working conditions were improved; and independent labor councils were set up. Again, it proved a pyrrhic victory. As the inexperienced government stumbled in managing the economy, and as it became desperate for revenue, it began delegating more and more to the private sector. And out of 300 labor councils in 1982, less than 80 remained active (Moaddel 1991: 320–36).

Socioeconomic offensives and reversals divided the Islamic Republican Party to the point where it could no longer function. To break the deadlock, Khomeini dissolved the party, in the summer of 1987, and created a new body, in February 1988, to resolve disputes between Parliament and the Guardian Council. The oddly named Majma-e Tashkhis-e Maslahat-e Nezam

(Regime's Expediency Discernment Council) was highly pragmatic. Its rulings were guided by whatever was in the immediate interest of the regime, and thus favored conservatives or radicals depending on the circumstances (Katzman 1993: 39–40). The regime was further stabilized via constitutional amendments in the summer of 1989—ratified weeks after Khomeini's death. The prime ministerial post was abolished and its powers reallocated to the presidency, in order to strengthen the elected executive, while the supreme guide's jurisdiction was expanded to balance the enhanced presidency. Yet despite these new prerogatives, Iran's twin rulers were hardly omnipotent. President Rafsanjani, elected in August 1989, failed to pass his economic liberalization program through Parliament. And the new supreme guide, Khamenei, was immediately criticized by clerics for failing to produce an acceptable doctoral thesis, and was compelled to conduct himself humbly among the clergy. Similarly, while the Guardian Council succeeded in winning the right to vet candidates for parliamentary elections, it still could not control legislation. After rejecting 1,060 out of 3,150 candidates in the 1992 elections, Parliament remained dominated by left-leaning statists (Axworthy 2014: 312–20). In sum, Iran's political elite remained divided between radicals, conservatives, and pragmatists, with each ensconced in its own institutional niche.

Eventually, politico-cultural differences compounded socioeconomic ones. The 1997 presidential elections was a tug-of-war between the reformist candidate, Muhammad Khatami, who promised to empower civil society and open up the political system—thus appealing to intellectuals, artists, activists, and Iran's cosmopolitan youth—and Ali Akbar Nateq-Nuri, a diehard defender of tradition—and thus a favorite among right-wing clerics. Both were regime insiders. Khatami had been minister of culture and Islamic guidance, and from 1992 ran the National Library. His father was an ayatollah; his brother was married to Khomeini's granddaughter; and he himself was close to Khomeini's son Ahmad. Nateq-Nuri had served as Parliament's speaker since 1992, and was President Rafsanjani's political ally. Khatami won two successive elections, receiving 70 percent of the vote in 1997, and 80 percent in 2001. But although reformers enjoyed a parliamentary plurality, traditionalists on the Guardian Council kept them in check. And because Khatami never disputed Khomeini's clerical-supremacy principle, his maneuvering space remained limited. The reformist Parliament was ultimately dismissed as "an ineffectual talking-shop," and traditionalists captured the 2003 Parliament (Axworthy 2014: 354).

Preferring to divide rather than crush opposition, the regime produced a curious presidential candidate: one that combined socioeconomic radicalism and politico-cultural traditionalism. Ahmadinejad was an engineering professor from a modest background. He made himself useful during Khomeini's purge of non-Islamist faculty members, and was rewarded with a provincial governorship (in Ardebil) between 1993 and 1997, before being elected mayor of Tehran in 2003. In the 2005 presidential elections, Supreme Guide Khamenei instructed Islamist militiamen and their dependents to mobilize support for Ahmadinejad. Yet he barely won, with the lowest percentage accorded to a presidential nominee (60 percent), and the lowest turnout (59 percent). The new president promised to redistribute oil wealth to the poor, and protect traditional religious values. But considering that his traditionalist supporters were also economic conservatives, he could only implement the latter part of his promise, and indeed ended up slicing oil subsidies and implementing International Monetary Fund (IMF) prescriptions (Axworthy 2014: 371–79, 397).

Ahmadinejad's lopsided platform rekindled both wings of the opposition: socioeconomic radicals and politico-cultural reformers (now calling themselves the Green Movement). The 2009 presidential elections registered a record turnout of 85 percent. Challenging the incumbent was Khamenei's former prime minister, Mir Hussien Musavi. And in a highly contested election, tainted by accusations of fraud (with militiamen stuffing the ballot box with rigged votes and security officials miscounting the votes), Ahmadinejad won a feeble 63 percent. Oppositionists took to the street on June 15, three days after the elections, but were quickly repressed. And when Ahmadinejad tried to placate them, in 2011, by removing the draconian Minister of Intelligence Heydar Moslehi, he was publicly rebuked by the supreme guide and almost faced impeachment (Axworthy 2014: 402–15).

With the Green Movement gathering support inside Iran and sympathy from the West, Khomeini's heirs refused to have their legs pulled. With impressive flexibility, the conservatives and traditionalists made a tactical retreat by not obstructing Hassan Ruhani in the 2013 presidential elections. The Scottish-educated Ruhani, a lawyer by training, was a moderate reformer, friendly to the West, and a regime insider. He had been at Khomeini's side in France; he was a Rafsanjani protégé, serving as his deputy speaker in Parliament, and deputy acting commander of the armed forces in the 1980s; he was secretary of the Supreme National Security Council between 1989 and 2005; and was appointed chief nuclear negotiator between 2003 and 2005. The fact that he resigned in protest of Ahmadinejad's bellicose behavior endeared him to the Green Movement and won him several friends in the West.

Ruhani's victory was followed by two landmark elections, in February 2016, which saw reformers sweep half the seats in Parliament, and 50 of them (including President Ruhani and former President Rafsanjani) elected for eight-year terms on the eighty-eight-member Assembely of Experts that will choose the new supreme guide (considering that the incumbent Khamenei is almost 80 years old). With well-balanced assemblies and a cabinet that includes both hawks and doves, Iran's political institutions seem to have managed "a deliberate return toward what one could regard as the Khomeini model of balance" (Axworthy 2014: 427).

Military: Return from Oblivion

The Imperial Armed Forces was virtually melting under the impact of purges and desertions. Six months after Khomeini landed in Tehran, almost 60 percent of the army had deserted (over 170,000 men); conscription was scrapped; and by the end of 1979, at least 10,000 military personnel were purged—a few dozen of them executed (Hickman 1982: 1). In the following months, half the old officer corps was sacked, some 17,000 men. The armed forces shrank to 120,000 men, a third of its pre-revolutionary size. And because foreign deliveries of spare parts and ammunitions were canceled, 30 percent of army equipment and 60 percent of air force and naval equipment became non-operational. Over the following five years, however, the numbers increased steadily, reaching 300,000 men in 1987, and conscription was reintroduced and extended to eighteen months (Schahgaldian 1987: 35; Ward 2009: 244). Two developments brought the military back from the abyss. Revolutionary chaos tempted separatist movements, so the army was called on to repress Kurds in the northwest, Arabs in the southwest, and Turkmen in the northeast. Then, of course, came the war with Iraq.

Having just seized power in a palace coup, Saddam Hussein hoped to begin his reign with a swift campaign to control the Shatt al-Arab waterway and the oilfields of the Arab-inhabited Khuzestan while Tehran was still putting its house in order. On September 22, 1979, Baghdad invaded. In terms of ground forces, Iran was seriously outmatched. Iraq had a 200,000-strong army, well equipped with tanks and artillery, while Iran had a force half that size, and its armory was crumbling. Hope rested on Iran's air force. With 450 aircrafts, including the formidable F-14 Tomcats, it was clearly superior to Iraq's 340 MiG and Mirage jets. Anxious about the imbalance, Saddam launched an early air strike aimed at destroying Iran's air force, as Israel had done to Egypt in 1967. He failed miserably: few runways and fewer aircrafts were damaged. Iran retaliated, the next day, with a devastating air attack, forcing Iraq to reallocate two-thirds of its jets to neighboring Arab countries (Axworthy 2014: 191–93). Aware of their limited combat experience, Iranian pilots steered away from conventional operations, such as dogfighting or providing air support to ground forces. Prudently, they targeted lightly defended civilian installations off the battlefield. Attacking the Iraqi interior minimized risk and maximized the strikes' political impact (Hickman 1982: 21). However, as the war went on, more and more of the Shah's pilots were released from prison (even those sentenced to death), and developed enough experience to be able to destroy Iraqi jets by a ratio of 10 to 1 (Axworthy 2014: 270). The Iranian navy also set to work immediately, engaging the Iraqis three times in the first ten days of war, but it soon abandoned direct combat—again due to incompetence—and focused on interrupting enemy commerce (Hickman 1982: 21).

Of course, Khomeini's men would not have deployed the military unless they felt reasonably secure. Losing a strip of land would have been preferable to losing the Revolution. Yet the purges of the first couple of years had tamed officers. Some were now openly religious (as well as opportunist "overnight Muslims"), but most become deliberately apolitical. And even though nationalism, not Islamism, continued to frame their professional worldview, Khomeini was shrewd enough not to stress the difference. He did, however, create a cleric-dominated Supreme Defense Council to oversee the armed forces. In addition, the Islamic Republican Party had attached a Political-Ideological Directorate to the Ministry of Defense, which dispatched commissars to every platoon to monitor officers and recommend promotions and transfers. Finally, the Islamist revolutionary militias had taken over urban centers, and pushed the regular forces to the borders or isolated barracks to further preempt coup plots (Schahgaldian 1987: 46–49; Ward 2009: 230). The new regime thus felt confident to empower professionals. After Mustafa Charman, the militiaman who headed the armed forces, was killed at the front in 1981, professional officers were promoted to the top, beginning with Ali Sayyid Shirazi, an artillery officer under the Shah, who became chief of staff in 1981, and Khomeini's representative to the Supreme Defense Council in 1986 (Katzman 1993: 28; Axworthy 2014: 220).

But besides wars against separatists and invaders, Khomeini's rehabilitation of the armed forces was essential to regime stability. The Bani-Sadr debacle was instructive. While revolutionary clerics glorified popular militias, President Bani-Sadr moved to the frontline, mingled with regulars, praised their heroism, and hoped to use them to consolidate power in Tehran (Hickman 1982: 23–26). And although officers did not rally to his support when he was removed, clerics realized the danger of abandoning the military to political contenders or, worse, a Persian Bonaparte. They also became wary of the growing power of militiamen, and saw the military as an essential counterbalance—just as the former had been conceived to counterbalance the latter (Axworthy 2014: 234). The immediate impact of this new balancing policy was to force regulars and militiamen to coordinate their battlefront operations, after months of leading fundamentally separate wars—thus allowing them to share the glory of protecting the homeland.

As a result, the republican military became much more popular than the imperial one. "For the first time since its creation in the early 1920s, the professional military is perceived by the people as essential to their continued safety and to Iranian territorial integrity" (Schahgaldian 1987: 37). The regular force also maintained its imperial size of 420,000.[3] It is true that after the war Tehran maintained a fairly low level of military spending of about 2 percent of GDP.[4] It is also true that while military service in the Islamic Republic still presented an avenue for social mobility, it no longer provided senior officers with the "astronomical bank accounts and seaside villas" they enjoyed under the Shah. But for what it is worth, this further shielded the military from public resentment (Schahgaldian 1987: 37)—something the security forces failed to achieve.

Security: The King Is Dead, Long Live the King

Unlike the armed forces, the security apparatus never had to stare at the precipice. Khomeini might not have intended to fight wars, but he certainly yearned for iron fist control. After some minor transfers, the national police and gendarmerie resumed their functions without much fuss. The only notable change was the 1990 merger of the 16,000-strong *komitehs* (revolutionary committees) with those regular forces (Katzman 1993: 43). And the aim was to rein in the irregulars rather than ensure the cooperation of the already loyal police and gendarmerie. The Ministry of Interior now employed 300,000 people, 60,000 of whom were officers.

Restructuring was limited to the intelligence sector, which today employs 30,000 operatives. The early defection of SAVAK leaders eased the institution's transition to SAVAMA—under the same director—then to VEVAK (Vezarat-e Ettela'at va Amniat-e Keshvar), or Ministry of Intelligence, in 1984, under Muhammad Reyshahri, a vicious member of the revolutionary tribunals. In 1989 the position was passed to Ali Fallahian, another zealous revolutionary. He remained in power until he clashed with President Khatami in 1998 (Axworthy 2014: 343). Another crucial expansion was that of prisons. The Shah's notorious Evin prison, which was designed to hold 1,500 prisoners, held 15,000 by 1983, and new prisons had to be built.

Of course, the most notable change was in the discourse of repression. Whereas the Shah's enemies were red (Communist) or black (Islamist), Khomeini invented an entirely new jargon, famously, *moharib* (a warrior against God), *mofsid* (a corruptor), and *monafiq* (a hypocrite). Security men would seize on these new categories in Khomeini's speeches and transform them into official crimes. Torture, officially banned in the 1979 Constitution, was renamed *ta'zir* (Islamic corporal punishment), and included religious-inspired innovations, such as "the coffin," where prisoners were locked until they repented (Axworthy 2014: 150, 285). Needless to say, security considerations trumped religious laws. For example, even though Ayatollah Shariatmadari outranked Khomeini in religious credentials, his critique of the new regime placed him under house arrest and stripped him of his jurist status—"an unprecedented act in Shi'a Islam, and in traditional terms, impossible" (Axworthy 2014: 225–26). And when Ayatollah Montazeri, the cleric designated to succeed Khomeini, spoke against repression, he was demoted in favor of Khamenei, who had not even produced a treatise to merit the rank of ayatollah (Axworthy 2014: 290).

Security control was essential to the Islamist regime. First, the peaceful opposition of liberal and leftist intellectuals who helped bring down the Shah was subdued. In April 1980 universities were closed pending an *enqelab-e farhangi* (cultural revolution) that cleansed the intellectual arena of foreign ideas. When reopened, in 1981, half of the faculty and thousands of students had been dismissed (Axworthy 2014: 313). Secular parties were banned and their leaders arrested, from the National Front in 1981 to the Communist Tudeh in 1983. There were also (real or fabricated) plots being uncovered all the time—notably, the one involving Foreign Minister Sadeq Qotbzadeh, who was dismissed for attempting to negotiate the release of the American hostages, and then executed in September 1982 for conspiring (with 170 accomplices) to overthrow the regime.

Violent opposition was much more dangerous, especially that of the leftist Mujahedin-e Khalq. In May 1979 Ayatollah Mutahhari, chairman of the Islamic Revolutionary Council, was assassinated. Disaster then struck, on June 28, 1981, with the bombing of the Islamic Republican Party's headquarters. The party's chairman, Ayatollah Beheshti, and seventy senior members were killed. Prime Minister Rajai and Parliament Speaker Rafsanjani had just left the premises minutes before the bomb went off. And the new chairman, Khamenei, was left with a permanent disability in his right arm when another bomb exploded during a press conference. The killing spree continued, claiming the lives of the chief of police, the head of Evin prison, the prosecutor general, and, most importantly, President-elect Rajai and his appointed premier. The reaction was brutal: by 1983, between 3,000 and 7,000 "terrorists" were killed on the streets or after summary trials, and by 1988, another 8,000 met the same fate (Ward 2009: 235; Axworthy 2014: 215, 285). A force of 7,000 Mujahedin reallocated to Baghdad and launched a desperate attack, in July 1988, on the eve of the Iran–Iraq ceasefire. Hundreds of militiamen were slain on the field, and the attack justified the execution of more than 5,000 Mujahedin (some estimate the figure to be as high as 30,000) in Iranian prisons—"It was the blackest episode in the record of the Islamic republic" (Axworthy 2014: 288–91).

Henceforth, the security apparatus was mostly occupied with reform activists. In the 1990s, security-hired thugs attacked reformist gatherings. President Khatami hoped to put an end to it by hiring a reformist interior minister, Abdullah Nuri, in 1998. But the latter was forced to resign after a few months, and received a five-year prison sentence for questioning the authority of the supreme guide. His successor, Abdulvahed Musavi-Lari, prudently kept his head down (Axworthy 2014: 341). VEVAK operatives then upped the ante by assassinating reformist intellectuals, in what became known as the Serial Murders Case of 1998. An infuriated Khatami cashiered the intelligence chief, Dorri-Najafabadi, and detained the operatives in charge. In retaliation, the head of Khatami's investigation committee on the murders, Said Hajjarian, was shot in March 2000. Security then clamped down on the pro-Khatami press, causing newspaper circulation to slump by 45 percent between 2000–2001 (Axworthy 2014: 345–52). Finally, repression of the 2009 protests against Ahmadinejad's reelection was ruthless, with hundreds reported dead, and many more detained and tortured (Axworthy 2014: 406).

The Revolutionary Guard

Discussion of the political, military, and security institutions under the new regime brings us to the crown jewel of Iran's institutional complex: the Sepah-e Pasdaran-e Enqelab-e Eslami (Islamic Revolutionary Guard Corps). Other revolutionary regimes have transformed their street militias into permanent fixtures, but very few of these militias performed the Guard's stabilizing role. This is because this remarkably independent organization has developed its own political, military, and security wings. It has become a "power triangle" all to itself. Khomeini officially inaugurated the Guard on May 5, 1979. But in reality, it had evolved spontaneously from the bottom up. It was not born out of a political party, as in the Nazi German and Communist Chinese cases. Nor did it rely on old regime officers, as in the French and Russian revolutionary armies. And the fact that it developed a complicated and permanent structure without sacrificing its revolutionary zeal owes much to this unique origin (Katzman 1993: 11–16; Ward 2009: 247). So where did the Guard come from?

To preempt being run over by leftist guerillas (the Mujahedin-e Khalq had 20,000 militiamen, and Tudeh could field 7,000 armed supporters), Islamists started organizing neighborhood *komitehs* (committees). Once the Shah abdicated, they took over local security. These 6,000 committeemen became the Guard's nucleus. Prominent cadres were disgruntled Marxists, who broke off from the old Mujahedin in 1977 to form an Islamic substitute, Mujahedin-e Enqelab-e Islami. Examples include Behzad Nabavi, founder of the dissident militia, who became the Tehran Guard commander, then minister of heavy industries (1981–1989); Ali Shamakhani, who served as Guard deputy commander, Guard minister, then regular navy commander; and the famous Mohsen Rezai, longest-reigning Guard commander (1981–1997), secretary of the all-powerful Expediency Discernment Council, and presidential candidate in 2009 and 2013. There were also members of the Islamic Nations Party, a rural guerilla group formed after the failure of the 1963 uprising, notably, future commanders Javad Mansuri, Abbas Zamani, and Kazem Bonjurdi. They were all young, typically in their mid-twenties, and most belonged to the urban lower-middle class. Funds initially came from mosques and clerical donations, before the state took over. In fact, despite centralization efforts, various regime strongmen financed their personal Guard companies until the mid-1980s. For example, Sadegh Khalkhali, a notorious revolutionary judge, used a few dozen as bodyguards. The new republic's first defense minister, Mustafa Charman, used his guards to control the Tehran airport. And the head of Evin prison, Asadollah Lajevardi, employed a 300-strong contingent (Schahgaldian 1987: 49; Katzman 1993: 28–33, 62; Ward 2009: 226).

The Guard swelled from 6,000 to 50,000 in two years, then jumped to 350,000 in the late 1980s (Ward 2009: 246). It expectedly contracted after the Iran-Iraq War to its present size of 125,000 men. And with size, of course, came responsibilities. The constitution charged the Guard with defending the Revolution. This open-ended mission evolved quite rapidly. The Guard initially took on "guarding" tasks: protecting official personnel (ministers, governors,

Parliament members) and public facilities (from ministries and prisons to banks and media stations). It also guarded public morality through patrols (the infamous white Toyota trucks of the Sarollah and Jondoallah in cities and villages, respectively). It then participated in the pacification campaigns against ethnic separatists, and helped collect taxes. With the war, it metamorphosed into a regular armed force, with a separate air force, navy, and military industry and procurement services. And soon, it also had its own intelligence agency, conducting domestic counter-intelligence, foreign espionage (with Guard spies planted in Iranian embassies), and exporting the Revolution abroad (via the Office of Liberation Movements and its striking arm, the 20,000-strong Qods Force). Finally, the Guard extended its political influence via an all-purpose propaganda arm, producing books, magazines, films, television programs, plays, and organizing rallies (Schahgaldian 1987: 74–75; Katzman 1993: 83–99; Ward 2009: 247).

The multiplication of tasks required an increasingly complex structure. The Supreme Council of the Revolutionary Guard, its highest executive body, started as a cabal of founding fathers. By 1984 its composition became defined by function rather than personalities; essentially, the Guard commander and his deputy, the Guard minister, and the commander of the Guard's central headquarters in Tehran. Three years later, it reinvented itself as the Joint Staff Council, and expanded to include the three service chiefs. Resisting government attempts after the war to create an integrated army-Guard joint staff, the Guard renamed its top body in 1989 as the Central Headquarters Staff. This top council received reports from eleven regional garrisons, and supervised fifteen departments, ranging from special operations, a security unit, intelligence and research, to women's affairs, ideological training, and cultural activities. The Guard also developed prestigious training centers, beginning with a makeshift Guard school on the grounds of the former U.S. embassy, followed by a high school (Imam Sadegh School) in 1982, and a university (Imam Hussein University) in 1986. It also founded specialized colleges for infantrymen, pilots, and marines, and a specialized think-tank, the Academy of Multilateral Defense and Strategy of the Revolutionary Guard. Finally, unlike those of the regular army, Guard barracks were placed in urban centers and recruits served in their home districts in order to further integrate them with the population (Schahgaldian 1987: 80; Katzman 1993: 81–105).

A crucial institutional coup was incorporating the Basij-e Mustazafin (Mobilization of the Oppressed) in January 1981. This curious body arose in response to Khomeini's call upon the occupation of the U.S. embassy to create a "popular army of 20 million" to deter Washington. A National

Mobilization Staff, a clerical-military body infused with guards, began training volunteers in Boy Scouts camps. Volunteers were heavily indoctrinated and lightly trained and armed (with a two-week standard course on grenades and automatic rifles). As volunteers, they relied on donations, not salaries. Their social composition differed from the Guard. They were mostly illiterate, poor rural folk varying in age from teenagers to senior citizens. They volunteered for three-month tours, usually off the agricultural season, between December and March. This is why estimations of their size vary. They started with 250,000 volunteers, and gradually expanded to 600,000 (by 1988), though during the eight-year war, some 3 million had seen action. Today, they make do with 90,000 active volunteers and 300,000 reservists, with a capacity to mobilize 11 million people. Their job in peacetime is to help with domestic security, and in wartime to prop up civil defense (Katzman 1993: 67–68; Ward 2009: 226–46).

The Basij were crucial to the Guard's early battlefield success against Iraq. Restrictions on imports of ammunition and spare parts undercut Iran's armory and artillery. And inexperience still hampered pilots and marines. Tehran was forced to turn to "an infantry strategy, one that relied on individual fervor to overcome staggering military odds" (Hickman 1982: 28). Hence came forth the famed "human waves" strategy. With a vast army of Basij cannon fodder, the Guard dispatched thousands of forerunners to clear the minefields (using their bodies to blow them up), advancing unhindered by artillery barrages (from both sides), and hurling themselves over Iraqi strongpoints. The unnerved Iraqis usually retreated to avoid hand-to-hand combat with these vicious zealots (Hickman 1982: 28; Axworthy 2014: 218). The Guard's first major military operation occurred in late 1981, and broke Iraq's siege of the city of Abadan (Katzman 1993: 85). Next came the Undeniable Victory offensive, in March 1982, in which 100,000 regular infantrymen, 30,000 guards, and 30,000 volunteers finally pushed Iraqi troops back across the borders (Hickman 1982: 29; Schahgaldian 1987: 87). That September, Iraq accepted a ceasefire.

The end of the occupation offered the regime a choice. The regular military wanted to stop. And Khomeini initially agreed. But, as Rafsanjani testified, Guard commanders, spearheaded by Mohsen Rezai, insisted in their critical meeting with Khomeini, on June 10, 1982, on punishing Saddam and installing a Shi'ite government in Baghdad. Khomeini acquiesced. Iraqi Shi'ites were invited to Iran to set up the Supreme Council for the Islamic Revolution in Iraq (SCIRI). A new war was declared to replace the Ba'ath Party with the SCIRI—a project that eventually succeeded in 2003 (Axworthy

2014: 227). Now that Saddam was fighting to survive, there could be no quick end to the war.

The Guard now had to think long-term. By the end of 1982, it developed air and naval services (formally inaugurated in 1985 and 1987, respectively). The rudimentary air force was based on the Shah's Imperial Civil Aviation, and used helicopters, training aircraft, and captured Iraqi jets. The Guard navy, launched out of the southern port of Bushehr, began by infiltrating enemy blockades, and ended up engaging U.S. oil tanker escorts in the celebrated Tanker War of 1987–1988. The Guard also established military industries, as early as 1984, to provide desperately needed small arms, Katyusha rockets, mortars, artillery shells, anti-chemical warfare, and communication equipment. As the war dragged on, the Guard introduced conscription, and in 1987, draftees formed 80 percent of its frontline troops (Katzman 1993: 86–90).

Unfortunately, none of this brought the Guard lasting territorial gains. Although its ground offensives expanded to include sometimes as many as 300,000 troops, it did not have the experienced artillery and armory support to hold the conquered positions. In time, the causality rate became inhibiting. For instance, the Guard lost 1,000 men, on average, every day in its three-week offensive, Operation Ramadan, in July 1982. "The outcome was a dreadful, drawn-out war of terrible conditions, terrible waste of human life, and a terrible, crippled failure to win decisive results" (Axworthy 2014: 229–31). With a million causalities, including 213,000 killed and 320,000 permanently disabled, and after squandering $200 billion, Tehran accepted a ceasefire in July 1988 (Axworthy 2014: 293–96).

Yet despite the absence of victory, the Guard's steadfastness throughout the war secured its position as a pillar of the republic. And immediately after the ceasefire, Guard commanders rushed to further institutionalize their power. Military ranks and a conventional order of battle were introduced in 1990. And although its ground forces remained the most effective, the Guard's air force and navy flourished. Today, for example, its pilots are trained in North Korea and fly advanced MIG-29s. Its navy uses the latest Chinese surface-to-surface Silkworm missiles. More surprisingly, it ring-fenced its military industry, leading the curve in missile production (famously, the long-range Shahab 3 missile, which can reach Europe), and, of course, nuclear research (Katzman 1993: 86; Axworthy 2014: 354).

Still, the Guard's greatest achievement was its successful defiance of civilian oversight. Initially, there had been *namayandeh-ye emam* (imam's representatives) attached to Guard units. At the end of the war, there were 300 of these clerical commissars (Schahgaldian 1987: 79). Yet heading the Office of the Imam's Representatives was a nightmare because members of the Guard were incredibly recalcitrant. Hassan Lahuti, its first occupant, lasted from May to October 1979. The Guard accused him of sympathizing with liberal Prime Minister Bazargan. Next came future presidents Rafsanjani and Khamenei. The former was tolerated for a month, and the latter until President Bani-Sadr's election in early 1980. Its longest surviving occupant, Fazlollah Mahallati, began with a short tenure, between the summer of 1980 and autumn of 1981, before being persuaded to return two years later. After his death in 1986, the position remained vacant until his deputy, Abdullah Nuri, agreed to take over in 1989. But only a year later, his centralizing ambitions provoked enough Guard members to have him replaced. His successor, Muhammad Araqi, lasted two years. And by 1992 the office became little more than a formality (Katzman 1993: 52–56, 121). There was also the Revolutionary Guard Ministry, established in 1982, to liaise between the Guard and politicians. Yet it was headed by Guard members: Mohsen Rafiqdust (1982-1988), then Ali Shamakhani until it merged into the new Ministry of Defense and Armed Forces Logistics in 1989. The merge really signified political frustration with any attempt to control the Guard from the outside. Even so, guards insisted on always having one of them appointed deputy defense minister, the first being Mahmoud Pakravan (Katzman 1993: 103; Axworthy 2014: 234).

Civilian authorities had early indicators of the futility of their task. Between March and September 1979, the Guard sufficed with de facto leaders. When President Bani-Sadr asked Abbas Zamani, one of the Guard's founders, to formally lead the Guard toward a merger with the regular military, Guard supporters forced Zamani to resign. When Bani-Sadr nominated Kazem Bonjurdi, another respectable Guard, he was rejected just for being a presidential nominee. Not being able to afford a leadership crisis at the war's outset, the president accepted the Guard's choice: Morteza Rezai, then his brother Mohsen. This early faceoff set the trend: the Guard picked its leaders (Ward 2009: 228). Indeed, most Guard commanders emerged from below. The bold and aggressive would win their comrades' admiration, and this "informal recognition is then affirmed by command superiors in a formal appointment" (Katzman 1993: 118). Autonomy allowed the Guard to achieve its most cherished goal: to preserve its own army, air force, navy, domestic security force, and intelligence unit.

Two reasons account for the Guard's effectiveness in snubbing civilian control. On the one hand, the Guard "developed out of revolutionary precursors which worked in parallel with, rather than subordinate to, Khomeini and his revolutionary clerical lieutenants"; and on the other hand, "Iran's cleric-dominated political leadership never organized itself into a cohesive, disciplined, party structure comparable to the Communist parties" (Katzman 1993: 123). The only alternative was to call on the regular military to destroy the unruly Guard. But Khomeini was practical enough to realize that tolerating the Guard outweighed the costs of trying to suppress it. If the military was unleashed against the Guard and failed, Iran would descend to civil war, and if it succeeded, his regime might become its hostage. And Khomeini's clerical successors prudently accepted that they could hardly succeed where their master failed. Unfortunately, just as civilian politicians were giving up on the attempt to control the Guard, the guards themselves began infiltrating civilian politics.

From the start, the Guard had a constitutional political mandate: to guard the Islamic Revolution. They first saw liberals as a threat, and decided to sabotage Prime Minister Bazargan's efforts to reach out to the West. This was accomplished by the occupation of the U.S. embassy. Although the operation was officially carried out by an obscure organization, Students in the Line of the Imam, the Guard's fingerprints were unmistakable: "Guards stationed around the Embassy had previously prevented a similar takeover by a militant leftwing, anti-US, but anti-Khomeini group in May 1979, yet the Guard did nothing to stop the Students that rushed the Embassy on November 4, 1979. Once the Embassy was seized, the Students officially thanked the Revolutionary Guard, essentially for not preventing the takeover . . . [and] after the failed U.S. rescue mission in April 1980, the hostages were moved to Revolutionary Guard installations" (Katzman 1993: 36). The Guard turned next to the leftist threat. It not only agitated against President Bani-Sadr until he was impeached, but it was also instrumental in defeating the Marxist militias. During the war, the Guard navy mined the Gulf's shipping lanes against the wishes of the civilian leadership, compelling the latter to turn to the regular navy to sweep the mines away. The Guard was involved in the Iranian pilgrims' protest in Mecca in July 1987, which ended with a massacre, to disrupt Speaker of Parliament Rafsanjani's attempt to improve relations with Arab Gulf countries in order to isolate Iraq. And when Rafsanjani became president and prepared a groundbreaking trip to France, Guard operatives assassinated former Prime Minister Bakhtiar in his Paris exile, leading to a cancellation of the planned presidential visit (Katzman 1993: 90, 136).

A more brazen episode of political brinkmanship occurred in September 1988. Preempting any attempt by civilians to blame the Guard for Iran's staggering losses during the war, numerous guards organized a massive Guard rally at Tehran's Azadi Stadium to renew their pledge to defend the Revolution. The images of this gathering were so visibly intimidating that "all those political leaders who addressed the Guard commanders' gathering pledged that the Guard would remain as a separate military force and prime guardian of the revolution. . . . Moreover, Khomeini publicly issued a statement of support for the Guard, directing political leaders not to take any steps to weaken it" (Katzman 1993: 59). Not a single commander was questioned, let alone dismissed. Indeed, many were promoted. It was Guard Minister Rafiq-Dust who took the fall, despite political support from Rafsanjani, his brother-in-law. The new minister was none other than the Guard deputy commander, Ali Shamakhani, who later combined command of the regular and Guard navies, despite his lack of naval expertise.

Instead of submitting to civilian control after the war, the Guard now influenced assignments in government. For example, Guard members and associates usually held key cabinet posts, especially in communications, construction, commerce, social affairs, culture, Islamic guidance, and foreign affairs. Many became ambassadors to countries such as the United Kingdom, Germany, and Pakistan. They served in local councils and held senior positions in parliamentary committees, including chairmanship of the defense committee (Katzman 1993: 124–30). Later, President Ahmadinejad rewarded the Guard for its support by choosing his minister of interior and minister of intelligence from among its ranks. Guard Commander Muhammad Ali Jafari was instrumental in suppressing protests against Ahmadinejad's reelection in 2009 and 2011 (Axworthy 2014: 405). In this and other instances, one must add, the Guard never awaited instructions from civilian politicians. It acted immediately (sometimes even proactively) to counter anti-regime stirrings.

Guard influence also spilled over to the economy, especially during the 2000s. A notable example was securing a controlling share in the state telecommunications monopoly in 2009. The $7.8 billion deal was the largest transaction in the history of the Tehran Stock Exchange. The Guard presently runs more than 100 companies in various sectors, particularly in construction and energy, generating an estimated $12 billion in annual revenue. Its economic prosperity owed much to international sanctions against Tehran. "Like Mafia-type organizations," they thrived on smuggling operations, while traditional businesses suffered from sanction-inflicted restrictions and inflation (Axworthy 2014: 387–408).

In short, the Guard today plays a greater role than any other post-revolutionary organization in Iran. It represses internal dissidents; mobilizes pro-regime supporters; deters foreign enemies; enforces Islamic values among Iranians and exports radicalism around the Muslim world; and, last but not least, it directs economic development, from construction to telecommunications and defense. Even back in 1987, observers saw the Guard as "the most powerful political and military organization in Iran," one that was so influential in the new regime that it might shape its "future nature and direction" (Schahgaldian 1987: 73). In June 2009 Ayatollah Montazeri, the cleric who was supposed to succeed Khomeini but was demoted for being too critical, denounced the Guard's repression of popular protests, complaining: "What we have is not an Islamic republic, but a military republic' " (Axworthy 2014: 408)—he died in his sleep in December 2009.

The Best of Enemies

If the growing influence of the Revolutionary Guard imperils the regime's power balance, geopolitics might prove the arbiter. The Revolution has placed Iran in a unique situation. A regime based on radical Shi'ism certainly alienated Iran's conservative Sunni neighbors much more than the Shah's Persian nationalism ever could. Tehran made this plain with an Office of Liberation Movements designed to export the Revolution. This Guard-run office (admirably renamed War on Satan Committee) won its first beachhead in Lebanon, when 1,000 Iranian guards helped the Shi'a of south Lebanon organize themselves in the face of civil war and Israeli occupation. Hence, Hezbollah was born in the mid-1980s. In the following years, Guard advisors propped up Shi'a groups in Afghanistan, Syria, Iraq, Yemen, Bahrain, and Saudi Arabia's Eastern Province. The Guard usually provided funds and weapons, but in a few instances, its elite Quds Force shouldered operational responsibilities (Katzman 1993: 99; Ward 2009: 267; Axworthy 2014: 222). Most operations were successful, leading Quds Commander General Qassem Suleimani to boast after reviewing his troops in Iraq in March 2015: "Today we see signs of the Islamic Revolution being exported throughout the region—from Bahrain to Iraq and from Syria to Yemen and North Africa" (Blair 2015: 28). Indeed, by 2015, four major Arab capitals (Baghdad, Beirut, Damascus, and Sana'a) lived in Iran's shadow. With such regional influence, Washington could no longer turn the other way.

Iranian-American relations had been severed after students occupied the U.S. embassy in November 1979 and held 52 Americans hostage for an incredible 444 days. Although the hostages were eventually released moments after Ronald Reagan took office, it was a vicious act of defiance—made worse by the botched attempt to save them.[5] Operation Eagle Claw strengthened the new regime's trust in divine favor in its fight against the *Shaytan-e Bozorg* (Great Satan) of world politics. In return, Washington supported

Baghdad during most of its eight-year war on its Persian nemesis. Yet there was a notable exception. Determined to support the Contras' war against the left-leaning Sandinistas in Nicaragua despite the refusal of Congress, Reagan sought a covert cash fund. Iran, at the same time, was in dire need of U.S. ammunition and spare parts. And Israel, which at this point feared Iraq more than Iran, was willing to mediate. Washington therefore ended up providing $500 million worth of secret military supplies to its sworn enemy, via Israel, in exchange for cash (Axworthy 2014: 208). What this notorious Iran-Contra affair revealed was that power politics could override the ideologically charged rhetoric in both capitals. This became even more necessary after 9/11.

America's war on terror brought it closer than ever to the Islamic Republic. Washington and Tehran were now fighting the same enemy: Sunni militants of the Wahhabi variant. And despite George W. Bush's inclusion of Iran in his 2002 Axis of Evil speech, what his administration inadvertently did was destroy Iran's two great enemies: the Afghani Taliban, and the Iraqi Ba'ath. Talks began less than a month after September 11. Ryan Crocker, then a senior State Department official, described how he flew secretly to Geneva to coordinate the attack on the Taliban with Iranians: "I'd fly out on a Friday and then back on Sunday, so nobody in the office knew where I'd been." He remembered how helpful Iranians were during these all-night meetings, helpful to the point of handing him a detailed map of the Taliban's strongpoints. Cooperation continued during the Iraq War, and afterward, as Crocker admitted, "The formation of the [Iraqi] governing council was in its essence a negotiation between Tehran and Washington" (Filkins 2013).[6]

Likewise, Barack Obama attacked the bloodstained Shi'ite regime in Damascus and the monopolistic one in Baghdad, but ended up launching strikes against their biggest rival: the Islamic State in Iraq and the Levant. In addition, Washington's dread of committing ground troops to these sectarian war zones forced it to rely on the Guard to do the dirty work. And in light of this undeniable coincidence of interests came the September 2013 phone call between the American and Iranian presidents, the first since the Revolution.

Yet what prevented this implicit alliance from becoming explicit is the Guard's most ambitious project: the nuclear program. The first enrichment plant was discovered at Nantz in 2002. Iran claimed the right to enrich uranium for peaceful purposes. Its rivals, especially Israel and Saudi Arabia, insisted that it sought nuclear weapons. While the stalemate persisted, Iranians suffered crippling international sanctions. As a presidential hopeful, Obama had pledged to negotiate a peaceful settlement with Iran. His administration's foreign policy, soon dubbed the Obama Doctrine, was that America's military strength had become so overwhelming that it could risk engagement with its former enemies, rather than isolating them, in hopes of encouraging friendlier regimes in countries like Iran, Cuba, and Burma. Negotiations with Iranian officials started in the autumn of 2013, and lasted over twenty-two months. The immediate result was a groundbreaking agreement, in July 2015, that conceded Tehran's right to produce nuclear energy for peaceful purposes and tied the phasing out of sanctions to Iranian compliance with international inspections. This in itself promised to inject billions of dollars into the Iranian economy in the form of renewed oil and gas exports, unfrozen assets, and foreign investment. Possibly more important is the change in American rhetoric. William Burns, the deputy secretary of state who kicked off the negotiations, praised his Iranian counterparts as "tough minded and skeptical as they were professionally skilled"—no more the outlandish mullahs they were routinely portrayed to be (Burns 2015). A CIA officer even described Qassem Suleimani, the zealous warrior who has led the Quds Force since 1998, as "the single most powerful operative in the Middle East" (Filkins 2013).

Nonetheless, it was Obama himself who revolutionized the discourse on Iran. In a televised and later published interview, he dismissed attempts to picture Iran as a dangerous enemy: "The truth of the matter is: Iran's defense budget is $30 billion. Our defense budget is closer to $600 billion. Iran understands that they cannot fight us." He sought to normalize Iran's image by committing the unthinkable: comparing it to the United States. "I think that it's important to recognize that Iran is a complicated country—just like we're a complicated country." He even went further and praised the Iranian leaders' "practical streak" and their "responsive[ness] . . . to their publics," and lauded the gallantry of the Iranian people who "withstood an eight-year war and a million people dead, [and] shown themselves willing . . . to endure hardship when they considered a point of national pride." And to his Arab allies' shock, Obama harshly criticized their hostility toward Tehran: "I think the biggest threats that they face may not be coming from Iran invading. It's going to be from dissatisfaction inside their own countries. . . . That's a tough conversation to have, but it's one that we have to have," and turned the screw further by welcoming the fact that "by virtue of its size, its resources and its people [Iran] would be an extremely successful regional power" (Friedman 2015).

Of course, when and how Iran normalizes its relationship with the United States and what type of regional map they agree on will help determine the power balance in Tehran. The increasingly complicated war against Sunni militants in Iraq and Syria enhances the value of the Revolutionary Guard and its Quds Force. But economic prosperity and political and cultural reintegration in the global community would strengthen the hand of reformers in the executive and legislative branches. There should be little doubt, however, that the presence of various alternatives to Iran's future is itself evidence to both the regime's decentralization and dynamism.

Conclusion

Parting ways with modernizing republics, the Pahlavi dynasty emulated Europe's absolutist monarchies. Although Iran's situation was very different from those it sought to resemble, the new shahs believed Persia's glorious past qualified it to play an assertive military role (as that of France), but because its progress had been delayed by a series of unfortunate reversal, it required an actively modernizing monarch to catch up (as European late modernizers had done). This decision might have been flawed on many levels (in light of the frailty of the army; economic backwardness; and an entirely different geopolitical settings), but it locked the country on the path of absolutist monarchies. Everything the Pahlavi shahs did was perfectly in line with this model. The problem was, of course, that this model belonged to a different time and place.

Absolutist monarchies were at bottom agrarian bureaucracies embedded in rural society and relying on the support of a landed aristocracy. This traditional structure was unsustainable in the age of industrial capitalism, with an economy dependent on oil revenues. Maintaining the dominance of landlords was exceedingly difficult by the 1970s, and empowering a petro-bourgeois required the monarch to abandon his top-down modernizing role.[7] Because the power formula sustaining active monarchies in Europe became untenable in the modern age, they were either thoroughly reformed or came down in pieces. Little wonder why Iran's Revolution fit the pattern of the "great historical social revolutions" (Skocpol 1994: 241). And because no such regime exists today, Iran's will likely remain the "Last Great Revolution."

Yet regimes do not simply collapse; they are either seized or overthrown. And this requires the disloyalty or futility of the agents of repression. So how can we account for their failure in the Iranian case? The answer is connected with another remarkable feature of royal absolutism: the dominance of the political apparatus (represented by the court) over the military and security organs. A hegemonic monarch keeps his military and security organs on a tight leash, and prevents them from developing an independent institutional identity. The inevitable result is paralysis once the monarch decides against bloodshed (in the Iranian case, it was to preserve the legitimacy of the Pahlavi dynasty and pass on the throne to the crown prince). The other two partners in the ruling bloc lacked the autonomy to act on their own behalf to save the regime. As Skocpol shrewdly noted—though without explaining why—Iran's officers "lacked the corporate solidarity to displace the Shah in a coup and save the state at his expense" (1994: 240). Regimes dominated by the political apparatus, as opposed to the military and security, are by definition the least capable of repression. It was the logic of absolutist monarchism that guided the building of subordinate coercive institutions, thus rendering them useless when the regime began to crumble.

Extending this argument to the present, one can attribute the strength of Iran's new regime to the balanced and thoroughly institutionalized ruling complex that emerged from the Revolution. But shifts in the balance of power result in regime change, even if this change was imperceptible at first. At the moment, it is the Revolutionary Guard that threatens the balance. This meta-institution, which gradually managed to accumulate political, military, and security functions, could override all other regime institutions and transform Iran from a popular theocracy to a military dictatorship, or worse, a police state. Iran could find itself on a similar trajectory to that of Turkey or Egypt—to which we turn next.

Notes

1. About eighty clerics are elected to the Assembly by popular vote (from clerical lists) for eight-year terms.

2. To finish off the left, the Communist Party, Tudeh, was banned and its leaders detained in the spring of 1983.

3. 350,000 ground forces; 52,000 air forces; and 18,000 navy (in 2013).

4. The percentage fell from 2.7 percent in 2003 to 1.8 percent in 2013 (as reported by Stockholm International Peace Research Institute, SIPRI).

5. Out of eight Sea Stallion helicopters launched from the U.S.S. *Nimitz* toward Tehran, on April 24, 1980, two were turned back by a sand storm, a third suffered irreparable malfunction, and a fourth crashed into an accompanying Hercules transport jet, killing eight American servicemen.

6. Of course, this did not prevent the tough-minded Quds Force from organizing resistance militias to expedite the U.S. pullback. Iranians typically "alternated between bargaining with the Americans and killing them" (Filkins 2013).

7. This discrepancy between the regime and its environment has bewildered Halliday (1979: 56), who thought "Iran is probably the only country in the world where the state has combined the vigorous promotion of capitalist development with a fully constituted monarchist regime." Iran was not a military dictatorship because its commanders were politically powerless (as opposed to regimes in Greece, Chile, and Indonesia). Nor was it Bonapartist or Fascist because it did not rely on conservative peasants or a petite bourgeoisie; it was not erected to suppress radical workers; it had no capitalist class; and it had no ruling party or ideology (Halliday 1979: 51–53). It was, in Skocpol's description, a unique "absolutist-monarchical military dictatorship" (1994: 240).

Bibliography

Abrahamian, Ervand. 1982. *Iran Between Two Revolutions*. Princeton, NJ: Princeton University Press.

Abrahamian, Ervand. 1989. *The Iranian Mojahedin*. New Haven, CT: Yale University Press.

Abrahamian, Ervand. 1999. *Tortured Confessions: Prisons and Public Recantation in Modern Iran*. Berkeley: University of California Press.

Acheson, Dean. 1969. *Present at the Creation*. New York: W.W. Norton.

Afary, Janet. 1996. *The Iranian Constitutional Revolution, 1906–1911: Grassroots Democracy, Social Democracy, and the Origins of Feminism*. New York: Columbia University Press.

Afary, Janet and Kevin B. Anderson. 2005. *Foucault and the Iranian Revolution: Gender and the Seductions of Islamism*. Chicago: University of Chicago Press.

Alam, Asadollah. 2008. *The Shah and I: The Confidential Diary of Iran's Royal Court, 1968–77*. New York: I.B. Tauris.

Algar, Hamid. 2001. *Roots of the Islamic Revolution in Iran*. New York: Islamic Publication International.

Arjomand, Said Amir. 1988. *The Turban and the Crown: The Islamic Revolution in Iran*. New York: Oxford University Press.

Arjomand, Said Amir. 2002. "Reform Movement and the Debate on Modernity and Tradition in Contemporary Iran." *International Journal of Middle East Studies* 34 (4): 719–31.

Axworthy, Michael. 2014. *Revolutionary Iran: A History of the Islamic Republic*. London: Penguin.

Azimi, Fakhreddin. 2004. "Unseating Mosaddeq: The Configuration and Role of Domestic Forces." In *Mohammad Mosaddeq and the 1953 Coup in Iran*, edited by Mark J. Gasiorowski and Malcolm Byrne, pp. 27–101. Syracuse, NY: Syracuse University Press.

Bani-Sadr, Abol Hassan. 1991. *My Turn to Speak: Iran, the Revolution, and the Secret Deals with the U.S.* New York: Brassey's.

Bayandor, Darioush. 2010. *Iran and the CIA: The Fall of Mosaddeq Revisited*. New York: Palgrave Macmillan.

Bayat, Asef. 1998a. "Revolution Without Movement, Movement Without Revolution: Comparing Islamic Activism in Iran and Egypt." *Comparative Studies in Society and History* 40 (1): 136–69.

Bayat, Asef. 1998b. *Street Politics: Poor People's Movements in Iran*. Cairo: American University Press.

Behrooz, Maziar. 2000. *Rebels with a Cause: The Failure of the Left in Iran*. New York: I.B. Tauris.

Benard, Cheryl and Zalmay Khalilzad. 1984. *The Government of God: Iran's Islamic Republic*. New York: Columbia University Press.

Bill, James A. 1988. *The Eagle and the Lion: The Tragedy of American-Iranian Relations*. New Haven, CT: Yale University Press.

Blair, David. 2015. "Deal for Peace in Our Time That Threatens a New Era of Turmoil." *The Daily Telegraph*, March 8, 2015.

Brzezinski, Zbigniew. 1983. *Power and Principle: Memoirs of the National Security Advisor, 1977–1981*. New York: Farrar, Straus, Giroux.

Burns, Gene. 1996. "Ideology, Culture, and Ambiguity: The Revolutionary Process in Iran." *Theory and Society* 25 (3): 349–88.

Burns, William. 2015. "The Fruits of Diplomacy with Iran." *New York Times*, April 2, 2015.

Byrne, Malcolm. 2004. "The Road to Intervention: Factors Influencing U.S. Policy Toward Iran, 1945–1953. In *Mohammad Mosaddeq and the 1953 Coup in Iran*, edited by Mark J. Gasiorowski and Malcolm Byrne, pp. 201–26. Syracuse, NY: Syracuse University Press.

Chubin, Shahram and Sepehr Zabih. 1974. *The Foreign Relations of Iran: A Developing State in a Zone of Great-Power Conflict*. Berkeley: University of California Press.

Cordesman, Anthony H. 1994. *Iran and Iraq: The Threat from the Northern Gulf*. Boulder, CO: Westview Press.

Cronin, Stephanie. 1997. *The Army and the Creation of the Pahlavi State, 1910–1926*. New York: Tauris.

Cronin, Stephanie. 2003. "Riza Shah and the Paradoxes of Military Modernization in Iran, 1921–1941." In *The Making of Modern Iran: State and Society Under Riza Shah, 1921–1941*, edited by Stephanie Cronin, pp. 37–93. New York: Routledge.

Cronin, Stephanie. 2010. *Soldiers, Shahs, and Subalterns in Iran: Opposition, Protest, and Revolt, 1921–1941*. New York: Palgrave Macmillan.

Dabashi, Hamid. 1993. *Theology of Discontent: The Ideological Foundations of the Islamic Revolution*. New York: New York University Press.

Daugherty, William J. 2001. *In the Shadow of the Ayatollah: A CIA Hostage in Iran*. Annapolis, MD: Naval Institute Press.

De Bellaigue, Christopher. 2004. *In the Rose Garden of the Martyrs: A Memoir of Iran*. New York: HarperCollins.

Eden, Anthony. 1960. *Full Circle*. London: Cassel.

Eisenhower, Dwight D. 1963. *Mandate for Change, 1953–1956*. London: Heinemann.

Filkins, Dexter. 2013. "The Shadow Commander." *The New Yorker*, September 30, 2013.

Foran, John. 2005. *Taking Power: On the Origins of Third World Revolutions*. New York: Cambridge University Press.

Friedman, Thomas. 2015. "Iran and the Obama Doctrine." *New York Times*, April 5, 2015.

Gasiorowski, Mark J. 2004. "The 1953 Coup d'État Against Mosaddeq." In *Mohammad Mosaddeq and the 1953 Coup in Iran*, edited by Mark J. Gasiorowski and Malcolm Byrne, pp. 227–60. Syracuse, NY: Syracuse University Press.

Gasiorowski, Mark J. and Malcolm Byrne (eds.). 2004. *Mohammad Mosaddeq and the 1953 Coup in Iran*. Syracuse, NY: Syracuse University Press.

Gharabaghi, Abbas. 1999. *Why Did It Happen?* Tehran: Arran Press.

Graham, Robert. 1978. *Iran: The Illusion of Power*. London: Croom Helm.

Halliday, Fred. 1979. *Iran: Dictatorship and Development*. New York: Penguin Books.

Harney, Desmond. 1999. *The Prince and the King*. New York: I.B. Tauris.

Heikal, Mohamed. 1981. *Iran: The Untold Story: An Insider's Account of America's Iranian Adventures and Its Consequences for the Future*. New York: Pantheon Books.

Hennawy, Noha, El-. 2011. "Critical Mass: Can a Radical Vanguard Have More Influence Than a Silent Majority?" *Egypt Independent*, December 1, 2011.

Hickman, William F. 1982. *Ravaged and Reborn: The Iranian Army*. Washington, DC: Brookings Institute.
Hoveyda, Fereydoun. 1980. *The Fall of the Shah*. New York: Wyndham Books.
Huwaidy, Fahmy. 1991. *Iran min al-dakhel* (Iran from the Inside). Cairo: Markaz Al-Ahram lel-Targama wal-Nashr.
Huyser, Robert E. 1986. *Mission to Tehran*. New York: Harper & Row.
Kamyabipour, Admiral Ali. 2011. Personal interview. Los Angeles.
Kapuscinski, Ryszard. 2006. *Shah of Shahs*. New York: Penguin Press.
Katouzian, Homa. 1999. *Musaddiq and the Struggle for Power in Iran*. New York: I.B. Tauris.
Katouzian, Homa. 2004. "Mosaddeq's Government in Iranian History: Arbitrary Rule, Democracy, and the 1953 Coup." In *Mohammad Mosaddeq and the 1953 Coup in Iran*, edited by Mark J. Gasiorowski and Malcolm Byrne, pp. 1–26. Syracuse, NY: Syracuse University Press.
Katzman, Kenneth. 1993. *The Warriors of Islam: Iran's Revolutionary Guard*. Boulder, CO: Westview Press.
Kazemi, Farhad. 1980. *Poverty and Revolution in Iran: The Migrant Poor, Urban Marginality, and Politics*. New York: New York University Press.
Keddie, Nikki R. 1981. *Roots of Revolution: An Interpretive History of Modern Iran*. New Haven, CT: Yale University Press.
Khomeini, Ruhollah. 1981. *Islam and Revolution: Writings and Declarations of Imam Khomeini (1941–1980)*. North Haledon, NJ: Mizan Press.
-Kian-Thiébaut, Azadeh. 1998. *Secularization of Iran: A Doomed Failure? The New Middle Class and the Making of Modern Iran*. Paris: Diffusion Peeters.
Kinzer, Stephen. 2003. *All the Shah's Men: An American Coup and the Roots of Middle East Terror*. Hoboken, NJ: John Wiley & Sons.
Kurzman, Charles. 2004. *The Unthinkable Revolution in Iran*. Cambridge, MA: Harvard University Press.
Louis, Wm. Roger. 2004. "Britain and the Overthrow of the Mosaddeq Government." In *Mohammad Mosaddeq and the 1953 Coup in Iran*, edited by Mark J. Gasiorowski and Malcolm Byrne, pp. 126–77. Syracuse, NY: Syracuse University Press.
Majd, Mohammad Gholi. 2000. *Resistance to the Shah: Landowners and the Ulama in Iran*. Gainesville: University of Florida Press.
Marashi, Afshin. 2003. "Performing the Nation: The Shah's Official Visit to Kemalist Turkey, June to July 1934." In *The Making of Modern Iran: State and Society Under Riza Shah, 1921–1941*, edited by Stephanie Cronin, pp. 99–115. New York: Routledge.
Martin, Vanessa. 2007. *Creating the Islamic State: Khomeini and the Making of a New Iran*. New York: I.B. Tauris.
Milani, Abass. 2008a. *Eminent Persians: The Men and Women Who Made Modern Iran, 1941–1979*. Vol. 1. Syracuse, NY: Syracuse University Press.
Milani, Abass. 2008b. *Eminent Persians: The Men and Women Who Made Modern Iran, 1941–1979*. Vol. 2. Syracuse, NY: Syracuse University Press.
Milani, Abass. 2011a. Personal interview. Los Angeles.
Milani, Abass. 2011b. *The Shah*. New York: Palgrave Macmillan.
Milani, Mohsen M. 1994. *The Making of Iran's Islamic Revolution: From Monarchy to Islamic Republic*. Boulder, CO: Westview Press.

Moaddel, Mansoor. 1991. "Class Struggle in Post-Revolutionary Iran." *International Journal of Middle East Studies* 23 (3): 317–43.
Moaddel, Mansoor. 1992. "Ideology as Episodic Discourse: The Case of the Iranian Revolution." *American Sociological Review* 57 (3): 353–79.
Moin, Baqer. 1999. *Khomeini: Life of the Ayatollah*. New York: St. Martin's Press.
Moshiri, Farrokh. 1991. "Iran: Islamic Revolution Against Westernization." In *Revolutions of the Late Twentieth Century*, edited by Jack A. Goldstone, Ted Robert Gurr, and Farrokh Moshiri, pp. 116–35. Boulder, CO: Westview Press.
Munson, Jr., Henry. 1988. *Islam and Revolution in the Middle East*. New Haven, CT: Yale University Press.
Musaddiq, Mohamed. 1988. *Musaddiq's Memoirs: The End of the British Empire in Iran*. London: JEBHE, National Movement of Iran.
Naraghi, Ehsan. 1999. *Min balat al-Shah ela segun al-thawra* (From the Palace of the Shah to the Prisons of the Revolution). Beirut: Dar al-Saqi.
Pahlavi, Mohamed Reza. 1967. *The White Revolution of Iran*. Tehran: Imperial Pahlavi Library.
Pahlavi, Mohamed Reza. 1980. *My Answer to History*. New York: Stein and Day.
Parsa, Misagh. 1989. *Social Origins of the Iranian Revolution*. New Brunswick, NJ: Rutgers University Press.
Parson, Anthony. 1984. *The Pride and the Fall: Iran 1974–1979*. London: Jonathan Cape.
Precht, Henry. 2004. "The Iranian Revolution: An Oral History Henry Precht, Then State Department Desk Officer." *Middle East Journal* 58 (1): 9–31.
Radji, Parviz. 1983. *In the Service of the Peacock Throne: The Diaries of the Shah's Last Ambassador to London*. London: Hamish Hamilton.
Rafsanjani, Akbar Hashemi. 2005. *Hayati* (My Life). Beirut: Dar al-Saqi.
Rahnema, Ali. 2000. *An Islamic Utopian: A Political Biography of Ali Shari'ati*. New York: I.B. Tauris.
Rajaee, Farhang. 2007. *Islam and Modernism: The Changing Discourse in Iran*. Austin: University of Texas Press.
Roosevelt, Kermit. 1979. *Countercoup: The Struggle for the Control of Iran*. New York: McGraw-Hill.
Rubin, Barry. 1981. *Paved with Good Intentions: The American Experience and Iran*. New York: Penguin Books.
Said, Edward W. 1997. *Covering Islam: How the Media and the Experts Determine How We See the Rest of the World*. New York: Vintage.
Saikal, Amin. 1980. *The Rise and Fall of the Shah*. Princeton, NJ: Princeton University Press.
Saleh, Haqi Shafiq. 2008. *Seqout 'arsh al-tawous: Enhiyar al-quwat al-musalaha al-Iraniya fei 'ahd al-usra al-Pahlaviya, 1941–1979* (The Fall of the Pahlavi Throne: The Collapse of the Iranian Armed Forces in the Reign of the Pahlavi Dynasty, 1941–1979). Cairo: Maktabat Madbouly.
Schahgaldian, Nikola B. 1987. *The Iranian Military Under the Islamic Republic*. Santa Monica, CA: RAND.
Schofield, Julian. 2007. *Militarization and War*. New York: Palgrave Macmillan.
Skocpol, Theda. 1994. *Social Revolutions in the Modern World*. New York: Cambridge University Press.

Sick, Gary. 1985. *All Fall Down*. New York: I.B. Tauris.
Sullivan, William H. 1981. *Mission to Iran: The Last US Ambassador*. New York: W.W. Norton.
Truman, Harry S. 1956. *Memoirs*. Vol. 2: *Years of Trial and Hope, 1946–1952*. New York: Doubleday.
Wahid, Latif. 2009. *Military Expenditures and Economic Growth in the Middle East*. New York: Palgrave Macmillan.
Ward, Steven R. 2009. *Immortal: A Military History of Iran and Its Armed Forces*. Washington, DC: Georgetown University Press.
Wright, Right. 2000. *The Last Great Revolution: Turmoil and Transformation in Iran*. New York: Alfred A. Knopf.
Zabih, Sepehr. 1988. *The Iranian Military in Revolution and War*. New York: Routledge.
Zegart, Amy B. 1999. *Flawed by Design: The Evolution of the CIA, JCS, and NSC*. Stanford, CA: Stanford University Press.
Zonis, Marvin. 1991. *Majestic Failure: The Fall of the Shah*. Chicago: University of Chicago Press.
Zubaida, Sami. 1988. "An Islamic State? The Case of Iran." *Middle East Report* 153: 3–7.

II | Turkey

THE LIMITS OF MILITARY GUARDIANSHIP

Even without an express prohibition it would appear doubtful whether officers as a type have the ability, the suppleness, the temperament, or the time for a continuous application to politics.

—*Vagts, History of Militarism, 1959*

DESCRIBING A REGIME TYPE is usually simpler than tracing its historical evolution. In the Turkish case, the opposite is true. Turkey's political trajectory is fairly straightforward. The founding coup of 1924 appointed the military as national guardian. Its mission was to protect not only the security, but also the secular and nationalist nature of the new republic. As such, the military as an institution (rather than a narrow coterie of officers) set the parameters of the political field, and delegated everyday governance and security to civilians. It only intervened when the rules of the game were violated, and invariably at the behest of civilian rulers or opposition. And this occurred four times in almost a century. Less obvious, is how to define Turkey today. The regime has all the features of a modern democracy: an open-market capitalist economy, a vibrant civil society, an effective secular constitution, and free and regular multiparty elections. Yet military guardianship, the authoritarian tendencies of civilian politicians, and the continuing ideological battle between secularism and Islamism mean that Turkish democracy remains relatively limited.

Scholars acknowledge this tension. One political scientist described Turkey as "a strange country that *swings constantly between democracy and militarism*" (Dagi 2008: 5). Another noted the paradoxical nature of civil–military relations in Turkey, where civilians have failed to subordinate the military entirely, even though the military recognizes the legitimacy of civilian oversight (Uzgel 2003: 179–81). In others words, according to yet another analyst, what distinguishes the Turkish military from interventionist militaries elsewhere "is its acceptance of the legitimacy of both democracy and civilian rule. . . . It is not praetorian; it has not tried to undermine democracy or usurp civilian authority" (Sakallioglu 1997: 153). This is why most students of Turkey agree that—regardless of occasional lapses to military rule—the country's trajectory could be characterized by its steady drive toward democratic consolidation (Kalaycioglu 2005: 197). As Perry Anderson concluded: "Turkey has on the whole been a land of regular elections, of competing parties and uncertain outcomes, and alternating governments. . . . [D]emocracy [has become] so entrenched that even serial military interventions could not shake its acceptance as the political norm in Turkey" (2009: 431–32).

However, the literature is divided over how this came about. Class analysts argued that compromise was always possible because the two forces struggling for dominance in Turkey are both conservative: nationalist conservatives led by the officer corps, and religious and economic conservatives represented by Islamist movements. Indeed, any historical survey of the Turkish political system would reveal that it "always worked in favor of the right" (Aksin 2007: 282). Again, quoting Anderson,

> [Turkey suffered from neither an] explosive class conflict to be contained, nor radical politics to be crushed. Most peasants owned land; workers were few; intellectuals marginal; a Left hardly figured. . . . In these conditions, there was small risk of any upsets from below. The elites could settle accounts between themselves without fear of letting loose forces they could not control. . . . Turkish democracy has been broken at intervals, but never for long, because it is anchored in a Centre-Right majority that has remained, in one form after another, unbroken. (2009: 433)

Still, one needs to understand why these conservative compromises became less military-dictated over time. After the full-blown coups of 1960 and 1971, and the particularly violent one in 1980, officers shifted to exerting pressure, as in the so-called soft coup of 1997, and their influence afterward diminished. A common explanation of officers' retreat from politics is geopolitics. While the North Atlantic Treaty Organization (NATO) was willing to accept (sometimes encourage) conservative coups in member states during the Cold War, the European Union (EU) has cited instances of military intervention to delay Turkey's accession. Officers therefore abstained from outright meddling in politics to avoid pubic blame for denying the country its hoped-for EU membership (Uzgel 2003; Karaosmanglu 2011).

Another explanation highlights the successful strategies of Turkey's conservative politicians, especially Islamists (Cizre 2008; Gürsoy 2011). After the military crushed their rebellions in the 1920s and 1930s, Islamists shifted toward electoral politics, first allying with traditionalist parties in the 1940s and 1950s, and then developing their own. Through a long and bitter "politics of engagement," they outmaneuvered, exhausted, and eventually reduced the influence of the armed forces (Turam 2007: 29). The most prominent author of Turkish Islamism, Necmettin Erbakan, had made such a prophecy himself in 1998, weeks before one of his numerous parties was suspended: "They have dissolved the MNP [his first party] so we created the MSP, which was much more popular and allowed Islamists to participate in government for the first time. Then they dissolved MSP, so we created Refah, which became the largest Turkish political party and led a coalition government. If they dissolve Refah, then our next party will dominate government alone" (Helal 1999: 220).

Two power strategies were particularly important to sociologists. The first is a popular strategy among Islamists in authoritarian settings, which is to mobilize supporters through the transformation of everyday social and cultural practices, rather than to directly contest the rules of the political game. The second strategy, a distinctive feature of Turkish Islamism, is to divide labor between several parallel social movements and political parties. This not only allows flexibility and innovation, but also rules out the possibility of a wholesale repression of Islamism (Mardin 1989; Zubaida 1996; Yavuz 2003: Tugal 2009a).

The problem here, of course, is that the other player, that is, the military, is treated as static, as permanently stuck in the mold shaped by the founders of the republic. But why would a professional war-making machine identify itself with a rigid cultural value such as secularism? Perhaps it fell hostage to its own revolutionary legacy as a modernizing force (Brown 1988: 140; Brooks 2008: 213; Güney 2002: 162), or perhaps Turkish officers, as most officers elsewhere, simply see themselves as "preservers of the status quo" (Harb 2002: 41). However, these wobbly justifications are based on a prevalent misperception of the military's actual strategy, one that conflates officers' vigilant secular rhetoric and their surprising pragmatism in dealing with Islamists. While most military interventions were "framed" in terms of safeguarding secularism, officers have, in fact, accepted the growth of Islamist power in order to check the rise of Communism and appease Western powers. Indeed, each intervention saw the "steady weakening of one of the [new republic's founding] pillars," starting with secularism (Anderson 2009: 442; see also Keyder 2004: 69).

Officers therefore were no blind custodians of a cultural dogma (Aydinli 2009; Heper 2011; Satana 2011). Their eagerness to control the political field followed from their institutional mission to privilege national security above all. In fact, all threats to the stability and territorial integrity of the state were treated similarly, whether secular-Islamist frictions, Communist intrigues, separatist actions (by Kurds and Alevis), or economic crises. A rare survey of Turkish officers in 2012 showed that only a quarter of them regarded secularism as the basis of the political system, while 73 percent highlighted the importance of unity, democracy, and the rule of law (Gurcan 2015).[1] As one general explained in his 1999 memoir, military actions were not meant to reinforce any particular social identity: "An officer is not a social scientist, he regards those who pose the threat as an 'internal enemy' who may even be more dangerous than external enemies" (quoted in Uzgel 2003: 187). As far as officers were concerned, Communists in the 1970s were Soviet proxies; Kurds were working hand-in-hand with Syria and Iraq; and Islamists were doing the bidding of the Saudis or the Iranians (Uzgel 2003: 187). What haunted them was not ideology, but the "Sèvres syndrome": the pathological fear that foreign powers are employing internal agents to partition Turkey, as they had attempted in the Treaty of Sèvres in 1920 (Yavuz 1999: 584). As Metin Heper and Aylin Güney indicated, "They were not in a *political* competition with the political elite. They considered themselves as nonpartisan arbiters, and not as rivals to the political elite. Most of the time they were on the sidelines and not in the political swirl, not because they have been forced to act in that manner, but because they thought it was proper for them to act in such fashion" (2004: 195). So despite their numerous interventions, Turkish officers were "reluctant participants" (Brown 1988: 143).

Because of their lack of interest in daily governance and policing, Turkish officers were open to domestic and geopolitical pressures to allow multiparty politics—granted they could always intervene to check excesses. And the establishment of a political space for parties to compete in began an interactive process (both collaborative and conflictive) between officers and politicians, with the former trying to preserve overall regime domination to better maintain social order, and the latter bent on expanding their autonomy by extending the margins of democracy. And it was a dialectical rather than a circular relationship: military interventions did not bring about full reversals, but instead reconstituted power relations in a way that surprisingly empowered politicians further. This was because the aim of each intervention was to render future interventions unnecessary. And being aware of that encouraged politicians to extract from officers as many concessions as possible. Gradually, military hegemony eroded, and the power balance shifted so markedly toward politicians that by the 2000s they felt confident enough to defy officers.

What about security? Owing to the unrivaled domination of the Turkish military during the founding years of the republic, it had for long incorporated domestic security in its portfolio. Historically, Turkey's police and intelligence agencies had been notably weak. They played no part in the establishment of the new regime, and scarcely figured as independent players in the power struggle between military officers and politicians. It was only after the 1980 coup that the army decided to unburden itself by rehabilitating the police force to carry out more extensive duties. But the decade that witnessed the expansion of the size and responsibilities of the security agencies was the same decade that saw the ascendancy of Turkey's most powerful political parties, which succeeded in winning the still emergent security establishment to their side. It thus seems that the security institution has simply shifted sides from the military to the political apparatus, though it remains a junior partner. Clearly, the absence of an invasive security machine goes a long way in explaining why Turkey succeeded in developing a somehow viable democracy.

6 The Founding Coup

MARCH 1924

TURKEY'S REVOLUTION FROM ABOVE IN the 1920s was described as the third attempt of its kind in a little under a century. Since the 1830s, modernizing Ottoman officers and bureaucrats championed Western-inspired reforms to reverse the decline of the caliphate. The first wave of reforms, known as the Tanzimat (1839–1876), produced a modern army and a constitution. Yet the reign of Sultan Abdülhamid II (r. 1876–1909) interrupted the process when he saw that instead of the reinvigorated empire promised by reformers, his realm had become besieged by internal crises, ravaged by military defeats, and teetering on the edge of bankruptcy. After the devastating loss to Russia in 1878 forced the sultan to forfeit the Balkans, he suspended the constitution, and reemphasized his symbolic role as caliph (religious leader of all Muslims). However, his rearguard action backfired. A cabal of junior officers and bureaucrats organized themselves into a Committee for Union and Progress (CUP), commonly known as the Young Turks. CUP attracted 850,000 members operating 360 branches across the country and was headed by a fifty-member Central Committee based in Salonika. Blaming the sultan's dictatorship for the recent military setbacks, the Salonika garrison fired the first shot in 1908, and mutiny soon spread to other garrisons. The sultan tried to rally the Istanbul garrison to defend the throne, but troops stationed in Macedonia marched on the capital to replace the obstinate monarch with his accommodating cousin Mehmed V Rasad (r. 1909–1918) and to transfer effective power to a CUP triumvirate composed of the ministers of war, navy, and interior: Enver, Cemal, and Talat, respectively (Yılmaz 2008: 2–3; Anderson 2009: 400–10).

The Young Turks were keen empire builders who hoped to jump back on the imperial bandwagon with other European powers. Although they espoused Turkish nationalism, they were set on reestablishing control over all those independence-seeking nationalist provinces: Greece, Armenia, the Balkans, and the Arab world. Their Westernizing reforms, however, failed to reverse their fortunes: between 1911 and 1912, Libya was lost to Italy, and the Ottoman armies were swept out of Greece and the Balkans. The venturesome triumvirate rashly gambled their last chip on the Great War. After initially approaching and being rebuffed by the Entente, the Young Turks threw their lot in with the Germans. The hope was that a Central Powers' victory would at least arrest Turkey's imperial collapse. But not only did the Entente hold its ground, and not only did Britain and France outflank the Ottomans by enlisting the support of their Arab subjects, and not only did the Ottomans fail to pay them back in kind by unleashing Indian Muslims against Britain, it also became obvious that the exhausted and overextended Ottoman armies were no match even for Russia—the weakest link in the Entente camp (Hopkirk 1994).

Yet despite their unconditional surrender in the autumn of 1918, the Ottomans were not totally vanquished. Their capital was safe after their heroic stance at Gallipoli, and—unlike tsarist Prussia, Russia, and Habsburg Austria—the regime remained relatively intact. Between September and October 1918, the CUP created Defense of Rights Committees to coordinate national resistance against any foreign occupation, and on the night of November 1, CUP leaders took a ship to Berlin to oversee resistance under the protection of Friedrich Ebert's new Social Democratic government (Rustow 1959: 542).

After the guns fell silent, the military situation was as follows: the empire's Arab provinces, including the strategic city of Mosul, were under either British or French control; the French also occupied Adana (Cilicia), Alexandretta, and eastern Thrace; the British took parts of eastern Anatolia and the Black Sea coast; the Italians landed in western and southern Anatolia; and the Greeks occupied Izmir (Smyrna) and other cities in western Anatolia, western Thrace, and the Aegean. In March 1919 the capital itself was placed under an Anglo-French authority, which proceeded to install a puppet sultan, Mehmed VI Vahideddin (r. 1918–1922), and forced him to accept the Sèvres Treaty in August 1920. The treaty not only formalized the victor's territorial gains, but also decreed the establishment of an independent Armenian state in northeastern Anatolia, and a Kurdish one in the southeast; granted all deported subjects (mostly Greek and Armenian) the right of return and financial reparation; demilitarized the Turkish Straits and placed them under international supervision; appointed a committee to manage the empire's finances; and permanently demobilized the Ottoman army, allowing only for rural and urban police forces.

Militarily speaking, however, there was still ground for hope. To start with, London and Paris failed to station enough troops in the Anatolian hinterland for logistical reasons (there was only one railroad in eastern Anatolia, a terrain otherwise inhospitable to troop movements). Control over Anatolia therefore remained effectively in the hands of seven Ottoman army corps: those based there during the war, and those returning from Arab and Caucasian provinces. Moreover, with eastern Anatolia neutralized on account of the Russian civil war, the Ottoman troops could afford to concentrate all their forces on the southwestern front on the borders with Greece (Walt 1996: 299–302; Fromkin 1989: 392–99).

And it was into this relatively favorable situation that an ambitious and handsome officer by the name of Mustafa Kemal made his entry. While stationed in Damascus in 1906, Kemal had founded the Fatherland Freedom Society, a Young Turk splinter group. He briefly joined the CUP, but remained aloof because he was not assigned the leadership position he believed he deserved. Nonetheless, he was invaluable to the Young Turk coup by personally directing the Macedonian regiments that suppressed the Istanbul garrison and ousted Sultan Abdülhamid II in 1909. Kemal achieved national eminence in Gallipoli, where he helped repel the Anglo-French landing on the Dardanelles, and later when he prevented a rout of the Ottoman armies in Syria. In fact, "no other military leader in 1919 could match Kemal's popularity or reputation of invincibility" (Rustow 1959: 537). Kemal returned to the capital after the armistice, and in the next six months used his connections at court (he had traveled to Prussia with the Sultan while he was still crown prince) to have himself appointed inspector of the Third Army in eastern Anatolia to (ostensibly) help demobilize the troops. He knew that the Greek occupation of Izmir (Smyrna) had sent shockwaves across Anatolia, further swelling the ranks of those bent on resistance. And he was determined to ride the crest of popular rage. After a two-month head start, in July 1919, Kemal resigned his post and called for a war of national liberation (Rustow 1959: 542).

The War of Liberation

A crucial difference between Kemal and his counterparts in Iran and Egypt was that his modernizing coup came on the heels of an immensely popular war of national liberation. Winning this war granted him more legitimacy than other coup-makers, thus allowing him to carry out a more sweeping revolution from above. But how did Kemal snatch victory from the jaws of defeat? From the very start, he excelled at "uniting his followers and dividing his antagonists" (Rustow 1959: 545). His success owed much to his ability to unite the home front, exploit geopolitical opportunities to the fullest, balance foreign powers against each other, and confront enemies one at a time.

The first step was to organize military resistance. Kemal drew inspiration from the French model of the National Guards, as popular militias embodying the will of the nation, yet he insisted on placing them under the supervision of the 50,000 nationalist officers he now led in Anatolia (Mango 1999: 229). In September 1919 Kemal integrated all Defense of Rights committees (volunteers led by village notables and intellectuals) into a central Committee for the Defense of Rights of Anatolia and Rumelia (i.e., Asiatic and European Turkey). Now that the military and political wings of his National Forces (Kuva-yi Milliye) were set, Kemal recruited two top generals to lead them: Mustafa Fevzi Çakmak, war minister between 1918 and 1920, and Mustafa Ismet Inönü, one of the ministry's young and bright undersecretaries. To enhance his popular legitimacy, Kemal convened a Grand National Assembly, half of which was officers and bureaucrats and the other half elected representatives, in Ankara in April 1920. And its first task, expectedly, was to elect him chairman and general commander of the National Forces (Rustow 1959: 542; Mango 1999: 276).

Kemal's monopoly over power was further guaranteed by the curious fact that between 1921 and 1922, the Armenian Revolutionary Party assassinated all CUP leaders who could have challenged his position, in retribution for the Armenian massacres committed during the Great War (Anderson 2009: 411–12). No less important was the European occupation of the capital, which justified his discrediting of the powerless sultan. So when the religious authorities excommunicated Kemal and his associates, he directed 250 clerics in Ankara to respond with a *fetva* (canonical decision) declaring that the current sultan was "the prisoner of the infidels, that it was the duty of the faithful to save him and his dominions, and that *fetvas* issued at the behest of enemy states lacked validity" (Mango 1999: 275). This is why a keen student of Kemal's coup noted, "Without the Western threat there probably would have been no revolution" (Trimberger 1978: 43). A situation of dual power now emerged, with a revolutionary regime in Ankara and a withering old regime in the capital.

To strengthen his hand, Kemal now sought international recognition. He understood that the Great War victors were too exhausted and divided to launch a concerted military campaign against him. They could, nonetheless, support a regional proxy. And Greece was the best candidate because of its territorial ambitions, and its close ties to British Premier David Lloyd George. Kemal's challenge therefore was to defeat Athens without provoking a confrontation with London (Mango 1999: 286). His Greek campaign benefited from three factors. First, Greek moves aggravated France and Italy, who saw Athens as little more than London's pawn. Second, the Greeks themselves were consumed by internal feuds between monarchists and their rivals, with Prime Minister Eleftherios Venizelos losing the 1920 election to those determined to reinstall King Constantine (Mango 1999: 306). But the third and most important card in Kemal's deck was Russian support. Moscow's new masters resented Athens for supporting their enemies during the civil war. With Russian-Turkish cooperation materializing into the Moscow Treaty, in March 1921, Western capitals immediately saw the danger of alienating Ankara. In this treaty, Kemal pledged to respect the Soviet Union's new borders, and to look favorably upon Moscow's interests in the Black Sea and the Caucasus in return for arms and funds (Ahmad 1993: 50 Walt 1996: 304–10). The ever shrewd Kemal, however, was not carried away by Russian generosity, and reassured the West that his rapprochement with the Soviets would not be at their expense if they recognized the Ankara regime (Mango 1999: 328).

With his cards carefully arranged, Kemal began his diplomatic maneuvers. Recognizing that France's primary concern was Syria and Lebanon, he sent emissaries to George Picot, who was then the French high commissioner in Syria and Armenia, advising him not to make enemies of Turks and Arabs at the same time, and proposing that a withdrawal of French troops from Cilicia would be matched by Ankara's relinquishing of all claims over these Arab provinces, a favorable compromise over the control of the disputed border districts of Alexandretta and Antakya, and a guarantee of French economic interests in Turkey. Kemal then lured the Italians with economic concessions, knowing full well that Rome viewed the Treaty of Sèvres with little enthusiasm because it favored the British. As a result, France and Italy broke ranks with Britain and signaled their intention to withdraw their troops from Turkey (Mango 1999: 259–60). Seeing that a wedge had been driven between the European allies, Lloyd George called for a conference in London in February 1921 to settle matters with Greece and Turkey. The London conference further exposed European discord, as Ankara's representatives convinced Paris and Rome to declare their impartiality in the Turkish-Greek dispute. Now that he had neutralized the Great Powers, Kemal turned his attention back to the Greeks (Ahmad 1993: 50; Mango 1999: 306–10).

Ankara's National Forces won two landmark victories against Greece: first in Sakarya in August 1921, followed by a rout of Greek forces in Anatolia in September 1922. The Turks initially crossed the Dardanelles in hot pursuit, but the sober Kemal realized that a Turkish invasion of Greece would certainly trigger British intervention, and so he recalled his troops, and then offered the British the oil-rich Iraqi province of Mosul and the international supervision they demanded over the Straits in exchange for a cessation of hostilities, which was finally achieved in October. Ankara's successful maneuvers encouraged British conservatives to withdraw from Lloyd George's wartime coalition, and elect a new government to negotiate peace at Lausanne in November 1922 (Walt 1996: 303–06; Mango 1999: 356–57).

Kemal seized the opportunity and abolished the sultanate on November 1, 1922, under the pretext that Turkey must speak with one voice during the coming negotiations. This had to be done tactfully considering that the oath each deputy took during the Grand National Assembly's opening ceremony stated that national resistance aimed to liberate the "fatherland, nation, sultanate, and caliphate from foreign rule" (Yılmaz 2008: 7). Kemal tried to ease the religious conscience of his deputies by claiming that the abolishment of the sultanate—the political wing of the caliphate—should not undermine the religious leadership of the caliph. When deputies seemed unconvinced, his tone turned threatening:

> Sovereignty and sultanate are taken by strength, by power and by force. It was by force that the sons of Osman seized sovereignty and the sultanate of the Turkish nation; they have maintained this usurpation for six centuries. Now the Turkish nation has rebelled, has put a stop to these usurpers, and has effectively taken sovereignty and sultanate into its own hands. This is an accomplished fact. . . . If those gathered here, the Assembly, and everyone else could look at this question in a natural way, I think they would agree . . . if they do not, the truth will still find expression, but some heads may roll in the process. (quoted in Yılmaz 2008: 8)

The law was passed, the last Ottoman sultan fled his capital in a British submarine, and the Assembly elected a compliant caliph, Abdülmecid Effendi, who—as it turned out—was also the last Muslim caliph. The Treaty of Lausanne, concluded in July 1923, established Turkey's modern borders, and cemented the legitimacy of its new rulers, now hailed as liberators.

Benign Dictatorship?

Those who studied the life of Mustafa Kemal had little doubt that he was "a rebel from within the ranks of the Ottoman establishment, not a popular revolutionary"; that his ultimate goal was "to bring order out of chaos" (Mango

1999: 242). This first required consolidating political control. The war of liberation helped him undermine the old Ottoman elite, but his concessions to Western powers provoked opposition within his own camp. Dissidents within the Grand National Assembly, unimaginatively calling themselves the Second Group, lobbied against the ratification of the Lausanne Treaty. Kemal's solution was simple. He dissolved the Assembly in April 1923; directed his delegation in Lausanne to sign the treaty in July; held fresh elections in August, while banning members of the Second Group from running; and had his new assembly of loyalists ratify the treaty on the same month. A few days later, Kemal organized these loyalists into the Republican People's Party (Cumhuriyet Halk Partisi, CHP), thus inaugurating the single-party rule that would last for over two decades (Trimberger 1978: 105–08; Yılmaz 2008: 9).

The incipient dictator then turned to his opponents, both regime insiders who opposed his personal autocracy, and the rural resistance, spearheaded by conservative peasants and Kurds, who opposed the secularism and Turkic nationalism of his regime. Kemal again carefully divided his battles. To appease intraregime contenders, he replaced his closest ally, Ismet Inönü, with a liberal figure (Ali Fethi Okyar) as head of the cabinet. He also allowed his opponents to form a new political party in November 1924, the short-lived Progressive Republican Party (Terakkiperver Cumhuriyet Fırkası). His real aim was to distract them for as long as he needed to pacify the countryside. In February 1925 Kemal crushed a Kurdish armed rebellion, while dissuading peasants and landowners from joining in the battle against him by repealing the tithe. Barely three weeks later, he reinstalled Inönü as premier, and passed two of his regime's most draconian laws: the Law for the Maintenance of Order, which granted the state dictatorial powers against whomever it deemed a public enemy; and the Independence Tribunals Law, which delivered swift justice to the regime's opponents, with no right of appeal—a mild version of the Jacobin Committee of Public Safety. These laws were then used to close down the Progressive Republican Party in June 1925, and prosecute its leaders: nineteen were sentenced to death, and seven were handed ten-year prison terms. Again, careful not to alienate all his rivals at once, Kemal coupled his suppression of political opponents with generous concessions to Turkey's urban intellectuals and rising bourgeoisie. In February 1926 the Assembly passed the Civil Code (almost translated to the last word from Swiss law), which expanded civil liberties, especially for women, followed by laws in April and May expanding capitalists' privileges, notably the Law for the Promotion of Industry, which provided cheap credit and tax exemptions (Yılmaz 2008: 11–12).

The unrivaled leader—who now took the name Atatürk (literally, "Father Turk")—finally used the 1935 CHP Congress to effectively merge state and Party, decreeing, for instance, that the CHP secretary-general should automatically become interior minister; heads of regional branches should become provincial governors; and all state officials should be Party members (Ahmad 1988: 754; Sakallioglu 1997: 154). Kemal, who began his reign with allusions to the French Revolution, now appeared to be infatuated with the totalitarian parties of the 1930s, both Fascists and Communists.

This was partly because Kemal's revolutionary project was not narrowly political, but socially and culturally transformative. And the most shocking act of Kemalism as a sociocultural creed was the abolishment of the caliphate—for the first time in Islam's fourteen-century history—on March 3, 1924, and the banishment of the members of the house of Osman, after their six-century rule. This was accompanied by the substitution of the longstanding office of *Seyhülislam* (the most senior Islamic scholar in the realm) with a state-run Directorate of Religious Affairs to manage mosques, appoint religious functionaries, and circulate authorized sermons. Sharīʿa laws were first confined to family law, before being entirely supplanted by Swiss-inspired civil codes. Private religious schools and Sufi orders were banned in 1925. And while Article 2 of the 1924 Constitution maintained that Islam was the religion of the state, this provision was removed in 1928, and a new clause, introduced in 1937, declared Turkey a secular republic. Also, the new Faculty of Theology at the University of Istanbul, charged with providing a modern interpretation of Islam, was transformed in 1933 into an Institute of Oriental Studies under the Faculty of Arts. Several Westernizing measures undermined Islamic culture further, famously the banning of the veil, enforcing European hats, adopting Latin script, prohibiting the Arabic call to prayer, and discarding the lunar calendar (Lewis 1952: 41). It is no small wonder that sociologist Serif Mardin judged Kemal's revolution as primarily cultural:

> The Turkish Revolution was not the instrument of a discontented *bourgeoisie*, it did not ride on a wave of peasant dissatisfaction with the social order, and it did not have as a target the sweeping away of feudal privileges, but it *did* take as a target the values of the Ottoman *ancien régime*. . . . [T]he symbolic system of society, culture, seems to have had a relatively greater attraction as a target than the social structure itself. And within culture, religion seems to have been singled out as the core of the system. (1971: 202)

Anderson similarly asserted that what was most astonishing about Turkey's transformation was that it culminated into "a cultural revolution without a social revolution, something historically very rare, indeed that might look *a priori* impossible" (2009: 414). Anderson convincingly explained the absence of anti-feudal, or even anti-capitalist impulse in the Turkish Revolution by the fact that the Ottoman social structure was based on an office-holding elite that had not been allowed to evolve into a powerful landowning class (2009: 415). But even if that was the case, why was Kemal so determined to achieve a wholesale transformation of Ottoman culture?

Some argue that secularism had been lurking in Turkey since the nineteenth century, and that Kemal only drove it to its logical end (Mardin 1971: 208; Helal 1999: 37). It was said that pious Muslims were "genuinely frightened by the agnosticism, not to say atheism, of leading CUP members" since 1908 (Mango 1999: 86). Ottoman modernizers, in general, and Young Turks, in particular, had for long turned their back on Islam as a binding identity, advocating instead "a common Ottoman citizenship and loyalty irrespective of religion or origin" (Lewis 1952: 38). So even though Kemal's subjects were 97 percent Muslim and less than 75 percent Turkic, his secular ethnic nationalism was in line with Turkey's intellectual developments in the last few decades (Kalaycioglu 2005: 2). Yet Atatürk's *kulturkampf* remains unprecedented in the Muslim world. As Anderson put it, "The scale and speed of this assault on religious tradition and household custom, embracing faith, time, dress, family, language, remain unique" (2009: 414). Why such audacity?

Barbara Ward (1942: 51) believed that Kemal was a faithful son of the Enlightenment. He was certainly never a man of faith, even during his youth, and thought of himself as an apostle of Western civilization, confiding to his diary months before his coup:

> If I ever acquire great authority and power, I think that I would introduce at a single stroke the transformation needed in our social life. I do not accept and my spirit revolts at the idea entertained in some quarters that this can be done gradually by getting the common people and the *ulema* to think at my level. After spending so many years acquiring higher education, enquiring into civilized social life and getting a taste of freedom, why should I descend to the level of the common people? Rather, I should raise them to my level. (Mango 1999: 176)

But there are reasons to believe that Kemal's secularism was largely instrumental. For one thing, Kemal did not shrink from employing Islam during the war of liberation. He embraced the title of *gazi* (Islamic conqueror), and glorified God in his speeches until 1924. Examples abound. On Kemal's orders, the opening ceremony of the Grand National Assembly was scheduled on a Friday, the day of Muslim congregational worship, and commenced with a procession from Hacı Bayram Mosque. "After prayers, a procession was formed, led by a cleric carrying a Koran on a lectern, while another man held above his head what purported to be a hair from the Prophet's beard. As a crowd of onlookers shouted '*Allahuekber*' (God is great), the deputies and accompanying officials walked to the ... meeting place of the assembly.... The procession stopped in front of the building, where more prayers were recited and sheep sacrificed." Kemal then delivered a long speech on how Islam grants "the greatest of authority to the united mass of believers." The following day, Kemal repeated in his first official proclamation, "We, your deputies, swear in the name of God and the Prophet that the claim that we are rebels against the sultan and the caliph is a lie" (Mango 1999: 277–78).

The reasons why Atatürk thought Islam would serve his purpose are too obvious. But why turn against it? Mardin suggested that Kemal saw Islam as a "mediating link between local social forces and the political structure," and knew that without disrupting this link, he would never be able to firmly control the state (1971: 205). In his memoirs, Inönü confessed that Kemal abolished the caliphate because he understood that in order to establish his rule: "The two-headed system had to go" (quoted in Mango 1999: 403). As Anderson commented: "The spirit in which Kemal made use of Muslim piety in these years was that of Napoleon enthroning himself with the blessing of the pope. But as exercise in cynicism they moved in opposite directions: Napoleon rising to power as a revolutionary, and manipulating religion to stabilize it, Kemal manipulating religion to make a revolution and turning on it once his power was stabilized" (2009: 417).

Of course, besides personal beliefs and the need to disrupt the traditional political structure, a third crucial reason for Kemal's cultural campaign was geopolitical. Kemal was a staunch realist, or as described by his biographer, "He was a practical man of action, a realist with a vision" (Mango 1999: 396). Considering that even before the Great War, the Ottomans had lost 83 percent of their provinces, Western powers recognized that if Istanbul kept up its Islamic leadership role, it might be tempted one day to recover its lost territories in the Balkans, Greece, and the Arab world, thus drawing their European patrons to war. Transforming the "very fundamentals of [Muslim] political existence" by introducing the "artificial state system" into the Muslim world was therefore high on their postwar agenda (Fromkin 1989: 17). And the twelfth point in U.S. President Woodrow Wilson's famous Fourteen Points emphasized the right to self-determination, which translated into "liberating" Muslim countries from the grip of the caliphate, as one of many colonial powers (Fromkin 1989: 258). In fact, when Ottoman radicals in Paris and Geneva before the war adopted the name "New Ottomans," their European hosts prevailed on them to use the term "Young Turks" instead (Rustow 1959: 516).

Kemal realized that—with Turkey under their mercy—there was no chance that the Great War victors would evacuate peacefully if they suspected Istanbul of expansionist yearnings. So in order to justify to his countrymen the surrender of the caliphate provinces in the Treaty of Lausanne, and to spare himself the burden of having to explain why he did not intend to reclaim them in the future, and—most important—to put the anxious Europeans at ease, Kemal had to substitute Islam with secular nationalism. So indeed it was the power structure that dictated secularism as an official ideology. Turkey's successive military defeats forced the new regime to "resolutely cast aside all dreams of imperial glory" (Rustow 1959: 551). Or as one insightful scholar remarked, the territorial unit that survived the collapse of the empire "turned out to be the Turkish nation," and this is all that the new regime felt it could defend (Dunn 1972: 179–80). As Kemal himself made clear: "Turkey does not desire an inch of foreign territory, but will not give up an inch of what she holds" (quoted in Shmuelevitz 1999: 300). In short, Turkey's Westernization campaign was "strongly bound to the goal of state survival" (Oguzlu 2003: 290–91).

So while many claim that if Kemal had failed to win the war of liberation, Turkey would never have become secular (Kalaycioglu 2005: 198), the opposite might be true: if Turkey had not become secular, Kemal would never have won the war. Factoring in this geopolitical dimension is important for two reasons. First, it underscores how secularism was not the product of internal sociocultural processes, but an ideology imposed from above as a national security imperative—a fact with far-reaching implications; and second, it justifies why adherence to secularism became less rigid among Turkey's military guardians with changes in the international context.

Depoliticizing the Military

Ottoman officers had spearheaded modernization since the 1830s, and—especially after the 1908 coup—became Turkey's dominant elite. Under their tutorship, junior officers were indoctrinated in the Young Turks' nationalist ideology—a doctrine intensified once these officers came face-to-face with the nationalist zeal of Arabs, Balkans, and Slavs in the Great War. This is why Kemal found dozens of supporters among army majors and captains, much more so that among senior officers (only seven brigadiers and three generals joined his camp). But though not everyone subscribed to Kemal's vision for Turkey, the officer corps was united in its frustration with the old regime's military sterility. This is why Kemal's faction enjoyed the tacit support of the War Office and the general staff from day one, and why he managed to win the backing of the forces stationed in Anatolia with relative ease (Rustow 1959: 534, 540).

The regular army was crucial to winning the war of liberation, and subsequently ousting the sultan and caliph. It also played a significant role in quelling provincial rebellions after the declaration of the republic, most famously, the 1925 uprising under the Kurdish Sufi Sheikh Said, which was crushed using 50,000 troops (half of the Turkish infantry at that point), and the 1937 Alevi revolt, which required heavy artillery and bombers, in addition to thousands of infantrymen. Nonetheless, the new regime was adamant about keeping officers out of politics. This presents one of the clearest points of contrast between civil–military relations under the Young Turks and under Kemal's emerging dictatorship: "The Young Turks, swept into power as champions of constitutional and parliamentary government, proceeded to concentrate power increasingly in military hands. . . . The Kemalist movement, starting from a military apex, worked hard to provide itself with a solid civilian base" (Rustow 1959: 544).

Before the first bullets were shot in the war of liberation, Kemal convened the Grand National Assembly to lay the foundations of civilian rule. That same year, he adopted a National Charter, which formed the basis of the 1924 Constitution. And later, he turned the Defense of Rights Committees into a civilian party, the CHP. He himself assumed the presidency of the republic from its establishment in 1923 until his death in 1938. Finally, Kemal sealed the new republic from the capriciousness of general commanders by providing a ruling creed for all to adhere to. This creed was elaborated in a series of ruling party congresses, beginning with his legendary six-day speech (*Nutuk*) in October 1927, which offered a proficiently doctored version of the Turkish Revolution, and culminating in the 1935 congress that produced the Six Arrows of Kemalism (republicanism, nationalism, populism, statism, secularism, and reformism), which were then incorporated in the 1937 Constitution. Kemal's ruling ideology was reinforced by a carefully cultivated personality cult, with equestrian statues of the beloved leader at every corner, and with the CHP posthumously declaring him Eternal Leader (*Ebedî Sef*) in a Party congress held after his passing under a slogan "very much reminiscent of the Nazis: One party, one nation, one leader" (Yılmaz 2008: 12).[2]

Equally important to civilian rule, of course, was Kemal's requirement that every officer involved in politics resign from the military, and his prohibition on the chief of staff's attending cabinet meetings (Helal 1999: 92; Wahid 2009: 66). This strict separation between military and government was attributed to Kemal's belief that it had been politicized officers who brought about Turkey's defeats over the last three decades. He was frequently quoted as saying, "As long as officers remain in the Party we shall never build a strong Party nor a strong Army" (Brown 1988: 132). A more sinister explanation is that the emerging dictator preferred to separate his increasingly long list of opponents from the army so that he could crush them without risking civil war (Rustow 1959: 545). In other words, removing officers from politics was not intended to establish civilian control in the Western sense, but rather to preclude the military from becoming a rival source of power to Kemal's ruling clique, which included both civilians and former officers (Sakallioglu 1997: 156). Regardless of the motive, Atatürk's revolution clearly included "a civilian component that militated against full-scale praetorianism" (Brown 1988: 140).

So what drove officers to intervene so often in future Turkish politics? The conventional response has been that while Kemal barred them from everyday governance, he entrusted them with guarding the overall character of the republic. In his last message to the armed forces, in October 1938, the leader beseeched his soldiers: "As you have protected and saved the country from oppression, catastrophe, and calamities ... [o]ur great nation and myself have complete trust and faith in your readiness and willingness to do your duty at any moment to protect the ... Turkish people against any danger from within or without" (quoted in Kili 2003: 153). According to this view, the military has not really been removed from politics, but promoted to a high-priest role. However, a careful examination of the causes of the military's recurrent coups reveals how they have been invariably propelled by threats to national security, and as such were directly linked to the interests and duties of the officer corps. In fact, it is clear that—rhetoric aside—officers have actually abandoned the principles of Kemalism, notably statism and radial secularism, to guarantee the country's security and stability.

What is most interesting about these interventions is that they were "conducted by the military-as-institution and led by its top leadership" (Harb 2002: 194). This is largely because the military structure that Kemal himself had set up in the 1920s produced a remarkably cohesive institution. The Defense Ministry and its head, supposedly the representatives of civilian authority, had no influence over the corps. The ministry was charged with minor administrative and financial duties, and generally deferred to officers' demands—in fact, the general staff dealt with the ministry as an adjunct (Brown 1988: 140). Moreover, although the defense minister was normally a civilian, officers colonized the ministry itself. As Defense Minister Ahmet Topalglu commented tongue-in-cheek in 1970: "In the Ministry of Defense, I am the only civilian person . . . the undersecretary is a general" (quoted in Sakallioglu 1997: 159). As late as 1989, the defense minister admitted in an interview with a foreign correspondent, "The Turkish general chief of staff establishes the priorities and presents the requirements and needs [so that] tasks are carried out by the Ministry of Defense according to the principles, priorities and major programs as determined by the general chief of staff" (quoted in Sakallioglu 1997: 159). The chief of staff and the service commanders thus remained autonomous. The chief of staff was appointed by the president from the list of generals who have commanded the land forces, though it was generally acknowledged that the incumbent chief of staff selected his successor and presented it to the prime minister to pass it on to the president *pour la forme*. The chief of staff reported directly to the prime minister after 1924 (except for a brief period between 1949 and 1961), and was solely responsible for choosing his commanders (Sakallioglu 1997: 159). This structure guaranteed the autonomy of the armed forces, and therefore helped officers develop their corporate agenda in a systematic manner.

Internal Security

One of Kemal's lasting influences was extending the army's responsibilities to domestic security. The police establishment he had inherited was rudimentary, to say the least. The first modern police force, established in 1845, was merely responsible for the capital, and within a year it was abolished and its duties transferred to the military-supervised gendarmes. A second police force was organized in 1879, again for the capital only, and in 1893 its purview was expanded to a handful of towns. The new force was made subordinate to the Ministry of the Gendarmes, which in turn reported to the Office of the Commander in Chief of the Ottoman Army. A decade before the war of liberation, in 1909, a General Directorate of Security (GDS) and an independent Ministry of Interior Affairs were created. But both were based in the sultan's capital, and so Kemal's government in Ankara could not trust them until it consolidated power. This is why the military, before and after the 1924 coup, assumed internal security duties (Caglar 1994: 117–18).

Eventually, however, combining war and security duties in one body undermined Kemal's hope to subordinate officers to civilian rule. Worse still, despite Kemal's remarkable feats, his personal style of government further weakened the political apparatus. Unlike Nasser in Egypt and the Shah of Iran, Kemal had no penchant for everyday governance, and from the late 1920s delegated control to weaker figures, such as his chief subordinate and future successor Ismet Inönü, so that he could devote his time to nocturnal adventures in the cabarets of Ankara and all-night gambling parties at his luxurious mansion on Çankaya Hill. By the 1930s, Turkey's chief politician had become an alcoholic, and soon the "pleasures of the will yielded to pleasures of the flesh." Kemal ultimately caught cirrhosis and died in 1938 at the age of fifty-seven. As Anderson rightly noted, Kemal was "a ruler who took to drink in despair at the ultimate sterility of his rule" (2009: 425). Maybe he sensed with his characteristic farsightedness that the tightly knit regime he had so carefully woven together would soon begin to unravel.

Notes

1. The survey and follow-up interviews included 120 officers from lieutenants to colonels in the summer of 2012.

2. A short-term flirtation with a loyal opposition party was attempted in 1930, with the Free Republican Party, but the idea was dismissed within months (Ahmad 1988: 754).

7 | The Corrective Coup
MAY 1960

KEMAL AND HIS MEN WERE the fourth generation of modernizing officers and bureaucrats.[1] Their success, where others have failed, was due in no small part to the opportunities provided by a radically different geopolitical context, defined by the Great War and its aftermath. And it was again geopolitics that prompted the Kemalist elite to loosen their grip on power less than a decade after the founder's passing. In fact, Turkey in the 1940s came under as much pressure to democratize as Southern Europe in the 1970s, Latin America in the 1980s, and Eastern Europe in the 1990s.

Democracy as a Security Imperative

Turkey's international standing was at its lowest ebb following the Second World War. President Ismet Inönü initially sought an understanding with Germany, and only when he came out empty-handed did he enter a defense treaty with the Allies. But once Hitler invaded Russia and realized he needed Ankara to protect his supply lines, Turkey immediately obliged. Inönü signed a nonaggression treaty with the Nazis in 1941, and dispatched his top generals (Emir Hüsnü Eriklet and Ali Fuad Erden) to Berlin to help the Führer conquer Russia by rallying the Turkic populations of the Soviet Union. However, when the pendulum swung against the Third Reich, Turkey returned to the Anglo-American fold—though refusing to declare war on Germany until February 1945, a week before the deadline for those willing to join the United Nations (Anderson 2009: 427–30).

In the postwar settlement, Moscow planned to swallow its treacherous neighbor. Stalin's condition for renewing Soviet-Turkish "friendship" was deploying Russian troops in the Straits. Ankara understood this as a prelude to a Communist takeover. Inönü poignantly confided to his diary: "The Russian forces would settle on the Straits area. Then Russia would keep coming up with new demands as the requirements of the joint defense. Their status in our country would be no different than their status in the eastern European countries which they had occupied. I made my decision immediately: Our answer would be no" (Yılmaz 1997: 4–5). Resisting Soviet domination, however, required American support.

But at this early stage of the Cold War—before NATO was established, or the Doctrine of Containment formulated—the price of joining the Western camp was to democratize. Propping up authoritarian regimes to block Communist advances had not yet become standard practice. And even if Washington was willing to grant an exception, Ankara's wartime double-dealing had cost it the goodwill of London and Paris. Turkey's rulers had to demonstrate their willingness to repent and transform. Their survival required opening up the political system, or at least pretending to do so. This link between Turkey's political reform and geopolitical desperation becomes clear when one considers that the first signals toward democratic change were made in April 1945, one month after Moscow tried to impose a joint defense agreement on Ankara, and days before the UN founding conference in San Francesco. The Turkish president, in fact, instructed his UN delegation as follows:

> The Americans may ask you when we will establish a multi-party regime. You will give the following answer to the question: "In the history of the Turkish Republic Atatürk was the great reformer. The role of Inönü will be to institutionalize reforms and to establish a full democracy, which was the intention of Atatürk himself". Inönü would like to have done this before. The many dangers and problems that came with the war held him back. It is the greatest desire of the President to achieve this goal as soon as the war will be over. (Yılmaz 1997: 7)

Turkey's opposition forces, composed of ruling party members whose views diverged from the Party line, harped on the same string. Adnan Menderes, one of the leaders of this faction within the ruling Republican People's Party (Cumhuriyet Halk Partisi, CHP), declared in a speech, in August 1945, "By ratifying the UN Charter we do not commit ourselves to anything that is not consistent with our Constitution. However, there are undeniable inconsistencies between our Constitution and the de facto state of affairs in the country. Hence, I wish we could use the ratification of the UN Charter as an opportunity to repeal these inconsistencies" (Yılmaz 1997: 8).

The masters of Ankara apparently hoped that a rigged election, such as the one held in 1946, was good enough to placate the West, particularly after the Truman Doctrine, in March 1947, promised to help nations threatened by Communism. What they failed to anticipate was the tirade of attacks on their autocratic regime during congressional debates on Truman's aid bill to Turkey in the summer of 1947. Members of Congress denounced the Turkish government so severely that the White House almost withdrew the bill, and it only passed on the condition that Congress would review it annually. Turkey's rulers could hardly imagine reliving this drama ever year, especially now that they had their eyes fixed on the lucrative Marshall Plan aid (another $574.3 million for Turkey), which was subject to the same conditions. They had to concede that tangible change was necessary.

But protection from Moscow and financial incentives aside, what truly unnerved the Turkish generals was fierce opposition to Turkey's joining NATO in 1949. Influential members, spearheaded by Britain, cited the country's autocracy to argue that it was an unreliable ally. And as the Turkish military expected, only after the opposition won its first election, in 1950, was Turkey's application finally accepted (Yılmaz 1997: 14–17). Officers now saw multiparty politics as a national security requisite. As Moscow's next-door neighbor, Ankara could not risk going it alone (Uzgel 2003: 197).

Of course, geopolitics alone does not explain Turkey's political opening. But it is worth observing that Turkey's domestic structure enabled it to respond to pressures to democratize more readily than other postwar fence sitters, who snubbed the Allies at their moment of desperation and were now struggling to rehabilitate themselves in the eyes of the West. Franco's dictatorship, for example, had only been consolidated in 1939 after a bitter civil war and was threatened by a resurgent republicanism. Salazar's Portugal faced strong Communist opposition and was set on preserving its African colonies (which it kept until 1974) despite internal opposition. The Turkish ruling bloc, by contrast, had been firmly installed in power for a quarter of a century by popular national liberators, such as President Inönü; it had no bourgeoisie to speak of after the deportation of its non-Turkic merchant class in the 1920s; and had a minuscule working class (its Communists were mostly intellectuals and students).[2] Again, Turkey was more vulnerable to Soviet invasion than Southern European autocracies, and was therefore more determined to secure Western protection (Yılmaz 2002: 80–81).

Needless to say, the transition to multiparty politics was carefully controlled from above. In June 1945 four ruling party leaders presented the Party with a list of reform proposals, later known as the Manifesto of the Four (Dörtlü Takrir). The principle defectors were Adnan Menderes, an affluent cotton planter who was in charge of CHP propaganda and education, and Celâl Bayar, who had been minister of the economy (1932–1938), and prime minister (1938), as well as the founder and governor of the state-owned Turkish Business Bank (Türkiye Is Bankası), the country's largest commercial bank (Yılmaz 2008: 15).[3] All they had initially hoped for was to replace the secular statist faction at the helm of the Party with a religiously tolerant and market-oriented one. Their demands were rejected. And at the November 1945 CHP Congress, Inönü announced that while autocracy was essential during the formative period of the republic, now those in opposition were free to break away and form their own party. So in January 1946, the signatories of the reform manifesto founded the Democratic Party (Demokrat Parti, DP), which formally adopted the Six Arrows of Kemalism, but was clearly determined to undermine two— statism and secularism—since its platform promised to curb bureaucracy, and reintegrate Islam into public life (Yılmaz 1997: 8). As Anderson noted, the DP formulated the general credo of its political heirs: "a liberal populism, combining commitment to the market and an appeal to tradition in equal measure" (2009: 433–34).

As mentioned before, the first national election, in July 1946, was unabashedly doctored: CHP won 85 percent of the vote, and the DP barely 14 percent. The ruling clique then began harassing DP deputies in the press to the point where they had to issue, in January 1947, an ultimatum, known as the Freedom Charter (Hürriyet Misakı), threatening to dissolve their party if government persecution continued. This coincided with the geopolitical indicators, discussed above, that a sham democracy would deprive Turkey of Western assistance. Recognizing that the geopolitical cost of repression was too high, the ruling bloc was forced to mend its ways. Inönü began extensive negotiations with Menderes and Bayar, culminating in the July 12 Declaration of 1947, which promised fair elections (Yılmaz 1997: 12–16; Karpat 1959; Eren 1963).

Doubtlessly, the CHP reckoned it was capable of maintaining its parliamentary majority in Turkey's first free elections. This misplaced confidence rested on one pillar: that the government had spared the country the ravages of war in 1939, unlike their predecessors in 1914. But gratitude is a fairly cheap currency in the political market. As future President and Premier Süleyman Demirel explained: "By the end of the war, the people were living in miserable conditions. . . . When the state leaders asked the people 'What do you want?' the answer they received was 'Bread'. To this, the state leaders replied, 'But at least you are alive, we saved you from the horrors of war'. But in the eyes of the people the war was a thing of the past" (Yılmaz 1997: 20). So in 1950, the DP won 54 percent of the votes, and the CHP came in second with 40 percent. Bayar became president, and Menderes headed an exclusive

DP cabinet for an entire decade. "The dictatorship Kemal had installed was over" (Anderson 2009: 431).

Turkey's democratic transformation was therefore spurred by political and military leaders responding to geopolitical dictates, rather than by pressure from below; and what it initially produced was a redistribution of power within the political elite. This view contradicts class-based explanations that portray Turkey's transformation as a bourgeois conquest supported by landlords. Advocates of this explanation highlight the rapid accumulation of capital during the war years (mostly through wartime profiteering), and the aggressive state actions against capitalists and landlords, exemplified by the postwar capital tax and the land reform bill of 1945 (Sunar 1974: 67–87; Keyder 1987: 113–17). The problem with this argument is that at this early stage of Turkey's socioeconomic development, the country's mostly commercial bourgeois had not yet crystallized into a "class-for-itself" in the Marxist lexicon, or a class capable of establishing "hegemonic" control, as Gramsci would put it. Only in the late 1980s did the Turkish bourgeoisie begin to develop the ideological and organizational capacity for class action against entrenched state elites. All that the merchants, small manufacturers, and landowners could achieve in the 1950s was to support one ruling faction against the other. Nor is there any evidence that the DP was a surrogate party that acted on behalf of the bourgeoisie. "The relationship between the DP and the Turkish bourgeoisie, just as the one between the DP and the [landowners and] peasant masses, was not one of political representation but a complete 'delegation of will' from the social support base of the party" (Yılmaz 1997: 21–22; see also Brown 1988: 134).

Be that as it may, DP fortunes began to wane. Its 54 percent of the votes in 1950 rose slightly to 57 percent in 1954, then dropped to 48 percent in 1957. By contrast, CHP's 40 percent fell to 35 percent in the next elections, then picked up again, by 1957, ending up where it had begun with 41 percent of the votes (Dodd 1969: 46). The reason for this reversal was primarily economic. Kemal had instructed his ministers to formulate a statist model inspired by Bolshevik industrialization in the 1920s but "detached completely from its ideological moorings" (Dunn 1972: 193). The Soviet example suited Kemal's autocratic dispositions, and his eagerness to govern a self-sufficient republic free from foreign impositions. It also reinforced the Turkish elite's hostility toward financiers and businessmen, who had been historically associated with foreigners and minority groups: Greeks, Armenians, and Jews (Roos and Roos 1971: 6, 17). DP leaders therefore banked on the tense relationship between bureaucrats and the private sector to score their remarkable electoral gains. But the Second World War had devastated the Turkish economy: soaring inflation called for subsidies, and unemployment forced many to seek public employment and welfare. The DP government used Western funds to provide peasants with cheap credit and buy their produce. It also boosted the cash-crop economy by building roads and importing modern farming equipment. However, lavish public spending relying on foreign assistance was naturally short lived. By the end of the 1950s, the budget deficit, external debt, inflation, and unemployment were running high (Anderson 2009: 434–35). Social unrest followed. And in response, the supposed harbingers of democracy turned to dictatorial measures. Menderes created parliamentary committees to investigate the "subversive activities" of his political enemies and imposed press censorship, and when riots continued, he closed down university campuses in Istanbul and Ankara, and declared martial law. After a whole month of disturbances, the military intervened (Harb 2002: 182).

The 1960 Coup: An Original Sin?

It can be argued that officers supported multiparty elections to guarantee Western military support in the face of what they perceived as an imminent Soviet threat (Bâli 2010). It can also be argued that many officers saw authoritarianism as politically destabilizing, and therefore a national security threat (Heper and Güney 2000: 637). But things had changed by 1960. Turkey had become firmly integrated in NATO. Relations with Washington have become fairly solid. And DP leaders had not only failed to maintain political stability, but were also introducing their own authoritarian measures. Even more disconcerting, the DP was undermining the Turkish military itself.

Back in the 1940s, scores of officers supported the DP for reasons specifically related to the military. First, they scorned the snubbing of military strongmen, such as Marshal Fevzi Çakmak, a hero of the war of liberation, and chief of staff for a record twenty-two years (1922–1944), who was forced to retire by President Inönü—his former subordinate—because he ran the army too independently. Officers equally resented the appointment of weak Inönü loyalists as military chiefs, as well as the 1949 law that subordinated the chief of staff to the defense minister rather than the prime minister. The DP had pledged to address military grievances and appoint Çakmak president if they controlled the government—a pledge that remained untested since the old marshal died in 1950 (Yılmaz 1997: 9–10). They did, however, renege on their other promise: to reorganize the army.

Junior officers resented Turkey's neutrality during World War II and placed the blame on their senior commanders—pejoratively dubbed "the

Prussians" for adhering to the old German school of thinking. Dazzled by the performance of the U.S. troops during the war, these young officers decided that the Turkish armed forces must embrace the American military doctrine. And they understood that opening up the political system was the price Washington demanded. Shortly after U.S. aid began pouring in, in 1947, junior commanders felt confident enough to defy the control of the Old Pashas. Representatives of this young cabal concluded a secret pact with DP leaders in 1950, guaranteeing military support for democratization (by preventing the use of the army in repression) in exchange for sweeping military reforms. And, indeed, two of these officers (Fahri Belen and Seyfi Kurtbek) were assigned cabinet posts in the first DP government, and the top brass was thoroughly purged. However, the new rulers did not keep their end of the deal. They feared that modernizing the military might empower it further. And so they dragged their feet, even when the two officers-turned-ministers resigned (Yılmaz 1997: 10–11). Officers felt double-crossed.

Worse still, Prime Minister Menderes displayed "a thinly veiled contempt" for officers, and allowed them no say in defense and foreign policy. And the DP continued the old practice of promoting loyalists, regardless of merit. But the straw that broke the camel's back was Menderes's frequent resort to martial law, which forced soldiers to clash with demonstrators, and thus tarnished the military's public image—a policy that pushed General Cemal Gürsel, the army chief and soon-to-be coup leader, to resign, on May 3, 1960 (Brown 1988: 134; Harb 2002: 181).

Unlike future interventions, it was junior officers this time who took the initiative. On May 27, 1960, DP leaders and cabinet members were arrested. Prime Minister Menderes and two of his ministers were hanged; President Bayar was only spared by former President Inönü's intercession; and DP loyalists in the armed forces were purged. The plotters did not have a clear political affiliation. Some were social radicals, others were nationalists, but most had no goal beyond restoring order and doing away with the troublesome DP (Anderson 2009: 435–36). Thus, when the thirty-eight-member National Unity Committee (NUC) was created to supervise political reform, it included two factions: fourteen junior officers, under Colonel Alparslan Türkes, wanted to remain in power until they were satisfied with the changes, and the majority, led by General Cemal Gürsel, wanted to withdraw rapidly from politics. Soon, the majority asserted itself, threatening to use the Third Army, based in eastern Anatolia, to crush the zealots. And at the beginning of 1961, the obstinate Colonel Türkes was exiled (Dodd 1969: 72; Harb 2002: 182).

A commission of professors and jurists, headed by the University of Istanbul's distinguished law professor Sıddık Sami Onar, were invited to draft a new constitution to be ratified by referendum. The constitution reestablished democracy, instating safeguards for civil liberties and freedom of the press. And by October 1961, the military returned to their barracks after having spent sixteen months in power (Anderson 2009: 435–36). By all accounts, the new constitution paved the way for a more stable democracy. It created a balance between Parliament, the government, and the presidency; introduced proportional representation and an upper chamber to review legislation; enhanced judicial independence and created a Constitutional Court; allowed the formation of unions, professional syndicates, and ideological parties. Another major difference between the 1961 Constitution and that of 1924 is that it laid the foundations of a welfare state, prepared to shoulder challenging socioeconomic responsibilities (Dodd 1969: 123; Caglar 1994: 113).

But even though the 1960 coup helped consolidate democracy, officers also established mechanisms to enable them to monitor politics in a legal manner without having to resort to armed interventions (Shmuelevitz 1999: 7; Aksin 2007: 268). The Internal Act of the Turkish Armed Forces stipulated in its Article 35 that "the military is responsible for defending both the Turkish Fatherland and the Turkish Republic as defined by the Constitution." And a National Security Council (Milli Güvenlik Kurulu, MGK) was set up to fulfill this duty through regular meetings between officers and civilians. MGK was composed of ten members: five civilians (the president, prime minister, ministers of war, the interior, and foreign affairs) and five commanders (the chief of staff and service chiefs), and met on a monthly basis (Heper and Güney 2000: 637). To formalize civil–military relations even further, the MGK introduced, in 1963, the National Security Policy Document (Milli Giivenlik Siyaset Belgesi, MGSB), aka the "red booklet," which is prepared by the military, intelligence, and foreign office, and defines threats and proposed responses. It is revised every December, and renewed every five years. And it soon became a key tool for officers to routinely sound their views on national policies (Uzgel 2003: 194). Finally, to guarantee a smooth transition, General Gürsel resigned from the military and served as president for one term only (1961–1966).

Despite all of these developments, once officers returned to their barracks, they had to withstand a hail of critiques from civilian politicians over their short sojourn in power (Dodd 1969: 61). Some lost patience. On February 22, 1961, sixty-nine junior officers and cadets of the Ankara War School, led by Colonel Talat Adyemir, drove a tank battalion onto the streets demanding the dissolution of Parliament. Their move was aborted in twelve hours by the solid refusal of their comrades to follow suit. The air force, under Air Marshal Irfan Tansel, even threatened to bomb the tanks if they did not turn back. Another coup attempt by the same Colonel Adyemir from the same Ankara War School, in May 1963, was aborted with similar ease. This one started with the arrest of ten officers—calling themselves the Young Kemalist Officers—at the naval and military schools in Istanbul for distributing pamphlets that praised Kemal's authoritarianism. On May 20 the now retired Colonel Adyemir donned his uniform and led officers and cadets from the Ankara War School in a second attempt to overthrow the government. This time there were causalities, as the rest of armed forces came down heavily on the conspirators, killing two of the cadets and losing six loyal troops. The punishment, naturally, was severe: 1,459 cadets were tried, 75 received four-year prison sentences; 93 received three-year terms; and the rest were acquitted; also 106 officers were tried, with 7 handed death sentences (though only 2, including Adyemir, were executed); 29 were imprisoned for life; and half of the remaining sentences were between four and five years (Dodd 1969: 61–62, 79–80; Aksin 2007: 269). The two failed attempts underscored the fact that the military did not tolerate, let alone encourage, full-fledged political interventions.

Secularism Loosens Its Grip

One of the most curious outcomes of the 1960 coup was that officers seemed to have become more accommodating of the role of Islam in society. By the late 1940s, it had become obvious to all that Islam was "too deeply rooted an element in the Turkish national identity to be lightly cast aside . . . [and] restoration of Islamic belief and practice [was perceived] as necessary" (Lewis 1952: 46). Even though members of the National Unity Council, which represented the coup makers, felt compelled to formally express their commitment to Kemal's secular principles, they did not back them up in practice. One of the junta members confirmed that "it is the greatest aim of the NUC to keep our sacred religion, which is the treasure of freedom and conscience, pure and unblemished, and save it from being a tool of reactionary and political movements" (Ahmad 1988: 755–56). Even before the coup, President Bayar had proclaimed: "The Turkish nation is a Muslim nation and will remain so"; and Prime Minister Menderes attacked secularism as "a means of provoking hatred and persecuting people" (Helal 1999: 79). The significance of these statements becomes obvious when contrasted with a much older statement by Interior Minister Shükrü Kaya, on December 3, 1934, in the Grand National Assembly, that began: "Religions have fulfilled their purpose and their functions are exhausted" (Ahmad 1988: 757). The contrast becomes clearer when compared to Kemal's notorious assertion in 1927: "I have no religion, and at times I wish all religions at the bottom of the sea. . . . Superstition must go" (Mango 1999: 463).

This change of attitude reflected the growing influence of Muslim activists. Of course, it mattered that Kemal's successor was personally "pious and conservative" (Anderson 2009: 426).[4] But there was also a reconfiguration of social forces during the drive to multiparty politics. With the dissolution of Sufi orders in 1925, popular piety was channeled toward underground religious communities, some of which were connected with the old orders, such as the Naqshbandis, but the more effective ones were new Sufi-inspired movements (Tugal 2002: 92–93). The most prominent in the 1950s was the Nur movement (Nurcu), a loosely organized network of the followers of Kurdish spiritual leader Bediüzzeman Said al-Nursi (1870s–1960).

From a very early age, Nursi had been distressed over the withering of Ottoman power. As a religious scholar, he drafted proposals on how to reconcile religion with modern, scientific thinking and presented them, in 1907, to Sultan Abdülhamid in person, only to be rejected and ushered to prison. The bitterness of this encounter converted Nursi to constitutionalism, and he thereby supported the Young Turk's modernizing regime, and enlisted in the army during the First World War. After a two-year stretch as a prisoner of war in Siberia, he returned to Allied-controlled Constantinople, in 1918, and the humiliation of defeat drove him to hastily join forces with Ankara's mutinous officers. Kemal invited him to address the Grand National Assembly, in 1922, at a time when the caliph still considered its members outlaws. But Nursi was soon disenchanted by the religious irreverence of the master of Anatolia and his coterie. He went into seclusion in the countryside, turning away from national politics to social reform. His goal now was to nurture a group of pious individuals with a correct understanding of Islam and a healthy appreciation for science and material success, what he frequently referred to as an "intellectually able group" (*entelektüel olarak yetkin*). Nursi began disseminating his writings (mostly in Arabic) among a select group of students. His prolific writings included religious commentaries, personal reflections, and the long speeches he improvised and delivered in court during his numerous trials, all collected under the title of *Risale-i Nur Külliyatı* (The Complete Epistles of Light). Nursi's work was interrupted by detention and trial on several occasions. But his suffering only enhanced his mystical aura and reinforced the commitment of his followers. Kemal's ban on the private publication of religious materials had a decisive influence on the character of the Nur movement. Transcribing, translating, and circulating handwritten copies of his commentaries cemented his network of students. Also, the fact that Nursi was kept almost permanently under house arrest impelled his expanding base of followers to organize themselves in the form of independent study groups (*dershane*).

As the republic moved toward a multiparty system, the Nur movement was the most well-organized section of Turkish civil society. At this point, Nursi encouraged his students to act as community activists, lending support to political leaders who uphold Islam without formally identifying with any particular party. This not only became the model for future Muslim activists, but it also made Turkish Islamism flexible enough to weather the storms of military reaction that swept away political parties between 1960 and 1997. The Nur network helped garner the votes that brought the DP to power in 1950—the party that was violently overthrown days before Nursi passed away in the summer of 1960. Afterward, the Nur study groups became more institutionalized, establishing branches all over the country (5,000 by the 1990s) and spreading abroad. Moreover, the diverse temperaments, backgrounds, and interpretations of Nur adherents (an estimated 6 million today) divided them into several groups rather than a single hierarchical organization, which made it impossible to repress them all (Yavuz 1999: 586–92; Abu-Rabi' 2003).

Indeed, long before Nursi's death, popular pressure convinced the rulers to offer a few valuable concessions: preachers returned to the army in May 1940; elected deputies debated reintroducing religion to public education in 1946; and by 1949 Islamic subjects were integrated into school curriculums. Following the DP's electoral victory, religious education became compulsory after the CHP had only made it optional the year before; Sufi orders were tolerated; calls to prayer were heard in Arabic again; and state radio aired Qur'an recitation (Lewis 1952: 40–43). DP leaders made sure to praise Nursi on every occasion, and frequently boasted about the number of mosques built under their watch (Ahmad 1988: 756). Most notable, however, was the fact that the 1960 coup was justified in terms of guaranteeing a stable democracy, not secularism.

Notes

1. The first three generations being the powerful Pashas of the Tanzimat (1839–1876); the Young Ottomans (1876–1878); and the Young Turks (1908–1918) (Yılmaz 2008: 2–3).

2. When Atatürk consolidated power, Turkey had perhaps 17,000 workers, and no industrialists to speak of (Fromkin 1989: 123). Until the late 1930s, Turkey remained an agricultural society with large and middling landowners dominating the countryside, and a small bureaucratic middle class in the towns (Mango 1999: 533).

3. The other two defectors (Refik Koraltan and Fuat Köprülü) were less prominent Party figures.

4. "In his private life, Inönü was a conventional Muslim, who carried a miniature Koran in his pocket. He saw to it that his children received private religious lessons" (Mango 1999: 529).

8 The Communiqué Coup

MARCH 1971

THE 1960 COUP INTRODUCED LEGAL and institutional changes, but it did not redraw the political map. The voting bloc that placed the Democratic Party (Demokrat Parti, DP) in power remained intact. So remnants of the dissolved DP regrouped, under the leadership of the American-educated engineer Süleyman Demirel, in a new party, the Justice Party (Adalet Partisi, AP), to cater to the same constituency. It was a signal perhaps that a more radical reaction was needed the next time Turkey's political process became deadlocked.

Resisting Restoration

In the first postcoup elections, held in 1961, the old ruling party (CHP) returned with 37 percent of the votes, followed by AP as a close second with 35 percent. The CHP advance was short lived. AP won the following two elections, with 53 percent of the vote (versus CHP's 29 percent) in 1965, and 47 percent (to CHP's 27 percent) in 1969. The 1960 coup had given way to a political "restoration" of sorts (Dodd 1969: 306). And, perhaps in response, the exiled Colonel Alparslan Türkes returned to form the Nationalist Action Party (Milliyetçi Hareket Partisi, MHP), a Fascist party with a Nazi-like militia, the notorious Gray Wolves, which terrorized leftists and minorities, although it received only 3 percent of the vote in its first electoral showing in 1969 (Heper and Güney 2000: 638).

Yet although AP inherited the DP's constituency, it did not reproduce its policies. The DP's plight dissuaded the new political rulers from clashing with the military. An additional deterrent was the fact that, during AP rule, the president remained a military figure: General Cemal Gürsel occupied the position until 1966, and was followed by Chief of Staff Cevdet Sunay (Harb 2002: 187). Economic policy represented another area of difference between AP and its predecessor. Although the new ruling party continued to dispense benefits to the countryside, its policies were much less market-oriented. AP supported state-led development and the import-substituting industrialization model enshrined in the 1961 Constitution (Yılmaz 2008: 2). The military itself became involved in economic development through the Armed Forces' Trust and Pension Fund (Ordu Yardimlasma Kurumu, OYAK), established in 1961 as a holding company run by civilians to invest 10 percent of officers' salaries in major industries (Uzgel 2003: 183).

However, Turkey was not spared the typical problems of late modernizers. The shifting of resources to manufacturing and artificial price controls weighed heavily on the agricultural sector. Two million peasant families, representing two-thirds of those engaged in farming, were forced to compete for industrial jobs with tens of thousands of landless rural laborers. Unemployment soared and wages fell (Dunn1972: 192). Workers became more susceptible to radicalization, and the state's loyal trade union, the Trade Union Confederation of Turkey (Türkiye Isçi Sendikaları Konfederasyonu, Türk-Is), no longer satisfied their needs. Many embraced Communism, and a Revolutionary Trade Union Confederation (Devrimci Isçi Sendikaları Konfederasyonu, DISK) came into being as an alliance of several militant unions (Tugal 2007: 9). At the same time, peasants and merchants in the countryside, and artisans and petite bourgeoisie in the cites drifted toward Islamism, which was about to form its first political party in 1970, the National Order Party (Milli Nizam Partisi, MNP), under an engineering professor by the name of Necmettin Erbakan.

Although members of the Nur movement provided solid support for the AP, and although the party's leader, Demirel, frequently professed his devoutness, remarking once for instance that "I was born into a family that does not sit down to breakfast before reading the Holy Koran," the moderate 1961 Constitution tempted some Muslim activists to organize their own parties, instead of influencing politics by proxy (Ahmad 1988: 764). This was a departure from the model set forth by Said al-Nursi, a departure that Islamists would come to regret in the 1980s and 1990s. Erbakan and his followers, hailing mostly from the Naqshabandi Sufi order, created an ideological party. Its first manifesto, the 1969 National View (Milli Görüs), placed Islam at the heart of Turkish identity, rejected Westernization, and called for stronger ties with the Muslim world.

The emergence of Fascists, Communists, and Islamists on the periphery of the political system polarized society, and the extremism simmering under the surface threatened the stable democracy that officers had hoped to establish through the 1961 Constitution. Workers paralyzed economic life through a series of strikes in the summer of 1970; students alternated between protests and urban warfare; political militants resorted to bank robberies to finance their activities; foreign dignitaries (mostly, American and Israeli) were kidnapped (Aksin 2007: 272). More dangerous still were reports that a Communist coup was in the offing, and a preemptive coup by the top brass was necessary to block it (Aksin 2007: 272).

Enter the Military

Alarmed that radicalism outside the corps might seep into and factionalize the armed forces, Chief of Staff Cemal Tural and the service chiefs decided to act (Dodd 1969: 308; Harb 2002: 44). On March 12, 1971, the high command issued a communiqué addressed to the president and speaker of Parliament "warning of dire consequences if civilians continued to jeopardize the state and law and order." When Demirel failed to respond, he was replaced by a technocratic government under former CHP functionary Nihat Erim, which amended the constitution to curb the influence of fringe political groups, and prepared for fresh elections (Harb 2002: 187–88). Meanwhile, martial law was declared, militants (especially from the left) were suppressed, and the Islamist MNP was dissolved. In addition, five generals, one admiral, and thirty-five colonels were cashiered (Kili 2003: 167; Aksin 2007: 272). A notable change to the mandate of the National Security Council (Milli Güvenlik Kurulu, MGK) was introduced, in 1973, allowing officers to not only share their views with politicians, but also present specific recommendations to the cabinet. More important, the military—increasingly distrustful of civilian politics—enhanced the autonomy of the chief of staff in formulating defense policy and budget (independent of Parliament), arms manufacturing and procurement, and personnel management (Sakallioglu 1997: 150).

In terms of security, the military continued to be responsible for internal stability and intelligence gathering. Article 85 of the revised Internal Service Regulations of the Turkish Armed Forces stated: "Turkish Armed Forces shall defend the country against internal as well as external threats if necessary by force" (Heper and Güney 2000: 637). It carried out this function through its own intelligence units, as well as working closely with the newly created (in 1965) National Intelligence Agency (Milli Istihbarat Teskilati,

MIT), which was supposed to report to the prime minister, but in reality was subject to military supervision. The MIT head and leading operatives (as well as half of its personnel) had been recruited from the army as a matter of course. And unlike its counterparts in the Middle East and Latin America, it did not establish much autonomy and remained attached to the military (Uzgel 2003: 181). Also, an anti-riot police was established for the first time in 1961 under the name of the Society Police (Toplum Polisi), though it would soon prove powerless without the direct support of military troops (Caglar 1994: 125).

Once the political arena was "judged sufficiently purged of subversion," democratic life was allowed to resume in October 1973, two and a half years after military rule (Anderson 2009: 438). This relatively minor regression revealed that the Turkish army was determined to keep political excesses in check. But as the next few years would prove, a more radical intervention would be needed to contain the social forces that multiparty politics had unleashed.

9 | The Passive Revolution

SEPTEMBER 1980

Unlike the 1960 coup, the 1971 intervention polarized the political landscape. Between January 1971 and December 1979, Turkey witnessed twelve coalition governments, with an average of one government every nine months (Helal 1999: 140). Most of these weak cabinets were headed by either Süleyman Demirel's Justice Party (Adalet Partisi, AP) or Bülent Ecevit, the professor of medicine who replaced Inönü at the helm of the Republican People's Party (Cumhuriyet Halk Partisi, CHP) in 1972, and included—as junior coalition partners—the Fascist Nationalist Action Party (Milliyetçi Hareket Partisi, MHP) and Necmettin Erbakan's new Islamist party, the National Salvation Party (Milli Selâmet Partisi, MSP). The inclusion of Islamists for the first time in government was a significant development, although their minor share in Parliament (12 percent in 1973; and 9 percent in 1977) still indicated that they did not carry real political weight, for although their social base was large numerically (artisans, small traders, peasants), their supporters were apolitical and geographically limited to the provincial towns of Anatolia (Narli 2003: 126).

Though these coalition governments signed on to the military's decision to invade Cyprus in 1974, under the pretext of protecting the Turkish minority against a Greek-inspired coup against Archbishop Makarios, they still challenged the military on several occasions. In 1973, for instance, Parliament rejected the general command's nomination of Chief of Staff Faruk Gürler for the presidency. Even though the latter resigned his army post to stand for elections, Parliament chose Admiral Fahri Korutürk instead (Aksin 2007: 274). Three years later, Prime Minister Demirel fought for the right to appoint service chiefs, though his attempt was overruled by the military's administrative court. Demirel was also openly critical of the officers' monopoly over the revising of the National Security Policy Document (MGSB), demanding that they consult the government before requiring any revisions (Sakallioglu 1997: 162; Uzgel 2003: 194). These and other incidents inflamed civil–military relations throughout the 1970s.

The economic situation was no less worrying. State-led industrialization halved agriculture's GDP share from 40 percent to 20 percent, but the import-substituting industrial policy harmed the economy without achieving the hoped for growth. While state-protected manufacturing and agriculture covered domestic needs, the two sectors failed to compete on the world market, causing a chronic shortage in foreign currency, which the state was then forced to borrow, thus accumulating huge debts. Fixing prices and exchange rates only made things worse, forcing consumers to turn en masse to the black market. To top it all off, Turkey imported close to 80 percent of its oil, and was therefore devastated by the quadrupling of oil prices after 1973. In short, the closed economy was driving the country to the abyss: inflation skyrocketed to 100 percent; the balance of payment deficit rose to $3 billion; and foreign debt reached $19 billion—from only $2 billion a decade before (Wahid 2009: 70–74). The obvious exhaustion of the import-substitution model combined with external shocks to paralyze the economy. A complete overhaul was due, and weak government coalitions lacked the political legitimacy to carry it out (Önis 1997: 749). Many considered a revolution from above necessary to reverse the country's economic collapse (Keyder 2004: 66). A more pressing cause was the "total collapse of civil peace" (Harb 2002: 189).

Rapid industrialization, and the economic crises it invited, provided a fertile ground for Communism. The expanding urban underclass swelled the ranks of the radical left. And the ethnically persecuted Kurds threw in their lot with them. Even policemen and junior military officers developed leftist sympathies. At this critical juncture, Greek Communists came to power in Athens and supported their counterparts over the border. Turkish Communists were now armed and ready. They had every reason to believe that Turkey was experiencing "an Allende moment" (Yılmaz 2009). Naturally, the rise of the left aggravated the Fascist squads. And the Gray Wolves began to attack Communists with impunity because their political representatives in government, the MHP, protected them from prosecution (Anderson 2009: 438–39).

At the same time, Islamists were gaining ground. Economic-driven migration from the countryside crowded the major cities with shantytowns. The new city dwellers remained rural in outlook, but without the dense communal bonds that sustained them in the village. Millions of peasants thus created "urban villages" and began to cluster around the Islamist MSP, which received the newcomers with open arms, providing them with welfare, job opportunities, social connections, and a voice in national politics (Ahmad 1988: 758). Islamists now grew defiant. In September 1980 a "Save Jerusalem Rally" organized in Konya (Erbakan's constituency) included demonstrators in traditional dress (including the banned fez), waving green flags, calling for a restoration of Shari'a, and refusing to sing the national anthem (Ahmad 1988: 750).

Just like the 1960s, polarization led to violence. But this time the violence was categorically different: clashes between Fascists, separatists, Communists, and Islamists gave way to kidnappings, bombs, and assassinations on an unprecedented scale. And the weak government coalitions and divided parliaments had no sway over the political street. Between 1975 and 1980, political violence claimed the lives of 5,000 people, and three times as many were wounded (Harb 2002: 91). Clashes escalated in 1978, when in less than nine months (between January and September) Turkey's witnessed 4,459 violent incidents, killing 711 people and injuring another 4,652. In this bleak year, authorities confiscated enough arms and ammunition to supply three military divisions (Shmuelevitz 1999: 121–31). A particularly shocking episode was the three-day confrontation between right-wing Sunnis and left-leaning Shi'is in the neighborhood of Kahramanmaras, in December 1978. After 109 people were killed, and after hundreds were injured on both sides, and after 500 houses and businesses were torched to the ground, the government (headed at this point by CHP's Bülent Ecevit) had no other choice but to deploy the army. The government and Parliament then agreed to declare martial law in thirteen provinces, including Ankara and Istanbul, in order to facilitate the army's mission (Shmuelevitz 1999: 12; Aksin 2007: 277).

This was a last resort measure after the police force proved utterly ineffective, even after its ranks were reinforced with 20,000 recruits in the summer of 1978, and another 5,500 the following summer (representing a total increase of 40 percent in personnel); and after the rural-based gendarmes were asked to help restore order in the cities; and after all the heads of the police and intelligence agencies were changed (Shmuelevitz 1999: 78). The police was not just unequipped, but because the constitution allowed officers to create independent professional associations, the police force was soon torn between two syndicates—the right-wing Police Unity (Pol-Bir) and the left-leaning Police Association (Pol-Der)—and this fragmentation made it difficult for policemen to unite behind the regime, or even their own institution (Caglar 1994: 152).

Unfortunately, even the military's "peacekeeping" units proved insufficient. Between December 1978 and September 1980, an average of twenty people were killed each day as a result of political violence (Aksin 2007: 279). With ideological, religious, and ethnic tensions spiraling beyond control, many believed that the country was slipping down the path of civil war (Wahid 2009: 70). A full-fledged military intervention seemed essential.

Yet the general staff was reluctant, issuing several communiqués warning against involving the army in political feuds. And the new Chief of Staff Kenan Evren, appointed in March 1978, backed this position (Shmuelevitz 1999: 81). However, polarization was creeping closer to the armed forces, prompting Evren to accuse political factions of trying to "split the Turkish army into pieces" (quoted in Shmuelevitz 1999: 117). The United States and NATO also promoted the military to intervene and preempt a Communist takeover, as had just happened in Greece and Italy, or an Islamist revolution, as in Iran (Yılmaz 2009).[1] After consulting with the field commanders and the service chiefs, and after several warning memos to civilian politicians, the army stepped in. On September 12 Evren announced in a short broadcast that the military invoked the power granted to it by the Internal Service Code to protect the republic from external and internal dangers, blamed politicians for failing to curb violence, and declared martial law (Sakallioglu 1997: 152).

Militarism and "Leftocide"

The military conducted itself in a remarkably cohesive manner. Six weeks after the coup, a new law (the Law on Constitutional Order) entrusted the military members of the National Security Council (Milli Güvenlik Kurulu, MGK), that is, chief of staff and service chiefs, with legislative and executive power, and delegated everyday governance to technocrats (Kili 2003: 170). The MGK was then reinvented as an emergency ruling body and pledged to return power to civilians after an estimated three-year transitional period, which it did. Evren repeatedly reminded the people that the aim of the intervention was "to avert civil war and to save democracy" (Harb 2002: 189). In one of his first declarations, he summarized the military's position as follows: "We have not eliminated democracy. I would particularly like to point out that we were *forced* to launch this operation in order to restore democracy with all its principles, *to replace a malfunctioning democracy*" (Brown 1988: 138). In a speech on July 24, 1981, Evren clarified: "I did not say 'return of democracy', but 're-founding democracy'. This is because 'return' would mean going back to pre-12 September [1980]. . . . [T]he bitterness of these days still burns in our hearts. Because of a degenerate democracy, democracy in name only, this nation suffered bigger casualties up to 11 September than it sustained in the Battle of Sakarya [the decisive battle against the Greeks in 1922]" (Shmuelevitz 1999: 168).

This "re-founding of democracy" involved brutal measures. Parliament was dissolved; municipal councils were dismissed; and prominent politicians (including all party leaders) were imprisoned or barred from politics for ten years. In a few months, 650,000 activists were detained, 230,000 were prosecuted, and among those 517 were sentenced to death (with 50 actually executed), and another 450 died in prison (presumably under torture); 14,000 were stripped of citizenship; and around 30,000 fled to exile (Helal 1999: 7; Sahin 2012: 2). In addition, more than 100 cadets were expelled from the army on account of their political affiliations. By the end of 1981, the MGK had passed 268 laws to regulate political life, signaling a complete overhaul of the system of government. And state security courts (two in 1984 and 128 three years later) administered swift justice to political dissidents (Ahmad 1988: 751–52; Aksin 2007: 280).

More important, the 1982 Constitution (still in effect today) institutionalized militarism in Turkish politics more than any other period since the birth of the republic. Article 118 obliged the cabinet to privilege, rather than just consider, MGK recommendations. And these recommendations, in turn, extended beyond security issues to school curriculums, television programs, and bureaucratic appointments (Heper and Güney 2000: 637). MGK now had a General Secretariat, headed by a military officer, to set the agenda for the monthly meetings and monitor the implementation of the council's decisions. The 1982 Constitution also decreed that in time of war, the chief of staff would assume the position of commander-in-chief on behalf of the president. In addition to these institutionalized mechanisms, it became normal, in the post-1980 years, for senior officers to issue statements on all matters of governance, sometimes even hold press conferences to publicize their views (Uzgel 2003: 191–95). Collectively, these changes were meant to provide the high command with a permanent veto power over government, and thus render "crude military intervention into politics redundant" (Sakallioglu 1997: 154).

Ironically, the 1980 coup and the repression that followed it were "not the gateway to a dictatorship in Turkey, but to a democratic catharsis" (Anderson 2009: 440). After the 1982 Constitution received 91 percent approval in a public referendum, martial law was lifted, in 1983, except in the southeastern Kurdish areas. Evren resigned his military commission and was elected president for a seven-year term. And parliamentary life resumed—albeit under new rules. The role of peripheral parties was limited by prohibiting those who received less than 10 percent of the votes from entering Parliament. The hope was to create a stable two-party system representing centrists on both left and right, rather than shifting coalitions between mainstream parties and extremists on the fringes. Moreover, the president was now entrusted with mediating between parties to grease the political machine if necessary (Harb 2002: 193).

The lasting effect of the 1980 intervention was the complete eradication of Communism—what Yılmaz bitterly described as "leftocide: a genocide of the Left" (Yılmaz 2009). But after the elimination of Communism achieved "a permanent alteration in the political landscape," there was a need to fill the void, especially given that the military's decision to liberalize the economy, to break away from the stagflation of the 1970s, was likely to provoke a fresh Communist onslaught. Here, Islamism proved useful. Empowering moderate Islamist parties promised to not only keep Communists in check, but also to prevent the rise of religious militants, such as the Turkish Hezbollah. Indeed, the Iranian Revolution, which occurred a year before the coup, pressed the urgency of using moderate Islamism to preempt Communists and radical Islamists. This is why the 1982 Constitution expanded the definition of Turkishness to include Islam, and urged the teaching of Islam in public schools (Tugal 2007: 9–11). Article 24 specifically stated: "Religious culture and moral education shall be compulsory in the curricula of primary and secondary schools" (Kili 2003: 172).

Of course, on the official level, the coup leaders criticized Islamists, and made several references to Article 163 of the Penal Code, which criminalized attempts to alter the secular character of the republic (Ahmad 1988: 750). In truth, however, the general's actions proved that they had effectively abandoned secularism in the interest of suppressing more dangerous creeds. Evren stated: "Laicism does not mean atheism" (Anderson 2009: 441), and many knew that despite his secular training in the army, his cultural background was "virtually the same as that of the people who are described as Islamists" (Ahmad 1988: 765). This is why repression against Islamists was minimal. Although the Islamist MHP was dissolved and its leader detained and barred from politics, Erbakan spent less than a month in prison, before being acquitted and returning to politics with a stronger party. In other words, after the generals dismantled the Islamist party, they winked at its members to try again.

This is why sociologist Cihan Tugal (2009a) saw the 1980 coup as a Gramscian "passive revolution," which defused popular revolutionary impulses through top-down reforms, as Europeans had done after 1815 to combat the spread of French revolutionary ideals. That being said, tolerating Islamism as an antidote to radicalism did not mean that the military renounced secularism.

Generals did not foresee Islamists' future success (Bâli 2010). Their attempt to enlist them in the battle against Communism was reminiscent of the strategy of Egypt's Anwar al-Sadat and Shah Muhammad Reza Pahlavi in Iran—and as was the case in both countries, things got out of hand.

Note

1. American blessing for the September 1980 coup is evident in the fact that U.S. military aid increased from $453 million before the coup to $688 million eight years after it (Wahid 2009: 81).

10 | The White Coup
JUNE 1997

After returning to barracks in 1983, the military was obviously reluctant to carry out another covert intervention; officers seemed willing to cede more autonomy to civilians. But instead of the stable two-party system the military envisaged, a much more fragmented political scene emerged from the rubble. What did this new scene look like? Before 1980, Turkey's two major parties were Kemal's original ruling party, the People's Republican Party (Cumhuriyet Halk Partisi, CHP), which represented the left-of-center after Bülent Ecevit took over, and the Justice Party (Adalet Partisi, AP), which represented the right-of-center under Süleyman Demirel. The military regime dissolved both parties and imposed a ten-year political ban on their leaders. However, the banned leaders defied military proscription and returned to politics, in 1987, via a popular referendum that rescinded the military ban. The problem was that when they resumed their activities, there were already two new parties occupying their former positions on the political spectrum: the Social Democratic Populist Party (Sosyaldemokrat Halkçı Parti, SHP), composed of the remnants of the CHP on the left, and Turgut Özal's Motherland Party (Anavatan Partisi, ANAP), the successor of AP on the right. Refusing to join one of these two, Demirel formed another right-wing party, the True Path Party (Dogru Yol Partisi, DYP), and Ecevit formed the Democratic Left Party (Demokratik Sol Parti, DSP). Now, there were two parties on the right-of-center, and another two on the left-of-center. Only Islamists maintained their ideology, members, and organization—albeit under a different name. Their banned National Salvation Party (Milli Selâmet Partisi, MSP), which had been the successor of the National Order Party (Milli

Nizam Partisi, MNP), was quickly reinvented as the Welfare Party (Refah Partisi, RP), under the leadership of the same man: Necmettin Erbakan. It was this political fragmentation that helped RP position itself as Turkey's mainstream party.

Another important factor had to do with changes within ANAP, the leading political party of the 1980s. While Prime Minister Özal headed the Party, he managed to keep the liberal and Islamist constituencies under the same roof through his unusual mix of economic liberalism and nationalism, on the one hand, and his strong ties to the Islamist movement, on the other.[1] That is why ANAP secured 45 percent of the votes in 1983, and 36 percent in 1987. ANAP, in fact, became so powerful that, in 1987, Prime Minister Özal appointed General Necip Torumtay as chief of staff against the wishes of the general command, and gloated in an interview, "No civilian government has appointed the general chief of staff itself. The position has been filled by automatic succession. From now on, this is going to be normalized. Governments should appoint the general chief of staff themselves according to merit" (Sakallioglu 1997: 161). In 1989, Özal himself became president despite the military's reservations, with them wanting to either extend to coup leader Kenan Evren a second term, or appoint a general in his stead. But when Özal became president and abandoned party politics, ANAP's new leader, Mesut Yılmaz, the representative of the liberal faction, failed to retain the Islamist base within the Party. Özal's ensuing death, in 1993, weakened the Party even further. And at the same time that ANAP was growing weaker, its most likely successor, Turkey's second right-of-center party, the DYP, was also losing ground. Süleyman Demirel's rise to the presidency in 1993 deprived this largely personalist party of its charismatic founder. Demirel's successor, economics professor Tansu Çiller, was much less appealing to voters. Finally, both ANAP and DYP lost Kurdish votes. That is because after the destruction of the left in the early 1980s, Kurds placed their trust in Özal and Demirel—personally, rather than as party leaders. As they suspected, once the founders existed the scene, their parties assumed a more nationalistic posture and rescinded their promises to relax constraints on Kurdish language and culture (Önis 1997: 751–57; Aksin 2007: 297).

In addition to the fragmentation of non-Islamist parties and the loss of their religious and Kurdish voters, RP's rise to power had to do with Turkey's new economic situation. Shortly before the 1980 coup, Prime Minister Demirel had decided to implement economic readjustments recommended by the International Monetary Fund (IMF), the so-called 24 January Decisions, and entrusted Turgut Özal with this sensitive task. Özal had served in the World Bank from 1971 to 1973, and was currently undersecretary for the

State Planning Organization. He continued his work for two years under the military government, which believed that his deflationary policy would bail Turkey out of its financial difficulties (Aksin 2007: 278). "Coming to power at the turn of the eighties, the hour of Thatcher and Reagan, he was the local equivalent in neo-liberal resolve" (Anderson 2009: 441). His job was much easier, though, than his Western counterparts because the military's crushing of left-wing opposition helped him cut down public spending, revoke price controls, and reduce wages without much fuss. But Özal's military-blessed economic liberalization reversed Kemalist statism almost completely. Turkey now adopted an export-oriented market economy, and dismantled the public sector. Employment in public sector factories fell from 250,000 to 100,000 between 1980 and 2000, at the same time that dozens of new export-oriented enterprises sprang up (Keyder 2004: 67). As in similar cases of economic liberalization, there were some indicators of recovery: GNP increased (by an average of 5 percent), industry overtook agriculture, and exports grew, especially after the local currency was devaluated. Also similar to other cases, income and wealth disparities increased, sparking social conflict. And both new opportunities in the cities and constraints in the countryside further fueled the continuing mass exodus from village to town (Önis 1997: 752).

Curiously, RP benefited from the negative as well as the positive effects of Turkey's neoliberal restructuring. As the republic underwent its most comprehensive economic shakeup, Islamism presented themselves as a substitute to both the social democratic politics of the left, and the conservative liberals on the right. Islamism differed from social democracy in its emphasis on free enterprise as the engine of growth, and from conservative liberals in its stress on social justice. As Islamists liked to portray themselves, they provided a third alternative to the merciless free market of capitalism and the suffocating state control of socialism. For the poor, the religious-inspired stress on social justice and Islamists' solid record as welfare providers were encouraging. For aspiring merchants and businessmen, the sanctity of private property and individual initiative in Islam legitimized their hoped-for growth—especially now that large, state-connected companies were losing out. For the middle classes, religious identity provided the basis of a class compromise among believers that could save Turkey from social strife (Önis 1997: 748–54).

But it was demography rather than economics that helped Islamism most. RP leaders encouraged their supporters to move from the countryside to the city to benefit from the new economic opportunities. The aim was to help them move up the social ladder so that they would have more of a say (and a stake) in politics. Islamists offered the newcomers food, casual employment, cheap credit, and hostels for temporary residence. By the 1990s, a new urban middle class had emerged in Istanbul; its members maintained strong links with the Anatolian towns they hailed from, and the medium-sized manufacturers and merchants who operated there (Narli 2003: 127).

These "Anatolian tigers" were key to the Islamist success story. Although perhaps 40 percent of the population was still employed in agriculture in the 1990s, the more active elements in the countryside—those with a "commercial impulse," as Barrington Moore would put it—devoted themselves to trade and industry. The violent elimination of the Greek and Armenian merchant class had first made their fortunes, allowing them to shift from farming to commerce. Turkey's economic liberalization and integration into the global market encouraged them to become manufacturers and exporters (through small- and medium-sized enterprises employing fifty workers or less). They began with textiles, though competition from China forced them to diversify their portfolio to iron and steel, chemical and metallurgical products, automotive parts, construction, food products, tourism, and finance. By virtue of their provincial piety and anti-statist bias, members of this class had supported Islamists since the 1970s. But it was only the liberalization of the economy and international trade that allowed them to accumulate enough capital to count politically (Önis 1997: 757–58; Narli 2003: 127). And they had one demand: the chance to grow without state constraints.

> The industrial structures of the developmentalist era had been characterized by the oligopoly of a few multi-tentacled holding companies, through which the import-substituting bourgeoisie of Istanbul, with their privileged access to policy makers in Ankara, had been able to maintain an iron grip over the economy. With the liberalization, a new breed of entrepreneurs emerged who had to compete in globalized markets, and indexed their behavior to commercial and consumer signals rather than bureaucratic decisions. . . . [A] number of smaller Anatolian cities with craft traditions and non-unionized workforces . . . began to emerge as regional industrial centers . . . [and their] businessmen contracted directly with retail chains and volume buyers in Europe. (Keyder 2004: 68)

Of course, they had already achieved much. Largely due to their efforts, Turkey's exports jumped from $3 billion in 1980 to $13 billion in 1990, and to the unfathomable figure of $50 billion by the end of the decade (Keyder 2004: 68). Yet bureaucratic obstinacy retuned after Özal died in 1993. The bureaucracy refused to abandon its role as primary provider of economic rents, promoting favored businessmen through export subsidies, public land allocations, construction permits, and sale of public enterprises (Wahid 2009: 75).[2] Because Islamists promised to end state patronage, the emerging business elite became adamant about ushering them to power.

What enhanced the political weight of this provincial business elite was not just their acute class consciousness, but also their rigorous organization. They combined their funds to form joint-stock companies that could compete with state-supported monopolies (Narli 2003: 128). Equally important was their creation of an independent business association. Big businesses were organized in the mainstream Turkish Industry and Business Association (Türk Sanayicileri ve Isadamları Dernegi, TÜSIAD), and so the middling bourgeoisie decided, in 1990, to establish an Independent Industrialists and Businessmen Association (Müstakil Sanayici ve Isadamları Dernegi, MÜSIAD). MÜSIAD's was exceptionally dynamic. Founded by a small group of young businessmen, its membership grew spectacularly, reaching 3,000 in a decade (and 4,900 by 2012), whereas TÜSIAD remained limited to 400 members. With the exception of a handful of large companies, most MÜSIAD members were small- and medium-sized businesses. And unlike its rival's members, who were concentrated in Istanbul and the surrounding Marmara region, MÜSIAD members came from both major metropolitan centers and small towns. The same applied to trade unions. While workers loyal to the state were members of the Trade Union Confederation of Turkey (Türkiye Isçi Sendikaları Konfederasyonu,Türk-Is), and the left-leaning ones preferred to join the Revolutionary Trade Union Confederation (Devrimci Isçi Sendikaları Konfederasyonu, DISK), Islamists created their own trade union: Confederation of Turkish Real Trade Unions (Hak-Is Konfederasyonu, HAK-Is). Expectedly, the members of these associations realized that to obtain a larger share of the economic pie, they had to support a political party that adopted their agenda. In the 1990s, this was the RP (Zubaida 1996: 13; Önis 1997: 758–60; Tugal 2007: 8–9).

One cannot deny that in addition to all these structural causes (political and economic), Islamists' success relied largely on their first-rate grassroots organization. Cihan Tugal's ethnography of Sultanbeyli, the first Istanbul district to vote for Islamists, revealed the importance of this aspect of their work. Until the mid-1980s, most of the district's residents were politically unaffiliated. As soon as Islamists set camp in this poor district, pious families in provincial towns and villages got wind of their educational and social initiatives, and began to pour into Sultanbeyli. The neighborhood expanded phenomenally, from 4,000 residents in 1985 to 80,000 four years later. RP activists organized the new residents into networks of family and kin, and linked them to other networks inside and outside Istanbul. By virtue of the welfare they provided, it was only normal for RP candidates to carry the district in every election in the 1990s. The Sultanbeyli model was replicated in dozens of neighborhoods. Thus, instead of relying on impersonal propaganda, Islamists adopted a strategy centered on transforming the everyday life of their voters through schools, mosques, hospitals, employment offices, and the like (Tugal 2009b: 432–36).

This does not mean that all those who voted for RP simply adhered to an instrumental rationality; Islamist activism also had a strong cultural component. Islamists managed to reconstitute identities and communal values by influencing everyday culture (Yavuz 2003: 23).[3] Their success not only affected pious Turks, but even seculars, who came to associate Islamists with social involvement and moral uprightness. Even more important was how this sociocultural campaign transformed the relationship between Islamists and the state. Increased exposure to Islamist soft power convinced state functionaries that Islamists were not determined to destroy the republic, and that they were willing to let themselves be influenced by the principles of the republic as well as help develop them. Islamists and bureaucrats began to "interact and reshape each other," and "an emerging *convergence*" slowly appeared on the horizon (Turam 2007: 4–9).[4]

It mattered, of course, that in the 1990s Islamists had the economic power to support these cultural activities. Özal's watch (as premier between 1983–1989, and president until 1993) witnessed the coinciding of civil society deregulation and the rise of Islamist capital in provincial towns. Özal himself had strong connections with the Naqshabandi Sufi order, and tolerated the spread of religious foundations and charities, as well as a vibrant Islamist press (Zubaida 1996: 11; Yavuz 1999: 585). Meanwhile, the budget of the Directorate of Religious Affairs increased sixteen-fold, and 5 million copies of the Qur'an were printed by the state (Anderson 2009: 442). Official figures also indicate that, by 1987, Turkey had more mosques than schools: 60,161, and 58,455, respectively (Ahmad 1988: 765).

Likewise, these cultural feats would not have been possible without an extensive religious education network. The state had permitted the teaching of the Qur'an in small mosques and private tutoring starting in the late 1940s. But the 1970s witnessed the dizzying proliferation of a new phenomenon: *imam-hatip okullari* (prayer leader-preacher schools), which taught students from the sixth through eleventh grades.[5] The official rationale for these schools, as their name indicates, was to produce religious functionaries. But in reality, restrictions on religious education in public schools propelled pious families to enroll their offspring in these schools to learn about Islam before continuing their education in secular universities (Aksin 2007: 304). So although the national "market" for religious functionaries required less than 3,000 prayer leaders and preachers every year, these schools produced annually more than 50,000 graduates, and in 1997, enrollment reached 1,685,000 students (Helal 1999: 209; Heper and Güney 2000: 640). Correspondingly, the number of *imam-hatip* schools jumped from 72 in 1970 to 389 in 1992. And Islamist charities, only too eager to help, provided scholarships, rented study halls, and subsidized schoolbooks. Graduates, who ended up working in the bureaucracy (notably, the police), the private sector, and civil society, maintained their Islamist connections, constituting a large body of well-educated intellectuals, business professionals, and state functionaries (Zubaida 1996: 13). No wonder why Erbakan described these schools as "the backyard of our party" (Aksin 2007: 304). The head of RP clearly understood that in time these graduates would represent "a religious middle class capable of competing with the secularist intelligentsia in economic, cultural, and political realms . . . [and that] this new avowedly Muslim intelligentsia would be a significant element in the construction of Islamism as a hegemonic alternative" (Tugal 2007: 10).

This pious middle class, spearheaded by the Anatolian business elite, presented themselves as "Islamic Calvinists" who lifted themselves from the ranks of peasants, tradesmen, and artisans through religious-inspired parsimoniousness, hard work, and moral righteousness (Ahmad 1988: 759; Yavuz 2010). So on the one hand, business ventures were buffeted by "a rhetoric emphasizing the need for the unity of believers against the nationalist and secularist bourgeoisie," and on the other hand, religion-based trust networks allowed these entrepreneurs to secure loans, hire trustworthy employees, and arbitrate trade disputes (Tugal 2002: 92).

For all the above reasons (structural and strategic), Islamists managed to double their share of the votes. Their signal success was in the municipal elections of 1994 and 1998, when RP carried Turkey's most important cities, including Istanbul and Ankara. These electoral victories "dramatically altered the previous image of the party in the public mind" from a parochial Anatolian party to a mainstream national party (Önis 1997: 743). Control of municipal administration, in turn, helped the Party redistribute funds to poor neighborhoods; provide welfare to the needy; distribute coal and clothing in the winter, and medicine and food all year round; improve infrastructure and services; pressure wealthy residents to donate generously to city-managed charities; and purge corrupt and unpopular state officials. Voters were also impressed by Islamists' institutional innovations, most notably the peoples' councils (*halk meclisi*), which allowed residents to communicate with local councilors routinely (Zubaida 1996: 12). Social activism in the 1980s, and successful municipal administration in the 1990s, increased Islamists' share of the national vote from 8 percent in 1987, to 17 percent in 1991, and 21 percent in 1995. Slowly but surely, RP moved from a junior partner in the cabinet to the leader of a government coalition. In June 1996 Erbakan became the first Islamist premier in the history of the republic (Heper and Güney 2000: 638; Narli 2003: 127–29).

Provoking a Soft Coup

When RP assumed power, which was more than what officers had in mind for Islamists, the military adopted a wait-and-see policy. By January 1997 intelligence reports accused Islamists of trying to erect a parallel state by packing the bureaucracy with likeminded employees, especially religious school graduates. Reports also indicated that RP was organizing a national campaign to reinstall Shari'a; that it was accumulating substantial funds through Islamist holding companies and banks; and that its rhetoric was becoming militantly anti-secular and anti-Western. Disturbing public statements by Party members substantiated this latter accusation. For example, a prominent RP deputy (Ibrahim Halil Çelik) threatened that if religious schools were closed down, "there would be bloodshed.... The army could not deal with even 3,5000-strong PKK [Kurdish militants]. How will it cope with six million Islamists?" Erbakan himself was quoted as reassuring his followers that Islamists would remain in power "either through normal channels or by shedding blood." And in defiance of decorum, Erbakan invited fifty-one Muslim clerics dressed in traditional garb to the prime minister's residence for *iftar* (the ceremonial breakfast banquet during the holy month of Ramadan) in January 1997 (Heper and Güney 2000: 640–42).

Furthermore, Erbakan tested military patience by trying to demote the position of chief of staff, subordinating it to the defense minister rather than the prime minster (Aksin 2007: 303). Failing to do so, he upped the ante and demanded full control over all decisions relating to military personnel.[6] Officers understood that Erbakan's aim was to prevent the generals from cashiering officers with Islamist sympathies because this disrupted his plan to Islamize the army. During a meeting with the general staff, on May 26, 1997, the prime minister was presented with a list of 141 officers who should be purged for promoting Islamism within the ranks. Erbakan stalled for as long as he could, and after he finally signed the decree, he tried to avoid future meetings at which such requests could be tabled. This might explain why the general command purged another 541 officers immediately after the RP was ousted (Helal 1999: 265; Brooks 2008: 215).

The Islamist prime minister then went further by meddling in the armed forces' most jealously guarded field: geopolitics. This the generals would not tolerate. As General Cumhar Asparuk, secretary-general of the National Security Council (Milli Güvenlik Kurulu, MGK), told the *Financial Times*, in December 1997, Turkey was "not ripe" for complete civilian control over national security issues (Brooks 2008: 223). So when the army launched Operation Poised Hammer against Kurdish separatists in Iraq, in May 1987, for instance, it did not wait for government permission, even though the operation involved some 50,000 troops; nor did it care to do so the following year when it threatened to invade Syria to pursue Kurdish militants. The most striking aspect of military autonomy in that field was its strategic alliance with Israel. The Turkish army concluded an agreement with its Israeli counterpart, in February 1996, before RP had even formed a government. It even compelled Erbakan to sign several complementary accords against his will. And when the frustrated prime minster tried to postpone the joint military exercises, scheduled for the summer of 1997, the Turkish army went ahead anyway (Aksin 2007: 309; Brooks 2008: 218–20). Still, Erbakan made it clear he wished to take Turkey in the opposite direction through highly publicized visits to Iran, Libya, and Pakistan—visits that infuriated the high command to the point where one general (Çevik Bir) described Iran as a terrorist state while Erbakan was in Tehran, just to embarrass him (Uzgel 2003: 204).

Military commanders now suspected that the RP was preparing for a head-on confrontation. But how far were Islamists ready to go? To test the waters, the high command demanded a small concession during an MGK meetings: enforcing obligatory eight-year attendance at public schools, which practically meant cutting two years from the religious schools. When rebuffed, the commanders expressed their alarm at the rising power of Islamism during another MGK meeting. President Süleyman Demirel duly noted their concern and sent a reproving memo to Erbakan. Weary of another civil–military showdown, Chief of Staff Ismail Hakki Karadayi reiterated publicly, on December 24, 1996, the importance of respecting secular democracy as defined by the existing constitution. Two days later, he stated clearly at an MGK meeting that the military would not remain idle if its warnings went unheeded. The chief of staff then organized briefings with journalists and bureaucrats to explain how Islamism was polarizing society in a way that threatened to revert the country back to the violence of the 1970s (Uzgel 2003: 184; Aksin 2007: 307).

President Demirel issued a final warning to Erbakan, in February 1997, asserting that "Article 2 of the Constitution stipulates that [the] Turkish Republic is a democratic, secular [state].... Threats the anti-secularist activities pose for the secular Republican State give rise to serious concern both in the society and in the state institutions. I would like to bring to your attention the need to implement intact those laws enacted to safeguard secularism ... and prevent the fundamentalist views from penetrating into schools, local governments, universities, the judiciary, and the military." But the RP remained undaunted. Accordingly, during the decisive February 28 MGK meeting, the commanders submitted the famous list of eighteen recommendations for immediate implementation by the government, including restrictions on religious schools, and controls against the spread of religious orders. Faced with an ultimatum, Erbakan decided to temporarily switch positions with Deputy Prime Minister Tansu Çiller—hoping that this game of musical chairs might get him off the hook. When this step proved too little too late and the high command was adamant about the implementation of its recommendations, Erbakan was forced to endorse them. Then when he later tried to maneuver, claiming that these measures were not binding on his government, the generals pressured RP's coalition partners to rebel, forcing Erbakan's resignation on June 18, 1997. President Demirel immediately appointed a new government under Mesut Yılmaz, of the Motherland Party (Anavatan Partisi, ANAP). On January 16, 1998, the Constitutional Court dissolved the RP on account of the anti-secular statements of its members, and banned Erbakan and four Party leaders from politics for five years (Heper and Güney 2000: 642–45; Aksin 2007: 306; Brooks 2008: 216).

An interesting question here is: Why did the military go to so much trouble to bring about the downfall of the RP government, rather than just oust it by force? There are several good explanations. Historically, this behavior fit the pattern that the Turkish military had set for itself since the birth of the republic, whereby direct action was considered always un-preferable (Heper and Güney 2000: 646). A more context-specific answer is that the military was embroiled in a vicious war against Kurdish separatists, between 1984 and 1999, and could not afford a full-scale intervention (Keyder 2004: 72). A third explanation is geopolitical. Turkey had applied for entry into the European Community in 1987, and although it was rebuffed in 1989, it was offered instead a free-trade customs union in 1995. The hope was to use this agreement to increase Turkey's chances of joining the European Union (EU). A coup at this point would have dealt the deathblow to Turkey's application (Anderson 2009: 442). Also, the officers who had led the transition from the German to the American model in the 1950s had come to occupy the top echelon in the 1990s,[7] and the Clinton administration had no wish to see a coup in Ankara—especially, in the absence of a militant Islamist or Communist threat (Uzgel 2003: 197).

All that being said, the military not only perceived its ultimatum to the RP as part of its constitutional duties, but it also believed it had the support of the people. Erbakan was politically weak, considering that his party's 21 percent of the national vote was hardly a popular mandate. At the same time, a national survey conducted by an independent institution, in October 1990, revealed that 92 percent of Turks considered the military as the most trustworthy institution in the state, and only 50 percent expressed trust in politicians.[8] Another survey in the mid-1990s showed that only 7 percent of the population sympathized with Islamism as an ideology. Also, by the end of 1996, both business and labor associations issued highly critical statements of RP's increasingly ideological politics. In other words, regardless of the fact that officers monopolized the means of violence, the popular balance of forces clearly tilted toward them (Heper and Güney 2000: 646; Brooks 2008: 213). But, of course, the situation was about to change.

Notes

1. Turgut Özal, an engineer by training, relied on Islamist support to transition to politics. His brother Korkut was one of MSP's leading figures, and managed to get him on the party's ticket in the 1977 municipal election in Izmir, but he lost. Months before the 1980 coup, another Islamist-friendly figure, Süleyman Demirel, appointed him to an economic post in the cabinet, and the military retained his services.

2. To cover these activities, the state borrowed heavily from the public, thus producing the staggering domestic debt and budget deficits that would eventually cause the economy to crash in 2001, the year the economy shrunk by 7.5 percent and foreign debt increased to over $100 billion (Wahid 2009: 75).

3. Several recent ethnographies have detailed their activities in this field (most famously, White 2002).

4. This is what Turam referred to as the *politics of engagement*: the "continuum of interplay between Islamic actors and state actors, ranging from contestation and negotiation to accommodation, cooperation and alliance" (Turam 2007: 13).

5. These schools began to appear in the 1950s under the auspices of the DP, and later the AP. Students are educated on two levels: intermediate (sixth to eighth years) and *lycée* (ninth to eleventh) (Aksin 2007: 304).

6. Officially, the Supreme Military Council, composed of fifteen generals, convenes annually under the chairmanship of the prime minister to make such decisions. The latter's role was traditionally to approve whatever the generals suggested.

7. Chiefs of Staff Necip Torumtay and Necdet Öztorun, for example, were awarded medals by President Ronald Reagan. And between 1984 and 1996, some 2,900 Turkish officers received training in the United States, and approximately 90 percent of the Turkish stockpile came from America.

8. The fact that the military was perceived as an embodiment of "all the cultural characteristics of the society" was reflected in the words of the Turkish minister of culture, who stated at a press conference in the summer of 1999, while introducing a new book on the history of the armed forces, "Turks have been known as a military-nation throughout history. The Turkish military is synonymous with Turkish national identity" (Altinay 2004: 1). The Turkish army therefore was not only seen as the guardian of republican principles, but also as a true representative of society. This sense of representation was reflected in its large size relative to the population: a 790,000-strong army in a population of 80 million (Wahid 2009: 73), in addition to its balanced social composition. An examination of officers' family backgrounds in 2000 showed that 25 percent came from a working-class background; 7.3 percent from peasant families; 10 percent descended from artisans or shopkeepers; 19 percent from bureaucrats; 10 percent from teachers; and 5 percent from professionals. These percentages have remained quite stable over time (Kili 2003: 159).

11 | Aborted Coups?

NOVEMBER 2002 AND AFTER

THE FIRST GENERAL ELECTIONS AFTER Turkey's "white coup" were held in 1999. In this election, the Democratic Left Party (Demokratik Sol Parti, DSP) of Bülent Ecevit secured a plurality. An all-inclusive coalition was formed between the left-of-center DSP, the right-of-center Motherland Party (Anavatan Partisi, ANAP) of Mesut Yılmaz, and the extreme right Nationalist Action Party (Milliyetçi Hareket Partisi, MHP), now headed by Devlet Bahçeli. This was the seventh coalition government since the beginning of the 1990s. The three odd partners wiggled on for three years before finally collapsing under the weight of their internal contradictions. It had become sufficiently evident that none of the parties that had governed Turkey in the past five decades had managed to secure a stable constituency. Most of them were, in fact, little more than "loose associations of interests without a stable political line" (Keyder 2004: 75). The new president, who succeeded Demirel in May 2000, was also a nonpartisan civilian, Ahmet Necdet Sezer, former head of the Constitutional Court (Aksin 2007: 313). The old parties seemed to have become politically bankrupt after the dizzying shifts and tactical alliances of Turkish politics since the 1940s. It was therefore unsurprising that in the watershed elections of 2002, almost all of the old governing parties failed to receive the 10 percent of the vote necessary to enter Parliament—except for the Republican People's Party (Cumhuriyet Halk Partisi, CHP), which barely secured 19 percent of the vote. In those elections, there was one big winner: the Justice and Development Party (Adalet ve Kalkınma Partisi, AKP).

The AKP, which was formed barely a year before the 2002 elections, won 34 percent of the vote. And after the gains of the parties that acquired less than the minimum 10 percent were allocated among the winners, AKP ultimately controlled 60 percent of the seats in Parliament—a majority unsurpassed since the 1950s. For the first time in almost two decades, a single party won enough votes to be able to form a government on its own. AKP's ascendency continued with a 40 percent win in the 2004 municipal elections, a 47 percent win in the 2007 national elections, and a landslide victory of over 50 percent of the votes in the 2012 elections—an ascendancy unheard of since the country's transition to multiparty politics. Equally significant was the election of the Party's Foreign Minister Abdullah Göl to the presidency, despite the fierce resistance of secular parties and the misgivings of top generals. This was again the first time since the 1950s that the president and prime minister belonged to the same party. Where did this new party come from?

A few weeks before the RP was officially dissolved, in 1998, another successor Islamist party was created to carry the torch: the Virtue Party (Fazilet Partisi, FP). The two were identical in ideology and membership, albeit the successor was more cautious about alienating the military. Still, in the 1999 elections, FP obtained barely 15 percent of the votes. Many young Party cadres saw this as an indicator of voters' weariness with ideological parties. After so much political turmoil, pragmatism and flexibility were what citizens sought. In short, young Islamist activists realized that they had to free themselves from "the clutches of an Islamic ideology in order to appeal to larger groups of the electorate" (Heper and Güney 2000: 649). When the youth of FP failed to impress this on their elders during the Party's 2001 Congress, they decided to break away and form their own party: the AKP. The new party's motto in the 2002 elections was "We have changed." Meanwhile, FP's insistence on avowedly Islamist politics prompted another court ban in 2001, and the rump of the Party regrouped in what turned out to be the last and weakest of Erbakan's chain of Islamist parties: the Felicity Party (Saadet Partisi).

In contrast to the ailing Erbakan and his associates, the leaders of the AKP were young, dynamic, professional, media savvy, and particularly attentive to business interests. Recep Tayyip Erdogan, AKP's charismatic prime minister, came from Istanbul's underprivileged Kasımpasa neighborhood. He was among the first-generation activists trained in religious schools. He then studied economics at Marmara University, and played soccer semiprofessionally for over a decade. At the same time, he became involved in grassroots organization with Erbakan's various parties starting in the 1980s. His working-class background, his rough character (honed through years on the soccer field), and his street activism distinguished him from other political leaders. At the age of 40, he became mayor of Istanbul (1994–1998), where he basically managed to turn the city around. His popularity soared when after his remarkable achievements as mayor, he was banned from politics for five years and sentenced to prison for ten months for reciting what were perceived as inflammatory verses in a public address in 1997.[1] The Party's second-in-command, Abdullah Gül, AKP foreign minister, and later president of the republic, came from a central Anatolian city (Kayseri) whose business community was archetypical AKP supporters: export-oriented medium-sized manufacturers. He studied economics in Istanbul and England, and worked at the Saudi-based Islamic Development Bank until 1991 when he entered politics. Thus, his social, educational, and professional background was particularly reassuring to Turkey's rising bourgeoisie (Aksin 2007: 308; Besli and Özbay 2011).

AKP's pragmatism was manifest in substituting Islamism as an ideology with what its leaders proclaimed was "conservative democracy"—a catch-all label meant to help the Party garner more votes by posing as "a corridor between Islamism and nationalism" (Bilici 2006: 4). And sure enough, by transcending its Islamist origins, AKP catered to a much broader constituency centered on middle-class business owners, though also including the lower classes in the city and countryside, in addition to religious and ethnic minorities and intellectuals opposed to the military's rigid definition of Turkish identity (Önis 2007). Yet despite this broad social base, AKP was not a standard populist movement—it could not have been so in light of its strict adherence to International Monetary Fund (IMF) guidelines and market liberalism. What distinguished its particular brand of populism was that it devised policies that addressed different social interests, rather than treating the masses as an undifferentiated bloc whose interests conveniently coincide with those of a reified state (Tugal 2002: 95). So who were its main beneficiaries?

Its core constituency was the Anatolian-based manufacturers-exporters. The Anatolian tigers preferred AKP to Erabakan's latest Islamist iteration because of the persistent tensions within the latter. Islamist parties, since the 1970s, catered to both capitalist entrepreneurs and their workers. And although it was wealthy provincials who generously financed these parties, electoral politics demanded that they appeal to the lower classes as well, especially after the crushing of the left made the votes of the poor available for the taking. Anatolian businessmen were becoming weary of Erbakan's emphasis on social equality, and his claim that Islam urges full employment and admonishes the accumulators of wealth. Suspicion of these "prosperity for all" slogans increased in the 1990s, when the growing army of informal laborers, having no Communist organ to turn to, swelled the ranks of the

RP, and Erbakan's government busied itself with reducing unemployment, raising wages, and fixing profit ceilings (Tugal 2007: 12–15).

This class-based polarization was reflected ideologically in the ongoing tension between proponents of "moral capitalism" and those of "alternative capitalism."[2] The first group accepted the free market, but hoped to use Islamic precepts to minimize its social damages: exploitation, consumerism, and wealth disparities. This group was also circumspect about joining the European Union (EU), preferring to create an Islamic common market through mechanisms such as Erbakan's short-lived exclusively Muslim Development-Eight (D-8) countries (designed to mirror the G-8).[3] The second group believed in the virtues of the open market and free trade, where middle-class entrepreneurs, protected from state intervention, would create wealth and provide social leadership. This view was advocated by the young Islamists who broke off to form AKP, and had, of course, the overwhelming support of the Muslim bourgeoisie in Anatolia. It eagerly pursued EU membership, and refused to anchor economic cooperation on religious identity.[4] According to this school of thought, Islam plays a role very similar to Weber's Protestant ethic, where religious affinity makes businessmen prudent and efficient (Tugal 2002: 98–100)—exactly the story that Anatolian businessmen were eager to promote.

What was certainly surprising, however, was AKP's popularity among the lower classes despite its faithful adoption of "a neo-liberal regimen with the fervour of the convert" (Anderson 2009: 449). This popularity was partly explained by Erdogan's native charisma, his humble origins, militant roots, common man piety, traditional Turkish machismo, and plain-talking populism—which created a powerful personality cult that inspired the masses. "In his person," noted Anderson, "[laid] a good deal of the symbolic compensation enjoyed by the mass of the party's electorate for any material hardships" (2009: 449–51). However, it was not all a matter of sentiments: AKP did actually provide "neo-liberalism with a human face"; it combined respect for market forces with systematic efforts to alleviate poverty and improve public services (Önis 2007: 24). And in engaging the bourgeoisie and urban slum-dwellers equally, AKP based its appeal on providing a voice to the voiceless, whether those who despite their business success remained excluded from the ruling circles, or those who did not share in the benefits of economic growth (Önis 1997: 748; Keyder 2004: 71).

Kurds also threw their lot with the AKP. War with the Kurdish Workers' Party (Partiya Karkerên Kurdistanê, PKK), which involved more than 250,000

Turkish troops and cost the Turkish taxpayer $6 billion annually, claimed the lives of some 30,000 people, and led to the internal displacement or deportation of 380,000 Kurds between 1984 and 1999. AKP promised to allow the use of the Kurdish language in private classes (though not public schools) and television programs. And in the summer of 2005, Erdogan began talking about the "Kurdish question"—"a phrase that is anathema to the national-secular establishment, as it implies a bigger problem than terrorism and poverty" (Tugal 2007: 23).

Apart from Kurds and other subaltern populations, Turkey's liberal and leftist intelligentsia, as well as human rights activists and academics, initially backed AKP because of its social activism and promise to extend the margins of democracy. All pro-democracy forces perceived AKP as the only effective weapon against the lurking authoritarian tendencies among Turkish elites, especially in the armed forces (Zubaida 1996: 15; Tugal 2007: 19). Ethnographer Berna Turam recorded: "In every visit to Turkey, I found an increasing number of educated people, professors, intellectuals, artists and businesspeople from secular circles appreciating AKP." Even more surprising, whenever these secular intellectuals referred to Erdogan, they insisted that he was not an Islamist, "He is *our* leader" (Turam 2007: 4–5). Another Turkish scholar captured this spirit in the following account:

> Some in Turkey and abroad are inclined to see the [AKP] as an Islamist movement, with a secret agenda to change the secular regime in Turkey. This is a fundamental misconception shaped by a false dichotomy of Islam vs. secularism. When one looks deeper at the AK party's social base, political program, their public discourse and performance in government, these do not confirm the assertion that the AK party is an Islamist party. Instead the AK party stands at the center-right of the political spectrum, representing, as did the earlier center-right political parties did in the 1950s, 1960s, and 1980s, the rising peripheral forces vis-à-vis the bureaucratic/authoritarian center. (Dagi 2008: 103)

AKP's ascendancy marked, for many Turkish intellectuals, the beginning of "a new phase in the struggle between the old Turkey and the new Turkey . . . with the AK Party on the side of the new Turkey" (Dagi 2008: 292; for similar views, see Radwan 2006; Yavuz 2006). Even nonpoliticized citizens appreciated AKP for sparing the country the political instability and economic mismanagement of the past decades (Kalaycioglu 2005: 190). In sum, all major classes and social groups "could see something for themselves in the AKP; this was, in the classical sense, a potentially hegemonic capitalist project" (Tugal 2007: 20). And by relying on a permanent majority, AKP was no longer hostage to the voter mood swings that had plagued Turkish politics for so long.

One must add here that a stellar economic record enhanced AKP's popularity. The decade before its rise to power was dismissed as "Turkey's lost decade" economically. Instead of an average 5 percent growth in the 1980s, the economy shrank by 9 percent in 2001; inflation hit 80 percent, and sometimes reached a three-digit figure; public debt comprised a shocking 150 percent of GDP; and the national currency was devaluated by 50 percent. Consequently, investments dried up, unemployment soared, there was an explosion of bankruptcies, and the country was sliding toward complete insolvency. No more capable of providing for the population, pre-AKP governments allowed education and health care to deteriorate significantly (their share in GDP in 2000 was 3.5 percent and 2 percent, respectively). Subsidies were first cut and then discontinued, and public expenditures reached their lowest ebb. By 2001 the Turkish economy had hit rock bottom. During its first term in power (2005–2007), AKP managed to reverse the country's economic deterioration, bringing down inflation to 8.8 percent; reducing the budget deficit to 1.2 percent; generating a 6 percent surplus, and an economic growth rate between 7 and 10 percent. At the same time, exports more than tripled from $30 billion to $100 billion (82 percent of which came from private manufacturers), and the ratio of exports to GDP rose from 14 percent to 21 percent (Keyder 2004: 75–77; Tugal 2007: 21; Anderson 2009: 450).

This successful performance continued during AKP's first decade in power. Between 2002 and 2010, the government sustained an average growth of 9 percent; reduced average inflation to 6.4 percent; reduced government deficit relative to GDP by more than half, and government debt relative to GDP from 74 percent to 41.6 percent; kept unemployment between 8 and 12 percent; increased foreign investments from $2 billion to $20 billion (three-quarters by European investors); and increased exports from $36 billion to $132 billion (half of which went to Europe). Even the global downturn of 2009, which slashed exports and foreign investments, did not damage the Turkish economy as it did in other countries. In 2009 the IMF decided that Turkey no longer needed international aid and could finally stand on its own two feet. And by 2010 Turkey had become the world's 17th largest economy (Pope 2010: 2; European Commission 2011: 111–15). More important, AKP's combination of sustained growth and low inflation expanded the base of social beneficiaries, boosting the Party's electoral fortunes (Önis 2007: 23).

Cultural Shift

An understanding of AKP power is not complete unless one appreciates how—compared to other Turkish parties—it "enjoyed an ideological hegemony over the whole political scene that none of them had ever possessed" (Anderson 2009: 447). AKP had indeed become so dominant that many criticized it for transforming the Turkish political system into "a one-dimensional democracy" (Önis 2007: 22). How did an Islamist-leaning party achieve cultural hegemony in such a sharply divided society? Of course, like any ideological hegemon, AKP presented its program as nonideological, but rather as pragmatic and sensible—or as Gramsci would put it: an expression of common sense. AKP advertised its platform as a perfect synthesis between everything that Turks cherished: economic liberalism and free trade, and the defense of national and religious values, that is, "a progressive and modernist vision with a conservative face" (Önis 2009: 22). Meanwhile, the Party gradually "instilled in ordinary citizens the desire to see pious rulers" take over, preaching the view that good, uncorrupt people should run the state, and that practicing Muslims are most likely to be so—an attempt to erode rather than abolish secularism (Tugal 2009b: 451). Finally, AKP, unlike its Islamist predecessors, dropped any hint of anti-Western or anti-capitalist rhetoric, which fit perfectly with Turkey's Westernized elite and export-oriented bourgeoisie (Anderson 2009: 447).

All that being said, AKP's intellectual edge would not have been possible without the success of the parallel and hugely influential social movement clustered around spiritual leader Fethullah Gülen and his "impeccably pro-business, pro-modern, pro-American" Islam, and his "Opus Dei-like empire" of social, financial, educational, and media networks (Anderson 2009: 455). From the day the republic had been founded, Turkish Islamists operated on two parallel fronts: loosely organized religion-based social movements (such as the Naqshabandi Sufi order, al-Nur movement, and finally the Gülen movement), and a series of political parties counting on their support (with AKP as the latest manifestation). The leaders of these social movements collected donations from an increasing pool of pious Muslims (millions of dollars in the case of the Gülen movement) and used them to offer health care, education, scholarships, stipends, lodging, religious study groups, and employment for their followers. They also helped arrange marriages, resolve family disputes, establish business contacts, and cement social trust (Yılmaz 2009). So although these movements were not officially entangled in electoral politics, they produced networks of likeminded Muslims, who then tended to act as a single voting bloc.

The founder of the most influential of these movements, the Service Community (Hizmet Cemaat), is Fethullah Gülen, a preacher (*hocaefendi*) born in the early 1940s in the eastern Anatolian town of Erzurum, home of Kemal's First National Congress, and a historically insecure frontier zone that cultivated the young preacher's appreciation of a strong military. The movement he founded evolved from the teachings of Said al-Nursi, though Gülen reformulated the master's ideas considerably, and combined them with Turkish nationalist and Western intellectual influences. The end result was an ideology that supported a strong state and military, a market economy, free trade, integration into the advanced (i.e., Western) world, and most important, Turkish nationalism and secularism. In other words, this neo-Nur movement interpreted Islam in a way that appealed to both the Kemalist establishment and the intellectual and business elites. Its celebrated "Turkish-Islamic synthesis" was perceived to have finally succeeded in establishing a modus vivendi between the country's religious population and nationalist military and elite.[5] It also helped that Gülen himself (who after 1999 moved to the United States) never criticized military intervention in politics.[6] With this attitude, the Gülen movement presented itself as "a bulwark against the populist and revolutionary interpretations of Islam," and then banked on its reputation for moderation to Islamize society (and eventually the state) in a nonconfrontational way (Tugal 2002: 93). But besides its potent ideology, the Gülen movement established its dominance through a formidable array of organizations, including a media empire, with a prominent daily (*Zaman*), several periodicals, television and radio stations, a first-rate public relations company (Gazeteciler ve Yazarlar Vakfi), and educational institutions (300 high schools, seven universities, and dozens of dormitories and summer camps)—all funded by a giant business network spearheaded by 2,000 members of the Business Life Cooperation Association (Is Hayatı Daynaısma Dernegi, ISHAD), and homegrown financial intuitions (such as Asya Finans, whose capital in the 1990s reached $500 million).

As such, the Gülen movement was in a position to both inspire and support the AKP during its first years in power (Yavuz 1999: 593–97; Aras and Caha 2003: 141–44: Yavuz and Esposito 2003). Theirs was a strategy to transform the system without attacking it, to renegotiate where the red lines should be drawn rather than to cross them in defiance. This roundabout strategy was the only available option to avert a direct military intervention.

Neo-Ottomans

AKP combined its political, economic, and cultural power to radically alter Turkey's foreign policy. Initially, the boldness of its geopolitical strategy not only increased its popularity at home and abroad, but also appealed to the Turkish armed forces. In 2002 AKP declared its intention to make Turkey a global power by 2023, the 100th anniversary of the establishment of the republic. This was a marked shift from Kemalist isolationism to what became known as "neo-Ottomanism" (yeni-Osmanlıcılık), an assertive foreign policy geared toward establishing Turkey as a global power (Murinson 2006: 946). AKP's ambition was not just to revive Turkish influence, but to also reclaim its regional hegemony, and thus symbolically "undo Napoleon's legacy" in the Middle East (Cagaptay 2012: 7).

The intellectual underpinnings of AKP's foreign policy had been provided by the Party's foreign policy architect, and future prime minister, Ahmet Davutoglu. The Strategic Depth (Stratejik Derinlik) doctrine articulated by this professor of international relations held that "strategic depth is predicated on geographical and historical depth," and that Turkey is uniquely positioned to benefit from both because it lies at the crossroads of several geopolitical spheres of influence, and its Ottoman legacy provides it with the historical ties to build on (Murinson 2006: 947). Davutoglu first expressed his views in an influential 1998 article, which analyzed the imbalances of the post–Cold War order and called on Turks to proactively establish their own power axis. Later, his book *Strategic Depth*, published in 2000, openly criticized Kemalism for failing to make use of Turkey's valuable geographic location and history. Davutoglu's goal was for Turks to "appropriate a new position: one of providing security and stability not only for itself, but also for its neighboring regions" (Davutoglu 2008: 79).

Davutoglu became chief foreign policy advisor to Prime Minister Erdogan, and later had a chance to implement his ideas as Turkey's foreign minister, and later as prime minister. This doctrine found particular resonance with Erdogan, who lent his personal dynamism and charisma to the cause. But what rendered this doctrine practical, unlike Nasser's pan-Arab ambitions for example, is the following: first, as with other AKP cadres, Davutoglu tempered his ambition with pragmatism, suggesting that in order for Turkey to become a global power, it needed "to practice caution and to calibrate Turkish foreign policy within the 'strategic parameters' set by the great powers" (Murinson 2006: 950); second, the geopolitical fluidity of the 1990s was unique, with the disintegration of the USSR and the Balkans, and the independence of a handful of Turkic republics. One could also add that the collapse of the Arab-Israeli peace process in 2000 and the destruction of Iraq in 2003 kept regional relations tense enough for Turkey to play the role of regional power broker. In short, the weakening of Turkey's neighbors provided Ankara with an enviable comparative advantage. Finally, while AKP's geopolitical project challenged the monopoly of generals over foreign policy, it intrinsically appealed to the prestige of the Turkish armed forces, and provided it with a popular justification to continue investing in military power in the post–Cold War era. Unlike officers in weak states with little more to do than bicker with politicians, the Turkish military was provided with an ambitious project at a time when NATO seemed to have lost its purpose (Uzgel 2003: 191–96; Kalaycioglu 2005: 12–13).

How did this new foreign policy manifest itself practically? AKP cemented relations with Israel during its first term. Party leaders visited Tel Aviv; businessmen close to AKP made profitable deals with their Israeli counterparts; and the government concluded more bilateral agreements with Israel than any other Turkish government. However, Erdogan was aware that his real power base was in the Muslim world, and that while he could be seen as mediating between Arabs and Israelis, he must not appear complacent with the latter (Pope 2010: 7).[7] One indicator of a more influential role in the Muslim world was that out of the thirty-three Turkish diplomatic missions opened under AKP rule, eighteen were in Muslim countries. And while the EU accounted for 56 percent of Turkish trade in 1999, its share dropped to 41 percent a decade later, at the same time that trade with Islamic countries climbed from 12 percent to 20 percent. The prime minister became very active in Middle East politics. He visited Tehran in the summer of 2004 to sign security cooperation and trade agreements, and mediated between Iran and the international community on the nuclear energy dispute. He also visited Syria (the first state visit by a Turkish official in fifty-seven years), Lebanon, and Saudi Arabia in 2006, and invited Hamas' political leader Khaled Mash'al to Ankara after his party's electoral victory that year. Erdogan was then invited to deliver the opening speech at the Arab League Summit in 2007, and returned the gesture by hosting a Gulf Cooperation Council meeting in Istanbul.

Then came the 2011 Arab revolts. For the proactive and increasingly aggressive AKP, this was a chance to reconfigure the regional power balance in Ankara's favor. It was a risky policy, considering the misgivings of world powers (especially Washington) and regional heavyweights (led by Saudi Arabia). But it initially yielded high dividends. AKP's popularity soared among Arabs, as evidenced by the exuberant millions who received Erdogan in Cairo that summer. Ordinary people embraced Turkish soft power (soap operas, music, tourism); and many rising politicians (particularly in Egypt and Tunisia) subscribed to the Turkish combination of Islam and democracy. More critically, AKP's financial and logistical support for Syrian rebels promised to install an incredibly grateful regime in Damascus.

However, AKP's most popular foreign policy was improving Turkey's chances of joining the EU. After the Customs Union Agreement between Turkey and the EU had come into effect in 1996, the Helsinki conference, three years later, designated Turkey as a candidate for EU membership. Within a month of AKP's 2002 victory, the Party scored a key diplomatic victory by getting EU leaders to commit to starting the negotiations for accession in 2005. The Party mobilized civil society and business associations to lobby Brussels, and carried out the required reforms with such scrupulousness that, in 2004, the EU announced that Turkey had met the union's political and economic standards, and no longer needed to be subject to continued monitoring (Davutoglu 2008: 83). To appreciate the importance of this aspect of AKP policy, one needs to remember that EU accession is arguably the only national project with overwhelming popular support in Turkey—in fact, opinion polls in the first decade of AKP rule showed that close to 75 percent of Turks were eager to join (Keyder 2004: 77–79). EU accession had for long been "a Turkish dream, a panacea for all ills" (Aksin 2007: 318). As Anderson explained:

> Entry into the EU had, indeed, to date been the magical formula of the AKP's hegemony. For the mass of the population . . . a Europe within which they can travel freely represents hope of better-paid jobs. . . . For big business, membership in the EU offers access to deeper capital markets; for medium entrepreneurs, lower interest rates; for both, a more stable macro-economic environment. For the professional classes, commitment to Europe is the gauge that Islamist temptations will not prevail within the AKP. For the liberal intelligentsia, the EU will be the safeguard against any return to military rule. For the military, it will realize the longstanding Kemalist dream of joining the West in full dress. In short, Europe is the promised land towards which the most antithetical forces within Turkey can gaze, for the most variegated reasons. In making its cause their own, the AKP leaders have come to dominate the political chequerboard more completely that any force since the Kemalism of the early republic. (2009: 449)

One of the reasons why AKP was so keen on EU membership was the realization that Turkish politicians needed concerted European pressure to keep the military in check (Keyder 2004: 77). Turkey thus provides a typical example of Adam Przeworski's (1991) famous model for democratic transition in countries where the ruling bloc is divided between a dominant and a weaker faction. Here, the weak faction lures the dominant one with external incentives to convince it to loosen its grip, then uses the political opening to consolidate its gains. The European Council's 1993 Copenhagen criteria, which required members to have stable democratic institutions, and respect for human rights and the rule of law, was welcomed by all those set on preventing another military intervention. At the same time, the EU's balanced mix of conditions and incentives was carefully designed not to alienate the generals. In short, joining the EU was no longer a foreign policy vocation, but "a must to establish and consolidate an 'open society' in Turkey" (Dagi 2008: 106).

In return, of course, Turkish Islamists had to demonstrate to Europe's satisfaction that they had become "good Muslim 'moderates'" (Tugal 2007: 17). Though European citizens showed little enthusiasm for closer ties with Turkey, EU leaders saw in the AKP-Gülen phenomenon a good model for Muslim immigrants in Berlin, Paris, and other European capitals. Europe's neighbor across the Atlantic thought likewise. In the post-9/11 security environment, Washington supported the AKP to prove that its war against terrorism was not a war against Islam or a clash of civilizations, and to be able to draw on Turkey's strategic location and regional influence to restructure the Middle East (Oguzlu 2003: 295–95). With Americans increasingly concerned about militant Islamism, moderate Western-friendly Islamists became highly valued. AKP's Turkey was framed by Washington as a "beacon of democracy in the Muslim world" (Keyder 2004: 84).

Notably, while Western relations with AKP and the Gülen movement thrived, U.S. relations with the Turkish military began to suffer, especially after the Soviet threat had sunk into the background. American support for the Kurds in Iraq, from the 1990 Gulf crisis onward, provoked several muted conflicts. Top generals suspected Washington of trying to offer autonomy to the Kurds on Turkey's southern borders (which became obvious after 2003). Tensions began as early as December 1990, when Chief of Staff Necip Torumaty resigned in protest of Turkey's support of an American war to weaken the central government in Baghdad (Güney 2002: 166). Washington, in turn, expressed its alarm over the Turkish army's shift from a defensive to an offensive strategy against the PKK, beginning in 1993, as well as the cross-border raids deep into northern Iraq to pursue PKK militants, which began in 1995 (with no less than 50,000 troops) and continue still (Uzgel 2003: 205). The high command certainly did not appreciate U.S. Secretary of State Madeline Albright's strict warning against a military coup in 1997. The office of the Turkish chief of staff published a pamphlet, in 1999, that carefully listed unfriendly actions by Washington, including opening up a Kurdish cultural institute before a Turkish one was established; encouraging Armenian and Greek lobbies in Washington to criticize Turkey; and including discussion of the Armenian genocide in American school textbooks (Bâli 2010).

In 2003 Chief of Staff Hilmi Özkök defended his country's successive wars against Greece (in 1974, 1987, and 1996) and the deployment of 30,000 troops in Cyprus, and warned that "if Turkey looses Cyprus, the process of the Turks' imprisonment in Anatolia would be completed," something the military will never allow, regardless of the opinion of Turkey's Western partners.[8] Turkish officers were infuriated by the way the U.S. invasion of Iraq in 2003 transformed the power balance between the army and the Kurdish militants almost permanently. Kurds were now no less important allies to the Americans than the Turkish military itself. Little wonder that it was the Turkish army that rejected U.S. use of Turkish territories and air space in its 2003 invasion of Iraq, while AKP leadership did not mind (Uzgel 2003: 200–02). The general staff's "deep disturbance" with the United States was displayed in a press conference by Chief of General Staff Büyükanıt, in April 2007, in which he criticized Washington for supporting Turkish Islamists and emboldening Kurdish separatists, claiming that such policies "will divide Turkey into pieces" (Dagi 2008: 44). In the same press conference, he attacked domestic forces for trying to undermine the military "under the façade" of meeting Western democratic and human rights conditions (Dagi 2008: 271). Turkish analyst Ihsan Dagi catalogued similarly sharp criticisms by top Turkish commanders against the West between 2006 and 2008, commenting at the end: "Common knowledge that the US and Turkey are allies does not hold entirely true in the eyes of the commanders. It seems that the 'comrades in arms' notion from the Cold War years is a thing of the past. What we see instead is a deep distrust. Turkish generals expect the worst from the Americans, including an outright occupation of Turkey" (Dagi 2008: 273).

The dilemma the military faced could be summarized as follows: "Democratization might increase state power in the international arena relative to other states [through EU membership and stronger U.S. support] but it could also decrease the power of the [military] in the domestic arena" (Yılmaz 2002: 75). This is why officers were becoming increasingly hesitant. Some were keen on deeper integration with the West, while others worried about how Islamists and ethnic minorities were manipulating Western countries to increase their political leverage. Either way, Turkey's generals came to realize that with the end of the Communist threat and the warm relations between AKP and the West, the international situation had become certainly unfavorable to a coup (Yılmaz 2009). "If there was a military coup in Turkey," Dagi wrote, "it would be not only against the government and Parliament but against the US and the EU" (2008: 45).

The Security Shifting Sides

Turkish security has not been a full partner in the ruling bloc since the birth of the republic. Security functions have been subsumed by the military according to the law. Police and civilian intelligence have acted as military aides in terms of urban security, while rural security has remained in the hands of the gendarmes, a military branch proper. The reasons for this odd arrangement are both historical and political. Historically, Ottoman security agencies were late and feeble creations (unlike the situation in Egypt, whose British colonial rulers created and supervised a first-rate police force during their eight-decade rule). Moreover, the rudimentary security structure that existed was based in Constantinople (the seat of the old regime) at a time when Kemal's revolutionary regime was centered in Ankara, and so the new rulers were forced to entrust security to the military (again unlike Nasser, who made immediate use of the security apparatus he inherited from the British in Cairo).

No less crucial in the Turkish case was that the early transition to multiparty politics placed the General Directorate of Security (GDS), which is part of the Interior Ministry, in the hands of elected politicians (rather than members of an authoritarian ruling party, as was the case in Egypt). The interior minister, an elected government appointee, held the GDS accountable for its actions, since he had to justify these actions to Parliament and respond to various public inquiries. In other words, the interior minister, as a representative of a political party in a competitive political system, had to rein in the security forces during his tenure if he wanted his party to win the next election. And political parties, for their part, practiced this right to the fullest, frequently reshuffling officers and reorganizing police work as they saw fit. One striking example suffices: when an internal change of leadership occurred in the ruling ANAP, in 1991, the new leader, Mesut Yılmaz, replaced the heads of all the police departments appointed by his Party predecessor (Caglar 1994: 139).

Turkish security agencies therefore could not develop a separate corporate agenda; their functions were usurped by the military, and their administration fell under whichever elected government was in power. This was entirely different from the case of the armed forces. Military guardianship over the national welfare, and responsibility for internal and external security were enshrined in all Turkish constitutions. Moreover, Turkish law gave full powers to the chief of staff and service chiefs over the military institution (though they nominally reported to the president), and the National Security Council (Milli Güvenlik Kurulu, MGK) involved them officially in policymaking.

Things began to change after the military expanded the Turkish security sector in 1980. Three important developments spurred this change: first, the dismal failure of the police to end political violence, in the late 1970s, forced the military into street clashes with protesters and ultimately a full-fledged coup; second, the start of the war against Kurdish separatists, in the early 1980s, promised to tie the military's hands for quite some time (the war officially ended in 1999, but operations continue until today); and third, this latter war drove thousands of Kurds and poor peasants from the southeast region to the big cities, where they joined the growing urban underclass in the shantytowns—itself a product of the economic liberalization of the 1980s—and all these factors coalesced, increasing the crime rate and terrifying the upwardly mobile middle class, let alone the upper classes. And the military, naturally, dreaded being dragged into petty law and order operations.

Accordingly, the high command announced in the Constitutive Assembly assigned to prepare the new constitution that the police forces would go through a comprehensive "re-organization project to effectually carry out its duties that will become heavier after the termination of the martial law." And verily so, the police sector experienced unprecedented "expansion and militarization, during which it was structurally and legally strengthened with the help of the military." The police budget was increased; its arsenal was reinforced; new police schools were opened around the country; and the force itself swelled from 50,000 officers in 1980 to 92,000 in 1991, and thousands more were added in 2002, 2005, and 2007 (Berksoy 2010: 137–43).

There were other important structural changes. These included the reorganization of the humble anti-riot units (Society Police) into the quasi-militaristic Active Force (Çevik Kuvvet), in 1982. The new force made use of sophisticated equipment, such as electrified truncheons, teargas bombs, machine guns, and armored vehicles. The following year, an anti-terrorism force, the

Special Operations Teams (Özel Harekat Timleri), was organized and trained by the vice-commander of the military's Special War Department, which was responsible for confronting armed guerillas, and was aided by a newly created Anti-Terrorism and Operations Department. A draconian anti-terrorism law (Law 3712 of 1991) defined a broad array of activities as terror, including counterfeiting documents, inciting youth against conscription, as well as the "intent" to commit violence. In 1993 motorcycle police units were introduced, with the aim of controlling the streets and collecting information in a systematic way. And finally, a sophisticated electronic surveillance system was set up in 2005 (Berksoy 2010: 140–47).

But the military's belated decision to empower the security apparatus coincided with its decision to advance Islamists in order to prevent a Communist resurgence. As a result, the purges that accompanied the 1980 coup removed police officers with leftist sympathies, and recruited Islamists in their place to act as a bulwark against the infiltration of Communism in the force. Surprisingly, the military's change of heart vis-à-vis Islamists, in 1997, did not affect the police, as evidenced by the fact that purges of military officers with Islamist sympathies after the 1997 soft coup did not extend to police officers (Tugal 2007: 11–16). Ali Caglar (2004), a sociologist who investigated the police force through employment data analysis and interviews, concluded that because of the low political value of the police force, the background checks carried out before admitting police officers were performed by "untrained, inexperienced and non-professional officers" and there were no systematic purges of politically affiliated members, and the few that were carried out targeted leftists not Islamists. In fact, since most police officers came from the same social background as religiously conservative citizens (the urban lower class and provincial middle class), piety became "very important in determining promotion prospects" (Caglar 2004: 357–61).[9]

But it was not just a matter of demography: the Gülen movement purposely infiltrated the police just around the time the force was expanding (Tugal 2002: 94). By the end of the 1990s, Islamists had turned the security apparatus into one of their "strongholds," and those who held top security positions recruited and encouraged likeminded Muslims. It was, in fact, reported that 700 of the 1,600 senior police chiefs were affiliated with Islamist parties, and that this explains why they were "zealous in suppressing unauthorized demonstrations by leftists and trade unionists, yet remarkably friendly to the unauthorized massive Islamist demonstrations" (Zubaida 1996: 12).

By the time AKP came to power, Islamists had succeeded in turning police officers into avowed supporters of the new ruling party (Tugal 2007: 5). AKP then used its leverage over the police force to improve the police's public image, and therefore the Party's own popularity. With Erdogan's trusted interior minister (Idris Naim Sahin), the police "engaged in 'proactive policing' and increased its surveillance capacity" in order to achieve security on the street without having to resort to repression (Berksoy 2010: 137). According to Amnesty International, police torture and other abuses decreased significantly after the AKP took power (Tugal 2007: 30). Other forms of state repression were done away with: state security courts were eliminated, the martial law declared in the Kurdish areas since 1987 was lifted, and the death penalty was abolished (Anderson 2009: 449).

AKP then turned the magic on the magician, and charged the police with investigating military officers. In 2006 the police announced it had found "secret official files" in the homes of recently retired army officers, detailing plans to destabilize AKP rule through random acts of violence and black propaganda. The files were then leaked to the public by the Gülen-connected newspaper *Zaman* (Dagi 2008: 55). In response, pro-military press accused "conservative religious elements in the police" of fabricating these secret files to implicate army officers. The ensuing drama revealed the depth of the "hitherto covert conflict between the military and the police" (Tugal 2007: 30). More importantly, it set the stage for an overdue confrontation between Islamists and officers.

Subordinating the Military

On the eve of AKP's rise to power, in 2002, opinion polls showed that the military was the most trusted institution in Turkey. The most recent poll, in 2011, was not as flattering: the percentage of citizens who still regarded the military in that way declined during that relatively short period from 90 percent to 60 percent (Tuysuz and Tavernise 2011: 5). It was therefore prudent of Islamists to avert an early clash with officers. As it worked tirelessly to consolidate power, AKP did not object to military operations against the Kurds, and readily deferred to generals in matters of national security. Erdogan also developed cordial relations with the "more liberal wing of the military," represented by Hilmi Özkök, who was chief of staff until 2006 (Tugal 2007: 27; Dagi 2008: 48).[10] Slowly but surely, however, AKP began curbing the military's political influence. In August 2003 the powers of the MGK were reduced: civilian members outnumbered generals with the addition of the ministers of finance and justice, and a representative of the Human Rights Coordinating High Council; MGK's secretary-general became a civilian; the council was no longer allowed to communicate with government departments directly to follow up on its decisions; and its meetings were now convened bimonthly rather than monthly. Taken together, these changes effectively recast MGK—the military's main mechanism for influencing politics—into a merely consultative body (Güney 2002: 174; Uzgel 2003: 192). AKP also cut the defense budget. In the decade before it came to power, the defense budget had increased steadily from $10 million to $16.4 million. By contrast, in the first four years of AKP rule, the budget shrunk back to $10.3 million. So although the Turkish economy was growing on an exceptional scale, "military expenditure declined substantially" (Wahid 2009: 84–85).

At the end of 2004, army officers reportedly contemplated a coup, but since the domestic and international situation did not allow for one, they needed a considerable amount of instability to justify a military intervention—even if they had to create it (Dagi 2008: 45).[11] In 2005 a series of bombs claimed the lives of several people in poor Kurdish towns, and police investigations implicated military officers. This was the beginning of what was later revealed to be an organized campaign of assassinations and random acts of political violence meant to embarrass AKP.[12] The general suspected of masterminding this terror campaign was the army's second-in-command, Yasar Büyükanıt. Erdogan asked the public prosecutor to take action against all those involved regardless of their status, but at the end the general was acquitted and two low-ranking officers assumed responsibility and were sentenced to prison. And in defiance of Erdogan, the high command insisted on appointing the suspect general, Büyükanıt, as chief of staff in 2006. Also, at the military's behest, Turkey's public prosecutor filed a lawsuit, in 2007, before the Supreme Court demanding AKP's dissolution on the grounds that it undermined the secular principles of the republic, but the case was dismissed for lack of evidence (Tugal 2007: 29–30).

AKP then announced it had uncovered another coup plot and put its protagonists on trial. The ruling party claimed that senior officers created a secret cabal, called Ergenekon (the mythical homeland of the Turkish nation), to destabilize the country and pave the way for military dictatorship (Dagi 2008: 5). This was followed with accusations that in 2008 an e-memorandum issued by a group calling itself the "Young Officers" expressed hostile intentions against AKP for colluding with Washington and Brussels to undermine the Turkish military (Dagi 2008: 48). The biggest revelation, however, made it to the headlines in January 2010. The liberal newspaper *Taraf* published documents exposing so-called Operation Sledgehammer (Bayloz Harekâtı) in which high-ranking officers, led by the then retired Chief of Staff Çetin

Dogan, had supposedly planned, back in 2003, to bomb mosques to create enough chaos to justify a coup. Arrests followed, and in a few months some 300 officers (including generals and admirals) were handed prison sentences. And to cover his back, Erdogan introduced constitutional amendments, in September 2010, that increased governmental appointees to the higher courts and the public prosecution office.

Belatedly, the general command decided to take a formal stance against the AKP. In the summer of 2011, Chief of Staff Isik Kosaner and the service chiefs submitted their resignations in protest of the prosecution of military personnel, including sixty generals, since AKP took power, on trumped up charges (Dombey 2012: 1). Yet in less than a week, AKP succeeded in appointing a new general command, headed by former commander of the military police (General Necdet Ozel), thus "decisively strengthening its control over its armed forces" (Arsu 2011: 3). For the first time, it was the prime minister who sat at the head of the table in the supreme military council's meetings. Observers agreed that the resignations and the ease with which AKP installed a new military leadership signaled that coups had become a remote possibility, even if the interests of the armed forces were at stake. As the outgoing chief of staff complained, the government had succeeded in creating the general impression that the Turkish army was "a criminal organization," and that he had regretfully failed to protect his men (Tuysuz and Tavernise 2011: 5).

Next, the unthinkable happened. In April 2012 AKP moved from defense to offense, prosecuting the two surviving generals of the five-member high command that carried out the 1980 coup. Kenan Evren (94 years old), former president and chief of staff, and Tahsin Sahinkaya (86 years old), former air force commander, were tried and found guilty for staging an extralegal takeover of power, even though neither could make it to the courtroom because of their poor health. The invincible Evren was demoted to the rank of private and sentenced to life imprisonment. He died a year later. The government's prosecutors followed through with a series of charges against the surviving leaders of past military coups. In May 2012 a Turkish court sentenced five generals, including the former head of the MGK, and the former heads of the army and the air force, to prison for staging the 1997 soft coup, and more than thirty officers have been held on that charge. Afterward, the recently retired (2008–2010) chief of staff, General Ilker Basbug, was arrested for leading a subversive organization aiming to spread chaos as a pretext to overthrow the government. In his court appearance, the embittered general commented: "Accusing the chief of the general staff of setting up an armed terrorist organization is the greatest punishment that could be given to me"

(Arsu 2011: 3). And in a sign of protest, as well as an indication of the waning prestige of the army, the Defense Ministry announced that between 2009 and 2013, an estimated 13, 751 officers and noncommissed officers (NCOs) had resigned their posts, and another 976 military administrators declined to renew their contracts.[13] The disgruntlement of officers was captured in a rare survey that indicated that 79 percent were unhappy with the way the army was being treated; 87 percent were pessimistic about the future of the armed forces; 95 percent disapproved of their offspring joining the ranks; and 100 percent thought they were not getting the respect they deserved from society (Gurcan 2015).

Finally, in the summer of 2013, Parliament amended the legal role of the army from guardian of the Turkish Republic to protector from foreign aggression. Prominent Turkish essayist Sahin Alpay hailed this "great achievement for Turkish democracy," and predicted that this mind-bending shift in civil–military relations meant that coups in Turkey were about to "take their place in the dustbin of history" (2012: 1). Former military officer Atilla Sandikli commented, "From now on, I believe that the army would not be able to dismiss any civilian authority" (Arsu 2011: 3). And Asli Aydintasbas, the Turkish columnist in the widely circulated daily *Milliyet*, concluded dramatically, "This is effectively the end of the military's role in Turkish democracy. This is the symbolic moment where the first Turkish republic ends and the second republic begins" (Tuysuz and Tavernise 2011: 5). Soon, however, the plot thickened.

The Great Unraveling

Trouble was simmering under the surface, and broke out in the tumultuous summer of 2013. A few months before, the government had authorized the building of a shopping mall with a façade replicating Ottoman-era barracks on Gezi Park, the tiny green patch abutting Taksim Square, Istanbul's secular cultural center. The project symbolized several ominous developments. Economically, it represented the hegemony of the new construction and commercial magnates who had made their fortunes under AKP rule. Culturally, there was the imposition of something so Ottoman-like at the urban hinterland of secular nationalist Turkey. Politically, how the decision was made reflected Erdogan's creeping authoritarianism: when a committee of urban planners rejected the destruction of the existing park, he simply replaced the committee with one composed of bureaucratic cronies (Hansen 2014). So on May 27, 2013, some fifty activists camped in the park to prevent the bulldozers from running over it. A couple of days later, the police assaulted their overnight vigil, burning tents and attacking the occupiers with tear gas and pepper spray. Repression had the opposite effect. By May 31 the few dozen protesters snowballed to hundreds of thousands; barricades were set up; and demonstrations spread to seventy other Turkish cities. In a belated attempt at damage control, Istanbul's administrative court suspended the building project. But although the park was saved, during the first ten days of June, an estimated 1.5 million Istanbul residents (some 16 percent of the city's population) participated in the demonstrations and the occupation of the park. And the police only resumed control on June 11 after violent street clashes (Yörük and Yüksel 2014).

The Gezi Park protest soon assumed its place on the honors list of new popular struggles, alongside Egypt and Tunisia, Greece and Spain, New York and Hong Kong. Like them, the nineteen-day protest was utterly leaderless; it relied on social media to mobilize supporters and popularize its cause globally; and it represented the high water mark in a cycle of protests.[14] There were also similarities in terms of class composition. Around 74 percent of the Gezi protesters were members of the working class (54 percent blue-collar laborers and 20 percent white-collar employees), though their rate of participation was low, well below 20 percent. The rest hailed from the new middle class (professionals, executives, small and medium capitalists), with a high rate of participation, of around 45 percent, which naturally made them more visible. In other words, they were not strictly united by class politics, but rather by a "popular movement driven by political demands, in which all social classes participated proportionally.... [T]he main target was not capital and its owners, but the Erdogan government." In fact, the participants were almost all political oppositionists: 80 percent were CHP voters, and another 10 percent voted for Kurdish parties (Yörük and Yüksel 2014).

As dramatic as the Gezi protests were, they proved to be the least of AKP's troubles. Despite police brutality, only one protester died of injuries; AKP won the municipal elections of March 2014, and five months later Erdogan became the first president elected by popular vote with a majority of 52 percent, and his loyal foreign minister, Ahmet Davutoglu, was installed in the premiership and chairmanship of the party without fuss. The real danger was the collapse of its unofficial alliance with the Gülen movement. It was like when "two pilots who are flying an airplane together start punching each other in the cockpit" (De Bellaigue 2014). The two political partners were suddenly embroiled in "an all out war." After their joint success in taming the Kemalist state and its military guardians, "the fight over the spoils became much more intense" (Tugal 2013). It is true that they had several disagreements along the way. The nationalist–Islamist synthesis at the heart of their ideological platform could not obscure the fact that the Gülenists were more wedded to nationalism, and the Erdoganists to Islamism. As such, the former resented the latter's tolerance of Kurdish autonomy demands and growing hostility toward Israel, and the latter accused the former of being too soft on militarism and pigheadedly opposed to active involvement in Middle East politics. Ultimately, however, they were both victims of their own success; they both believed the time was ripe to make their bid for absolute power.

AKP dealt the first blow. In the summer of 2011, dozens of Gülenists were removed from the Party's electoral lists and the bureaucracy. The response came in February 2012 when the Gülenist prosecutor general (Celal Kara) subpoenaed Hakan Fidan, Turkey's spy chief and Erdogan's confidant, for secretly negotiating with Kurds in Oslo since 2009, thus exposing and embarrassing the government. The Gülen-affiliated media went further by celebrating and lionizing the Gezi Park protests in the summer of 2013. Weeks later, AKP announced it was forcing Gülen-operated schools to either shut down or submit to government monitoring by September 2015. The bill threated some 350 college-exam preparation schools (*dershanes*), a main source of recruitment and a multimillion-dollar industry (De Bellaigue 2014; Hansen 2014).

Gülenists upped the ante, unleashing their mighty network of police officers and prosecutors.[15] On December 17, 2013, the police raided the houses of fifty suspects in bribery and graft cases, including the sons of three cabinet ministers (interior, economics, environment and city planning), the head of the state-owned Halkbank, and three AKP-affiliated construction tycoons. There were calls for Erdogan to resign. Instead, the wily prime minister convinced the implicated ministers to resign, then openly declared war against Gülen's "parallel state": the public prosecutor in charge of the investigation was reassigned; the policemen who led the raids were arrested; a witch-hunt targeting reporters and media executives in Gülen flagships began; an extradition order against Gülen was filed; and eventually, some 40,000 civil servants, judges, and policemen were either dismissed or relocated (Karaveli 2014). The government also orchestrated a run on deposits in the Gülenist Bank Asya, depleting its holdings by 46 percent between December and February, in hopes of crippling the movement's finances. Then, on February 15, Parliament passed legislation tightening government control of the judiciary, after a heated twenty-hour session that ended—amusingly—with a fistfight. Bloodied but refusing to bow down, Gülenist media outlets hinted that the police had several dossiers and tapes (including sex tapes) incriminating AKP officials, and leaked a tape, on February 24, of Erdogan instructing his son Bilal on how to dispose of $37 million. Two million people heard the conversation on the very day it was uploaded on YouTube (Tugal 2013; De Bellaigue 2014). In a swift response, the government drafted a new law that expanded the power of the intelligence service (MIT) over the police. And when Erdogan's trusted National Intelligence Agency (Milli Istihbarat Teskilati, MIT) chief, Hakan Fidan, resigned his post to run for Parliament, in February 2015, the embattled leader forced him to withdraw his resignation days later.

After years of silence, the elusive Fethullah Gülen himself penned an op-ed in the *Financial Times* warning Turks that "a small group within the government's executive is holding to ransom the entire country's progress," and explaining the goals and limits of his past partnership with AKP: "After decades of coups and political dysfunction, the ruling AK party's attempt to end military interference in domestic politics was necessary. . . . But the dominance in politics that was once enjoyed by the military now appears to have been replaced by a hegemony of the executive. A dark shadow has been cast over the achievements of the past decade" (Gülen 2014). Indeed, faced with extreme adversity, Gülenists appealed indirectly to the military. In June 2014 suspects in the Sledgehammer coup plot were released pending retrial, and then acquitted in March 2015, on the eve of the watershed national elections.

As the elections drew near, the economy showed signs of cooling down. AKP's first decade in power had generated breakneck expansion. Between 2002 and 2012, the economy grew by 230 percent to become the world's 17th largest economy, with an average yearly growth rate of 5.2 percent. Inflation fell from 30 percent to 7 percent, and the budget deficit from 10.2 percent to 2.8 percent of GDP during the same period (Çarkoglu 2014). In the next three years, the indicators were much less encouraging. GDP grew at a little over 3 percent in 2015, down from 8.8 percent in 2011; unemployment stood at its highest level in five years, at 11.3 percent; and the Turkish Lira lost perhaps 30 percent of its value. The immediate cause seemed to be excessive dependence on foreign trade, which suffered as a result of the economic turmoil in Europe and the Middle East, Turkey's main trade partners. But the downturn might have been a symptom of a larger structural distortion. AKP's neoliberal policies channeled wealth to upper-middle-class entrepreneurs at a much faster pace than it could provide welfare relief to the growing sector of casual laborers, now composing 55 percent of the workforce (Yörük and Yüksel 2014). More dangerous still, AKP had transformed Anatolia's middling merchants and manufacturers into giant capitalists, who now exacted a higher price in return for their continued support. The government's notorious urban renewal projects, such as the Gezi Park mall, were just one example (Tugal 2014). Another was Erdogan's persistent meddling in the economy on behalf of Turkey's new fat cats; notably, harassing the banking sector to cut back interest rates, and denouncing those who disagreed (including the governor of the central bank) as agents of foreign governments and their "interest rate lobby" in Turkey—a rhetorical ruse invoking the memory of the Western speculators who supposedly wrecked the finances of the Ottoman Empire (Akkoc 2015).

Perhaps less worrying to average citizens than the economy, but still problematic enough to be held against AKP in the elections, was its perceivably reckless geopolitics. After a decade of receiving praise for reestablishing Turkey's role as regional leader, AKP's policies starting in 2011 had proved to be too adventurous. Erdogan had gambled and lost. He believed his ironclad support for revolutionaries in Egypt and Syria would create two grateful allies. Instead, his Islamist comrades in Cairo were violently overthrown, and his old friends-turned-enemies in Damascus preferred to see the country burn than surrender power. So rather than emerging as the patron saint of new Islamist democracies in the Middle East, the Turkish president had antagonized the largest Arab country, and brought war and terrorism to his 900-kilometer border with Syria. Moreover, his failure to control the stream of Islamist militants to Syria and Iraq had tested the patience of his Western allies to the limit.

Problems with Washington have been even worse. Tactical differences gave way to a serious strategic conflict on how to reorganize the Middle East. The first signs of disagreement arose when Ankara denied the Bush administration the right to use Turkish territory in its 2003 Iraq War (though Erdogan himself did not mind). American soldiers responded by arresting Turkish military personnel in northern Iraq and interrogating them for three days before releasing them. This incident exposed the increasing tension between the two allies regarding Kurds. AKP asked the U.S. Army to prevent Kurdish militants from using Iraqi territories to launch attacks against Turkey, but Washington was too preoccupied with the Sunni insurgency to act on this request. In return, AKP later ignored American pleas to convince Damascus to halt the passage of Sunni insurgents to Iraq. Erdogan's surprisingly combative rhetoric against Israel did not help. His newfound affection toward the Palestinians further emboldened Hamas and infuriated Congress. Barack Obama's election and his 2009 address to the Turkish Parliament promised to turn a new page in the troubled relationship. But although Obama pledged to negotiate a deal with Iran (and eventually did), Ankara tried to force his hand. It voted against additional sanctions on Tehran and joined an initiative with Iran and Brazil to end the sanctions. However, the greatest crisis in Turkish-American relations occurred in Syria. After its decade-long alliance with Damascus and Tehran, the AKP government took an astonishingly radical stance against the rulers of Syria and their Iranian defenders once the Syrian rebellion began—so radical that they pressured Washington to topple the Assad regime by force on behalf of the Syrian rebels. As the conflict spiraled out of control, with a massive influx of Syrian refugees to Turkey and devastating terrorist attacks on its border towns, Erdogan blamed the hesitant Obama for his woes, especially after he personally beseeched the U.S. president to act during their meeting in Washington in May 2013. America's refusal to condemn the Egyptian military's overthrow of the Muslim Brotherhood president in Cairo convinced Erdogan that Turkey and America are on the opposite sides of history: one backing democratic transformation, and the other yearning for the safety of authoritarian rule. Conflicting approaches to the 2014 rise of Daesh, the militant make-believe caliphate in Iraq and Syria, accentuated this difference. Ankara insisted that only the creation of (preferably Islamist) democratic regimes could eliminate the root cause of Islamist militancy. Washington sought an immediate and pragmatic solution in the form of propping up strong (albeit authoritarian) regimes to eradicate militants, and blamed Turkey for stoking the flames of unrest (Kanat 2015b).

Compounding AKP's domestic and geopolitical difficulties is the problem of Erdogan himself. Even for one of the region's most successful politicians, Erdogan's megalomania seems excessive. When elected president, he installed himself in a specially built billion-dollar White Palace (Ak Saray) in the forests of Ankara—now the world's largest residential palace with 1,000 rooms built on an estate four times the size of Versailles. On the eve of the elections, he had his face emblazoned next to the prime minister's on a 4709-square-meter poster, which eventually entered the Guinness World Records as the largest-ever poster. Other monumental images of his characteristic face appear everywhere, on freeway billboards, on residential buildings, in all sorts of public transit vehicles—all showing him in "purposeful motion, like an action hero ... [an] evocation of 1930s-era masculinity" (Hansen 2014). He had also become markedly irritable: lashing out at journalists and media outlets by name; denouncing imaginary foes in increasingly long and fiery speeches; and banning Twitter and YouTube whenever his paranoia gets the best of him. Riding roughshod over his own party, Erdogan pushed aside Abdullah Gül, his longtime friend and very successful president, and secured the premiership and AKP chairmanship for his devoted foreign minister, Ahmet Davutoglu, after informally conferring with Party cadres (rather than risk a Party election), only to dismiss him unceremoniously, in May 2016, for being too independent. He then placed his son-in-law (Berat Albayrak), known associates, and media sycophants on the Party's electoral list and eventually in cabinet. Furthermore, he snubbed the existing constitution, which raises the president above the political fray, by interfering in everyday governance and campaigning personally to amend the Constitution. All this alienated voters during the summer of 2015, especially after he declared his intention to win a parliamentary majority to revamp the Turkish political system by turning its ceremonial presidency into an all-powerful imperial presidency with him as a second founder, an Islamist Kemal, a fountainhead of a new hegemonic ideology: Erdoganism (Akyol 2015). It is no small wonder that Turks initially shrunk from providing him with the majority he demanded in the national elections held in June 2015.

With 41 percent of the vote, AKP failed to secure an outright majority and lost its thirteen-year-long hold on Parliament, and with it the chance to amend the constitution to Erdogan's liking. The Party lost 9 percent of its 2011 supporters, an estimated 2.7 million voters. And considering that the president treated the election as a referendum on his new vision for Turkey, he seemed to come off worse than his party, losing 11 percent of his past supporters in the August 2014 presidency. A closer look at the election results reveals the curious fact that AKP lost most of its seats to parties from opposite ends of the political spectrum, and for the same reason: the Kurdish question. Erdogan's much-publicized Kurdish Opening negotiations antagonized both Turkish nationalists and Kurds. The nationalists turned to the right to preempt any future deal between Turkey's Islamists and Kurds, thus pushing the ultra-nationalist MHP to third place with 17 percent of the vote, while the Kurds turned away from AKP in frustration with its stalling tactics, and voted for a left-wing newcomer, the People's Democratic Party (Halkların Demokratik Partisi, HDP), raising it above the 10 percent voting threshold necessary to enter Parliament (Tanchum 2015).

With 12.5 percent of the vote, HDP was arguably the biggest winner in the June 2015 elections. This Kurdish party, founded only in 2012, successfully presented itself as a progressive "rainbow coalition" of ethnic and religious minorities, as well as representative of the feminist and LGBT communities (its electoral list showed a 50 percent quota for women, and another 10 percent for LGBT candidates). Its youthful and combative leader Selahattin Demirtas had symbolically challenged Erdogan for the presidency a few months earlier, and received 10 percent of the vote. Sensing the public mood, the HDP campaigned directly against the president, and offered itself as the focal point of resistance against Erdogan's unbridled authority. As such, its voters came form all sorts of backgrounds: Islamists affiliated with the Gülen movement, Kemalists frustrated with the CHP's limitations; leftists fueled with optimism by the Gezi protests; all those persecuted on sectarian or gender grounds, including, of course, Kurds.

It is therefore clear that both MHP's increased clout and HDP's symbolic victory were largely reflections of Erdogan's failure to settle the Kurdish issue. The secret AKP-Kurdish negotiations in Oslo in 2009 had collapsed shortly after they started, as a result of the Gülenists' exposure of them. And a military enraged by AKP's treachery made 2012 one of the bloodiest year since its war on the Kurds began. AKP tried again in the spring of 2013, sending emissaries to jailed PKK leader Abduallah Öcalan. But the government's passivity—some say complicity—during the militant Islamists' attacks on Kurdish villages in Syria and Iraq (most famously, the village of Kobani at the end of 2104) alienated Turkish Kurds. The nationalist MHP seized the opportunity to campaign against the rising militancy of Kurds on Turkey's southern border, and found favor with those loath to negotiating with Kurds from a position of weakness. Meanwhile, the HDP promised an alternative route to Kurdish emancipation, that is, through a democratic parliamentary struggle, rather than shabby political deals. Either way, the hope elicited by AKP's electoral stumble drove one Turkish political scientist to declare exuberantly: "Erdogan's new Turkey has lost, and the new Turkey of Gezi Park has won" (Letsch 2015). This was clearly an exaggeration. AKP's reversal was relative, limited, and—as it turned out—temporary.

Rather than accepting loss, and learning to conduct himself more modestly, the ever-defiant Erdogan gambled his political future—and won. The president bungled his party's attempt to negotiate a coalition government by refusing to concede key ministries and demanding a retraction of corruption charges against his family and supporters. When his crippling conditions were rejected, Erdogan called a snap election in four months, in November 2015. If AKP had ended up losing more votes, there is little doubt that the Party would have ostracized its power-hungry president. But in the election, AKP was in for a stunning comeback. With an exceptionally high turnout, over 85 percent of registered voters, Erdogan's party regained its majority, with 49.4 percent of the vote, only 13 parliamentarians short of the supermajority required to amend the constitution. This 8.5 percent increase in its share of the vote meant that AKP attracted an additional 4.5 million voters in just four months. And a district-by-district analysis shows that these extra votes came from all across the country. Mustafa Kemal's old CHP remained in second place with a quarter of the vote, largely the same percentage as recorded in June. But both MHP and HDP came off worse: the former shed half of its seats and fell to 11.9 percent, and the latter lost a quarter of its seats, barely making it back to Parliament with 10.6 percent (Kanat 2015a).

How could we explain this quick reversal? To start with, the president ended talks with the Kurdish PKK and adopted a hard-line nationalist line that brought back right-wing voters. At the same time, the street activism of an HDP emboldened by its summer victory frightened its left-of-center supporters. Perhaps most important were two suspiciously timed terror attacks, the first bombing killed 34 people and injured 100 in Suruç on the Syrian-Turkish borders in July, barely a month after the first election. The second was the deadliest bombing in Turkish history, killing 103 people and injuring 400 in the capital Ankara, just one month before the November election. Even those considerably wary of Erdogan's drive toward unbridled authority saw the need for a strong executive to stop this wave of violence in its track (Tanchum 2015)—though, of course, the bombings continued after AKP was returned to power.

An exuberant Erdogan now believed he had the mandate to rule unequivocally. And to the alarm of many, he began to turn increasingly to the security sector to repress opponents. Three months after his electoral victory, several television channels were closed, dozens of journalists were imprisoned or denied accreditation citing security concerns, and the bestselling daily *Zaman* was raided by the police and placed under the control of court-appointed trustees (Butler 2016). It is true that the results of the 2015 elections were a testament to the robustness of Turkish democracy, which despite meddlesome generals and highhanded politicians continues to revolve around the ballot box. Yet the ruling party's attempt to silence critics and sideline the military by empowering the security establishment might spell the doom of this still evolving democracy—as happened in Egypt under Nasser and his successors.

Conclusion

The early hegemony of the armed forces over the Turkish Republic proved to be a blessing in disguise. Because this hegemony implied the appropriation of domestic security duties, the security apparatus—usually the strongest advocate of authoritarianism—remained feeble and fragmented for decades. And because professional officers are naturally disinclined to handle everyday governance, they responded positively to internal and external pressures to allow multiparty politics. Finally, because the military was the most powerful player in the political system, it developed the confidence and the discipline to act as a united institution with a clear corporate agenda—it was neither subjugated and corrupted by autocratic rulers, nor penetrated by security agents. The military was the nation's guardian. But what did that mean exactly?

In contrast to the common belief that the military has always intervened in Turkish politics in defense of Kemalism, the founding ideology of the republic, or secularism, in particular, a close historical analysis reveals that whenever the military acted, it did so mainly to defend its autonomy or the state's national security (as defined by the high command). And the reason why the military intervened so frequently in politics was because Turkey did, in fact, suffer from domestic instability and was often involved in high-stake geopolitical confrontations. On the one hand, separatist and radical political movements produced enough turmoil to force civilian politicians to summon the military to restore order on several occasions. And, on the other hand, the country's NATO-assigned role as a bulwark against Communism during the Cold War; its numerous armed confrontations with Greece over Cyprus and the islands of the Aegean; and the protracted confrontation with Kurdish militants in the south (especially after the collapse of Iraq)—all have combined to justify military intervention in politics from a national security viewpoint.

Unfortunately for officers, the price of turning away from routine governance and direct everyday administration was reallocating more and more power to those who were ready to shoulder this hefty burden: civilian politicians. After every intervention, Turkey's generals did their best to create a more stable political system so that they would not have to re-intervene in the future. The unintended consequence of their institutional reforms was the creation of stronger political parties. Predictably, these parties acquired the stamina and experience to beat the masters at their own game. Political leaders fine-tuned their ideologies to suit the temperament of Turkish society; formulated and re-formulated their socioeconomic programs several times to capture as much votes as possible; divided labor scrupulously with civil society groups; allied themselves to forceful class players; learned the ropes of international politics; and negotiated smartly with the military. The most developed version of Turkey's ruling political parties, the Justice and Development Party (Adalet ve Kalkınma Partisi, AKP), not only curbed the military's political influence, but also resolved to punish officers for their past sins—the hunter has become the hunted.

Is this trend reversible? Will the military somehow regain the upper hand and resume its guardianship role in Turkish politics? Perhaps. But if it did, it would be because of political failure, because the ruling party overshot the mark. If there is a present threat to Turkish democracy, it is the AKP's arrogance of power—an arrogance that has already begun to alienate considerable segments of the Party's broad consistency. Political jealousy is another source of threat. Constant failure to unseat AKP through the ballot box might tempt other political factions to (temporarily) betray democracy and rally around the armed forces in an attempt to undermine their mighty rival. Yet the clearest and most present danger is Erdogan's attempt to extend his authority by empowering the security sector to repress political opponents and counterbalance the military. This is the policy that transformed Egypt into a police state—and despite the considerable differences between the two, no country is immune to its dangers. The future of Turkish democracy thus remains uncertain. The only thing for sure is that overall military control over the Turkish regime in its formative years has allowed this democracy to evolve, albeit at a high cost for all involved.

Notes

1. The poem penned by Turkish nationalist Ziya Gökalp had religious overtones. It read: "The mosques are our barracks, the domes our helmets, the minarets our bayonets and the faithful our soldiers." Although it was approved by the Ministry of Education and taught at schools, the court deemed it as inciting religious hatred.

2. A third, radical group saw capitalism as inherently immoral, but it remained small and ineffective.

3. Curiously, he wanted to name it M-8 (with "M" for Muslim), but on Egypt's insistence changed it to D-8.

4. A representative of this school, Ali Bayramoglu, president of MÜSIAD, proclaimed that the only war between Muslims and Westerners is a "war of brand names" not a "war of civilizations," and that "capital cannot be classified as pious and irreligious. The objective of capital is making profit" (Tugal 2002: 100).

5. One should note that this "Turkish-Islamic synthesis," which had become a "textbook doctrine" by the late 1990s (Anderson 2009: 441), was not entirely new. Even before the birth of the republic, it was broadly perceived that "despite secularism, the older idea that Muslim equals Turk and non-Muslim equals non-Turk persisted" (Lewis 1952: 39). And in the 1960s, Colonel Alparslan Türkes, the leader of the Fascist MHP, promulgated similar ideas (Ahmad 1988: 760).

6. With regard to the military-Islamist showdown in 1997, for instance, he was quoted as saying: "The MGK is a constitutional institution. It is a part of the state.... In an enlightened era which has experienced democracy and secularism, it is impossible for the Turkish people to go back" (Aras and Caha 2003: 147).

7. The prime minister's theatrical outburst at the 2010 Davos summit during a discussion with the Israeli president can be seen in this light. On this occasion, the Turkish premier publicly denounced the Gaza blockade and the Israeli commandos' surprise night attack on the *Mavi Marmara*, the leading vessel in the Turkish aid flotilla, while it was still in international waters, killing nine Turkish citizens. Erdogan flew back to Ankara that night to a cheering crowd of tens of thousands of Turks, and thousands demonstrating in several Arab capitals in his support—a public relations coup de grace of the first order (Pope 2010: 7).

8. The United States had responded by banning the sale of Cobra attack helicopters to Ankara in 1974, and took similar punitive measures against Turkey whenever it renewed attacks against Greece and Cyprus (Uzgel 2003: 205).

9. A police survey in 2000 showed that 80 percent of police officers were the sons of workers, small tradesmen, merchants, and farmers, and 82 percent of them came from villages and small provincial towns. This in why despite the fact that 41 percent of arrests and prosecution against demonstrators between 1994 and 2000 occurred against Islamists, there is still a "widely-held perception that the police is more tolerant of religious groups" (Uysal 2010: 196–202).

10. Özkök's colleagues criticized him for being "too soft" on AKP, and blamed this on his long tenure as military attaché in Brussels, where he probably came under persistent pressure from EU governments (Dagi 2008: 48).

11. Sener Eruygur, an army general, was the main culprit, and after retirement he went on to head the Kemalist Thought Association (Atatürkçü Düşünce Derneği, ADD), a Turkish political think-tank (Dagi 2008: 49).

12. The weekly news magazine *Nokta* also revealed, in March 2007, that the military was profiling media personnel to decide which elements to employ in its propaganda campaign against AKP. The military responded not with a denial but rather by launching an investigation to discover who leaked these reports, raided the magazine's headquarters, closed it down, and confiscated its documents (Dagi 2008: 36–38).

13. Abd-Almajeed, Sayyed. 2013. "Al-jaish al-Turkey wal-ekhtenaq fei da'rat al-zel" (The Turkish army suffocating in the shadows), *Al-Ahram*, March 19, 2013.

14. Turkey witnessed 100 protests in December 2012; 150 in January; 200 in March; 250 in May; and 400 in June 2013 during and after Gezi (Yörük and Yüksel 2014).

15. For discussion of Gülenists' infiltration of the police force and other law-and-order bodies, see Letsch 2014, and Ahmet Sik's extensive study *The Imam's Army* (2011).

Bibliography

Abu-Rabi', Ibrahim (ed.). 2003. *Islam at the Crossroads: On the Life and Thought of Bediüzzaman Said Nursi*. Albany: State University of New York Press.

Ahmad, Feroz. 1988. "Islamic Reassertion in Turkey." *Third World Quarterly* 10 (2): 750–69.

Ahmad, Feroz. 1993. *The Making of Modern Turkey*. New York: Routledge.

Akkoc, Raziye. 2015. "How Turkey's Economy Went from Flying to Flagging?" *The Daily Telegraph*, May 30, 2015.

Aksin, Sina. 2007. *Turkey from Empire to Revolutionary Republic: The Emergence of the Turkish Nation from 1789 to Present*. New York: New York University Press.

Akyol, Mustafa. 2015. "Is 'Erdoganism' a Threat to Turkey's Islamism?" *Al-Monitor*, March 31, 2015.

Alpay, Sahin. 2012. "Settling Accounts with a Brutal Coup." *Today's Zaman*, April 9, 2012.

Altinay, Ayse Gül. 2004. *The Myth of the Military-Nation: Militarism, Gender, and Education in Turkey*. New York: Palgrave Macmillan.
Anderson, Perry. 2009. *The New Old World*. New York: Verso.
Aras, Bulent and Omer Caha. 2003. "Fethullah Gülen and His Liberal 'Turkish Islam' Movement." In *Revolutionaries and Reformers: Contemporary Islamist Movements in the Middle East*, edited by Barry Rubin, pp. 141–54. Albany: State University of New York Press.
Armstrong, H. C. 1933. *Gray Wolf: The Life of Kemal Atatürk*. New York: Capricorn Books.
Arsu, Sebnem. 2011. "With Four Names, Turkey Marks a New Era." *New York Times*, August 4, 2011.
Aydinli, Ersel. 2009. "A Paradigmatic Shift for the Turkish Generals and an End to the Coup Era in Turkey." *Middle East Studies* 63 (4): 581–96.
Bâli, Aslı. 2010. Interview with author. Los Angles, May 25, 2010.
Berkes, Niyazi. 1964. *The Development of Secularism in Turkey*. Montreal: McGill University Press.
Berksoy, Biriz. 2010. "The Police Organization in Turkey in the Post-1980 Period and the Re-construction of the Social Formation." In *Policing and Prisons in the Middle East: Formations of Coercion*, edited by Laleh Khalili and Jillian Schwedler, pp. 137–56. New York: Columbia University Press.
Besli, Hüseyin and Ömer Özbay. 2011. *Recep Tayyip Erdogan: Bir Liderin Dogusu* (Recep Tayyip Erdogan: Story of a Leader). Beirut: Arabic Scientific Publishers.
Bilici, Mucahit. 2006. "The Fethullah Gülen Movement and Its Politics of Representation in Turkey." *The Muslim World* 96: 1–20.
Brooks, Risa A. 2008. *Shaping Strategy: The Civil-Military Politics of Strategic Assessment*. Princeton, NJ: Princeton University Press.
Brown, James. 1988. "The Politics of Disengagement in Turkey: The Kemalist Tradition." In *The Decline of Military Regimes: The Civilian Influence*, edited by Constantine P. Danopoulos, pp. 131–46. Boulder, CO: Westview Press.
Butler, John. 2016. "Turkey's Climate of Fear." *The Spectator*, January 30, 2016.
Cagaptay, Soner. 2012. "The Empire Strikes Back." *New York Times*, January 14, 2012.
Caglar, Ali. 1994. "Recruitment, Occupational Consciousness and Professionalism in the Turkish Police." Unpublished diss., University of Surrey.
Caglar, Ali. 2004. "Recruitment in the Turkish Police." *Policing & Society* 14 (4): 348–64.
Çarkoglu, Ali. 2014. "Turkey Goes to the Ballot Box: 2014 Municipal Elections and Beyond." Turkey Project Policy Paper 3. Center on the United States and Europe at Brookings Institution, Washington, DC, March 2014.
Cizre, Umit. 2008. "The Justice and Development Party and the Military: Recreating the Past after Reforming It." In *Secular and Islamic Politics in Turkey: The Making of the Justice and Development Party*, edited by Umit Cizre, pp. 132–71. London: Routledge.
Dagi, Ihsan. 2008. *Turkey between Democracy and Militarism: Post-Kemalist Perspectives*. Istanbul: Orion.
Davutoglu, Ahmet. 2008. "Turkey's Foreign Policy Vision: An Assessment of 2007." *Insight Turkey* 10 (1): 77–96.
De Bellaigue, Christopher. 2014. "Turkey Goes Out of Control." *New York Review of Books*, April 3, 2014.

Dekmejian, Richard H. 1982. "Egypt and Turkey: The Military in the Background." In *Soldiers, Peasants, and Bureaucrats: Civil Military Relations in Communist and Modernizing Societies,* edited by Roman Kolkowicz and Andrzej Korbonski, pp. 28–52. London: Allen & Unwin.

Dodd, C. H. 1969. *Politics and Government in Turkey*. Manchester, UK: Manchester University Press.

Dombey, Daniel. 2012. "Turkey Arrests Ex-Army Chief on Charge of Leading a Terrorist Organization." *Financial Times,* January 7, 2012.

Dunn, John. 1972. *Modern Revolutions: An Introduction to the Analysis of a Political Phenomenon*. Cambridge, UK: Cambridge University Press.

Eren, Nuri. 1963. *Turkey Today and Tomorrow: An Experiment in Westernization*. New York: Praeger.

European Commission. 2011. *Turkey's 2011 Progress Report*. Brussels.

Fromkin, David. 1989. *A Peace to End All Peace: The Fall of the Ottoman Empire and the Creation of the Modern Middle East*. New York: Henry Holt.

Gülen, Fethullah. 2014. "Turkey Needs a New Constitution to Save Its Democracy." *Financial Times,* March 10, 2014.

Güney, Aylin. 2002. "The Military, Politics and Post-Cold War Dilemmas in Turkey." In *Political Armies: The Military and Nation Building in the Age of Democracy,* edited by Kees Koonings and Dirk Kruijt, pp. 162–78. New York: Zed Books.

Gurcan, Metin. 2015. "Opening the Black Box: A Research on Attitudinal Differences among the Officer Corps in the Turkish Military." Unpublished paper.

Gürsoy, Yaprak. 2011. "The Impact of EU-Driven Reforms on the Political Autonomy of the Turkish Military." *South European Society and Politics* 16 (2): 293–308.

Hansen, Suzy. 2014. "Whose Turkey Is It?" *New York Times Magazine,* February 5, 2014.

Harb, Imad K. 2002. "Military Disengagement and the Transition to Democracy in Egypt and Turkey." Unpublished diss., University of Utah.

Helal, Reda. 1999. *Al-Saif wa al-Helal. Turkiya min Ataturk ela Erbakan: Al-Sera' bein al-mu'assasa al-'askariya wa al-Islam al-siyassi* (The Sword and the Crescent. Turkey from Atatürk to Erbakan: The Struggle between the Military Institution and Political Islam). Cairo: Shorouk Books.

Heper, Metin. 2011. "Civil-Military Relations in Turkey: Towards a Liberal Model." *Turkish Studies Special Issue* 12 (2): 241–52.

Heper, Metin and Aylin Güney. 2000. "The Military and the Consolidation of Democracy: The Recent Turkish Experience." *Armed Forces & Society* 26 (4): 635–57.

Heper, Metin and Aylin Güney. 2004. "Civil-Military Relations, Political Islam, and Security: The Turkish Case." In *Civil-Military Relations, Nation-Building, and National Identity: Comparative Perspectives,* edited by Constantine P. Danopoulos, Dhirendra Vajpeyi, and Amir Bar-or, pp. 183–98. Westport, CT: Praeger.

Hopkirk, Peter. 1994. *Like Hidden Fire: The Plot to Bring Down the British Empire*. London: Kodansha International.

Kalaycioglu, Ersin. 2005. *Turkish Dynamics: Bridge Across Troubled Lands*. New York: Palgrave Macmillan.

Kanat, Kilic Burga. 2015a. "The November 2015 Elections in Turkey: Stability and Return to the Center." Foundation for Political, Economic and Social Research (SETA) Analysis, Washington, DC, November 2015.

Kanat, Kilic Bugra. 2015b. "Turkey and the U.S.: The Longest Two Years of the Relations." Foundation for Political, Economic and Social Research (SETA) Analysis, Washington, DC, June 2015.

Karaosmanglu, Ali. 2011. "Transformation of Turkey's Civil-Military Relation: Culture and International Environment." *Turkish Studies Special Issue* 12 (2): 253–64.

Karaveli, Halil. 2014. "Erdogan Loses It." *Foreign Affairs*, February 9, 2014.

Karpat, Kemal H. 1959. *Turkey's Politics: The Transition to a Multi-Party System*. Princeton, NJ: Princeton University Press.

Keyder, Çaglar. 1987. *State and Class in Turkey: A Study in Capitalist Development*. London: Verso.

Keyder, Çaglar. 2004. "The Turkish Bell Jar." *New Left Review* 28: 65–84.

Kili, Suna. 2003. "Role of the Military in Turkish Society: An Assessment from the Perspective of History, Sociology and Politics." In *Military Rule and Democratization: Changing Perspectives*, edited by Asha Gupta, pp. 145–83. New Delhi: Deep and Deep Publications.

Kinross, Lord. 1964. *Atatürk*. New York: William Morrow.

Kinross, Lord. 1977. *The Ottoman Centuries: The Rise and Fall of the Turkish Empire*. New York: William Morrow.

Lerner, Daniel P. 1964. *The Passing of Traditional Society: Modernizing the Middle East*. New York: Free Press.

Letsch, Constanze. 2014. "Turkish Police Caught in the Middle of War." *The Guardian*, February 9, 2014.

Letsch, Constanze. 2015. "Election Result Heralds a New Turkey." *The Guardian*, June 8, 2015.

Lewis, Bernard. 1952. "Revival in Turkey." *International Affairs* 28 (1): 38–48.

Lewis, Bernard. 1969. *The Emergence of Modern Turkey*. Oxford: Oxford University Press.

Mango, Andrew. 1999. *Ataturk: The Biography of the Founder of Modern Turkey*. New York: Overlook Press.

Mardin, Serif. 1989. *Religion and Social Change in Modern Turkey: The Case of Bediüzzaman Said Nursi*. Albany: State University of New York Press.

Murinson, Alexander. 2006. "The Strategic Depth Doctrine of Turkish Foreign Policy." *Middle East Studies* 42 (6): 945–64.

Narli, Nilufer. 2003. "The Rise of the Islamist Movement in Turkey." In *Revolutionaries and Reformers: Contemporary Islamist Movements in the Middle East*, edited by Barry Rubin, pp. 125–40. Albany: State University of New York Press.

Oguzlu, H. Tarik. 2003. "An Analysis of Turkey's Prospective Membership in the European Union from a 'Security' Perspective." *Security Dialogue* 34: 285–99.

Önis, Ziya. 1997. "The Political Economy of Islamic Resurgence in Turkey: The Rise of the Welfare Party in Perspective." *Third World Quarterly* 18 (4): 743–66.

Önis, Ziya. 2007. "Conservative Globalism at the Crossroads: The Justice and Development Party and the Thorny Path to Democratic Consolidation in Turkey." *Mediterranean Politics* 14 (1): 21–40.

Pope, Hugh. 2010. "Pax Ottomana? The Mixed Success of Turkey's New Foreign Policy." *Foreign Affairs*, vol. 89, no. 6 (November–December) 2010, pp. 1–9.

Przeworski, Adam. 1991. *Democracy and the Marker: Political and Economic Reforms in Eastern Europe and Latin America*. Cambridge, UK: Cambridge University Press.

Radwan, Walid. 2006. *Turkeya bein al-'Almaniya wa al-Islam fei al-Qarn al-'Eshrin* (Turkey between Secularism and Islam in the Twentieth Century). Beirut: Sharekat al-Matbu'at.

Roos, Leslie L. and Noralou P. Roos. 1971. *Managers of Modernization: Organizations and Elites in Turkey (1950–1969)*. Cambridge, MA: Harvard University Press.

Rumford, Chris. 2003. "Resisting Globalization? Turkey-EU Relations and Human and Political Rights in the Context of Cosmopolitan Democratization." *International Sociology* 18: 379–94.

Rustow, Dankwart A. 1959. "The Army and the Founding of the Turkish Republic." *World Politics* 11 (4): 513–52.

Sakallioglu, Ümit Cizre. 1997. "The Anatomy of the Turkish Military's Political Autonomy." *Comparative Politics* 29 (2): 151–66.

Sarigil, Zeki. 2011. "Civil-Military Relations beyond Dichotomy: With Special Reference to Turkey." *Special Issue: Civil-Military Relations in Turkey. Turkish Studies* 12 (2): 265–78.

Satana, Nil. 2011. "Civil-Military Relations in Europe, the Middle East and Turkey." *Turkish Studies* 12 (2): 279–92.

Shankland, David. 1999. *Islam and Society in Turkey*. Cambridge, UK: Eothen Press.

Shmuelevitz, Aryeh. 1999. *Republican Turkey: Aspects of Internal Affairs and International Relations*. Istanbul: Isis Press.

Sik, Ahmet. 2011. *The Imam's Army*. Istanbul: Postaci.

Sunar, Ilkay. 1974. *State and Society in the Politics of Turkey's Development*. Ankara: Ankara Üniversitesi Siyasal Bilgiler Fakültesi.

Tanchum, Michael. 2015. "Turkey's Rough Ride." *Foreign Affairs*, October 28, 2015.

Tatari, Eren. 2005. "Islamic Social and Political Movements in Turkey." *American Journal of Islamic Social Sciences* 24 (2): 94–106.

Trimberger, Ellen Kay. 1978. *Revolution from Above: Military Bureaucrats and Development in Japan, Turkey, Egypt, and Peru*. New Brunswick, NJ: Transaction Books.

Tugal, Cihan. 2002. "Islamism in Turkey: Beyond Instrument and Meaning." *Economy and Society* 31 (1): 85–111.

Tugal, Cihan. 2007. "NATO's Islamists: Hegemony and Americanization in Turkey." *New Left Review* 44: 5–34.

Tugal, Cihan. 2009a. *Passive Revolution: Absorbing the Islamic Challenge to Capitalism*. Stanford, CA: Stanford University Press.

Tugal, Cihan. 2009b. "Transforming Everyday Life: Islamism and Social Movement Theory." *Theory and Society* 38: 423–58.

Tugal, Cihan. 2013. "Towards the End of a Dream? The Erdogan-Gülen Fallout and Islamic Liberalism's Descent." *Jadaliyya*, December 22, 2013.

Tugal, Cihan. 2014. "Stillbirth: The New Liberal-Conservative Mobilization in Turkey." *Jadaliyya*, May 15, 2014.

Tughian, Sherif. 2011. *Recep Tayyip Erdogan: Mu'azen Istanbul wa muhatem al-sanam al-Ataturki* (Recep Tayyip Erdogan: The Preacher of Istanbul and the Destroyer of Atatürk's Idol). Damascus: Dar al-Ketab al-Arabi.

Turam, Berna. 2007. *Between Islam and the State: The Politics of Engagement*. Stanford, CA: Stanford University Press.

Tuysuz, Gul and Sabrina Tavernise. 2011. "Top Generals Quit in Group, Stunning Turks." *New York Times*, July 30, 2011.

Uysal, Aysen. 2010. "Riot Police and Policing Protest in Turkey." In *Policing and Prisons in the Middle East: Formations of Coercion*, edited by Laleh Khalili and Jillian Schwedler, pp. 191–206. New York: Columbia University Press.

Uzgel, Ilhan. 2003. "Between Praetorianism and Democracy: The Role of the Military in Turkish Foreign Policy." *Turkish Yearbook* 34: 177–211.

Wahid, Latif. 2009. *Military Expenditure and Economic Growth in the Middle East*. New York: Palgrave Macmillan.

Walt, Stephen M. 1996. *Revolution and War*. Ithaca, NY: Cornell University Press.

Ward, Barbara. 1942. *Turkey*. Oxford: Oxford University Press.

Weiker, William F. 1963. *The Turkish Revolution, 1960–1961: Aspects of Military Politics*. Washington, DC: Brookings Institute.

White, Jenny B. 2002. *Islamist Mobilization in Turkey: A Study in Vernacular Politics*. Seattle: University of Washington Press.

Yavuz, Hakan. 1999. "Towards an Islamic Liberalism? The Nurcu Movement and Fethullah Gülen." *Middle East Journal* 53 (4): 584–605.

Yavuz, Hakan. 2003. *Islamic Political Identity in Turkey*. New York: Oxford University Press.

Yavuz, Hakan (ed.). 2006. *The Emergence of a New Turkey: Democracy and the AK Parti*. Salt Lake City: University of Utah Press.

Yavuz, Hakan. 2010. Interview with author. San Diego, November 19, 2010.

Yavuz, Hakan and John Esposito (eds.). 2003. *Turkish Islam and the Secular State: The Gülen Movement*. Syracuse, NY: Syracuse University Press.

Yılmaz, Hakan. 1997. "Democratization from Above in Response to the International Context: Turkey, 1945–1950." *New Perspectives on Turkey* 17: 1–38.

Yılmaz, Hakan. 2002. "External-Internal Linkages in Democratization: Developing an Open Model of Democratic Change." *Democratization* 9 (2): 67–84.

Yılmaz, Hakan. 2008. "The Kemalist Revolution and the Foundation of the One-Party Regime in Turkey: A Political Analysis." In in *Ergun Özbudun'a Armagan, Cilt I, Siyaset Bilimi*, edited by Serap Yazıcı, Kemal Gözler, and Fuat Keyman, pp. 535–64. Ankara: Yetkin Yayınevi,.

Yılmaz, Hakan. 2009. Interview with author. Istanbul, August 3, 2009.

Yörük, Erdem and Murat Yüksel. 2014. "Class and Politics in Turkey's Gezi Protests." *New Left Review* 89 (September–October 2014).

Zubaida, Sami. 1996. "Turkish Islam and National Identity." *Middle East Report* 199: 10–15.

III | Egypt
THE POLITICS OF REPRESSION

One does not establish a dictatorship in order to safeguard a revolution; one makes the revolution in order to establish the dictatorship.

—*George Orwell, Nineteen Eighty-Four,* 1949

OBSESSION WITH THE MALICIOUS role of the military in Egyptian politics has resulted in a dogma that defies rational discussion. Country experts insist that the regime has maintained its military character from the time of Colonel Gamal Abd al-Nasser's coup in 1952 to General Abd al-Fattah al-Sisi's power seizure six decades later. In fact, some of the best studies of contemporary Egypt were devoted to documenting military hegemony over politics (Springborg 1989; Cook 2007; Droz-Vincent 2007). And recent additions to this growing literature extended the analysis to how generals manipulated and eventually crushed the 2011 revolt (Frisch 2013; Grawert and Abu al-Magd 2016). What underlies this claim is a belief that once an officer, always an officer. In other words, even if members of the armed forces moved on to become intelligence operatives, businessmen, bureaucrats, governors, ministers, or even presidents, they invariably retain a primal loyalty to their mother institution.

The strength of this dogma is evident by the fact that it has scarcely been challenged. Students of the Egyptian regime prefer to work around, rather than confront it. Most try to highlight political aspects of the regime, such as the presidency (Kassem 2004; Owen 2012); the political economy of regime maintenance (Mitchell 2002; Richter 2007; Blaydes 2011); and the role of opposition, whether Islamists (Mahmood 2005; Masoud 2014: Wickham 2015), workers (Beinin 2012; Alexander and Bassiouny 2014), or civil activists (Osman 2013; Abdelrahman 2014). Very few bother with the security sector, and those who do adopt a purely historical perspective (Khalili and Schwedler 2010; Sirrs 2010).

My analysis, by contrast, suggests that power relations between Egypt's military, security, and political institutions are far too volatile and complicated for any of them to singlehandedly direct the regime one way or another. The 1952 coup produced an internally differentiated regime whose components oscillated between cooperation and competition over the next few decades. The military dominated at first, but the overall trajectory was one whereby the political and security institutions gradually coalesced to sideline their third partner. By the 1970s, after a series of wars, conspiracies, coup plots, and socioeconomic transformations, the balance within this tripartite alliance tilted heavily toward the security apparatus, with the political leadership living contentedly in its shadow, and the military subordinated, if not totally marginalized. Egypt had metamorphosed into a police state—the type most difficult to change.

It is true that the regime had remained authoritarian throughout. But to appreciate important variations in the form and degree of authoritarianism, and, by the same token, missed opportunities for change, one must be able to identify the separate agendas of the key players, and trace their interactions over time. The 2011 revolt provides the latest example. The popular uprising was initially successful because it (inadvertently) disrupted the delicate balance between the ruling institutions. Had the revolutionaries consciously exploited these institutional tensions, they might have accomplished some of their goals. Similarly, the conflict-ridden partnership between military officers, security men, old regime networks, and their general-turned-president passes unnoticed in the course of denouncing the 2013 counter-revolution. Indeed, this false perception of a unified elite ruling under military tutelage is itself a constitutive element of regime resilience. Exposing its credulity is one of the main objectives of this part of the study.

12 | Militarism and Its Discontents

MARCH 1954

THE FREE OFFICERS WERE YOUNG military men who grew up in a country occupied by the British in 1882 under the pretext of protecting the Egyptian sovereign from his own army. The colonial power exploited Egypt's resources, manipulated monarchs and cabinets, and kept the army understaffed and unequipped. Parliamentarian politics, launched at earnest after Egypt was allowed a constitution in 1923, was little more than a cat-and-mouse game between the liberal Wafd (the majority party) and royalist parties supported by the young King Farouk—a perfect setting for British divide-and-rule tactics. Political futility was compounded with social disparities. Over half of Egypt's 21 million inhabited the countryside: 11 million were landless, while a mere 12,000 large and middling landowners (crowned by 147 families) controlled a third of arable land. Merchants had been fortunate because of the inflation caused by the American Civil War and the two world wars, but London dissuaded them from making the transition to industry. In the 1950s, manufacturing barely contributed 8 percent to the national income, and the country's 1.3 million wageworkers were mostly artisans. One might have expected the country's nascent industrialists to pray for a revolution from above to dislodge the landed class, repress popular radicalism, and end foreign domination. But most capitalists believed there was still time for reform. The proletariat was small and dispersed. Peasant revolts were unlikely because the Egyptian state (comparable to Russia in 1905, and unlike France in 1789) controlled the countryside. Like their Russian counterparts in 1917, Egyptian capitalists worried that a revolt against the landowning class might ultimately ruin them (Al-Rafe'i 1989: 61–63; Al-Bishri 2002: 79–80; Abdel-Malek 1968: 14, 39).

Yet the officer corps itself was becoming increasingly bourgeois. The gathering storms of Nazism persuaded the British to prepare a more functioning force for the dark days ahead. The sons of middling landowners, professionals, and merchants were men who could actually fight. On the eve of the Second World War, the army expanded from 3,000 to 100,000 men, and dropped back after the Second World War to the still high figure of 36,000 men (Al-Bishri 2002: 539–41). Many of the Free Officers belonged to the first group of middle-class youth who had entered the Military Academy in the late 1930s. They were ideologically eclectic: a few were Islamists; some were socialists or Fascists; many were liberal pragmatists; and the majority did not think beyond removing the corrupt rulers and returning to the barracks. All, however, were professionally demoralized for three reasons: humiliation at home and abroad; the transfer of control over military affairs from Parliament to the monarch; and their employment in domestic repression.

First, there was the debacle of February 4, 1942, when officers stationed around the royal palace watched helplessly as British tanks forced King Farouk at gunpoint to replace his Nazi-sympathetic cabinet with one led by the liberal Wafd. With bruised pride, 400 officers, including the Free Officers' leader, Lieutenant Colonel Gamal Abd al-Nasser, met three days later to formulate a response. A delegation, led by another Free Officer, Major Salah Salem, relayed to the monarch their willingness to target British troops, but his chamberlain cautioned them to back off (Aly 1994: 50). The whole incident turned them irrevocably against the cowardly king who obeyed foreign dictates, the opportunist majority party that accepted foreign tutelage, and of course the bullying British. In a letter to a school friend, Nasser bemoaned: "I am ashamed of our army's powerlessness" (Aburish 2004: 18–19). Major General Muhammad Naguib, who eventually spearheaded the Free Officers' coup, described how this bitter incident convinced him that a regime change was necessary (Naguib 1984: 66–67).

But as distressing as this episode had been, real disaster struck six years later. Dozens of officers volunteered to help prevent the wholesale dispossession of their Palestinian neighbors, but they were reluctant to engage the Zionists in a formal war. The military was unprepared, having last seen combat in 1882. King Farouk, however, wanted to regain his lost prestige by playing a leading role in Arab politics. He therefore vetoed his generals and sent his men to their doom. Military disgruntlement was such that between September and December 1948, 28 officers and 2,100 soldiers were arrested on the battlefield for mutiny (Heikal 2003: 407). Tragedy turned to scandal when the Egyptian press revealed that European governments offered royal courtiers substantial commissions to help them unload their defunct stockpiles from both world wars. To add insult to injury, Nasser was included in the delegation sent to Rhodes in February 1949 to negotiate the first Arab-Israeli truce, a political defeat no less humiliating than the military one. It was no coincidence that the Free Officers' first pamphlet, distributed in November 1949, was a condemnation of the Palestine catastrophe, and their first communiqué after the coup denounced those who had stabbed the army in the back (Ahmed 1993: 73). Again in a letter to his school friend, Nasser evocatively described how "soldiers were dashed against fortifications .... using defective arms which had been purchased by the king's cronies, a collection of petty crooks who profited from the war" (Aburish 2004: 24). Naguib, who was injured twice during the war, concluded that the real enemy resided in Cairo (Naguib 1984: 72). More disasters loomed as the king pressured his government, in 1950, for the right to name the war minister, chief of staff, and to install a confidant as commander-in-chief to oversee promotions. The list of incompetents he chose to lead the army included his diplomat brother-in-law, and a corrupt prison warden. His intention to place a malicious border patrol officer (who barely survived assassination by Nasser) at the head of the military was among the immediate triggers of the 1952 coup. In Naguib's words, the high command was becoming a gallery of arms dealers, land speculators, and criminals (Naguib 1984: 67).

The situation became intolerable when defeated officers came back to find thousands of their countrymen locked up. The court saw the war as a good opportunity to silence opposition, and ordered the army to join in repressing demonstrators, especially after the police proved unreliable—in October 1947, 7,000 police officers organized anti-government strikes, which continued intermittingly until 1952 (Al-Bishri 2002: 292–95). Adding fuel to the fire, the government abrogated the 1936 Anglo-Egyptian Treaty in October 1951. The treaty had legitimatized British presence around the Suez Canal, but now Britain had no legal cover. This placed the military in an awkward position. In their rhetoric, politicians encouraged citizens to attacks British installations, but then required the army to prevent them from doing so. Expectedly, British forces scourged villages that aided "terrorists." Officers petitioned the king to permit them to defend national sovereignty, but were ignored. The police stepped in. On January 25, 1952, some 7,000 British troops occupied the city of Ismailia against police resistance. In total, 50 police officers were killed and 80 injured. The occasion was marked as Police Day, and from then on January 25 was celebrated to honor police martyrs (the 2011 revolt was scheduled on that day to highlight the disparity between the police of yesteryear and that of today). The next morning, rioters set downtown Cairo on fire. The army was asked to restore order. Officers were becoming the henchmen of a regime that was losing legitimacy—as evidenced by the fact that four cabinets ruled in quick succession between January and July 1952 (Aly 1994: 63). Clearly, there was a power vacuum that no political force was ready to fill since all thought of power in terms of "the force of numbers, the force of the masses, and never the force of arms" (Botman 1988: 116).

Institutional grievances thus explain why the coup was endorsed by the armed forces, regardless of the motivations of the ringleaders. For scores of officers, the coup did not disrupt military discipline but reestablished it. The aim was to erect an independent civilian regime that would enhance military power. It was neither to assume political power nor preside over socioeconomic modernization. The rapid turnover of military juntas in Iraq (between 1936 and 1941) and Syria (between 1949 and 1951) was alarming enough. Nasser and his associates, however, thought otherwise. Captivated by the Turkish experience in the 1920s, they hoped the coup would usher in a transformative revolution from above. Herein lies the root of the struggle that would consume the country over the next months.

Opening the Floodgates

On July 23, 1952, eighty mid-ranking officers seized the leadership of the armed forces, arrested generals, and cashiered all brigadiers and lieutenant colonels who did not participate. Without his army, King Farouk was powerless. He abdicated and left for exile on August 2, and a republic was declared the following summer. A fourteen-member Revolutionary Command Council (RCC) took over. Though it included all branches, real power lay with the infantry, whose three representatives would shortly control the political, military, and security institutions. These were future President Gamal Abd al-Nasser; Abd al-Hakim Amer, soon-to-be army chief; and Zakaria Muhi al-Din, the architect of Egypt's new security apparatus. It was also infantry Captain Salah Nasr who coup-proofed the military. Nasr, the future intelligence czar, compiled a list of officers he considered security threats: 800 were purged; 2,700 were reassigned to administrative duties; 329 were placed under surveillance; and another 71 died in "accidents" between March and December 1953 (Nasr 1999a: 156, 186). The RCC also created the Republican Guard, in June 1953, which, according to its first chief Abd al-Muhsen Abu al-Nur, was charged with defending the rulers against the rest of the military (Abu al-Nur 2001: 34). Finally, conscription was introduced, in 1955, and noncommissioned officers (NCOs) were promoted to the corps, since large armies were more difficult to enlist in a coup. Firmly in control, the coup makers debated the future. The rift between those who wanted to return to the barracks and those who aspired to revolutionize society from above ran from the RCC downward. Those favoring withdrawal found support in General Naguib, the council's nominal leader, and Khaled Muhi al-Din, its most progressive member, in addition to the critical mass within artillery and cavalry, the professional-minded elite services. Advocates of continued rule organized around Nasser, the RCC's effective leader, and his infantry colleagues. The outcome of their two-year confrontation shaped the new regime.

Nasser articulated the position of those officers adamant to stay in power in his speech to factory workers, in December 1953: "[We] did not carry out this revolution to govern or lead.... [O]ne of our first goals was to restore genuine representative life ... but we were appalled by the bargains, demands, maneuvers, and deceit.... [W]e decided that this country should not be ruled by a class of political mercenaries" (Al-Rafe'i 1989: 53–54). This is what diffident officers, like Naguib, refused to understand. Nasser had sought the support of this decorated general because his junior co-conspirators were neither known to the public, nor held authority among apolitical officers. Knowing that figureheads usually develop an appetite for power, Nasser planted confidants in Naguib's entourage. He also held informal meetings with RCC members to coordinate their stances before convening under Naguib (Nasr 1999a: 226). Besides these containment tactics, Nasser built his grand strategy on three pillars: building an entrenched security force; replacing the existing power centers with a new political apparatus; and garnering geopolitical support.

The instinctively paranoid Nasser created a hydra-headed security community. He began with the interior ministry, which he personally led after the coup, before passing it to his security wizard, Zakaria Muhi al-Din, in October 1953. Relying on military associates, Muhi al-Din refashioned the police, purging 400 of its 3,000 officers (Sirrs 2010: 37). The Special Section, established by the British in 1911, was transformed into a first-class intelligence organ: the General Investigations Directorate (GID)—renamed in 1971: the State Security Investigations Sector (SSIS). The British-designed City Eye surveillance system, basically a network of informers, was enhanced. Detention centers were expanded, whether desert-located (Huckstepp, al-Tur, al-Wahat), or urban (Tura, Abu-Za'bal, al-Qanater). Again, the British had built these in the 1930s to intern as many as 4,000 oppositionists. Now, their capacity was stretched to 25,000 detainees, and during Nasser's eighteen-year rule, some 100,000 citizens passed through them (Gorman 2010: 158–69).

Combining his ministerial position with that of director of the Military Intelligence Department (MID), Muhi al-Din reoriented this agency as well toward internal political security, that is, spying on Egyptians not just foreign armies (Abu al-Fadl 2008: 87). He then used a handful of MID officers to create Egypt's first civilian intelligence agency: the General Intelligence Service (GIS), in December 1953. Muhi al-Din also converted a group of military captains into security agents to run Nasser's personal intelligence unit—soon to be known as the President's Bureau of Information (PBI). In short, Muhi al-Din built a "veritable pyramid of intelligence and security services . . . [whose] labyrinthine complexity and venality" became the mainstay of Egypt new political order (Vatikiotis 1978: 164–65).

Of course, foreign expertise was crucial. Americans provided a $1 million worth of surveillance and anti-riot equipment immediately after the coup. They also introduced a whole range of electronic equipment and techniques for bugging hotel rooms, army halls, homes, and automobiles (Copeland 1970: 82). Charles Cremeans, future head of the CIA's Office of National Intelligence Estimates, explained how to prepare intelligence estimates. But Nasser wanted more. In October 1952 he requested CIA training for his men. Soon, a troika of intelligence operatives arrived in Cairo. James Eichelberger, Miles Copeland, and Frank Kearn had all served in the U.S. Army Counter-Intelligence Corps, and later witnessed the transformation of the Office of Strategic Services (OSS) into the CIA. Their contact in Egypt was Captain Hassan al-Tuhami, another Nasser loyalist, who now administered an overseas training program. The CIA recruited instructors from the SS and Gestapo to lend a hand (Sirrs 2010: 32–34).[1] In April 1958 Egypt also signed a training agreement with the KGB, and a decade later with East Germany's Stasi (Nasr 1999a: 158).

If Muhi al-Din did Nasser's bidding in the security sector, Abd al-Hakim Amer was expected to do the same in the army. Nasser insisted that Naguib's first presidential decree, in June 1953, would be to promote Amer from major to major general, and appoint him commander-in-chief of the armed forces. Nasser preferred direct control from above to attaching political commissars to army units, as the Communists did. Amer was not only Nasser's best friend since college, but also the only RCC member whom Naguib trusted, since he had served as his chief of staff during the 1948 war. Naguib's press secretary Riyad Samy said the president would not have surrendered the army to anyone else (Samy 2004: 21). To control the army, Amer turned to the conspicuously labeled Office of the Commander-in-Chief for Political Guidance (OCC), another of Nasser's creations. Salah Nasr, the man who purged the military after the coup, headed the OCC and staffed it with Free

Officers. As a political watchdog, it ferreted out troublemakers and dispensed patronage, and did so mainly through a secret network of politically ambitious officers who did not participate in the coup but were eager to improve their prospects by securing it. By 1967 the members of this network exceeded 65,000 officers (McDermott 1988: 16).

Nasser also appreciated the importance of political mobilization. While Naguib rested on his sensational popularity, Nasser built concrete organizations. In November 1952 he unveiled a new Ministry for National Guidance, named his RCC colleague Salah Salem minister, and asked him to keep Naguib away from the limelight, and later to tarnish his reputation. Here too, Nasser relied on foreign expertise, notably Paul Linebarger, America's leading black propagandist; Leopold von Mildenstein, Joseph Goebbels's Middle East information director; and SS black propaganda expert Johannes von Leers (Sirrs 2010: 45). By January 1953 Nasser had replaced all existing political parties with a mass-based Liberation Rally, basically a platform for pro-regime demonstrations. Nasser was secretary-general, though he delegated power to Majors Ibrahim al-Tahawi and Ahmed Te'ima. The Rally's cannon fodder were enthusiastic students, as well as peasants and workers sent by their masters in hope of currying favor with the regime's strongman (Hafez 2010: 108–11).

The final component of Nasser's power strategy was to secure geopolitical support for his faction. The United States was the main candidate. Washington's Middle East policy was to encourage independence movements to curtail British and French hegemony, and then draw the new nations to its orbit through military and economic aid. In 1951 Secretary of State Dean Acheson had formed a special committee on the Arab world to search for "an Arab leader who would have more power in his hands than any other Arab leader ever had before, 'power to make an unpopular decision' . . . one who deeply desires to have power, and who desires to have it primarily for the mere sake of power" (Copeland 1970: 48–49). The sentiment was made explicit in a British Foreign Office memo, on December 3, 1951, which summarized the American-British view: "The only sort of Government with which we can hope to get an accommodation is a frankly authoritarian government . . . both ruthless and efficient. . . . We need another Mustafa Kemal. . . . Even though Egyptians are not Turks, and men like Mustafa Kemal cannot be ordered *à la carte*!" (Turner 2006: 96).

In February 1952 the CIA's Kermit Roosevelt traveled to Cairo to find an Egyptian Atatürk. Through Ambassador Jefferson Caffery's good offices, he held three meetings in March 1952 with members of the Free Officers, including Nasser (Copeland 1970: 51–53). The focus, according to one participant, was how Americans could convince their Anglo-Saxon partners to keep their hands off Egypt in exchange for Nasser's guarantee to modernize the Egyptian economy and suppress Communists (Hammudah 1985: 88–89). Three nights before the coup, Nasser asked Free Officer Ali Sabri to liaise with U.S. Assistant Military Attaché David Evans. Truman immediately welcomed the coup, warned the British not to intervene, and directed his ambassador in Cairo—who infamously referred to the Free Officers as "my boys"—to support the new rulers (Aburish 2004: 43). Kermit Roosevelt met Nasser's delegates shortly after the coup to discuss future cooperation. This was followed by a series of sessions between Nasser and CIA operatives James Eichelberger and Miles Copeland at the residence of the Cairo CIA station chief, Colonel William Lakeland (Copeland 1970: 63).

There were also political meetings at the house of Abd al-Moun'em Amin, another Free Officer Nasser charged with contacting the Americans. RCC member Khaled Muhi al-Din, who attended a couple of those meetings, remembered how the Americans pressed for land reform (Muhi al-Din 1992: 188). Convinced that the Bolshevik and Chinese revolutions relied on deprived peasants, they saw land redistribution as indispensable to fighting Communism. On August 20, 1952, Washington sent a telegram to its ambassador in Cairo stating that "the Government of the United States will give encouragement and assistance to land reform ... to lessen the causes of agrarian unrest and political instability" (Ahmed 2007: 131). Three weeks later, the RCC issued a hastily prepared agricultural reform law.

Nasser also hoped the United States could assist with the British evacuation. Eisenhower dispatched Steve Meade to evaluate the power balance within the RCC. Meade reported back, in May 1953, that Nasser dominated the council. Secretary of State John Foster Dulles, the first high-ranking official to visit the new republic, seconded the report the following month (Copeland 1970: 64–65). Afterward, Washington exerted so much pressure on London that Churchill protested in a letter to Eisenhower, on June 12, 1953, that America's bias to Nasser "in spite of the numerous far-reaching concessions which we made" was surprising and frustrating, and concluded dramatically, "We should not think we had been treated fairly by our great Ally" (Turner 2006: 116).

True to its Cold War conviction that military strongmen were more reliable than erratic civilians, Washington spurned Naguib's promise to reinstate democracy. Indeed, a week after the coup, Dean Acheson confided to his Cairo ambassador that officers were easier to handle than parliamentarians (Ahmed 2007: 19–20). Kennedy's special assistant Arthur Schlesinger defended this doctrine, citing support for Nasser as one of its prominent instances:

> [Democratizing coup-installed regimes] would only alienate those who held the real power—the military—and open the door to incompetent liberals who would bring about inflation, disinvestment, capital flight, and social indiscipline and would finally be shoved aside by the communists. . . . [T]he process of development was so inherently disruptive that the first requirement had to be the maintenance of order. The basic issue is not whether the government is dictatorial or is representative and constitutional. The issue is whether the government, whatever its character, can hold the society together. . . . [C]ivilian government tended to be unstable and soft; military governments were comparably stable and could provide the security necessary for economic growth. (Schlesinger 1965: 186–87)

While Nasser was busy erecting a new order, Naguib continued to invest in the old. Still hoping to reinvigorate Egypt's constitutional democracy, Naguib snubbed Nasser's security coterie and surrounded himself instead with constitutional lawyers, notably, Abd al-Razeq al-Sanhouri, who was asked to draft a new constitution, and Suleiman Hafez, who penned the monarch's abdication letter. Appointing Hafez as interior minister, in September 1952, was a big mistake. Although Naguib intended to signal his respect for the law, he unwittingly helped Nasser take over the ministry, in June 1953, with the reasonable excuse that this time of crises needed a firmer grip than that of a lawyer. Naguib also entrenched himself with the landed elite. Yet Egypt's sociopolitical structure was designed to keep those mostly absentee landlords dependent on whoever ran the state—as Nasser diligently did. Another mistake: Naguib capitalized too much on his folk hero image; "People lost control when they saw him, applauding, chanting, and throwing themselves on his car" (Younan 2008: 25). He traveled around the country to galvanize the masses, and used his military associates, Riyad Samy and Muhammad Riyad, as press secretaries, not spies as Nasser had done. Finally, he flirted with the Muslim Brotherhood to further cultivate popular support (Abu al-Nur 2001: 41–43). What the president failed to understand, in contrast to his sober rival, was how mercurial popularity was as a political asset.

Naguib was even worse in attracting foreign support. Too worried about tarnishing his reputation, he countered Nasser's aggressive tactics with a roundabout approach. Instead of employing loyal officers, he relied on Muslim Brothers. Between May 1953 and January 1954, Brothers Munir Delah and Saleh Abu-Raqiq conducted two rounds of talks with Trefor Evans and Michael

Creswell of the British Embassy, in which they vouched for Naguib's democratic credentials (Al-Rafe'i 1989: 130–34). Another seven rounds were held with U.S. officials between May and August 1953, with the participation of the Brotherhood's General Guide Hassan al-Hudaybi himself. In one meeting, Brother Mahmoud Makhlouf claimed that "Naguib would be willing to sign a secret understanding with the US. . . . [But] Opposition might be encountered from Abdel Nasser." In another, the general guide endorsed Naguib's agenda for withdrawing the military from government and empowering "a coalition of 'good men' from the various political parties" (Allam 1996: 548, 556). Of course, this was exactly what Western powers were against. And the fact that Naguib avoided direct contact with them did not help.

Naguib's main problem, however, was that he ignored the army and security. It is true that many officers supported his democratic stance, but instead of organizing a network of supporters, he preferred handing down orders through official channels. Even when artillery and cavalry officers begged him, in August 1952, to lead a corrective coup, he refused to fracture the ranks. As Naguib confided to the head of the Republican Guard, it was beneath him as president and RCC chair to conspire with junior officers (Abu al-Nur 2001: 41–43). He also refused to believe, according to his memoir, that Nasser, a colonel with an "undistinguished public presence," could turn the officers against him (Naguib 1984: 211). In short, Naguib counted on the support of the people, rather than the military, security, or foreign powers. But Egyptians yearned for a strongman—as they did in 2013. Naguib himself later confessed: they wanted "an Egyptian Ataturk," a role he was unwilling to play (Naguib 1984: 181).

Between Two Mutinies

Comparing Nasser and Naguib's power strategies tempts one to conclude that the latter was outmaneuvered from the start. However, Nasser had to face down two daring mutinies in the artillery (January 1953) and cavalry (March 1954). Artillery and cavalry officers believed their role was to reform democracy, not replace it. Moreover, politically motivated purges offended their professional temperament. Artillery officers also held a grudge against Nasser, who had placed their cherished Colonel Rashad Mehanna under house arrest, in October 1953, for conspiring with Muslim Brothers (Nasr 1999a: 167).

On December 14, 1952, artillery Captains Muhsen Abd al-Khaleq and Fathallah Ref'at submitted a petition to Nasser demanding the reconstitution of the RCC to allow each service equal representation. The petitioners warned that they had not overthrown one king to be ruled by fourteen (RCC members). Nasser asked them to sketch a blueprint of the political system they envisaged at Military Intelligence headquarters. They did not take the bait. Instead, artillerymen and cavalrymen met in secret, between December 30 and January 7, to plot a counter-coup, with the blessing of the Muslim Brothers. The plan was to arrest RCC members (except Naguib) during their weekly meeting using the 1st Artillery Brigade, which was stationed across from RCC headquarters, then seize control of the capital using the 2nd Artillery Division and Artillery School companies, before declaring a short transitional period, under Naguib, to prepare for elections. Samy Sharaf, an artillery lieutenant whose brother was one of the conspirators, tipped off the MID, and was rewarded with employment by the agency. On January 16 Zakaria Muhi al-Din apprehended thirty-five culprits, tried them summarily, and sentenced twelve of them to prison, including Mehanna (Muhi al-Din 1992: 222). As soon as the ringleaders were detained, 500 artillerymen threatened to use force to free their colleagues. Muhi al-Din calmed them down by promising to release them shortly, which he did not (Hammad 2010: 714). Now, a much bigger munity was in the works.

Tensions were rising between Naguib and Nasser. After Naguib complained during an RCC meeting, on December 20, that the media was ignoring his speeches, members accused him of hijacking the Revolution. Then on February 23, 1954, RCC members met in Nasser's office and asked the chair to go home, hoping he would accept his figurehead status. Instead, Naguib resigned, declaring that he could no longer preside over "a state of informants" run by CIA and ex-Gestapo operatives (Naguib 1997: 186–87). Naguib's goal, as he later admitted, was to arouse citizens and soldiers (Hafez 2010: 117). Nasser called his bluff, not only accepting his resignation, but also placing him under house arrest. OCC Director Nasr, and head of the Republican Guard Abu al-Nur replaced the guard unit stationed outside Naguib's house with Nasr's 13th Infantry Battalion, and detained those who resisted (Nasr 1999a: 228–32; Abu al-Nur 2001: 58–64).

Nasser did not expect that Naguib's resignation could trigger another mutiny, followed by a mass uprising. When Naguib stepped down, on February 26, cavalrymen sent a delegation, under Captains Ahmed al-Masri and Farouk al-Ansari, to express their wish for Naguib to head an interim civilian government to organize elections. Nasser warned that premature elections would bring back reactionary forces. At this point, the delegation withdrew from the talks and called for a sit-in at the cavalry's Green Mess Hall. Three hundred officers showed up, and units from the 4th Armored Division surrounded the nearby military general headquarters (GHQ). Mutineers demanded Naguib's reinstatement, Amer's dismissal, the RCC's dissolution, and an immediate return to democracy. Nasser rushed to the hall to reason with them. Following a heated debate, the encircled Nasser exclaimed: "Who gave you the right to speak for the people," to which one of the cavalrymen responded: "We are the parliament of the people until a parliament is formed." Thoroughly intimidated, especially after hearing tank movements outside the hall, Nasser agreed to form a transitional government under Naguib and cavalry's RCC representative Khaled Muhi al-Din. He then returned to RCC headquarters, and dispatched Khaled to fetch Naguib, in the early hours of February 27, so that the two could take charge (Muhi al-Din 1992: 270–73). Nasser was so disturbed that he asked his family to hide because, as his wife Tahiya recorded, cavalrymen might bomb their house (Abd al-Nasser 2011: 80).

It seemed for a moment that it was all over. But the tide soon turned. "It took only one hour," as Khaled bitterly reported, "for the situation to reverse completely. It was during the sixty minutes that passed between my trip to Naguib's house and back that everything turned upside down" (Muhi al-Din 1992: 277). It was security men, fearing that democracy would cut their new careers short, that saved the day. Gamal Hammad, the infantry officer who drafted the Free Officers' first communiqué, was present at GHQ as events unfolded and described Nasser as a mere spectator (Hammad 2010: 886–88). This was also the view of the three men at the receiving end of this security counter-attack: Naguib, Khaled, and cavalry mutiny leader Ansari. Naguib noted how the press was already documenting human rights violations and asking for reprisal. It was only natural for security officers, he wrote, to understand that democracy "would mean their end, that they will be held accountable for what they did" (Naguib 1984: 240). Khaled recalled warning Nasser that an intramilitary confrontation could escalate into a bloodbath, but the latter responded submissively: "I no longer understand what is going on" (Muhi al-Din 1992: 277–79). Ansari, in a letter from prison to Hammad, blamed himself for underestimating the ferocity of the new security elite who stood to lose from democracy (Hammad 2010: 938–39). Indeed, future President Anwar al-Sadat had always claimed that Nasser defended democracy during the first RCC meeting, in July 1952, but it was the power-hungry security coterie whom he thought would protect the Revolution that ended up controlling it (Sadat 1978: 157).

So if it was not Nasser who called the shots, then who did and how? Emphasizing how desperate times call for desperate measures, two of these officers-turned-security operatives, Shams Badran and Abbas Radwan, convinced a reluctant Nasser to allow them to offer the imprisoned artillery officers their freedom in return for helping to put down the cavalry uprising. The two quickly sealed the deal and informed their boss, OCC Director Salah Nasr, that artillery was at his service. Nasr sent agitators to other services to portray cavalry's call for democracy as a Communist ploy (Nasr 1999a: 236–39)—then made his move:

> I ordered my old 13th Infantry Battalion to surround cavalry headquarters, and the freshly released artillery officers to block tank outlets. I then asked [air force Captain Ali] Sabri [who joined the security apparatus] to send jets roaring at low altitudes over the besieged officers for intimidation. Meanwhile, I dispatched Tuhami [another security associate] and five intelligence officers to detain Naguib at artillery headquarters. When Amer discovered I had ordered troop movements without his approval, he called me into his office, grabbed my shirt, and screamed hysterically, with his gun pointed at me: "I will kill you! I will not allow the country to descend to chaos! I am the commander-in-chief not you!" But as soon as I assured him that everything was under control, and that the revolution was now safe, he calmed down. At this point, Khaled dashed into the office, asking who ordered the siege against cavalry. I asked him to warn his colleagues that if they did not disperse they will be bombed to the last man. Finally, I ordered the Military Police to storm in and detain ringleaders. By the end of the day, the situation was resolved. I ordered Radwan, my assistant, to keep an eye out and went home to get some sleep. (Nasr 1999a: 240–43)

To everyone's surprise, however, the pendulum swung back in the opposite direction. Few Egyptians were aware of the overnight military confrontation, but when they awoke to a communiqué announcing Naguib's removal, thousands—spurred by the Muslim Brothers—took to the streets shouting, "To prison with Nasser! No revolution without Naguib!" The size of the uprising was too overwhelming for Nasser's security acolytes (Game' 2004: 51). A cornered Nasser was forced to reinstate Naguib. But it was not back to square one. Naguib's triumphant return on a crest of popular revolt and with military backing provided him with a golden opportunity to eliminate his rivals. Yet he preferred reconciliation, and appointed Nasser as prime minister to demonstrate his goodwill. It was his undoing.

The New Regime Crystallizes

Immediately after the pro-Naguib demonstrations subsided, the security force rounded up thousands of participants, including the leaders of the Muslim Brothers. Nasser then pulled out his greatest bluff in the form of the

March 5 Decrees, which called for the election of a Constitutive Assembly in three months to draft a democratic constitution, and lifted restrictions on political activity and the press. This sudden change of heart aroused Naguib's suspicions. To secure himself, he demanded, on March 8, the right to appoint senior commanders (to undercut Amer); the right to veto cabinet decisions (to check Nasser); and a referendum on his presidency (to legitimize his post). Nasser not only accepted, but also issued the March 25 Decrees that revoked all restrictions on old regime parties, and prohibited Free Officers from partaking in elections (Naguib 1984: 247–50). Officially, the decrees aborted Nasser's hoped-for revolution. In reality, they were a call to action to all those who stood to lose by the restoration of the old order: officers who participated in the coup and feared punishment; peasants who benefited from land redistribution; workers who preferred dictatorship to liberal capitalism; the petty bourgeois that had barely begun to dream of social mobility. Even Naguib's allies felt cheated. Muslim Brothers feared the return of the liberal Wafd. And pro-democracy officers and activists aspired to create a new democracy, not return to the old one. Again, the most vulnerable stratum was the security elite, for as soon as censorship was lifted, the press launched a concerted campaign against their abuses (Hammad 2010: 1028). Indeed, Nasr confessed in his memoir to masterminding the March decrees to provoke "a revolution against the [pro-democracy] revolution" (Nasr 1999a: 262).

Nasr then advised Nasser on how to preempt another popular uprising. The first step was to neutralize the Muslim Brothers. Nasser had disbanded the movement and arrested the general guide and 540 senior members, in January 1954, to clear the ground for his showdown with Naguib the following month. The detainees were now released, and Nasser paid homage to the general guide at his house, on March 26. Lured by this new alliance, the Brothers abandoned Naguib. At the end of March, the general guide held a press conference to denounce the old party system, and thereafter refused to return Naguib's calls—causing the latter to sardonically comment that the general guide seemed never to leave the bathroom (Naguib 1984: 252). Following this fake rapprochement, Nasser asked Ibrahim al-Tahawi and Ahmed Te'ima, his security lieutenants at the Liberation Rally, to organize a general strike on March 27. With sufficient bribes to union leaders, 1 million workers brought the country to a standstill. That same day, the Liberation Rally organizers and the military police bussed thousands of peasants to Cairo, chanting, "No parties! No parliament! No elections!" (Vatikiotis 1978: 142–45). Meanwhile, the security trio of Nasr, Badran, and Radwan collected signatures for military and security petitions to remove Naguib and retract the March decrees. Officers were reminded that the return of the old regime might cost them their jobs, possibly their lives. The petitions were then read on public radio to signal that the coercive organs now stood united behind Nasser. On March 29 Nasser announced that—having heard the "impulse of the street"—the March decrees would be revoked, but that to maintain order, all strikes and demonstrations were now banned (Hammad 2010: 1069–79, 1167). It was another of those Napoleonic moments when a democratic revolution gives way to a military dictatorship by mobilizing citizens, then dismissing them. It would happen again in 2013.

Naguib tried to fight back. He asked the interior minister to crack down on the Liberation Rally demonstrations, but Zakaria Muhi al-Din requested signed authorization to use violence. Naguib, of course, hesitated. He next turned to his cavalrymen supporters, but they warned him that their intervention might lead to a massacre. Again, he refused. The only option he had was to stoically accept that if he was not willing to risk civil war, he must retire. "I was as exhausted as a boxer in the final round; I was not yet knocked out, but had lost too many points throughout this long game" (Naguib 1984: 257–63). Naguib's associates likewise threw in the towel. His closest advisor (Suleiman Hafez) resigned, on March 26; his aide-de-camp (Muhammad Riyad) escaped to Saudi Arabia the next day; and his RCC cavalry contact (Khaled Muhi al-Din) took refuge in Switzerland. When his esteemed constitutional lawyer Abd al-Razeq al-Sanhouri offered some resistance, military police officers assaulted him in his State Council office, on March 29. And between April and June, 177 pro-Naguib officers were purged (Vatikiotis 1978: 142–45).

The security then turned to civilian institutions. Anyone who held office before the coup was stripped of political rights; syndicates and student unions were dissolved; armored vehicles surrounded universities and other public assembly sites; and employees, professors, and students were forced to spy on their colleagues (Abdallah 1985: 122). Nasser now assumed full executive power, while President Naguib rarely left his house, confiding to his journal that "Egypt has now entered a dark age of injustice and terror" (Naguib 1984: 266). Within weeks, Nasser's men secured "total control of the armed forces . . . the neutralization and eventual destruction of other existing loci of political power . . . the control of education, the media, professional syndicates, trade unions, the rural structures in the countryside, the religious institutions and orders, the administration and bureaucracy, eventually, the whole society" (Vatikiotis 1978: 127).

Nasser then proceeded to tie his loose ends with the Muslim Brothers. After a highly suspicious attempt on his life in Alexandria, on October

26, 1954, when Brother Mahmoud Abd al-Latif supposedly shot him nine times at close range but missed, the greatest crackdown in the history of the Muslim Brothers began. Over 20,000 Brothers were shipped to concentration camps; 1,050 were officially tried, and among those, 6 leaders were executed, and the rest, including the general guide, received long prison sentences. The movement was again disbanded, its property confiscated, and the slightest expression of sympathy with it outlawed—a chilling prequel to the 2013 campaign. On November 14 the security force announced an alleged conspiracy between the Brothers and the besieged president. Naguib was placed under house arrest in a heavily guarded villa on the outskirts of Cairo, where he would remain for the next eighteen years. In his memoir, Naguib expressed no pity for the Brothers who, in his view, were blinded by greed from the obvious fact that the military was using them to consolidate power (Naguib 1984: 253)—again, a remarkable repeat of their ignoble performance after the 2011 revolt.

In the summer of 1956, Nasser was elected president (by 99.9 percent); the RCC was dissolved; and a new constitution was approved. The March 1954 crisis thus set the new regime on its authoritarian trajectory. If Naguib had won, Egypt might have followed the Turkish path, with the military presiding over a limited democracy. Nasser's creation of an enhanced security apparatus made all the difference. Between 1952 and 1954, the new security elite developed enough to realize that its interests were not the same as those of the military, and that democracy would bring their careers to an abrupt end. While the military dragged its feet—as in any large and internally stratified institution—the sharp-minded security operatives moved unfalteringly to rule out the hope of a military-ushered democracy. However, this was not the end. The way the new regime crystallized set the stage for a grander confrontation between Nasser (the chief politician) and Amer (the chief general). And it would be the various factions of the sprawling security community that would have to arbitrate.

Note

1. These included Lieutenant General Wilhelm Farmbacher of the German Wermacht; two SS operatives, Otto Skorzeny and Oskar Direwanger; and four Gestapo officers, Leopold Gleim, Franz Buensch, Joachim Deumling, and Alois Anton Brunner (Copeland 1970: 87; Sirrs 2010: 33).

13 | Blood, Folly, and Sandcastles

JUNE 1967

One of the remarkable things about Egypt's new regime was that it was a "dictatorship without a dictator" (Aburish 2004: 56). It was the security aristocracy that ruled. Citizens lived under constant surveillance: phones, offices, and homes were bugged; mail was regularly checked; neighbors, colleagues, even siblings could not be trusted. Suspect behavior invariably invited "dawn visitors," who could detain people for indefinite periods and force them to confess to whatever crime they fancied through unspeakable torture. Neither Nasser nor Amer could rein in the leviathan they had unleashed. And indeed both blamed Egypt's misfortunes on the "*mukhabarat* (intelligence) state." As a matter of fact, what appeared to be a personal battle between the president and his field marshal, between 1956 and 1967, masked a power struggle within the security community. The security elite, which stood united against Naguib, was now divided into two competing factions: those attached to Nasser's political apparatus, namely, the Ministry of Interior with its General Investigations Department (GID), and the President's Bureau of Information (PBI); and those attached to Amer's military, that is, the Office of the Commander-in-Chief for Political Guidance (OCC), the Military Intelligence Department (MID), and the General Intelligence Service (GIS). It was a struggle for supremacy that ended with disaster on the morning of June 5, 1967. But its first round commenced in October 1956, during the Suez Crisis.

Military Defeat, Political Triumph

The road toward the Suez War did not begin with the nationalization of the Suez Canal in July 1956, but two years earlier over a military-related dispute. Since most officers supported the 1952 coup because of their resentment of the army's unpreparedness, it was only natural that procuring advanced weapons was at the top of Nasser's agenda. He initially turned to Washington. In October 1954 a meeting was held at security operative Hassan al-Tuhami's apartment between Nasser and Amer, the CIA's Miles Copeland, and U.S. Generals Albert Gerhardt and Wilbur Eveland. An agreement was reached to provide Egypt with $20 million worth of weapons. But the following month, Washington only announced an economic aid package of $40 million. America first wanted Egypt to join the Baghdad Pact, a pro-Western regional defense alliance. Nasser refused, warning the CIA's Kermit Roosevelt that he might negotiate instead with the Eastern bloc (Copeland 1970: 123–33, 148). With Israel stepping up its raids against Palestinians in the Egyptian-controlled Gaza Strip, Nasser was forced to conclude the famous Czech Arms Deal with Moscow in September 1955. That month, he delivered a speech blaming the West: "When we carried out the revolution we turned to every country . . . to arm our forces, we turned to England, we turned to France, we turned to America . . . [but] we only heard demands [that undermine] Egypt's dignity" (Al-Rafe'i 1989: 199). Before the Americans knew what hit them, Nasser went further by recognizing Red China, in May 1956. The United States retaliated by withdrawing its offer to help build the High Dam, a hydroelectric project that promised to double Egypt's industrial capacity. A furious Nasser responded by nationalizing the Suez Canal in front of an ecstatic crowd, on July 26, 1956, to boost national revenue to finance the dam and purchase weapons.

Instead of just aggravating the United States, Nasser's decision provoked three odd partners to invade Egypt, in what became known as the Tripartite Aggression. Britain, France, and Israel had different reasons. Nasser threatened Britain's conservative Arab allies (Jordan, Iraq, Aden, and the Gulf sheikhdoms), and now his control of the strategic waterway placed a quarter of British imports and three-quarters of its oil needs under his mercy (Johnson 1957: 11–14). France not only resented Cairo's support of the Algerian revolt, but also the French-run Suez Canal Company was the "last great international stronghold of French capital" (Turner 2006: 187–93). Israel, for its part, wanted to nip in the bud its western neighbor's drive for military parity, and thus seized on the French invitation for a joint assault (Turner 2006: 260–64). The plan, as set in the Sèvres Protocol, on October 24, 1956, was to topple Nasser and reestablish control over the Suez Canal in three stages. First, Israeli forces would roll into Sinai to draw in Egypt's army, then British and French paratroopers would occupy the canal under the pretext of protecting the international waterway, and finally, a full-fledged invasion would install a new government in Cairo.

As agreed, Israel's armored brigades stormed across the border, on October 29, 1956. Two days later, a Franco-British airstrike paved the way for an invasion by the "largest amphibious fighting force since the end of the Second World War" (Turner 2006: 1). Egypt's military command was naturally startled. When Nasser got to GHQ, on October 31, he was asked to surrender to spare the military total destruction. Amer suffered a nervous breakdown, bewailing how the attack "will send the country back a thousand years" (Imam 1996: 53). The president rebuked his top commander's "unmanly" behavior, and threatened to court martial him if he continued to "mope like an old hag" (Aburish 2004: 119). He then benched Amer and took control: planning a meticulous withdrawal from Sinai; sinking cement tanks to obstruct navigation in the canal; and rallying Egyptians for popular resistance from the pulpit of al-Azhar mosque (Al-Gamasy 1993: 13). However, it was ultimately the Great Powers' opposition that tipped the scales. Washington could not tolerate a reassertion of European imperialism in a region it had begun to consider its own, and Moscow treated an assault on a country it was courting as an unforgivable insult. The belligerents withdrew under international pressure, and Egypt had to accept a UN peacekeeping force, and allow Israeli navigation in the Red Sea.

So while the Egyptian military was defeated, the Suez War was hailed as a political triumph. And while Nasser's political agility was celebrated, Amer's military shortcomings were exposed. Amer was supposed to reshuffle his incompetent commanders. But his security associates were eager to safeguard their patronage network within the army, and thus warned him that purging loyal subordinates would weaken his position—especially after the military prowess Nasser displayed during the crisis. In a stormy meeting, on November 15, 1956, an audacious Amer rejected Nasser's pleas for changes in military leadership, refusing even to transfer the scandalously inept air force commander, Sedqi Mahmoud, because he was his man. In fact, the terribly insecure Amer promoted himself to field marshal (Abu Zikri 1988: 71). A wedge was driven between the longtime comrades.

The Dark Years

The Suez War debacle and the ensuing confrontation convinced the president to remove his friend from military command. This was easier said than done. Amer's security aides, led by OCC strongmen Salah Nasr and Abbas

Radwan, placed him at the center of an elaborate patronage network within the corps: distributing honors, granting favors, hosting all-night parties, and keeping the "field marshal's men" untouchable (Hammad 2010: 1330–40). Soon thereafter, Amer became the army's Santa Clause. Colonel Muhammad Selim recounted one telling incident: "A junior officer once walked up to Amer as he was about to leave GHQ and complained that he was forced to use public transportation to commute to work everyday. Amer tore the top part of his cigarette packet and wrote on its back: 'Dear Fiat manager, dispense a car immediately to the bearer of this message.' The field marshal did not even ask for his name; the fact that he donned the uniform and came to him for help was enough" (Selim 2009).

The president's security men were also at work. PBI Director Samy Sharaf suggested creating a secret pro-Nasser network within the army. And because the officer corps was effectively sealed off by Amer's security apparatus, Sharaf decided to focus on the Military Academy, which was headed by a relative of his, future War Minister Muhammad Fawzy. Sharaf recruited six cadets and instructed them to lay low until they graduated. After a few meetings with his sleeping cell, however, the field marshal's men picked them up. And an embarrassed Nasser had to disclaim them. Another PBI operative, Hassan al-Tuhami, bugged Amer's phones on his own initiative. Again, the field marshal's alert security apparatus found out, and Tuhami was exiled to Vienna for a decade (Sharaf 1996: 456).

The two old friends were now embroiled in a cat-and-mouse game. Amer's military security men wanted to extend their control to the civilian security institutions. OCC Director Salah Nasr lobbied to have himself appointed head of the GIS in May 1957, and his OCC deputy Abbas Radwan as interior minister in October 1958. In return, Nasser employed former GIS Director Aly Sabri at PBI to capitalize on his contacts at the agency to neutralize Nasr. The president also anticipated Nasr's official takeover in May by appointing two confidants (Amin Huwaidi, and Sha'rawi Gomaa) to senior positions at GIS in February. He then convinced Amer to appoint Shams Badran as new OCC director. Badran had been liaising between the presidency and the military, and Nasser hoped he would deliver the military back to him. Nasser was further reassured by the fact that the loyal Zakaria Muhi al-Din, the architect of the entire security apparatus, was unofficially supervising all civilian security agencies, regardless of who was in charge at GIS or the Interior Ministry. The president's safeguards, however, came to naught. Sabri clashed with PBI Director Sharaf and had to be reallocated, and the shrewd Nasr isolated GIS from Zakaria, transferred Nasser's men, Huwaidi and Gomaa, to the PBI, and proceeded to ally GIS with the military-based OCC. Worse still, the field marshal won over Badran, Nasser's spy, through his lavish, laissez-faire management style (Huwaidi 2002: 195). Now, all security organs—except for the president's own PBI—came under Amer's control.

When Egypt and Syria merged, in 1958, into a United Arab Republic, the president seized the opportunity to kick his friend-turned-rival upstairs by appointing him governor of Syria. The field marshal agreed, believing he would now have his own country to run. But the union was dissolved in three years. Amer felt particularly responsible because it was his Syrian aide-de-camp (Abd al-Karim al-Nahlawy) who organized the anti-Egyptian coup. In the heat of the moment, he resigned all official positions, to Nasser's great relief. The president moved quickly, reappointing Muhi al-Din interior minister, demoting Radwan to minister without portfolio, and was about to remove Nasr from the GIS. But in January 1962, Muhi al-Din and PBI's Sharaf uncovered an OCC coup plot to reinstate Amer, and Nasser thought it wise to beat a tactical retreat and recall his old friend (Fawzy 1990: 33).

The president soon came up with a new ploy to lure Amer away from command. In September 1962 he convinced Amer that they should rule collectively through a presidential council. To ascend to this political position, however, Amer would have to hand over the military to Muhammad Fawzy, the Military Academy director—and Sharaf's relative (Fawzy 1990: 33). Believing he was being promoted to co-president, Amer went along. During the council's first meeting, on September 18, Nasser announced the appointed of Aly Sabri, his former security associate, as prime minister, and reminded Amer to submit his resignation as agreed. Instead, OCC Director Shams Badran came to see Nasser the next day to inform him that the field marshal had decided to remain in his position. When Nasser insisted that Amer carry out his part of the deal, Badran returned in a couple of months with the field marshal's letter of resignation. Skimming through it, the president immediately realized he was being set up. In the letter, which Badran insinuated might leak to the press, Amer accused Nasser of becoming a dictator: "What you should be working for now is democracy. . . . I cannot imagine that after all this time, after eradicating feudalism and manipulative capitalism, after the masses have placed their trust in you unreservedly you still fear democracy." That morning, a shocked Nasser saw armed paratroopers demonstrating outside his house. PBI also warned him that Nasr at GIS was plotting something big with military commanders. Soon, Badran conveyed another ominous message: Amer would only resign if Nasser established democracy. A meeting was organized on December 11. The field marshal stressed that the political loyalty of the army depended on him personally, and any attempt to remove him would trigger a coup. Nasser again recoiled (Sadat 1978: 208). He thought he extracted a concession from Amer when he pressured him to appoint Fawzy chief of staff, after he had denied him general command. But although the field marshal acquiesced, he ended up restricting Fawzy to administration, and improvised a post in the chain of command (ground forces commander) to carry out the chief of staff's operational duties (Fawzy 1990: 54).

At this point, Nasser regretted his neglect of political organization. If he had formed a proper ruling party, he could have riddled the military with political commissars, as in Russia and China. Instead, he chose to control the military through a secret network of loyal officers. Now their loyalty shifted to Amer, and he no longer knew their identities.[1] Amer's security ensemble (OCC and Military Intelligence) had made the military their powerbase, and established beachheads in the civilian security sector (through GIS). And Nasser's security organs (PBI and the Interior Ministry) were constantly outclassed. But perhaps it was not too late. If Nasser revamped the political apparatus, maybe he could reduce the relative weight of the military in the ruling bloc. The idea of the Arab Socialist Union (ASU) was thus born. PBI Director Sharaf admitted as much, "We suffered an imbalance; the weight of the military was growing beyond control. Nasser created the ASU as a political counter to the army" (Sharaf 1996: 228–29).

Counterweighing the Military

Nasser built on what he had. The chaotic Liberation Rally had given way, by 1958, to the pyramid-shaped National Union (NU). But both were interest networks with no capacity for ideological mobilization. The passing of the socialist laws of 1961, which Nasser used to broaden his mass base, provided the occasion to reorganize the political apparatus. The 1962 National Charter introduced the ASU, an organization meant to embody the popular will. It was structured along two axes: profession, with committees for workers, peasants, intellectuals, soldiers, "patriotic" capitalists, and a socialist youth organization for students; and residence, with branches in cities and villages. The ASU was tasked with producing ministers, parliamentarians, governors, university deans, and the like, as well as driving legislation and policy. In short, it was the seat of political power.

Nasser's ruling organization was supposed to act as a popular vanguard. In a meeting with ASU executive, in January 1966, the president explained: "We cannot succeed unless we understand the masses. We must take their ideas and opinions, study it, organize it, reflect it back to them, and then point them in the right direction" (Abd al-Nasser 1966: 14–16). But the ASU was not equipped for this role. In his enthusiasm to copy the organization of Communist parties, the president overlooked one crucial ingredient: Communism. Nasser did not adhere to any ideology. He was a pragmatist with lofty ideas about social justice. And without ideology there can be no ideological indoctrination. So all the ASU could do was link various groups to the regime through material temptations rather than ideological commitment. This was good enough to achieve Nasser's overriding goal: to balance the military—a goal sometimes expressed rather crudely, as, for example, when a 1964 ASU summer camp chose the following topic for discussion: "How should ASU youth resist a possible coup?" (Imam 1996: 90).

The absence of ideology and the obsession with neutralizing the army condemned the ASU from the start. The organization regulated rather than mobilized society. And it did so by presenting itself as the fastest road to social mobility and the safest way to alleviate suspicions of dissent. Many of its 6 million members were opportunists who were delighted to learn that one no longer had to be an officer to benefit from the Revolution; a civilian route had just opened up. Worse still, the deeply embedded security character of the regime seized the ASU. The Interior Ministry vetted members and kept them under surveillance. Intelligence officers, such as Abd al-Fatah Abu al-Fadl, were planted at ASU to monitor its performance (Abu al-Fadl 2008: 223). And indeed, the organization itself assumed security tasks; its members not only preached political obedience, but also reported dissidents. By 1966 its archives held more than 30,000 secret reports on military officers alone (Sirrs 2010: 88). Nasser himself encouraged this role. During the same January 1966 meeting, he urged ASU members to act as informers: "You must be courageous enough that when you notice the deviation of another member to bring it to the attention of the office" (Abd al-Nasser 1966: 13). The ASU became so proficient in collecting information that Nasr at GIS complained to Nasser that it was spying on his own spies (Heikal 1990: 401).

This security role reached its zenith with the creation of the Vanguard Organization (VO), a secret body within the ASU designed to help with indoctrination, but that rapidly degenerated into a full-fledged intelligence organ. The idea behind the VO, as Nasser explained during the founding meeting in June 1963, was to form secret cells of carefully selected ASU cadres to penetrate public institutions (Sharaf 1996: 183–91). Nasser hoped the VO would become the political nucleus of his regime—a civilian equivalent to the Free

Officers. But its 30,000 members were preoccupied with security from the beginning. The VO itself operated in secret (its existence was only revealed in 1966); two of its four founding members were PBI operatives (Sharaf and Sabry); its leader was Interior Minister Sha'rawi Gomaa; and its charter decreed that: "each member is obliged to present [security] reports . . . to his superiors." This was not far from what Nasser intended. In a meeting with VO members, in March 1966, he said: "We need supporters within the executive branches and administration . . . [for] surveillance and oversight" (Ahmed 1993: 764–71). He was specifically worried about the military, adding in that same meeting that "I believe that it would be impossible for the army to prepare for a coup [without political support]" (Ahmed 1993: 786). The VO thus infiltrated universities, factories, unions, the media, and the bureaucracy, to report on suspicious activities. In the words of one member, it had become a "political Gestapo" (Hosni 2007: 20–22).

To the extent that the ASU and VO had a social power base at all, it was the aspiring rural middle class and its urban offshoot in the state bureaucracy. These formed the backbone of Egypt's ruling party until the end of Mubarak's rule. The 1952 coup had taken place in a society where 2,500 large landowners (with 147 elite families) and 9,500 middling owners controlled a third of arable land, next to 2.5 million small holders, and 11 million tenant farmers and landless peasants. Though land redistribution granted poor peasant barely enough to subsist on, they were sufficiently grateful to the Revolution to form a solid base for popular mobilization. But the apprehensive Nasser feared their revolutionary enthusiasm might get out of control, and preferred to keep them tied down under village notables. So he placed middling landowners at the apex of the control networks that had been run for decades by rural magnates (Binder 1978: 344; Yunis 2005: 69). In other words, land reform shifted power from large landlords to a class of *kulaks*. Security considerations were again prioritized over the potential for mass mobilization.

The July 1961 Socialist Laws further enhanced the economic power of the rural middle class by undermining that of the wealthy urban stratum. The laws themselves also had something to do with security. Intelligence czar Zakaria Muhi al-Din reported that a group of thirty senior military officers were courting Egyptian capitalists to help them replace Nasser with Amer. The report highlighted how two-thirds of the economy was still in private hands, and how half of Egypt's workers were employed by private businesses. A swift move was therefore necessary. In October 1961 Muhi al-Din arrested 40 prominent investors, and in mid-November sequestrated the financial assets of another 767 (Abdel-Malek 1968: 160). The next logical step was to eliminate the private sector in banking, international trade, heavy industry, transportation, and the media. Even in medium industries and commercial companies—the last domain of private enterprise—the public sector became a controlling shareholder (McDermott 1988: 121–22).

The expansion of the urban managerial class offered the middling landowners an opportunity to extend their influence to the city. They pushed their offspring to join the bureaucracy and public sector companies. And accordingly, the sons of rural notables dominated the state bourgeoisie, which exceeded 1 million employees in 1967 (Yunis 2005: 66–67). Soon these rural-minded bureaucrats transformed the public sector into a financial fiefdom to supplement the agricultural fiefdoms of their fathers. Strategically placed in the city and the countryside, this new elite became the bulwark of the ASU and VO. To rely on conservative village notables and civil servants seemed much safer to Nasser's security coterie than to mobilize urban activists or unruly peasants. That is not to say that these strata became a ruling class. Their role was rather to sustain those in power, and therefore represented a "second stratum of the ruling class," one that mediates between rulers and society (Binder 1978: 13).

The fingerprints of Nasser's security elite appear all over this power-building process, even when the president aspired for a wider popular base. For example, he pledged that 50 percent of ASU members would be workers and peasants. Yet his security advisors managed to include middling landowners in the peasant category, and public sector employees in the labor one (Abd al-Mo'ty 2002: 78). And when Nasser wanted conservative elements filtered out during the transition from the NU to the ASU, his security men rejected only 1.5 percent of NU applicants to the ASU. In fact, 78 percent of those in charge of NU village units, and 60 percent of those heading NU urban offices occupied the same posts under the ASU (Binder 1978: 309–15). As one intelligence official noted, ASU was not formed of the same social forces as that of the NU, but of actually the same people (Abu al-Fadl 2008: 226).

It is this group of middle-class opportunists that propped the ruling party for the next five decades—although it would have to share the spoils with affluent businessmen after the 1970s. Eventually, this security–political alliance would marginalize the military, as Nasser had planned. But for the moment the field marshal's men still hoped to reassert their power. And it was this attempt that set the stage for the final showdown.

The Military Needs a War

For such a brief encounter, the 1967 Arab-Israeli War remains one of history's most consequential confrontations. In Egypt, the defeat was "so unexpected in its totality, stunning in its proportion, and soul-destroying in its impact" (Aburish 2004: 249). How could we explain the astonishing sequence of events that led up to this defeat? How could the politically astute Nasser act so belligerently when he had so little control over his army? Egyptian analysts blame an American plot to destroy Nasser. Israelis claim that he thought he could actually destroy Israel. Others highlight how Arab states (especially Syria and Jordon) dared Nasser to act on his virtuoso rhetoric.[2] Perhaps the true motivation will remain hidden forever, but the logic of the intraregime power struggle provides an explanation that best incorporates the available evidence. And this logic points to only one direction: that the effectiveness of Nasser's counterbalancing strategy convinced Amer's men that if the military does not accomplish something spectacular soon, it would lose its place at the epicenter of power.

Of course, Amer knew beyond the shadow of a doubt that the army was not prepared for war, even as he pretended to provoke one. In December 1966 he received a report by the military's high command advising against any confrontation with Israel. The report was based on the disastrous effects of the Yemen War. The Egyptian army had sent instructors to support Yemeni nationalists in 1962. Amer had embraced this opportunity to boost the military's image in a short and effortless campaign against promonarchy bandits (Fawzy 1990: 24–26; Sadat 1978: 211). His plan almost worked, since U.S. President Kennedy supported the Yemeni republicans. However, Britain and Saudi Arabia, who supported the monarchists, persuaded Lyndon Johnson to change sides (Schlesinger 1965: 523). The Egyptian army was now trapped in an unconventional war against Western-funded guerillas. Its few hundred instructors swelled into a 70,000-strong force by 1965 (Vatikiotis 1978: 162). The 1966 report assessed the impact of this regional "Vietnam": how military discipline suffered from the exigencies of guerilla warfare; how pilots forgot the basics of dogfighting after years of aimless strikes against a country with no air force; and how equipment and ammunition were depleted. Moreover, budget constraints forced the military to discharge thousands of reservists and freeze conscription. And so by May 1967—the month Amer began to agitate for war—the army suffered a 37 percent shortage in manpower, 30 percent shortage in small arms, 24 percent in artillery, 45 percent in tanks, and 70 percent in armored vehicles; and trained pilots were fewer than the available aircraft. Another report described 1966–1967 as the worse training year in the army's history (Al-Gamasy 1993: 39–40; Dunstan 2009: 26).

What made this unmistakably bleak picture bleaker still was Nasser's warning to Amer of an imminent U.S. plot (Fawzy 1990: 10). Washington believed that Egypt's socialist nationalism was as dangerous as Communism. Keen to allay such fear, Nasser responded warmly to Kennedy's 1961 circular to Arab leaders, triggering a two-year personal correspondence. Relations remained cordial because Kennedy believed a cornered Nasser might be more aggressive (Schlesinger 1965: 522–23). This changed with Johnson, who believed that force was the only language Nasser understood. Being a Texan congressmen also meant he had particularly intimate relations with oil conglomerates and Israel supporters, who both loathed Nasser. Johnson first charged the CIA's Robert Komer to turn Egypt's Yemen adventure into a quagmire. Next, he suspended American wheat shipments to Cairo. But something more devastating was underway. Toward the end of 1966, former World Bank President Eugene Black informed Nasser that Washington was planning to "unleash Israel" against him. Nasser's closest advisor Mohamed Hassanein Heikal confirmed that an American-Israeli committee, under Walt Rostow, was considering plans to remove him from power, via so-called Operation Turkey Shoot (Heikal 1990: 361–74). In fact, on the first day of the 1967 war, Rostow prefaced his report to Johnson as follows: "Herewith the account . . . of the first day's turkey shoot" (Dunstan 2009: 72).

Now, if Amer had a clear picture of the dismal state of the army, and if he had been forewarned about the American-Israeli intentions, why did he undertake such an incredible gamble in the summer of 1967? The answer lies in Nasser's success in counterbalancing the military. The president's security team decided, in 1962, that it was impossible to depose Amer's men, and thus shifted from frontal assault to siege warfare. Since access to the military was blocked, they focused on building new political organizations and controlling the executive. The ASU was created in 1962, followed by the VO in 1963, and Nasser's security loyalists led the cabinet: Sabri between 1962 and 1965, and Muhi al-Din between 1965 and 1967, and the ratio of officers in the cabinet was cut from 52 percent in 1961 to 36 percent in 1964 (Dekmejian 1982: 31).

Driven by insecurity, Amer's security aides took preventive measures. In the summer of 1966, OCC Director Shams Badran purged 173 officers, and reshuffled another 300 in the most extensive reorganization since 1952. The aim was to advance loyal officers to field commands to oversee troop movements (a hectic job, one they usually snubbed), and recall neutral officers to GHQ under the watchful eye of the OCC (Al-Gamasy 1993: 83; Hammad 2010: 1380–83). And in September 1966, Badran himself was promoted to war minister. Afterward, Amer issued two crucial decrees: one expanding the jurisdiction of the war minister, and the other shrinking the responsibilities of Nasser's ally, Chief of Staff Muhammad Fawzy (Fawzy 1990: 37–38). Still, they did not feel safe. In November 1966 Murad Ghaleb, Egypt's longtime ambassador to Moscow, overheard Intelligence Director Salah Nasr explaining to Amer's lieutenants that as long as Nasser controlled the executive, their position would remain vulnerable (Ghaleb 2001: 101). Badran therefore demanded the premiership, which Nasser flatly rejected. Tensions rose and a compromise was reached whereby Sedqi Suleiman, a reputably unaligned officer, replaced the president's ally, Muhi al-Din, as premier. The field marshal then reversed the declining ratio of officers in the cabinet from 36 percent under Muhi al-Din to 55 percent under Suleiman (Dekmejian 1982: 33). In return, Nasser asked for a neutral officer to head Military Intelligence, and both sides agreed on Muhammad Sadeq, Egypt's military attaché to Bonn (Sirrs 2010: 95).

Amer's men, however, believed that these maneuvers only bought them time. If the military did not pull off a dramatic feat soon, its relative weight within the regime would continue to diminish. After the Yemen debacle, the army had to prove itself in the arena that no one else could claim: on the battlefield—for as Hobbes once proclaimed "There is no honour Military but by warre" ([1651] 1968).

"At Dawn We Slept"

It all started in December 1966, when Amer telegrammed Nasser from Pakistan demanding the deployment of his troops into Sinai to silence Arab critics who accused them of hiding behind the United Nations Emergency Forces (UNEF) positioned there since 1956. The president ignored Amer's plea. But on May 14, 1967, acting on unconfirmed Russians reports that Israel was mobilizing against Syria, the field marshal went ahead with his plan, later justifying his decision to Nasser by citing the Egyptian-Syrian defense pact concluded a year before. The president was frantic. He had specifically instructed Amer the night before to double-check the Soviet report before taking action. Nasser quickly dispatched his trusted Chief of Staff Fawzy to Damascus to check claims of an imminent Israeli attack. The latter reported back to Amer, on May 15, that the Soviet report was baseless. However, as Fawzy recalled: "The field marshal made no reaction. . . . I began to suspect that the alleged [Israeli] troop concentrations was not the principle reason for his mobilization order" (Fawzy 1990: 72). Moreover, on May 2, the Jordanian monarch had delivered a warning through the future Egyptian chief of staff, General Abd al-Mon'em Riyad, that America and Israel planned to drag Egypt into a devastating war. Riyad submitted a full report to Amer. But the report was concealed from Nasser until the army had crossed into Sinai (Heikal 1990: 439–40). In a desperate attempt at damage control, the president asked Amer for the draft letter he intended to send to UNEF. He received Arabic and English versions, and amended the Arabic one to request a redeployment rather than withdrawal of UN troops. But, on May 16, Amer called to apologize: the un-amended English version was mistakenly submitted, requiring a full UN withdrawal. Nasser tried to retract the letter, but UN Under-secretary General Ralph Bunche, possibly under American pressure, refused (Brooks 2008: 90–91).

With the army deployed in Sinai, Amer raised the stakes by demanding, on May 21, a block on Israeli navigation in the Red Sea. Nasser pointed out that this was a *casus belli*, to which Amer retorted that his men could not sit on their hands as Israeli flags flashed before them, and that if his wish was not granted, they might start shooting Israeli vessels. When Nasser asked him if he was ready for war, Amer famously responded: "My neck is at stake" (Brooks 2008: 92). To silence the president, Badran claimed that during his recent visit to Moscow, the Soviet defense minister pledged to defend Egypt should the Americans come to Israel's aid—a claim the Soviets vehemently denied after the war, and their denial was corroborated by the Egyptian ambassador to Moscow (Ghaleb 2001: 107). Relying on his own intelligence sources, Nasser rounded up the high command, on June 2, to let them know that Israel was planning to attack from the air in seventy-two hours, and to ask them to fortify air force squadrons in Sinai to prevent a repeat of the Suez War, when jets were destroyed on the ground. The president also advised against striking first, lest Egypt loses international support, which proved crucial in 1956 (Browne 2009: 75). The next day, Nasser reiterated in an interview with British journalist Anthony Nutting that Egypt "planned no further escalation" (Brooks 2008: 65). In a final effort to avert war, he asked Muhi al-Din to travel to Washington, on June 5, to find a way out. It was too late. June 5 was the day Israel attacked.

Around dawn, an Israeli armada of 196 fighter-bombers (approximately 95 percent of the Israeli Air Force) headed toward Egypt. Before noon, 85 percent of the Egyptian air force (304 planes) was destroyed. Over the next six days, Egypt lost 700 tanks, 450 field guns, 17,500 soldiers (11,500 killed and the rest injured or captured), and out of its 300,000 men in arms, only half remained in formation. Yet the "volume of the losses," as future War Minister Abd al-Ghany al-Gamasy bitterly noted, "betrays the immensity of the disaster" (Al-Gamasy 1993: 79). Amer was bluffing, and Israel called his bluff.

All the evidence suggests that the field marshal's men never imagined that their grandstanding would trigger a war. Indeed, when Amer's frantic chief of operations told him that the army was in no condition to engage Israel, he responded nonchalantly: "There is no need to worry. This is nothing but a military demonstration" (Al-Gamasy 1993: 22). GIS director Salah Nasr admitted after the war that the troops were mobilized for a "political purpose, which was to demonstrate military strength [at home]" (Imam 1996: 159). The "demonstration" aspect of the whole episode was clear enough when Amer marched his troops through the streets of Cairo, parading their weapons and chanting patriotic songs, even though 80 percent of his force in Sinai was undrilled reservists, hastily marshaled to the front in their civilian garments. Although the size of the fully mobilized army never exceeded 130,000, Amer claimed he commanded 2 million. Also, a whole squadron of planes, as well as dozens of tanks, and hundreds of boxes of small arms and ammunition remained locked in warehouses until the end of the war (Huwaidi 2002: 191). Moreover, despite threats to attack, Egypt's only military plan (Plan Qaher) was purely defensive (Brooks 2008: 86).

The high command's actions after their final meeting with Nasser show how dismissive they were of the possibility of war. To start with, they ignored his warning of an Israeli air strike in three days. Soon-to-be War Minister Amin Huwaidi attested: "Our fighter jets remained exposed on the front, even though rudimentary concrete shelters could have been built in a couple of days" (Huwaidi 2002: 191). The commander of the air force in Sinai only learned of Nasser's warning after the defeat (Imam 1996: 143). Even more incredible was the fact that, after the meeting, Military Intelligence sent a circular to units in Sinai affirming that Israel would never attack. One day before the war, a lieutenant crossed the peninsula to deliver anti-tank ammunition to a forward border post. The post commander was surprised: "We don't need any ammunition. There isn't going to be a war" (Dunstan 2009: 15). Then came Amer's disastrous decision to fly with his staff to the front in an unarmed transport on June 5, the very day Nasser predicted Israel would attack. So when the war started, Egypt's entire high command was divided between those suspended in midair with Amer, and those who were either seeing him off in Cairo or waiting to receive him at the airport in Sinai. Naturally, air defense units were ordered to hold their fire until the field marshal's plane landed safely, and Amer could not revoke these orders once the attack began because if he had broken radio silence, he might have been shot down (Al-Gamasy 1993: 50).

Next came the ultimate testimony to Amer's unpreparedness for battle: his demand for a Soviet-endorsed ceasefire one hour after the commencement of hostilities, followed by his tragic order of a general retreat from Sinai (Sadat 1978: 228). The ground forces had been offering considerable resistance. Egyptian troops performed best when entrenched in defensive strong points; this was the tactic that required the least training—only bravery. The soldiers stalled Israel's advance to allow the high command to overcome the shock and take charge. The sensible thing to do was to fall back to Sinai's naturally fortified Mitla and Gidi Passes, block the Israeli ground invasion, and then counter-attack (Dunstan 2009). This was Nasser's advice when he dropped by GHQ on the afternoon of June 5: to dig-in around the passes (Sadat 1978: 229). But on the second day of the war, Amer gave Chief of Staff Fawzy twenty minutes to draft a withdrawal plan. "I was astounded. . . . The field marshal was psychologically worn out and seemed on the verge of a nervous breakdown. . . . The land forces . . . were holding out steadily, and there seemed to be no reason whatsoever to consider a withdrawal." Nonetheless, Fawzy prepared a rough plan for a four-day pullout with enough delaying tactics to keep the army intact. Amer stared at him blankly and said he had already issued an order to withdraw in twenty-four hours (Fawzy 1990: 151–52). Catastrophe followed: tens of thousands of soldiers abandoned their equipment and withdrew in chaos only to find themselves stranded in the scorching desert under the mercy of marauding Israeli fire power. Amer's unilateral decision to withdraw was doubtlessly the single most important cause of the 1967 defeat. Gamasy summed up what he saw at the front:

> I watched a heavy flow of troops move westward [away from Sinai]. It was completely disorganized. . . . Could a retreat take place in this manner, when it normally required extreme discipline and precision and, according to the doctrine of war, should take place while the fighting still continued. . . . The [high] command had given up control of its forces at the most critical time. . . . [T]he situation can neither be explained nor excused . . . troops withdraw[ing] in the most pathetic way . . . under continuous enemy air attacks . . . an enormous graveyard of scattered corpses, burning equipment, and exploding ammunition. (Al-Gamasy 1993: 64–65)

A rather conclusive piece of evidence of how military mobilization that fateful summer was plainly a bluff comes from Badran's confession during his trial, in February 1968: "We were 100 percent sure that Israel would not dare to attack" (Al-Gamasy 1993: 76). Clearly, the field marshal's men thought that they could wipe out the effects of the Suez War (by removing UN observers, and reestablishing Egypt's control over Red Sea navigation) by simply intimidating Israel. All the military needed was to appear formidable. And that it did. With all eyes fixed on the army's gallant march into Sinai, Amer could "return to the center stage of . . . politics after he thought he was so close to the exit" (Heikal 1990: 818). Little did he suspect that the exit door had just opened up. The defeat finally provided Nasser with the opportunity to reclaim the military.

The Showdown

After Israel occupied Sinai, Nasser told Amer he was announcing their collective resignation in a televised speech. Amer conceded, provided that his faithful security man (and current war minister) Shams Badran became president. But on June 9, Nasser's primetime speech only mentioned his own resignation and named security czar Zakaria Muhi al-Din as his successor (Sadat 1978: 232). Hundreds of thousands immediately flooded the streets, protesting Nasser's decision and pledging to fight Israel under his banner. Their spontaneity was contested since ASU had the capacity to spark mass demonstrations with great speed. In February 1967 Aly Sabri used the ASU to mobilize 100,000 people in ten hours. A later experiment mobilized 40,000 people in three hours (Yunis 2005: 7–8). The fact that these drills took place three months before the June 9 demonstrations makes it clear that regardless of the spontaneity of some, ASU was the mastermind. It also helped that the police did nothing to repress them. In fact, Interior Minister Sha'rawi Gomaa warned Muhammad Hassanein Heikal, Nasser's confidant, that unless the president retracted his resignation, his men would not hold back the crowds (Heikal 1990: 851). Amer's resignation was only announced at the late-night news bulletin after the masses had already taken to the streets to prove that they only wanted Nasser's return. The choice of Zakaria Muhi al-Din as successor seems to have been also well calculated. As Amer rightly noted: "A fetus in his mother's womb was bound to reject Zakaria," the feared security baron (Ahmed 1993: 913).

The field marshal's main security ally, GIS Chief Salah Nasr, carried to Nasser the military's rejection of any changes in the high command. Nasser rejected this veiled threat. On June 11 he returned to office and put Fawzy in charge of the military. Four days later, he invited Amer to his house to let him know he would not be reinstated (Heikal 1990: 875–86). The field marshal's men responded with a fierce defamation campaign among the ranks, blaming Nasser—an egoistic and obsessive adventurer—for all the military setbacks in Syria, Yemen, and Sinai (Al-Gamasy 1993: 35). The message, in the words of one field commander, was that the president keeps "throwing an army that cannot swim into the sea, and then punishing it for drowning" (Abu Zikri 1988: 380–97). Some even claimed that Nasser engineered his army's defeat to rein it in—like a merchant who burns his shop in the hope of a fresh start (Al-Sanhouri 2005: 314; Ghaleb 2001: 124). Security officials distributed Amer's 1962 letter of resignation to show how the field marshal had implored his friend to renounce dictatorship before it ruined the country (Sharaf 1996: 160–61).

Compared to this efficient pro-Amer offensive, Nasser's associates seemed at a loss, partly because the latter hoped to appease Amer, Badran, and Nasr, "the unholy trio who ran a government within the government in Egypt without his knowledge or approval," with ceremonial posts—in Amer's case: the vice presidency (Aburish 2004: 267). The president's hesitance encouraged Amer's faction to move from slander to action. The field marshal's security wizards (Badran, Nasr, and Abbas Radwan) plotted a coup to restore their patron. The paratroopers' commander, General Osman Nassar, summarized their motive: "We implore you [Amer] not to give this man [Nasser] power over us. . . . [H]e will not shrink from humiliating and destroying us" (Hosni 2008: 155). On June 10 Nasr hid Amer in an intelligence safe house until Badran and Radwan had turned his Cairo residence into a fortress guarded by two platoons with artillery guns, and 300 militiamen from Amer's hometown in Upper Egypt. On June 11, 600 officers (among whom were fifty brigadiers and generals) drove twelve armored vehicles into GHQ, chanting "There is no leader but the field marshal!" before turning to Amer's house to pledge their allegiance (Fawzy 1990: 166–68). And on June 26, Nasr sought the CIA's blessing for his plan to topple Nasser (Sirrs 2010: 105). The plan was to sneak Amer to the Suez Canal, where the army was mostly concentrated, while paratroopers neutralized the Republican Guard, and GIS operatives rounded up Nasser and his associates. Amer would then address the nation, detailing the president's responsibility for the defeat, and declaring war under his command to liberate Sinai (Hammad 2010: 1345; Ahmed 1993: 925–33). The plan was sound, but the field marshal delayed its execution upon receiving Nasser's invitation for a meeting to reach an accord. Against the advice of his security men, Amer accepted. After missing his chance to act, it was now Nasser's turn.

It was days before the plot was scheduled to unfold that Nasser's security men got wind of it. The president's PBI was tipped off by a GIS operative, four officers, and Amer's cook. To plan a counterattack, Zakaria Muhi al-Din formed a taskforce composed of PBI Director Samy Sharaf, Interior Minister Sha'rawi Gomaa, and former intelligence operative Amin Huwaidi. Meetings were held after midnight at a sporting club to avoid GIS surveillance, and soon Nasser was presented with Operation Johnson. Amer was to be lured out of his stronghold and detained. Republican Guard forces would storm into his house to allow Interior Ministry officers to arrest the conspirators. Huwaidi would then take over both the War Ministry and the GIS to administer a sweeping purge of military and intelligence personnel. The end goal was to depoliticize the military and redirect intelligence from domestic to external espionage (Sharaf 1996: 160–75).

The plan was implemented successfully. Amer arrived at the presidential residence, on the night of August 24, 1967. Muhi al-Din escorted him to an undisclosed location. The field marshal's villa was occupied after a four-hour siege and a brief skirmish. His followers were shortly apprehended. At dawn, Huwaidi reached GIS headquarters, and immediately issued orders to place 148 military officers and 18 intelligence operatives (including the agency's chief Nasr) in custody. On September 13 Amer supposedly committed suicide (Fawzy 1990: 175–74; Huwaidi 2002: 249–275).

It is no mystery why the military did nothing to save its beloved leader and his men. A colonel, who served at the front in 1967, captured the general mood within the ranks, "Soldiers abandon their leaders [in peace] when their leaders abandon them in war" (Al-Beteshty 2006: 17). A brigade commander in 1967 and future war minister, Kamal Hassan Aly, described how he and his comrades regarded Amer's men less as fellow officers than as "security agents similar to the political commissars of the Soviet army . . . a new ruling class within the army" (Aly 1994: 117). So even though Amer's security elite bought off the loyalty of many officers, a critical mass within the armed forces saw clearly how the politicization (and straightforward corruption) of the military had hurled their institution to the abyss.

Now, it was Nasser's chance to reverse the military politicization trend he had in 1952 ushered in. Acting in his dual capacity as war minister and GIS director, Huwaidi launched an investigation into the cause of defeat, and concluded that it was "the political leadership's loss of control over the military and security agencies" (Huwaidi 2002: 190–91). Between November 1967 and February 1968, Muhi al-Din supervised a comprehensive purge of Amer loyalists: 1,000 officers and 300 intelligence operatives were discharged, and 90 conspirators, including Nasr, Badran, and Radwan, and Amer's supreme commanders were handed long prison sentences (Hosni 2008: 143, 151). The percentage of officers in the cabinet decreased from 66 percent in 1967 to 21 percent, and those in the ASU from 75 percent in 1962 to 43 percent (Hammad 1990: 35–36). The number of generals was cut in half. Service chiefs were asked to report directly to the president. The OCC—the nerve center of Amer's security network—was dissolved. And the National Defense Council, composed of the president and his top ministers and security advisors, was formed in 1969 to take over the responsibility of determining Egypt's national security interests from the Supreme Council of the Armed Forces. Finally, Huwaidi devoted a special section within GIS to carry out the role of the now-dissolved OCC in monitoring political trends within the armed forces (Huwaidi 2002: 305, 438–51).

The president followed this dramatic restructuring with the March 30 Manifesto, which blamed the 1967 defeat on the military–intelligence complex, and vowed to open up the political system through a new permanent constitution, which was drafted in 1970, and ratified the following year. But—good intentions aside—Egypt's institutional set-up barred this option. It is true that military-based security organs were either dissolved (the OCC) or redirected toward external enemies (Military Intelligence). It is also true that the civilian intelligence (GIS) was now restricted to counterintelligence and foreign espionage. But the security shakeup left three formidable institutions standing: the Interior Ministry with its dreaded General Investigations Department (GID), the president's homegrown intelligence agency (PBI), and the security-oriented ASU, and its secret VO. After a brief soul-searching journey, Nasser was swayed by his security advisors toward maintaining authoritarianism, and only substituting military protection for that of a devastatingly effective civilian security system. The president took a huge step in that direction by creating the Central Security Forces (CSF) at the beginning of 1969. These anti-riot shock units (numbering 100,000 in 1970) were composed of military conscripts placed under the control of the Interior Ministry—a most unusual arrangement. If GID and PBI were now solely responsible for surveillance and investigations, neither of them had the capacity to repress demonstrations, a task previously handled by the military. Nasser therefore supplied them with a paramilitary police force to do the job. The CSF, in other words, was specifically designed to "obviate military involvement in riot control" (Springborg 1989: 101).

There was also a geopolitical element to the continued dominance of security men. The military launched a war of attrition against Israeli forces in Sinai between July 1967 and August 1970. These intermittent battles, as well as the preparation for the upcoming war of liberation, required foreign aid. Convinced that what happened in 1967 was "an Israeli execution of an American war," Nasser abandoned his balancing strategy and aligned himself with Moscow (Heikal 1990: 914). The Soviets provided advanced weapons (T-62 tanks, Tu-16 bombers, MiG-21 fight bombers), and an air defense system (centered on SAM-6 missiles) without which Egypt could not have entered another war, and—in "an unequivocal military gesture"—sent their own pilots, technicians, and instructors to help rebuild the army and handle its defense (Al-Gamasy 1993: 117). The Soviets promoted the rise of Egypt's new security triumvirate: Sharaf, Gomaa, and Sabri—whom citizens now referred to as the "centers of power" (Hammad 2008: 1). Of course, Moscow was typically obsessed with security control, but the three men also advanced themselves as guarantors of a continued Soviet alliance against the vacillation of democratic (i.e., pro-Western) forces within and outside the regime.

The question one must confront at this point is why the defeat did not spur a popular revolt, perhaps supplemented by a few mutinous regiments, as happened in Russia and Prussia following the Great War? The part concerning the military is relatively easy to answer. For one thing, the army was in a state of shock. After all, it was defeated in six short days, rather than four years of drawn out battles. Also, unlike the war-hardened soldiers of Europe's two great land powers, Egyptian soldiers scarcely saw combat during these days. Finally, a decade of politicization and security control—something without parallel in the armies of the tsar or the kaiser—kept them loyal. As for the people, they did, in fact, revolt in two waves of massive student and worker uprisings, in February and November 1968—for the first time since 1954. Military tanks surrounded the protesters and helicopters hovered over their heads, but they were only present to intimidate. It was the Ministry of Interior that was now expected to restore order, and it did so with a vengeance: the police used live ammunition, killing 21 people, injuring 772, and detaining 1,100 (Abdallah 1997: 27–45, 149–53). Again, almost two decades of security control prevented university and labor activists from developing the organizations necessary for a full-scale revolt—a phenomenon replicated in 2011. But as ineffective as the 1968 demonstrators were, they legitimized the security branch's anti-democracy campaign—as re-occurred in 2013. Opposition cannot be tolerated in times of national crisis. Once more, the opportunity to open up the political system had come and gone. The first time, in 1954, it was demanded by officers concerned about the negative effects of immersing the military in politics. In 1967 their fear were vindicated, and the demand for democracy should have been even more resounding. In both cases, however, security forces won the day.

Notes

1. The 1967 trials revealed how OCC Director Badran had charged members of his cohort in the class of 1948 with managing these cells (Sharaf 1996: 359–60).

2. For Egyptian interpretations, see Abu Zikri (1988) and Heikal (1990); for Israeli ones, see Eban (1992), Oren (2002), and Segev (2007); and for Western analysis, see Kerr (1969), Nutting (1972), Brecher (1974), Parker (1993), Boyne (2002), and Brooks (2008).

14 | Becoming a Police State

OCTOBER 1973

NASSER'S PREMATURE DEATH, IN SEPTEMBER 1970, sent shockwaves across the country, especially because he had not groomed an appropriate successor. Vice-President Anwar al-Sadat was perceived as weak and unpopular. Before the 1952 coup, Sadat had joined the least significant army service, the Signal Corps. During the 1948 war in Palestine, he was a runaway from prison, where he had been interned for Nazi sympathies. King Farouk reincorporated him into the corps after agreeing to join the ill-reputed Iron Guards, secret assassins of royal enemies. On the night of the coup, Sadat famously went to the cinema and picked a fight with an audience member that ended up at the police station. His co-conspirators suspected he was planning to use the theater tickets and police report as alibis had the coup failed. Nonetheless, Nasser found Sadat's cunning useful. And it was the insecure president's habit of rotating the vice-presidency between nonthreatening candidates that placed Sadat—barely a few months in office—on Nasser's throne.

With the military counting down to war to liberate Sinai from Israeli occupation, officers feared that Sadat's feeble personality and lack of combat experience would drive him to sue for peace. Yet his presidency sat well with Egypt's so-called centers of power: Aly Sabri, who dominated the Arab Socialist Union (ASU); Sha'rawi Gomaa, interior minister and head of ASU's secret Vanguard Organization (VO); and Samy Sharaf, director of the President's Bureau of Information (PBI), who also held sway in the military and intelligence through his relative Muhammad Fawzy, the war minister, and his protégée Ahmed Kamel, director of the General Intelligence Service (GIS). Ruling in the shadow of a ceremonial president suited these security magnates. And Sadat seemed the safest bet: he had no following in the military or security, he held no executive position between 1956 and 1969, and was one of the least popular politicians within ASU. Yet to keep him under their thumb, Sabri was promoted to vice-president, and Sharaf to minister of presidential affairs. Still, Sadat was not completely powerless. As secretary-general of the National Union (1957–1961), and speaker of Parliament (1961–1969), he acquired valuable experience in the political machinations of the state. More important perhaps was his particular skill at divide-and-conquer tactics. Drawing advice from the indispensable newspaper editor Muhammad Hassanein Heikal, Egypt's unrivaled *Machtpolitik* strategist, Sadat patched together a coalition of Republican Guard members, policemen, and professional officers to outmaneuver his rivals.

Eradicating the Centers of Power

Before the centers of power put their house in order, Sadat revived plans to merge with Syria, Libya, and possibly the Sudan into an Arab federation. His aim was to justify an institutional overhaul. But his opponents moved swiftly. The ASU vetoed the presidential proposition, on April 21, 1971, citing the results of a military survey opposing any such union because it would postpone the war (Sadat 1978: 299). A few more skirmishes convinced the centers of power that Sadat must go. Yet they differed over how. A replacement coup seemed implausible. They army would not intervene in a political battle in Cairo while Israel was still in Sinai, especially because the president let it be known that he was eager to wage war if it were not for the quibbling of his egoistical rivals (Hamroush 1987: 30). So when War Minister Fawzy devised a coup plan, it backfired. On April 21 he asked Chief of Staff Muhammad Sadeq to prepare an emergency strategy to secure the capital, adding suspiciously that once a state of emergency was declared, soldiers should only receive instructions from him (Fawzy), Gomaa, and Sharaf. Instead of following orders, Sadeq warned the president (through Heikal) and offered to swing the officer corps in his favor, in addition to his friend Al-Lethy Nassef, head of the Republican Guard (Heikal 1983: 40–41). Determined not to lose another battle to Israel, the chief of staff was infuriated by the continuing intrigue at a time when all effort should be directed to war preparation (Hammudah 1985: 173). The centers of power now considered a political coup: to oust Sadat through the ASU, as the Soviet Communist Party had done with Khrushchev six years earlier. To provide a pretext, ministers and ASU executives would collectively resign in protest of Sadat's autocracy; ASU and VO would then bring about a government shutdown through strikes in the bureaucracy and the public sector; state media would propel the masses into the streets to force the military to intervene (Binder 1978: 389)—a strategy strikingly similar to that of the 2013 crisis.

May Day 1971 provided a dress rehearsal. Osman Ahmed Osman, soon to be the richest man in Egypt and Sadat's closest friend, described the scene: "I noticed how the centers of power handed out Nasser's pictures to the workers and strategically distributed their loyalists around the hall to shout pro-Nasser slogans, casting doubt over Sadat's legitimacy" (Osman 1981: 402). Sadat stood his ground, concluding his speech with a resounding condemnation of the centers of power: "No group has the right to impose its will on the people through centers of power. . . . [T]he people alone are the masters of their destiny" (Mansour 2009: 142). The following day, he dismissed Sabri from the ASU and the vice-presidency.

As the confrontation became public, the battle lines were drawn. One figure returning from the shadows was Hassan al-Tuhami, Nasser's veteran intelligence operative who had left the country at Amer's request. Tuhami, a friend of Sadat's since the 1940s, hoped to take over from Sharaf as PBI director. Another security ally was Hafez Ismail, who had been banished to the Foreign Ministry after clashing with Amer, and rewarded with the GIS directorship during Nasser's final days. Ismail held a grudge against Sharaf because he had replaced him at GIS with his student Ahmed Kamel, and was grateful to Sadat for naming him as national security advisor. Although Ismail's days at GIS were few, the contacts he had developed proved useful during the coming clash. Then a precious prize fell into Sadat's lap on May 11: audiotapes detailing his rivals' conspiracy, and thus allowing him to charge them with treason. Sharaf had ordered PBI and GIS to spy on both Sadat and his own co-conspirators, and Gomaa had the Interior Ministry's GID tap his conversations with state officials, including his collaborators. But who turned the tapes in? Sadat claimed it was Captain Taha Zaki, a family friend in the police (Sadat 1978: 304). Sharaf said it was a GIS informant who worked for Tuhami or Ismail (Sharaf 1996: 457). Recent evidence suggests it was a CIA officer by the name of Thomas Twetten (Sirrs 2010: 120).

CIA involvement made sense because of the geopolitical aspect to Egypt's domestic struggle. Sabri was known as Russia's man in Cairo; Gomaa headed the Leninist-style VO, which the Soviets cherished; Fawzy was exceedingly grateful for Russia's military support; and Sharaf, as it turned out, was probably a KGB asset.[1] In fact, the day the centers of power offered their resignations, Russia's top military representative dined at Sharaf's house (Game' 2004: 151). Sadat, on the other hand, presented himself to Donald Bergus, the CIA official in Cairo, as the man prepared to cut the Soviets loose—as he eventually did (Sharaf 1996: 401).

With incontrovertible evidence of a conspiracy at hand, Sadat removed Gomaa from the Interior Ministry and VO, on May 13. The governor of Alexandria, Mamduh Salem, took over as interior minister before Gomaa learned of his dismissal. Salem had begun his career with the British-controlled secret police in the 1940s, and then headed GID's Alexandria office after the coup (Sirrs 2010: 21, 53). Not wanting to rely solely on Salem's contacts in the Interior Ministry, Sadat sent a detachment of the Republican Guard to secure his safe entry to the ministry (Mansour 2009: 431). Knowing he was next in line, Sharaf made his way to the military's general headquarters, where he found Gomaa waiting for the war minister to wrap up a meeting with his commanders. Fawzy pleaded with the high command to remove Sadat on account of his secret dealings with the Americans. But Chief of Staff Sadeq stood his ground: "[There is no way] the Egyptian armed forces would get mixed up in politics while we are preparing for war" (Heikal 1983: 41). Once the angry Fawzy left GHQ, Sadeq called the president to assure him of the army's neutrality. He was immediately named war minister. That evening, May 14, Ashraf Marawan, Nasser's son-in-law and Sharaf's right-hand man at PBI, defected to the president's camp. He turned over Sharaf's secret dossiers, and was rewarded with the PBI's directorship (Game' 2004: 168). Before that fateful night ended, Sadat appointed Ahmed Ismail GIS director. Ismail served twice as chief of staff under Nasser, but was fired both times for incompetence, and so naturally resented Nasser's men. The centers of power threw their last card. On May 14 they announced their collective resignation on state television, hoping to incite popular rebellion. Instead, they made it easier for Sadat to eliminate them. On May 15 the president carried out his "corrective revolution." He arrested ninety-one officials, including six ministers (among them Sharaf, Gomaa, and Fawzy), the GIS director (Kamel), twenty ASU executives, twenty-three VO cadres, four members of Parliament, and six senior bureaucrats. Hassan al-Tuhami, the returning security maverick, chaired an emergency court that imposed long sentences on the ringleaders. Sadat handed over the ASU and leadership of Parliament to his friend and in-law Sayyid Mar'ie. He then reorganized the security community.

While Nasser believed in the multiplication of security officers, Sadat preferred ironclad control. The two men were insecure in their own ways—as veteran conspirators usually are. Nasser's constant thirst for information made him spread his sensors as wide as possible. The over-anxious Sadat, by contrast, favored consolidation. After 1967 Nasser had dissolved the OCC and redirected Military Intelligence and the GIS toward foreign espionage. Sadat continued the job by abolishing the security-oriented VO, and reinventing the PBI as an information secretariat, which merely summarized government memos. He then reinforced the Interior Ministry with a dozen more departments in order to allow the GID to devote itself to political policing, rather than organized crime. The Free Officers had remained suspicious of the Interior Ministry's investigative agency despite the purges that accompanied its 1952 transformation from the secret police to GID. After all, the secret police had been the bastion of royalist intrigue for decades. For political security, therefore, Nasser relied on the PBI and GIS; and Amer had his OCC and Military Intelligence. Under Sadat, however, the agency reclaimed its former position as the leading security institution. It was rechristened as Mabaheth Amn al-Dawla (State Security Investigations Service, SSIS). Egypt's most powerful security organ thus came into being.

How could we explain Sadat's victory over those who dominated most state institutions? Conventional histories emphasize his exceptional cunning. Yet scheming alone was not enough. The truth is, the centers of power were divided. After finally wresting power from Amer's faction, in 1967, they began to negotiate a pecking order. Nasser's premature death, in 1970, caught them unprepared. The problem was how to establish a hierarchy between three equally powerful players. Sabri, Gomaa, and Sharaf balanced each other too well for a coalition leader to emerge. In fact, it was this deadlock that brought Sadat to the presidency; they needed a lame-duck president until they sorted things out. When Sadat dismissed Sabri, his comrades were happy to deal with one less contender. However, they shot themselves in the foot because Sabri's experience as prime minister (1962–1965), ASU secretary-general (1962–1969), and vice-president (1970–1971) made him the strongest candidate for the presidency. Gomaa might have controlled the Interior Ministry, but it was only after Sadat that it had become the central pillar of power. And the VO, which he also headed, was essentially an espionage organ. Finally, Sharaf was let down by his allies. The war minister learned the hard way that wartime militaries have little appetite for political intrigue. And the GIS director failed to penetrate the agency deep enough during his few months in office. And when it appeared that the military and intelligence support he counted on would not be forthcoming, his deputy at PBI turned against him.

In sum, the president's opponents were not a unified camp, but disparate centers scrambling to consolidate their power. Sadat's triumph paved the path for the rise of Egypt's police state under the rapidly evolving Interior Ministry, and its SSIS spies. But first there was a war to be fought. Sadat's road to power had to pass through occupied Sinai.

The Road to October

The post-1967 de-politicization of the military was still raw. Defeating Israel militarily threatened to bring the army back to the center stage. Losing a new war meant political suicide. The middle road was narrow and thorny. It required waging a successful war without re-empowering the officer corps politically. This could only be achieved if the military victory was limited and faceless. No popular war heroes could be allowed to emerge—heroes who might convert their popularity into political capital. Liberating Sinai had to be perceived as a political rather than military triumph; war had to appear secondary to politics. This compelled the president to employ Egypt's best generals for limited tasks before deposing (and preferably defaming) them.

It began in May 1971 after Sadat imprisoned War Minister Muhammad Fawzy for treason despite his efforts in rebuilding the army after 1967. Muhammad Sadeq, who took his post, was determined to win the next war. This is why, as Military Intelligence director, he sided with Nasser against Amer, and, as chief of staff, helped Sadat eradicate the centers of power. For chief of staff, Sadat made a controversial choice, promoting the audacious head of the Commando Corps, Saad al-Din al-Shazly, over the heads of thirty senior generals. The president wanted to assert his right to choose (or dismiss) commanders regardless of military regulations. He also recognized that Egypt needed the fearless Shazly in the first stages of the war. The problem was that the high command doubted the president's devotion to a decisive military victory. Capturing the general mood, Mohamed Hassanein Heikal, a close advisor to Sadat and Nasser before him, commented: "The chasm between arms and politics widened in Egypt. It became apparent that neither politics trusted the ability of arms, nor did arms trust the competence of politics" (Heikal 1993: 262). The dispute centered on the war plan. The generals believed that an attack must be "forceful and unlimited: a clean, swift sweep through . . . all our occupied territories" (Shazly 1980: 25). At minimum, the high command agreed in their meeting on January 2, 1972, that the offensive must reach the Sinai Passes (Brooks 2008: 132). This was also the view of the now-imprisoned former War Minister Fawzy. Egypt's first line of defense extended from its borders with Israel to the Sinai Passes; the second line of defense stretched from the passes to the Suez Canal; and third line was the canal itself. Egypt's army was presently stationed along the third line of defense, and at minimum had to advance to the second line, which was the passes (Fawzy 1990: 101).

Why were the passes so important? A veteran of the 1948 war described them as nature's gift to Sinai's defense (Hammudah 1985: 137). Military historians believed the passes were simply "impassible" (Insight Team 1974: 70). Every Egyptian cadet was taught that controlling the passes was the key to defending Sinai (Heikal 1983: 60). These were the passes that Nasser advised Amer to dig into in 1967 to halt the Israeli advance. And these were also the passes that Moshe Dayan asked the Israeli forces to occupy because they provided "much better defense lines than the canal" (Golan 1976: 147). Israeli Commander and future Prime Minister Ariel Sharon remembered vividly how well the passes served Egyptian troops in 1956: "The Israeli air attack had failed to dislodge defenders cocooned in rifle pits dug along the tops of ridges and in caves cut into the steep walls of the pass. For the Egyptians it was like shooting at a fairground target. . . . The only way I could see to defend ourselves was to move into the pass and take up positions there, where the steep cliffs and narrow defiles would give the oncoming Egyptian tanks no room for maneuver" (Turner 2006: 317–19). In fact, Israel had to build the Bar-Lev defense line along the canal because—away from the passes—Sinai's open terrain offered no other point of defense. As summarized by one American expert: with Sinai being "an exposed killing ground," any battle over it was simply "a two-way race for the passes" (Cordesman 2006: 201–02). And in his colossal, military-endorsed history of the 1973 war, General Gamal Hammad concluded that asking the army to turn from offense to defense before reaching the passes amounts to surrendering the initiative to the enemy (Hammad 2002: 52–54).

Now, although Sadat assured the high command that he intended to seize the passes during the first wave of attack, his generals doubted him because he wanted to launch war before receiving the weapons necessary for such a sweeping assault. Sadat's unilateral decision to ask Soviet experts, in July 1972, to leave the country shocked his generals. War Minister Sadeq criticized him for alienating Egypt's only arms supplier (Al-Gamasy 1993: 141–45). A stunned Shazly tried to reason with him: "You must realize how dangerous this decision is. . . . There is no question that it will affect our capabilities" (Shazly 1980: 111). Tension reached a climax on the night of October 24, 1972. Sadat had asked the war minister to prepare for an attack in November; an order Sadeq duly ignored because a premature attack limited to crossing the Suez Canal without seizing the passes would be disastrous. So while Sadat thought he was meeting his generals to review the final preparations for war, they were there to protest his plan. According to the minutes of the meeting, Sadat began by denying rumors that he was "selling the country to the Americans," and seeking peace with Israel (Sabri 1979: 31). The war minister, his deputy, and the navy commander questioned the president's decision to "go to war with whatever weapons we had." Clearly enraged, Sadat responded that none of them had "the right or the competence" to second-guess him (Sadat 1978: 319–21). The adamant deputy war minister insisted that a limited war would quickly descend into a hopeless defense of a few insignificant bridgeheads on the banks of the canal. Sadat barked: "I know what I am doing. It is none of your business. Make one more objection, and you will be asked to stay home. . . . Shame on you! Learn your place! You are a soldier, not a politician." When the navy commander said it was inappropriate for the president to scold his generals in this degrading manner, Sadat gave him a piece of his mind, too. At the end of the meeting, an indignant Sadeq asked Sadat why he had opted to meet with his generals if he was not willing to listen to them. The president's response came a few days later: the war minister was placed under house arrest for plotting a coup; every general who had pressed him was sacked; and over a hundred senior officers were purged (Sabri 1979: 65–67; Shazly 1980: 122–23). To justify himself, Sadat portrayed the dismissed high command as "a group of childish pupils, [composed of] a deceived leftist, an ailing psychopath, a mercenary, a traitor to Egypt, a conspirator" (Mansour 2009: 335–36).

In response, dozens of officers formed the Save Egypt Movement to prevent the president from pushing them into war unprepared. It was led by no less than the commander of the Central District (Cairo), the Military Intelligence chief, two divisional commanders and chiefs of staff, and a commando unit head. And it was the SSIS that uncovered the plot—one of the first instances of the Interior Ministry spying on the army (Shazly 1980: 129; Brooks 2008: 121). Pulling no punches, the president took another controversial decision by appointing Intelligence Director Ahmed Ismail as war minister on October 26, 1972.

Ismail was a timid 56-year-old general who was fighting a losing battle with cancer. His overcautious nature had kept him from joining the Free Officers in 1952. His performance during the 1948 and 1956 wars was quite unremarkable. He was relieved twice from duty for incompetence, as a divisional commander in August 1967, and as chief of staff in September 1969 (Sirrs 2010: 121). And his physicians warned that he could not handle a stressful job (something Sadat himself knew about Ismail); in fact, he took to his bed in the middle of the war (Mansour 2009: 367). What distinguished Ismail was that his service history and medical condition made it impossible for him to nurture a following among officers. More important, he was the known arch-enemy of Chief of Staff Shazly. The two had remained on nonspeaking terms ever since their fistfight in Congo in 1960, when Ismail tried to flaunt his authority as Egypt's military attaché in the face of Shazly who served with the UN peacekeepers. The young Captain Shazly refused to obey Brigadier Ismail not just because he had no jurisdiction over him, but also because he thought Ismail blatantly inept. In fact, Shazly had resigned in March 1969 as head of the Commando Corps when Nasser appointed Ismail chief of staff, but before his resignation was considered, Ismail was dismissed once more. Indeed, when Sadat consulted Shazly on Sadeq's replacement as war minister, he advised that anyone other than Ismail would do. When the president appointed him anyway, Shazly was appalled: "Mr. President ... I have a history of disagreement with Ahmed Ismail. . . . It would be impossible to work in harmony." Sadat shrugged, "I know all that" (Shazly 1980: 124–25). Finally, he was the only man among Egypt's unyielding generals who accepted the president's still hidden plan to wage a limited war as a catalyst for political settlement (Heikal 1983: 64).

Still, any war was risky, whether limited or otherwise. Another defeat would be politically disastrous. At the same time, a straightforward victory would create military heroes who could then challenge Sadat. The examples of Naguib and Nasser were instructive. Even though Egypt lost in 1948, the two men's gallant performance gained them enough legitimacy within the ranks to defy the king. To avoid this risk altogether, Sadat first explored the option of liberating Sinai without a war—a purely political triumph. He hoped for a repeat of the 1956 Suez War, minus the war. On that occasion, Egypt had secured an astonishing political victory away from the battlefield (Sabri 1979: 54). In Sadat's mind, the party that delivered that victory on a silver platter was the United States. He often recalled how Eisenhower "transformed [Egypt's] military defeat into political victory." He also saw Nasser's decision, in 1967, to hand power to the pro-American Zakaria as an admission on his part that "there was one power that ruled Egypt and the world, that is: America." Summarized in his favorite aphorism: "America holds 99 percent of the cards" (Sadat 1978: 194, 232, 390). Accordingly, Sadat embarked on a private war to win over America.

Sadat's first move after becoming president was to appeal to Washington's envoy to Nasser's funeral to "try him out" (Sadat 1978: 296). He then sought the support of congressional members during their visit to Cairo in March 1971. He also tried to appease the United States by removing his anti-American Foreign Minister Mahmoud Riyad (Hamroush 1987: 17, 40–46). Before that, he had asked a former Free Officer, Abd al-Mon'em Amin, to befriend the U.S. chargé d'affaires in Cairo, Donald Bergus. Amin brandished the new president's anti-Communism and apologized for Nasser's unwarranted hostility toward Washington, adding shamelessly that "[he] did everything for his own glory, and believed that defying America would elevate him." When Bergus mumbled tactfully that Nasser was also a great leader, Amin retorted: "He was only great because he brought great disasters upon his country" (Heikal 1993: 758–60). When the Americans remained uninterested, Sadat sought the help of his longtime friend Kamal Adham, the chief of Saudi intelligence. Adham installed a hotline between the presidency and the CIA's Cairo station, but also advised Sadat to stop talking and do something tangible. So Sadat expelled Moscow's 15,000 military experts, in July 1972 (Heikal 1983: 445; Sirrs 2010: 121). President Richard Nixon still ignored him, for as the U.S. national security advisor explained to Egypt's UN representative: "Why pay for something offered freely"? (Abd al-Magid 1998: 121).

Eventually, Sadat realized that these sporadic attempts were useless, and decided to refocus all his energy on the man he believed could deliver Sinai: Henry Kissinger. In February 1973 the president dispatched his national security advisor, Hafez Ismail, to meet Kissinger at the Connecticut home of Pepsi-Cola Chairman Donald Kendall (Heikal 1993: 235, 270–71). Sadat finally got his secret backchannel to the White House. Ismail immediately laid his cards on the table, declaring that his boss was the first Arab leader willing to "enter into a peace agreement with Israel" (Burr 2004: 41). Kissinger was impressed by Sadat's eagerness, but—as he wrote in his memoir—he believed that a long-term Egyptian-American alliance required Cairo to acknowledge the following reality: "that Israel was too strong (or could be made too strong) to be defeated even by all of its neighbors combined, and that the . . . key to the Middle East, therefore, resided in Washington" (Kissinger 1994: 737). In his estimation, Sadat recognized the second fact, but he still needed to accept the first. So, as he later confessed, "What did I do in those conversations? I talked with [Sadat's envoy] about the weather and every other subject in the world. . . . I played with him. I toyed with him. My aim was to gain time and postpone the serious stage for another month, another year" (quoted in Golan 1976: 145). Ismail reported back that Kissinger could not do much for a defeated country. He highlighted a section in the minutes of his last meeting with Kissinger, in May 1973, where the latter had said: "I have told you last time, and I will continue to say that there is no better position for the Israelis than the one they are in right now. . . . As long as Israel feels it could preserve its position, we do not think, honestly, that it will pull back" (Burr 2004: 37, 47). The message was clear: war could no longer be postponed.

"The Victory Egypt Threw Away"

As America seemed reluctant to furnish Sadat with a purely political settlement, he was now forced to walk the delicate path of unleashing the military, on the one hand, and curbing its success, on the other. While his generals aspired to liberate Sinai by force of arms, the president wanted to trigger negotiations through a symbolic act of military defiance. His aim therefore was to cross the Suez Canal and establish a beachhead on the East Bank. His alibi to the army would be that Egypt had been forced to fight a limited war because it could not secure enough Soviet weapons, and that the United States would not allow Israel to lose (Brooks 2008: 104). So his strategy, as one U.S. military expert put it, was a "demilitarized [war] strategy [which] manifested itself as a diplomatic offensive pegged to a military attack" (Schofield 2007: 98). The problem was that the armed forces understandably rejected his aim for "a diplomatic rather than a battlefield victory" (Schofield 2007: 109). They hoped that once the war started, they could see their mission through with minimal interference from the capital. However, Sadat's tight-leash control over operations eventually led to what was described variously as Egypt's "Lost Victory," by the *Sunday Times* (Ghaleb 2001: 213); "The Victory Egypt Threw Away," by the team of international experts who studied the war (Insight Team 1974: 219); Egypt's road "From Victory to Self-Defeat," by a Western scholar (Barnet 1992: 128); and, more evocatively, as the "savage struggle that Egypt . . . had little hope for winning but nonetheless came very close—perhaps within hours—to doing so," by a renowned military historian (Boyne 2002: xiv).

As mentioned before, victory hung on reaching the Sinai passes. Egypt lacked Israel's *blitzkrieg* capacity for mobile war, but it could achieve a "static victory" by holding the perfectly defensible passes (Insight Team 1974: 86). This was the centerpiece of Plan 200, formulated by War Minister Fawzy, and initially presented to Nasser and Sadat, in March 1970 (Fawzy 1990: 12, 365). Updates by Chief of Staff Shazly never altered the central aim. Infantrymen and armory would cross the canal and storm the Bar-Lev fortifications under the cover of artillery and air raids, then march quickly to the passes and dig in until the high command reassessed the viability of further advance. Meanwhile, the Syrians would attempt to regain the Golan Heights, and thus divide Israel's attention (Shazly 1980: 18; Al-Gamasy 1993: 138–39).

Before dawn on October 6, frogmen sabotaged the underwater oil pipes that Israel planned to turn ablaze if Egyptians attempted to cross the canal. At 2:05 P.M. an armada of 222 jets bombed Israeli airfields and missile sites in Sinai, and artillery barrages covered the crossing of infantrymen in rubber dinghies and floating bridges. The troops overran the Bar-Lev Line's fortifications, and established five bridgeheads on the East Bank. By nightfall, Egyptians had just achieved "the largest crossing in military history," with 100,000 troops armed with anti-tank missiles, 1,000 tanks, and 13,500 armored vehicles (Shazly 1980: 157). Under the protection of a dense umbrella of SAM air-defense batteries, the Egyptian army proceeded to destroy 49 Israeli planes and 500 tanks. And while the high command prepared to lose 10,000 soldiers in the crossing, only 200 were actually killed. With Israel's air force and armory temporarily neutralized, Egypt dominated the battlefield and was in a position to advance to the passes before the Israelis knew what hit them (Al-Gamasy 1993: 226, 250). As an Israeli historian was forced to admit, "Military history offers few parallels for strategic surprise as complete as that achieved by Egypt" (Shlaim 1976: 348). Even the Israeli Defense Minister Moshe Dayan complained in his first wartime press conference, "I doubt whether there is another place in the entire world that is protected by such a dense array of modern missiles. I doubt whether there is a place in Russia or Vietnam that is equipped like . . . the Egyptian front at the canal" (Insight Team 1974: 189). Israeli commanders understood that if Egypt kept the initiative, they would be dragged into a drawn-out war of attrition in Sinai. In fact, Dayan confided to his staff that "there was not a single tank between Tel Aviv and the Israeli lines in the Sinai" (Boyne 2002: 58).

Israeli reporter Matti Golan captured the mood in Tel Aviv during those first several days: "[Prime Minister] Mrs. Meir, Dayan, and Chief of Staff [David] Elazar were so tired and pessimistic that they were ready to throw in the towel" (Golan 1976: 66). At the same time, a *New York Times* war correspondent summarized the spirit on the Egyptian front in one sentence: "The Aim of Every Egyptian Soldier: To Advance Eastward."[2] The international team of experts who studied the war thus concluded: "[I]f the Egyptians chose to press on, it did not look as if Israel—even with its reserves—would be able to do other than fight a continuing rearguard action" (Insight Team 1974: 191). Indeed, by October 8, Egypt had amassed a fighting force of 100,000 men a few kilometers away from the passes, backed up by four divisions and two armored brigades. It was time to move forward.

But instead of advancing to the passes, Egypt decided to "hand over [its] brilliantly won initiative to the Israelis" (Insight Team 1974: 226). As future War Minister Kamal Hassan Aly reported, despite the military's plea for a rapid advance, Sadat simply halted the offensive on October 9 (Aly 1994: 319). Abd al-Ghany al-Gamasy, the chief of operations, begged him to understand that an offensive now would be carried out "Under the best conditions for us and the worst for them" (Al-Gamasy 1993: 264). Gamasy turned to War Minister Ismail, Sadat's ally, "I beg you to remember that . . . the principle of proceeding eastward to the passes was predetermined and there was no disagreement over this." It was a political decision, Ismail replied (Al-Gamasy 1993: 265–66). The Military Advisory Board reduced its recommendations to the president to only one: "Advance to the passes" (Heikal 1993: 438). Situation Report No. 4 from Egypt's field commanders stressed that the Israelis had redirected their energy away from the Egyptian to the Syrian front, and that this was the best time to develop the attack. Two days later, on October 11, Situation Report No. 6 warned that an Israeli counterattack was expected in forty-eight hours, and that the chance for an advance was slipping away. The War Ministry reported that Sadat's halt had caused confusion on the front, and that it had become the sole subject of discussion among officers and soldiers (Heikal 1993: 396–422). A cable sent by the U.S. Interests Section in Cairo to Washington indicated that Egypt would surely seize the passes right away (Burr 2004: 151). Pentagon analysts thought Egypt was mad to cross the canal and then just sit still (Hamroush 1987: 184). The Russian ambassador personally told Sadat that reconnaissance revealed there were only two Israeli brigades blocking his way, and estimated that he could seize the passes in a few hours (Heikal 1993: 392–93). The Russians also informed Egypt's foreign minister that his country's slowing down at this point was military suicide (Ghaleb 2001: 213). According to Soviet generals, to stop now amounted to "throw[ing] away all that had been won" (Boyne 2002: 96). Yet to no avail. When former Prime Minister Mahmoud Fawzy relayed to the president the concerns of Egypt's allies and neighbors with this unwarranted halt, Sadat responded: "Rest assured, everything is in my hand" (Heikal 1993: 419).

The president's decision was catastrophic because while Egyptian bridgeheads stretched 200 kilometers across the canal, they were only a little over 10 kilometers deep—almost half the distance between the canal and the passes. And because of his "ultimately fatal" decision, Cairo practically "frittered [its] gains away" (Insight Team 1974: 135, 172, 232). So what was he up to? Unbeknownst to his high command, a mere twenty hours after his troops had crossed the canal, and while they continued to advance successfully, Sadat sent a secret cable to Kissinger to assure him that "Egypt had no intention of intensifying the engagements or widening the confrontation" (Al-Gamasy 1993: 237). This was the first of thirty-eight secret cables, transmitted between October 7 and 29, in which Sadat desperately sought Kissinger's help in getting Israel to agree to a political settlement (Heikal 1993: 792–858). Sadat's war decisions therefore had nothing to do with battlefield developments, but rather with his campaign to enlist Kissinger's support in achieving his ultimate goal of a political solution aided only partially by a modest military operation.

Instead, Kissinger summoned Israeli Ambassador Simcha Dinitz to inform him of Sadat's pledge not to extend his narrow foothold on the East Bank (Burr 2004: 126). Since Israel did not have the resources to engage both the Egyptian and Syrian fronts simultaneously, the Pentagon had advised Israeli Chief of Staff David Elazar to freeze one front, and concentrate all effort on the other, before turning back to finish off the first (Al-Gamasy 1993: 247–48). Knowing that Egyptians were not planning to advance made Israel feel secure enough to turn its attention to the Syrians (Boyne 2002: 45). So suddenly the Syrians, who were on the verge of liberating the Golan, found themselves overwhelmed (Aly 1994: 319).

As Gamasy later noted in his memoir, when the Americans eventually declassified Sadat's secret cables, he finally understood why political directions seemed constantly "out of step with the military achievements." But it was hard for him to overcome the shock that while Egypt's troops were dying on the battlefront, "the political leadership had divulged its military intentions" to a country that was actively assisting its enemy (Al-Gamasy 1993: 240, 272). Heikal's remarks were more dramatic: "This was the first time in history that a country at war disclosed its intentions to its enemies, and gave them a free hand on the political and military fronts" (Heikal 1993: 360).

The American contribution to the Israeli war effort surged after it became clear that Israel's heavy losses during the first days of the war had crippled its offensive capabilities. Kissinger convinced Nixon that if the Arabs won, they would be impossible to negotiate with (Kissinger 1992: 481–82). "Without [an] airlift," he added, "Israel would be dead" (Burr 2004: 207). Nixon, in turn, had no reservations. Recalling his reaction a few months later in a gathering of American Jewish leaders, the U.S. president asked his secretary of state: "Henry, do you remember that on that fourth day [of the war] you came and suggested that I send five planes?—and I said if it's all right to send them five, let's send them fifty" (Golan 1976: 49). So on October 9, Nixon instructed his national security team "that Israel must not lose the war . . . and that Israel be told that it could freely expend all of its consumables . . . in the certain knowledge that these would be completely replenished by the United States without any delay" (Boyne 2002: 75–79).

Rearmed and ready, Israel blunted the Syrian attack, between October 8 and 14, while Egyptians stayed put, then counter-attacked in Sinai. This was when Sadat, again defying the entire high command, ordered an advance. Why the sudden change of heart? His official justification was that he wanted to provide relief to the Syrians. This is a curious explanation considering that the decimation of Syrian forces had only been possible because of his week-long halt. A better explanation could be derived from Kissinger's aloofness during the past few days. Sadat's domestic situation was becoming critical as Israeli fighters began bombing Egyptian cities. But as the tone of his letters to Washington became frantic, Kissinger's responses were patronizing and dismissive, claiming, for example, that the United States "is not following the Israeli operations in detail, nor does it get informed of them in advance," and so there was nothing it could do to stop them (Heikal 1993: 426). Sadat assumed that a resumption of the offensive might unnerve Washington. As befitting a soldier who never saw combat, he walked blindly into a trap. Israel had contained the Syrians, rearmed its troops, and came back with a vengeance.

The military leadership anxiously sought to prevent the coming disaster, one no less fatal than the unwarranted halt, albeit in the opposite direction. The Military Advisory Board strenuously objected to the belated advance, which now had a mere 20 percent chance of success (Heikal 1993: 438). Shazly, Gamasy, and other commanders tried to impress on the president that the window of opportunity had closed, and that Egypt's only option at this point was to defend the bridgeheads as best as it could until a ceasefire was reached. They specifically warned that a break in the lines now would allow the enemy to penetrate (Shazly 1980: 166; Al-Gamasy 1993: 271). The two field commanders tendered their resignation—though the war minister refused to accept them, insisting they had to follow orders (Heikal 1993: 432). Still enjoying the role of armchair general, Sadat ordered the two armored divisions on the West Bank of the canal to cross over to the East to back up the offensive. Now his generals became positively livid. These two divisions represented Egypt's strategic reserve. If they relinquished their position on the West Bank, Israel could invade the Egyptian mainland. Again, the president would have none of it. As expected, the ill-conceived attack, on October 14, cost the army 260 tanks (to only 10 Israeli ones) and had to be called off on the same day after one of the two field commanders suffered a heart attack (Boyne 2002: 128). One of the most bizarre reactions to this whole debacle occurred at 3 A.M. on October 18, when fifteen junior officers showed up at the presidential palace, and demanded to see Sadat. The baffled president received them in his bedroom in pajamas. The officers told him the army was boiling over with anger because of his inexplicable decisions, and that "crazy ideas" were spreading among their colleagues. Sadat thanked them for their honesty and promised to get back to them—which of course he never did (Heikal 1993: 487).

Worse still, as the generals had predicted, the advance opened a gap wide enough for Israel to slip behind Egyptian lines and cross the canal to the now exposed West Bank. Again, America's role was vital. Kissinger postponed a ceasefire until Israel "either ousted the Egyptians from the east bank . . . or made their position there untenable" (Boyne 2002: 102). Once Sadat threatened in his correspondence with Kissinger to escalate matters on the front, a U.S. reconnaissance Blackbird mapped the battlefront, on October 13 and 15 (the day before and after the Egyptian advance), to uncover whether troop movements had created a breach. One was indeed located at a juncture called Deversoir (Aly 1994: 361). Kissinger warned Israel to move quickly if it wished to finish "on top" (Kissinger 1979: 522–23). On October 15 Israeli forces made their way across the canal. A week later, they commanded seven brigades on the West Bank. Now, Kissinger called for a ceasefire (Al-Gamasy 1993: 282).

The breach offered one positive advantage for Sadat: a pretext to remove Shazly and destroy his legacy. Sadat really had no choice, considering that since Amer no other officer had enjoyed such charismatic authority inside and outside the ranks. A Western diplomat described him as "Egypt's Dayan . . . a hero to the Egyptian public even before the October war—a model of the 'new Egyptian officer.'" Folk tales circulated about how he saved his men from destruction by the Nazis in 1942; how bravely he conducted himself in Palestine in 1948; how his paratroopers performed brilliantly in Yemen in the 1960s; and particularly how he returned his men unscathed to Cairo in 1967, an episode that had become "encrusted with legend" (Insight Team 1974: 226–28).

So, on October 18, the president charged his chief of staff to travel to the front to stop the flow of Israeli troops. Shazly concluded that unless four brigades fell back from the East to the West Bank to counter the Israelis, the breach would widen (Al-Gamasy 1993: 290). Sadat exploded in his face, "Why do you always propose withdrawing our troops. . . . If you persist in these proposals I will court martial you. I do not want to hear another word" (Shazly 1980: 172). War experts agreed that Shazly's proposal was "the biggest threat to an Israeli victory. . . . It was Israel's good fortune that . . . his recommendations had been rejected" (Boyne 2002: 180–84). Shazly himself described Sadat's obstinacy as "a combination of madness, ignorance, and treason" (Shazly 1980: 180). It was, in the words of one Western historian, "a self-inflicted Stalingrad" by a man who had gambled away his army "in the hope that he could still pull off a diplomatic coup" (Boyne 2002: 201). Nonetheless, Sadat got what he wanted. It was "very easy to liquidate the breach," he claimed, but Shazly "wasted valuable time gathering information" (Sadat 1978: 348). Shazly supposedly returned "trembling, and told me . . . we have to withdraw all our troops from Sinai. . . . That night, I removed him and appointed Gamasy in his place" (Sadat 1978: 349). Except for Air Force Chief Hosni Mubarak, all the other witnesses refuted Sadat's story (Al-Gamasy 1993: 282).

In December 1973 Shazly was dispatched to Europe to serve as military attaché, before being sacked in 1978 for publishing his memoirs, which began as follows: "I have written it with reluctance, with sorrow and with anger . . . at the man who is currently the President of my country," a man responsible for the "wholesale distortion of the achievements of the armed forces" (Shazly 1980: 9–10). Shazly exposed Sadat's deceitful behavior during the war "to preserve a regime of autocratic privilege, which it upheld by lying to its citizens and then spying on them to see if they believed the lies. Even if the price were the failure of our assault on the enemy, the regime was determined to keep the armed forces subservient to that real, secret end" (Shazly 1980: 96). He then moved to Algeria to form the Egypt National Liberation Front, a movement dedicated to overthrowing the regime. In 1992 Shazly returned to Egypt and was immediately seized at the airport and taken to prison. A couple of years later, he was released and subsequently retired from public life. The top brass never abandoned him, though. According to his family, Mubarak's Defense Minister Hussein Tantawy regularly checked on his health, and helped clear his name in court in 2005 (Badr al-Din 2011: 20–23). It was Mubarak, following in Sadat's footsteps, who considered him an enemy until the last day. Shazly lived through the January 2011 revolt, but died one night before the military forced the president to step down. A few weeks after, his thus far banned memoirs were published in Egypt and widely distributed—a symbolic gesture from the military to its cherished commander.

Refusing to admit his mistakes, Sadat dismissed the breach as a "circus show aimed at television audiences" (Mansour 2009: 235). But he then quickly accepted the ceasefire. Like all his previous decisions, accepting a ceasefire-in-place was hotly disputed. Even Hafez Ismail, his loyal national security advisor, was startled by his unconditional compliance. He begged his chief to insist on an Israeli pull-out from the West Bank—which was already a huge concession from Egypt's initial position that fighting would continue until Israel withdrew to the 1967 borders: "Mr. President, there is no need for this rush. . . . I honestly believe that the armed forces could still confront the situation." When his calls fell on deaf ears, Hafez Ismail took a step that would cost him his job. Instead of explaining the rationale behind Egypt's acceptance of the ceasefire to bewildered cabinet members, on October 24, he lost his nerve and disowned the president's actions (Heikal 1993: 524–27, 569). Finally, Sadat met his high command, on November 21. He thanked them all for their great service to the country, and declared that he now considered the war over and expected the armed forces at this point not to meddle in politics, adding that the upcoming disengagement talks are "a political matter. Whether they reach an agreement or not is nothing to you. You must mind your own business" (Shazly 1980: 195).

There was no one to challenge Sadat. The short list of officers who wielded some influence within the corps was getting even shorter. One month before the war, Republican Guard Commander al-Lethy Nassef was mysteriously pushed off a balcony in London. Two months after the war, Chief of Staff Shazly and all the field commanders were assigned to civilian jobs (Shazly 1980: 202). War minister Ismail died of cancer a few months later, as Sadat had anticipated. It was inconceivable for Sadat to act otherwise. He intended for the military to pave the road for a political settlement, not in the Clausewitzian sense, where war accomplishes political ends, but rather by proving itself incapable of achieving what only the political leader could achieve.

Twilight of the Generals

By the time the war ended, only one of its authors was left standing: Chief of Operations Gamasy. He took over what Sadat had renamed the Defense Ministry. And it was now his turn to fall. Gamasy enjoyed immense prestige as the architect of the gallant Suez Canal crossing, and was a persistent critic of the way the president ran the war. Moreover, he would have certainly objected to Sadat's plan to redirect the army away from combat toward economic projects. Gamasy attributed the 1967 defeat to such misuse of military energies, "The armed forces became involved in land reclamation, housing, the national transport system. . . . [This] was detrimental to its main responsibility, which was to be a fighting force" (Al-Gamasy 1993: 85). Letting him go at this stage was therefore dangerous. He had to become tainted with the unpopular peace talks first. He had to sign on the dotted line.

Against his will, Gamasy was charged, on October 28, with the thankless task of heading Egypt's delegation to the first direct Egyptian-Israeli negotiations, held in a tent on the Cairo-Suez road with the goal of disengaging the belligerents in Sinai. Israeli officers could not help but notice how "demonstratively somber" he appeared (Golan 1976: 116). Gamasy was then asked to receive Kissinger, on January 11, to lay the ground for peace talks. But as soon as the meeting started, Kissinger stunned everyone by announcing that Sadat had already agreed to permanently limit the Egyptian presence in Sinai to 7,000 troops—down from 100,000. Gamasy lost control:

> "You are giving Israel what would guarantee the security of its forces and denying us everything that would safeguard our forces. I do not approve of this and I cannot . . . justify this to our forces." . . . I left the meeting room angry, with tears in my eyes. . . . I had appreciated the enormous effort and the sacrifices in the war, and there seemed to be no need for this huge concession which might endanger our armed forces. . . . There was no need—politically or militarily—to accept this reduction in troops. (Al-Gamasy 1993: 335–37)

The next day, Sadat scolded Gamasy. His promises to Kissinger must be fulfilled, and he did not need to consult the military before making decisions (Al-Gamasy 1993: 335–37). Two months later, in March 1974, a rebellion broke out among the soldiers besieged in Sinai in protest of Sadat's proposed reduction, though there was little they could accomplish considering they were cut off from the rest of the country (Brooks 2008: 121). In June 1975 forty-three officers were arrested for planning an anti-Sadat coup. Then between February and April 1976, a large number of officers (which remains unspecified) resigned in protest of his policies. Again, several senior commanders were sacked, in 1977, for supporting an attempted coup by naval officers. This was followed by the arrest of fourteen paratroopers and a major shake-up of the army, in July 1977, when paratroopers planned to remove the man they now saw as a treacherous dictator (Dekmejian 1982: 38–39).

Apparently, the military's outrage was not all gung-ho. Foreign Minister Ismail Fahmy, who handled the political side of the negotiations, noted how Sadat's concessions shocked both Kissinger and the Israelis (Fahmy 1985: 117). Kissinger described to the Israeli cabinet how the president constantly rebuked his military and diplomatic advisors. He would actually ask them to leave the room and then apologize to his American guests, "Gamasy and Fahmy were good men but did not understand [anything]." On the issue of troop reduction, for example, Gamasy insisted that Egypt could not protect Sinai without at least 250 tanks. Kissinger's aim was to shrink this figure to 100 tanks. When he met Sadat, he started with the implausible number of 30 tanks, with the hope that Egypt would then agree to 100. To his surprise, Sadat immediately agreed to the lesser number. Kissinger tried his luck once more. Israel had requested a withdrawal of the SAM air defense umbrella 20 kilometers away from the canal. Gamasy said it was impossible to pull it back more than 5 kilometers. Kissinger then appealed to Sadat, who instantly approved—with one request, though: that the "details of the thinning out of forces and arms restrictions be spelled out in . . . private letters sent by President Nixon to him" so that the public would not know about it (Golan 1976: 160–65).

What was Sadat trying to accomplish? In a private conversation with newspaper editor Ahmed Bahaa al-Din, he explained: "My generals . . . are wasting time over . . . trivial details. They do not understand that I was not negotiating disengagement with Israel, but rather with America. When I went to war, I did not go to war against the Israeli army, I was fighting to shake the convictions of all the American institutions: the Presidency, Congress, the CIA, the Pentagon . . . and their businessmen as well" (Bahaa al-Din 1987: 158). In a conversation with Heikal following his first encounter with Kissinger, Sadat relayed proudly how he began the meeting: "I told him Henry, do not waste your time with details. . . . You are a man of strategy, and so am I, so let us not be held back by details. . . . The future hangs on one question: Can we be friends? I want us to become friends, and if Egypt becomes your friend, then the whole region will open up to you." It was two years later, in September 1975, during a dinner at the Georgetown house of presidential speechwriter Joseph Kraft that Heikal learned that Sadat had also asked for the United States to "secure him personally and his regime" because there were many people plotting against him "inside his own country" (Heikal 1993: 675–80).

This was normal considering the harsh judgments of his national security team that saw things differently. Foreign Minister Fahmy concluded in his memoirs that Sadat squandered all that the Egyptian military had managed to achieve during the war (Fahmy 1985: 118). Murad Ghaleb, Egypt's wartime foreign minister, lamented how Sadat's blind trust in Washington "cost us the glory we achieved during the crossing" (Ghaleb 2001: 215). It was only normal that his attitude would hit the military hardest. One general complained, "Sadat had single-handedly given away all that the Egyptian army had won with great sacrifice. Without consulting anybody, he had caved in to the Israeli request that the Egyptian military presence east of the canal be reduced to nothing" (Brooks 2008: 141). Or as Shazly poignantly noted, "The President had thrown away the greatest army Egypt had ever assembled" (Shazly 1980: 184). With such bitterness, Egypt's senior commanders had to go. On October 5, 1978, the entire leadership of the October War was replaced.

Gamasy's successor was hardly more fortunate. Just like Ahmed Ismail before him, the new defense minister, Kamal Hassan Aly, had been appointed intelligence director for a brief period to prepare him for the top military post. Also, similarly to Ismail, his job was to keep the army from politics (Sadat 1978: 242). However, Aly understood professionalism as rooting out mediocre officers. He still advocated a strong military, with some say in national security policy. And so he was reassigned a few months later to the Foreign Ministry, and charged—just like Gamasy before him—with developing peaceful relations with Israel, a task that could have hardly endeared him to the troops (Aly 1994: 441–44).

Aly's replacement in the Defense Ministry scarcely survived over a year in office. On March 2, 1981, Defense Minister Ahmed Badawy, another influential officer, was killed in a helicopter crash with thirteen senior commanders. The official story was that the helicopter's tail became tangled in an electric wire. The pilot had a different story though, asserting that the engine suddenly lost power.[3] Moreover, one of the survivors recalled hearing an officer cry out before the crash: "There is something wrong with this plane" (Al-Banna and Bakry 1981: 3). These testimonies were not the only reason why the public became suspicious. Some asked why the defense minister and his top lieutenants would all be on the same helicopter, and how could the pilot responsible for transporting such a distinguished group drive his helicopter into an electric wire in broad daylight. Eyebrows were raised once more when the pilot, who mysteriously survived the crash, was shot a few months later at his apartment (Al-Baz 2011: 9). More significantly though, Badawy had made controversial remarks in Parliament weeks before his death, insisting that "peace should not lead to any change in the nature or mission of the armed forces."[4] But there was even more to the story. Alwy Hafez, a Free Officer, member of Parliament, and close friend of the deceased minister, accused Sadat and his sidekick Mubarak of killing Badawy and his colleagues because they threated to expose the corrupt arms dealing with Washington made possible by the sidelining of the military. Badawy had confronted Sadat with what he knew a fortnight before his death, but the president not only ignored him, but also turned the conversation into how a new round of purges was needed to keep the military loyal. The infuriated defense minister declined, reminding his boss that those he proposed to remove were among Egypt's best officers. Afterward, according to Hafez, the defense minister became convinced that the political leadership must be overthrown (Sha'ban 2011: 54–55). After the 2011 revolt, Ahmed Abdallah, a ruling party cadre and a relative of Badawy, confirmed that the latter had indeed met Sadat forty-eight hours before the accident and threatened to resign because of the president's insistence on corrupting and downgrading the army (Al-Baz 2011: 9). An indignant Sadat responded, in the leading daily *Al-Ahram*, that such conspiracies occur within shabby regimes like those in Syria and Libya, not in Egypt (Nafe' 1981: 1).

With the character (or literal) assassination and dislodging of almost all officers who carried some weight in the armed forces, military presence in politics diminished significantly. The ratio of officers in the cabinet fell from 66 percent in 1967 to 9 percent in 1977. While some 10 percent of Nasser's ambassadors were officers, Sadat completely blocked their access to the diplomatic corps. And while twenty-two of Egypt's governors were officers in 1964, only five held that post in 1980 (Springborg 1989: 95–96; Brooks 2008: 119). Sadat finally dealt his military a most cunning blow, in May 1979, in the form of Presidential Decree 35, which stated that "officers who occupied the most senior posts in the armed forces, in operations, and as commanders of the main branches of the forces in the 6 October 1973 war shall remain in service in the armed forces for life. . . . They will remain military advisors for life, loyal to the armed forces. They shall not occupy military posts in the organizational structure of the armed forces so that honoring them and benefiting from their unique experience will not run counter to the principles of renewal and continuity" (Al-Gamasy 1993: 404). The decree sealed the fate of the entire "October Generation." It condemned the war-seasoned leaders to a surreal existence, a state of limbo whereby they could neither occupy military commands, nor move to civilian politics. Sadat then chose a vice-president (Hosni Mubarak) from Egypt's weakest service and the one least capable of plotting a coup: the air force. Sadat thus effectively banished Egypt's great fighting generals to a no man's land between politics and the military, to a twilight zone from which they could never return. The president then redirected the military as a whole from a combat-oriented to an economic institution, famously declaring that October 1973 was Egypt's last war and that the army should now direct its energy toward the "war of economic development."

Season of Migration to the West

With the military effectively demobilized and de-politicized, the regime relied on security and political organs to control the populace. Sadat, however, sought to complement domestic control with external support. And he naturally chose the United States. Not just because the Russians never trusted (or respected) him, but also because, by the mid-1970s, the USSR seemed to be struggling to catch up. A unipolar world was emerging, and Sadat wanted to end up on the winning side.

But worming himself into Washington's good graces required several military concessions. Demilitarizing Sinai was one. It provided Israel with a buffer zone, and denied Egypt control of the most strategic part of the country. Another was substituting the United States for Russia as the main supplier of weapons and training, despite Washington commitment to Israel's security. Arranging joint exercises with U.S. troops (the annual Bright Star maneuvers) to familiarize them with desert wars was a third offering of friendship. A final, confidential concession was abandoning Nasser's efforts to develop nuclear weapons (Riedel 2010: 8). There were also a few cherries on top, sudden bouts of generosity, such as the handing over of a battery of Soviet SAM-6 anti-aircraft missiles—which kept Egypt's skies safe—to the U.S. Army so it could explore ways of neutralizing it (Cooley 2000: 35–36).

There were political concessions as well; concessions that drove three foreign ministers to quit their job between 1972 and 1978, and forced Sadat to reshuffle his cabinet four times between 1978 and 1980. To begin with, Sadat surrendered totally to the machinations of U.S. Secretary of State Henry Kissinger, despite his role in reversing Cairo's military fortunes during the war. He rebuked his aides for questioning Kissinger, and referred to him fondly as "the man who never lied to me, or ever betrayed his promises" (Sadat in Mansour 2009: 240), a man who represented "the real America . . . that stands by every country in need of assistance to help establish a better world" (Sadat 1978: 366). Even though Kissinger's "shuttle diplomacy," between 1973 and 1975, came to nothing, Sadat continued to place all his eggs in the American basket. He unilaterally annulled the Egyptian-Soviet Friendship Treaty, in March 1976, and humiliated Moscow on every occasion to please Washington; even though his foreign ministers explained that this meant placing Egypt under Israel's mercy (Kamel 1983: 26; Fahmy 1985: 108).

For his diplomatic aides, however, the straw that broke the camel's back was his November 1977 visit to Jerusalem. A month before, Sadat received a note from Jimmy Carter conditioning U.S. support on "a bold, statesman-like move to help overcome the hurdles" facing the peace talks (Brzezinski 1983: 110). Egypt's top editor, Ahmed Bahaa al-Din, recalled that Sadat waved the note and bragged: "You see, the American president is begging me," and I cannot let him down (Bahaa al-Din 1987: 161). The president informed his military and diplomatic staff that he intended to travel to Israel and address the Knesset. Foreign Minister Fahmy warned that recognizing Israel was Egypt's last card to play. He pleaded with Sadat not to throw it away before securing a return to the 1967 borders. If the president recognized Israel unilaterally in hopes of shaming the world, dazzling the Americans, and exposing Israeli intransigence, then Egypt would be completely naked in any future negotiations. War Minister Gamasy was less subtle than his diplomatic counterpart: "[He] raised his hands and screamed: 'The Knesset no! There is no need'" (Fahmy 1985: 386–97, 398). Sadat proceeded with his plan anyway. When Fahmy and several senior diplomats resigned, he searched for a replacement from outside the diplomatic corps. He appointed Cairo University Professor Boutros Ghali (future UN secretary-general) minister of state for foreign affairs, and longtime friend Muhammad Ibrahim Kamel as foreign minister. Kamel remembered Sadat telling him: "I allowed myself to appoint you without consulting you first because I consider you my son, and I need someone I can completely trust" (Kamel 1983: 41). And Ghali knew he was chosen because he was already stigmatized: he descended from an aristocratic family with close links to the monarchy; he was a Christian married to a Jew; and he was avidly pro-Western (Ghali 1997: 19).

Carter's National Security Advisor Zbigniew Brzezinski wrote that, to America's delight, Sadat's initiative fit perfectly with Israel's goal "to confine the peace process to a separate Israeli-Egyptian agreement, which would split the Arabs while letting Israel continue its occupation of the West Bank and Gaza" (Brzezinski 1983: 235). But as Fahmy predicted, Sadat's Knesset pledge of peace and recognition gave Israel no reason to offer concessions. A year following this historic visit, negotiations were still stuck; Israel was still occupying over half of Sinai; and Egyptian troops were still deployed on the West Bank of the canal—exactly where they had been since 1967. Carter now proposed a peace summit at Camp David. The goal, according to Brzezinski, was to limit Sadat's choices to either walking out on the United States or accepting whatever the Israelis offered—and, as Brzezinski duly noted, "Sadat chose the latter" (Brzezinski 1983: 274). Gamasy suspected that Sadat intended to demilitarize Sinai and warned him that this was "unacceptable from a military perspective" (Al-Gamasy 1993: 141). It was not that the officer corps was vying for another war, but their support of peace did not mean that they could "accept strategic inferiority" (Cordesman 2006: 202). So Sadat simply traveled to Camp David without Gamasy or any other military representative, and removed the war minister and his high command two weeks after retuning (Brooks 2008: 136).

One has to admit that the pressure on Sadat was unbearable. He never expected that after all his concessions and flirting with Washington, the United States would still adopt the Israeli position to the letter. Two days before the signing of the Camp David Accords, Sadat threatened to withdraw, but then Carter paid him a visit: "I actually went and changed my clothes so that I would look more formal. . . . I asked him to step inside. He looked extremely drawn and nervous. . . . I then said to him, 'I understand you're leaving. . . . [This] will mean first of all an end to the relationship between the

United States and Egypt.' . . . Sadat looked absolutely shaken," and decided to stay on (quoted in Brzezinski 1983: 271–72). Not only that, he actually gave Carter a "carte blanche for his subsequent negotiations with the Israelis" (Brzezinski 1983: 283). To justify this unwarranted submission to his aides, Sadat claimed that Carter wanted to corner Begin and show the world that Israel was against peace. In reality, as William Quandt, a member of the U.S. team at Camp David, confided to Ghali, Sadat assured Carter that he had no problem accommodating Israel, but wanted his subordinates to think he did so reluctantly. Kamel and Ghali recounted that whenever they pointed out that a certain concession threatened Egypt's interests, Sadat would shrug and say: "Let's just do this one for Carter's sake" (Kamel 1983: 603; Ghali 1997: 149). Naturally, the Egyptian delegation saw the settlement, and the demilitarization of Sinai in particular, as "a humiliation to Egypt" (Ghali 1997: 149, 153). Moreover, concluding a separate peace with Israel undermined Egypt's regional influence. Kamel immediately resigned: "I almost died of disgrace, disgust, and grief as I witnessed this tragedy unfold" (Kamel 1983: 515).

Sadat's subordinates were not that far out of line, considering that Brzezinski himself was amazed with how "excessively deferential [he was] to American concerns and needlessly irritating to the rest of the Arab world," and how he overruled his delegation in front of the Americans and Israelis for trying to say so (Brzezinski 1983: 238). In fact, Sadat was so compliant that the Americans became concerned of "the possibility of something unpleasant occurring" to him at Camp David, and asked security to "instigate tighter controls over access to Sadat's cabin" (Brzezinski 1983: 265). On the last day of the negotiations, Brzezinski wrote in his diary, "We might get a compromise agreement today, though the burden will fall on Sadat's shoulders. It will be hard for him to justify it" (Brzezinski 1983: 270). What Egypt's negotiating team failed to grasp, according to Brzezinski, was that their boss "saw the peace process as an opportunity to fashion a new American-Egyptian relationship . . . to becoming America's favorite statesman" (Brzezinski 1983: 236, 265, 270).

A young diplomat by the name of Nabil al-Araby tried, in a desperate attempt, to alert the president to the danger of investing so much in Carter. Sadat responded: "As you have seen, I have heard you out without interruption so that my critics would stop spreading rumors about how I do not listen to anyone or read anything. But what you have just said has entered my right ear and exited from the left one. You people in the Foreign Ministry believe you understand politics, but the truth is: you do not understand anything. I can no longer concern myself with your advice or memos. I am a man who is following a grand strategy that none of you is capable of perceiving or comprehending. I have no more need for your sophistry and petty reports" (Kamel 1983: 607–08). Notably, al-Araby became Egypt's first foreign minister after the 2011 revolt, and the only two diplomats who complied with Sadat (Ahmed Maher and Ahmed Abu al-Gheit) served as Mubarak's last two foreign ministers.

Besides military and political concessions, Sadat also agreed to close security cooperation with his new partner. Because the CIA had come under Congressional attack during the Nixon years, the Carter administration decided to outsource black-ops. So in 1976, the heads of U.S and French intelligence met in Cairo with four of their Middle East counterparts (Egypt, Iran, Saudi Arabia, and Morocco) to establish the Cairo-based Safari Club, a secret organization aimed at countering Communism in Africa, starting with the Congo, Ethiopia, and Somalia (Cooley 2000: 24–27). The Shah's overthrow, in 1979, allowed Egypt to serve as America's foremost regional security partner. Its most spectacular task was to subvert the Soviets in Afghanistan. Brzezinski's plan to mobilize Islamist zealots was unveiled in Cairo, in January 1980 (Brzezinski 1983: 444–54). Sadat agreed to recruit a volunteer army; supply it with small arms from Egypt's depots; and ship it to Afghanistan on Egyptian cargo planes (Cooley 2000: 31–32). These were the militants who returned to terrorize Egypt in the 1990s, and eventually took their militancy globally through al-Qaeda.

In return for all these concessions, Washington promised protection for him and his regime. Intelligence operative William Buckley put together a CIA-managed program of personal security with an annual budget of $20 million. U.S. anti-terrorism experts trained Sadat's bodyguards. And when the increasingly unpopular president signaled his need to travel by helicopter—unlike his predecessor who traveled in an open motorcade—he received three U.S.-funded Westland helicopters. Drawing on American support, Sadat also expanded the Republican Guard from an infantry battalion to a brigade of special troops, equipped with tanks and armored vehicles. Most importantly, Washington boosted Egypt's security organs: the Ministry of Interior capacity for telephone-tapping increased from 1,200 lines in 1971 to 16,000 in 1979; street cameras were introduced; and mobile listening posts helped monitor opposition meetings (Sirrs 2010: 137, 153).

Apparently Sadat's contemporaries disagreed over why he offered so many concessions to the Americans? Kissinger told Israeli leaders that "Sadat had fallen victim to human weakness. It was the psychology of a politician who wanted to see himself—and quickly—riding triumphantly in an open car . . . with thousands of Egyptians cheering him" (quoted in Golan 1976: 152–53).

Brzezinski noted in his Camp David diary, "My worry is that Sadat does not seem to differentiate clearly between fact and fiction," most of his facts were "simply untrue" (Brzezinski 1983: 93). Heikal agreed, "Sadat the escapist became Sadat the dreamer; Sadat the dreamer became Sadat the actor. Most of his life Sadat was acting a part—or sometimes several parts at the same time" (Heikal 1983: 13). Fahmy also registered how unsettling it was to work for someone who fabricates facts and then believes them (Fahmy 1985: 13). Kamel judged his old friend as a "unique psychological case," a man living in a make-believe world, who confuses dreams with reality (Kamel 1983: 189). Game', another intimate friend, confessed that Sadat's "excessive egoism" blinded him (Game' 2004: 191). Soviet officials saw him as megalomaniac (Boyne 2002: 94). Even the military historians who studied the October War described Sadat as "a somewhat repressed man, prone to swoops between euphoria and depression" (Insight Team 1974: 46). In short, Sadat's entourage—whether friends or subordinates, military or civilian, domestic or foreign—attributed his decisions to some psychological disorder.

The problem is: they measured his actions on the wrong scale, that of national achievement. But Sadat was acting as a strategic player in an intra-regime struggle that had consumed Egypt since 1952. His aim was to augment the power of the political apparatus, which he represented, against the most troublesome partner in the ruling bloc: the military. And on that scale, Sadat fared quite well. Sadat's substitution of U.S. protection for that previously provided by the military was a well-calculated power strategy. Reliance on the military left the political leadership vulnerable to the convulsions of the officer corps. In contrast, the United States offered stable support with only a few strings attached: peace with Israel, friendship with the West, subscription to the global war against Communism (and later Islamism), and transition to capitalism. None of these demands jeopardized Egypt's political rulers. Indeed, Sadat spelled out his strategy in a conversation with Bahaa al-Din, who had just retuned from a visit to Tehran in 1974:

> You know, for a long time I have considered the Shah of Iran my role model among Third World leaders. Your non-aligned leaders whose clamor had occupied the world for years: Nehru, Nkrumah, Sukarno, even Abd al-Nasser, even Tito who is still alive, where are they now? Some died, some were defeated, some were overthrown, and some shrank in their borders like Tito. Only one member of this generation remains on his throne, with all its power and glory, and with the whole world seeking his friendship: this is the Shah of Iran. And the reason is simple. While all those other leaders believed the world has two great powers, Russia and America, and tried to deal with them on par, the truth

> could not be farther; there is only one great power, which is America. . . . It was the Shah of Iran who realized that. So what did he do? He sat on America's lap, and clutched its coattails. And as you see, while all your friends are gone, America fulfilled the Shah's needs. A revolution erupted [under Mosaddeq], and he escaped to Italy. The Americans brought him back, and installed him again on the throne. . . . That is why I think he is a brilliant and extraordinary man. (Bahaa al-Din 1987: 68–69)

Ironically, the Shah—deposed by his people, and abandoned by the United States—was forced to spend his last days in Cairo, enjoying the hospitality of his secret admirer, Sadat. Commenting on the Egyptian president's reception of the fallen Persian monarch, one observer remarked in *The New York Times* how amusing it was to see "the new Shah embracing the old Shah" (Ibrahim 1980: 3).

Back to the Home Front

Although American protection substituted the *function* of the military in the ruling alliance, in a tripartite regime reducing the *weight* of one institution (in this case, the military) requires increasing that of the other two (the political and security institutions). Empowering the Ministry of Interior to handle domestic repression was straightforward enough. Less obvious, however, was how to strengthen the ruling party. The Arab Socialist Union (ASU) could no longer rely on civil servants and middling landlords. For one thing, public employees (some 3.2 million in 1978) usually remain neutral when their employers bicker, as in May 1971, when the president and his ministers fought it out and the bureaucracy remained paralyzed. Also, village notables (an estimated 3,600 families) are too provincial in outlook. They could deliver votes, but lacked the interest or capacity to intervene in national politics. The ruling party now needed a new social elite that identified its interests with those of the Party and was ready to fight for them when necessary. Because Sadat wanted a social base that owed nothing to Nasser, and because he knew that economic liberalization was nonnegotiable to Americans, he supported the emergence of a capitalist elite. In other words, "since his rivals were on the left and his potential support on the right, a rightward course which would win over the power bourgeoisie made the most sense" (Hinnebusch 1990: 192–93).

How could Sadat produce this new elite? The class that controlled the means of production was the state bourgeoisie (some 34,000 public sector managers, and 11,000 senior administrators). Wartime deficits had forced them into shabby deals with private investors in return for bribes and commissions. Yet Sadat saw these corrupt functionaries as the basis of his new class; "With a foot in high state office and assets in private society, this group was not only the most strategic social force, but the one most prepared to accept his leadership" (Hinnebusch 1990: 192–93). Hence, between 1971 and 1980, and despite all talk of economic liberalization, state employment grew by 70 percent (Brooks 2008: 115). Their role now was to subcontract projects to private entrepreneurs in order to transform landowners, merchants, and contractors into a coherent capitalist bloc that owed its existence to the ruling party. By controlling the allocation of foreign trade and building permits, tax exemptions, public loans and lands, the ruling party turned bureaucrats into middleman between public resources and acquisitive capitalists. It was less state-fostered capitalism than "state-fostered corruption" (Saleh 1988: 16). Even workers and peasants joined the bonanza. The oil boom that followed (and was partly caused by) the October War triggered an exponential growth in the migration of poor Egyptians to Libya, Iraq, and the Arab Gulf, from 58,000 migrants in 1970 to 5 million in 1980 (Abd al-Fadeel 1983: 11). Migrants invested their funds back home, and eventually returned to join the expanding business class. Then came Law 43 of 1974, which officially inaugurated Infitah ("opening the door") by abolishing Nasser-era restrictions and opening up the country to foreign investments. The number of agents for foreign companies surged from a few dozen in 1974 to 16,000 by 1981 (Abd al-Mo'ty 2002: 105, 191). "Cairo became a city of middlemen and commission agents for Europeans and Americans . . . shuttling between luxury hotels and government ministries, wheeling and dealing on an ever-increasing scale." In a country that had no millionaires in 1970, more than 17,000 sprang into existence by 1980 (Heikal 1983: 183–91).

American investors were both the architects and primary benefactors of these developments. By his own admission, Sadat's primary economic advisor was David Rockefeller. Sadat not only bragged about how the world-famous magnate was his "friend"—just like Kissinger and Carter before him—but also gave him full access to Egypt's economic data and consulted him on every major decision (Bahaa al-Din 1987: 114). Naturally, as soon as the Egyptian market opened up, American merchandise began pouring in. Between 1974 and 1984, Egypt imported $2.8 billion worth of American goods, constituting 33 percent of all Egyptian imports, while Egyptian exports to the U.S. market were a meager $33 million, representing only 8 percent of total Egyptian exports. And, indeed, 85 percent of Egyptian exports to the United States represented only one item: oil (Al-Mashat 1986: 61). This, of course, made sense considering that American investors secured 70 percent of the profits made in the oil sector in Egypt. But it was U.S. banks that made the highest returns. Between 1974 and 1980, private banks in Egypt increased from zero to 56, and many of these were American. By 1985 U.S. banks had already drawn $9.9 billion worth of foreign currency deposits, and the bulk was transferred abroad (Handoussa 1990: 122). During the period between 1974 and 1984, the United States also offered $15 billion in the form of loans and aid. This was the first installment in the massive United States Agency for International Development (USAID) program that began supplying Egypt with $2.3 billion annually after 1979. Ostensibly meant to boost the Egyptian economy, USAID conditions required the Egyptian government to hire "excessive US consultancy services . . . [and purchase] overpriced American goods and services," in addition to sustaining the inflated USAID bureaucracy (1,030 employees in Egypt in the 1970s compared to only 4 in Israel). Further, the United States retained the right to determine investment priorities, leading some to treat the USAID as Egypt's shadow cabinet. So although Egypt desperately needed to develop its industries to satisfy its growing market and increase its exports, Washington directed 82 percent of its aid, in 1978, to the oil sector, which primarily served American companies, and spent less than 4 percent on industry. "On balance, therefore, it would seem fair to say that American aid to Egypt has reaped substantial American dividends in terms of investment and trade" (Handoussa 1990: 110–17). Sadat himself lobbied on behalf of American investors. For example, when his cabinet turned down Rockefeller's offer to open up a branch of the Chase Manhattan bank, the president overruled his ministers and ordered a merger between Chase and Egypt's National Bank. And when Egypt Air decided to reject an overly expensive offer from Boeing, it received the following memo: "Dear Sir, the president has given orders that the agreement with Boeing and the accompanying financial arrangements should be signed immediately" (Heikal 1983: 82–83, 185). Finally, against the advice of his ministers, Sadat authorized the formation of the first business lobby in the country, the American Chamber of Commerce in Egypt (AmCham). With direct links to the presidency, AmCham became key to shaping economic policy rather than just removing obstacles to U.S. investments (Kandil 1986: 103–04).

As the 1980s dawned, Egypt was effectively locked into the course that Sadat had set. Domestically, Infitah had made the regime dependent on a new capitalist elite, a class which "devoted their activities to short-term trade, reaping high cash profits that have ... often been hoarded in the form of cash or jewelry, or spent on unnecessary luxuries, lavish consumption, or otherwise invested or saved abroad" (Oweiss 1990: 34). Heikal drew a stark comparison between them and the pre-July 1952 elite: "The old feudal class ... was small and exploiting, but at least its wealth and ambitions were based on land ownership. Its stake in the soil of Egypt meant that it was never wholly alienated, never devoid of fundamental patriotism, which comes from planting down roots. But the new rich had no roots" (Heikal 1983: 87). This was Nasser's greatest fear: "an unpatriotic, corrupted wealthy class which contributes nothing substantial to the product of the country and which is inclined to export its profits to Switzerland" (Copeland 1970: 216). Ignoring Nasser's admonition, Sadat infested the ruling party with the germ whose future covetousness would eventually pull down the roof in 2011. As Heikal sardonically concluded, with the new "supermarket economy ... Egyptian society was now divided between "the 'fat cats' and their hangers-on, perhaps 150,000 people at most, on one side, and the rest of the population on the other" (Heikal 1983: 86–88). Still, Sadat had his new, pyramid-shaped elite, with state-nurtured capitalists on top, ASU cadres and their rural allies in the middle, and public employees and workers at the base. What was needed now was a political vessel to bring them together. Hence, the National Democratic Party (NDP) was born.

In 1976 Sadat formed three *manabir* (platforms) representing the left, right, and center within the ASU. Prime Minister (and former Interior Minister and State Security officer) Mamduh Salem was put in charge of the centrist platform. The three platforms were transformed into political parties the following year, with the centrist platform becoming the new ruling party, the NDP. Sadat subsequently decreed that a Political Parties Committee chaired by NDP's secretary-general must approve any new party. He thus constructed a system with one hegemonic party flanked by loyal opposition from left and right. And while the ASU was officially dissolved, what really happened was that its 6 million members simply transferred to the NDP, which even occupied the same headquarters and regional offices. The primary difference, of course, was that the new party elite included businessmen. But the revamped ruling party could barely operate without Interior Ministry protection. Security officers screened NDP applicants and monitored members; subdued dissent at universities, factories, and villages; rigged parliamentary, student, and syndicate elections to guarantee a NDP majority. In short, NDP rule was only possible under the shadow of a full-fledged police state.

The fact that the Interior Ministry replaced the military at the center stage naturally provoked mutual hostility. While ASU leaders had come from a military background, the NDP elite was born under the watchful eyes of a police officer: Mamduh Salem. Sadat also hired more policemen as provincial governors. More disturbing was the amount of power accrued by interior ministers under Sadat, especially the notorious al-Nabawi Ismail. Ismail was one of the few policemen who opposed Naguib and helped organize the March 1954 anti-democracy demonstrations. After two decades with the secret police, he became chief aid to Salem, the first police officer to hold the post of interior minister, in 1971, and prime minister, in 1976. Sadat then appointed Ismail interior minister in 1977, and the latter became so powerful that he controlled the nomination of future cabinet members, including the prime minister (Ismail in Fawzy 2008: 49, 86–90).

But what drove military officers through the roof was that they now came under the purview of the Interior Ministry's SSIS. Former chief of staff Shazly recalled chairing a military appraisal committee, in 1972, to recommend promotions. But Sadat's war minister struck out a few names in compliance with SSIS reports. That same year, Egypt received a shipment of advanced Russians tanks (T-62s), but although the high command dispatched them immediately to the front, the tanks remained in Cairo until tank brigade leaders were cleared by security. Again, in a meeting between the president and his commanders, he accused senior officers of inciting soldiers against him, and when they denied this, he produced an SSIS operative from an anteroom to elaborate on the charges (Shazly 1980: 83–99). A more dramatic example was Sadat's dismissal of War Minister Sadeq and his senior aides when security reported that he had become too popular within the ranks and too critical of presidential policies (Sirrs 2010: 127). The president also entrusted his security aide, Ashraf Marawan, rather than a military officer, with negotiating arms imports (El-Sayed 2007: 2). Security control became so pervasive that Sadat asked SSIS Deputy Director Fouad Allam to investigate an alleged plot by mid-ranking officers, in March 1981 (Allam 1996: 413).

As the competition between the military and the Interior Ministry intensified, the two were severely tested by the January 1977 riots. As part of Sadat's economic liberalization, the government decided to halve its subsidies on basic commodities. Millions took to the streets. The January 18–19, 1977, food riots were the largest since and most violent since 1952, so violent that Sadat had to escape in a helicopter before his house was attacked. Knowing that the police were not yet equipped to deal with such massive riots, Sadat was forced to call in the army. War Minister Gamasy, however, asked him first to rescind his unpopular decision, and the cornered president conceded (McDermott 1988: 54). Meanwhile, Sadat ordered the SSIS to keep track of every army vehicle and officer on the street because he suspected his war minister of planning a coup. The lesson learned was that marginalizing the military required militarizing the police (Genedi 2011: 154).

The Interior Ministry was asked to devise Plan 100, which was a plan to respond to another popular revolt—this is the very plan that failed miserably in January 2011. The paramilitary Central Security Forces (CSF) were rapidly inflated from 100,000 to 300,000 troops, in 1977, and their arsenal was upgraded from batons and rifles to tear-gas canisters and armored vehicles (Fawzy 2008: 154–56). In 1979 alone, the United States supplied the CSF with 153,946 tear-gas bombs, 2419 automatic guns, and 328,000 rubber bullets (Al-Mashat 1986: 65). CSF was meant to obviate the need to call on the military to restore order. As one analyst put it, "If SSIS comprised the eyes, ears, and interrogator of the regime, the CSF was its instrument of brute force" (Sirrs 2010: 162). Expectedly, the degree of mistrust between Sadat and his army deteriorated to the point where he asked the Interior Ministry to handle his personal safety inside the Defense Ministry and other military bases (Hammudah 1986: 239). Colonel Muhammad Selim captured the mood of the officer corps thus:

> We understood that the general strategy was to weaken the army and strengthen the police force. This began with Mamduh Salem in 1971, but it picked up only after al-Nabawai Ismail took over the Interior Ministry in 1977. We lived to see the day when the Interior Minister became the most powerful man in Egypt. We also followed how the CFS was being propped up to take over riot control. We were quickly becoming dispensable. And there was nothing we could do about it. (2009)

At this point, the Interior Ministry decided to flex its muscles. Drunk with power, al-Nabawi Ismail decided, in September 1981, to detain 3,000 of the country's leading intellectuals, journalists, clerics, priests, and oppositionists, to teach them to respect their president. In fact, SSIS Deputy Director Allam admitted that the original list included 12,000 dissidents, but the ministry thought it impractical (Allam 1996: 269). Two days after the mass arrests, Sadat delivered a fiery speech in Parliament, celebrating what he called the "September revolution"; gloating that one of the detainees (a revered Islamist preacher) was "rotting in prison like a dog"; and yelling at his petrified audience: "Beware! I will no longer show mercy towards anyone!" (Hammudah 1986: 65).

The Closing Act

On October 6, 1981, Egyptians followed the annual victory parade celebrating the crossing of the Suez Canal on the first day of the 1973 war. They knew that this one was different—though little did they realize how different. It was supposed to be a spectacular parade exhibiting the American weapons that Egypt had recently acquired. All the country's leaders and dozens of foreign dignitaries were seated in the review stand around the president in his Prussian-style military uniform covered with ribbons and stars, which he had awarded himself. Officers and cadets marched in their shiny uniforms; files of tanks and artillery guns trailed along; and fighter jets thundered above, spewing trails of colored smoke. The parade was supposed to symbolize Sadat's achievements during his decade-long tenure. How it ended was no less symbolic. At the precise moment that Sadat was gazing above at the new jets, an armored vehicle broke formation and drove toward him. Four assassins launched from the vehicle throwing grenades and firing their rifles. In forty seconds, the president was gunned down with nine others, and another twenty-eight were injured. Although a record thirty-nine shots pierced Sadat's body, medical examiners attributed his death to nervous shock.[5] And expectedly so: this was the first time Egyptians had assassinated their pharaoh. To add insult to injury, very few people bothered to attend his funeral—forcing American television presenter Barbra Walters to speculate that if Sadat was watching from above how little Egyptians cared for him, he would have died a second time out of grief (Hammudah 1986: 18–25, 233).

Sadat's assassination is one of the least examined episodes in Egypt's history. The assassins' ties to the military have been regularly downplayed, and its context blurred. These omissions, however, cannot be sustained in light of the following. First, the assassins had all served in the military: the ringleader (Khaled al-Islambouly) was an artillery lieutenant, another was a national guard sergeant and former infantry marksman, a third was a reserve lieutenant, and the last was a former air defense officer. Second, the assassination was masterminded by a renegade colonel in military intelligence and an October War hero (Abbud al-Zumur), who was instantly released by the military following the 2011 revolt after three decades in prison. Third, the assassination took place during a military parade in a military-secured zone (with three checkpoints to ensure that no live ammunition entered the parade ground). Fourth, Interior Minister al-Nabawi Ismail revealed that the original plot involved a fighter jet crashing into the review stand—kamikaze style—which means that the plotters had links with air force pilots (quoted in Fawzy 2008: 119). Fifth, the assassins asked the defense minister and other military leaders to step aside, yelling that their target was the president and his interior minister. Sixth, although the lead assassin was marked as an Islamist radical by Military Intelligence (he was interrogated in October 1980, but the investigation had been shelved), and although his brother was detained a few days before the parade for the same charge, he was still allowed to participate in the parade (Hammudah 1986: 28, 78). Seventh, the assassination was meant to spark a popular-instigated coup because it was believed that the military was no longer invested in the regime, as in 2011 (Abd al-Hafeez and Khayal 2011: 7). Eighth, Fouad Allam, SSIS deputy director, said that investigations revealed a coup by mid-ranking officers was actually planned in March 1981, but his men had preempted it (Allam 1996: 413). Ninth, former Chief of Staff Shazly observed in an interview with *Newsweek* following the assassination that the officers he knew viewed the assassination as a step in the right direction (Hammudah 1986: 50–52). Finally, many of the reasons the plotters gave for killing Sadat were military-related. Following his release from prison, in March 2011, al-Zumur admitted: "We assassinated Sadat because he accepted an end to the military conflict between the Arabs and Israel" (Abd al-Hafeez and Khayal 2011: 7). To top it all off, the interior minister had confided to the prime minister the night before the assassination that he was almost sure the president would not survive the parade because of the radicalism lurking within the ranks, and that he had warned Sadat that he would be particularly vulnerable in a military-controlled zone, but the president brushed his warning aside (Fawzy 2008: 110–14). Intriguingly, SSIS got definite word regarding the assassination two hours beforehand, and quickly dispatched an envoy to evacuate Sadat, but military police prevented him from reaching the president or the interior minister (Fawzy 2008: 123; Allam 1996: 312).

While none of the above implicates the entire officer corps, they do indicate three incontrovertible facts: that several officers were involved in planning, executing, and covering up the assassination; that the assassins were confident the military was hostile toward Sadat; and that, in the light of the above two facts, it was clear yet again that the military could not be trusted.

So why then did the attempt to seize power fail? Clearly, the plotters undermined the other coercive apparatus in the ruling bloc, the junior partner that had come of age under Sadat: the security institution. The army played no major role in preserving order. It was the Interior Ministry that apprehended the plotters; protected government buildings; and investigated the military's negligence or complacency in the assassination (Sirrs 2010: 149–51). The two-month SSIS investigation resulted in court marshal for six artillery officers and dismissal of an undisclosed number of officers (Allam 1996: 284). For Interior Ministry officers, this was baptism by blood. And they passed with flying colors. The CSF chief, General Abd al-Rahman al-Faramawy, recalled proudly how effective the ministry was:

> On the day Sadat was assassinated, I was at CSF headquarters. Without waiting to hear from the Interior Minister, I immediately put Plan 100 into effect. The plan arranged for CSF units to secure strategic sites, such as the television building and the major ministries, to preempt any possible coup. Over the next two days, I dispatched CSF troops to the south to deal with the threat of an Islamist insurgency down there. We were forced to rely on the military for transportation, especially since we needed helicopters. But we did not call on the army's help because it was then under SSIS investigations. Sadat was assassinated in a military-secured zone without a policeman in sight. It was widely believed during those early days that the officer corps was involved. We will never be completely sure, however, because the outcome of the investigations remains classified. (2009)

By the time Mubarak began his long tenure, the course had already been set: the military had been politically marginalized and suspect; the security had proven to be loyal and reliable; and the new NDP business elite had come to represent the regime's strongest social base. But there was one more challenge Mubarak had to overcome. Apparently, the army still had some fight left in it.

Notes

1. In 1974 a KGB officer revealed how he recruited Sharaf in 1958. Sadat cited this revelation in a speech in 1974 and added that Sharaf had confessed to him in a letter from prison that he had developed a "special relationship" with Moscow (Barron 1974: 51–53; Hammad 2008: 58–59, 71; Sirrs 2010: 64–65).
2. *Al-Ahram* 31718: 3. Cairo (10/13/1973).
3. *Al-Akhbar* 8965: 3. Cairo (3/6/1981).
4. *Al-Akhbar* 8963: 7. Cairo (3/4/1981).
5. The medical report was printed in *Al-Akhbar* 9149: 3. Cairo (6/7/1981).

15 | The Long Road to a Short Revolution

OCTOBER 1981–JANUARY 2011

HOSNI MUBARAK RULED LONGER THAN his two illustrious predecessors combined. His reign brought good tidings to the net beneficiaries of the regime: a political class plundering with impunity, and security men who became, in the words of one of their own, "masters of the country."[1] It was, however, a time of great uncertainty for the people, and the army.

The Military's Final Stand

Egypt's fourth president was the first not to belong to the Free Officers Movement, although he became an officer three years before the 1952 coup. He spent his junior years as an air force instructor. And during the 1967 war, he famously aggravated Nasser by alleging that American jets participated in the strike against Egypt without producing tangible evidence. Nasser reassigned him to an administrative job as director of the Air Force Academy, but his fortunes changed under Sadat, who favored low-profile officers. He was appointed air force commander in 1972, and promoted to vice-president in 1975. Unlike most of Sadat's military and political subordinates, he never questioned the president's wisdom, especially regarding the United States. In fact, he concluded one of his first interviews after taking office, by saying: "Without the United States it would have been difficult, if not impossible to achieve what President Sadat achieved. I am very comfortable about dealing with the United States, and I will continue to do so."[2] Barely a month in office, he confessed to veteran editor Mohamed Hassanein Heikal, "I do not know why Nasser befriended those impoverished Russians. Sadat [rightly] favored the lavish Americans. Nasser's biggest mistake was to defy the Americans. Besides, President Anwar [Sadat wisely] chose peace with Israel. President Nasser should have known that fighting Israel was hopeless. Jews control the whole world, as you know. Take it from me, no one can cross America" (Heikal 2012: 65).

By the time Mubarak came to power, the military had been considerably tamed. The purges of the 1950s and 1960s had removed politicized officers, while those of the 1970s removed anyone who became too popular. Defense Minister Abd al-Halim Abu Ghazala initially seemed to be none of the above. He was only two years younger than Mubarak, though unlike the president, he had joined the Free Officers, participated in the 1948 and 1956 wars, and was not involved in the 1967 debacle. Abu Ghazala also played a field role in the 1973 war as artillery commander, rather than spend the war by Sadat's side in Cairo like Mubarak. Also unlike Mubarak, he was a military scholar who authored several books on warfare with an eye toward improving the combat performance of the Egyptian army. But since Abu Ghazala shunned politics, he seemed nonthreatening. Moreover, he served as military attaché to Washington, between 1977 and 1980, where he played a crucial role in setting up Cairo's new alliance with the Pentagon. Yet like everyone who assumed the top military post, from Amer to Hussein Tantawy (Mubarak's last defense minister), Abu Ghazala chose the military over political loyalty. Instead of guarding the president's back, he sought to empower the armed forces.

To start with, Abu Ghazala raised his men's wages, upgraded military facilities and uniforms. Soon, soldiers began comparing him to Amer in his generosity and camaraderie (Aly 1986: 3). And sure enough, the relationship between Mubarak and Abu Ghazala became as strained as that of Nasser and Amer before them. The new field marshal, however, was subtler than the old. He had no taste for rows or emotional outbursts. He sidestepped, rather the confronted the president, and continued to nurture his power base. He raised no objections, for instance, against Mubarak's reshuffling of the high command, in 1983, without consulting him. Nor did he complain when he was removed from the ruling party, in 1984, to maintain a distance between military and politics (Al-Mashat 1986: 67). Also, Abu Ghazala proved more successful than Amer in pandering to the masses. He contrasted Mubarak's "unhesitating preference for secularism" by cultivating "an image of devoutness" (Springborg 1989: 100). For example, in a televised interview in 1986, he stressed the importance of faith to his soldiers, snubbing calls to secularize the army (Abd al-Quddus 1986: 3). A year later, he claimed in the daily *Al-Ahram* that his military doctrine was "inspired by the Qur'an" (Abdallah 1990a: 27). More dangerous still, Abu Ghazala repeatedly attacked the security's draconian methods against Islamists, leading the Muslim Brothers to praise him as one of the few officials who appreciated "the Islamic impulse in Egyptian society" (Abdallah 1990: 16). It also helped that his wife donned the veil, and that his close friend was a renowned Islamist. Naturally, Mubarak felt that removing such an immensely popular figure might require a " 'corrective' revolution of at least the magnitude that Sadat launched in May 1971" (Springborg 1989: 102, 124–25). That is, of course, unless Abu Ghazala committed some major blunder. Unfortunately, he committed two.

The first blunder was agreeing to pull back his troops after being fully deployed to quell the Central Security Forces' (CSF) munity, in February 1986, without bargaining to increase the army's leverage. Aggravated by rumors of a one-year extension to their three-year service term, and infuriated by the abusive treatment of police officers, 17,000 CSF conscripts took to the streets, burning and looting indiscriminately throughout Cairo. The Interior Ministry was helpless. Fear of fraternization prevented CSF Chief General Abd al-Rahman al-Faramawy from sending in other CSF units. "We were in a fix," Faramawy explained, "the CSF was the striking arm of the police force, and now that its troops were out of control, who could rein them in" (2009). To his great apprehension, Mubarak was forced to call in the army. Abu Ghazla's troops made short work of the mutineers, killing 107 and injuring 715 in two days. But instead of seizing the opportunity to reestablish military dominance—as his successor did in 2011—the field marshal shepherded his men back to the barracks. To Mubarak's dismay, Abu Ghazala's popularity soared after his men saved the capital. And the field marshal, naturally, became overconfident. Days after the munity, he told veteran editor Mohamed Hassanein Heikal that if he wanted the presidency, he could have dispatched "one officer no more (even a lieutenant) to the television and radio studios to deliver a communiqué on my behalf. The whole story would have been over in five minutes. And the people would have welcomed [my coming to power]" (Heikal 2012: 143). As it turned out, this was the military's last chance—until 2011.

Now, the ambitious field marshal committed his second, and fatal blunder. The blow came in September 1988, when the Israeli daily *Yediot Aharonot* reported that the Egyptian defense minister smuggled missile parts and technology from America without the Pentagon's permission. The missile in question was a Scud-B variant that Abu Ghazala was hoping to reverse-engineer. To make matters worse, the newspaper also exposed his secret exchanges with North Korea on missile technology, and his attempt to develop chemical weapons behind Washington's back. Mubarak realized this was his chance to dismiss his friend-turned-rival (Al-Baz 2007: 78–81). In April 1989 Abu Ghazala was demoted to presidential aide, and persuaded to resign in February 1993. To preempt his entry into civilian politics, the Interior Ministry implicated him in an explosive sex, bribery, and political abuse scandal that rocked Cairo in April 1993. The humiliated field marshal subsequently withdrew from public life. Remarkably though, during Egypt's first multicandidate presidential elections, in 2005, there was a popular demand for Abu Ghazala to run. But hours before he was scheduled to announce his candidacy, on June 29, Mubarak paid him a visit and asked him to back down. Abu Ghazla never spoke again in public. He died three years later (Al-Baz 2007: 166). His fall from power ended the era of eminent generals. From this point onward, as one writer noted sardonically, "The most popular military officer on billboards in Egypt [was] Colonel Sanders of Kentucky Fried Chicken" (Shatz 2010: 6).

Abu Ghazala's replacement was Youssef Sabri Abu Taleb. This was a shrewd decision on Mubarak's part for two reasons. First, Abu Ghazala had been his subordinate throughout the 1970s, forcing the embittered Abu Taleb to resign the day his assistant was promoted over him. Second, the new defense minister had served in a civilian post, as Cairo's governor, for the past six years, and the grudge he openly held against Abu Ghazala kept his contact with officers to a minimum. Determined to wipe out his predecessor's legacy, Abu Taleb alienated officers further by terminating the controversial R&D infrastructure Abu Ghazala had laid down for missile production (Eytan, Gazit, and Gilboa 1993: 140). Mubarak's final coup de grace was to appoint Hussein Tantawy, the head of the Republican Guard, the new defense minister in May 1991. Tantawy served him faithfully for twenty years before defecting in 2011.

Military Privileges under Mubarak

Political–military tensions at the beginning of Mubarak's reign forces one to wonder: What did the military have to complain about? Did it not control a lucrative niche of the economy? Did its members not enjoy various privileges? Was it not being trained and armed by the world's only superpower? Surely, these perks were enough to buy off the army. The problem was, however, that these benefits masked a number of troubling issues—especially if one accepts the premise that the military actually cares about acting as a military.

To start with, military spending fell from 33 percent of GDP in the mid-1970s to 19.5 percent in 1980 and further down to 2.2 percent of GDP in 2010—the lowest level in the country's history. In money terms, defense expenditures oscillated between \$2.4 and \$4.2 billion under Mubarak, regardless of inflation or the tenfold increase in Egypt's GDP from $17.8 to $188 billon.[3] Moreover, the celebrated $1.3 billion provided annually by Washington had depreciated by at least 50 percent since 1979. Rather than basking in prosperity, the military lived under the fear of having to "slash military salaries severely" (Frisch 2001: 2). Indeed, the situation was so dire that Israeli strategists remarked, "A striking factor about the Egyptian Armed Forces' combat arsenal is that a portion of it, including aircraft, is kept in storage . . . [because of] budgetary constraints" (Eytan, Heller, and Levran 1985: 91), and that because of these constraints "cost-effective simulation training took priority over live training" (Eytan and Levran 1986: 131). In terms of the arms industry, the ambitious joint venture, involving Saudi Arabia, Qatar, and the United Arab Emirates (UAE), lost much of its capital when the Gulf sponsors withdrew in protest of Egypt's 1979 treaty with Israel. More injurious to military pride, the goal of the Arab Organization for Industrialization (AOI) was no longer to secure Egypt's independence—as Nasser had originally intended—but to make it a regional arms dealer. And even here, the presidency reaped the gains. It was Mubarak, his close friend, and intelligence veteran Hussein Salem who handled arms exports (Murad 1986: 15).

More revealing still is the truth behind the famed military–industrial complex. In 1978 Sadat officially redirected the army toward economic projects through the National Service Projects Organization (NSPO). Under Mubarak, the NSPO employed perhaps 100,000 people in enterprises as diverse as construction, land reclamation, and agro-industries. The appropriateness of reinventing the military as an economic player provoked public debate in the mid-1980s. Army spokesmen responded by first clarifying that this was a purely *political* decision, and then explaining that the government wished them to become financially self-sufficient and to help development by providing cheap goods and services (Farahat 1984: 7; Fakhr 1985: 9). A 2008 report by the Central Auditing Authority confirmed that the military's economic activities covered its bare necessities without generating much surplus (Farouk 2008: 288). And in March 2012, General Mahmoud Nasr, the assistant defense minister for financial affairs, revealed that the total worth of the military's economic complex in 2011 was roughly $1 billion, and that profits accumulated during Mubarak's three-decade tenure were $1.2 billion—relatively modest figures (Gamal 2012: 2).

Over and above everything else, Mubarak's privatization policy in the 1990s and his son's neoliberal policies in the 2000s further reduced the army's economic role (Marshall 2015). No wonder why the high command "fiercely resented Gamal Mubarak . . . [who] preferred to build his influence through business and political cronies rather than through the military, and those connected to him gained huge profits from government monopolies and deals with foreign investors" (Goldstone 2011: 13). A member of the Policies Committee, who defected to the opposition, prophesized in 2010: "Gamal's support comes from people in the business elite. . . . But if his father dies tomorrow, they [the Army] will shut him out. . . . [W]ithin five or six minutes of his death, you'll see tanks in the street" (Frisch 2013: 187). Yet ruling party capitalists took no heed. When U.S. Ambassador Francis Richardoni relayed to one of them Defense Minister Tantawi's concerns, he scoffed: "Tantawi is not stronger than Abu-Ghazala" (Heikal 2012: 305). It therefore seems, as the *Financial Times* reported in 2011, that the army's "reputed economic 'empire' . . . is considerably more modest in volume than is commonly believed, and has probably shrunk in proportion to a national economy that has grown by more than 3 percent annually since 2003 . . . [and] although a few generals are rumored to have become rich, the main purpose [behind the military's economic activities] . . . is to ameliorate the impact of a rapidly privatizing economy on the living standards of officers" (Sayigh 2011: 11).[4]

This last point is crucial. While Mubarak's inflationary policies eroded the value of all government wages, civil servants moonlighted and took bribes to supplement their shrinking incomes. Officers, however, were stuck with their paychecks. In addition, the subsidized services they received were humble by upper-middle-class standards (Al-Baz 2007: 70). A casual observer could not fail to note how shabby military discount stores, automobiles, housing complexes, and beach cabins were when compared to those enjoyed by Egypt's upper-middle class—who, as a matter of course, never joined the ranks. As a result, the majority of Egypt's active forces (let alone reserves) suffered manpower quality problems because of their low educational and health standards. The fact that the army's improved performance in 1973 was attributed to the inclusion of educated middle-class elements did not prevent Sadat from revising the conscription formula after the war, presumably to free this class to join the private sector. College graduates now served for only nine months, and once again the army was stuck with illiterate peasants who could mostly handle menial duties. When the high command asked for special funds to retain qualified conscripts, Mubarak saw no national emergency to justify increased spending (Barnet 1992: 143–44; Cordesman 2006: 159–62). In 1996 the frustrated generals began sending recruiting delegations to Egypt's expatriate communities, but very few were attracted to a low-paying military career (Frisch 2001: 5–6). Worse still, Mubarak asked State Security to monitor those who stood out. And these security reports often sent good officers packing, usually with a decent retirement package (Selim 2009).

What about American patronage? Though any type of foreign military assistance comes with strings attached, the reason why the military regarded

American aid as particularly problematic was the specific constraints that came with it. Four years after leaving office, Abu Ghazala revealed that officers were frustrated by having to rely on a country committed to keeping the military power of all Arab countries behind Israel (Al-Baz 2007: 206–08). This commitment was demonstrated on several occasions. For instance, the number of Egypt's F-16 fighter jets was kept to less than two-thirds of Israel's. When Cairo demanded the Advanced Medium-Range Air-to-Air Missile (AMRAAM), which Washington readily provided to the UAE, the Pentagon rejected the request, citing Israeli objections. Also, although the United States furnished Israel with 70 percent of the development costs of Arrow missiles, it refused to help Egypt build an advanced missile program. So while the arsenal in both countries had many types of weapons in common, Israel's lot was better in quantity and quality, and its indigenous manufacturers benefited from U.S. assistance to remain ahead (Frisch 2001: 3–5). Even when Egypt asked the Russians to upgrade its air defense system with S-300 missiles, which were particularly effective against Israel's cruise missiles, the Pentagon blocked the deal (Cordesman 2006: 175–77). One needs to remember that Abu Ghazala lost his job when a reluctant Pentagon drove him to smuggle American missile technology and deal with North Korea to make the Egyptian army better than Washington would allow for. And even Mubarak's ever-cordial Defense Minister Tantawy complained of American limitations on the armed forces (Essam al-Din 2011: 1). Indeed, the funds were spent on American equipment, and much of it had little operational utility. A case in point is tanks—not a very important item for a country not planning to wage large-scale conventional wars. Under U.S. guidance, Egypt compiled an arsenal exceeding those of all Latin American and sub-Saharan African militaries combined. Attempting to make use of this bloated stockpile, Tantawi suggested exporting some of Egypt 1,100 M1 Abrams to post-Saddam Iraq. Washington refused. Months later, General Dynamics sold 140 M1 Abrams to Iraq for double the price Cairo offered, and Egypt was persuaded to buy yet another 125 tanks (Marshall 2013). Finally, the 1979 peace treaty, upon which U.S. military assistance was based, "sat poorly with many of Egypt's senior officers" from the very start, largely because it de-militarized Sinai (Waterbury 1983: 376). Indeed, one of the first steps the military took after the 2011 revolt was to revise constraints on its deployment in Sinai.

Besides Israel, the United States was a superpower that vigorously defended its hegemony throughout the region and did not welcome Egypt's projection of military power in any direction. Even when Egypt was summoned to facilitate America's liberation of Kuwait, it was not allowed to play a more active role afterward in Gulf security via an Arab defense force. The Egyptian military was basically expected to pose as a "deterrent force situated in the background" (Frisch 2001: 6). To add insult to injury, it paid handsomely for its marginalization, since American aid was expensive. It only cost $1.7 billion worth of Russian weapons to fight the Suez War (1956), the Yemen War (1962–1967), the 1967 Arab-Israeli War, the War of Attrition (1967–1970), and the October War (1973). Compared to its two-decade relationship with Moscow, the first five years of Egypt's U.S. alliance left it in debt for $6.6 billion, even though it neither went to war, nor planned to do so (Handoussa 1990: 114).

To conclude, Mubarak's military suffered from "rank disequilibrium": a psychological dissonance that spreads among members of an institution whose position becomes at odds with their original duties (Al-Mashat 1986: 64). Officers trained for war, while knowing full well that they were never meant to fight one; they were asked to defend the nation while being deprived of suitable manpower; and they were exclusively dependent on a country sworn to preserve their rival's superiority. It did not help that Mubarak frequently asserted his conviction that "war had become outdated." Since wars invariably end with a peaceful settlement, he argued, why not cut to the chase and go straight to negotiations. It is difficult imagine officers warming up to these pronouncements, especially given that their sage of a president was not so pacifist in dealing with his countrymen. Apparently, "police wars" were not yet outdated in Mubarak's dictionary.

Placing the Police on a Pedestal

As the army's power declined, the Interior Ministry grew into a formidable empire. With military spending at a record low, the security budget increased sevenfold from $583 million to $3.3 billion between 2002 and 2008 (Frisch 2013: 183). The police force swelled from 150,000 men in 1974 to over a million in 2002, representing an increase from 9 to 21 percent of state employment. This is, of course, in addition to the 450,000 CSF conscripts (the numerical equivalent of 20 army divisions) who served for three years, and the 60,000 national guard and 12,000 border patrol soldiers who reported to the ministry (Farouk 2008: 275–81; IISS 2009: 33). Overall, during the final decade of Mubarak's tenure, the Interior Ministry mammoth encompassed perhaps 2 million security personnel in a population of perhaps 83 million (Sayigh 2015: 7).[5] To grasp the enormity of this figure, one should remember that the Soviet police force under Stalin in the 1930s was a mere 142,000 men (Skocpol 1979: 226); that today 142 million Russians suffice with a 200,000-strong security force (Soldatov and Borogan 2010: 80); that the entire Chinese army in 2009 numbered only 2.3 million in a population of 1.3 billion (Brendon 2010: 12); and that Egypt's own army in 2010 was no more than 460,000. Another interesting fact: counter-insurgency experts estimate the ratio of officers-to-citizens needed to contain insurgencies on the scale of those raging in Iraq and Afghanistan at 20 officers per 1,000 citizens (O'Hanlon 2010: 75); in Mubarak's Egypt, the ratio was 25 security men to every 1,000 citizens. At the same time, Interior Ministry expenditures increased from 3.5 percent of GDP to almost 6 percent, between 1988 and 2002. In money terms, it increased from L.E 260 million to L.E. 348 million during the first four years of Mubarak's tenure. Thereafter, police wages multiplied almost fourfold, from L.E. 819 million in 1992 to L.E. 3 billion in 2002. The real increase in police revenue, however, came from the government's tacit consent to the extortions they imposed on citizens from the 1990s onward (Suleiman 2005: 84–86; Farouk 2008: 285).

This was not the worst of it. Beginning with the 1984 parliamentary elections, repression took a new turn when the police hired criminals to manhandle opponents. This notion of "outsourcing repression" harks back to the 1970s, when Sadat's Interior Ministry supplied Islamists with knives and metal bars to terrorize opposition groups. It also employed thugs to sabotage civil society meetings criticizing the president (Abdallah 1985: 198; Heikal 1983: 213). With the weakening of opposition, through decades of repression, the Interior Ministry's last challenge was to suppress Islamist militants between 1992 and 1997, which it did at the cost of 2,000 killed and another 47,000 detained (Kepel 2006: 276–99). Afterward, it saw no signs of trouble on the horizon, and consequently delegated everyday repression to seasonally hired thugs in order not to implicate (or bother) the police. Criminal investigation units would nominate petty criminals to State Security officers, who would then prep and turn them over to the CSF. Thugs would help CSF conscripts by starting brawls outside polling stations; beating up demonstrators; menacing strikers; driving peasants off their land. The downturn, however, was that the police could scarcely prevent these thugs from bullying citizens during their off-duty hours. "The secret business relationship between the thugs and State Security officers ... provided the former with protection on the streets, thus transforming them into unleashed and undeterred monsters" (Omar 2011: 5). Police-linked thugs extorted money from the wealthy, harassed shopkeepers, and molested females on crowded boulevards. Citizens had become fair game.

In time, policemen themselves began acting like thugs. One observer noted, "The average Egyptian can be dragged into a police station and tortured simply because a police officer doesn't like his face" (Shatz 2010: 8). This was again a Sadat-era phenomenon. Between 1974 and 1976, newspapers reported for the first time cases of criminal (not political) suspects being tortured by the police to confess to the crimes they committed (or did not commit). Torture was so brutal that sometimes suspects admitted to murder (a crime punishable by death) only to discover afterward that their alleged "victims" were still alive. So now it was citizens, rather than activists, being tortured to confess to crimes, rather than dissent, by criminal investigators, rather than secret police officers, in police stations, rather than isolated detention centers. From that point forward, police violence became endemic. It was no longer just about extracting confessions, but also to force citizens to pay bribes, withdraw complaints, sign business contracts, or just to make them learn their place. Indeed, torture transcended the boundaries of "frequent practices" to become "standard behavior ... [something] applied automatically without effort or reflection, something that does not require full consciousness or focus or planning; violence had become a second nature" (Abd al-Aziz 2011: 45–46). But if one might expect regimes to act violently against contenders, why was there so much violence against the "apolitical and peaceful citizen" (Abd al-Aziz 2011: 9–10). As one analyst concluded, it was because policemen had been transformed from instruments of authority to *authority itself,* that is, from regime supporters to its principle beneficiaries. Hence, the relationship between policemen and citizens had been reformulated into that of master and slave. "The new masters could bestow their protection on whomever they choose, and they could also deprive anyone of dignity, pride, liberty, confidence, respect, or any human value" (Abd al-Aziz 2011: 61).

At the same time, the State Security Investigations Sector (SSIS) developed into a "a state within the state." It dwarfed all other government institutions; it scrutinized nominees for cabinet positions, Parliament seats, governorships, university chairs, editorial boards, public sectors companies and banks, and, of course, the military. It constantly monitored society through informers and electronic surveillance, and ran large detention centers—with the number of political detainees oscillating between 15,000 and 40,000 during Mubarak's tenure. Evidence for how tightly SSIS managed political life was revealed after the Muslim Brothers secured 20 percent of the 2005 Parliament—an unparalleled achievement. Asked three years later if he expected comparable success in the next elections, the Brotherhood's general guide said he was not sure because in the previous elections "State Security gave us a list of districts to run in, and promised to let us win in most. They have not contacted us so far about next year." When the dumbfounded interviewer asked him to clarify this statement, he explained that the George W. Bush administration was pressuring Egypt to democratize after 9/11, and the SSIS wanted to scare them a little, and his organization did not mind getting a few more seats (Al-Galad, al-Masry, and al-Khatib 2009: 11). And surely enough, when State Security turned against the Brothers in the 2010 elections, their share fell from 88 seats to zero. Parliament Speaker Fathy Sourur recalled his shock upon hearing the results: "I have worked with the president for twenty-five years, but lately I felt that the Interior Ministry was running the country" (Muslim 2011b: 10).

Ultimately, it was the appointment of Habib al-Adly as interior minister, in 1997, that gave Egypt's police state its final form. Adly served in State Security from 1965 to 1993, then as its director in 1996, before becoming interior minister. As a testament to his central role in the regime, Adly occupied this post for fourteen years, whereas his predecessors from 1952 onward served, on average, for 3.2 years. One of the reasons why is because he forged intimate relations with the businessmen-dominated Policies Committee of the ruling party (Omar 2011: 5).

Changing of the Guard

Police empowerment did not rule out the need for an entrenched ruling party. The structure and function of this party had remained consistent since the 1950s. It was always pyramid-shaped with a wide base in the countryside, which narrowed down as one moved to the cities. And its role was to organize the regime's social bases. These were basically rural notables and public employees, whether white-collared or workers. What changed was the social composition of the party elite. Under Nasser, some 1,000 military officers controlled the key political posts (Perlmutter 1974: 112). With Sadat's economic liberalization, a new class of state-nurtured businessmen emerged. By the turn of the twenty-first century, this stratum gave way to monopoly capitalists, who perhaps relied on state contracts at the beginning, but were now too wealthy to be controlled from above. It was these billionaires who now led the National Democratic Party (NDP). For the first time since 1952, economic elites were manipulating the state rather than being manipulated by it.

Mubarak did not intend for economic magnates to colonize the NDP. He hoped for businessmen to represent one of many interest groups within the Party. When he ascended to office, he replaced seven of the thirteen-member politburo, sixteen of the twenty-three-member secretariat, and nine of the chairs of the NDP's fifteen standing committees, in a move calculated to purge business oligarchs, such as Osman Ahmed Osman. The president concurrently promoted Party apparatchiks. Youssef Wali, an agro-bureaucrat, became NDP secretary-general, assisted by Kamal al-Shazly, who had served in all post-1952 political organizations. The remaining NDP capitalists responded by extending patronage to state bureaucrats (3.5 million in the 1980s) to guarantee sustained access to public resources, such as cheap land, state credit, trade monopolies, tax and tariff exemptions (Springborg 1989: 87, 137, 158–69). With this powerful combination, the ruling party continued to gravitate into the orbit of big business.

The social consequences were grave. To start with, the new businessmen did not generate enough jobs; the state remained the primary employer, with the bureaucracy swelling to 5.5 million and public factory workers to 600,000 by the end of Mubarak's reign (Abd al-Fadeel 1983: 124–25). What economic liberalization did produce was acute social inequality. World Bank statistics, in 1980s, showed that the richest 5 percent of the population controlled 22 percent of the national income, while the share of the poorest 20 percent was merely 5 percent (Oweiss 1990: 12). Mubarak was temporally saved by the oil boom of the 1970s, which increased state revenue from oil exports, remittances of Egyptians working in oil-rich countries, and traffic in the Suez Canal. One-third of the public revenue came from these external rents, as opposed to less than 50 percent from taxes. Oil prices, however, plummeted from $36 a barrel in 1980 to $12 in 1986. This immediately caused a sharp decrease in foreign currency reserves—a crippling disaster in a country with a high import bill. Inflation skyrocketed to 23 percent, and unemployment to 19 percent. Washington chose this moment to suspend its aid to Egypt pending the application of International Monetary Fund (IMF) reforms (Suleiman 2005: 54). A devastating debt crisis ensued. In 1989 Egypt filed for bankruptcy and thus became ineligible for those international loans it so desperately needed to meet its domestic obligations.

It was only by joining the war against Iraq in 1991 that the country could start running again, since its biggest creditor, the United States, conditioned pardoning half of its debt, as well as convincing European and Arab countries to follow suit, on its participation (Bush and Scowcroft 1998: 412). But despite the elimination of half its foreign debt, Egypt still lost the remittances coming from Iraq and other Gulf countries as a result of the war. Foreign aid was also reduced since Egypt now had to compete with dozens of former Communist European countries after the collapse of the Berlin Wall (Wahid 2009: 133). And a condition of any such foreign funds was to comply with IMF recommendations.

So regardless of the dire social situation, Mubarak adopted, in 1991, an IMF structural adjustment program based on reducing subsidies and the privatization of state assets. By 1999, 76 percent of subsidies were slashed, including the state duty to hire university graduates. And the public sector was restructured into 314 holding companies, of which 124 were sold (Ghoneim 2005: 86, 158). The share of the public sector fell from 54 percent of GDP, and 70 percent of total investment, to 28 percent of GDP, and 44 percent of investments (Adly 2009: 11). Egypt's finances improved—on paper. During its first decade (1991–2001), IMF reforms reduced the deficit from 15.3 percent to 3 percent of GDP, and achieved a 5 percent growth rate (Mitchell 2002: 272).

However, economic liberalization did not deprive the ruling party of its most salient asset: its ability to tap into various types of rents and then redistribute them in ways that allowed it to maintain power. Political autonomy was first guaranteed by the fact that the state did not rely heavily on taxation, but rather on extracting rents, a third of which came from two public enterprises, the Suez Canal Company and the Egyptian General Petroleum Corporation. The state also managed the allocation of foreign aid. But one of the least studied sources of rent was land. Egyptians inhabit only 4 percent of their territory, with the rest classified as public land. The ruling party could therefore assign lots to property developers, hotel magnates, or realtors at whatever price and under whatever conditions. Under Mubarak, the state actually allotted 67,200 square kilometers—an area the size of Palestine, Lebanon, Kuwait, Qatar, and Bahrain combined—worth L.E. 800 billion to handpicked businessmen (Al-Gahmy and Abd al-Qawy 2011: 7). NDP-linked businessmen dug assiduously into this gold mine: beginning from the 1990s, gated compounds, masquerading as American-style suburbs, mushroomed around the capital; holiday resorts spread over tens of thousands of acres on the Mediterranean and Red Sea coasts; and real estate speculation became the most lucrative investment in town. Indeed by 2002, real estate had replaced agriculture as the third largest nonoil investment sector, way ahead of manufacturing. Instead of generating an export boom, economic liberalization generated a building boom. Egypt was paving over its arable land, while its people were forced to import their food from the West (Mitchell 1999: 29, 274–81).

Political power was similarly manifest in the privatization program. To begin with, while the government estimated the value of the public sector at L.E. 124 billion in 1991 (though independent consultants insisted it was closer to L.E. 500 billion), by 2000 almost half of the public sector was sold for a meager L.E. 15.6 billion to favored investors, after the government retroactively adjusted its estimation to the absurd amount of L.E. 28.8 billion (Ghoneim 2005: 93–95). A bigger problem was that on the eve of the IMF program, 260 out of the 314 state-owned companies were actually profitable, and overall annual profits (an estimated $550 million) more than compensated for the losses (only $110 million). The real concern was public banks, which held 60 percent of national deposits, and provided 50 percent of loans. Over 30 percent of these loans, however, were nonperforming—and most of these had been acquired without collateral by state-connected businessmen (Mitchell 2002: 276–82). Specifically speaking, by the late 1990s, twenty-eight NDP-endorsed businessmen received 13 percent of the total public credit with an average of L.E. 1 billion each. And in 2002, twelve of them were responsible for 18 percent of nonperforming loans in public banks (Adly 2009: 11–12). So the government used 40 percent of its proceeds from privatization to bail out its cronies, rather than provide welfare. In short, "The reform program did not remove the state from the market or eliminate profligate public subsidies. Its main impact was to concentrate public funds into different hands, and many fewer" (Mitchell 2002: 282). The concentration of economic power in the hands of a few tycoons had profound political consequences. With so much accumulated capital, they were no longer satisfied with living in the state's shadow. They wanted to rule.

So who were these new capitalists? At the beginning of the new millennium, the Egyptian economy was dominated by less than two dozen family-owned conglomerates. The founders of these dynasties had a lot in common: most had their roots in construction; their businesses were kicked off through state contracts; they drew funds freely from public banks; they paid very little taxes (business taxes constituted only 6 percent of public revenue between 2008 and 2012); they partnered with foreign (especially American) investors; they employed a relatively small working force (3,000, on average); and their products catered to the needs of the affluent. This class fragment certainly did not represent the Egyptian bourgeoisie in its entirety, but it was the fragment off which the rest of the class members made their living, and the one none of them could hope to compete with or dislodge. Directly below these super-rich businessmen, another 5 percent of the population enjoyed modest affluence, with the rest of society divided neatly between the relatively poor, and the 50 percent living below the poverty line (less than $2 a day). Among the latter group, perhaps 10 million dwelled in shantytowns on the outskirts of the capital, "slums with no schools, hospitals, clubs, sewage systems, public transportation or even police stations . . . a Hobbesian world of violence and vice" (Ibrahim 1996: 39–41; Singerman 2004: 161).

With such a socioeconomic imbalance, Mubarak flinched from sharing power with the new mega-capitalists. The stability of the 1952 regime, he surely recognized, rested on the exchange of social rights for political ones. According to this unwritten social contract, the state provided employment, education, health care, and subsidized goods and services to its citizens, in return for their forgoing of their right to participate in politics. Unfortunately, this arrangement required a solvent state. Until 1971 sequestered land and financial assets, nationalized businesses, and cheap Soviet aid sufficed. Nasser believed that before these resources dried up, state-led industrialization would generate the surplus needed to carry on. However, Sadat's partnership with the United States replaced affordable Soviet assistance with expensive and conditional American aid, and his open door policy squandered state wealth. More important, the wedding of business and politics—so actively encouraged by Sadat—allowed capitalists to entrench themselves too deeply in the bureaucracy and ruling party to be purged. Ultimately, Egypt's deteriorating finances and sustained pressure from the world capitalist centers propelled Mubarak to rely more and more on private investors.

Politically speaking, however, this new stratum was the most dangerous of all the economic elites of the post-1952 era because it was the only one that combined alliances with global capitalists with alliances with state rulers and functionaries. More crucial still: they were also avid organizers. In the 1990s, they established a joint committee linking the Egyptian Businessmen Association (EBA), their formal platform since 1979, and the cabinet. They also infiltrated state-run economic bodies, such as the chambers of commerce and industry, and used them to promote their interests (Bianchi 1990: 215). With successful lobbying tactics, they dared to devise a grander strategy. They now clustered around a young investment banker, who had begun his career in the Bank of America and worked in London for a while before returning to Cairo in 1995. The young man had two enticing assets: he was politically ambitious, and he was the president's son. In 2000 Gamal Mubarak and his new best friends established the Future Generation Foundation (FGF), a civil association designed to promote Gamal's image as Egypt's youth leader. That same year, Mubarak appointed his son to the NDP's general secretariat, as head of the Youth and Development Committee. And in 2002, Gamal created and chaired a new political body within the Party: the Policies Committee (PC): a crystallization of capitalists and self-styled neoliberal intellectuals. The PC became the throbbing heart of the ruling party and the embodiment of its "New Thinking"—the NDP's 2002 convention slogan (Shatz 2010: 9–10). People referred to the committee mockingly as "Gamal's cabinet," not knowing that soon enough its members would, in fact, form the country's first "businessmen cabinet."

On the morning of July 14, 2004, unsuspecting Egyptians woke up to the news that a computer engineer, Ahmed Nazif, was charged with forming a government stacked with Gamal's crony capitalists and neoliberals. The cabinet included six monopoly capitalists who were put in charge of ministries directly related to their business portfolios, in addition to a number of prominent neoliberal thinkers. A few examples suffice. Ahmed al-Maghraby, owner of the tourism conglomerate Accor Hotels, was appointed minister of tourism, and a year later minister of housing and construction; Rashid Ahmed Rashid, head of the regional affiliate of the multinational Unilever, became minister of industry and trade; Mohamed Mansour, chairman of Al-Mansour Motor Group, was charged with overseeing the Ministry of Transportation; Youssef Boutros Ghali, longtime IMF executive, was entrusted with the Treasury; and Mahmoud Muhi al-Din, a Cairo University professor who was later elected executive director of the World Bank, handled economics and investment. All of these men were, of course, members of the PC. What followed afterward was nothing less than a full-fledged "bourgeoisification" of the leadership of the ruling party. NDP businessmen more than doubled their share of Parliament seats, and controlled key parliamentary committees. Most significantly, iron and steel tycoon Ahmed Ezz, Gamal's mentor and closet associate, became Parliament majority leader and chair of the Planning and Budget Committee (Muslim 2011a: 7). And in 2006, Gamal himself became NDP assistant secretary-general. It was only natural that his business cronies now flirted with the idea of pushing him to the presidency.

The NDP's old guard, of course, resisted. Parliament Speaker Fathy Sourur shared his frustration with reporters after the 2011 revolt: "Their [the businessmen's] entry into the cabinet was a big mistake, especially that they were put in charge of the fields they specialized in, which caused a contradiction between public and private interests, and I said this more than once . . . to the party, but no one listened" (Muslim 2011c: 9). Many probably blamed these changes on the proud father who wanted to pass the mantle to his son (under the insistence of the mother, some might add). But a few objective conditions made the NDP reliant on Gamal's capitalists— chief among these were solvency and geopolitics.

Between 1992 and 2002, state revenue declined from 30 percent of GDP to 20 percent, and domestic debt increased from 67 to 90 percent of GDP. The state was, in fact, running on debt. And since the ruling party lived off state finances, it too was running on debt. But who were the creditors? Half of the debt came from public sector banks, which had little choice but to obey the rulers. A second source was treasury bills, though raising money through this route was cumbersome and time-consuming. The most readily available way to keep the political machine solvent was to count on the generosity of regime-friendly capitalists (Suleiman 2005: 192–96, 218). At the beginning, they offered commissions in return for state contracts. Donations also paid part of the bill. But as monopoly capitalists began to take charge of the ruling party and government, they assumed financial responsibilities as well: they funded NDP conventions; they launched media campaigns; they paid bribes to stifle opposition; they bought votes and organized pro-regime demonstrations (Biblawi 2012: 16). In addition, their business partnerships with global investors eased pressures on the regime to democratize. They even accompanied Mubarak during his annual pilgrimage to Washington to sing his praises (Amin 2009: 93).

In return for their valuable services, the economic magnates now demanded a full neoliberal restructuring. A new tax regime, which gradually materialized between 2002 and 2010, imposed 60 percent of the tax burden on the general population via indirect taxes and tariffs. At the same time, taxes on business revenues were sliced in half from 40 to 20 percent. In addition, the tax-collecting authority was quite lenient on tax evasion, allowing businessmen—if caught—to pay the amount due plus a small fine without the prospect of imprisonment (Suleiman 2005: 207–17). Then there were the ever-increasing price levels. In January 2003 the government floated the currency exchange rate, causing the value of the Egyptian pound to lose 25 percent of its value vis-à-vis the U.S. dollar. The decision was justified by the need to improve Egypt's balance of trade. What happened instead was that importing activities persisted at the same level, while the price of imports and domestic products that relied on imported components skyrocketed. Egyptians now experienced the smoldering effects of stagflation.

The Time Bomb

Egypt's dark days got darker. Between 2000 and 2009, the GDP increased from $92.4 billion to $187.3 billion, and economic growth increased from 3.2 to 5 percent. But the economic growth achieved during that decade (mostly due to the doubling of oil prices after the invasion of Iraq, and the increase in foreign investments) did not alleviate citizens' lives. In 2006 World Bank reports indicated that 47 percent of the population was living on less than $2 a day (Wahid 2009: 134–42). In 2010 unemployment was estimated at 26.3 percent

(Shatz 2010: 6). More than 3 million people joined the underground economy. Education spending consumed less than 5 percent of GDP; food subsidies were reduced by 20 percent, causing the price of various food items to increase threefold; and while the rich decorated their lavish compounds with artificial lakes and swimming pools, 79 percent of Egyptians had no access to clean drinking water and a proper sewage system (Abd al-Aziz 2011: 90–91).

The countryside suffered through counter-reforms that abrogated the gains the peasantry had made since 1952. Rent regulations expired, and 1.2 million tenants had to negotiate new contracts. Considering that 7 million peasants and their families lived off these lands, protests soon erupted. Land seizures and sabotage of agricultural equipment became so rampant that the government deployed the CSF to subdue angry peasants (Ghoneim 2005: 113–15). Likewise, privatization provoked numerous labor strikes, notably the violent April 6 national strike of 2008. In fact, between 2001 and 2011, perhaps 2 million workers participated in strikes. And in 2010 alone, there were over 700 strikes (Benin 2011). Even within the traditional bastion of state power—the bureaucracy—things were going downhill. Only the top 0.2 percent, a little over 8,000 officials, were well paid (some receiving six-figure salaries), while the rest of the 5.5 million employees gradually descended to the ranks of the proletariat (Ghoneim 2005: 142).

Of course, the ultimate guarantor of the regime could not have stood by idly as billions were passing from hand-to-hand under its nose; it had to be given a piece of the action. Post-2011 investigations revealed that the Interior Minister Habib al-Adly and his immediate family owned nine villas, seven apartments, thirteen construction sites, substantial agricultural tracts, a shopping mall, four Mercedes automobiles, and had made significant deposits to their bank accounts. His total personal wealth amounted to L.E. 8 billion (Al-Geziry 2011: 1). State Security laid claim to a vast plot of (military) land in the buzzing Cairo neighborhood of Nasr City to establish its new headquarters. In Alexandria, thirty-eight State Security officers acquired 750,000 square meters of land for L.E. 13 per meter in 2000, when the real price exceeded L.E. 300 per meter. And after the uprising, the courts froze the assets of fifty-two senior police officers on charges of corruption (Sabri 2011: 6).

Needless to say, neoliberal restructuring pushed the regime further into the Interior Ministry's iron cage. Egypt's capitalists-turned-ministers realized that they were now beholden to the police forces more than ever. The social unrest resulting from the shrinking of social benefits, the steady rise in price levels, the laying off of thousands of workers required constant repression. Little wonder why Gamal's PC was expanded to include the interior minister in 2005. The fortunes of the political and security apparatuses remained symbiotically linked until the very last day.

As the countdown to the Revolution began, it was clear that the regime was losing its traditional social bases: the rural and urban middle class. Rural notables had become dispensable because the outright rigging of elections (financed by direct handouts from ruling party capitalists and carried out by the Interior Ministry) rendered its political control function in the countryside superfluous. Now they could be pressured to sell their land to satisfy the appetite of the superrich for giant agro-industrial projects. The wells of the state bourgeoisie were also drying up since the dismantling of the public sector diminished their middlemen role between aspiring businessmen and public resources. Added to the woes of the middle class were those of the petty businessmen of the late 1970s and 1980s. Ruling party tycoons raised market entry barriers and eliminated competitors with relative ease. Tolerance for small fish in the business world was shrinking by the moment. Finally, staggering unemployment and inflation rates made life impossible for educated youth who realized that their diplomas carried no weight in Egypt's neoliberal economy. In the end, only the tiny fragment linked directly to the political apparatus (the uppermost crust of the bourgeoisie) remained loyal, while the majority of the middle-class fragments resented the regime for abandoning them. Revolt, in this case, seemed the only way out of their suffering. With the clock ticking away toward September 2011, the date the president was supposed to pass on power to Gamal and his capitalist allies, the middle class expected nothing but total ruin. When a call went out to make a final stand against the regime on January 25, 2011, they had only their chains to lose.

Notes

1. The security chief of one of Egypt's governorates made this comment in 2011 (Hassan 2011: 3).

2. *Al-Ahram* 34634: 5. Cairo (10/9/1981).

3. The figures are based on Shtauber and Shapir (2005: 113–16); Cordesman (2006: 157–63); Wahid (2009: 137–41); Khalaf and Dombey (2011: 3); and Gamal (2012: 2).

4. The *Washington Post* summarized the vagueness of present assessments by observing that "economic experts estimated the military's holdings anywhere between 5 and 60 percent of the economy" (Hauslohner 2014).

5. These included 850,000 policemen and staff; 100,000 State Security officers and associates; 450,000 anti-riot forces; and some 400,000 paid informers and thugs (Sayigh 2015: 7).

16 | The Resilience of Repression

JANUARY 2011 AND AFTER

THE SNOWBALL STARTED ROLLING FROM the west. When a policewoman slapped an unemployed college graduate for working as a street vendor without permit, the indignant young man set himself on fire, triggering a massive uprising that overthrew the country's political leadership in three weeks. This all occurred in a country with strikingly similar circumstances to Egypt: Tunisia. Unlike the monarchies of Morocco and Jordan, where the army is loyal to the sovereign, and the tribal societies of Libya and Yemen, as well as the monarchial-tribal societies of the Gulf, where the reigning tribe controls the military leadership whereas the rank-and-file come from lesser tribes, the Egyptian and Tunisian armies were drawn from ethnically and religiously homogenous populations and swore allegiance to modern republican constitutions. Also, contrary to the army-controlled regimes of Syria, Algeria, and the Sudan, the two countries had metamorphosed from coup-installed military regimes into police states. In the process, armies in both countries were gradually sidelined by a suspicious political elite in favor of an expansive security institution, and thus grew eager to alter the political formula once circumstances allowed. Finally, the lower classes in both states suffered from an exploitative and corrupt state-nurtured business elite with strong ties to global investors. Tunisia was, of course, considerably smaller than Egypt in area, population, and the size of its police and military forces, but its experience had a crucial demonstrative effect for Egyptians. It showed them that the unthinkable was, in fact, thinkable. Now, Egyptians started moving, and the military realized that at last the external factor they hoped would shift the stagnant power balance to its favor began to materialize.

18 Days

The year (2011) was the year of the purported succession from father to son. The day (January 25) was Police Day, a national holiday honoring police heroism against the British in 1952—a day that always highlighted the dark contrast between what the police used to be and what it had become. But on January 25, 2011, Egypt had no organized opposition to speak of. Disgruntled activists joined several united fronts. The new ones were Kefaya (Enough), a movement founded in 2004 to despose Mubarak, and the National Association for Change, which began in 2010 canvassing for election of Mohamed ElBaradei, former director of the International Atomic Energy Agency (IAEA), to the presidency. And, of course, there were still the old opposition parties representing liberals and leftists, as well as the Muslim Brotherhood, the Islamist movement invariably manipulated by the regime (to scare liberals in the 1950s; leftists in the 1970s; militant Islamists in the 1990s; and Americans throughout Mubarak's reign) before being cast aside (usually to prison) once it has served its purpose. But the youth movements that captured the world's attention were the April 6 Youth Movement, whose name commemorates the failed national strike on that day in 2008, when striking workers were repressed using live ammunition; and the We Are All Khaled Said Facebook page, named after the Alexandrian boy whose head was smashed on the pavement in 2010 because he exchanged words with police hoodlums. The fact that the latter, which was created by the 30-year-old Google marketing executive Wael Ghonim, drew over half a million members in three months indicated how Egyptians identified with the murdered youth. Citizens felt that no matter how compliant they were, no one was safe. In short, the Egyptian opposition on the eve of the revolt was little more than an amalgam of loose platforms with overlapping memberships and political affiliations. And even though the participants had become increasingly vocal since 2005, politicians and security men saw no cause for concern. This relaxed attitude was brilliantly captured in Mubarak's satirical side comment during the inauguration of the 2010 Parliament (a month before the revolt), "Let them [opposition forces] entertain themselves."

This is why no one thought much of the call to demonstrate on January 25 by the April 6 Youth Movement and We Are All Khaled Said Facebook page. On the designated day, some 20,000 activists demonstrated in front of the Interior Ministry, three blocks away from Tahrir Square in downtown Cairo. They were quickly repressed using tear gas and water hoses, thirty activists were detained, and a university student was killed. Over the next two days, the marches persisted, attracting more and more participants and spreading throughout the country. The police escalated its actions, arresting 4,000 demonstrators (including Wael Ghonim), and adding rubber bullets to its gas-and-water cocktail (killing four people and injuring over a hundred). But instead of scaring activists away, the embattled activists appealed to the people through social media to join them for a Day of Rage on Friday, January 28. Egyptians hesitated. With succession around the corner, their lives would probably deteriorate. Yet a potentially devastating clampdown unnerved many. That morning, the security network cut off cellphone and Internet communication services, and flooded the streets with anti-riot police. Many would have preferred to stay home that day if they were not obliged to attend Friday prayers. The euphoria of the last three days apparently inspired the country's timid preachers to denounce dictatorship and urge defiance. Fired up by religious sermons and besieged by a sea of angry demonstrators pouring out of Cairo's 300,000 mosques, common folk were carried away; their minds were finally made up. Thus began the march to Tahrir Square.

Policemen were exhausted on their fourth day of street skirmishes, but they still resisted. They fired live ammunition; ran over demonstrators with armored vehicles; drowned them in a fog of tear gas; drove them back with high-pressure water hoses—but to no avail. Equipped only to repress a handful of urban protesters, they now faced millions. Following heroic battles around Cairo's downtown neighborhoods and Nile bridges, where hundreds were killed, and the ruling party headquarters was set ablaze, security forces threw in the towel. The road was finally clear. At this point, the activists-turned-revolutionaries had to decide where to go: leftward to the state media building, and the adjacent Foreign Ministry; or rightward to the seat of Parliament, the cabinet, and the Interior Ministry; or straight ahead to Tahrir Square. They opted for the latter, providing the regime with valuable time to fortify these strategic sites by nightfall.

Why did the protesters choose a giant public square (approximately 490,000 square feet that could hold perhaps a million people) rather than sensitive state organs? Seizing a downtown plaza could hardly stifle life in a sprawling city like Cairo. And unlike the teeming alleyways and buildings crammed in the capital's popular neighborhoods, the exposed square offered no protection. The only advantage was *visibility*. Activists drew inspiration neither from the revolutionaries of nineteenth- and early-twentieth-century Europe, nor from their neighbors in Libya and Syria. They did not grasp the necessity of creating a situation of dual power by occupying government buildings, entrenching themselves in crowded neighborhoods, seizing towns, and using all of these actions to incrementally supplant the regime. Instead, they drew inspiration from Eastern Europe in 1989. They were dazzled by how peaceful demonstrators could overturn their regimes by occupying plazas to galvanize public opinion and dare their oppressors to shoot them in front of television cameras. Tahrir Square fit this strategy perfectly. And it worked—for the moment.[1] For a few valuable hours, the demonstrators controlled the streets, and the chant that had come to define the uprising reverberated across the country: "The People Demand to Overthrow the Regime!"

Waiting in the wings were the armed forces. As it became clear that the Interior Ministry was unable to stem the uprising, the cornered president summoned his gravediggers in a final attempt to restore order. An army that had been subdued by its other two ruling partners for four decades rolled confidently into the streets. The fact that members of the high command were doubtlessly loyal to Mubarak did not prevent them, under the weight of general opinion within the corps, to abandon their old political master to his fate. Acting otherwise risked fracturing the army that seemed visibly supportive of the revolt. On that first night, soldiers were seen on television smiling and hugging demonstrators. Tanks paraded scrawls that read "Down with Mubarak" and the demonstrators chanted: "The People and the Army are One Hand." The message was unmistakable. Even before the military knew how massive or persistent the uprising was, it was here to see it through.

At the end of this bloody day, U.S. President Barack Obama expressed concern at the use of violence against protesters. Still, Mubarak had to try. The seasoned dictator mixed sticks with carrots during his first address to the nation after the revolt, close to midnight on January 28. The president dismissed the "businessmen cabinet" and the interior minister and appointed a vice-president for the first time in thirty years. But his audience was shocked to learn that this vice-president was none other than the fearsome intelligence chief Omar Suleiman, and that the new cabinet would be formed under Mubarak's friend Ahmed Shafiq, the civil aviation minister, who planned to retain fifteen other ministers of the just dismissed cabinet. In response, demonstrators declared a permanent sit-in in Tahrir and other squares around Egypt until Mubarak stepped down. Field hospitals, open-air theaters, gigantic television screens, food vendors, garbage collection services, and even barbershops were set up for the comfort of the demonstrators. From this point on, it was a waiting game.

On January 31 the Supreme Council of the Armed Forces (SCAF) issued its first communiqué, asserting that officers should not use force against demonstrators. Mubarak's speaker of Parliament admitted that during a meeting he had attended with the president, Defense Minister Hussein Tantawi made it clear that: "The soldiers are not going to strike against demonstrators; that they were there to protect not assault them" (Sourur in Muslim 2011c: 9). As one member of SCAF later explained, "The armed forces took charge before the president stepped down in accordance with the communiqué that stated that the military acknowledges the legitimacy of the [demands of the] Egyptian people" (Osman 2011: 8).

So the following day, Mubarak had to try harder. Vice-president Suleiman held secret talks with two representatives of the Muslim Brothers, future President Mohamed Morsi, and future Speaker of Parliament Saad al-Katatni. They were promised a political party and a bigger share of Parliament if they could help diffuse the revolt—which they accepted. Later that night, Mubarak delivered an emotional speech in which he pledged that neither he nor his son would run in the next election, and hinted at fundamental changes in the ruling party and an investigation of police violence. Many were swayed by his sentimental plea. Less than twenty-four hours later, however, regime thugs dashed into Tahrir on camels and horses, whipping protesters and chasing them around the square, and showering them from surrounding rooftops with Molotov cocktails. Activists fought back with hastily built barricades and stones. After a sixteen-hour battle, the attackers withdrew. The notorious "Battle of the Camel" incident, on February 2, sealed Mubarak's fate. However, he continued offering concessions: a committee to amend the constitution was set up; the National Democratic Party (NDP) secretary-general and leading cadres, including Gamal Muabarak and his chief lieutenant, Ahmed Ezz, were removed from power; the infamous Policies Committee (PC) was dissolved; the interior minister and the businessmen-ministers of the dismissed cabinet would be interrogated by the general prosecutor; a handful of activists were released, including Wael Ghonim, who broke down in tears in a television interview, winning more sympathy for the revolt; and it was agreed that Mubarak would travel to Germany for medical checkups. But the protesters remained adamant. And beginning from February 8, sit-ins were supplemented by labor strikes.

Finally, on February 10, SCAF convened without its supreme commander (the president) in what was perceived as a soft coup. State television announced that the president was going to make an important statement. CIA Director Leon Panetta said in Congress that Mubarak was going to step down. Demonstrators prepared for the party of a lifetime. Instead, the president gave a pedantic and anticlimactic address, concluding with his decision to temporarily delegate power to the vice-president. Stunned demonstrators began screaming and hurling shoes at the television screens in Tahrir Square. As soon as it was over, hundreds of thousands marched to the presidential palace, 40 kilometers from downtown, and surrounded it by the dawn of February 11. Later in the afternoon, a helicopter transported Mubarak and his family to the Red Sea resort of Sharm al-Sheikh, and the vice-president announced that Mubarak had surrendered authority to SCAF. The high command promised to withdraw from politics after a six-month transition period, which would supposedly end with power handed over to an elected authority. After eighteen days of popular defiance and over 1,000 martyrs, a new chapter had begun.

Interregnum

Despite the fact that millions of Egyptians participated in the uprising, decades of effective repression prevented the emergence of an organized revolutionary movement to lead the way. If the military had not refrained from using violence, the revolt might not have lasted long. And if it were not for the tension within the ruling bloc, officers would not have abandoned their allies. In fact, the *Daily Telegraph* revealed how in 2010 the high command had charged Chief of Military Intelligence (and future President) Abd al-Fattah al-Sisi with drawing up "a blueprint for the army to seize power in case of revolution," and his proposal was "putting troops on the streets and saying [the army] stood with the Egyptian people" until Mubarak and his associates stepped down (Spencer 2014). After being sidelined by the security and political institutions for years, the military saw the revolt as an opportunity to outflank its unruly partners and get back on top. If anything, the revolt exposed how security really constituted the backbone of Mubarak's regime. Once the Interior Ministry was paralyzed, politicians hardly put up a fight. The president, his family, and top aides were arrested on financial and criminal charges; the ruling party was dismantled; the Parliament and municipal councils were dissolved; and the constitution was replaced by a SCAF-issued Constitutional Declaration, approved overwhelming by referendum in March.

The general's main priority now was to rein in demonstrations. Military Police, back in action for the first time since 1967, violently dispersed Tahrir Sqaure sit-ins in March and April, unleashed the Interior Ministry against demonstrators, starting from June, and used security-hired thugs to protect the Defense Ministry in July. Thereafter, military–security violence became systematic, occurring once a month in more or less the same pattern: police assaults on demonstrators following skirmishes by hired thugs; the rallying of thousands of activists to repulse the attack; and the inevitable dragging of the military into the fray. State brutality reached a particularly high pitch in the last two months of 2011 when nerve gas and live ammunition were used, killing some 100 activists. And in February 2012, thugs killed 74 anti-police soccer fans (the so-called Ultras), during a game in Port Said, with security blocking the escape routes. In short, although SCAF decapitated the political institution, it refused to carry out revolutionary changes. As assistant defense minister for legal affairs explained:

> Some believe that the armed forces took charge by virtue of revolutionary legitimacy, but what happened was that ... when the armed forces found the country collapsing, they intervened by virtue of being the only power on the ground capable of protecting the country.... What happened in 1952 in fact had been revolutionary legitimacy, because the Free Officers ... carried out the revolution and seized power.... Now we have a different situation, where those who revolted on January 25, 2011 were not the ones who seized power. (Osman 2011: 8)

What the general did not explain was why the army could not pursue a revolutionary course. The interests of the officer corps were not necessarily inconsistent with the democratic ideals of the 2011 revolt. Contrasting the status of armies under authoritarianism and democracy makes this much clear. Typically, suspicious dictators keep their militaries on a tight leash through constant security surveillance, promoting mediocrity, fostering divisiveness, weeding out popular figures, and ignoring military input during policy formulation. Many democracies, by contrast, shower their armies with privileges, celebrate military heroes, encourage retired generals to pursue lucrative careers in the private sector or to run for office, and involve the chiefs of staff in national security decisions. The truth is that armies tend to thrive in democracies and wither under the shadow of dictatorship.

However, striving to improve one's position within the pecking order of an authoritarian regime is one thing, and democratizing society to maximize the interest of one's institution is another. The latter path was evidently beyond the grasp of a military caste that could not even begin to imagine what free governance looks like. Yet it was not only a failure of the imagination. Three reasons explain why the military held back. First, the sealing of officers from politics, through security monitors, prevented the emergence of the likes of Nasser's Free Officers. SCAF had neither a political vision nor an adequate understanding of the political landscape. Second, contrary to the rudimentary security infrastructure that fell into the coup makers' laps in 1952, the military now faced a hydra-headed establishment capable of guarding its autonomy with great ferocity. Third, the level of socioeconomic deprivation left by the old regime convinced generals that opening up political life might cause unfathomable turmoil—especially since the chaotic revolutionary scene produced no leaders capable of harnessing popular energy. The absence of a revolutionary vanguard to stabilize the street meant that if the floodgates of democracy were open, waves of angry citizens might sweep the country. Owing to their combat training and heavy equipment, the military could scarcely police Egypt's chock-full alleyways and rambling shantytowns. SCAF therefore flinched from undermining security control, opting instead for a tactical alliance.

This was indeed the Interior Ministry's strategy. To weather the revolt unscathed, the security apparatus refused to deploy its troops for months, biding time and delaying the gratification of total pacification until diehard revolutionaries and officers alike learned that chaos was the only alternative to police repression—the famous *après moi, le déluge* strategy. But it did not remain entirely passive. Rather, it provoked and ambushed protesters at carefully selected times and places, engaging them in short, brutal battles, and leaving dozens of bodies behind. Each time, investigations were conducted, mercurial third parties blamed, and the entire matter conveniently shelved. Intolerant to violations of public order, military officers were driven into the arms of their haughty security partners. So despite the arrest of the interior minister, the heads of the SSIS, the CSF, general security, as well as the chiefs of security in five governorates, and fourteen high-ranking officers—all of whom would eventually walk free—the Interior Ministry was not held accountable for a single violation before or after the revolt. Officers close to retirement age were sent off with full benefits; trifling reshuffles were carried out here and there; and Egypt's infamous State Security was simply renamed National Security, while repression and torture—the defining features of authoritarianism—continued.

A Second Revolt?

Although the military's role was enhanced, and that of the omnipotent security establishment hardly touched, the political seat remained vacant after Mubarak's political apparatus had been deposed. Revolutionary activists, Islamists, and old regime loyalists scrambled to fill it. The problem was that the Egyptian revolt had become trapped in a *balance of weakness*. None of the political players had the power to consolidate a new regime, nor even resurrect the old. And none of them wanted to make strategic alliances to break the stalemate. A game of musical chairs thus ensued under the fretful gaze of officers.

The military's preference was for a junior, inexperienced partner who would govern in its shadow. The revolutionary activists seemed like a safe choice. They were naïve, small in number, and unorganized. A few appointments could appease them, and their presence in government would assure the angry protesters that the Revolution had, in fact, succeeded. So on March 3, 2011, SCAF assigned the first transitional government to a man from a list submitted by the young revolutionaries. Cairo University Professor Essam Sharaf was lifted over the shoulders of a jubilant crowd in Tahrir Square, after delivering his famous "I draw my legitimacy from you" speech. His government included longtime opposition figures, and the decisions they took—in economics, social welfare, political rights, and culture—were refreshingly progressive. Yet this "revolutionary" cabinet lasted for less than eight months. And it was the revolutionaries who brought it down. For one thing, they resented the idea of cooperating with officers in principle. Liberals upheld the axiom of civilian control, and leftists saw the military as a servant of the ruling class. Also, activists expected their government to function while strikes and demonstrations continued to press for faster and more radical changes. And because Sharaf had no real authority over them, the military and security had to step in, and in an exceedingly violent fashion, which, in turn, deepened mistrust between activists and their seemingly complacent government. Unable to either stop or protect his supporters, Sharaf resigned in November, and SCAF appointed a caretaker government under a former prime minister pending parliamentary elections.

Islamists were next in line. From a military perspective, they presented a good balance. They were less chaotic than revolutionary activists, but not as organized as the old regime networks waiting in the wings. And they had considerable influence over the street, yet seemed willing to abide by the military's roadmap. Also, world powers would never completely trust Islamists at the helm, and would therefore welcome a prudent guardian to check their excesses—and who is more responsible than the high command? Finally, Islamism's grand geopolitical designs could furnish the army with the kind of rhetoric needed to expand its influence, and play a more active regional role. Likewise, the security institution saw Islamists as repression-friendly. Years of underground operations have made them paranoid and willing to see conspiracies everywhere, and their moral reform agenda required constant policing. Most importantly, Islamists were primarily interested in using their political gains as platforms for cultural transformation. And until enough Egyptians convert to their ideological project, they were not likely to challenge the military and security.

So in the autumn of 2011, SCAF allowed Islamists to consolidate control over the first post-revolt Parliament. The Muslim Brothers' new Freedom and Justice Party secured about 46 percent, and al-Nur, the largest of the recently established parties representing fundamentalists (*salafis*), won around 25 percent. The Brothers now decided to push their luck and run for the presidency. SCAF accepted the appointment of Mohamed Morsi, in July 2012, but dissolved the Islamist-dominated Parliament on the eve of the election, on a legal technicality, to hedge their influence. A month later, the new president demonstrated his good will through a reshuffle of the high command designed to please the military. The aging Defense Minister Hussein Tantawi and Chief of Staff Sami Anan were decorated with medals and appointed presidential advisors. Other high-ranking officers were even better remunerated: the outgoing navy commander was charged with administering the Suez Canal; the air defense commander was named head of the army's industrial complex; and SCAF strongman Muhammad al-Asar became assistant defense minister. To further emphasize his unwillingness to rock the boat, the president chose their replacements from a list of senior commanders. Director of Military Intelligence Abdel Fattah al-Sisi was handed the defense portfolio, and field commander Sedqi Sobhy was promoted to chief of staff. And on the night these measures were announced, the president promised, in a highly indicative speech, to respect the independence of the military, and provide it with weapons and training from diverse sources, that is, not just America.

Appeasement, however, was not the only thing the military was looking for in a political partner. Officers were eager to relieve themselves of the burden of everyday governance. But Islamist incompetence tested their patience. Particularly troubling was the Islamists' inability to contain their political rivals. Sisi offered to mediate on the heels of massive anti-Islamist protests six months after Morsi came to power. Yet by December 2012, the Brotherhood was already flexing its muscles: snubbing military mediation and employing armed supporters to repress opposition. As polarization threatened to rip the country apart, the defense minister issued a stern warning to all parties to settle their differences through dialogue. A gathering protest, which took the name *Tamarod* (Rebellion), called on Egyptians to take to the streets on June 30, 2013, to remove Morsi. All non-Islamist forces endorsed the rebellion (old regime and revolutionary alike), as did the largest section of Egyptian society: its decidedly apolitical citizens.

The political impasse forced the military and security to make a choice. SCAF was unwilling to impose outright military rule. Its intervention would have to be carried out in conjunction with whichever political faction was capable of restoring stability. Shoring up the Islamist president was one option—and a perfectly viable one. Brothers never hinted at reducing military privileges. In fact, they courted military protection. Their 2012 Constitution handled the military with kid gloves: the defense minister had to be an officer; commanders represented a veto-wielding majority in the National Defense Council; civilians could be tried in military tribunals while officers were immune from civilian courts; and the scale of salaries, benefits, and pensions was maintained. Yet the military worried that supporting the Brothers might entail massive repression of their increasingly restive opponents. A more seemly option was to lend the military's weight to anti-Islamist forces. But could they really command the street? The generals had to wait and see.

Similarly, the security institution had little to complain of when it came to Islamists. The Brothers had offered them nothing less than unconditional support throughout the transitional period. Pleas to overhaul the security agencies before proceeding to elections were rejected as delaying tactics. Brothers not only endorsed the repression of attempts to reignite the revolt, but they actually blamed the victims of police assault, sneering tactlessly on each occasion: "What sent them there [to the street]?"—meaning those troublemakers got what they deserved. The Islamist-controlled Parliament spared no opportunity to praise the gallant law enforcers. Indeed, it approved a 300 percent pay raise for security forces; and when it amended the 1971 police authority law, it enhanced the autonomy of the Interior Ministry by terminating the president's tutelary role as head of the Higher Police Council, shielding security operations from civilian watchdogs, and transferring judicial oversight from military tribunals to an Interior Ministry disciplinary board. And when Morsi became president, he asserted in a televised interview that the Interior Ministry had been rehabilitated and was performing the most patriotic of duties. He muted Justice Ministry demands to impose harsher penalties for torture, and shelved a fact-finding commission report that accused security agents of killing demonstrators in 2011. The president even had the audacity to extol policemen for being "at the heart of the 25 January 2011 [uprising]." Needless to say, security violations surged under Morsi, with 359 cases of torture, resulting in 217 deaths during his 365 days in office (Sayigh 2015: 8–14). But then again, while Brothers hoped to convert them to the "good cause," old regime elements cajoled them to stick with the devil they knew. Just like the military, security men needed time to assess the dowry and choose a bride. Morsi's first interior minister, Ahmad Gamal al-Din, was particularly torn because he had not severed his ties with the old regime. He appeared before court as a defense witness during Mubarak's trial, and his uncle had been NDP parliamentary majority leader. When protesters besieged the presidential palace, in December 2012, police protection was unmistakably fickle. And after being forced into a humiliating backdoor escape, Morsi assigned the top security position to another policeman, Muhammad Ibrahim, whom the Brotherhood hoped would be more sympathetic.

In short, the Muslim Brothers' allegation that their attempt to govern democratically was disrupted by a counter-revolution was not entirely accurate. Brothers were single-mindedly devoted to appeasing the army and security. It is unlikely they intended to dismantle Mubarak's authoritarian regime and submit themselves to the swinging moods of democracy; they merely wanted to replace the old regime at the pinnacle.

It was therefore under the shadow of Egypt's mighty coercive institutions that Brothers, activists, and old regime networks jockeyed for the political slot. Let us start with the old regime. Although the ruling party was dismantled, decades of cooperation left a solid network of political associates. At the top were the monopoly capitalists and senior officials of the now dissolved NDP, who all received acquittals during Morsi's tenure, and the body was composed of the same bureaucrats and village notables who had served the regime since 1952. Upon Morsi's election, this formidable network launched a concerted campaign to win the minds (though not the hearts) of the revolutionary activists. They convinced them to abandon their vendetta and unite with their enemy's enemy to save the country from religious rule. Yet the most persuasive argument for such a peculiar alliance came from Islamists themselves. In sermons and talk shows, Islamist preachers could barely contain their excitement about the approaching crusade to rid the country of infidel influences, that is, liberal and leftist activists. Disenfranchised revolutionaries were hardly expected to go down without a fight. They would rather see the Revolution aborted than hijacked. So they threw in their lot with old regime elements in hopes that they had reformed themselves. And with a solid revolutionary cover, remnants of the old regime pursued a Trojan horse strategy, sabotaging Morsi's attempt to govern through their clients in the bureaucracy, state unions and media, and the judiciary. The president's gambit to wrest power via an autocratic Constitutional Declaration, in November 2012, backfired, providing the perfect pretext for a well-orchestrated battle to end his rule through rallies and media campaigns.

To prevent being outflanked, the Brothers needed to drive a wedge between the old regime and the revolutionaries by locking in an alliance with one of them. But each alliance carried a hefty price tag. Compromising with secular activists would discredit the Brothers ideologically, costing them the conservative vote. At the same time, a deal with the old regime would be materially taxing. Like Brothers, the old ruling party managed an extensive patronage network of businessmen, rural leaders, and bureaucrats. Sharing power meant dividing the already small pie of public resources. Morsi, an incurable victim of wishful thinking, hoped that appointing old regime technocrats might do the trick. In six months, he appointed two cabinets, both under Hisham Kandil, an Irrigation Ministry employee, and both sated with old regime functionaries. In addition, peace offers were made to old regime associates in jail or exile. But as endearing as the Brothers' opportunism was to old regime members, the hopelessly romantic activists had an even greater advantage: utter disorganization. So while Brothers wasted time analyzing the costs and benefits of each prospective alliance, the old regime gradually enveloped the embittered revolutionaries.

It is important to note here that the state of disarray that characterized the 2011 revolutionaries showed no sign of abating. Activists were still considering their options two years after the uprising. Some preferred to join one of the many competing parties that sprang into existence after the revolt. Others banked on their recent celebrity to act as independent politicians. Still, others could not be tempted to leave the streets. Even labor activists seemed to be distracted by conflicting and myopic demands. The problem with these self-styled revolutionary youth was not that they had run out of steam. It was the exact opposite: they had too much steam for their own good, and thus kept running around in circles. Observers have marveled at the way social media leveled the playing field by establishing horizontal networks under the nose of the state, and mobilizing citizens at dizzying speed. Activists were no longer compelled to go through the arduous and dangerous process of creating a revolutionary movement. And agitprop could be disseminated at the click of a bottom. But the democratization of revolution had its cost: the temptation of *permanent subversion*. Why waste time formulating programs, electing leaders, or building organizations if one could destabilize a regime now and worry about it later? Of course, overthrowing a regime without considering the alternative is common in revolutions. But even then, identifiable factions would form before the revolt (as with the Sons of Liberty, and Bolsheviks) or shortly afterward (as with the Roundheads, and Jacobins) to vie for power. Amongst Egypt's media-savvy youth, however, no such faction emerged.

Grown-ups were no less efficient in dispersing their energies. After having reinvented themselves as revolutionaries, old-time opposition figures remained set in their ways: quarrelling over breadcrumbs and nurturing rival niches. They still preferred ad hoc cooperation through popular fronts, just as they had done under Mubarak. The 2012 version was labeled the National Salvation Front (NSF)—and, as soon became clear, never has such a grand name been assumed by such a mediocre body. The NSF brought together the same colorful personalities that have featured in every united front, before and after the revolt. It paraded three high-profile oppositionists. Mohamed ElBaradei was an international diplomat and Nobel laureate, who spent most of his life abroad. He was often censured for his unfamiliarity with Egyptian politics, but the revolt also revealed his lack of strategy, initiative, and organization. And though he possessed the air of a detached intellectual, ElBaradei was neither a philosopher, like Václav Havel, nor a weathered sage of the stature of Gandhi or Mandela. ElBaradei's primary (possibly only) asset was his cosmopolitan image, which appealed to Western powers and the country's upper-class urbanites. Next in line was a local diplomat. After serving Mubarak for two decades as Egypt's foreign minister and Arab League secretary-general, Amr Moussa presented himself as a longtime closet oppositionist. Unlike ElBaradei, he took his chances and ran for president in 2012 and came out fifth—a rather embarrassing performance. Moussa's main talents were a facility for hard work and an inflated view of his legacy. His main asset: optimism. His strategy was to be there when fortune smiles. And to make sure he was present on the political scene at the right time, he tried his best to be on it all the time. One must add that ElBaradei and Moussa created rival parties in 2012, and neither proved successful. The third, slightly less satirical figure was Hamdeen Sabahi, a man who had at least established his own political party before the revolt. As one of the leading lights of the pro-Nasser student movement in the 1970s, and a member of Parliament under Mubarak, Sabahi understood domestic politics inside out. He came out third in the presidential race, and tried to capitalize on his ballot box gains by founding yet another youth movement: al-Tayar al-Sha'bi. What Sabahi lacked was an alternative. His political program could be summed up in one word: nostalgia—which probably explains why his greatest enthusiasts were artists. Sabahi promised to revive Egypt's past glory under Nasser, but without retracing any of Nasser's steps—and without ever explaining how. And while the potential of each of these leaders was modest, their synergy proved even worse. They failed miserably to unite the revolutionary camp despite the rising cost of fragmentation. It is worth remembering that over 50 percent of Egyptians voted for a revolutionary candidate during the presidential elections. The tragedy was that there were six of them, which divided the votes and left the country with none other than the Jekyll and Hyde of

Mubarak's Egypt: the old regime and its alter ego, the Muslim Brothers. And with their persistent inability to get their house in order, the country's self-proclaimed revolutionaries relegated themselves to the role of kingmakers—which is precisely what they did in 2013. To legitimize Sisi's seizure of power, ElBaradei served as vice-president in the post-Brotherhood government; Moussa chaired the Assembly that drafted the new constitution; and Sabahi proved a good sport by losing the presidential election to Sisi.

But before any of this could happen, the masses had to vote Brothers out with their feet. The popular mobilization in the summer of 2013 was unprecedented. Millions of people (35 million according to enthusiasts) took to the streets, not once, but three times in the period of a month: rebelling against Morsi on June 30; celebrating his overthrow on July 3; and expressing defiance against Islamist threats on July 26. It is true that some protesters had been paid off by the old regime; others brainwashed by anti-Islamist media. Still, six decades of political bribes and propaganda scarcely brought out a fraction of this number. At the height of his power, and in his moment of final desperation, Mubarak failed to lure more than a 100,000 supporters. And those demonstrating on behalf of the old regime in the months following Mubarak's downfall hardly exceeded a few thousand. The reality is: Islamists alone could claim credit for this unsurpassed popular wave.

So why did Islamists make so many enemies in such a short time? Old regime elements and revolutionary activists had a clear motive: the former were not sure the Brothers were willing to share the spoils of Egypt's patronage state, and the latter resented their opportunism. Islamists focused on wining over the agents of coercion, but failed to appreciate that their dilly-dallying could drive their political opponents into a tactical alliance against them, and that such an alliance would force the custodians of violence to revise their stance. It is therefore the Brothers' ineptness and overreliance on repression that gave the impetus to Egypt's second revolt. But there would never have been enough foot soldiers had the common folk abstained. So perhaps the Brothers' cardinal mistake was to dismiss their usually indifferent subjects. As stubborn and scornful of the people as Mubarak was, he was wise enough to grasp that concessions were necessary to deprive his challengers of popular support. And in each of the speeches he delivered during the 2011 revolt, he relinquished significant ground: dismissing the cabinet; purging the leadership of the ruling party; dissolving the infamous PC; forming a committee to amend the constitution; and pledging that neither he nor his son would run in the coming election, which was only nine months away. Morsi, in contrast, would not yield—not even offering to reshuffle the cabinet or shore his legitimacy via popular referendum. When warned of the gathering rebellion, he put down his opponents as a handful of scoundrels, and delivered an incredible three-hour speech ridiculing some of these imaginary foes by name—and laughing repeatedly at his own jokes. After being shown footage of the millions that demonstrated against him on June 30, he still insisted it was a "Photoshop revolution." Morsi then went on to deliver his second (and, as it turned out, last) record-breaking speech, where he waved his fist belligerently and repeated he was Egypt's legitimate leader ninety-eight times in forty-five minutes. What his audience saw was not the arrogance of power, but the vanity of a fool.

The question the Brotherhood should have asked itself is what drove Egypt's overwhelmingly apolitical citizens to reject the group with such vigor—a possibly historic decoupling of Islam and Islamism in the popular psyche. Two motivations animated ordinary people: secular and religious. As citizens, they were appalled at the Brothers' incompetence in government; and as Muslims, they were outraged at how their religion was being manipulated to explain away this incompetence. They no longer saw Brothers as god-fearing underdogs who strove for power to uphold Islam, but another breed of corrupt politicians using religion to stay in power. This was confirmed after Morsi's forced dismissal. Angry Islamists camped outside Rab'a al-Adawiya mosque in the Cairo suburb of Nasr City. And for forty nights, Egyptians would tune in (or stroll by) to see and hear what Islamists were doing. And what they witnessed steeled their will to rebel. They heard threats of violence by Brotherhood supporters: youth were encouraged to blow themselves up (Cairo's first ever car bomb exploded on September 5), and seasoned militants vowed terrorism would persist unless Morsi was reinstalled. Opponents were religiously denounced; comparisons with Prophet Muhammad's conquests against infidels were conjured; and children marched with coffins and white shrouds to express their readiness for martyrdom. Following the violent clearing of the sit-ins on August 14, at the cost of over 600 lives, Egyptians followed with amazement how Islamists chose to retaliate: attacking churches and monasteries, looting museums, and shooting bystanders.[2] Particularly symbolic was the ransacking of the farmhouse of Mohamed Hassanein Heikal, Egypt's foremost writer since the 1950s and a Sisi advisor, and the burning of 18,000 volumes from his rare book collection. Above all, many were struck by the Brothers' doublespeak: their bigotry at home and meekness aboard; preaching religious war in Arabic, and mounting a peaceful democratic crusade with the foreign press. Suddenly, the Brothers' fine-tuned narrative of victimhood lost its appeal. When the new government declared them a terrorist organization—something even Nasser dared not attempt—many were willing to consent.

Egyptians, who are naturally suspicious of state media, would never have believed their government when it cried wolf, unless they had looked the wolf in the eyes and felt its bite. They knew that Morsi was no more Egypt's Allende than Sisi was his Pinochet, and preferred the risk of backtracking to military rule to the certainty of sliding into religious Fascism.

Popular outrage was central to military–security calculations. In meetings with oppositionists at Cairo's Navy Officers Club, both said they would not intervene unless protests threatened security and stability (Levinson and Bradely 2013). Sisi's statements in the weeks before the uprising expressed similar reluctance. On May 15 he warned: "The notion of inviting the army into the country's political life again is extremely dangerous. It could turn Egypt into another Afghanistan or Somalia" (Eleiba 2013). Four days later, he added: "No one should think that the solution is with the army. . . . The army is fire. Do not play against it and do not play with it." As the stalemate persisted, he issued his penultimate warning, a week before the scheduled revolt: that the army will not stand by and watch the country "slip into a conflict that will be hard to control" (Lesch 2014). In private, he urged Morsi to offer concessions to preempt protests. Morsi assured him that no such protests would occur. And when millions eventually marched against him, on June 30, the Brotherhood president remained unfazed. So, on July 1, the military gave all political factions forty-eight hours to hammer out a compromise. When the ultimatum expired, the generals made their move. Their justification, as spelled out by Sisi, was: "We believed that if we reached civil war, then the army would not be able to stop it" (Lesch 2014).

Officers recognized that Morsi's refusal to budge was based on his belief that the agents of coercion could be used to suppress protests. And if they held back, Islamist militants would be called upon to finish the job. Officers reviewed their options. Remaining neutral in the face of the anti-Islamist uprising meant standing by and watching the country slide into civil war (as in Lebanon). Repression on behalf of Islamists meant identifying with a narrow religious regime (as in Iran). Intervention thus seemed the best way to safeguard the country's security. And accusations of coup plotting were much preferred to those of impotence or Fascism. They chose the best of three evils.

On July 3 Morsi was removed to an undisclosed location, and Sisi unveiled a roadmap to democratic transition, originally endorsed by the 2011 revolutionaries: a transitional presidential team headed by the chief of the supreme constitutional court; a neutral technocratic government; a committee of legal experts to prepare the constitution; an appointed committee representing all social forces to discuss it; and a popular referendum to approve it before conducting parliamentary and presidential elections. Naturally, supporters of the 2011 revolt thought the military was finally taking their side. More important, Sisi proved he had the backing of the entire military. Upon Morsi's dismissal, Brothers tried to sway the lower ranks through religious appeals and heart-wrenching accounts of army brutality. At the same time, there were rumors that pro-Brotherhood foreign capitals had made generous offers to any senior officer willing to displace Sisi. With the armed forces subject to temptation from above and pressure from below, the sensible thing to do was to keep them locked up in distant garrisons. Instead, Sisi fully deployed his forces to protect the demonstrations he personally called for, on July 26, without fearing that some might either join Islamists or march to the Defense Ministry and arrest him. Not a single defection occurred.

However, following the military intervention, the self-righteousness of the activists who supported the anti-Islamist revolt led them to believe that they could delegate the dirty business of seeing it through to officers, and then reinvent themselves as advocates of reconciliation. At this moment of national crisis, the wavering of civilians convinced many Egyptians that only officers were bold enough to take decisions and stick with them. Comparisons were drawn between the 60-year-old Sisi and Nasser—still a popular idol. Whether he planned it all along, or was merely stepping into a power vacuum, the ambitious general now eyed the presidency. And what hastened his decision was seeing the old regime resurgent. Because as Brothers committed political suicide, old regime elements immediately turned against their latest allies: revolutionary icons were hounded (and many imprisoned); and the loyal oppositionists of the Mubarak era relinquished their revolutionary pretensions and fell in line. Old regime officials now moved in for the kill.

Commentators, eager to preach wisdom to Egyptians from the pulpit of European history, rushed in to draw analogies between Cairo's June Days in 2013 and those of Paris in 1848. In both instances, they claimed, liberals panicked when they saw that the freedoms they demanded had empowered radicals, and immediately implored the army to rein them in. Doubtlessly, liberals made a paradoxical appeal to military men in both cases; but this is where the resemblance ends. In France, they had dominated the Assembly, and when challenged by a radical mob, chose to preserve order with bullets and bayonets. By contrast, the threat in Egypt did not come from radicals, but rather from conservatives (political, socioeconomic, and religious conservatives neatly wrapped together). Nor did the threat materialize in the street: Egypt's reactionaries dominated the legislative and executive branches for a whole year, and tried to enlist the support of the army and police. It was liberals who mobilized the masses and led street protests. Because of their weakness, they had to rely on old regime networks to spark their revolt, and on the agents of coercion to complete it. If there is one more commonality between France of 1848 and Egypt of 2013, it was the attitude of liberals in the post-June Days. Morally indignant, they bowed out of the scene as soon as they realized what they had done, effectively surrendering power to the forces of order without a fight—yet another reminder that idealists who get too carried away with their own principles might be a noble breed, but they are certainly terrible revolutionaries. Their ends are always greater than their means; and their moral scruples narrow down the options they have to augment such means. Theirs is always a blind gamble, justified by a romantic faith in popular wisdom, which invariably lets them down. French peasants crowned a second emperor; and those in Egypt wanted Islamism out at any price—even if it required a Faustian deal with their past tormentors.

Sisi's Way

With Muslim Brothers behind bars and revolutionary activists banished to the political wilderness, the road was clear for the old regime to recapture Parliament and the presidency and restore "Mubarakism without Mubarak." But the return of those experienced political handlers, as thick as thieves as they were with security, would force the military back to square one. The generals would be gently and gradually cheated out of their brief sojourn on top. To prevent being outflanked, the military had to cut them off at the path to the presidential palace. And so the high command met in January 2014 to nominate Sisi for the presidency, in hopes of blocking the restoration of Mubarak's men.

Sensing there was little they could do to stem the tide, old regime representatives were prudent enough to decide that if you cannot beat them, join them. If reestablishing their monopoly over political power proved elusive perhaps they could share it. Better yet, perhaps they could stroke Sisi's inflatable ego enough for it to soar over the political theater and then rule in its shadow. In fact, manufacturing a Sisi cult would turn him into a lighting rod for popular criticism while the counter-revolution proceeded unhindered. So, with full old regime support, Sisi was voted president in the summer of 2014 by 97 percent, compared to Morsi's meager 51 percent in 2012. And the new constitution won 98 percent approval, dwarfing the 64 percent endorsement of the Islamist one.

But if remnants of the old regime were willing to relinquish the presidency, they were adamant about dominating Parliament, which thanks to the constitution they helped draft would wield greater power than Mubarak's old assemblies. The new Parliament combined the authority of the lower and upper houses; could withdraw confidence from the cabinet by simple majority; could override presidential vetoes by a two-thirds vote; and could not be prematurely dissolved without a referendum. To keep Sisi the only visible symbol of the new regime, Mubarak-era parliamentarians opted to run as independents rather than regroup in another ruling party. Their allies in the political and judicial fields therefore tailored the electoral law in favor of wealthy, independent candidates, with only 21 percent of Parliament going to party-list candidates, compared to 66 percent in the 2012 Assembly. With Islamist parties (except the fundamentalist al-Nur) outlawed, and independent Islamists short of funds and banned from campaigning, an old regime takeover seemed inevitable.

Sisi, of course, had other plans. It is true that he was partly elected to watch the military's back, but he was not simply their patrol officer at the presidency. He would never return to the corps. Nor was he planning to retire soon. His principle preoccupation, naturally, was to carve his own legacy—as president, not former officer. For this he needed a loyal political machine. But where could he get one? One option was to rely on the military as a quasi-political party, as Nasser had done. And indeed, seventeen of the first twenty-seven provincial governors Sisi appointed were military officers (and only two were policemen). Yet Nasser had learned the hard way that political and military priorities frequently conflicted, and that a president could fall hostage to his generals unless he balanced the officer corps with a political party—something Sisi seemed reluctant to do. His initial hope—again a throw-back from Nasser's time—was to de-politicize government, to turn politics into management. Institutionally, this meant taking decisions at the presidential level, rubber-stamping them in Parliament, and delegating their execution to battalions of technocrats orchestrated by a proficient state-trained administrator, such as Sisi's first and second prime ministers: long-time managers of the state-owned Arab contractors, and the national energy sector, respectively.

Vested interests in Parliament, however, would disrupt this immaculate scheme. And this is why the president stalled divesting legislative power to old regime parliamentarians. As one of his confidants related to the popular daily *Al-Ahram*, Sisi was "apprehensive ... of the hegemony of businessmen over parliament" (Dunne 2015: 9). Elections were therefore pushed from 2013 to 2015. And days before they were scheduled, in March 2015, the Supreme Constitutional Court postponed them yet again, citing irregularities in the electoral law. Judges were equally helpful in disqualifying the iron-and-steel tycoon and old ruling party's majority leader, Ahmed Ezz, from running on a technicality. Meanwhile, Sisi instructed his supporters, in a January 2015 meeting, to organize themselves into a single electoral list, with the tacky title Fei Hub Masr (In Egypt's Love), which would then operate as a unified voting bloc, under the even less inventive name of 'Etelaf Da'm Masr (Egypt's Support Coalition), with guidance from Sisi henchmen, such as former Military Intelligence General Sameh Seif al-Yazal.

In the event, the turnout for the 2015 parliamentary elections was embarrassingly low, 22 percent of registered voters nationwide, and barely 20 percent in Cairo. Activists, intellectuals, and political oppositionists associated with the 2011 revolt were practically eliminated, as was the fundamentalist al-Nur Party, now representing all Islamists with less than 2 percent. On the other hand, the scions of the counter-revolution became the dominant force. And although Sisi's electoral list secured 20 percent of Parliament, the majority of seats (over 62 percent) went to independents, largely old regime businessmen, village notables, and professional politicians. And in the first battle of wills, it was the old regime men who came out victorious, rejecting Sisi's Civil Service Bill to reduce and reform the bureaucracy. The president recognized that the country's 7.2 million employees (according to the latest World Bank figures) formed the backbone of the old regime patronage structure. He tried to break it, but lost to his political rivals, now entrenched in Parliament.

Political squabbles aside, however, Sisi understood from the very beginning that his success relied chiefly on his ability to salvage the economy. In order to leverage his legitimacy and distinguish himself from Mubarak's exclusionary capitalists, Sisi needed to broaden his network of social beneficiaries. Half of the population he inherited was poor; the middle class (an estimated 44 percent) was fast eroding; and only 7 percent of his subjects could call themselves wealthy. Moreover, youth unemployment was over 26 percent, a dangerous indicator for a man keen on marginalizing angry young activists. Political expediency dictated that he increase public spending. And this explains why public subsidies increased by a staggering 300 percent during Sisi's second year in power, despite his desperate attempts to slash them during his first year (ESCWA 2013; Sayigh 2016). But fiscal conditions were dire: public debt constituted 94 percent of GDP, and foreign reserves had severely fallen from $35 billion in 2011 to $15 billion in 2015. At the same time, inefficiency and corruption hampered the state's capacity to levy direct taxes or prevent shifting the burden of indirect taxes to the already suffering consumers. So where would the money come from?

The president first pursued private donations. After Morsi's ouster, the government launched the fundraising campaign 306306, a nod to the anti-Islamist uprising on June 30. And upon his election, Sisi inaugurated and personally supervised the Tahya Masr (Long Live Egypt) fund to raise $13 billion. He then urged leading businessmen, in several heated sessions, to pay their due—a price for the stability he provided. Yet until 2016, the former campaign barely collected $140 million, and the latter fund some $880 million. Sisi responded with new taxes on capital gains and dividends; wealth taxes for millionaires; wage-ceilings for top public executives; and a steep reduction in energy subsidies, which mostly benefited big factories (forty-five factories receive two-thirds of energy subsidies). These largely punitive measures proved insufficient. So the president next appealed to Egyptian's sense of patriotism. To finance a major extension of the Suez Canal, his government offered $9 billion worth of investment certificates, restricted to Egyptian nationals. They sold out in eight days. However, it turned out that patriotism could only be spurred by a higher rate of return than any offered in the market. At 12 percent interest, public subscription proved expensive. Sisi had to look elsewhere.

Having served as military attaché in Saudi Arabia, the new president had a keen understanding of Arab Gulf politics. Saudi leadership was propped up by the Emirates and Kuwait, and challenged by the small but ambitious Qatar. Since the first three were longtime supporters of Mubarak, feisty Doha—by default—found itself on the side of the Egyptian opposition. So although the Muslim Brothers had historically relied on Saudi and Kuwaiti goodwill, and had nothing to do with Qatar, Brothers and Qataris oddly found themselves allies. It began in 1991, when the Brothers double-crossed their Gulf patrons by supporting Saddam Hussein, while Mubarak rallied to their side. Pro-Saudi sheikhdoms subsequently shunned the Brothers and invested heavily in Egypt, and Mubarak, in turn, eschewed the defiant Qataris. The 2011 revolt offered Doha an opportunity to dislodge its Gulf rivals and entrench itself with Cairo's new rulers, who turned out to be the Brothers. And with Cairo's rapprochement with Tehran, the Riyadh faction became entirely encircled. Sisi's presidency therefore benefited the Saudi camp in two ways: it secured their continued access to the Egyptian market, and promised to hedge Iranian hegemony. In fact, Sisi publicly pledged to militarily protect his Gulf allies, and proved as good as his word by allowing the United Arab Emirates (UAE) to use Egyptian air bases to strike Libya in the summer of 2014, and joining Riyadh's expansive campaign against the pro-Iranian insurgency in Yemen the following year. Could this lucrative partnership supply the president with the funds he so desperately needed?

Initially, this seemed to be the case. Saudi Arabia, the Emirates, and Kuwait furnished Cairo with a $20 billion stimulus package in 2013 to meet urgent popular demands: supplying fresh water and natural gas, developing shantytowns and poor villages, building hospitals and schools. In addition, an Emirati company undertook a $40 billion project to build 1 million low-income houses. And in December 2015, Saudi King Salman pledged another $8 billion worth of investments over five years if Cairo joined his military crusade against militant Islamists and, more importantly, Shiites. Not wishing to limit himself exclusively to Arab aid, Sisi also organized an extraordinary international investment conference, in the spring of 2015, which secured $36.2 billion in investment deals and $5.2 billion in loans. He also convinced Russia, during Vladimir Putin's much publicized visit to Cairo, to invest in heavy industries, and concluded, during his own visit to China, contracts for new power stations and a high-speed railroad. No less important was maintaining American aid, which should have been suspended—according to U.S. law—following the military's political intervention. Sisi knew how to stroke Washington's security concerns. For one thing, he demonstrated his ability to find other military suppliers. *TIME Magazine*'s February 2015 report on Cairo's purchase of French Rafale jets worth $5.9 billion rightly concluded that the deal had "nothing to do with France, and everything to do with the United States." The fighter jets were too sophisticated for counter-insurgencies (compared to U.S. Apache helicopters), and too expensive for Egypt's budget-strapped government. But it was an act of defiance against Washington. And reviving military cooperation with Moscow was another age-old tactic (Rayman 2015). Indeed, Sisi's quid pro quo attitude was glaring enough during his first American television interview, on September 23, 2014, on *CBS News*. When prompted by Charlie Rose to support Washington's campaign against Islamist militants, he replied: "Give us [first] the Apaches and F-16s that you have been suspending for over a year-and-a-half now." And it worked. In March 2015 Obama lifted the freeze on aid to Egypt, recanting his promise to maintain it until Cairo demonstrated "credible progress" toward democracy, and linking his decision instead to "the interest of U.S. national security" (Baker 2015).

With an inflow of foreign finance and indigenous donations, Sisi strove to wrest economic control from old regime oligarchs. This required positioning the military as a direct recipient of funds and then rechanneling these funds to small- and medium-sized businesses through subcontracting and joint ventures. And accordingly, the public tender law was amended to allow the state to award contracts without competitive bidding. Part of the reason why Sisi took this action was so that the efficiency and productivity of military outfits, with their free-labor conscripts, would surpass the corrupt and incompetent bureaucracy, with its links to business cronies. With the military spearheading a conservative alliance of small- and medium-sized companies, Sisi could achieve fairly distributed economic growth—and the military could reestablish its economic leadership in the process. So following Botherhood's dismissal, the Sisi-dominated interim government assigned construction projects worth $770 million to military ventures. Sisi then announced a number of military-supervised mega projects, including the creation of a new capital (a pipedream of sorts); a massive land reclamation scheme to extend the Nile Valley and build some fifty new cities; in addition to the Suez Canal project, which involved drilling a parallel canal, widening the existing one, and transforming the canal zone into a trade and manufacturing hub.

Yet when all is said and done, it will be difficult to cut the tycoons off completely. For one thing, they control telecommunications, tourism, and commerce, and crowd the army out in construction, manufacturing, and agriculture. After years of speculation, hard data have finally become available on the military's relative economic weight vis-à-vis the private sector. According to the 2015 annual statement issued by the Agency for National Services Projects, the holding company that runs most of the military's businesses, its share across the economy was well below 10 percent: in land reclamation, it was 1.2 percent of the total surface reclaimed; in wheat production, Egypt's strategic crop, it was less than 1 percent; in red meat and dairy products, it was 0.2 percent and 0.4 percent, respectively; in industry, it has remained around 3 percent for the past decade; in construction, its share rose to only 10 percent; and in telecommunications, the country's most lucrative sector, it was close to nil, while in that other notoriously lucrative sector, tourism, the military owned only 4 of the 128 resorts on the Mediterranean coast and even fewer on the Red Sea. It is true that after the ouster of the Muslim Brotherhood in 2013, the military undertook mega projects, for a total of 5.5 billion Egyptian pounds, but this, in fact, represented 10 percent of total public investment that year. Even the army's largest construction project, the New Suez Canal, has been largely subcontracted to over seventy private companies, including giants such as Orascom, the company run by the politically ambitious Sawiris family. And while it is true that the military derives rent through its regulatory control over the allocation of desert land, one should remember that it shares this privilege with other civilian agencies responsible for housing and urban development (Barayez 2016). Finally, the military's decision to gear its economic activities toward stabilizing the political situation after 2011 has not been particularly rewarding. Short-term loans to the state, road construction, bread distribution, fixing rundown electric power plants to overcome chronic shortages, and so on imposed costs rather than generated profit.

Of course, none of this rules out the military's appetite to expand economically now that it has secured political leverage, but the facts show that the military is far from capable of overtaking the old regime's business oligarchs. Dispossessing or prosecuting them would scare away investors, and hanging them out to dry would be time-consuming because the capital they accumulated under Mubarak allows them to flourish without state patronage. In fact, in 2014, *Forbes* reported that the five wealthiest men in Egypt belonged to two families (Sawiris and Mansour), whose combined wealth represented 6.25 percent of the country's GDP. Moreover, Sisi's gamble on foreign investment will likely fail considering that for the last two decades, foreign direct investment (FDI) accounted, on average, for less than 1 percent of GDP, and was mostly concentrated in the energy sector. With the world still recovering from the 2008 financial crisis, and oil prices plummeting dramatically from $140 to $40 a barrel between 2009 and 2016, the prospects seem bleak. And, of course, the import restrictions Sisi imposed to stop the depletion of his foreign currency reserves are isolating Egypt even more. More importantly, even if foreigners prove unexpectedly forthcoming, they would prefer to work with well-established private sector companies rather than the military. So whether as domestic investors or partners to foreign investors, old regime capitalists seem irreplaceable. And if Sisi casts them out politically, they could sabotage his economic recovery (Adly 2014a; 2014b; 2015). The president's task therefore is to renegotiate turfs in a way that appeases generals and businessmen, without antagonizing his restless population—a thankless task by any measure. But until such task is accomplished (if ever), security control cannot be compromised.

Legitimizing Revolution, De-Legitimizing Revolutionaries

While politicians maneuvered, security forces methodically closed down all venues of opposition. While officially praising the 2011 revolt, their overriding aim was to prevent its repetition. Quickly and imaginatively, they fashioned a more authoritarian political space than that of the darkest days of the 1960s. Overthrowing the Muslim Brotherhood was the first step. As a critical Reuters News Agency report disclosed: "It was widely assumed that Egypt's military leaders were the prime movers behind the country's counter revolution. But dozens of interviews with officials from the army, State Security and police, as well as diplomats and politicians, show the Interior Ministry was the key force behind removing Egypt's first democratically elected president." Security officers organized consultations with secular activists. Interior Ministry personnel collected anti-Morsi petitions, and eventually joined the protests against him. The interior minister wormed himself into Sisi's good graces, flattering him in corridor talks as the country's savior. Mid-ranking police officers dined frequently with their military counterparts to hammer home the message. According to one security officer who attended these informal chats: "[We] spoke a lot about the Muslim Brotherhood. We had more experience with them than the army. We shared those experiences and the army became more and more convinced that those people have to go." And as popular agitation against Morsi became rampant, "Pressure from the Interior Ministry on Sisi and the military grew." Finally, two weeks before the 2013 uprising, the Interior Ministry hosted a meeting for 3,000 senior police officers at one of its social clubs to flesh out what they described as "the revolution of the state" (Al-Sharif and Saleh 2013).

Within nine months of Morsi's ouster, some 2,500 people were killed in clashes with the police and another 17,000 injured; 16,000 oppositionists were officially arrested (independent sources documented over 41,000 detentions); hundreds of death sentences were handed down (1,000 in March 2104 alone); and thousands of civil associations were dissolved (380 in March 2105 alone), notably the April 6 Youth Movement, which spearheaded the 2011 revolt and was now accused of espionage and its leaders imprisoned. A series of draconian laws restricted protests; eliminated pre-trial detention limits; and expanded the definition of terrorism to encompass any disruptive activity. More alarming still, extrajudicial killings and "disappearances" (i.e., undocumented detentions) became almost a matter of routine. And despite a farcical law, in December 2014, criminalizing any critique of the 2011 revolt, a security-instigated change of guard in broadcast media dislodged pro-revolution presenters, from satirists to newscasters. And the new constitution granted the Interior Ministry an effective veto over police affairs (Dunne and Williamson 2014; Dunne 2015; Sayigh 2015: 15). The security sector's institutional autonomy was further enhanced by a key substitution at the top: in March 2015 Interior Minister Muhammad Ibrahim, who came from the ministry's indecorous prison sector, lost his job to longtime State Security's operative, Magdi Abd al-Ghaffar.

Worse still, the proliferation of Islamist militants, domestically and regionally, has boosted the security force's legitimacy. By any account, this is the "deadliest and most complex insurgency in [Egypt's] modern history" (Awad and Hashem 2015). While the previous Islamist insurgency killed

391 police officers in thirteen years (1986–1999), the current one killed double that number, over 700 officers, in only two years (2013–2015). And what makes it even more difficult to tackle is that the insurgent landscape is markedly diverse. At the center lies the Sinai-based Ansar Beit al-Maqdis, active since 2011, and gaining considerable traction after pledging alliance to Daesh (ISIS) in November 2014 and becoming its Sinai Province. Its most spectacular operation was the downing of a Russian jet carrying 224 tourists from the Red Sea resort of Sharm al-Sheikh. There are also groups affiliated with al-Qaeda operating in the western desert and the populous Nile Valley. And, of course, the competition between Daesh and al-Qaeda over recruits is likely to escalate the violence even further. No less dangerous is the plethora of revolutionary fighters who turned to violence in reaction to police repression. Though amateurs with no combat experience, they are highly motivated and perceive themselves as legitimate heirs to the 2011 revolt. Their targets include anything from police stations, army checkpoints, university campuses, to official buildings and personnel, such as the public prosecutor, slain in the summer of 2015 (Awad and Hashem 2015).

Naturally, Egypt's "war on terror" provided the perfect environment for the security apparatus to thrive. Perhaps there is no better example of how state institutions succumbed to security's worldview than the court ruling exonerating Mubarak, his interior minister, and top security chiefs from violently suppressing the 2011 revolt. The highlight was the justices' acceptance of the "truthful testimony" of "the sages of the nation," such as Mubarak's intelligence czar Omar Suleiman and his two successors, the current head of State Security, and the last three interior ministers, that "an axis of evil composed of America, Israel, Iran, Turkey, and Qatar," working through its foot soldiers "the Brothers ... Hezbollah and Hamas," set out to destroy Egypt under the guise of "an American project for democracy" so that "the Zionist entity [Israel]" would maintain its regional hegemony. These plotters, the November 2014 ruling concluded, were the true perpetrators of violence, and the security apparatus acted legitimately in defense of the state (*Tebian* 2014: 107–11).

Even more striking is the change that occurred in the security's role with regard to parliamentary politics. Under Mubarak, the Interior Ministry rigged elections, and afterward State Security officers blackmailed the odd parliamentarian who crossed the line. In the 2015 elections, however, the boundary between politics and security was practically erased. Campaign strategies were devised in the offices of State Security and civilian intelligence. Candidates received instructions on where to run and which lists to join. And after the elections, security officers actually helped organize the various voting blocs. Not only that: the unthinkable happened, in February 2016, when rabble-rouser Tawfik 'Ukasha, who had received the highest number of votes during the elections, was voted out of Parliament for jeopodizing state security (Al-Sayyad 2015; Al-Sinnawi 2015; Abd al-'Azim 2016). As summarized by a former parliamentarian, Mubarak's last two Parliaments were run by businessmen; the current one is being run by security men (Al-'Elemy 2015).

Conclusion

The outcome of a revolution rarely corresponds with the intentions of those who carry it out. The unhappy fate of the Egyptian Revolution of 2011, like so many other revolutions, was to produce a reconfigured old regime. A final balance sheet will take years to tally. But a few results are already in. The military was doubtlessly the greatest winner. It reasserted itself as a combat force against global Islamist militancy: firing missiles into Libya and Yemen, and launching an extensive counter-insurgency at home. It reversed its economic decline, which had begun in the 1990s and accelerated in the 2000s. And it exerted its autonomy vis-à-vis the United States, demonstrating conclusively that Washington needed Egyptian generals more than the other way round. The security institution came in a close second. It not only managed to land on its feet, but also augmented its power and legitimacy. With Islamists branded as terrorists, secular activists as spies, and the whole Revolution as a foreign conspiracy, the Interior Ministry reclaimed its 1960s role as the nation's shield during a time of crisis. Old regime politicians did relatively well. Even without a ruling party, their carefully entrenched networks weathered the storm. Longtime parliamentarians, businessmen, bureaucrats, village notables, journalists, and judges coordinated their efforts admirably. And the Revolution taught them that they were perhaps better off operating as ostensibly independent politicians, state officials, and patriotic citizens than through an unpopular ruling party. The greatest losers, obviously, were the revolutionaries. The activists who triggered the revolt seemed to have succumbed to the lethargy of defeat, and the Islamists who joined them in hopes of quick gains languish in prison or exile.

At present, Egypt remains a police state. The future looks uncertain. Sisi continues to strive to institute populist governance, as evident in his hypernationalist rhetoric; censoring of opponents; claims that politics is a luxury Egypt can ill afford; and calls for loyal technocrats and honorable citizens to serve their country selflessly as administrators and philanthropists under his wise leadership. The president's former employers hope to bring the country back under military stewardship. If the two join forces, Egypt would effectively become a military dictatorship. Remnants of the old regime are hot on their heals, vying for a place on the political bandwagon, with the sure knowledge that their strength in the economy, the bureaucracy, and the countryside guarantees they will not be left behind. And regardless of who wins the race to the top, security will certainly be happy to offer its services in the hope of eventually tilting the regime in its favor. In short, what Egypt has to look forward to is one form of authoritarianism or another: either a reversal to the Nasser-Amer cocktail of presidential populism spurred by military dominance, or the persistence of the police state variety introduced by their successors.

Notes

1. Of course, the missing ingredient was geopolitics. With the Soviet patron of the ailing Communist regimes of Eastern Europe retrenching, and the anxious United States and European Union determined not to allow the chance of freedom to slip away, demonstrators in 1989 received sustained media attention and Western support. The Egyptian regime, by contrast, had been aligned with global powers, and after the initial wave of international support subsided, the new rulers were allowed to liquidate the revolt. Tahrir Square now became an open-air prison, where demonstrators could be sealed off and ignored until the revolutionary steam ran out.

2. An official fact-finding committee report estimated the number of deaths at 693 civilians and 10 policemen, and injuries at 1492 civilians and 170 policemen. Some 64 churches and monasteries were also attacked (according to *Al-Taqrir*).

Bibliography

Abdallah, Ahmed. 1985. *The Student Movement and National Politics in Egypt, 1923–1973*. London: Al Saqi Books.

Abdallah, Ahmed. 1987. "Siyasiun wa 'askariun" (Politicians and Military Men). *Al-'Arab*, December 21, 1987.

Abdallah, Ahmed. 1990a. *Al-Jaysh wa al-Dimuqratiyah fi Masr* (The Military and Democracy in Egypt). Cairo: Sina lel-Nashr.

Abdallah, Ahmed. 1990b. "Al-qwat al-musalaha wa tatwer al-dimuqratiyah fi Masr" (The Armed Forces and the Development of Democracy in Egypt). In *Al-Jaysh wa al-Dimuqratiyah fi Masr* (The Military and Democracy in Egypt), edited by Ahmed Abdallah, pp. 9–28. Cairo: Sina lel-Nashr.

Abdallah, Ahmed. 1997. "Rad fe'l al-shabab iza' al-hazima" (Youth Reaction towards the Defeat). In *Harb yunyu 1967 ba'd thalatheen sana* (The June 1967 War after

Thirty Years), edited by Lutfi al-Khuli, pp. 21–46. Cairo: Markaz al-Ahram lel-Targama wal-Nashr.
Abd al-Azim, Hazem. 2016. "Shehada fei haq al-Parlaman" (A Testimony on Parliament). *Masr al-Arabiya*, January 1, 2016.
Abd al-Aziz, Basma. 2011. *Eghraa al-sulta al-mutlaqa: Masar al-'unf fei 'elaqat al-shurta bei al-muwaten 'abr al-tarikh* (The Temptation of Absolute Power: The Course of Violence in the Relationship between the Police and the Citizen Across History). Cairo: Sefsafa.
Abd al-Fadeel, Mahmoud. 1983. *Ta'amulate fei al-mas'ala al-eqtesadiya al-misriya* (Reflections on the Egyptian Economic Question). Cairo: Dar al-Mustaqbal al-Arabi.
Abd al-Fattah, Essam. 2009. *Muhammad Naguib: Al-Raful alazi sana'etthu wa damaratthu aqdara* (Muhammad Naguib: The Man Made and Unmade by His Destiny). Cairo: Kenouz lel-Nashr wel-Tawzee'.
Abd al-Hafeez, Mohamed Saad and Mohamed Khayal. 2011. "Abbud al-Zumur yakshef asrar gadida" (Abbud al-Zumur Reveals New Secrets). *Al-Shorouk*, March 16, 2011.
Abd al-Magid, Esmat. 1998. *Zaman al-enkesar wa al-entesar: Muzakerat diplomacy masri 'an ahdath masria wa 'arabia wa dawlia: Nesf qarn men al-tahawulat al-kubra* (The Time of Defeat and Victory: Memoirs of an Egyptian Diplomat regarding Egyptian, Arab, and International Events: Half a Century of Great Transformations). Cairo: Dar al-Shorouk.
Abd al-Mo'ty, Abd al-Baset. 2002. *Al-tabaqat al-egtema'iya wa mustaqbal misr: Etegahat al-taghir wa al-tafa'ulat, 1975–2020* (Social Classes and the Future of Egypt: Trends of Change and Interaction, 1975–2020). Cairo: Merit lel-Nashr wal-Ma'lumat.
Abd al-Nasser, Gamal. 1966. "Hadith Gamal Abd al-Nasser al-tanzimy fei al-mu'tamar al-awal le-'ada' al-makateb al-tanfiziya fei al-muhafazat 'an eslub al-'amal fei al-etehad al-eshteraky" (Gamal Abd al-Nasser's Organizaitonal Talk at the First Congress of the Members of the Provincial Executive Offices regarding the Working Methods at the Arab Socialist Union). *Al-Tali'ah* 2 (2): 11–18.
Abd al-Nasser, Gamal. 1991. *Wathaiq thawrat yulyu* (The July Revolution Documents). Cairo: Dar al-Mustaqbal al-Araby.
Abd al-Nasser, Tahiya. 2011. *Zekrayaty ma'ahu* (My Memories with Him). Cairo: Dar al-Shorouk.
Abd al-Quddus, Mohamed. 1986. "Awlad al-balad, Ta'zim salam lel-mushir" (Countrymen, Salute the Field Marshal). *Al-Sha'b*, vol. 3, October 4, 1986.
Abdel-Malek, Anwar. 1968. *Egypt: Military Society*. New York: Random House.
Abdelrahman, Maha. 2014. *Egypt's Long Revolution: Protest Movements and Uprisings*. London: Routledge.
Abu al-Fadl, Abd al-Fatah. 1967. "Hawl al-etehad al-eshteraky: Takwinuh wa ahdafuh" (Concerning the [Arab] Socialist Union: Its Composition and Goals). *Al-Tali'ah* 3 (3): 89–98.
Abu al-Fadl, Abd al-Fatah. 2008. *Kunt na'iban le ra'is al-mukhabarat* (I Was Deputy Director of Intelligence). Cairo: Dar al-Shorouk.
Abu al-Nur, Abd al-Muhsin. 2001. *Al-Haqiqa 'an Thawrit 23 Yulyu* (The Truth about the July 23 Revolution). Cairo: Al-Hay'a al-Masriya al-'Ama lel-Kitab.
Aburish, Said K. 2004. *Nasser: The Last Arab*. New York: St. Martin's Press.
Abu Zikri, Wagih. 1988. *Mazbahat al-abriya' fei 5 yunyu 1967* (Massacre of the Innocent on June 5, 1967). Cairo: Al-Maktab al-Masry al-Hadith.

Adel, Hammoudah. 1987. *Eghtiyal ra'is: Bei al-watha'iq: Asrar eghtiyal Anwar al-Sadat* (The Assassination of a President: With Documents: Secrets of Anwar Sadat's Assassination). Cairo: Sina lei al-Nashr.

Adly, Amr. 2014a. "The Economics of Egypt's Rising Authoritarian Order." Carnegie Middle East Center, Beirut, June 2014.

Adly, Amr. 2014b. "The Future of Big Business in Egypt." Carnegie Middle East Center, Beirut, November 2014.

Adly, Amr Ismail. 2009. "Politically-Embedded Cronyism: The Case of Post-Liberalization Egypt." *Business and Politics* 11 (4): 1–26.

Ahmed, Mohamed Abd al-Wahab Saiyyd. 2007. *Al-'Alaqat al-masriya al-amrekiya men al-taqarub ela al-taba'ud, 1952–1958* (Egyptian-American Relations from between Proximity and Distance, 1952–1958). Cairo: Dar al-Shorouk.

Ahmed, Ref'at Sayyed. 1993. *Thawrat al-general: Qesat Gamal 'Abd al-Nasser kamila min al-milad ela al-mout (1918–1970): Mawsu'a fikria wa siassia* [The General's Revolution: Gamal Abd al-Nasser's Complete Story from the Cradle to the Grave (1918–1970): An Intellectual and Political Register]. Cairo: Dar al-Huda.

Al-Akhbar. 1981a. "Al-Akhbar tuhaqeq hadith al-ta'era" (Al-Akhbar Investigates the Plane Incident). March 6, 1981.

Al-Akhbar. 1981b. "Al-Shahid al-Badawy men aqwaluh" (The Martyr al-Badawy in His Words). March 4, 1981.

Alexander, Anne and Mostafa Bassiouny. 2014. *Bread, Freedom, Social Justice: Workers and the Egyptian Revolution*. London: Zed Books.

Allam, Fouad. 1996. *Al-Ikhwan wa ana* (Al-Ikhwan and I). Cairo: Akhbar al-Youm.

Aly, Kamal Hassan. 1994. *Mashawir al-'umr: Asrar wa khafaiya sab'een 'aman min 'umr masr fei al-harb wel-mukhabarat wel-siyasa* (Life Journeys: Secrets of War, Intelligence, and Politics during Seventy Years in Egypt's Life). Cairo: Dar al-Shorouk.

Aly, Sa'id Isma'il. 1986. "Haza al-nigm al-sati'" (That Shinning Star). *Al-Ahali*, October 8, 1986.

Amin, Galal. 2009. *Misr wa al-misrieen fei 'ahd Mubarak, 1981–2008* (Egypt and the Egyptian during Mubarak's Reign, 1981–2008). Cairo: Dar Merit.

Ashour, Omar. 2015. "Collusion to Crackdown: Islamist-Military Relations in Egypt." Brookings Center Analysis Paper 14, Doha, March 2015.

Awad, Mokhtar and Mostafa Hashem. 2015. "Egypt's Escalating Islamist Insurgency." Carnegie Middle East Center, Beirut, October 21, 2015.

Badr al-Din, Hany. 2011. "Harb October: Al-umniya al-akhira lel-Shazly" (The October War: Al-Shazly's Last Request). *Al-Ahram Al-Araby*, vol. 729, March 3, 2011, pp. 20–23.

Bahaa al-Din, Ahmed. 1987. *Muhawarati ma'a al-Sadat* (My Dialogues with Sadat). Cairo: Dar al-Helal.

Baker, Peter. 2015. "Obama Removes Weapons Freeze Against Egypt." *New York Times*, March 31, 2015.

Al-Banna, Ragab and Khamis al-Bakry. 1981. "Secertair al-mushir yarwi tafasil al-lahazat al-akhirai" (The Field Marshal's Secretary Recounts the Details of the Final Moments). *Al-Ahram* 34416: 3, May 3, 1981.

Barayez, Abdel-Fattah. 2016. "This Land Is their Land: Egypt's Military and the Economy." *Jadaliyya*, January 25, 2016.

Barnet, Michael N. 1992. *Confronting the Cost of War: Military Power, State, and Society in Egypt and Israel*. Princeton, NJ: Princeton University Press.
Barron, John. 1974. *KGB: The Secret Work of Soviet Secret Agents*. New York: Reader's Digest Press.
Al-Baz, Muhammad. 2007. *A-Mushir: Qesat so'ud wa enhiar Abu Ghazala* (The Field Marshal: The Story of the Rise and Fall of Abu Ghazala). Cairo: Kenuz lel-Nashr wal-Tawzee'.
Al-Baz, Muhammad. 2011. "Eteham Mubarak bei eghtiyal al-mushir Ahmed Badawi bei sabab kashfu fasad safaqat al-selah fei al-gish" (Mubarak Accused of Assassinating Field Marshal Badawi Because He Exposed the Corruption of Arms Deals in the Military). *Al-Fajr*, August 22, 2011.
Beinin, Joel. 2012. "The Rise of Egypt's Workers." Carnegie Endowment for International Peace, Washington, DC, June 2012.
Al-Beteshty, Abd al-Aziz. 2006. *Al-Tha'abin* (The Snakes). Cairo: Al-Maktab al-Masry al-Hadith.
Bianchi, Robert. 1990. "Interest Groups and Politics in Mubarak's Egypt." In *The Political Economy of Contemporary Egypt*, edited by Ibrahim M. Oweiss, pp. 210–21. Washington, DC: Center for Contemporary Arab Studies, Georgetown University.
Binder, Leonard. 1978. *In a Moment of Enthusiasm: Political Power and the Second Stratum in Egypt*. Chicago: University of Chicago Press.
Al-Bishri, Tareq. 2002. *Al-haraka al-siyassiya fei masr, 1945–1953* (The political movement in Egypt). Cairo: Dar al-Shorouk.
Blaydes, Lisa. 2011. *Elections and Distributive Politics in Mubarak's Egypt*. New York: Cambridge University Press.
Botman, Selma. 1988. *The Rise of Communism in Egypt*. Syracuse, NY: Syracuse University Press.
Boyne, Walter J. 2002. *The Two O'clock War: The 1973 Yom Kippur Conflict and the Airlift That Saved Israel*. New York: Thomas Dunne Books/ St. Martin's Press.
Brecher, Michael. 1974. *Decisions in Israel's Foreign Policy*. New York: Oxford University Press.
Brooks, Risa A. 2008. *Shaping Strategy: The Civil-Military Politics of Strategic Assessment*. Princeton, NJ: Princeton University Press.
Browne, O'Brien. 2009. "Six Days of War Spark Forty Years of Strife." *Quarterly Journal of Military History*, 22 (1): 70–79.
Brzezinski, Zbigniew. 1983. *Power and Principle: Memoirs of the National Security Advisor, 1977–1981*. New York: Farrar, Straus and Giroux.
Burr, William. 2004. *Asrar harb October fei al-watha'eq al-amrikiya* (Secrets of the October War in the American Documents). Translated by Khaled Daoud. Cairo: Markaz Al-Ahram lel-Targama wel-Nashr.
Bush, George and Brent Scowcroft. 1998. *A World Transformed*. New York: Vintage Books.
Cook, Steven A. 2007. *Ruling But Not Governing: The Military and Political Development in Egypt, Algeria, and Turkey*. Baltimore, MD: John Hopkins University Press.
Cooley, John K. 2000. *Unholy Wars: Afghanistan, America, and International Terrorism*. London: Pluto Press.
Copeland, Miles. 1970. *The Game of Nations: The Amorality of Power Politics*. London: Weidenfeld and Nicolson.

Cordesman, Anthony H. 2006. *Arab-Israeli Military Forces in an Era of Asymmetric Wars.* Westpoint, CT: Praeger.

Dekmejian, Richard H. 1982. "Egypt and Turkey: The Military in the Background." In *Soldiers, Peasants, and Bureaucrats: Civil-Military Relations in Communist and Modernizing Societies,* edited by Roman Kolkowicz and Andrzej Korbonski, pp. 28–42. Boston: Allen & Unwin.

Droz-Vincent, Philippe. 2007. "From Political to Economic Actors: The Changing Role of Middle Eastern Armies." In *Debating Arab Authoritarianism: Dynamics and Durability in Nondemocratic Regimes,* edited by Oliver Schlumberger, pp. 195–214. Stanford, CA: Stanford University Press.

Droz-Vincent, Philippe. 2011. "A Return of Armies to the Forefront of Arab Politics?" Istituto Affari Internazionali Working Papers 11, 21, pp. 1–10.

Dunne, Michele. 2015. "Egypt's Nationalists Dominate in a Politics-Free Zone." Carnegie Endowment for International Peace, Washington, DC, April 2015.

Dunne, Michele and Scott Williamson. 2014. "Egypt's Unprecedented Instability by the Numbers." Carnegie Endowment for International Peace, Washington, DC, March 2014.

Dunstan, Simon. 2009. *The Six Day War 1967: Sinai.* London: Osprey.

Eban, Abba. 1992. *Personal Witness: Israel Through My Eyes.* New York: Jonathan Cape.

Eleiba, Ahmed. 2013. "Military Messages." *Al-Ahram Weekly,* May 15, 2013.

Al-'Elemy, Ziad. "Hewar" (Interview). *Al-Shorouk,* November 3, 2015.

ESCWA. 2013. *Arab Middle Class Report.* New York: UN Economic and Social Commission for Western Asia.

Essam al-Din, Gamal. 2011. "Al-Mushir al-samet Tantawy" (The Silent Field Marshal Tantawy). *Al-Tahrir,* vol. 80, p. 1.

Eytan, Zeev and Aharon Levran. 1986. *The Middle East Military Balance.* Jaffee Center for Strategic Studies. Boulder, CO: Westview Press.

Eytan, Zeev, Shlomo Gazit, and Amos Gilbo. 1993. *The Middle East Military Balance.* Jaffee Center for Strategic Studies. Boulder, CO: Westview Press.

Eytan, Zeev, Mark A. Heller, and Aharon Levran. 1985. *The Middle East Military Balance.* Jaffee Center for Strategic Studies. Boulder, CO: Westview Press.

Fahmy, Isma'il. 1985. *Al-tafawed min agl al-salam fei al-sharq al-awsat* (Negotiating for Peace in the Middle East). Cairo: Maktabet Madbouli.

Fakhr, Ahmed. 1985. "Al-fikr al-'askari al-masri wa idarit al-sira': Al-ahdaf al-istratigia lel-'askariya al-masriya" (Egyptian Military Thinking and Conflict Management: The Strategic Goals of Egyptian Militarism). *Al-Jumhuriya,* vol. 9, January 20, 1985.

Farahat, Mohamed Nur. 1984. "Hawl hukm al-mu'asasat wa tahakum al-mu'asasat" (Concerning the Rule of Institutions and the Autocracy of Institutions). *Al-Ahali,* vol. 7, December 19, 1984.

Al-Faramawy, Abd al-Rahman. 2009. Interview with author. Cairo, June 5, 2009.

Farouk, Abd al-Khaleq. 2008. *Guzur al-fasad al-edari fei misr: Be'at al-'amal wa si-yasat al-ugur wa al-muratabat fei misr* (The Roots of Administrative Corruption in Egypt: The Working Environment and the Policies of Wages and Incomes in Egypt). Cairo: Dar al-Shorouk.

Fawzy, Mahmoud. 2008. *Al-Nabawi Ismail wa guzur manaset al-Sadat* (Al-Nabawi Ismail and the Roots of Sadat's Review Stand). Cairo: International Language Home.

Fawzy, Mohamed. 1990. *Harb al-thlath sanawat, 1967–1970: Muzakirat al-fariq awal Mohamed Fawzy* (Three-Year War, 1967–1970: Memoirs of Lieutenant General Mohamed Fawzy). Cairo: Dar al-Mustaqbal al-Araby.
Frisch, Hillel. 2001. "Guns and Butter in the Egyptian Army." *Middle East Review of International Affairs* 5 (2): 1–14.
Frisch, Hillel. 2013. "The Egyptian Army and Egypt's 'Spring.'" *Journal of Strategic Studies* 36 (2): 180–204.
Al-Galad, Magdi, Charles Fouad al-Masry, and Ahmed al-Khatib. (2009). "Mahdi 'Akef fei awal hiwar sahafi ba'd azmat al-insihab" (Mahdi 'Akef in His First Newspaper Interview Following the Withdrawal Crisis). *Al-Masry Al-Youm*, October 24, 2009.
Al-Gamasy, Mohamed Abdel Ghani. 1993. *The October War: Memoirs of Field Marshall El-Gamasy of Egypt.* Cairo: American University in Cairo Press.
Game', Mahmoud. 2004. *'Araft al-Sadat* (I Knew Sadat). Cairo: Al-Maktab al-Masry al-Hadith.
Genedi, Assem. 2011. "Ada' gihaz al-shurta" (The Performance of the Police Force). In *Thawrat 25 Yanaier: Qera'a awaliya wa ru'iya mustaqbaliya* (The January 25 Revolution: A Preliminary Reading and Future Prospects), edited by Amr Hashem Rabie', pp. 251–88. Cairo: Al-Ahram Center for Political & Strategic Studies.
Al-Geziry, Kamal. 2011. "Mumtalakat al-Adly" (Al-Adly's Possessions). *Al-Shorouk*, March 26, 2011.
Ghaleb, Murad. 2001. *Ma'a Abd al-Nasser wa al-Sadat: Sanawat al-intesar wa ayam al-mehan: Muzakirat Murad Ghaleb* (With Abd al-Nasser and Sadat: The Years of Triumph and the Days of Trial: Memoirs of Murad Ghaleb). Cairo: Markaz Al-Ahram lel-Targama wel-Nashr.
Ghali, Boutros Boutros. 1997. *Tariq masr ela al-Quds: Qesat al-sera' men agl al-salam fei al-sharq al-awsat* (Egypt's Road to Jerusalem: The Story of the Struggle for Peace in the Middle East). Cairo: Al-Ahram lel-Targama wel-Nashr.
Ghoneim, Adel. 2005. *Azmat al-dawla al-misriya al-mu'asera* (The Crisis of the Contemporary Egyptian State). Cairo: Dar al-'Alam al-Thaleth.
Golan, Matti. 1976. *The Secret Conversations of Henry Kissinger: Step-by-Step Diplomacy in the Middle East.* New York: Quadrangle/The New York Times Book Co.
Goldstone, Jack A. 2011. "Understanding the Revolutions of 2011: Weakness and Resilience in Middle Eastern Autocracies." *Foreign Affairs*, vol. 90, no. 3, pp. 8–16.
Gorman, Anthony. 2010. "Confining Political Dissent in Egypt Before 1952." In*Politics and Prisons in the Middle East: Formations of Coercion*, edited by Laleh Khalili and Jillian Schwedler, pp. 157–73. New York: Columbia University Press.
Grawert, Elke and Zeinab Abul-Magd. 2016. *Businessmen in Arms: How the Military and Other Armed Groups Profit in the MENA Region.* New York: Rowman & Littlefield Publishers.
Hafez, Suleiman. 2010. *Thekrayati 'an al-thawra* (My Memories of the Revolution). Cairo: Dar al-Shorouk.
Hammad, Gamal. 2002. *Al-Ma'arek al-harbiya 'ala al-gabha al-misriya* (The Military Battles on the Egyptian Front). Cairo: Dar al-Shorouk.
Hammad, Gamal. 2008. *Al-Hukuma al-khafiya fei 'ahd Abd al-Nasser wa asrar masra' al-mushir Amer* (The Invisible Government during the Reign of Nasser and the

Secrets of Field Marshal Amer's Death). Cairo: Al-Shareka Al-Mutaheda lel-Teba'a wel-Nashr wel-Tawzee'.
Hammad, Gamal. 2010. *Asrar thawrat 23 yunyu* (Secrets of the July 23 Revolution), Vols.1 and 2. Cairo: Dar Al-'Ulum.
Hammad, Magdi. 1990. "Al-muasasa al-'askariya wa al-nizam al-siasi al-masri" (The Military Institution and the Egyptian Political Regime)." In in *Al-Jaysh wa al-Dimuqratiyah fi Masr* (The Military and Democracy in Egypt), edited by Ahmed Abdallah, pp. 29–50. Cairo: Sina lel-Nashr.
Hammudah, Adel. 1986. *Eghtiyal ra'is: Belwatha'eq asrar eghtiyal Anwar al-Sadat* (A President's Assassination: Documented Secrets of the Assassination of Anwar al-Sadat). Cairo: Sina lel-Nashr.
Hammudah, Hussein Mohamed Ahmed. 1985. *Asrar harakat al-zubat al-ahrar wa al-Ikhwan al-Muslimeen* (Secrets of the Free Officers' Movement and the Muslim Brothers). Cairo: Al-Zahraa lel-'Ilam al-Arabi.
Hamroush, Ahmed. 1987. *Ghorub yulyu* (July's Sunset). Cairo: Dar al-Mustaqbal al-Arabi.
Handoussa, Heba. 1990. "Fifteen Years of US Aid to Egypt—A Critical Review." In *The Political Economy of Contemporary Egypt*, edited by Ibrahim M. Oweiss, pp. 109–24. Washington, DC: Center for Contemporary Arab Studies, Georgetown University.
Hassan, Bahie. 2011. "Naql mudir amn al-Behera le-tatawulhu 'ala al-sha'b" (Transferring al-Behera's Security Chief for His Insulting the People). *Al-Shorouk*, March 26, 2011.
Hassan, Khalaf Aly. 2011. "Taqasi al-haqa'eq: Al-watani shakal tanziman shebh 'askari lel-baltagia" (Fact Finding [Commission]: The National [Democratic Party] Formed a Paramilitary Organization of Thugs). *Al-Masry Al-Youm* 2475: 4, March 24, 2011.
Hauslohner, Abigail. 2014. "Egypt's Military Expands Its Control of the Country's Economy." *Washington Post*, March 16, 2014.
Heikal, Mohamed Hassanein. 1983. *Autumn of Fury: The Assassination of Sadat*. London: Andre Deutsch.
Heikal, Mohamed Hassanein. 1990. *1967: Al-Infegar* (1967: The Explosion). Cairo: Markaz Al-Ahram lel-Targama wa-Nashr.
Heikal, Mohamed Hassanein. 1993. *October 1973: Al-Selah wa al-siyasa* (October 1973: Arms and Politics). Cairo: Markaz Al-Ahram lel-Targama wa-Nashr.
Heikal, Mohamed Hassanein. 2003. *Seqout nizam: Lemaza kanet thawarat yulyu 1952 lazema?* (Regime Fall: Why Was the July 1952 Revolution Necessary?). Cairo: Dar al-Shorouk.
Hinnebusch, Raymond A. 1990. "The Formation of the Contemporary Egyptian States from Nasser and Sadat to Mubarak." In *The Political Economy of Contemporary Egypt*, edited by Ibrahim M. Oweiss, pp. 188–209. Washington, DC: Center for Contemporary Arab Studies, Georgetown University.
Hobbes, Thomas. [1651] 1968. *Leviathan*. London: Penguin Classics.
Hosni, Hamada. 2007. *Abd al-Nasser wa al-tanzim al-tale'i, 1963–1971* (Abd al-Nasser and the Vanguard Organization, 1963–1971). Beirut: Maktabat Beirut.
Hosni, Hamada. 2008. *Shams Badran: Al-ragul alazi hakam misr* (Shams Badran: The Man Who Ruled Egypt). Beirut: Maktabat Beirut.

Huwaidi, Amin. 2002. *Khamsin 'am min al-'awasif: Ma ra'ituh qultuh* (Fifty Stormy Years: I Told What I Saw). Cairo: Markaz Al-Ahram lel-Targama wa-Nashr.
Ibrahim, Saad Eddin. 1996. *Egypt, Islam, and Democracy*. Cairo: American University in Cairo Press.
Ibrahim, Youssef M. 1980. "U.S. Stake in Egypt Rests on One Man—Anwar el-Sadat." *New York Times*, March 30, 1980, p. E3.
Imam, Abdallah. 1996. *Nasser and Amer: Al-Sadaqa, al-hazima, al-entehar* (Nasser and Amer: The Friendship, the Defeat, and the Suicide). Cairo: Dar al-Khayal.
Insight Team of the London *Sunday Time*. 1974. *Yom Kippur War*. New York: Doubleday.
International Institute for Strategic Studies (IISS). 2009. *The Military Balance 2009: Annual Assessment of Global Military and Defense Economics*. London: Routledge.
Isma'il, Hafez. 1983. *Amn Misr al-qawmy* (Egypt's National Security). Cairo: Maktabet Madbouli.
Johnson, Paul. 1957. *The Suez War*. London: Macgibbon & Kee.
Kamel, Mohamed Ibrahim. 1983. *Al-Salam al-da'ie fei Camp David* (The Lost Peace in Camp David). Cairo: Ketab al-Ahaly.
Kandil, Amani. 1986. "Al-tatawer al-siyasi fei misr wa son' al-siyasat al-'ama: Derasa tatbiqiya lel-siyasa al-eqtesadiya" (Political Development in Egypt and the Making of Public Policy: An Empirical Study on Economic Policy). In *Al-Tatawer al-demokraty fei misr: Qadaya wa munaqashat* (Democratic Development in Egypt: Issues and Debates), edited by Ali al-Din Helal, pp. 87–114. Cairo: Maktabet Nahdet al-Sharq.
Kassem, Maye. 2004. *Egyptian Politics: The Dynamics of Authoritarian Rule*. London: Lynne Reinner.
Kepel, Gilles. 2006. *Jihad: The Trial of Political Islam*. London: I.B. Tauris.
Kerr, Malcolm H. 1969. *The Arab Cold War: Gamal Abd al-Nasir and His Rivals, 1958–1970*. New York: Oxford University Press.
Al-Kholi, Lutfi. 1966. "Thermometer Kamshish" (The Kamshish Thermometer). *Al-Tali'ah* 2 (6): 5–9.
Al-Kholi, Lutfi. 1976. "Democratiyat al-manaber, Democratiyat al-ta'adud" (The Democracy of Platforms, The Democracy of Pluralism). *Al-Tali'ah* 12 (6): 5–12.
Kissinger, Henry. 1979. *White House Years*. New York: Little, Brown and Company.
Kissinger, Henry. 1992. *Years of Upheaval*. New York: Little, Brown and Company.
Kissinger, Henry. 1994. *Diplomacy*. New York: Simon & Schuster.
Lesch, Ann M. 2014. "Playing with Fire: The Showdown in Egypt between the General and the Islamist President." Foreign Policy Research Institute E-Notes, March 2014.
Levinson, Charles and Matt Bradely. 2013. "In Egypt the 'Deep State' Rises Again." *Wall Street Journal*, July 19, 2013.
Mahmood, Saba. 2005. *Politics of Piety: The Islamic Revival and the Feminist Subject*. Princeton, NJ: Princeton University Press.
Mansour, Anis. 2009. *Min awraq al-Sadat* (From Sadat's Papers). Cairo: Dar al-Ma'aref.
Marshall, Shana. 2013. "Cashing in after the Coup." *Foreign Policy*, July 18, 2013.
Marshall, Shana. 2015. "The Egyptian Armed Forces and the Remaking of an Economic Empire." Carnegie Middle East Center, Beirut, April 2015.
Al-Mashat, Abd al-Mone'm. 1986. "Al-'Awamel al-kharegiya wa al-tatawer al-demokraty fei misr" (External Factors and the Democratic Development in Egypt). In *Al-Tatawer al-demokraty fei misr: Qadaya wa munaqashat* (Democratic

Development in Egypt: Issues and Debates), edited by Ali al-Din Helal, pp. 53–78. Cairo: Maktabet Nahdet al-Sharq.

Masoud, Tarek. 2014. *Counting Islam: Religion, Class, and Elections in Egypt.* Cambridge, UK: Cambridge University Press.

McDermott, Anthony. 1988. *Egypt from Nasser to Mubarak: A Flawed Revolution.* London: Croom Helm.

Mitchell, Timothy. 1999. "Dreamland: The Neoliberalism of Your Desires." *Middle East Report* 210: 28–33.

Mitchell, Timothy. 2002. *Rule of Experts: Egypt, Techno-Politics, Modernity.* Berkeley: University of California Press.

Muhi al-Din, Khaled. 1992. *Al'an atakalam* (Now, I Speak). Cairo: Al-Ahram lel-Targama wel-Nashr.

Murad, Mohamed Helmi. 1986. "Al-riqaba al-gha'iba 'ala al-infaq al-'askari wa al-tafwidat al-laniha'iya le-safaqat al-silah wa mizaniyat al-qwat al-musalaha" (The Absent Oversight of Military Spending and the Limitless Authorizations Regarding Defense Contracts and Budgets). *Al-Sha'b*, September 9, 1986.

Muslim, Mahmoud. 2011a. "Al-Masry Al-Youm wagahat Fathy Sourur bei al-etahamat fakashaf asrar khatira, al-halaqa al-ula" (Al-Masry Al-Youm Confronted Fathy Sourur with Accusations, so He Revealed Dangerous Secrets, Part One). *Al-Masry Al-Youm*, March 24, 2011.

Muslim, Mahmoud. 2011b. "Al-Masry Al-Youm wagahat Fathy Sourur bei al-etahamat fakashaf asrar khatira, al-halaqa al-thaniya" (Al-Masry Al-Youm Confronted Fathy Sourur with Accusations, so He Revealed Dangerous Secrets, Part Two). *Al-Masry Al-Youm*, March 24, 2011.

Muslim, Mahmoud. 2011c. "Al-Masry Al-Youm wagahat Fathy Sourur bei al-etahamat fakashaf asrar khatira, al-halaqa al-akhirah" (Al-Masry Al-Youm Confronted Fathy Sourur with Accusations, so He Revealed Dangerous Secrets, Final Part). *Al-Masry Al-Youm*, March 24, 2011.

Nafe', Ibrahim. 1981. "*Hal al-hadeth mudabar*" (Was the Accident Fixed?). *Al-Ahram*, March 6, 1981.

Naguib, Muhammad. 1984. *Kunt ra'isan lei masr* (I Was President of Egypt). Cairo: Al-Maktab al-Masry al-Hadith.

Naguib, Muhammad. 1997. *Kalimati lel-tarikh* (My Word for History). Cairo: Dar al-Kitab Al-Jami'i.

Nasr, Salah. 1999a. *Muzakirat Salah Nasr (al-guze'al-awal): Al-Sou'd* [The Memoirs of Salah Nasr (Part One): The Rise]. Cairo: Dar al-Khayal.

Nasr, Salah. 1999b. *Muzakirat Salah Nasr (al-guze'al-thani): Al-Entilaq* [The Memoirs of Salah Nasr (Part Two): The Launch]. Cairo: Dar al-Khayal.

Nutting, Anthony. 1972. *Nasser.* London: E.P. Dutton.

Omar, Nabil. 2011. "Habib al-Adly: Asrar rehlat al-so'ud ela 'arsh al-dakhliya" (Habib al-Adly: Secrets of the Rise to the Throne of the Interior [Ministry]). *Al-Ahram*, March 14, 2011.

Oren, Michael B. 2002. *Six Days of War: June 1967 and the Making of the Modern Middle East.* New York: Presidio Press.

Osman, Ahmed Osman. 1981. *Safahat min tagrebati* (Pages from My Life Experience). Cairo: Al-Maktab al-Masry al-Hadith.

Osman, Dalia. 2011. "Musa'ed wazir al-defa' lel-sho'un al-qanuniya wa al-desturiya fei hewaruh" (Undersecretary for Defense for Legal and Constitutional Affairs in His Interview). *Al-Masry Al-Youm*, March 17, 2011.

Osman, Dalia and Pasant Zein al-Din. 2011. "Masdar 'askari: nabhath ta'dil mu'ahadat al-salam" (A Military Source: We Are Looking Into Modifying the Peace Agreement). *Al-Masry al-Youm*, August 29, 2011.

Osman, Tarek. 2013. *Egypt on the Brink: From Nasser to the Muslim Brotherhood*. New Haven, CT: Yale University Press.

Oweiss, Ibrahim M. 1990. "Egypt's Economy: The Pressing Issues." In *The Political Economy of Contemporary Egypt*, edited by Ibrahim M. Oweiss, pp. 3–49. Washington, DC: Center for Contemporary Arab Studies, Georgetown University.

Owen, Roger. 2012. *The Rise and Fall of Arab Presidents for Life*. Cambridge, MA: Harvard University Press.

Parker, Richard B. 1993. *The Politics of Miscalculation in the Middle East*. Bloomington: Indiana University Press.

Perlmutter, Amos. 1974. *Egypt: The Praetorian State*. New York: Transaction.

Quandt, William B. 1992. "Lyndon Johnson and the June 1967 War: What Color Was the Light?" *Middle East Journal* 46 (2): 198–228.

Al-Rafe'i, Abd al-Rahman. 1989. *Thawrat 23 yulyu 1952: Tarikhna al-qawmi fei saba' sanawat, 1952–1959* (The Revolution of July 23, 1952: Our National History in Seven Years, 1952–1959). Cairo: Dar al-Ma'aref.

Rayman, Noah. 2015. "The Real Reason Egypt Is Buying Fighter Jets From France." *TIME magazine*, February 14, 2015.

Richter, Thomas. 2007. "The Political Economy of Regime Maintenance in Egypt: Linking External Resources and Domestic Legitimation." In *Debating Arab Authoritarianism: Dynamics and Durability in Nondemocratic Regimes*, edited by Oliver Schlumberger, pp. 177–94. Stanford, CA: Stanford University Press.

Sabri, Ahmed. 2011. "Zuwar al-fajir estawlu 'ala mumtalakat al-sha'eb" (Dawn Visitors Appropriated the People's Properties). *Sout al-Umma*, March 12, 2011.

Sabri, Musa. 1979. *Watha'eq harb October* (October War Documents). Cairo: Akhbar al-Youm.

Sadat, Anwar. 1978. *Al-Bahth 'an al-zat* (In Search of Identity). Cairo: Al-Maktab al-Masry al-Hadith.

Saleh, Amani Abd al-Rahman. 1988. "Usul al-nukhba al-siyasiya al-misriya fei al-sab'inat: Al-nash'a wa al-tatuwer" (Origins of the Egyptian Political Elite in the Seventies: The Birth and Development). *Al-Fekr al-Strategy al-Araby* 26: 9–50.

Samy, Riyad. 2004. *Shahid 'ala 'asr al-ra'is Muhammad Naguib* (A Witness to the Reign of President Muhammad Naguib). Cairo: Al-Maktab al-Masry al-Hadith.

Al-Sanhouri, Abd al-Razeq. 2005. *Al-Sanhouri min khilal awraquh al-shakhsiya* (Al-Sanhouri through His Personal Diaries). Cairo: Dar al-Shorouk.

Sayed, Abdel-Rahman, El-. 2007. "Shrouded in Mystery." *Al-Ahram Weekly*, July 5, 2007.

Sayigh, Yazid. 2011. "Egypt's Army Looks Beyond Mubarak." *Financial Times*, February 3, 2011.

Sayigh, Yezid. 2015. "Missed Opportunities: The Politics of Police Reform in Egypt and Tunisia." Carnegie Middle East Center, Beirut, March 2015.

Sayigh, Yezid. 2016. "Chasing Egypt's Economic Tail." Carnegie Middle East Center, Beirut, January 2016.

Al-Sayyad, Ayman. 2015. "Parlaman 2015: Qera'a fei Suwar" (2015 Parliament: Reading Pictures). *Al-Shorouk*, December 27, 2015.

Schlesinger, Arthur M. 1965. *A Thousand Days: John F. Kennedy in the White House*. Greenwich, CT: Fawcett.

Segev, Tom. 2007. *1967: Israel, the War, and the Year That Transformed the Middle East*. New York: Metropolitan Books.

Selim, Muhammad. 2009. Personal interview. Los Angeles, March 7, 200.

Sha'ban, Mohamed. 2011. "Man qatal Ahmed Badawi" (Who Killed Ahmed Badawi). *El-Shabab*, vol. 410, September 2011, pp. 54–55.

Sharaf, Samy. 1996. *'Abd al-Nasser: Keif hakam masr?* ('Abd al-Nasser: How He Ruled Egypt?). Cairo: Madbouli al-Saghir.

Al-Sharif, Asma and Yasmine Saleh. 2013. "The Real Force behind Egypt's 'Revolution of the State.'" Reuters, October 10, 2013.

Shatz, Adam. 2010. "Mubarak's Last Breath." *London Review of Books*, vol. 32, no. 10, pp. 6–10.

Shazly, Saad El-Din. 1980. *The Crossing of the Suez: The October War (1973)*. London: Third World Centre for Research and Publishing.

Shlaim, Avi. 1976. "Failures in National Intelligence Estimates: The Case of the Yom Kippur War." *World Politics* 28 (3): 348–80.

Shtauber, Zvi and Yiftah S. Shapir. 2005. *The Middle East Military Balance, 2004–2005*. Jaffe Center for Strategic Studies. Brighton, UK: Sussex Academic Press.

Singerman, Diane. 2004. "The Networked World of Islamist Social Movements." In *Islamic Activism: A Social Movement Theory Approach*, edited by Q. Wiktorowicz, pp. 143–63. Bloomington: Indiana University Press.

Al-Sinnawi, Abdallah. 2015. "Marakez al-Quwa al-Jadidah" (New Power Centers). *Al-Shorouk*, December 22, 2015.

Sirrs, Owen L. 2010. *A History of the Egyptian Intelligence Service: A History of the* Mukhabarat, *1910–2009*. New York: Routledge.

Skocpol, Theda. 1979. *States and Social Revolution: A Comparative Analysis of France, Russia, and China*. New York: Cambridge University Press.

Spencer, Richard. 2014. "How Sisi Plotted to Save Army Rule Even While Hosni Mubarak Was in Power." *Daily Telegraph*, June 1, 2014.

Springborg, Robert. 1989. *Mubarak's Egypt: Fragmentation of the Political Order*. Boulder, CO: Westview Press.

Springborg, Robert. 1990. "Agrarian Bourgeoisie, Semiproletarians, and the Egyptian State: Lessons for Liberalization." *International Journal of Middle East Studies* 22 (4): 446–72.

Springborg, Robert. 2011. "More Pressure Needed." *New York Times*, February 14, 2011. http://www.nytimes.com/roomfordebate/2011/02/10/what-will-the-egyptian-military-do/watch-the-rank-and-file (accessed May 13, 2011).

Steinberg, John W. 2010. *All the Tsar's Men: Russia's General Staff and the Fate of the Empire, 1989–1914*. Baltimore, MD: Johns Hopkins University Press.

Suleiman, Samer. 2005. *Al-Nizam al-qawi wa al-dawla al-da'ifa: Edaret al-azma al-maliya wa al-taghir al-siyasi fei 'ahd Mubarak* (The Strong Regime and the Weak

State: Managing the Financial Crisis and Political Change in Mubarak's Reign). Cairo: Dar Merit.

Taqrir al-naha'i lelagnat taqasi haqa'eq 30 yunia (Final Report of the Fact-Finding Commission concerning [the] June 30 [Revolt]). Cairo, November 26, 2014. http://www.shorouknews.com/news/view.aspx?cdate=26112014&id=2b3e50b2-52aa-47d4-a929-8dba01128e6f.

Tebian min mahkamet al-qarn (The "Century's Court Case" Statement). Cairo, November 29, 2014. http://www.almasryalyoum.com/news/details/587974.

Turner, Barry. 2006. *Suez 1956: The Inside Story of the First Oil War*. London: Hodder & Stoughton.

Vatikiotis, P. J. 1978. *Nasser and His Generation*. London: Croom Helm.

Wahid, Latif. 2009. *Military Expenditure and Economic Growth in the Middle East*. New York: Palgrave Macmillan.

Waterbury, John. 1983. *The Egypt of Nasser and Sadat: The Political Economy of Two Regimes*. Princeton, NJ: Princeton University Press.

Wickham, Carrie Rosefsky. 2002. *Mobilizing Islam: Religion, Activism, and Political Change*. New York: Columbia University Press.

Wickham, Carrie Rosefsky. 2015. *The Muslim Brotherhood: Evolution of an Islamist Movement*. Princeton, NJ: Princeton University Press.

Younan, Ref'at. 2008. *Muhammad Naguib: Za'im thawra am wagehat haraka?* (Muhammad Naguib: A Leader of a Revolution or the Figurehead of a Movement?). Cairo: Dar al-Shorouk.

Yunis, Sherif. 2005. *Al-Zahf al-muqadas: Muzaharat al-tanahi wa tashkil 'ebadet Abd al-Nasser* (The Sacred March: The Resignation Demonstrations and the Shaping of the Cult of Abd al-Nasser). Cairo: Dar Merit.

Conclusion

REVOLUTION, REFORM, AND RESILIENCE

"The coup d'état from which the state is born," wrote Bourdieu "attests to an extraordinary symbolic act of force . . . the idea that . . . there is one point of view that is the measure of all points of view, one that is dominant and legitimate" (2014: 69). The real coups that underlie this symbolic foundation involve three consecutive processes: first, concentrating power in the hands of a few agents; second, the differentiation and distribution of power among a few ruling institutions "tied by the organic solidarity implicit in the division of the work of domination"; and third, the development of this "relatively autonomous bureaucratic field" into a "site of competitive struggles" between institutional agents over how to exercise power over society (Bourdieu 2014: 376). Foucault similarly described how power relations in many societies are anchored in a relationship of force established through (internal or external) war at a given historical moment. The establishment of a new regime, though ostensibly ushering a "reign of peace," actually inscribes the domination of the victors in state institutions. The new regime thereafter represents this "perpetual relationship of force" together with the clashes, shifts, and reversals intended to modify it (Foucault 2004: 15–16).

The present study examined these multiple processes in Iran, Turkey, and Egypt. It began with the coups that founded their various regimes and the division of power between military, security, and political institutions, then traced the collaboration and competition of these institutions across decades, and concluded that regime change is often the by-product of their attempts to modify the power balance. This final section reviews the literature on coups and compares the Iranian, Turkish, and Egyptian trajectories to consider why one experienced revolution, the other evolved via reform, and the third remains resilient.

Genesis: Founding Coups

We are often told that officers should defer to politicians, that their job is to defend, not shape regimes, and that their institutional demands must be expressed through legal channels, either through lobbying or bureaucratic bargaining (Huntington 1957: 81–83; Kolkowicz 1978: 9–13; Allison and Zelikow 1999: 5). Even regimes that fail to establish professionalism in the ranks still manage to impose civilian rule through various "coup proofing" mechanisms (Brooks 1998; Cook 2007; Droz-Vincent 2007). But this norm has often been violated. An exhaustive dataset on coups from 1950 to 2010 recorded 457 coup attempts, half of which were successful, and three dozen occurred quite recently, between 2000 and 2010 (Thyne and Powell 2011: 249–55).[1] In fact, more than two-thirds of non-Western countries experienced coups in the second half of the twentieth century (Nordlinger 1977: 191). And in the Middle East alone, a quantitative study registered eighty-nine coups between 1950 and 2013 (Albrecht 2014). Students of civil–military relations bickered over the explanation.

Marx's account of Louis Bonaparte's 1851 coup in the wake of the failed 1848 Revolution led modern-day class analysts to consider "Bonapartism" a symptom of repressed revolutions. Officers supposedly act on behalf of the ruling class (Wolpin 1981: 12; Hobsbawm 2001: 231). Yet Marx himself had allowed for the possibility of officers serving their own ends:

> [W]ere not barrack and bivouac, saber and musket, moustache and uniform finally bound to hit upon the idea of rather saving society once and for all by proclaiming their own regime as the highest, and freeing civil society completely from the trouble of governing itself. . . . Should not the military at last one day play state of siege in their own interest and for their own benefit? ([1852] 1963: 35)

Under Napoleon III, Marx noted, "The state machine has consolidated its position so thoroughly" that it could act independently ([1852] 1963: 122). Another sign of incongruence between class and military intervention is that middle-class officers often act in the interest of the underprivileged classes. Decades before Pinochet's coup, upper-class Chilean officers, provoked by the economic elites' control of the booming nitrate-export economy under the powerless President Alessandri, took power to enact social reform and empower labor organizations (Agüero 2002: 112–15). In fact, Latin American officers habitually shifted alliances between conservative and progressive groups, often undermining the very group they once helped install (Lieuwen 1965: 65–66). It is not therefore unreasonable to believe that military professionalization "declasses" officers (Chorley 1973: 37; Needler 1975: 67; Ricks 1998).

Postwar liberals countered Marxist pessimism by emphasizing the progressive potential of coups in postcolonial societies. Nineteenth-century colonial powers built modern indigenous armies to maintain order. Native officers thus became the most advanced social force in the colonies, and felt obliged to modernize their societies from above (Janowitz 1960; Pye 1962; Shils 1962; Huntington 1968; Welch 1976a). Trimberger famously christened these coups as "revolutions from above," and saw them as preferable to popular revolutions because they seize power with minimum violence, and implement sweeping social changes in a pragmatic and gradual manner (1978: 3, 105–07). The Indian and Japanese trajectories verified this thesis. Establishing an effective Indian bureaucracy under British tutelage set the pattern for a "crushing civilian dominance" over an outsized Indian army (Cohen 1976: 45–47). In contrast, the underdevelopment of Tokugawa Japan forced Meji Restoration modernizers to turn to the new national army (Buck 1976: 149–52).

The Middle East was a case in point (Vatikiotis 1961; Halpern 1963; Sharabi 1966). In the absence of developed political institutions, newly politicized forces in the Middle East drifted toward a surrogate institution: the army (Huntington 1968: 193–99). At first glance, the coups of Reza Shah (1921), Mustafa Kemal (1924), and Gamal Abd al-Nasser (1952) offer paradigmatic examples. The three young officers saw and eventually used their armies as tools for modernization: building roads and factories, breaking up large landholdings, overseeing a secular and national education system, and so on.

However, advocates of the modernizing role of the army in undeveloped countries expected officers to return to barracks after fulfilling their mandate, and re-intervene only when summoned by their political masters to avert chaos—as when Mao called on the army to reestablish control over his party after the ill-fated Great Leap Forward (Chang 1976: 128; Shichor 2004: 90). But coup makers frequently proved unwilling to withdraw from politics. And while some did modernize their countries, almost all coup-installed regimes remained far from civilian-controlled. Liberals soon realized that "praetorianism"—a concept coined by Finer (1962)—tends to reproduce itself. "The aftermath of military intervention is military intervention" (Nordlinger 1977: 207). Or as Perlmutter put it: "Praetorianism begets praetorianism" (1982: 317).

Indeed, many area specialists rejected the Marxist and liberal contention that civilian control is the mark of "normal" politics. In sub-Saharan Africa, for instance, "quasi-permanent military rule" was accepted as a feature of tribal politics, and therefore a normal facet of everyday government (Decalo 1998: 1–7; Spiro 1967). In Latin America, decades of European-styled professionalization did not inhibit military intervention in the politics of Chile, Brazil, Argentina, and Peru between 1964 and 1989 (Nunn 1992; Agüero 2002). Israel, the most institutionally developed Middle East state, had "no clear-cut dichotomic distinction between 'civilianism' and 'militarism'" (Horowitz 1982: 79).

Clearly, civil–military relations were more problematic than Marxists or liberals assumed. Because officers were typically preoccupied with their corporate interests, rather than class or nation, military intervention in politics should not be treated as a temporary transgression. From an "institutional-interest perspective," even when officers claim to be defending society, it turns out that—seen through military eyes—this defense "consists in the first instance of the defense of national security, and thus entails the maintenance of a strong military"; and when officers press for economic growth, it is mostly because a prosperous economy permits a sizeable defense budget (Needler 1975: 67–71). Officers are therefore not "obediently enacting ... roles assigned to them by vague and impersonal systematic forces"— such as class or nation (Thompson 1975: 459–66). They are power players in their own right. This is why, as Chorley proclaimed, "To fit professional fighting forces into the body politic has always been a dangerous and anxious task" (1973: 15).

In that sense, both the occurrence and absence of coups merit explanation—for as Mann put it: "In principle, all well-organized militaries could seize power," even if "only a few actually do so" (2004: 64). Moreover, studies of military influence should not rest on the most flagrant instances, such as coups. Cohen warned that the belief that "if there is no fear of a coup there can be nothing seriously amiss with civil-military relations is one of the greatest obstacles to serious thinking about the subject" (2003: 242). Liddell Hart incisively maintained that "a volcano is still a volcano even when it is not in eruption" (foreword in Chorley 1973: 10). And Welch (1976a: 3–5), Finer (1962: 282–83), and Colton (1978: 63–64, 71–72) helpfully mapped civil–military relations on a continuum, whose poles—complete civilian or military control—are little more than ideal types.

Ironically, the theorist on whom liberals drew most to formulate their principle of military subordination to politics had spent his life arguing for their interconnection. Clausewitz famously declared that war was an instrument of policy, but the policy he had in mind was one that "fights battles instead of writing notes." His ideal statesman was one who commands enough military knowledge to be able to direct the army himself: solider and statesman "combined in one person." Far from arguing for the separation of political and military power, Clausewitz emphasized the "intimacy of their connection" (1988: 255–67). Cohen rightly pointed out that the Clausewitzian view is not only "incompatible with the doctrine of professionalism codified by the 'normal' theory of civil-military relations," but his views on the intersection of political and military spheres are "far more radical ... than is commonly thought" (2003: 7–8). Without an active partnership between statesmen and generals (such as that which developed between von Moltke and Bismarck), war preparation and conduct could drive a wedge through the ruling bloc, with politicians wary of military hawkishness, and officers resentful of civilian ignorance and hesitance. Cohen's study of civil–military relations confirmed how "closely and inseparably linked" they remain across various contexts (2003: 84–85).[2]

Gramsci arrived at the same conclusion through a slightly different route. He started by highlighting how numerous regimes were, in fact, military-dominated "even if the army as such does not take part in it." These regimes carefully conceal the role of officers, even when the army "determines the [regime's] situation and dominates it" (1971: 211–15). Gramsci then made the strikingly original claim that even the military's nonintervention in politics is a political act par excellence:

> [I]t is not true that armies are constitutionally barred from making politics; the army's duty is precisely to defend the Constitution—in other words the legal form of the State together with its related institutions. Hence so-called neutrality only means support for the [regime]. ... The military are the permanent reserves of order and conservation; they *are* a political force. (1971: 211–15, emphasis added)

Overt intervention, or "Caesarism" in Gramscian lexicon, denotes a stalemate. It reflects a situation in which the "forces in conflict balance each other in a catastrophic manner; that is to say, they balance each other in such a way that a continuation of the conflict can only terminate in their reciprocal destruction." And it is during this "equilibrium of forces heading towards catastrophe" that a military strongman emerges to save the regime by either preserving or transforming it. Gramsci indeed recognized that "there can be both progressive and reactionary forms of Caesarism" (1971: 219). In other words, the military is not simply a proxy for class or nation. The causes and consequences of each military intervention must be contextualized.

Drawing on cases spanning seventeenth- to twentieth-century England, France, Italy, Spain, Russia, and Germany, Chorley (1973: 184) confirmed this Gramscian insight. Military power provides the ultimate sanction of any regime—a fact "kept discretely in the background" in everyday democratic politics. And, as Gramsci previously concluded, this "convenient fiction" of military neutrality collapses during crises, when officers either defend or change the regime (Chorley 1973: 177). But as accurate as these observations might be, the question is: Why is military influence so persistent?

Many scholars traced this back to the military origins of modern states. Anderson described Europe's first centralized states as "machines built overwhelmingly for the battlefield" (1974: 32). Tilly famously quipped: "War wove the European network of national states, and preparation for war created the internal structures of the states within it" (1990: 76). Howard broadened this further: "It is hard to think of any nation-state . . . that came to existence before the middle of the twentieth century which was not created . . . by wars, by internal violence, or by a combination of both" (1983: 39; see also Paret 1992: 221). Or as Foucault put it: "War obviously presided over the birth of states: right, peace, and laws were born in the blood and mud of battles" (2004: 50–51). This bloody genealogy obviously cast a long shadow. As Mann observed: "Despite the formal incorporation of military power into the state . . . military caste autonomy and segmental power *increased*"—a most "surprising [and] paradoxical trend" in his view (1993: 403).

Part of the reason for Mann's surprise is that the military's historical role cannot fully account for its present impact. This is why a few students of military power emphasized instead how the military's peculiar organization makes it difficult to desist from interregime struggles. To start with, it is unreasonable to organize the military into an ironclad caste with monopoly over violence, and then expect it to remain politically passive. The tension arising from having strong corporate interests and a capacity to impose them, yet refraining from doing so, provides fertile ground for continued intervention (Vagts 1959: 295). And attempts to counter this by civilianizing the army (through conscription, hiring civilian administrators, etc.) are generally futile. As Clausewitz explained, "No matter how we see the citizen and the soldier in the same man, how strongly we conceive of war as the business of the entire nation . . . the business of war will always remain individual and distinct. Consequently . . . soldiers will think of themselves as members of a kind of guild, in whose regulations, laws, and customs the spirit of war is given pride of place" ([1832] 1989: 187). Second, politicians themselves (incumbents and challengers alike) frequently solicit the support of this "single most powerful group in society" (Nordlinger 1977: 13, 46). It is enough to consider here the intensity of military cohesiveness and institutional differentiation relative to other groups. Unlike classes or political parties, the military chain of command allows the "small group of men who hold the chain's uppermost links . . . [to] maneuver the whole enterprise" with relative ease. This capacity is enhanced by the military's separateness from society, a separateness that conveys to officers that they are above society and its petty quarrels, that they might be sometimes obliged to step in to save society from politicians who "work for party not country . . . operate chiefly through words . . . waste time . . . [and have] no taste for the prime political resource, organized violence" (Poggi 2001: 183–88, 197). This is why Nisbet dismissed the assumption that an institution with such "size, reach, and sheer functional importance" can abstain from politics as "sheer fantasy" (1981: 146–49; see also Cohen 2003: 242). In Nietzsche's lucid prose: "To demand of strength that it *not* express itself as strength, that it *not* be a desire to overwhelm, a desire to cast down, a desire to become lord . . . is just as nonsensical as to demand of weakness that it express itself as strength" ([1887] 1998: 25).

Building on this logic, my analysis of the coups in Iran, Turkey, and Egypt went beyond the economic and political motivations of the coup makers themselves to why the rest of the armed forces went along with them. Why officers and soldiers allowed these coups to become the foundation of new regimes rather than simply shoot the perpetrators for treason? The reason in all three cases was that the corporate interests of the army (or the strongest services within it) coincided with those of the coup leaders. And these interests were always expressed in terms of how to make the army a better fighting machine.[3] What this meant exactly differed in each case. The Turkish and Egyptian armies blamed their monarchs for their tragic defeats in 1918 and 1948, respectively. Only a complete overhaul of the regime, they believed, could endow them with the fighting effectiveness necessary to deal with the grave postdefeat challenges, the dismembering of the Ottoman Empire, and the implanting of a Zionist state at the heart of the Arab world. And although Iran, by comparison, neither had a modern national army nor suffered a major defeat, the officers in charge of its various militias were consumed in internal rivalries. The Cossacks who supported the coup hoped to steal a march on the gendarmes and unify all of Iran's fighting forces under their command—which they eventually did. So regardless of the aims of the handful of politicized officers who spearheaded the coups, they were only successful because they appealed to the institutional interests of the corps. But after their colleagues helped place them in power, the coup makers' individual differences and the varying structures they inherited forced them to fashion their new regimes in very different ways.

Formation: New Regimes

Once in power, the military could enshrine its guidelines for running the state in a constitution, hand power to civilians, and re-intervene only when necessary. These regimes typically institute joint civilian–military decision-making bodies (usually a national security council) to allow officers to voice their policy concerns, and veto undesirable ones. And they usually experience corrective coups to oust uncooperative politicians, and put the state back on track. This "guardian" model represents the "normal course" for militarism because officers quickly despair of day-to-day governance (Hobsbawm 2001: 212). Inverting Weber's depiction of politics as a vocation, Nordlinger points out that officers consider government a part-time "avocation" (1977: 139–42). Their hope is to be able to "rule without governing" (Cook 2007). And, in fact, large quantitative studies of officers' attitudes following military interventions show "little systematic evidence that coup leaders have an interest in running the country.... [C]oup leaders opt to turn over leadership as soon as a legitimate government can be put in place given their lack of ambition for continued rule" (Thyne and Powell 2014: 6; see also Geddes 1999: 123).

Sometimes, however, coup makers hope to install themselves permanently in power, not as members of a military junta, but as "governors" in the Foucauldian sense. Governance in the modern world entails what Foucault describes as the reinvention of the social body in line with the "military dream of society," a society whose subjects are "meticulously subordinated cogs of a machine" laboring under the gaze of "technicians of discipline" in an elaborate system of "permanent coercions" (1979: 169). This process could be achieved by extremely subtle mechanisms in democracies (and this is what Foucault mostly studied). But the ambition of total social subjugation occasionally tempted the much less subtle—and certainly less effective—coup leaders. Their instruments included a fledging political apparatus to manage the population, and an entrenched security force to police it and keep it under surveillance. The political wing is typically constituted of a corporate ruling party, attached to a massive bureaucracy and propaganda organs, and overseen by a presidency or politburo. The security sector includes a regular and secret police, intelligence agencies, and paramilitary forces. Together, they penetrate and control the social body.

This type of authoritarian regime borrows heavily from totalitarians, whether Fascist or Communist. Authoritarian rulers first eliminate independent power centers: the economic ruling class is incorporated or undermined; civil associations are dismantled or heavily regulated; the media is censored or turned into mere propaganda; and police repression traverses the entire social body (Arendt [1951] 1994: 419–20; Nordlinger 1977: 26–27; Thomas 1984: 89–92). Authoritarians then amalgamate state and party, as was the case in Bolshevik Russia (Trotsky [1937] 2004: 69–72) and post-Risorgimento Italy (Gramsci 1971: 228). And to further ensure party dominance, rulers multiply state offices and foster competition between the different branches by assigning them similar or overlapping tasks. Nazis, for instance, shifted security responsibilities from the Sturmabteilung (SA) to the Schutzstaffel (SS), and finally the Sicherheitsdienst (SD), without any of them being abolished (Arendt [1951] 1994: 400–04).

The centrality of the security apparatus here cannot be overstated. As the always eloquent Arendt put it: "Above the state and behind the façades of ostensible power, in a maze of multiple offices, underlying all shifts of authority and in a chaos of inefficiency, lays the power nucleus of the country, the superefficient and supercompetent services of the secret police" ([1951] 1994: 420). If power is essentially that which represses, then the security apparatus is "power's Homeric epithet," according to Foucault (2004: 15). Herein lies the center of gravity of authoritarian rule. And this is where coup makers part ways with the army officers who put them in power.

For as imperative as it is to the coup itself, the military is unsuited for continuous domestic repression. Its training and weaponry are geared toward defense against foreign armies, perhaps domestic insurgents, but not civilian opposition. Police power, in contrast, is "coextensive with the entire social body" (Foucault 1979: 213). And because authoritarians feel more threatened by their citizens than by foreign enemies, the security force is their weapon of choice (Arendt [1951] 1994: 420–21). Army officers might be willing to repress limited segments of the population for limited periods. But authoritarian rule requires permanent repression, simply because the social and political antagonisms it creates are never truly resolved (Trotsky [1920] 1961: 54; Gramsci 1971: 222). Indeed, preserving a perpetual relationship of force vis-à-vis the population requires constant vigilance: the regime must preempt and neutralize all forms of resistance before they materialize (Foucault 2004: 17). Security prerogatives are justified by what Agamben described as a "permanent state of emergency," where what was once presented as exceptional circumstances is gradually replaced by "an unprecedented generalization of the paradigm of security as the normal technique of government" (2005: 2, 14, 87). Eventually, Arendt concluded, the security apparatus becomes the regime's "true executive branch," the "only openly ruling class" ([1951] 1994: 425–30).

In this type of police state, deterrence is vital. Like armies in the battlefield, security triumphs by killing a few, and intimidating millions (Trotsky [1920] 1961: 58). The punishment of dissidents is designed to leave "a memory" in the minds of all citizens; "Punishment *tames* man," as Nietzsche put it ([1887] 1998: 53–56). But fear is not enough. The best form of repression, Foucault insisted, is that which "coerces by means of observation," where "each gaze would form a part of the overall functioning of power" (1979: 168–71). Effective surveillance is multilayered. It "leaves no zone of shade and constantly supervises the very individuals who are entrusted with the task of supervising" (Foucault 1979: 176–77). It therefore requires "drafting the entire population . . . [for] voluntary espionage services." And in such as society, a "neighbor gradually becomes a more dangerous enemy to one who happens to harbor 'dangerous thoughts' than are the officially appointed police agents" (Arendt [1951] 1994: 422). The fact that anybody may be an informer paralyzes opposition.

This ubiquitous system was first devised in revolutionary France, when Jacobins set up popular surveillance committees to ferret out counterrevolutionaries. The idea then spread to Communists, Fascists, and postcolonial autocrats (Puddington 1988: 87). In Stalin's Russia, for instance, commonplace informers were as important as NKVD officers (Chase 2001: 405). Nazi Germany created multiple networks of security agents, each spying on the other (Arendt [1951] 1994: 403). The Brazilian SNI maintained an office in every government department to monitor personnel (Stepan 1988: 19). Milder versions were adopted in Western democracies during the Cold War (Nisbet 1981: 147), and received a new lease-on-life with the war on terror, with the individualization of war rendering citizens potential suspects (Beck 2003: 261–66).

In coup-installed regimes, the military, above all, must remain under scrutiny. Coup makers owe their power to the military, but they also have firsthand experience with what rebellious officers, like themselves, are capable of. Their hypersensitivity to the dangers of Bonapartism leads to "a *de facto* takeover by the police" (Hobsbawm 2001: 214). Security agents become the ruler's eyes and ears within the officer corps, and balance against the military's institutional power. The secret police monitors army meetings, inspects officers' files, taps phone lines, and hires informers within the ranks. Security reports become a major criterion in promotion, rotation, bonuses and perks, retirement packages, as well as purges (Nordlinger 1977: 15; Rapoport 1982: 258–59; Lawson 2007: 109–10). Revolutionary France again provided the inspiration, with a *représentant en mission* in almost every army unit—an invention later copied in most revolutionary regimes, and perfected in Russia and China. Because Trotsky relied on imperial officers to create the Red Army, he needed "political officers" to guarantee Bolshevik control (Wolpin 1981: 74–75). Mao readily understood that "political power comes out of the barrel of a loaded gun," and was determined "to have the Party control the gun and never allow the gun to control the Party" (Kolkowicz 1982: 233).

Besides security measures, authoritarian rulers ensure military compliance through coup-proofing strategies, most commonly, divide-and-rule practices between services, and creating loyal elite units. Middle East authoritarians embraced both options, but leaned mostly toward the second, with the notorious spread of republican guards from Egypt to Yemen to Iraq and the Levant. Rulers also used economic enticements. Under feudalism, military commissions usually went to the sons of wealthy families. As military and social statuses became separated, rulers were eager to convince their officers that their corporate interests were well served by the regime. Military spending would be initially increased; officers would get to travel abroad (with lavish allowances) for training; they would run major economic projects; and they would regularly receive various perks and tax exemptions (Droz-Vincent 2007: 198–211).

So why did the Turkish coup leaders adopt the guardian model, and their Egyptian counterparts prefer the governor one? And why did the humble Iranian Cossacks feel they could afford neither? There were certainly differences in the dispositions of the coup makers in each country, but let us start with the structural variations. At the moment of birth of the three new regimes, the Turkish military was by far the strongest: it had governed a world empire (albeit a disintegrating one) for almost six centuries; it had carried out several palace coups (the last of which occurred in 1908); it had been a full contestant in the Great War (although on the losing side); and it had prevented Turkey's absolute subjugation by the war victors. Moreover, political power was centered on the caliphate, which has been destroyed by the war, and dealt the deathblow by the army itself. On account of its perceived strength and legitimacy, once the army seized power, it did so confidently, conceiving itself as above politics, as the nation's guardian. The Egyptian army was in a much less secure position, considering its diminished status following its defeat under Muhammad Ali in 1840 (a full century before it carried out the coup); its humiliating subordination to the British after 1882, and failure to carry out a national liberation war; and its catastrophic defeat in the 1948 Palestine war to Zionist "gangs." Egypt's coup makers could not rest on their laurels—simply because they had none. Also, political power was not just concentrated in the monarchy, which they immediately abolished, but for three decades had been shared between the king and several party leaders and parliamentarians, which meant that the threat was more diffuse and hence securing the regime more complicated. Egypt's Free Officers therefore felt compelled to erect a pervasive security apparatus to maintain control over not only politics, but also an officer corps naturally loath to everyday politicking. Fortunately, they had inherited a well-functioning secret police (compliments of the British colonizers). All they needed was to expand and reorganize it. Iran, in contrast to both, had neither a viable military nor a security establishment to speak of, and therefore naturally continued the ancient monarchical tradition to guarantee popular obedience.

Moreover, there were important personal distinctions between the three coup chiefs. Kemal and Nasser were hailed as war heroes (albeit in lost wars), and both capitalized on their status to organize political cliques within the armed forces to help them seize power. Reza Khan, by contrast, was a lone wolf; an obscure and apolitical Cossack colonel handpicked by the British to bring order to a country they believed was slipping into chaos. Also, unlike the charismatic generalissimos of Ankara and Cairo, with their fiery speeches and grand popular gestures, the brutish, half-literate master of Tehran could hardly impress his subjects. It is no small wonder that the former two felt assured enough to abolish monarchism and establish their own political parties, while the latter continued to rely on a medieval-style court with its mystical allure. And, in fact, it was Reza Khan's decision to extend monarchical rule, rather than adopt the modern republicanism of his illustrious counterparts that set Iran's trajectory apart. Finally, one should note here that a similar embrace of republicanism and modernity did not mean that Kemal and Nasser shared a similar worldview. Kemal had always been a staunch Europeanist, who longed to align Turkey with the Western camp. Nasser, on the other hand, mistrusted the imperial West, and developed close affinities with the totalitarian regimes of the East. It is not entirely surprising that Kemal tried to institute a military-dominated democracy, while Nasser inadvertently laid the foundation for a police state.

Transformation: Three Trajectories

The captivating images associated with mass uprisings lead many to believe that when "the people" have finally had enough, they could rise together and force political change. The Iranian Revolution of 1979, Egypt's inspiring

Tahrir Square occupation in 2011, and even Turkey's more limited Gezi Park protests of 2013 initially corresponded with this romantic imagery, best captured in Trotsky's evocative exposé:

> The most indubitable feature of a revolution is the direct interference of the masses in historic events. In ordinary times the state ... elevates itself above the nation, and history is made by the specialists in that line of business.... But at those crucial moments when the old order becomes no longer endurable to the masses, they break over the barriers excluding them from the political arena, sweep aside their traditional representatives, and create by their own interference the initial groundwork for a new regime.... The history of revolution is for us first of all a history of the forcible entrance of the masses into the realm of rulership over their own destiny. ([1930] 1980: 17–18)

There were many such moments in the decades that followed the founding coups in Iran, Turkey, and Egypt: great popular upheavals, major insurgencies, and other forms of street politics. Students of regime change, however, agree on little else other than the fact that change cannot be forced from below if officers are willing and capable of repression (Chorley 1973: 20; Johnson 1982: 94; Hobsbawm 2001: 226–27). Plainly stated, "There has not been a single instance in which civilians alone demonstrated the strength to overthrow [a] regime backed by a unified officer corps intent upon retaining power. They simply do not have sufficient numbers, organization, and weapons" (Nordlinger 1977: 139). Or as Schmitt grimly stated: "The endeavor to resist the leviathan, the all powerful, resistance-destroying, and technically perfect mechanism of command, is practically impossible.... It is 'utopian' in the true sense of the word" ([1938] 2008: 46). The hope is for oppositionists to capitalize on struggles between ruling institutions, or better yet, find powerful allies within them (Tilly 1990: 100; Skocpol 1994: 7). Understanding divisions within the ruling bloc is therefore essential to revolution.

One of the most divisive issues for any ruling group is how to respond to popular opposition (Skocpol 1979: 47; Goldstone 2003: 13). This is where tensions between the military, security, and political institutions come to the fore. These ruling partners are neither equally invested in regime survival, nor are they equal in power. Politicians are naturally reluctant to relinquish their authority, but they have to rely on coercive institutions to thwart domestic and foreign threats. The military controls the most devastating means of violence, but it gets weary of the adverse effects of direct governance on its corporate interests. Meanwhile, the security apparatus compensates for its lack of equally destructive power as that of the military by sustaining the regime through active, day-to-day protection. Among the three, the security is likely to suffer most from a transition to democracy. While most politicians are granted amnesty, security crimes (illegal surveillance, torture, executions, etc.) rarely go unpunished. Also, unlike the universally esteemed officer corps, security privileges are substantially deflated in democracies.

Regime resilience is largely determined by the interplay of these three institutions—asymmetrical in power and desire to rule. One possible outcome is that the military turns against the regime, usually through a corrective coup that (at least superficially) adopts popular demands. In the face of sustained popular opposition, officers dread transforming the military into an instrument of repression: a despised, second-rate gendarmerie too preoccupied with domestic control to prepare for war. This was the case in several Latin American regimes, where rulers fostered professionalism out of fear that the "militarism that had given them power might take it away," while forgetting that once officers recognized soldiering as "a full-time job that left no room for doubling in politics," they were less likely to support them (Lieuwen 1965: 151–53). Indonesia provides another example of military weariness of politicization (Nordholt 2002: 136–52). Military defeat usually reinforces this feeling. Regime change in Pakistan (1971), Greece (1973), and Argentina (1982) followed their failure on the battlefield (Danopoulos 1988: 14–17). The growing power of the security apparatus is another reason for military frustration and ultimate abandonment of the regime—as in Brazil (1985) with the *abertura* (Coelho 1988: 164–66; Stepan 1988: 32–58).

In fact, one of the widest datasets on military intervention in politics from 1950 to 2010 confirmed that "empirical analyses strongly support the argument that coups promote democratization, particularly among states that are least likely to democratize other wise" (Thyne and Powell 2014: 1; see also Geddes 1999). Another extensive analysis of the military's role in regime change revealed that in 63 percent of the 229 cases studied, officers preferred to pass power to a civilian authority with some semblance of popular legitimacy, and only in 7 percent of the cases were they forced to do so by popular uprisings (Maniruzzaman 1987: 21). This is why Geddes (1999) repeatedly cited, in her authoritative survey of regime transitions, the military's role in democratization. Again, this is not because officers respect democracy, but because a controlled democracy usually proves to be the lesser evil from a military standpoint; and because whenever officers make that decision, they are the most capable of loosening the grip of authoritarianism.

Turkey provides a textbook example. Its founding coup placed the military—as an institution—in a guardian role: as an overseer, not enforcer. Officers presided over the creation of a competitive political arena, and undertook overall regime security. The security sector, which regularly identifies with and supports authoritarianism, remained a weak player. It is true that the military intervened repeatedly to defend its autonomy and the state's national security (usually intertwined in the military mind), but it promptly withdrew after each intervention and reformed the political system in a way that would make future interventions unnecessary. Inevitably, and despite setbacks and reversals, this strategy allowed the development of strong and competitive political parties, which managed, in the fullness of time, to broaden their popular and geopolitical support and with them the margins of democracy. The latest version is the Justice and Development Party (Adalet ve Kalkınma Partisi, AKP), which finally managed to curb military influence. The future, as always, remains uncertain. AKP had become a victim of its own success: its attempt to monopolize political power and build a loyal security apparatus is obviously alarming. Yet, its relatively humble showing in the 2015 elections, together with the impressive gains of a just-formed party, demonstrates the continued vitality of Turkish democracy.

Egypt falls on the other end of the spectrum. Entrusting the fortunes of the new regime to a voracious security apparatus, and the gradual marginalization of the military, set the tone for authoritarian resilience. And the reduction of politics to the machinations of one oversized and corrupt ruling party further commended the regime to the mercy of the security barons. The popular revolt against this parasitic police state in 2011 was partly successful because of the support for an embittered military. But the constrictive structure of Egypt's authoritarian regime ruled out transition to some form of limited democracy. It is true that the upper echelons of the ruling bloc are presently in flux, with a president striving to stand on his own two feet without a ruling party, longtime politicians (and their business cronies) set on returning to the center stage; a military determined not to be sidelined again (and indeed compensate for its past losses), and an omnipotent security apparatus still holding the regime to ransom. But regardless of the new power configuration being currently negotiated, Egypt will most likely continue to be an authoritarian police state.

The Iranian trajectory placed it somewhere in the middle. Its founding coup created neither a military-dominated regime capable of gradual reform, nor a resilient police state. It was probably the last modern instance of what Weber (1978: 231) referred to as *sultanism*: "When domination develops an administration and military force which are purely personal instruments of the master," that is, when military and security officers are reduced to "household staff." By investing in an almighty royal court that overshadowed all other regime institutions, the Pahlavi dynasty ended up weakening, and eventually alienating the agents of coercion. The two Pahlavi monarchs attempted some reforms, with passive support from the newly established military and a security apparatus that clumsily came to existence in the late 1950s. But their rigid, out-of-date belief in an all-powerful king and his loyal vassals could hardly withstand the winds of change that overtook the regime in 1979. The Iranian Revolution succeeded largely because regimes centered on a monarch tend to collapse when he loses nerve. The Shah's voluntary abdication dealt the deathblow to his regime, as did the abdication of Charles X (1830) and Louis-Philippe (1848) to their respective regimes in France. But a military and security paralyzed by their master's vacillation between repression and compromise could have rallied to the regime's defense (before, or especially after the Shah abdicated) if they had the will and capacity to do so. In the event, the former raised the white flag and the latter defected to the revolutionaries. Iran's new rulers declared a republic (although an Islamic one) and built a well-balanced and relatively dynamic (albeit exclusive) regime. Fears of slipping into autocracy surface whenever the proclaimed defender of the Revolution, the ominous Islamic Revolutionary Guard, reasserts its power over other regime sectors. But hopes that Iran's uniquely balanced regime would persist are renewed with the small triumphs of reforming forces in parliamentary and presidential elections, and the presence of a relatively independent and nationalistic military.

None of these three trajectories was determined at the first instance, or in the early days of regime formation. The detailed study of decades of interaction of military, security, and political institutions shows the importance of timing, strategy, personalities, geopolitical changes, and historical contingencies. But understanding the genesis of each new regime and the logic of power it initiates is as important as tracing the shifts and turns that follow. And even though the Iranian, Turkish, and Egyptian regimes continue to change, in one form or another, their history continues to weigh them down.

Notes

1. According to Thyne and Powel (2011: 255), most of these coups happened in Africa (36.5 percent) and Latin America (31.9 percent), followed by the Middle East (15.8 percent), and Asia (13.1 percent), and very few in Europe (2.6 percent).

2. Cohen's (2003) work examined civil–military relations under Abraham Lincoln, George Clemenceau, Winston Churchill, David Ben-Gurion, Lyndon B. Johnson, George H. W. Bush, and George W. Bush.

3. As Clausewitz plainly stated: "The end for which a soldier is recruited, clothed, armed, and trained, the whole object of his sleeping, eating, drinking, and marching *is simply that he should fight*" ([1832] 1989: 95).

Bibliography

Abella, Alex. 2009. *Soldiers of Reason: The Rand Corporation and the Rise of the American Empire*. New York: Mariner Books.

Addi, Lahouari. 2002. "Army, State and Nation in Algeria." In *Political Armies: The Military and Nation Building in the Age of Democracy*, edited by Kees Koonings and Dirk Kruijt, pp. 179–203. New York: Zed Books.

Agamben, Giorgio. 2005. *State of Exception*. Chicago: University of Chicago Press.

Agüero, Felipe. 2002. "A Political Army in Chile: Historical Assessment and Prospects for the New Democracy." In *Political Armies: The Military and Nation Building in the Age of Democracy*, edited by Kees Koonings and Dirk Kruijt, pp. 111–34. New York: Zed Books.

Albrecht, Holger. 2014. "The Myth of Coup-proofing: Risk and Instances of Military Coups d'état in the Middle East and North Africa, 1950–2013." *Armed Forces & Society*: 1–29.

Allison, Graham and Philip Zelikow. 1999. *Essence of Decision: Explaining the Cuban Missile Crisis* (2d ed.). New York: Addison Wesley Longman.

Anderson, Perry. 1979. *Lineages of the Absolutist State*. London: Verso.

Arendt, Hannah. [1954] 1994. *The Origins of Totalitarianism*. New York: Harcourt.

Baaklini, Abdo I. 1976. "Civilian Control of the Military in Lebanon: A Legislative Perspective." In *Civilian Control of the Military: Theory and Cases from Developing Countries*, edited by Claude E. Welch, pp. 255–83. Albany: State University of New York Press.

Bacevich, Andrew J. 2007. "Elusive Bargain: The Pattern of U.S. Civil-Military Relations Since World War II." In *The Long War: A New History of U.S. National Security Policy Since World War II*, edited by Andrew J. Bacevich, pp. 207–64. New York: Columbia University Press.

Beck, Ulrich. 2003. "The Silence of Words: On Terror and War." *Security Dialogue* 34: 255–67.

Bourdieu, Pierre. 2014. On the State: Lectures at the College de France, 1989–1992. Cambridge, UK: Polity Press

Brooks, Risa. 1998. *Political-Military Relations and the Stability of Arab Regimes* London: Institute for Strategic Studies.

Brzezinski, Zbigniew. 1954. *Political Controls in the Soviet Army*. New York: Research Program on the USSR, East European Fund.

Buck, James H. 1976. "Civilian Control of the Military in Japan." In *Civilian Control of the Military: Theory and Cases from Developing Countries*, edited by Claude E. Welch, pp. 149–86. Albany: State University of New York Press.

Castro, Celso. 2002. "The Military Politics in Brazil, 1964–2000." In *Political Armies: The Military and Nation Building in the Age of Democracy*, edited by Kees Koonings and Dirk Kruijt, pp. 90–110. New York: Zed Books.
Chang, Parris H. 1976. "The Dynamics of Party-Military Relations in China." In *Civilian Control of the Military: Theory and Cases from Developing Countries*, edited by Claude E. Welch, pp. 123–48. Albany: State University of New York Press.
Chase, William J. 2001. *Enemies Within the Gates? The Comintern and the Stalinist Repression, 1934–1939*. New Haven, CT: Yale University Press.
Chorley, Katharine. 1973. *Armies and the Art of Revolution*. Boston: Beacon Press.
Clausewitz, Carl von. [1832] 1989. *On War*. Princeton, NJ: Princeton University Press.
Clausewitz, Carl von. 1988. *War, Politics, and Power: Selections from* On War, *and* I Believe and Profess. Washington, DC: Regnery Gateway.
Coelho, Edmundo Campos. 1988. "Back to the Barraks: The Brazilian Military's Style." In *The Decline of Military Regimes: The Civilian Influence*, edited by Constantine P. Danopoulos, pp. 147–71. Boulder, CO: Westview Press.
Cohen, Eliot. 2003. *Supreme Command: Soldiers, Statesmen, and Leadership in Wartime*. New York: Simon & Schuster.
Cohen, Stephen P. 1976. "Civilian Control of the Military in India." In *Civilian Control of the Military: Theory and Cases from Developing Countries*, edited by Claude E. Welch, pp. 43–64. Albany: State University of New York Press.
Colton, Timothy J. 1978. "The Party-Military Connection: A Participatory Model." In *Civil-Military Relations in Communist Systems*, edited by Dale R. Herspring and Ivan Volgyes, pp. 53–78. Boulder, CO: Westview Press.
Cook, Steven. 2007. *Ruling But Not Governing: The Military and Political Development in Egypt, Algeria, and Turkey*. Baltimore, MD: John Hopkins University Press.
Danopoulos, Constantine P. 1988. "Military Dictatorships in Retreat: Problems and Perspectives." In *The Decline of Military Regimes: The Civilian Influence*, edited by Constantine P. Danopoulos, pp. 1–24. Boulder, CO: Westview Press.
Decalo, Samuel. 1998. *Civil-Military Relations in Africa*. Gainesville: Florida Academic Press Inc.
De Kadt, Emanuel. 2002. "The Military in Politics: Old Wine in New Bottles? An Attempt at Stocktaking." In *Political Armies: The Military and Nation Building in the Age of Democracy*, edited by Kees Koonings and Dirk Kruijt, pp. 313–32. New York: Zed Books.
Droz-Vincent, Philippe. 2007. "From Political to Economic Actors: The Changing Role of Middle Eastern Armies." In *Debating Arab Authoritarianism: Dynamics and Durability in Nondemocratic Regimes*, edited by Oliver Schlumberger, pp. 195–214. Stanford, CA: Stanford University Press.
Engels, Frederick and Karl Marx. 1968. *Selected Works*. London: Lawrence & Wishart.
Epstein, Alek D. and Michael Uritsky. 2004. "Questioning the Role of Army in Nation-Building: The Development of Critical Discourse on Civil-Military Relations in Israel." In *Civil-Military Relations, Nation-Building, and National Identity: Comparative Perspectives*, edited by Constantine P. Danopoulos, Dhirendra Vajpeyi, and Amir Bar-or, pp. 169–82. Westport, CT: Praeger.
Finer, Samuel E. 1962. *Men on Horseback: The Role of the Military in Politics*. London: Pall Mall Press.

Finer, Samuel E. 1982. "The Morphology of Military Regimes." In *Soldiers, Peasants, and Bureaucrats: Civil Military Relations in Communist and Modernizing Societies,* edited by Roman Kolkowicz and Andrzej Korbonski, pp. 281–309. London: Allen & Unwin.

Fisher, Sydney N. 1963. *The Military in the Middle East.* Columbus: Ohio State University Press.

Foucault, Michel. 1979. *Discipline and Punish: The Birth of the Prison.* New York: Vintage Books.

Foucault, Michel. 2000. *Power: Essential Works of Foucault, 1954–1984.* New York: The New Press.

Foucault, Michel. 2004. *Society Must Be Defended: Lectures at the Collège De France, 1975–76.* New York: Penguin Books.

Geddes, Barbara. 1999. "What Do We Know about Democratization after Twenty Years?" *Annual Review of Political Science* 2: 115–44.

Goldstone, Jack. 2003. *Revolutions: Theoretical, Comparative, and Historical Studies.* Belmont, CA: Thomspon-Wardsworth.

Goodwin, Jeff. 2001. *No Other Way Out: States and Revolutionary Movements, 1945–1991.* New York: Cambridge University Press.

Gramsci, Antonio. 1971. *Selections from the Prison Notebooks.* New York: International Publishers.

Gupta, Asha. 2003. "Evolving Role of the Military." In *Military Rule and Democratization: Changing Perspectives,* edited by Asha Gupta, pp. 1–24. New Delhi: Deep & Deep Publications.

Halpern, Manfred. 1963. *The Politics of Social Change in the Middle East and North Africa.* Princeton, NJ: Princeton University Press.

Hobsbawm, Eric J. 2001. *Revolutionaries.* New York: The New Press.

Horowitz, Dan. 1982. "The Israeli Defense Forces: A Civilianized Military in a Partially Militarized Society." In *Soldiers, Peasants, and Bureaucrats: Civil Military Relations in Communist and Modernizing Societies,* edited by Roman Kolkowicz and Andrzej Korbonski, pp. 77–108. London: Allen & Unwin.

Howard, Michael. 1983. *Clausewitz.* New York: Oxford University Press.

Huntington, Samuel. 1957. *The Soldier and the State: The Theory and Politics of Civil-Military Relations.* Cambridge, MA: Harvard University Press.

Huntington, Samuel. 1968. *Political Order in Changing Societies.* New Haven, CT: Yale University Press.

Ibn Khaldun, Abd al-Rahman. [1377] 1977. *Al-Muqaddimah lei kitab al-'ibar wa diwan al-mubtada' wa al-khabar fei ayam al-Arab wa al-Berber wa man 'asarahum min zawi al-sultan al-akbar* (The Prolegomena). Alexandria, Egypt: Dar Ibn Khaldun.

Janowitz, Morris. 1960. *The Professional Soldier: A Social and Political Portrait.* New York: Free Press.

Janowitz, Morris. 1967. "The Military in the Political Development of New Nations." In *Garrisons and Government: Politics and the Military in New States,* edited by Wilson C. McWilliams, pp. 67–79. San Francisco: Chandler.

Joas, Hans. 2003. *War and Modernity.* Cambridge, UK: Polity Press.

Johnson, Chalmers. 1982. *Revolutionary Change.* Stanford, CA: Stanford University Press.

Johnson, Chalmers. 2004. *The Sorrows of Empire: Militarism, Secrecy, and the End of the Republic*. New York: Henry Holt.

Johnson, Chalmers. 2008. *Nemesis: The Last Days of the American Republic*. New York: Henry Holt.

Johnson, John J. 1964. *The Military and Society in Latin America*. Stanford, CA: Stanford University Press.

Kennedy, Hugh. 2001. *The Armies of the Caliphs: Military and Society in the Early Islamic State*. New York: Routledge.

Kestnbaum, Meyer. 2009. "The Sociology of War and the Military." *Annual Review of Sociology* 35: 235–54.

Khuri, Fuad I. 1982. "The Study of Civil-Military Relations in Modernizing Societies in the Middle East." In *Soldiers, Peasants, and Bureaucrats: Civil Military Relations in Communist and Modernizing Societies*, edited by Roman Kolkowicz and Andrzej Korbonski, pp. 9–27. London: Allen & Unwin.

Kimmel, Michael. 1990. *Revolution: A Sociological Interpretation*. Syracuse, NY: Syracuse University Press.

Kolkowicz, Roman. 1967. *The Soviet Military and the Communist Party*. Princeton, NJ: Princeton University Press.

Kolkowicz, Roman. 1978. "Interest Groups in Soviet Politics: The Case of the Military." In *Civil-Military Relations in Communist Systems*, edited by Dale R. Herspring and Ivan Volgyes, pp. 9–126. Boulder, CO: Westview Press.

Kolkowicz, Roman. 1982. "Toward a Theory of Civil-Military Relations in Communist (Hegemonial) Systems." In *Soldiers, Peasants, and Bureaucrats: Civil Military Relations in Communist and Modernizing Societies*, edited by Roman Kolkowicz and Andrzej Korbonski, pp. 231–51. London: Allen & Unwin.

Koonings, Kees and Dirk Kruijt. 2002a. "Introduction." In *Political Armies: The Military and Nation Building in the Age of Democracy*, edited by Kees Koonings and Dirk Kruijt, pp. 1–8. New York: Zed Books.

Koonings, Kees and Dirk Kruijt. 2002b. "Military Politics and the Mission of Nation Building." In *Political Armies: The Military and Nation Building in the Age of Democracy*, edited by Kees Koonings and Dirk Kruijt, pp. 9–34. New York: Zed Books.

Koonings, Kees and Dirk Kruijt. 2002c. "Epilogue—Political Armies between Continuity and Demise." In *Political Armies: The Military and Nation Building in the Age of Democracy*, edited by Kees Koonings and Dirk Kruijt, pp. 333–47. New York: Zed Books.

Lawson, Fred H. 2007. "Intraregime Dynamics, Uncertainty, and the Persistence of Authoritarianism in the Contemporary Arab World." In *Debating Arab Authoritarianism: Dynamics and Durability in Nondemocratic Regimes*, edited by Oliver Schlumberger, pp. 109–28. Stanford, CA: Stanford University Press.

Lenin, Vladimir. 1987. *Essential Works of Lenin: "What is to be done?" and Other Writings*. Chicago: University of Chicago Press.

LeoGrande, William M. 1978. "A Bureaucratic Approach to Civil-Military Relations in Communist Political Systems: The Case of Cuba." In*Civil-Military Relations in Communist Systems*, edited by Dale R. Herspring and Ivan Volgyes, pp. 201–18. Boulder, CO: Westview Press.

Lieuwen, Edwin. 1965. *Arms and Politics in Latin America*. New York: Praeger.

Luxemburg, Rosa. [1925] 2006. *Reform or Revolution and Other Writings*. New York: Dover.

Machiavelli, Niccolò. [1532] 2004. *The Prince*. New York: Pocket Books.

Maniruzzaman, Talukder. 1987. *Military Withdrawal from Politics: A Comparative Study*. Cambridge, MA: Ballinger.

Mann, Michael. 1986. *The Sources of Social Power.* Vol. I: *A History of Power from the Beginning to A.D. 1760*. New York: Cambridge University Press.

Mann, Michael. 1993. *The Sources of Social Power.* Vol. II: *The Rise of Classes and Nation-States*. New York: Cambridge University Press.

Mann, Michael. 2004. *Fascists*. New York: Cambridge University Press.

Marx, Karl. [1852] 1963. *The Eighteenth Brumaire of Louis Bonaparte*. New York: International Publishers.

McWilliams, Wilson C. 1967. "Introduction." In *Garrisons and Government: Politics and the Military in New States*, edited by Wilson C. McWilliams, pp. 1–44. San Francisco: Chandler.

Michaels, Albert L. 1976. "Background to a Coup: Civil-Military Relations in Twentieth-Century Chile and the Overthrow of Salvador Allende." In *Civilian Control of the Military: Theory and Cases from Developing Countries*, edited by Claude E. Welch, pp. 283–312. Albany: State University of New York Press.

Mills, C. Wright. [1956] 2000. *The Power Elite*. New York: Oxford University Press.

Morris, James Winston. 2009. "An Arab Machiavelli? Rhetoric, Philosophy, and Politics in Ibn Khaldun's Critique of Sufism." *Harvard Middle Eastern and Islamic Review* 11: 1–31.

Mosca, Gaetano. 1939. *The Ruling Class*. New York: McGraw-Hill.

Moten, Matthew. 2010. "Out of Order: Strengthening the Political-Military Relationship." *Foreign Affairs*, vol. 89, no. 5, pp. 2–8.

Mufti, Malik. 2009. "Jihad as Statecraft: Ibn Khaldun on the Conduct of War and Empire." *History of Political Thought* 30 (3): 385–410.

Needler, Martin C. 1975. "Military Motivations in the Seizure of Power." *Latin American Research Review* 10 (3): 63–79.

Nelson, Anna Kasten. 2007. "The Evolution of the National Security State: Ubiquitous and Endless." In *The Long War: A New History of U.S. National Security Policy Since World War II*, edited by Andrew J. Bacevich, pp. 265–301. New York: Columbia University Press.

Nietzsche, Friedrich. [1887] 1998. *On the Genealogy of Morality*. Indianapolis, IN: Hackett.

Nietzsche, Friedrich. [1906] 2006. *The Will to Power*. New York: Barnes & Noble.

Nisbet, Robert. 1981. *Twilight of Authority*. New York: Oxford University Press.

Nordholt, Nico Schulte. 2002. "The Janus Face of the Indonesian Armed Forces." In *Political Armies: The Military and Nation Building in the Age of Democracy*, edited by Kees Koonings and Dirk Kruijt, pp. 135–61. New York: Zed Books.

Nordlinger, Eric A. 1977. *Soldiers in Politics: Military Coups and Governments*. Englewood Cliff, NJ: Prentice Hall.

Nun, José. 1967. "The Middle-Class Military Coup." In *The Politics of Conformity in Latin America*, edited by Claudio Véliz, pp. 66–118. London: Oxford University Press.

Nunn, Frederick N. 1992. *The Time of the Generals: Latin American Professional Militarism in World Perspective.* Lincoln: University of Nebraska Press.

Odom, William E. 1978. "The Party-Military Connection: A Critique." In *Civil-Military Relations in Communist Systems,* edited by Dale R. Herspring and Ivan Volgyes, pp. 27–52. Boulder, CO: Westview Press.

O'Donnell, Guillermo. 1973. *Modernization and Bureaucratic Authoritarianism: Studies in South American Politics.* Berkeley: University of California Press.

O'Donnell, Guillermo, Philippe Schmitter, and Lawrence Whitehead (eds.). 1986. *Transitions from Authoritarian Rule.* Baltimore, MD: Johns Hopkins University Press.

Palmer, R. R. 1958. *Twelve Who Ruled: The Year of the Terror in the French Revolution.* Princeton, NJ: Princeton University Press.

Paret, Peter. 1992. *Understanding War: Essays on Clausewitz and the History of Military Power.* Princeton, NJ: Princeton University Press.

Perlmutter, Amos. 1982. "Civil-Military Relations in Socialist Authoritarian and Praetorian States: Prospects and Retrospects." In *Soldiers, Peasants, and Bureaucrats: Civil Military Relations in Communist and Modernizing Societies,* edited by Roman Kolkowicz and Andrzej Korbonski, pp. 310–31. London: Allen & Unwin.

Poggi, Gianfranco. 2001. *Forms of Power.* Malden, MA: Polity Press.

Poulantzas, Nicos. 1975. *Political Power and Social Classes.* London: Verso.

Prados, John. 2007. "Intelligence for Empire." In *The Long War: A New History of U.S. National Security Policy Since World War II,* edited by Andrew J. Bacevich, pp. 302–34. New York: Columbia University Press.

Przeworski, Adam. 1995. *Sustainable Democracy.* New York: Cambridge University Press.

Puddington, Arch. 1988. *Failed Utopias: Methods of Coercion in Communist Regimes.* San Francesco: Institute for Contemporary Studies.

Pye, Lucian W. 1962. "Armies in the Process of Political Modernization." In *The Role of the Military in Underdeveloped Countries,* edited by John J. Johnson, pp. 85–100. Princeton, NJ: Princeton University Press.

Rapoport, David. 1982. "The Praetorian Army: Insecurity, Venality, and Impotence." In *Soldiers, Peasants, and Bureaucrats: Civil Military Relations in Communist and Modernizing Societies,* edited by Roman Kolkowicz and Andrzej Korbonski, pp. 252–80. London: Allen & Unwin.

Ricks, Thomas E. 1998. *Making the Corps.* New York: Simon & Schuster.

Roxborough, Ian. 1994. "Clausewitz and the Sociology of War." *British Journal of Sociology* 45 (4): 619–36.

Rudolph, Lloyd I. and Susan Hoeber Rudolph. 1967. "Generals and Politicians in India." In *Garrisons and Government: Politics and the Military in New States,* edited by Wilson C. McWilliams, pp. 130–49. San Francisco: Chandler.

Schlumberger, Oliver. 2007. "Arab Authoritarianism: Debating the Dynamics and Durability of Nondemocratic regimes." In *Debating Arab Authoritarianism: Dynamics and Durability in Nondemocratic Regimes,* edited by Oliver Schlumberger, pp. 1–20. Stanford, CA: Stanford University Press.

Schmitt, Carl. [1932] 1996. *The Concept of the Political.* Chicago: University of Chicago Press.

Schmitt, Carl. [1938] 2008. *The Leviathan in the State Theory of Thomas Hobbes: Meaning and Failure of a Political Symbol.* Chicago: University of Chicago Press.

Segell, Glen. 2004. "The Nation-State, Nationalism, and Civil-Military Realtions Theory." In *Civil-Military Relations, Nation-Building, and National Identity: Comparative Perspectives,* edited by Constantine P. Danopoulos, Dhirendra Vajpeyi, and Amir Bar-or, pp. 51–66. Westport, CT: Praeger.

Sharabi, Hisham B. 1966. *Nationalism and Revolution in the Arab World.* Princeton, NJ: Princeton University Press.

Sharabi, Hisham B. 1967. "Parliamentary Government and Military Autocracy in the Middle East." In *Garrisons and Government: Politics and the Military in New States,* edited by Wilson C. McWilliams, pp. 183–202. San Francisco: Chandler.

Shichor, Yitzhak. 2004. "Military-Civilian Integration in China: Legacy and Policy." In *Civil-Military Relations, Nation-Building, and National Identity: Comparative Perspectives,* edited by Constantine P. Danopoulos, Dhirendra Vajpeyi, and Amir Bar-or, pp. 83–106. Westport, CT: Praeger.

Shils, Edward. 1962. "The Military in the Political Developments of States." In *The Role of the Military in Underdeveloped Countries,* edited by John J. Johnson, pp. 7–68. Princeton, NJ: Princeton University Press.

Skocpol, Theda. 1979. *States and Social Revolutions: A Comparative Analysis of France, Russia, and China.* New York: Cambrdige University Press.

Skocpol, Theda. 1994. *Social Revolutions in the Modern World.* New York: Cambrdige University Press.

Spiro, Herbert. 1967. "The Military in Sub-Saharan Africa." In *Garrisons and Government: Politics and the Military in New States,* edited by Wilson C. McWilliams, pp. 264–72. San Francisco: Chandler.

Stepan, Alfred. 1988. *Rethinking Military Politics: Brazil and the Southern Cone.* Princeton, NJ: Princeton University Press.

Thomas, Clive T. 1984. *The Rise of the Authoritarian State in Peripheral Societies.* New York: Monthly Review Press.

Thompson, William R. 1975. "Regime Vulnerability and the Military Coup." *Comparative Politics* 7 (4): 459–87.

Thyne, Clayton L. and Jonathan M. Powell. 2011. "Global Instances of Coups from 1950 to 2010: A New Dataset." *Journal of Peace Research* 48 (2): 249–59

Thyne, Clayton L. and Jonathan M. Powell. 2014. "Coup d'état or Coup d'Autocracy? How Coups Impact Democratization, 1950–2008." *Foreign Policy Analysis* 10 (2): 1–22.

Tilly, Charles. 1990. *Coercion, Capital, and the European State, AD 990–1990.* New York: Basil.

Trimberger, Ellen Kay. 1978. *Revolutions from Above: Military Bureaucrats and Development in Japan, Turkey, Egypt, and Peru.* Brunswick, NJ: Transaction Books.

Trotsky, Leon. [1920] 1961. *Terrorism and Communism.* Ann Arbor: University of Michigan Press.

Trotsky, Leon. [1930] 1980. *History of the Russian Revolution.* New York: Pathfinder.

Trotsky, Leon. [1937] 2004. *The Revolution Betrayed.* New York: Dover.

Vagts, Alfred. 1959. *A History of Militarism: Civilian and Military.* New York: Meridian Books.

Vatikiotis, P. J. 1961. *The Egyptian Army in Politics: Pattern for New Nations?* Bloomington: Indiana University Press.

Weber, Max. 1978. *Economy and Society: An Outline of Interpretive Sociology*. Berkeley: University of California Press.

Welch, Claude E. 1976a. "Civilian Control of the Military: Myth and Reality." In *Civilian Control of the Military: Theory and Cases from Developing Countries,* edited by Claude E. Welch, pp. 1–42. Albany: State University of New York Press.

Welch, Claude E. 1976b. "Two Strategies of Civilian Control: Some Concluding Observations." In *Civilian Control of the Military: Theory and Cases from Developing Countries,* edited by Claude E. Welch, pp. 313–28. Albany: State University of New York Press.

Wolfers, Arnold. 1962. *Discord and Collaboration: Essays on International Politics.* Baltimore, MD: Johns Hopkins University Press.

Wolpin, Miles D. 1981. *Militarism and Social Revolution in the Third World.* Totowa, NJ: Allahnheld, Osmun & Co.

INDEX